THE PASSION OF INGMAR BERGMAN

THE PASSION OF INGMAR BERGMAN

FRANK GADO

Duke University Press
Durham 1986

To my wife Gunilla,

and to our children, Anna, Tobias, and Carin.

They paid the price while I rendered years into pages.

Contents

Acknowledgements

In valediction while releasing the manuscript to the typesetter, I would like to express my gratitude to:

John Stenman, my father-in-law, for faithfully sending me clippings from Swedish newspapers for seventeen years;

Ingmar Bergman, for permitting me to quote from his published and unpublished works, and for granting the use of family photographs;

Margareta Bergman Britten Austin, for correcting biographical errors into which previously published accounts had led me, for generously supplying additional information, and for allowing me to quote a long passage from her novel *Karin*;

Else Fisher-Bergman, for confiding in me, and for sending me the photograph of herself as Beppo;

Ingrid Karlebo Bergman, for providing published scripts, and for mediating with her husband to assist in my obtaining his permissions;

Richard Vowles, for his extraordinarily kind words, for his interest, and for his suggestions;

Marsha Kinder, for sharing with me unpublished material in her possession;

Svensk Filmindustri, Sveriges Radio-TV, and Svenska Filminstitutet, for their cooperation;

Thora Girke, as valued a friend as a secretary, for her unstinting willingness to furnish help beyond the boundaries of duty;

Union College, for grants through its Humanities Development Fund which made it possible for me to be relieved of teaching obligations during two sabbaticals;

George Puleo, for helping me launch my research at a time when my knowledge of Swedish was still scant;

John Benedict, for his belief in the merits of my approach to an interpretation of Bergman;

Reynolds Smith and Robert Mirandon, my editors at Duke University Press, for their sensitivity and patience;

and to George Metes, William Thomas, S. O. A. Ullmann, Camille Qualtere, Thomas Di Salvo, Frank Coppay, James McCord, Michael Shinagel, and Stanley Kaminsky, each of whom read portions of my manuscript during its long evolution and offered suggestions for its improvement.

Finally, I would like to pay homage to the memory of Samuel B. Morrell, a man of rare wit and a complete friend. Despite his denigration of cinema as a bastard pretender to the majesty of theater, he offered painstaking critiques of my first drafts and tried to train my views. Although I have rewritten almost every paragraph since his death, and although I am certain he would object as strenuously to this last version as to the first, he has a remained a constant companion in the enterprise.

Preface

When film was mute, the story, in its strictly verbal mode, lay in the scenario, at one remove from the film itself; the audience encountered the word only as a printed intrusion on the pictorial experience—an expedient testifying to the limitations of the camera as a narrative instrument. Application of literary criticism to a patently nonliteral artifact seemed inappropriate, and, indeed, most serious studies of the cinema during the silent era concerned theoretical approaches to the medium. With the development of sound, film drew closer to the drama; even so, the filmscript never rose to the status of literature enjoyed by the text used in the theater. Although a play is predicated upon its performance (even if its stage is only the reader's mind), it also exists as a literary entity apart from its interpretation in any particular enactment. In contrast, our experience of the filmscript is fixed to a single mise-en-scène, dominated, moreover, by the composition of specific images extending far beyond the indications of the writer's words. Significantly, when the founders of the New Wave sank the footings for a systematic film criticism by posing analogies to literature, they assigned the role of author to the director.

Yet, if it would be absurd to exclude the manner of visual presentation from evaluation of the cinema, it is equally absurd to confine all examinations of that multifarious art to a grammar of images. At issue is not the rival claims for the primacy of the word or picture but the recognition that both serve within a narrative context. First and last, the fictive film tells a story. Although numerous mediate acts affect it aesthetically, its radical meaning, like that of a story related through any other medium, resides in its metaphoric character as a fiction. Notwithstanding the objections lodged by the school of film criticism that insists on inventing wholly idiosyncratic principles, or, from the opposite quarter, the cavils of etymological purists who would reserve the term to traditional forms of literature, inquiry into how that meaning is made manifest through story is a function of literary criticism.

The argument for employing a "literary" perspective becomes all the more cogent when the filmmaker is Ingmar Bergman. Cinema, like the theater, is a collaborative enterprise in which the writer and the director are the principal architects of a work's statement. In most instances, these roles are quite distinct—thus allowing for separate evaluation of their contributions. (Indeed, the *politique des auteurs* movement fastened on the fact that, under the studio system, a director often rendered a personal statement from the cliché-ridden scripts to which he was assigned; accordingly, much like the assembler of collages who transforms his materials, he was the real artist.) In contrast, Bergman, with few exceptions, has worked from his own scripts; the reification of his words before the camera represents a later phase of a continuous creative act, a refinement of a single text by its single author.

For altogether different reasons, critics have been referring to Bergman as a literary filmmaker ever since he sprang to the world's notice in the mid-'fifties; what they have meant by that description, however, has shifted over the years. Initially, it indicated his interest in the kinds of questions traditionally explored by major writers; such films as *The Seventh Seal* seemed better suited for comparison with Goethe, Dostoyevski, Strindberg, Kierkegaard, and Camus than with the ephemera of popular culture produced by the motion picture industry. Next, when the revolutionary films of Antonioni and the younger generation of French directors had set the fashion among intellectual film buffs at the start of the 'sixties, calling Bergman literary was a disparagement that underscored his continuing indebtedness to the theater. The subsequent change in his approach to cinema—evident first in *The Silence* and then, emphatically, in *Persona*— undermined the criticism, yet the label survived. His films after the mid-'sixties reduced action to a minimum and subordinated it to the camera's intense study of the face during long monologues; thus, "literary" now implied his concentration on words at the expense of a rhetoric of images.

Although there is a measure of misassessment—and, following the

first phase of his international success, of invidious bias—in the critics'
judgments, they nonetheless point to a fundamental truth: that Bergman's
films witness his conception of himself as a writer. From his adolescence through his twenties and early thirties, even as he pursued his
first career as a director in the theater, Bergman nurtured the dream that
he would be the new Strindberg; only after it became apparent that his
hopes as a dramatist and novelist would never be realized did he commit himself to motion pictures as something more than an opportunity
to invest the excess of his creative energy. Even then, filmmaking did not
actually displace his initial ambitions; in effect, the camera became an
extension of his pen.

Over four decades, Bergman's fictions have displayed remarkable
variety: their settings range from the newly Christianized Sweden of the
thirteenth century to the war-ravaged landscape of a near future; their
protagonists, from adolescents struggling for a place in the bewildering
world of adults to an old man revisiting his youth in the course of
weighing his life's worth; their styles, from low and high comedy to
slow-moving modern versions of religious drama. Yet, throughout this
diversity, the operation of a singular imagination is evident. Numerous
critics have tried to identify the thematic nexus that distinguishes his
work, and, depending on which aspects they choose to stress, they have
written about the search for God or the flight from God; the pleading for
the alienated artist or the attack on art for its vapidity; the horror over
the apocalyptic disintegration of our society or the morbid fascination
with its decline; the veneration of the Female or the essential misogyny
in his portrayal of women; the rejection of bourgeois values or the
nostalgia for the vanished milieu they once governed. Although this
study comments on these same recurring (and apparently contradictory)
motifs, it also recognizes them as surrogates for conflicts lodged deep in
Bergman's personal history. The relationship of that inner drama to the
artistic creation agitated by it is my central subject.

In proposing examination of the artist in order to understand the art,
I am not arguing that Bergman's artistic achievements will thereby be
enlarged or diminished, or that his films are aesthetically incomplete
without knowledge of the circumstances giving rise to them. But our
critical attentions to a work are not solely devoted to its evaluation, and
our curiosity neither starts nor stops at the discovery of how the processes of art integrate the elements of an isolated composition. When an
initial exposure to an artist engages our interest, we seek out his other
works. If we are at all alert, each succeeding encounter should train our

sensitivity to the concerns of his art; we become aware of his evolution in refining both what he wants his content to express and the formal means to render it. Gradually, the dichotomy between the artistic act and its reception by us as audience fades as we begin to enter the work from its maker's perspective and attempt to account for the peculiar features of his creation; on the one hand, study of the art yields insight into the artist; on the other, knowledge of the artist guides the inquiry into the art.

In the case of Bergman, the critical commentary has tended to view the films in the light of the filmmaker's life ever since he began his career. He invites the practice, for even though he has not adopted autobiography as a generic model for cinema in the manner of a Fellini or a Truffaut, the autobiographical impulse has been unmistakable: the preoccupation with adolescent revolt in his early films (and with the problematical relationships of children and parents in his later ones) obviously derives from his own troubled passage through the early years of his life; the attraction to theological questioning seems a natural consequence of being the son of one of Sweden's most prominent ministers; the recurrent scrutinizing of the artist vis-à-vis society clearly reflects both an aggressive justification of his profession and a profound doubt about its value in the contemporary world. Moreover, throughout a lifetime of interviews and other public statements, Bergman has not only confirmed the self-portraiture in these broad strokes but also freely indicated details from his past that have been seminal in the development of scripts. Yet merely to note the biographical correlations, as previous studies have done, has a limited usefulness: although it furnishes a gloss to the content of his fictions, it overlooks the more intriguing questions pertaining to the complex involvement of the self in the operation of that content as metaphor and in the relationship of metaphor to form.

In beginning this project seventeen years ago, I intended to write a series of related essays that, in tracing Bergman's career and artistic development, elucidated the construction of meaning in each of his works. I had no preconceived method to impose, no single critical theory to illustrate, no thesis to ride. In general, I have persisted in that original intent to allow Bergman's own practice, rather than a particular interpretive framework, to determine the course of my attentions; even so, a central conception evolved. I realized early on that whatever the concerns of Bergman's dramatic material may outwardly appear to be, they conceal a rudimentary personal myth, akin to dream in its symbolic language. As the study progressed, I concluded that no attempt to explain the dynamics of his fictions, even in their public aspect, could ignore the elementary psychic fantasy at their core. To the extent to which I focus on this internal symbolism, the book is psychoanalytically oriented.

The justification for any critical exercise, of course, consists in its contribution to our understanding of its subject. Although my analysis of Bergman's works, in almost all instances, yields interpretations that diverge markedly from those offered by other critics, the motivation was not to arrive at provocatively novel results but to raise to higher relief the design that steered their maker's imagination. With this in view, even such often-discussed films as *Smiles of the Summer Night*, *Wild Strawberries*, *Through a Glass Darkly*, and *Cries and Whispers* reveal quite different contours of meaning, and films that have been dismissed as aberrant bagatelles (like *Not to Speak of All These Women*) fall into place as expressions of the same abiding myth.

But my approach does not only serve to clarify the individual films; it also illuminates what underlies the various phases in Bergman's career. That his films show a sudden artistic maturation at the start of the 'fifties is not entirely (or even principally) because he at long last masters his cinematic craft. Although the early films build on psychological conversions of his personal experience, they are like daydreams, too close to that experience to liberate the artist; in contrast, the conscious striving for the resonance of art in his plays releases the unconscious, from which pours the true dream—or, more accurately described, the nightmare. The death of his aspirations as a playwright makes possible the rebirth of the artist in the filmmaker.

For the remainder of this decade—the eight years from *Evening of the Jesters* through *The Virgin Spring*, which many still consider his finest period—the energy of his films is produced by a tension between the destructive, nihilistic dream vision and the artistic contrivance that offers rescue from despair. For Bergman, the making of fiction becomes a kind of magic, generating consoling illusions even though the magician remains all too aware that they are only tricks. But by the end of the 'fifties, the magic no longer works, and the filmmaker, for the first time in his films, begins to use art as a means not of escaping from the horrorscape of the dream but of expressing it. This courageous effort culminates in *Persona*, a masterpiece in which the art consists of art destroying its very possibility of being. Thereafter, as Bergman himself concedes in film after film, he can only show the fragments.

The Early Years

The Depths of Childhood

"To make films," Bergman has repeatedly said, "is to plunge into the very depths of childhood."[1] The fullest representation of that childhood occurs in *Fanny and Alexander*, which he meant to be both a summation of four decades in cinema and a symbolic loop joining the grand, final expression of his art to the origins of the artist. With evident fascination, he re-creates there a sensitive boy's feelings of wonder as he watches the unfolding dramas of a Swedish clan similar to Bergman's own. To be sure, the Ekdahls in that film are not a direct transcription of the Bergmans, but young Alexander Ekdahl unmistakably corresponds to young Ingmar, and the family revels that the filmmaker depicts at great length evoke the warm memories of a period he has often described as happy and privileged.

In attributing his creativity to childhood, however, Bergman is not referring to an external reality which the filmmaker could imitate or reshape but to the psychological forces which stimulated his imagination and set the patterns of its operation. And despite the many occasions on which he has remembered his early years as a golden time, he has spoken more frequently, and more vividly, of their horrors — of systematic humiliation, of an abiding guilt, of painful insecurity and profound feelings of rejection. That he somehow managed to survive, he has said, was close to a miracle; when he at last won independence from his parents, "it was like emerging from an iron lung and finally being able to breathe for oneself."[2] The mood at the beginning and end of *Fanny and Alexander* may reflect the kindest of Bergman's memories, but the Gothic central section in this portrayal of the artist-in-the-making is a plunge into that interior of consciousness which has been at the center of virtually every story, play, and film he has written.

Bergman states that an examination of his films, "from one end to the other," will show "what I have always strongly felt": that "the practice of art is an exorcism, a ritual act, an intercession, a satisfaction of the inner need."[3] Close examination of the metaphoric patterns through which those functions are expressed will also show that what needs to be exorcized, ritualistically mediated, or satisfied traces back to his relationship with his parents. No factor in Bergman's life has had a greater or more persistent effect on his dreamlike creativity. If any attempt to understand the imagination at work in his films must lead to his childhood, the understanding of that childhood leads to his parents.

His father, Erik Bergman, was the son of a pharmacist who died while Erik was still a boy. That death and the subsequent death of a younger sister seem to have had a pronounced effect not only on Erik's temperament but also on his choice of profession. Intrigued by the solemnity of the burial rite, the lonely boy made playing minister at pretend funerals his favorite game; eventually, the game matured into a determination to study theology.

After enrolling at the University of Uppsala, he paid a call on the Åkerbloms, relatives who lived in town, and quickly fell in love with his second cousin Karin. It would not be an easy courtship.

Although both had similar ancestries — grandfathers and great grandfathers on each side had been pastors and distinguished schoolmen — the Åkerbloms were a rung above the Bergmans on the social ladder. Karin's mother, Anna, who taught French in Uppsala at one point, was an unusually intelligent woman with a deeply religious personality.* The man she married, a widower, twenty years her senior, with three sons, was an enterprising businessman: among his other accomplishments, Johan Åkerblom had built the South Dalarna Railway. The obstacle to the divinity student's suit was not social, however. From the start, Anna Åkerblom deeply disliked the young man who was calling on her daughter — and he reciprocated her feelings. When Karin and Erik began

---

*Among Anna's family were several intellectuals. Her father, Ernst Gottfried Calwagen, a descendant of the Walloons who had emigrated to Sweden in the seventeenth century, had been a distinguished linguist and grammarian. From him, she inherited not only a facility for languages but also the traits which have given the Swedish Walloons a reputation for cleverness and industry.

thinking of marriage, the mother's objections went beyond personal antagonism. Johan Åkerblom was afflicted with a rare progressive muscular atrophy, a hereditary disease also present in Erik's family. A marriage between these cousins would increase the odds that the trait would surface in their children. (In fact, Erik carried the disease, which manifested itself in his later life and eventually led to his death. And Anna's concern would prove prophetic: Dag, the couple's first child, fell victim to the disorder and sat totally paralyzed for nearly twenty years before he died of it in 1984.) In addition, the family showed a disquieting history of "nervous instability." One of Johan Åkerblom's sons by his first marriage, also named Johan, had fallen in love with his stepmother during his adolescence; schizophrenia developed, and for the rest of his life he suffered from delusions of grandeur. But Karin would not be swayed, and in the end, virtually defying her mother, she accepted Erik's proposal. After his ordination, they married when he secured a post as a chaplain in Forsbacka, a small community of ironworkers near Gävle—a town in which he had spent much of his childhood.

A few years later, the couple left the rural village for Stockholm, where Erik was employed as a curate in the Östermalm district's grand Hedvig Eleonora church. For him, being in the capital meant an exciting change, and he derived great satisfaction from his work. For Karin, however, these were trying years. Although she knew she could always count on financial support from her mother in Uppsala, her husband's salary could just meagerly support the family that slowly grew. In addition, the World War caused a food shortage in Sweden—a land that then, even more than now, depended on imported commodities; rations were so tight that parts of the country suffered severe hunger. To be sure, the Bergmans were more fortunate than most. After the birth of their second child, Ernst Ingmar, on July 14, 1918, the christening was celebrated at Våroms, Anna Åkerblom's country villa, where there were plenty of eggs for the cake.* Even so, the consequences of these depressing conditions on the young clergyman's parishioners taxed his energy. And the devastating effects of the worldwide influenza epidemic that struck in three waves between June 1918 and February 1919 were far worse: in the fall and again in the winter, Erik Bergman was steadily engaged in visiting the sick and consoling the families of those he buried.

Within a few years the marriage was showing signs of internal strain. In church, Erik Bergman won everyone's affection. He was the town's

---

*Although his parents were living in Stockholm, Ingmar was born in the Academic Hospital in Uppsala, a short walk from his grandmother's flat.

best-loved minister as well as a handsome man who attracted the admiration of women of all ages. At home, he was the subordinate figure: it was his wife "who first and last ran everything"—although "always within the constrained framework placed on everything by [his] work and status."[4] Their fundamentally dissimilar emotional and intellectual characters exacerbated tensions. A novel by Ingmar's sister Margareta captures the atmosphere in a passage she introduces as "a sort of folksong about primaeval post-war Östermalm":

> Both Father and Mother were artistically gifted. Mother could —should—have been a tragedienne, Father a poet. Two incompatible temperaments! Two desperately unhappy, imperfect human beings, either of whom, alone or with some other life-partner, could perhaps have been brought to marvellous fruition; but whose talents were stunted, etiolated, watered down and crushed by the mutually destructive life-style they created for themselves....
>
> Should it ever cross my mind to send my folksong to the printer's, I should first have to explain to the gentle reader how Father's days usually started in a state of incomprehensible gaiety. Splashing, whistling, jubilantly singing fragments of seasonal chorales. *A rose from Jesse's rod has blossomed* or *Now in this lovely summer time* as the case might be, he'd take an ice-cold shower, shave, and brush his teeth with the same frenzy as other men in quite different cultural and social circles pass the early morning hours enjoying their wives or mistresses. Probably the comparison isn't as outrageous as it may seem. Because year in and year out poor Father, clergyman of the State Lutheran Church as he was, lived on a minimum erotic subsistence level.
>
> But Mother, she suffered from insomnia. After spending half the night indulging one of her few vices—reading—and having managed during the small hours with the aid of sleeping tablets to scrape together a few hours sleep, she'd come stumbling in to breakfast only half-awake and in a state of extreme nervous irritability, there to find her freshly-washed, matitudinally cheerful husband standing as hungry as a hunter behind his chair at the breakfast table, gold watch in hand and waiting for the porridge to be served up, followed by a hash of ham and fried potatoes with fried eggs and pickled beetroot etc., to say nothing of Lalla's witches' brew known as coffee. Nine o'clock, on the dot! Set on so fateful a collision course, the impact as these two heavenly bodies met was

stupendous—and unavoidable. Sometimes, it's true, God intervened and averted it. But mostly His mind, alas, seemed to have wandered to other matters. And then, between these two diametrically opposed morning temperaments, arose an unbearable tension. Controlled at first by Mother's yawns and Father's ever more forced and brittle cheerfulness, it gave rise, sooner or later, to an—for us children —unbearable silence: a silence which in turn, as the meal approached its end, would explode into a grandiose quarrel, of which Malin and I were doomed to be witnesses or—even worse—be dragged in as participants; cross-examined as to *who* had said this or *who* had said that—*who* was in the wrong and who in the right?*[5]

Given force by the pressure of hiding her unhappiness under the facade of being a minister's contented wife, Karin's passionate nature eventually found release in love for Torsten Bohlin—another minister, who would later become a bishop and a theologian of some renown. The romance burst into the open around 1925. (Emotionally, it was a wrenching year for Karin. Ernst, her only full brother, was killed in an airplane crash in August.) For a while there was a possibility that she and Bohlin would run off together, and in tempestuous clashes the Bergmans talked of a divorce. But her lover, perhaps assessing the damage that would ensue, appears to have had second thoughts, and she also understood the consequences a divorce would have for her children and what the taint of scandal would mean for someone from her social background. The emotional breach between husband and wife did not heal quickly, however. Erik, a hypersensitive man already exhausted from carrying a heavy burden of clerical duties, became "pathologically jealous" and suffered a grave nervous breakdown that continued to affect his health for the next five years. Karin also contin-

---

*I am deeply indebted to Margareta Bergman, not only for permitting quotation of a long passage from her novel but also for reading the penultimate draft of this biographical chapter. She has corrected numerous mistakes concerning the family that were gleaned from published accounts. Most generously, she has also supplied additional information.

Miss Bergman cautions readers of her novel to bear in mind that it is not autobiography but a work of fiction "which among other things includes a tragi-comic picture of a family which have much in common with the Bergmans." The section above quotes those lines marked by Miss Bergman in a photocopy to indicate what "really can be said to apply to our parents." Next to the word "tragedienne," however, she notes: "not actress, rather 'producer'"—presumably meaning not a theatrical producer but a writer of tragedies.

On the side steps of the Sophiahem parsonage. Karin Bergman holds Ingmar (then called "Putte" by the family) on her lap; Dag is standing at the rail.

Karin Bergman's last passport photograph.

Photograph of Erik Bergman accompanying his obituary in the *Hedvig Eleonora Församlingsblad.*

ued to feel the repercussions. Margareta remembers that both parents were "frequently absent for longish periods at a time, my father in nursing homes; likewise my mother. The psychoneurotic storms of that time must have been terrible indeed."[6] A diary found among her clothes in a drawer after her death in 1966 would disclose the anguished thoughts of the woman who struggled to play her part as a minister's wife. On reading these painful confessions, Ingmar marveled at "how she hid and endured her weariness, her desperation, her boredom and despair . . . [which] she had recorded in greatest secrecy, day by day, concisely, cryptically with abbreviations and microscopic illustrations. And in another diary, predating this one, she had for several years written even more secret notes telling, with daring candor, of her innermost, guilt-ridden feelings."*[7]

Shortly before the romance between Karin and Bohlin erupted, a major change had occurred in the family's circumstances after the Queen, impressed by a sermon she had heard Erik Bergman preach, recommended that he be installed as chaplain at Sophiahemmet. Since this private hospital had maintained ties to the Royal Family from the time of its founding in the eighteenth century, the appointment implied future promotion for the minister. Of greater immediate importance, the post furnished the family with their first parsonage in Stockholm. Though only a short walk from the heart of the city on what was then its outermost rim, the house had a commodious farm kitchen, a great living room hearth, and an almost rural setting within the hospital park that adjoined Little Jan's Wood.

But Ingmar's recollections of the ten years spent at Sophiahemmet are less colored by its idyllic surroundings than by an aching loneliness, by the feeling that he was conspicuously different from other children, by unhappy submission to the protocol his father's office imposed on the family, and, above all else, by a sense of dread. Sophiahemmet could supply a child's imagination with ample cause for fright. One of its buildings stored corpses until they were taken away for burial, and in the hospital's basement the boy watched as bins of arms, legs, and organs gathered from the surgeries were dumped onto the glowing coals of the incinerator. These sights, however, he found morbidly fascinating. His fears focused instead on the parsonage, which darkness transformed into a theater for his insecurity and guilt.

---

*Margareta persuasively denies that her brother ever read the intimate, second diary, which she says was left, wrapped in brown paper, "explicitly 'to Margareta after my death, or to be burnt.'"[8]

The nursery had an ordinary black blind which, when drawn, made everything alive and frightening: the toys changed and became unfriendly or just unrecognizable. It was a different world without mother—a noiseless, isolated, lonely world. The blind did not exactly move and no shadows showed on it. Even so, there were figures there. Not any special kind of little men, or animals, or heads, or faces, but *something for which no words existed.* In the glimmering darkness, they crept out of the curtains and moved toward the green lampshade or to the table where the drinking water stood. They were quite ruthless. They were relentless and powerful, and they disappeared only if it became really dark or very light, or when sleep came.[9]

Even more terrifying was a wardrobe in the upstairs hallway. According to him, a teenage girl who came to the house had told him it concealed a tiny dwarf with sharp teeth that gnawed off the feet of misbehaving children. Ingmar believed every word: "Nothing made me so ready to beg forgiveness for anything at all or confess to any transgression as a few hours' imprisonment in that dark wardrobe beside the stairs to the attic."[10]

Allusions to this "torture chamber" recur again and again in his films and in interviews; it has become a centerpiece of personal myth. His unvarying accounts of punishment describe confusion on being caught in what his father called a lie, unspeakable fright while incarcerated in the wardrobe, physical pain from a caning administered by his father, and then, after the instruction to beg forgiveness from his mother, joy when she responded with kisses. Whether Ingmar ever suffered exactly the treatment he insists was administered with ritualistic regularity, however, is questionable. His brother Dag, four years his senior, often incurred his father's ire (although Margareta has no memory of the story Ingmar has told on Swedish television of Dag's being so badly flogged by his father that his mother had to bathe his welts to ease the pain and reduce the swelling). A gifted child who reacted to the strife between his parents by showing an indifference to his studies, Dag once brought home the lowest possible grades. With good reason, his father was exasperated: in the Sweden of that era, school grades had the force of doom in determining a child's future. Moreover, Karin favored Dag above the other children (for which Ingmar never completely forgave her), and Erik was inclined to transfer onto her darling the anger he felt against his wife. The fact that Dag bore his punishments stoically further vexed his father. But Ingmar had an altogether different temperament; according to Margareta, he avoided challenging his father head-on and soon developed a skill for mollifying his wrath. In a memoir written for his daughter in 1941, Erik recorded the consternation his second son had caused him:

> Ingmar was a good-natured child, cheerful and friendly. It was utterly impossible ever to be stern with him. . . . None of you other children has ever caused us such misery and worry as Ingmar has. He's easily led. When I write these lines I have behind me many depressing experiences of his violent temper and unbalanced temperament. At one moment he can be so frightfully hard and unfeeling. The next, he's as soft and sensitive and helpless as a little child. I can only leave this inexpressibly beloved child in God's hands. Myself I can do no more, so worried and tormented am I on his behalf.[11]

Margareta is quite certain that Ingmar's legendary imprisonment in the wardrobe occurred only once, that no beating attended it, and that it was their grandmother—not father—who locked him in. Erik was a loving, sensitive soul, "really rather a weak or anyway easily frightened man" whose nervousness made him vulnerable to provocation. If, like most Swedish fathers in that period, he believed he had a duty to administer corporal punishment, he "panicked too easily to be a dictator."[12]

But even if the infamous wardrobe story is a complete fabrication, its Dickensian horror does express a psychological "truth" about his childhood. Bergman has compared the "official existence" of being the chaplain's son to "living on a silver salver" (a phrase his mother often uttered):

> [We were] subjected to painful inspection and a continuous cross-current of comments. . . . My brother, my sister, and I were never proper minister's children, and our upbringing was beset by [our parents'] hysterical desperation, arising from their forlorn and withering hope that we might become good citizens, a credit to them in the eyes of the congregation and their circle of friends. Our parents' fear of what people would say was equalled only by the force of their will. Wholly in the thrall of a frantic need to assert authority and pitiably motivated by what they thought best for the children, they committed (completely unconsciously, to be sure) one uncon-

scionable assault on us after another. The threat of punishment lay over everything, and punishment was meted out with relentless precision.[13]

Worse than the punishment itself was the emotional detachment with which it was inflicted and the silence that followed until the child begged forgiveness. If, at times, Bergman has excused his parents for "unconsciously" causing psychological damage, he has also shown less charity. In an interview on Swedish television after his father's death in 1970, he stated, "My parents did their best to destroy the lives of their children."

Such public statements and the picture of his mother and father reflected in his films have shocked and angered not only family members but also their close friends whose memories differ sharply from his. During that same interview, Bergman recalled his parents' attempt to cure him of his persistent bedwetting by forcing him to wear a red shirt the next day as a badge of shame. Margareta, however, has registered "extreme scepticism" about the episode: "That would have been a bit mad and downright sadistic."[14] Why would Bergman retail imaginary events and then allude to them in his films? Apparently, because these inventions serve to confirm the nightmare brewed in his psyche. Else Fisher, Bergman's first wife, has theorized that, from childhood, he developed a tendency to convince himself of the lies he told: "Ingmar still has the capacity of making up and believing his own truths." In support of her view, she quotes one of his earliest playmates: "Ingmar never could distinguish between lie and truth, fantasy and reality."[15]

Margareta has been particularly upset by her brother's portrait of their father as a harsh authoritarian.

Sometimes it seems to me that Ingmar is behaving in retrospective imagination toward his father as Lear's daughters did toward Lear! What he is above all doing is "denying" (in the psychoanalytical sense) the power exerted over us all by our mother (perhaps by "displacing" it onto our father, who was really a weak or anyway easily frightened man). . . .
    Ingmar was his father's preferred son, and in his eyes always forgivable. . . . [He] had a genius for evading punishment if such was in question. He was charming and ingratiating, to an extent which sometimes infuriated me—though I was his playmate—and probably also Dag. He was in no sense a "victim"—

except of the chronic tensions and anxiety which we all three suffered from.[16]

Summers offered some relief from those tensions. Like most Swedish families of their class, the Bergmans fled the city—in their case, to a house in Dalarna built by Karin's father. (Historic and picturesque, the region rather resembles New England in its terrain and in the independent, democratic temper of its people. Until recently, it was the only part of Sweden where the informal "you" was in universal use; its natives proudly boasted that they said *du* even to the King.) Ingmar loved the place. Whereas Stockholm connoted winter, constraint, classroom regimen, uneasy dealings with schoolmates, and a world ruled by religion, Dalarna implied freedom from social scrutiny, the almost unending daylight of the long Northern summer, the multiplicity of nature, and the maternal *lares*. Not surprisingly, Ingmar regarded the province as his spiritual home.

The other house over which Anna Åkerblom presided had an even stronger influence on him, despite the relatively little time he spent there. This fourteen-room flat in Uppsala was situated amid storybook surroundings. One block away, a hillside of lawn led up to the sixteenth-century castle, flanked by cannon and the historic Gunilla Bell that chimed the start and close of day. A few hundred feet to the north, the twin spires of Uppsala Cathedral rose above the twisting streets connecting the old town and one of Northern Europe's earliest universities. Closer by in the other direction lay the Swan Pond, bounded on one end by Flustret, an ornate nineteenth-century inn. Between the Cathedral and Flustret, the Fyris River flowed by the relics of Uppsala's storied past—the pump over the martyred St. Erik's well, the medieval student jail, the old academy water mill.* And if the past did not suffice in providing the boy with the stuff of fantasy, one of Sweden's very first movie theaters was around the corner. Most engaging of all, however, were Grandmother Åkerblom in her tightly bunned hair, starched white collar, and traditional black dress, and the flat where time seemed to have frozen when she and her husband moved there from Dalarna in the 1890s.

A woman who cared little for girls and not much more for the society of women, Anna Åkerblom took special delight in Ingmar, making him feel like a young prince in enchanted surroundings.

*This is the area shown in *Fanny and Alexander*, where the mill, now a museum, serves as the Bishop's house.

There were all sorts of mysterious objects: the ice box, the firewood bin, the colored glass panels of the kitchen door, the steps to the attic where it always squeaked, wheezed, and crackled. There was the ticking of the clocks, the chandelier crystals casting their refracted beams, the enormous china closet with its inexhaustible number of stories about the tiny folk who lived within its depths. There was the smell of birch logs and newly-baked bread, of Grandmother's rosewater, and of freshly-scrubbed floors. There was also a great sense of security. Grandmother bedded her guest down on the ottoman in the dining room, and when the gaslights from the street shone at night, they drew ships, forests, and strange moving vegetation on the ceiling. In the wallpaper patterns, there were also faces, but at Grandmother's place [unlike at home], they were never dangerous.[17]

Everything seemed touched by a benign magic. Once, he imagined that an alabaster replica of Venus came to life; another time, as the Cathedral bells rang and a piano played a waltz in a nearby flat, he was convinced that the sunlight dancing over a painting of Venice had turned into sound, that the figures in the painting were gesticulating and conversing, the canals were flowing, and the Piazza San Marco pigeons taking flight.[18]

Yet, even though Bergman's writing frequently refers to the dreamily carefree summers in Dalarna and to the fantasies licenced by the Uppsala sanctuary, and even though these reprieves played an important part in the boy's life, the essential clues to his imagination lie in the intimate psychological drama set in the parsonage. Within that small cast, mother acted several parts, the most crucial role being that of the inamorata incessantly courted by her son.

As a child I was in love with my mother. I found her beautiful, desirable, and unattainable. I did almost anything to purchase her tenderness. It was no easy matter. She had been raised in a convention which dictated that small boys should be shaped into strong, brave men in society. I didn't understand that; I was a coward, evasive, given to lying, diffusive, and generally thirsting for love. Most of all, I wanted to play with dolls. I was afraid of other boys. I wanted to be somewhere away from the uproar and where one conversed in calm, soft voices. I wanted to be caressed and touched. I remember that mother strictly admonished me not to behave like a girl. I never understood why I couldn't, since it really was much more pleasant.

> I am certain that mother had a great talent for tenderness. But a severe upbringing and a lifelong impossible marriage hindered that talent. Mother became rather rough with both her sons. Her warmth could emerge in flashes, suddenly and, to me, incomprehensibly. Then I would let myself be filled with it, blinded and stunned by it. Just as quickly, that flash of warmth could turn to ice. Then one was completely shut out.[19]

Once, when he was six and his mother was preparing for a trip, he threw a tantrum. Such outbursts were frequent and, given the mother's iron resolve, futile. But on this occasion, Bergman recalls, something inspired him to feign illness; to his delight, her will melted. "I got to sit on her lap, a rare favor. I was permitted to be with her when she combed her long, dark brown hair; she embraced me and looked at me for a long time with concern. It was my secret pleasure—I still remember it today."[20]

Unquestionably, her influence outweighed all others in the development of her son's literary and artistic interests. In telling him stories while nursing him through his illnesses and in orchestrating the family's fireside Sunday entertainment, during which she would read aloud from such authors as Zacharias Topelius, Hans Christian Andersen, and Selma Lagerlöf, she encouraged his fantasy and displaced the father as the model for emulation. In addition to steering him toward his career, she also profoundly affected the content of his art and its figures of meaning. Woman, in the world of his imagination, possesses magical power: repeatedly, women who brace the dual functions of mother and mistress offer escape from tragic reality through illusion.

Margareta remembers her mother as the dominant parent, much more frightening at times than her father, but in Ingmar's imagination Karin Bergman was linked to the qualities of delight and mercy, while his father symbolized punishment and justice—associations made all the more vibrant by Erik Bergman's profession. Outside the troubled confines of the parsonage, however, there were moments of delectable intimacy. Among the sweetest of Bergman's childhood memories were the hours he spent journeying with the minister on bicycle trips to the countryside churches in Uppland. "My father would teach me the names of the flowers, plants, and birds. We would pass the day in each other's company without the annoying intrusion of external agitations."[21] But he also remembers these feelings of closeness slipping away when it came time for the father to conduct the service. While Ingmar planted himself back of the pews or roamed the balcony, often musing over the late medieval wall paintings typical of these churches, the man at the altar or in the pulpit became a stranger, lost to the congregation, speaking in a different language of a distant God.

Initially, in the child's mind, father loomed as God's surrogate; then, gradually, God became the extension of father—and thus the object of both a longing and a resentment that, in his films, focuses on Christ's cry to his Heavenly Father at the Crucifixion, "Why hast thou forsaken me?" But if Bergman identified the abandoned Jesus with himself, he also conceived a bitterness toward the Jesus who was confident of the Father's love, and on whom his own father lavished the professions of love Ingmar felt should have been directed at him. (In this respect, Tomas's "jealous hatred of Jesus" as a rival for the attention of "an entirely private, fatherly God" in *The Communicants* resounds as Bergman's personal confession.) When Erik Bergman took on the responsibility of preparing his son for confirmation, the clash of ambivalences produced Ingmar's first faith crisis.

The demand for attention and reassurance which underlay the boy's envy of Jesus also prodded his imagination. Continually reminded of his vulnerability and inadequacy, he sought means to assert his power and worth.

> I remember from my very early childhood my need to show off what I had accomplished: my proficiency in drawing, my knack for bouncing a ball off a wall, my first strokes when I learned to swim. I remember having a strong need to attract the notice of adults to these signs of my presence in this world. I could never get enough attention from my peers. Therefore, when reality no longer sufficed, I started imagining, entertaining friends of my own age with unprecedented stories of my secret feats. These were troublesome lies, soon hopelessly dashed against the sober scepticism of those around me. Finally, I withdrew from the community and kept my dreams to myself. A kid seeking human contact and possessed by fantasy rather quickly turned into a hurt, sly, and suspicious dreamer.[22]

Bergman's first significant steps in converting daydreams into art were primitive theatrical experiments: upended and draped with cloth, a table in the children's room was transformed into a stage, and dolls and cut-out cardboard figures were made to serve as actors. The "theater" had been started by Margareta and her friend Lilliane Åhgren, but once Ingmar was introduced to the game, his interest in it became consuming.

At the age of twelve, he saw his first play, a children's story directed at Dramaten (the Royal Dramatic Theater) by Alf Sjöberg—man who, ironically, would film Bergman's first screenplay thirteen years later. Overwhelmed, he tried to approximate the wonder of the experience. Along with Margareta, his closest companion, he developed meticulously planned productions, complete with phonograph music. Year by year, the "theater" grew more elaborate and its repertoire so sophisticated that it included dramas by Strindberg and Maeterlinck, among others. More than a hobby, this involvement with drama took on the aspects of apprenticeship.

The closest competition to the miniature stage as a field for his imagination came from the movies. Taken to see *Black Beauty* when he was about six, he was so distressed by the fire scene that it brought on a fever. That same susceptibility to illusion, however, also made the stories on the screen unusually compelling. Soon he was tagging after his brother Dag to attend the nature films regularly shown for children on Saturday afternoons and stealing into the projection room at the *Slotts Bio* on visits to Uppsala. By his early teens, Bergman had graduated to more exciting fare. Although the horror pictures of the early 'thirties were often clumsy and, in Sweden, heavily censored, *Frankenstein*, *The Mummy*, and other films featuring their misshapen kin strongly affected a mind already disposed to seeing demons. One can well believe his testimony that the visions they induced haunted him through sleepless nights, yet, when the monsters returned in sequels and imitations, he marched off to meet them. In deputizing for the terrors of the child's psyche, they were in a sense more "real" than the surface reality of everyday life. (When, for a series at the Swedish Film Institute in the late 'sixties, a group of directors was asked to name the films that had personally influenced them, Bergman chose *Frankenstein*.)

Although the magic lantern he was given in 1927 was an inferior substitute for the excitement of the movie theater, it offered the dual advantages of availability and, more important, obedience to his control. As a powerless witness to the real-life drama of both the family and the parishioners who laid their troubles at the parsonage door, Bergman has said, he felt a special need to give concrete form to the "forces" manipulating the scenes. The "little tin box" served as his famulus. From the plates that told the story of "Little Red Ridinghood," he inferred a metaphysical allegory in which the wolf was "a devil without horns but with a tail and gaping red jaws; a devil curiously palpable and yet inapprehensible, the representative of evil and seduction on the flowered wallpaper of the children's room."[23]

Within a year, the marvel of the lantern paled before the splendor of a movie projector Dag received as a Christmas gift from a relative. Ingmar, feeling that the projector had been presented to the wrong brother, sacrificed most of his tin soldier army in a swap to adjust the matter. The first film strip he acquired—three meters in sepia showing a woman awakening in a field, stretching, and disappearing off the frame's right edge—so entranced him that he projected it over and over until it was beyond repair. The home movie theater was soon absorbing as much time as the doll theater. When a larger apparatus replaced the rudimentary device, he cadged coins and saved from his allowance money until the hoard could be spilled on the counter of the old Jewish shopkeeper who sold films on Kungsgatan in Uppsala. But Ingmar did not just show these simple films; he also wanted to make them. His first "film" consisted of snapshots that he and Lilliane Åhgren's brother Rolf pasted together. (Rolf Åhgren still has it in his possession.) Later he discovered that celluloid could be glued. Gathering a batch of reels he had tired of viewing, he snipped the strips into pieces and spliced the rearranged sequences to create his own story. Another expedient involved soaking exposed film in a soda solution to remove the emulsion, and then drawing in India ink directly on the frames to produce a crude animation.

Almost all children indulge in make-believe, and many devise ingenious means to express it. The psychological pressures within the Bergman family that propelled his fantasies are also quite common. What makes Bergman's make-believe unusual is the intensity with which he pursued it and its persistence long past the time when an adolescent begins reorienting himself toward adjustment to the reality of the outside world. Reflecting on the burst of creative energy that marked his twenties, Bergman attributed it to "the dammed-up hunger of the child."[24] Although the critics' frequently lodged charge that his early scripts were "pubescent" infuriated him, he would on occasion admit that they were his means of acting out his own delayed maturation.

When he was sixteen, the family moved a short distance to the fashionable apartment house district of Östermalm, where his father had succeeded to the pastorate of Hedvig Eleonora (a position which, because of the church's association with the royal house, led directly to his appointment as Royal Chaplain). New surroundings, however, only accentuated his isolation. His upbringing in a clerical home bore the stamp of a cultural milieu at least a generation behind that of the rest of society, and he was keenly aware of being peculiar. He was not allowed to stay out late at night. He loved classical music, but the jazz that had become the fad among the young mystified him. Other boys showed off their daring in the water; he, afraid to dive, stayed back. Other boys displayed their muscles on the tennis court; he was embarrassed by his bony frame. He stammered (or so he recalls; Margareta has no memory of her brother's suffering from a speech impediment). He felt lost in trying to impress and attract girls: he did not know how to dance, and his interests were scarcely of a sort to make conversation easy. In recent years, he has talked about his sexual initiation with a schoolmate. She was a fat girl, as lonely as he, and no nimbus of romance adorned their purely physical encounter; but, he says, she earned his everlasting gratitude for reassuring him of his masculinity and preserving his sanity.

To be sure, he probably did not appear nearly as peculiar as he thought, but in his mind's eye he was the ugly duckling. Retreating into himself, he listened to plays on the radio or worked with his doll theater, hid in the darkness of the movie theater, or took his regular seat in the third row of the opera and followed the performance with libretto in hand. Private yearnings fed on a heavily Romantic diet: his passion for Strindberg, unquestionably the greatest literary influence on his life, continued to grow, along with an abiding love of Wagner. Nietzsche was a new discovery, which he pursued with the zeal of a convert. A good friend recalls Ingmar quoting his vatic writing at every turn, apparently needing "to comfort himself with the thought of being an Übermench."[25]

Against this background, his month-long trip to Germany in 1936 in conjunction with an exchange program for Christian youth acquires heightened significance. A political innocent when he arrived, he at first made nothing of the Nazi trappings in the pastor's house where he stayed; soon, however, he was exuberantly breathing Hitler's afflatus. The village, perhaps because it evoked memories of the farm community in Dalarna, was a welcome contrast to Stockholm, and he made friends with members of the Hitler Youth—among them, Hannes, one of the sons of his German host. The presence everywhere of the music and myth of his idol Wagner also contributed to his exhilaration, but it was the nation's energy and sense of purpose that made the deepest impression. Years later, in viewing the films of the concentration camps and seeing the ravaged survivors who found haven in Sweden, Bergman could guess the fate met by the Jewish banker's daughter with whom he had been briefly infatuated; he felt such crushing guilt and shame after the war that he repressed the memory of the sojourn for the next three decades. In the 'thirties, however, he found the Nazi fanfaronade most inspirating theater.

Compared to the summers in Germany, the gymnasium years at Palmgrenska School were oppressively tedious. The master for his class remembers Bergman as a pleasant, able student, but his own reports describe searing contests of will and a pedantic rote learning quite hostile to his temperament. "I hated school as an institution, as a system, and as a principle," he later wrote to an old school friend. It was an ill-suited environment for "a problem boy, lazy, talented (rather), a dreamy bohemian at first satisfied with the school but then angry, genial in the manner of Strindberg, soundly reactionary, an immature teenager want-ing to impress his hatred. . . . lacking poise and social adaptability, a cream puff: weltschmerz of a typically egocentric sort."[26] Even so, he conformed to his parents' expectations and scored top grades. (His only deviation was a failing examination in Latin, his favorite subject —attributable to emotional upset from the day before when his parents had insisted on his attending a clergyman's funeral.)

By the time Bergman passed the examinations that marked the end of gymnasium and qualified one for entrance to the university, he had already fixed on a vocation in theater as a director. (According to him, the decision dated from his seeing Olof Molander's production of *A Dream Play* in 1935—a classic interpretation of Strindberg that remained the definitive version until Bergman staged the play a quarter of a cen-tury later.) But two obligations stood in the way of his embarking on that career. One, an interchapter in his life, was compulsory military service. With the knack for incongruity apparently typical of the military in all countries, the army assigned the young man with delicate hearing to the artillery. Mercifully, a doctor diagnosed stomach problems (probably the start of an ulcer that would plague him in later years), and he was sent home. Bergman recalls his army days as opéra bouffe in which he played the part of soldier very poorly, yet friends claim that his military service, in liberating him from his parents' domination and giving him a measure of physical confidence in himself, was not an altogether sorry experience.

The second obligation was to enter the university. The obvious choice should have been Uppsala, not only because of his earlier attachment to the city and the precedent of his father's having taken his degree there but also because, as the Swedish equivalent of Oxford, it enjoyed the greatest prestige. Instead he enrolled at Stockholm (then technically not a university but a "high" school). This may have been due to the financial advantage of being able to live at home, or perhaps he was swayed by the presence of the renowned Strindberg scholar Martin Lamm on its faculty, but whatever the reason for his choice, the institution did not hold his interest long; although he enlisted as a student in the literature and art history departments, the closest he got to a degree was the submission of a long directorial analysis of Strindberg's *The Keys to the Kingdom of Heaven* in a seminar. Within a year of his matriculation, he was busily working with actors rather than concentrating on books and examinations — to the dismay of his parents, who clearly had a different future in mind for their son.

A Foothold in Theater

Although Bergman's fame outside of Europe rests entirely on his cinema, in Sweden (and, more recently, in Germany), his production of a play commands at least as much attention as the release of a new film. He himself has always stressed that he is above all a man of the theater. During the late 'fifties, he was fond of telling the foreign journalists who paraded to Stockholm for interviews that, while "film is a mistress, theater is a loyal wife." In the light of the filmmaker's astounding international celebrity at the time, the statement seemed a bit quaint — and therefore highly quotable — but it rather accurately described the division of his interests up to that point. Most of his year was devoted to the stage; cinema occupied him mainly during the summer months, when the theaters were closed.

That the unscholarly university student would eventually beat his way into theater was inevitable; as it happened, a path opened for him. In the Old City quarter of Stockholm, the Mäster Olofsgården youth mission which had begun an experiment with amateur dramatics was already failing in its first project. Invited to rescue the venture, Bergman immediately accepted. Although he had never worked with live actors before and, at twenty, was not much older than those in his company, his puppet shows had served as a rehearsal for real theater. Perhaps more important, his childhood had prepared him psychologically. The need to control circumstances, to exact respect, and to stand in the center of activity found ready satisfaction in the role of director.

For much of his career, Bergman would be known as "the demon director"; he began earning that epithet right from the start. Lacerating criticism alternated with soothing words until the actors, caught between their anger and their apologies, were rendered malleable. Hard as he was on them, he was doubly severe with himself. Not even a high fever kept him from rehearsals, and for all the screaming at others, he accepted every failure as ultimately his own. A company gradually took shape.

The performance of their first play in late May 1938 received both a warm public response and short, charitable notices from the reviewers for the Stockholm papers. The most important members of the audience for Bergman, however, were his parents, whom he was trying to convince that the investment of time and labor at the expense of his university studies was justified. If, as has been reported, the minister and his wife enjoyed the evening, their pleasure was surely hostage to the hope that their son would soon be spending more of his energies on pursuing his degree. He, of course, had other ideas.

To blame theater exclusively for the rift between son and parents would be inaccurate; rather, the theater became the symbol of ever-widening differences in their values and attitudes. The inevitable rupture was violent. A quarrel between father and son came to blows; when the mother sought to separate them, Ingmar slapped her. Suddenly realizing the significance of that act, he immediately packed his belongings and moved in with Sven Hansson, the man who had engaged him at Mäster Olofsgården. The break was not quite total—the parents continued to provide small sums toward his upkeep, and some messages still flowed between them through Hansson—but for four years, they neither met nor spoke. Clearly, the achievement of independence from his mother was necessary, for she had made arrest of his maturation a condition of their relationship. "Mamma was so terribly strong-willed," the sympathetic Hansson later stated, "he had to cut himself free or else he would have become a namby-pamby, socially an undeveloped person."[1]

The most important of his productions with the Mäster Olofsgården company was *Macbeth*, for which he abandoned the mission's theater and rented a high school auditorium. The march of German troops across Europe had Sweden wondering nervously whether its traditional neutrality would be respected. *Macbeth*, he claimed, was no Renaissance museum piece but a timely parable, an "anti-Nazi" drama exposing "the springs of evil." How deep his indignation at the Nazis was, however, is open to question. At the outbreak of the Winter War in Finland, when many of his countrymen were adopting youngsters surrendered by their Finnish parents to save them from the devastation of their land, he was quoted as saying, "It doesn't matter what government is in power, so long as it is possible to go on performing theater."[2] His concern during rehearsals focused not on Hitler's victims nor on Swedish collusion with the German war machine but on how war jitters might affect the performance; just before opening night, when rumors of invasion resulted in the call-up of the draft-age males in the company, he got Hansson to contact their commanding officer and arrange for leaves to keep Hitler from "spoiling my premiere."[3] Actually, practical not political motives appear to have governed the program: it was obvious that a well-executed Shakespearean tragedy would enhance both the company's credentials and his own, and he thought *Macbeth* the most manageable. And perhaps, too, as his commentary on the play implies, there may have been a personal reason for selecting this story about how "a mighty autocrat is cut to pieces" and the psychological complexities of "unjust seizure of power . . . hysterical desperation, fear of death and longing for death, and eventual bloody reconciliation."[4] Bergman himself appeared in the role of Duncan.

The success of *Macbeth* may be gauged by a review in a leading Stockholm daily which not only praised the young director's imagination, energy, and good taste but also pronounced the company Sweden's best amateur group. With such notices to swell his chest, Bergman began to find the affiliation with Mäster Olofsgården too constricting. One route from the mission led back to the university—or, more accurately, to one of its satellite worlds. The editor of *40-tal* (*The 'Forties*), the major journal of the rising literary generation, had been so impressed by Bergman's *Macbeth* that he invited the director to meet with the Consonants, a gathering of student intellectuals; from this circle came the opportunity to direct, first Strindberg's *The Pelican* and next his *The Father*, for the Student Theater. Within the following year, the dining hall that did double duty as the company's playhouse had become his home base.

At the same time, Bergman edged into professional theater by persuading the library system to sponsor Sagoteatern, a company under his direction which would perform children's plays within Stockholm's Citizens' Hall. His enthusiasm for exposing children to the wonders of the stage was genuine, but, in the back of his mind, he also had grander plans for the ninety-nine seat auditorium placed at his disposal. Shortly after his debut with *The Tinderbox*, a dramatic version of Hans Christian Andersen's tale, he announced the formation of the Citizens' Theater, an experimental repertory company. So certain was he of success that he recruited professional actors (without obtaining official approval) and announced a schedule for the season—launched, of course, by a

Strindberg play (*Ghost Sonata*). He even assured "Stockholmers of all classes, ages, and kinds" that they would soon attend premieres of "a pair of very powerful new plays by two of our best authors who are interested in the company."[5] But *Ghost Sonata* failed to draw an audience, and when an abridged version of *A Midsummer Night's Dream* three weeks later fared no better, the Citizens' Theater quickly perished.

Sagoteatern, which would survive to the end of the season, affected his future in another way, however. In March 1942, Else Fisher, a twenty-three-year-old dancer, had just returned to Stockholm after a month-long engagement in occupied Copenhagen. Seeking rehearsal space in which to create new dances, she went to a school in her neighborhood and waited outside the headmaster's office. Minutes later, Bergman exited. Although they had become acquainted when she had done the choreography for Topelius's *Blue-Bird* at Sagoteatern the previous fall, this was an awkward moment to strike up a conversation. But as she and the headmaster walked down the hall to find a room that might be suitable for her purpose, the young director in the frayed corduroy trousers stood watching. "Suddenly," she remembers,

> I felt Ingmar writing a big question mark on the back of my black furcoat. He must have been asking himself: "Can I perhaps use her for my theater's last program in May?" That was exactly what he asked me the same evening, when he phoned. He wanted me to create a pantomime for Sagoteatern. I was very happy indeed and asked him to pay me a visit in order to discuss ideas. "I can offer you a cup of tea," I said. "Fine, I'll bring some biscuits with me," he answered.[6]

Bergman surely thought he had discovered a kindred soul as Else talked of inventing plays for a home theater when she and her younger sister Randi were teenagers. Even though the plays had never been written down, she could describe them precisely; one in particular —about a beautiful tightrope walker (whom the sisters portrayed as dancing on a skip rope laid across the floor), a clown who loves her, and a villain named Bofvén (i.e., Scoundrel)—struck her as an excellent basis for a pantomime. Bergman agreed, and she began elaborating the simple "Circus Ballerina" into the four acts of *Beppo the Clown; or, The Kidnapped Camomilla.*

> In our [original] play, the villain kidnapped the Clown. Transform-ing that idea, I found it much more dramatic to give the leading

Else Fisher in her costume as Beppo.

part to the Clown: rather stupid but very much in love with Camomilla, he does not give up in his efforts to rescue the kidnapped dancer. [And by] giving Mr. Bofvén the ability to change himself through magic, I saw a possibility of different kinds of choreography in different surroundings. The first act [was set] in the Circus. [In the second,] Bofvén had a shop for toys in which Camomilla was his finest doll. The third act took place in the palace of an oriental Pasha. And in the fourth, Bofvén had brought Camomilla to his home among the stars at 53 Winter Street.* There, Beppo wins a terrible fight with Bofvén and is able to bring his darling home to the Circus together with the captured Bofvén —who, after promising to be a kind, not dangerous, traditional magician, is engaged at the Circus.[7]

An immediate success, the pantomime was presented at matinees for a month. Else, who made a specialty of comic solo performances (a reviewer would later describe her as "Sweden's only female clown"), danced the role of Beppo while Bergman sat beside the phonograph, changing the 78 rpm records every few minutes.

*Vintergatan, literally "Winter Street," is the Swedish name for the Milky Way.

For Else, professional admiration and personal fondness had quickly ripened into love. But Bergman seemed to regard her only as a trusted comrade; she did not know that he had begun to reciprocate her feelings. Nor did she know that he was sharing a Södermalm apartment with a woman he had met through the Consonants a year earlier. A published poet with a yearning for adventure—she reputedly had camped with soldiers in the Spanish Civil War, lived within the walls of a French religious order, and, later in her short life, became the mistress of a Sicilian mafioso—Karin Landby fascinated the young man who was fighting to overcome his bourgeois upbringing. She also answered a deeper need by shoring up his confidence and encouraging him to believe in his dreams of a great career. The survival of Sagoteatern owed almost as much to her energy as to his: in addition to acting (she had played the witch in *The Tinderbox*), she took charge of publicity, promoted interest in the venture among the schools, and managed the administrative chores. (Ironically, it was she who had engaged Else Fisher for *Blue-Bird*.)

By the spring of 1942, however, Bergman was growing restive under their arrangement. While rehearsing *Beppo*, he told his collaborator that working with Landby had become difficult. "Well, then, why don't you fire her?" Else asked. "I can't," he replied. "She's indispensable to the theater." Actually, the problem had little to do with the theater, and her hold on him involved much more than her "indispensability" to its operation. Later, in an article about his portrait of Karin Landby as Rut Kohler in *Woman Without a Face*, he would call this "puma's" real-life counterpart a "debauched, sadistic being" who aroused his pity and disgust; privately, he deprecated her "nymphomania."[8] There may have been some basis for these aspersions: besides her sexually uninhibited behavior, she is reported to have been hospitalized for mental illness. Yet, if Bergman found her character so reprehensible, why had he allowed their affair to last as long as it did? And why, several years after its termination, should he have felt compelled to conduct what was tantamount to a public exorcism in *Woman Without a Face*?

The evidence embedded in his fictions—especially in *Hour of the Wolf*—suggests that what initially attracted him to Karin Landby also led him to vilify her. The infernal creature he saw in her reflected his own sexual guilt and served to confirm his sense of himself as a damned soul; for someone haunted by self-accusation, abandonment to lust furnished a perverse relief. But it did not remove the guilt which had caused his psychological distress. When Else Fisher entered his life, she represented nothing less than the promise of a spiritual regeneration. To reach for the vision of childlike innocence she offered, he not only had to shed the other woman but also to repudiate the debased self that she mirrored. Karin Landby thus assumed the guise of witch whose erotic spell had held him captive.

Perhaps significantly, Bergman invited his mother and sister to one of the last performances of *Beppo* and introduced them to Else. As a daughter of the middle class (her father, who had died in 1929, was a Norwegian engineer; her mother, a teacher of textile design at the School of Industrial Art), she reflected a background compatible with that of the Bergmans, and her personality and values were sure to earn the family's approval. Even though he had not yet confessed his love to Else, he may already have been anticipating a proposal of marriage. As soon as *Beppo* ended its run, he fled the Södermalm apartent and moved into a room provided by friends in Östermalm. The dancer was now the focus of his thoughts. Three years later, he would tell her that, for him, she would always be the incarnation of Beppo; conceivably, he may have seen himself in May and June 1942 as Bofvén, conquered by the gentle clown, shorn of his evil identity, and ready for employment as a good magician.

The summer began on a dismal note. When the final curtain came down on *Beppo*, it marked the end of Sagoteatern; the project had been close to Bergman's heart, and he felt very disappointed that it was not renewed for another season. Also dampening his mood was the fact that none of the many open-air theaters in Sweden's "folk parks" had offered him a job—while Else had been hired to dance in a touring folk musical. (At one point, feeling sorry for himself—and perhaps a bit jealous—he remarked, "You have a profession, but I have none.") For a few weeks, he pondered over his future and wrote letters to Else which arrived at every stop in her tour. Then, around Midsummer Day, he made a decision. Traveling to Else in Jönköping, he mustered the courage to ask the question which had been dominating his thoughts: "Do you dare to marry me?" It was the first time he had let her understand that his affection extended beyond warm feelings for a friend and colleague.

The phrasing of the proposal may have expressed more than insecurity. In July, when Else's tour took her to Dalarna, she visited the Bergmans at Våroms, where his mother gladly received her prospective daughter-in-law. The young couple then went for a walk; as they crossed a meadow, Else remembers, he solemnly declared, "You will surely go to Heaven, but I am going to Hell." His letters to her over the remainder of the summer contained a similar intimation: the handwriting was an almost illegible scrawl, yet he often took the trouble to draw a little devil beside his signature. Else could only guess at its meaning: "That didn't look very friendly, but perhaps he wanted me to see the diabolic side of my future husband."[9] There may well have been something of a childish game in this: a boy instinctively feels that the way to win the well-mannered good girl's sympathy is to parade his horridness—and although Ingmar and Else were twenty-four, the child in each continued to reside not far beneath the surface. Nevertheless, Bergman seems to have been convinced of a demonic force in his being which, if she "dared" marry him, might destroy her happiness.

The second half of the summer brought Else another surprise. One day in July, the familiar envelope from Dalarna was unusually thick. Bergman's letter announced that he had decided to become a playwright and was enclosing his first effort—a drama based on Hans Christian Andersen's tale "The Travel Companion"—for her assessment. In this story about a young man who journeys through life accompanied by his shadow, Death, Bergman found a metaphor which would often recur in his later writing—most overtly, in *The Seventh Seal*. To Else, the drama expressed a terror of death that Ingmar had never revealed in their discussions. Other plays followed ("some of them," Else remembers, "difficult to understand"); several featured a character named Jack Kaspersson, whom Else recognized as his persona, and incorporated the puppet theater conceit which particularly fascinated him at this time. Although, in the future, Bergman would exaggerate the number of plays he finished that summer, he may have written as many as eight. Not all were full-length dramas, and only two were ever staged; still, by any measure it was a prodigious output. In addition, he asked Else to read a short story written in a blue school notebook (an indication of an earlier vintage.) She liked it and urged him to develop it further. Two years later, this story about a student and a cruel Latin teacher who were in love with the same woman would be the springboard giving rise to one of the great careers in the history of cinema.[10]

Bergman's immediate objective in writing his plays was to interest the Student Theater in letting him direct one of them at the start of the fall season. He succeeded: *The Travel Companion* was scheduled for a September presentation. Practically on the eve of rehearsals, however, he canceled the drama based on Andersen and substituted a wholly original script he composed in a few days. Else Fisher's account of a conversation they had just after he had finished his draft of the new play conveys a sense of his boiling creativity in that period. The couple were in her mother's parlor, discussing God. "I told Ingmar how I imagined God when I was six years old: 'He was a kind old man with a beard, sitting on a white cloud on a rococo stool like that one'—and I pointed to a little stool. 'That inspired me,' Ingmar later said."[11] Bergman went home and hastily revised the play.*

The Death of Punch, a two-act play with choreography by Else Fisher, opened on September 24. It would prove a momentous premiere. If the twenty-four-year-old author was a bit disappointed that, in general, the reviewers moderated their praise, he could take solace in the fact that the most enthusiastic of them was also the most influential. Sten Selander of *Svenska Dagbladet* detected a debt to Strindberg and Lagerkvist but lauded the new dramatist for developing a personal vision that went beyond his sources:

> There is not the slightest doubt that no other debut in the Swedish theater for quite some time has given such promise for the future. At least one scene in his play . . . is completely original and displays a macabre humor of rather high caliber. The dialogue is handled with sureness throughout and is satisfyingly natural. The author undoubtedly has an imagination for which the theater is the natural playfield.

As it happened, it was not the Swedish theater which immediately sought to exploit that promise but the renascent Swedish film. Although Sweden had been a pioneer in the early development of motion pictures and had produced two of the silent film's major directors in Mauritz Stiller and Victor Sjöström, the industry slid precipitously during the 'thirties (in part because internal bickering and jealousies led to the emigration of much of its best talent; in part because the advent of sound curtailed its foreign market). The appointment in 1942 of Carl-Anders Dymling as head of Svensk Filmindustri, the dominant company, began a process of rejuvenation. Dymling recognized an opportunity in the Second World War. Not only did the war boost all entertainment business by stimulating escapism, but it also provided a special benefit to the Swedish cinema by restricting competition from the combatant nations. Dymling was not just looking to immediate gains, however. A number of the expatriated Swedes had returned home from film centers

---

*A quarter century later, Bergman would have Bibi Andersson recount this story in *A Passion*.

abroad; by gathering them at SF, Dymling hoped to patch a broken tradition and foster the rise of a new generation.

Recognizing that a major weakness of Swedish film in the 'thirties had been its insipid stories, Dymling stressed the importance of recruiting fresh literary talent. On reading the reviews of *The Death of Punch*, he spoke to Stina Bergman, the head of the script department, and instructed her to investigate.* The young playwright was rather cool to her inquiries, however. And when he finally did appear for an interview, he showed no respect for the protocol of the occasion. "Shabby and coarse, rude and unshaven, with a laugh out of the darkest corner of hell," she wrote in her notes of this first meeting, "yet a real clown with an unstudied charm so killing that, after a couple of hours of conversation, I had to drink three cups of coffee to get back to normal."[12] Nevertheless, impressed by his intensity, she offered him a job.

Bergman procrastinated. He had set his eyes on a career in theater, not in film, and several encouraging developments argued for staying on his original course. Having just obtained permission to stage Soya's *When the Devil Makes an Offer* at the Student Theater—which would be the first Swedish production of this leading Danish dramatist—he wanted to make the most of the opportunity. Furthermore, the favorable reviews of *The Death of Punch* led him to question the wisdom of diverting his creative energies to the script department, where he would have to serve an apprenticeship as a midwife to other people's stories. But the chief reason he hesitated was that he had obtained employment as third assistant director at the Royal Opera. Though a lowly post—he was expected to fetch beer and snacks in the rehearsal breaks as well as to cue entrances during the performances—it provided financial security and promised advancement through the directorial ranks at the most prestigious opera house in Scandinavia. Then Dymling himself approached the reluctant candidate and argued his case. Bergman had to admit that, if he was serious about developing his talent as a writer, cinema presented an opportunity he should not ignore. Moreover, he

---

*Stina Bergman was the widow of Hjalmar Bergman, a major novelist and, after Strindberg, the most promnent Swedish dramatist of this century. (The two Bergmans are not related. The name is common in Germanic Europe.)

There are rather obvious affinities between the literary interests of the two Bergmans (most notably, in their fascination with the puppet theater as a metaphor for life). For this reason, the link provided by the widow was especially prized by Ingmar. The next year, following his production of two Hjalmar Bergman one-acts at the Dramatist's Studio, Stina Bergman, as though recognizing a line of succession, awarded Ingmar her husband's silver pen.

and Else would soon be setting up a household, and SF was offering a monthly salary of five hundred crowns. At last he decided to take the chance and forsake a future at the Royal Opera for one in film. The contract, initially for a year, called for him to begin his duties in January.

Meanwhile, he and Else had been planning for their marriage. Although she had had some concern about how a conservative Christian family would react to having a dancer as daughter-in-law, the Bergmans quickly put her fears to rest. When the engagement was announced in October, his mother gave Else her sapphire ring as a keepsake to mark the occasion. Setting a date for the wedding had to be deferred, however, until an apartment could be obtained in housing-scarce Stockholm. Four months later, they found a two-room flat, and on March 25, 1943, the ceremony was held in Hedvig Eleonora, Pastor Bergman's church.* After a reception in his parents' home, the couple left for a brief honeymoon in Gothenburg—a place chosen because it offered the best theater in Sweden.

Else, who had made her debut in February at Stockholm's Konserthus (the principal recital hall—and the site of the annual Nobel Prize ceremonies), immediately became pregnant and had to interrupt her career. (Their daughter Lena was born three days before Christmas.) While she was confined to their tiny apartment, her husband spent his days working at SF and his nights at theater rehearsals. One might suppose that, as an ambitious artist, she would have resented the unfairness, but she was very much in love, and a storybook happiness filled the hours they reserved to themselves. Some time during the year, Bergman supplied most of the dialogue for the conversion of *Beppo* from a pantomime into a play (which, within a few years, would become a staple in the repertory of Swedish theater). Even though they were man and wife, the authors maintained an existence that seemed as innocent as the tale which had brought them together. Ingmar's teddy bears lay scattered throughout the tiny apartment, and the couple's favorite amusement consisted of reading *Winnie-the-Pooh* aloud to each other.

Bergman's schooling at SF began with the adaptation of novels; having demonstrated that he had talent for screenwriting, he was then told to develop a script from an original idea. He chose the story of the Latin teacher. Apparently, the completed assignment received no more consid-

---

*Among the guests was Max Goldstein, one of several German Jews whose escape from Hitler had been abetted by Erik Bergman. Goldstein, who adopted the professional name Mago, would later be intimately associated with Bergman as his costume and set designer.

eration than any other exercise, but Bergman had faith in the script and eventually enlisted the interest of Victor Sjöström, Sweden's most eminent film director during the silent era whom Dymling had installed as artistic supervisor. With Sjöström's support and Dymling's prodding, *Torment* was added to SF's 1944 production schedule. In little more than a year, an utter novice had become a full-fledged screenwriter. And that rapid progress encouraged another ambition: not content to write films, he also wanted to direct them.

Theater, however, remained his prime objective, and if 1943 laid the foundation for his work in cinema, it was even more important to his building a stage career. Before touring the parks that summer with a revival of *Little Red Ridinghood* (which he had previously directed at Sagoteatern), he mounted three new productions. Two—Soya's play and a drama about the Nazi Occupation—were presented at the Student Theater; the third, Rudolph Värnlund's *U 39*, at the Dramatist's Studio, Brita von Horn's brave enterprise dedicated to the twin goals of developing interest in native playwrights and stirring opposition to the Nazis. Directing at the Studio represented a long step up from university theater. Originally, Värnlund's play was in the hands of Per Lindberg, one of the triumvirate of directors who had ruled over Swedish theater since the 'thirties. Then Lindberg fell ill. Perhaps on the advice of Stina Bergman, Lindberg's sister, von Horn decided to engage the "crazy lad" whose energy seemed surpassed only by his fervor. It was a bold gamble. But such is the stuff of theatrical legends. The ovation Bergman received on opening night raised the twenty-four year old to the level of the illustrious director he had replaced.

That fall, he returned to the Student Theater to tend the bud of his reputation as a playwright with *Jack Among the Actors*. But then military conscription of key cast members after rehearsals had started forced him to substitute another of the plays he had written the previous summer. Composed of four distinct segments unified only by theme and locale, *Tivoli* permitted greater flexibility with his actors, yet it was a poorer play than *Jack Among the Actors* and less interesting than *The Death of Punch*. Reviewers expressed their disappointment. Bergman's successes that season more than compensated for this one mild rebuff, however. Shortly before *Tivoli*, his production at the Studio of Kaj Munk's *Niels Ebbesen*, a trenchant attack on the Nazis disguised as a medieval drama, had evoked even higher praise than his work with *U 39*. And his production of two Hjalmar Bergman one-act plays at the Studio early the next year secured his reputation as the brightest young director in the capital.

Through a combination of hard work, daring, and luck, Bergman had managed a steep climb in a remarkably short time; still, the immediate prospect seemed to offer little beyond the plateau he had reached. Power and influence in European theater flow from appointments at the state-established theaters; because of the country's small population, there were few such positions in Sweden, and when a vacancy occurred, the competition practically excluded the young. But luck once again favored Bergman.

Five hundred miles south of Stockholm, the Hälsingborg City Theater teetered on the edge of collapse. The most modern theater in Europe had just been erected in Malmö, Sweden's third largest city, and the government, confident that this new facility would serve the entire region, withdrew its subvention from nearby Hälsingborg. Hoping Stockholm could be moved to reverse its decision, the city council gambled on subsidizing the theater for one year. To its embarrassment, however, no director seemed willing to risk affiliation with a dying enterprise. When Herbert Grevenius, a writer and critic (and later Bergman's collaborator) recommended Bergman, the council was skeptical that a twenty-five year old could command a theater; yet they could ill afford to disregard any possibility. On the same day they made their phone call to Stockholm, Bergman took the night train south and outlined his proposal en route. At 8:07 P.M. on April 7, 1944—the city newspaper recorded "for future scholars should it prove 'an historic moment' for the Hälsingborg City Theater"—Bergman signed a contract making him "Europe's youngest theater chief."

Else shared his excitement. Together, they chose the actors for the company, discussed the selection of plays, and planned a New Year's Eve revue for which they would compose sketches and dances. Bergman's revival of *Beppo* for a short tour of the city's parks further reflected their partnership. But then, after packing their belongings, Else fell ill with a high fever. Tests soon indicated tuberculosis—the same disease that had stricken her father. Instead of leaving for Hälsingborg, she arranged for a nurse to care for their baby daughter Lena in her mother's home and entered a sanitorium.

For the next six months, she wrote her husband daily, but no letters arrived from him. Odd as this seemed, she read newspaper reports of the City Theater's resurgence and told herself that his responsibilities were absorbing every minute of his time. Even more peculiar was his response to her news in February 1945 that she had recovered and eagerly anticipated the resumption of their family life: rather than force a readjustment at a difficult moment, he said, it would be better if she and the baby stayed with her mother in Stockholm. Still, she suspected nothing. Then, in May, she learned the real reason for his keeping her at a distance. He wanted a divorce so he could marry Ellen Lundström —the choreographer that Else, just before entering the sanitorium, had recommended he hire as her substitute.* Though deeply wounded, Else refused to engage in recriminations. "Of course I have asked myself why such things happened," she would reflect in 1985. "Were Ingmar and I too happy? (Sometimes in a too childish way.) Was it too much of an idyll for him? I [now] understand that it was time for him to exchange the rather shy and innocent woman with the figure of a boy for a more feminine and sexy one."[13]

But more than the attraction to Ellen Lundström doomed the marriage. Years later, Bergman would tell his first wife that he had had several marital partners because "I have so many lives."[14] From the moment he assumed his post in Hälsingborg, it seems, Else Fisher already belonged to the past. He had a mission—not only to save the City Theater but also to compel Sweden to take notice of his talent. Over the next two years, he achieved a small miracle—partly through the impressive produc- tions he staged at a dizzying pace, partly through a genius for self-promotion.

Appealing shamelessly to local pride, he opened the season with Brita von Horn's new play about Margareta von Ascheberg, an eighteenth- century female colonel who had filled an unreasonable conscription quota decreed by Stockholm. The regional press quickly spotted the parallel between the gallantry of the woman who "had shown the gentle- men of the Capital what she could accomplish" and the "sacrifices of a new regiment in the theater raised with the hope that not only will the theatrical life of the town be saved but also that those in power in Stockholm will know the City Theater is worthy of the state's confi- dence."[15] *Lady Ascheberg at Widtskövle* flopped when the author herself presented it in a Stockholm premiere during the same season; in Hälsingborg, it was such a success that additional performances had to be scheduled at odd hours to accommodate the rush. Soon, Bergman was boasting to the press, "I'd like to see a Stockholm theater draw one-sixth of the city's population in a month."[16]

---

*One of the matters that had to be settled during the divorce was ownership of the rights to *Beppo*. Since Bergman had written most of the dialogue, Else offered him the copyright, but he nobly insisted that the play was essentially hers. Later, she wrote other plays and served on the board of the Swedish Dramatists' League.

The first step in restoring the City Theater to financial health, Bergman recognized, required the cultivation of regular attendance by the bourgeoisie, yet he also exerted himself to make good his proclamation that he would build "a theater for everybody." In addition to running the theater, Bergman directed ten productions within two seasons. For the children ("the only real theatrical audience"), he installed a program of Saturday matinees—launched by *Beppo*. For the town's intellectual elite, he staged *Macbeth* and Strindberg's *The Pelican*. And for the patrons who felt too comfortable in his flattery of their vanities, he offered *Rabies*, Olle Hedberg's dramatization of his novel scathing the middle class.

Not content to let the plays speak for themselves, he made a practice of addressing the public directly via a page-long column in the program in which he jabbed hard enough at their sensibilities to make them feel the point but not so hard as to provoke outrage. Usually taking the form of self-interviews, these commentaries on the productions and on his theatrical aspirations often used members of the theater board and the chief accountant (a stagestruck haberdasher whom Bergman himself had selected) as lumpish foils to his reckless genius. Theater resulted from the encounter of icons and iconoclasts; if it was to live, it must be "a pulpit from which to preach; a barricade against idiocy, idle-mindedness, cowardice, crassness, apathy, crudity, and boredom; a playground, battlefield, bordello, trouble spot, and bathhouse."[17] He obviously enjoyed the pose of enfant terrible. "The devil is my potentate," he cried over a signature ending with a small sketched devil as a flourish. "One can't help sympathizing with him despite his tail, one-leggedness, and horns."[18]

That a young director who commanded only a three-hundred-seat theater should swagger so grandly before the public was comical, yet, remarkably, he generated an excitement from this outpost on the southern border that reached all the way to the capital. Among those making the pilgrimage to Hälsingborg was Alf Sjöberg, one of the truly great directors in Swedish theatrical history who was then serving as the chief of the Royal Dramatic Theater (Dramaten); his comment to the press could not have been more laudatory:

It has been a long time since I've seen such a performance in theater. . . . I'll leave immediately for Stockholm to sound the alarm. One of my colleagues was saying that Swedish theater lacked stimulation nowadays. Even if I have to pay his fare, he must come to Hälsingborg. . . . This success is proof of the great soul who rules over this ensemble. . . . I didn't know much about Bergman's equipment as a director, but what I saw was absolutely overwhelming.[19]

Given that Sjöberg, while making *Torment* at the end of the previous winter, had schooled Bergman in the art of cinema direction, his remarks might be discounted as a show of professional courtesy, but others who were under no such obligation voiced similar judgments. When Bergman announced his departure in 1946 to join Torsten Hammarén's theater in Gothenburg, he had ample warrant to congratulate himself on his accomplishment. "Confess that the City Theater has been a good platform," he reflected in print. "What were you before coming here? A guy on the periphery. But now your name is on people's lips. Isn't that a good feeling?"[20]

The road to Gothenburg seemed certain to lead very shortly to a glory beyond his imagining when he first took the train to Hälsingborg, but the next six years would prove difficult. Gothenburg, Sweden's second largest city, took a rather haughty pride in its theater, and its critics seemed determined to show the brash young director that they could not be as easily impressed as their counterparts in little Hälsingborg. Bergman's debut with *Caligula* was disparaged as too ostentatious and frenetic; his second production, *Macbeth*, drew fire for Anders Ek's incongruously "Marxistic" interpretation of the title role. Eventually, Bergman earned the critics' respect—*A Streetcar Named Desire*, his last production while under contract, and Valle-Inclán's *Divine Words*, which he presented as guest director at the beginning of the next season, won extraordinary acclaim; even so, he never completely forgave them for their hostility. The deeper hurt, however, was caused by tensions within the organization. Working under Hammarén meant not only sacrificing the prerogatives he had enjoyed as theater chief but also adjusting to a new approach to theater. Bergman was accustomed to trusting his intuition; Hammarén prepared meticulously in regard to even the slightest detail. Bergman had acquired a reputation as a bully who would thunder at his casts to get the effect he wanted; Hammarén, who always kept his emotions under control, stressed the importance of listening to the actors' opinions and of trying to facilitate their work. Perhaps the best illustration of their clashing temperaments is furnished by an anecdote: when Bergman smashed a cup in anger, Hammarén calmly made a note of the damage and informed him that it would be deducted from his pay. Although Bergman later praised the methodical Hammarén effusively for having taught him the discipline of theater during his three years at Gothenburg, at the time he felt as though he were being systematically humiliated. What followed was worse. In partnership with Lorens Marmstedt, he founded a theater in Stockholm (named the Intimate in honor of Strindberg), but neither the critics nor the public were impressed, and the venture ended abruptly when Marmstedt fired him after only three productions. Two engagements as a guest director the next year (the first at Dramaten; the second in Norrköping) were almost as disappointing. Bergman was plainly off-stride. It was a period, he later said, in which everything was going to hell

Then, in 1952, Malmö selected him as its new chief. The appointment contained a double irony: it had been the presumed deathblow to Hälsingborg from the construction of the Malmö theater that had created his grand opportunity; as chief at Hälsingborg, his job was to prove that the small city's theater had a right to exist in the shadow of the colossus. Yet, once the colossus was in operation, it seemed to have been a gigantic mistake: every director looked upon its elephantine, technically super-sophisticated stage as a wild beast. Now Bergman's challenge was to tame it and show that it was useful theater after all. He succeeded brilliantly. During his six-year tenure, he developed the best acting company and consistently fashioned the most exciting productions anywhere in Sweden: achieving on the grandest scale the objectives he had announced in Hälsingborg, he created a theater for every taste, ranging from *The Merry Widow* and *The Teahouse of the August Moon* to *Ghost Sonata*, *Don Juan*, and *The Castle*. By the time he took his place as chief at Dramaten in 1963, he had already established himself as the preeminent figure in Swedish theater. For all its prestige, Dramaten needed him more than he needed Dramaten.

Several of cinema's most prominent filmmakers—including two of its greatest innovators, D. W. Griffith and Sergei Eisenstein—were trained in the theater, and numerous directors, especially in Europe, have alternated between stage and screen. No major filmmaker, however, has remained as closely tied to the theater as Bergman or achieved a comparable level of distinction in his stage career. From his earliest days on the fringes of the professional theater, he has consistently shown daring in his mise-en-scène and forcefully imposed a personal stamp on the plays he has presented; many of his productions have set the standard by which subsequent versions have been measured—at least in Scandinavia. Almost inevitably, one mode of interpretive art has affected the other, and Bergman maintains that the principal influence has flowed from his work in theater to his work in film; indeed, on several occasions, he has even suggested that his artistic evolution as a film director can be traced more readily through his stage productions than through the films themselves. In addition, it was his theatrical companies that, with a few notable exceptions, furnished and schooled the personal troupe so closely identified with his films. And perhaps most important of all, his background in theater is reflected in the dramatic structure of his screenplays—rather obviously during the crucial middle phase of his career, more subtly after the middle 'sixties.

The focus of this study, however, is not on Bergman as a director or even on the cinematic aspect of his films; rather, it is on the imagination expressed through his extensive dreamwork of fictions spanning five decades. That inquiry properly begins with *Torment*, the first of those fictions to reach the screen and the base from which much of the rest would rise.

The 'Forties Films

Learning to Make Movies

Considered in either of two respects, the thirteen films between 1944 and 1950 that carry Bergman's name in the credits define a period. Most obviously, the 'forties were a time for the young director to pass from apprentice to journeyman, for him to learn the idioms of cinema and to wean a personal style from the paradigms of others. Yet Bergman was also a writer using film as one of two principal means of "publication." This literary aspect only tangentially relates to his evolution as a director; his five original screenplays (plus a sixth which, though an adaptation, was so radically altered it virtually falls within that category) retrace the same preoccupations, and whether the direction was entrusted to him or assigned to Sjöberg or Molander makes little difference to an understanding of the psychological forces manipulating their content.

Despite a tendency to see *Torment* as Bergman's film, his contribution beyond supplying the script was so slight as to be unmeasurable. He was nominally the assistant director, but "script girl" would have described his duties more accurately: the true purpose of his assignment was to gain practical experience in the regimen of filmmaking by rubbing elbows with Alf Sjöberg. Carl-Anders Dymling had realized that, if Svensk Filmindustri (SF) were to recover from its malaise, it would have to spawn a new generation of directors; Bergman's record in theater clearly indicated he might have a future beyond the script department boiler room. But the intention misfired. Bored and occasionally resentful in his role as underling, he resisted the valuable lessons Sjöberg was demonstrating. Even though Bergman's films in the latter half of the decade would reveal a pronounced eclecticism, none would draw from Sjöberg to any significant degree.

Nevertheless, *Torment* figures prominently in Bergman's rise as a director in that its enormous (and completely unexpected) success convinced studio heads they had stumbled onto a spokesman for the younger generation. The same instincts that had led to a profitable script, they reasoned, might also flourish if theater's new wunderkind took his place behind the cameras. Curiously, Dymling dismissed the possibility of using one of Bergman's own stories for his directorial debut; instead, he prescribed a sentimental Danish comedy (which, coincidentally, Bergman had included on the roster of plays while he was chief at Hälsingborg). *Crisis* was clearly chosen as a training exercise: it could be shot very inexpensively, and (given a relatively large provincial market) its homily of rural values further reduced the financial risk. But the results upset these calculations. Not only was the direction flaccid, but the public found the story confusing and critics denounced its moral values as the "garbage" of an adolescent mind. Worst of all, Dymling felt betrayed. Instead of sticking to the simplicity of the original material, Bergman, without consultation, had sought to transform it into a parable of evil more congenial to his interests. When the studio announced its plans for the following year, the production schedule revealed that the "unreliable" Bergman had been exiled to the script department.

Fortunately for the crushed neophyte, an independent producer thought SF had been too hasty. An impassioned roulette player, Lorens Marmstedt liked to gamble in business as well: discerning a talent in Bergman—and an incipient shift in public taste toward the relatively erotic subject matter Bergman had presented in *Torment* and *Crisis*—he engaged him to adapt and direct a Norwegian play about a pair of shopworn lovers. Once again, Bergman stumbled: *It Rains on Our Love* failed to recover even its very low costs. Yet the film shows a small measure of progress, not in its script (as clumsy, in its own way, as *Crisis*) but in its recognition of the need for a cinematic style.

In a lecture on "Cinema's Artistic Suicide" delivered in May 1946, Bergman had warned that faithful adherence to the conventions of realism would spell a moribund future for the industry. Salvation, he told the Uppsala student audience, lay in recapturing the spirit of fantasy that had characterized the silent era: film should build on the tradition "started by Georges Mélies, continued by the Swedes Sjöström and Stiller, and resumed by Chaplin, Disney, and the best of modern

French cinema, particularly Carné."[1] *It Rains on Our Love*, released six months after that address, illustrates the precept. Although typical of many 'forties films in its mood and theme, the treatment strains to imitate the French school of the 'thirties—most of all, Carné, whose realistic films Bergman admired for being "always a quarter turn from reality." (Carné was his favorite director during his Mäster Olofsgården days. Despite his hard-driving schedule, he would occasionally suspend a rehearsal to drag the entire cast to a Carné film.)

"Reality" in *It Rains on Our Love* is severe. In the Stockholm train station, David, an ex-convict, meets Maggi, a pregnant, unwed country girl about to return home with shattered hopes of an acting career. "Do you think I can be picked up by the first guy who comes along?" Maggi asks. "Not by the first," David answers like a young Bogart, "but by the best." As trust gradually displaces suspicion, they dare to expose their vulnerability to each other, and eventually they decide to form a league of two against the world. But the world is an unremitting adversary: the pettifogging clergy impedes their plans to marry; David's start at a job leads to trouble with the employer; a government official evicts them from the small house they have bought; and Maggi loses her baby.

As this brief synopsis should suggest, one of the film's two cardinal faults lies in reliance on a mere addition of difficulties to substitute for dramatic complexity and development of the characters; the woeful succession quickly becomes boring and the attack on society it is meant to justify loses force through repetition. The other problem owes entirely to Bergman's "quarter turn" from this heavy-handed social criticism. The separation of the scenes with cartoon title cards, obviously meant to evoke the playfulness of the silent films, undermines whatever pathos the film may achieve. Even more incongruous is the hovering presence of two vaguely supernatural characters: a good spirit (an elderly man with an umbrella—his parachute from heaven, as it were) and his curmudgeonly, apparently infernal counterpart. At David's trial for hitting the eviction officer which ends the film, the good spirit becomes an angelus ex machina who delivers the couple from their plight.* To succeed, such juggling of naturalism and whimsy requires the very sure hands of a master—which Bergman, at this stage, certainly did not have.

---

*Although some of the script's weakness may be blamed on Oscar Braathen's play, and some on Herbert Grevenius, Bergman's partner in the adaptation, Bergman assumed the full responsibility for the trial scene—a diatribe against society too ponderous to be lifted by the seraphic wings that beat at the finale.

Marmstedt accepted his losses and, the next year, patiently assigned another play to Bergman. *Ship to India*, by the Swedish-Finn Martin Söderhjelm, is strongly reminiscent of two of Bergman's favorite playwrights, Eugene O'Neill and Tennessee Williams; more important, its central conflict had affinities with the psychological tensions Bergman had experienced with his own parents.* Alexander Blom, the captain of a salvage boat, dreams of escape to exotic places aboard an oceangoing vessel; the signs of encroaching blindness intensify this urge to burst from his trap before it is too late. His wife Alice, fearing his primitive energy, welcomes the blindness as a form of gelding that will tame him and force retirement to a country cottage where he would be under her control. Johannes, their son, also yearns for freedom—in his case, from the domineering father who has retarded his development toward manhood.

These opposing desires explode when Blom brings home a vaudeville performer and announces they will run away together. Sexually aroused by the girl, Johannes tries clumsily to take her by force; he fails, but later, in an old mill away from the Captain's influence, each discovers the child in the other and they become lovers. When Blom learns that his son has defeated him by winning the girl's affection, he forces Johannes to dive to the wrecked ship he has been trying to raise, then cuts his oxygen hose. As the salvage crew works frantically to rescue Johannes, Blom flees to a private room he has maintained apart from his family, destroys the model ship that has been his symbol of escape, and attempts suicide by lunging through a window.

The major change Bergman made in his adaptation was to set the whole of Söderhjelm's story as Johannes's flashback to events seven years in the past. Thus, the film begins with Johannes's return from his years at sea to lift his beloved out of the degradation into which she has fallen during his absence and ends with his whisking her off to happiness in a foreign land. Ostensibly, the flashback device was designed to supply the happy ending which audiences would presumably demand, but another, perhaps more compelling reason for Bergman was to shift the focus from the oppressing Captain Blom to the oppressed Johannes —and thereby transform the film into a more personal statement. (The striking similarity between Bergman's metaphor of his childhood as life

*The tyrannical father in Söderhjelm's play, however, is a man of iron will. In Bergman's own fictions, the father figures are essentially weak men who strike a resolute pose to compensate for their weakness; the role of the truly powerful, authoritarian father is assumed by God.

in an iron lung and the image of Blom's trying to kill his son by depriving him of oxygen needs no elaboration. Nor does the coincidence of Oedipal conflicts.) The alteration, however, severely damaged the excellent possibilities of the original material. Aside from being dramatically unearned, the happy ending introduces unanswered questions. Why, one wonders, has Johannes waited seven years to rescue the girl? Why, indeed, did he abandon her in the first place? Also, in running off with his father's paramour, Johannes vicariously fulfills Blom's plan; surely some recognition of that irony is in order, yet the film ignores it. But the frame's most disorienting effect owes directly to the son's supervention of the father as protagonist. It is, after all, Blom's tortured desire that propels the drama, and it is his discovery of his monstrosity, manifested in the attempted suicide, that brings the drama to a formal resolution; Johannes's fate (or, for that matter, the girl's) is quite irrelevant to the central motif.

If, from one perspective, the film is defective because Bergman yielded to the urge to personalize it, from another it suffers because he had not yet developed his own cinematographic style. Although *Ship to India* abandons the notion of interweaving realism and fantasy, it continues to show the persistent influence of the French. A borrowed style, to be sure, is better than none at all, and this imitation did have the advantage of familiarity (no less a critic than André Bazin praised it for its "purity"—no doubt because it reminded him of his compatriots). Even so, in viewing the film one is conscious of a style being imposed rather than generated from within, and the various sequences do not knit well. When the film was shown as a Swedish entry in the Cannes Film Festival, some members of the audience hooted, "Carné, Carné!" Bergman, sitting in the theater, cringed.

Ship to India found little favor in Sweden and failed to attract much popular attention abroad, but Marmstedt was still unwilling to cast Bergman adrift. In *Music in the Dark*, however, he exerted much greater control over his director. Dagmar Edqvist's novel, a tearjerker about a blinded young musician's struggle to accept a woman's love, had enjoyed a very large sale, and Marmstedt, not wishing to have Edqvist's formula tampered with, assigned the screen adaptation to her. Through daily supervision on the set, he also made sure that Bergman shot exactly what the producer wanted, and he freely exercised his privileges in the editing process. Although Bergman disliked both the script and the producer's interference, his back was to the wall. Once, in a cocky moment at the outset of his career, he had piously vowed never to make a film "calculated to tickle the tear ducts of lonely old dames," but now he had a string of three money-losing pictures behind him and two families to support.

Almost every meeting between these two men with such different personalities saw tempers flare. Bergman wrote letters denouncing Marmstedt as "a vulgar, snobbish playboy [who] should tend to his vices and his booze and not meddle in art, of which he knows nothing." The "playboy" responded by calling his director a pretentious, nasty, incompetent amateur, self-deluded into thinking he was Marcel Carné, and an exhibitionist bent on recklessly squandering other people's money to expose his soul. Yet, privately, Marmstedt defended Bergman as a prodigious talent. Bergman, too, concealed a deep respect for his "antagonist." Years later, he would confess his gratitude to Marmstedt for "teaching me thoroughly . . . how to look coldly and objectively at my own rushes, . . . to ask myself whether or not I'd realized my intentions. . . . He was stimulating. He drove me and upbraided me, yet he was enthusiastic."[3]

In 1948 the most immediate reason for Bergman to be grateful to him was that Marmstedt made the formula work; and because *Music in the Dark* earned a profit, SF was willing to repatriate him as a director. Bergman hoped for a chance to direct with his own material, and the fact that the company also bought his new screenplay encouraged him. But because *Woman Without a Face*, acquired a year and a half earlier by SF, had become a profitable film under Gustaf Molander's direction, Dymling wanted to try that lucky combination again by placing *Eva* in Molander's hands. Bergman next submitted a proposal for *Prison*, but Dymling rejected it as an impossible film. When Bergman asked what SF had in mind, he was given the thick manuscript of an Olle Länsberg novel and the instruction to render it into something manageable for the screen. *The Gold and the Walls* became *Port of Call* within a few months, and Bergman had another financial success.

The story of Berit (a girl with a past) and Gösta (a seaman who enters her life on the day she attempts suicide, falls in love with her after they have spent a night in bed, and then must decide whether he can live with the knowledge of her former lovers) required extensive rewriting —which Bergman was quick to point out to the studio in arguing that advertisements should attribute the film to him, not to Länsberg. And indeed, several scenes (such as one in which Berit meets a fay lover) are distinctly typical of Bergman. Even so, the film remains a hammer-and-saw reworking within another man's conception, and if, in its social protest, *Port of Call* superficially resembles other Bergman filmscripts of this period, it is because the theme was in the air (especially in cinema) during this second burst of Social Democracy in Sweden. Moreover, despite the pride he took in his adaptation, the screenplay is crude carpentering that retains the episodic looseness of the novel and that, in its varied declamations for social justice, takes leave of dramatic considerations.

The direction in *Port of Call* is only slightly less clumsy than the script. Prepared now to move away from Carné's influence, he fell under the spell of Italian neorealism, particularly of Rossellini: in *Open City*, the young Swede said, he heard "the melody of postwar thought." Before shooting began, he let Länsberg guide him around Gothenburg, a city Bergman so disliked during the two years he had lived there that he remained a stranger to it. Fascinated by his discovery of the currents flowing beneath the urban surface, he decided to imitate the new Italian directors by freeing the camera from the studio to show the city's inner vitality. The political, social, and economic conditions of postwar Italy from which neorealism sprang, however, were not easily exportable —least of all to Sweden; consequently, Bergman's imitation achieved only the faintest echoes. Even the mobility of the camera that critics have praised as the sign of a new freedom in his work is evinced in only a few illustrative shots, periodically interjected among sequences where the motion picture frame is still employed as though it were a compressed stage. Ironically, the grab at realism in the exterior shots only accentuates the cramped and artificial quality of the action filmed in the studio.

While laboring over Länsberg's sprawling novel, Bergman did not forget *Prison*; Dymling's rejection only whetted his eagerness to see it before the cameras. Once again, he turned to Marmstedt, who agreed to finance the film even though he believed—accurately, as it turned out —that it would be a commercial failure. (Perhaps he wanted to pave Bergman's return route from SF if *Port of Call* should fail; perhaps, more generously, Marmstedt simply believed in Bergman and felt that *Music in the Dark* had put him in his "prodigy's" debt.) But Marmstedt took care to minimize his stake. The budget was set at about $30,000— roughly half of what SF allotted to a film—which meant, among other economies, that *Prison* was shot in the astonishing time of eighteen days.

As the first film to be both written and directed by Bergman, *Prison* has been elevated to a special niche and praised as the first of his works to show the sign of his genius. The claim is overblown in almost every respect. Bergman had already directed five films and sold original scripts for three others; the mere fact that writer and director finally coalesced in *Prison*, although obviously a matter of pride to Bergman, imbued the product with no magical properties. (Besides, its distinction as a "first" is somewhat compromised by his refashioning of *Crisis* to tell his own story two years earlier.) And tempting though it may be to use the conditions under which it was made as an excuse to diminish its faults and magnify its as-yet protean virtues, Marmstedt's pinchpenny budget was not responsible for its fundamental weaknesses. Quite simply (as the next section should demonstrate), Bergman tried to pack too much into his story; seeking support for a grand pronouncement, he proliferated detail.

A similar trust in profusion mars the direction. Earlier in the year, he had amassed a small collection of film prints in which the German masters were heavily represented.* The impress of Wiene and Pabst on *Prison* is rather obvious. But so, too, is Cocteau's. And interleaving these influences is Rossellini's. Although one critic was sufficiently impressed by this patchwork to crow that *Prison* was the first film in twenty-five years to place Sweden "at the forefront of international developments," the judgment reflects the dearth of adventurousness in the Swedish films of the 'forties more than it does any genuine thrust into the avant-garde by Bergman.

The artistic breakthrough he had strained to achieve in *Prison* actually came a few months later, working with a script in which he was only indirectly involved. "I began to find my own paths," Bergman later commented. "Here and there in *Thirst*, the medium began to work for me."[4] One reason for this success may have been that his cinematographer was Gunnar Fischer, with whom he had earlier joined in *Port of Call*. Bergman learned to trust Fischer and to rely on him (the two would form a team for most of the next decade). Another reason may have been the subject matter: Bergman was at last stepping beyond the lower-class world in which most of his previous films were mired and into a milieu he knew intimately. Much of the film deals with dancers—and, of course, both of his wives were dancers. Moreover, its motif of conjugal conflict found a personal

---

*The money to buy the films had been a binder paid to him by David O. Selznick for an adaptation of *The Doll's House*. Selznick wanted Alf Sjöberg to direct Bergman's treatment of Ibsen's play, but nothing came of their collaboration. In concluding that Hollywood could never understand Ibsen, the two Swedes nevertheless enjoyed a laugh at its "spendthrift" ways.

reference point in the bitter dissolution of his marriage to Ellen Lundström.

Whatever the precipitating cause, the result was a sudden, new understanding of how to use the camera as a narrative instrument. The methodical development of the opening scene in a Basel hotel room, for example, in which the neurotic yet sympathetic character of the protagonist is revealed before she speaks a line, is quite unlike any sequence in his previous films. So, too ("here and there," to use Bergman's phrase), is his deployment of background against foreground, not merely for the purpose of decoration or to present information but as an indication of psychological complexity; beyond its function as a two-dimensional representation of three-dimensional reality, the screen develops an interior in which to situate ideas.

Memories differ as to how much Bergman contributed to the screenplay, but he at least discussed the project with Herbert Grevenius, the good friend who wrote the adaptation of the Birgit Tengroth short stories on which the film is based. Aspects of the film's theme as well as some of the inserted episodes strongly suggest Bergman's influence. Tengroth's stories implicitly blame the callousness of men for the unhappiness of their women; although this attitude survives in the film, it meets a Strindbergian misogyny often manifested in Bergman's early work. The twining of the two strands creates a despair which, of his 'forties films, only *Prison* matches. The sexes in *Thirst* are locked in the mutual infliction of suffering, yet the alternative, loneliness, is worse than pain: hell together, the film concludes, is bearable because it is better than hell alone.

The theme emerges from the juxtaposition of two stories. In one, Rut and her husband Bertil are returning to Stockholm from a summer vacation in Sicily; in their confinement to hotel rooms and train compartments, they behave like pitted birds. Rut is the more aggressive in her clawing because she is more conscious of being trapped. Age is threatening her career as a ballerina, and her sterility, caused by an abortion before marriage, rules out the compensation of motherhood. Seeing no other escape, she thinks of leaping from the moving train. Bertil's wish for freedom expresses itself as the train is crossing the Swedish border: realizing that the couple's reimprisonment in their daily routine is just hours away, he dreams of murdering his wife. When he awakes to find Rut still alive, he feels a rush of elation. Neither the husband nor the wife will change as a result of the journey, however, for neither has illusions about their future. They simply accept their anguish

—not as a punishment for their faults or even as the cost of love, but as the condition of an existence in which freedom is a dangerous mirage.

The second story, framed by the first, illustrates the desolation beyond such mutual toleration of despair. Viola (linked with Rut in that she is both a dancer and Bertil's former wife) runs from her psychiatrist when he cynically proposes sexual intercourse with him as a palliative for her inevitable insanity. Among the Midsummer Eve celebrants in the street, she meets a former classmate who was expelled despite her superior talents as a ballet student. Viola accepts the friend's invitation to have a drink in her apartment and eventually broaches the question she has been wrestling with in her own life: How has this spirited woman managed to survive without the psychological support of either marriage or a profession? When the friend's answer soon becomes evident through an attempt to seduce her into a lesbian relationship, Viola's shock at having been so cruelly deceived causes her to flee to the waterfront, where she then commits suicide by dropping into the sea.

By even a rude gauge, *Thirst* falls far short of elegance in either its dramatic or its cinematic composition. The first story revolves around Rut, yet its resolution fixes on Bertil. The relationships between the film's two sets of characters seem too obviously a contrivance to lace separate stories, and Rut's sighting of the lover responsible for her sterility as two trains pass each other unnecessarily strains the use of coincidence. The many water images (among others: the title superimposed on a shot of a whirlpool; the attention to a water carafe in the first scene; Bertil's possession of a coin with the face of Arethusa; the crossing of the strait toward an acceptance of life in one story coupled with the suicide by drowning in the other) seem to indicate a complex symbolism, but they never connect in a pattern of meaning that develops as the stories progress. Similarly, a scene in which Rut passes food to people gathered outside the train in a war-ravaged German town, although it is one of the most moving in the film, creates a specious parallel between her emotional starvation and Germany's hunger. And occasional lapses into unintended comedy (such as occur when a glazier who is incidentally present punches the psychiatrist for his ungentlemanly behavior toward Viola, or when the lesbian seems to acquire hairy horns in revealing her desires) undercut the story's essential pathos.

Yet, despite its awkward moments, *Thirst* was a pivotal film—and not just in terms of Bergman's education as a director. Dealing with the Tengroth material forced him to shift his imagination into new areas which subsequently nourished his own growth as a writer. It was the first of his films to assume a woman's perspective. Equally important, Grevenius's effort to relate the two stories thematically, though sometimes heavy-handed, seems to have alerted Bergman to the possibilities of counterpoint and melodic variation as cinematic techniques. More narrowly, such devices as the use of the journey to represent an internal process of discovery; of the world of ballet, with its emphasis on youth, to illustrate the menace of aging; of the train compartment, paradoxically joining confinement and motion, as an analogue to life; and of the bloom of summer as emblematic of the delusory happiness that an autumnal truth will inevitably sere—all of which occur initially in *Thirst* —would soon become prominent features in his screenplays.

As the decade was ending, however, one could scarcely have predicted much of a future for Bergman in cinema. *Thirst* had been hurriedly made while its director was shuttling between its set in Stockholm and the Gothenburg City Theater, where he was staging *A Streetcar Named Desire*. The film's marginal success at the box office boded no marked improvement in his working conditions at SF. Indeed, two of his labors for the studio during the next year signaled the danger of sinking to the level of a hack. His sale of an outline for the wretched *While the City Sleeps*, based on Per Anders Fogelström's novel, can be dismissed as a bit of moonlighting forced on him by financial problems in the wake of his divorce, but capitulation to the same pressure in making *Such Things Don't Happen Here* was less excusable. This adaptation of an espionage thriller (in which he assisted—even though he chose to shun the credit) embarrassed him even while he was shooting it. To be sure, in spinning a silly story calculated to exploit the Cold War mood of 1950, the film managed to be a fairly slick imitation of the Hitchcock manner. But it was, after all, a strictly commercial, routine assignment —and it must have occurred to him that reliance on such "junk" to pay the bills could easily become his fate.

To Joy, which actually preceded the thriller but was released after it, offers more poignant testimony of his dejection. Bergman had begun working on an outline in the early summer of 1949. Severely disappointed by the reception of *Prison*, emotionally spent as a result of the breakup of his second marriage, and exhausted from his double duties in theater and cinema, he accepted an invitation from Birger Malmsten, his favorite leading man in those days, to share a vacation on the French Riviera. But the holiday only increased his unhappiness: feeling out of place in the Mediterranean sun, bothered by the insects, bored by the conversation of the people he met, and overcome by loneliness, he fell to brooding.

> I was homesick and I started to romanticize my marriage.... I became a little sentimental, and so I fell to thinking about my time in Hälsingborg, about how much fun it was, about the symphony orchestra, and [about my discovery] that I wasn't quite the genius I had imagined myself to be. Those first real setbacks had begun to affect me.[5]

Some of that listlessness seems to have carried to his direction of the film. Although there are passages in which he takes full advantage of the camera's unique dramatic properties—such as when the protagonist's aged mentor, about to visit the young couple, realizes while pausing at the door that he would be intruding on the intimacy of their silence, and leaves; or when, in the daring, long concluding sequence, Bergman relies solely on facial expressions and the orchestra's playing of Beethoven to convey his meaning—*To Joy* generally retreats from the visual artistry occasionally displayed in *Thirst* or the misguided array of effects that burst in *Prison*. Here the camera tends to trail the story, recording the action before it without insight.

The most telling evidence of blunted ambition, however, lies in the story itself. The tale of a musician who dreams of triumphs but then has to settle for an ordinary future after botching his chance as a soloist, it is a transparent version of Bergman's reflection on his own life and career during the 'forties. He had decided that, "even if one is a mediocrity, one has to go on functioning. I developed a kind of comfort from this notion —that in the ranks of culture, it is the infantry which is important and not the more glamorous cavalry."[6] After the film's premiere, Bergman's old irascibility flared at the reviews, but even in anger, he was defending his "mediocrity." One reviewer had laughed at the pretension of mixing Beethoven into a "Hearts and Flowers" story and advised a long rest for the filmmaker; others pronounced similar judgment, though in less scathing language. In response, Bergman assailed his detractors for their ivory tower smugness: "I'm not a shitty snob who makes films for a clique of withdrawn aesthetes."[7] Unfortunately, the masses whom he believed he was serving ignored the film. Although he would later damn the sentimentality that had flowed from a nakedly autobiographical impulse, in 1950 he was stunned by its disaster.

Fictions About the Self: "A Shorter Tale"

Six of Bergman's 'forties filmscripts invite closer scrutiny, not for the part they played in his career as a filmmaker but for what they reveal about the psyche that infused their rather naive, commonplace plots. Despite the fact that the success of *Torment* subsequently prompted Bergman to rewrite it as a play, neither it nor any of the others hints at Bergman's later emergence as one of our most literary filmmakers.* (Certainly, none would tempt a producer into investing in a remake.) All churn quite similar material—there was more than a little truth in the sarcasm of the Swedish critics of the 'forties who soon labeled Bergman "the puberty crisis director." Yet it is precisely as expressions of "delayed adolescence" that they provide the essential clue to the mature artist.

Perhaps the best prism for separating the pulp magazine content of these filmscripts from their personal underside is one of Bergman's very few published attempts at short fiction. "A Shorter Tale About One of Jack the Ripper's Earliest Childhood Memories" appeared in *40-tal*, the organ of the 'Forties-ist literary movement; unlike the drab realism of the 'Forties-ists' vaguely "existentialist" outcries against society, however, Bergman's 2,600-word piece about stock figures of the puppet theater has the Expressionistic nature of a dream.

Linked with the story's final sentence, the headnote constitutes the outermost of four concentric time rings. The author's presentation of the central character suggests Bergman himself: "a man who stands outside the gallery and, mostly by mistake, has landed among the actors. This is Jack the Ripper, not to be confused with his English namesake although he too is a man with a past. He is a tall, dark ectomorph who gains everyone's confidence and, in addition, has a knack for getting involved in the affairs of others." Theobald Gangster, another of the "puppet" characters, seems to be Jack's artistic alter ego; if the full story were told, Bergman says, it would "relate why Gangster writes poetry." (This is in keeping with the implication of the title: a "shorter" tale not just because it is an excerpt but also because it metaphorically compresses something longer—presumably Bergman's own life story.)

At the outset, Theobald is urging his drinking partner to tell his story, but Jack hesitates until Theobald, "rather pleased without knowing why," remarks that his wife, Elin Gangster, is eavesdropping. This loos-

---

*The stage version of *Torment* was directed by Peter Ustinov in London and by Per Gjoersoe in Oslo in early 1948.

ens Jack's tongue, but even then, he cannot begin directly; instead, he talks about a clock he owned long ago when he was rich. (The feminine gender of "clock" in Swedish lends itself to his description of "her" as though she were a woman.) Eventually, he mentions Marie, his mistress in those days—although, he fastidiously insists, they slept in separate beds. Marie lived in the room with the clock. One "blue and violet night," she woke him, screaming that someone was inside the clock. Jack grabbed his favorite penknife (which "knew everything about men a little knife needs to know"), tiptoed to the clock, and discovered to his astonishment that the clock had stopped. Suddenly, an officious-looking, ten-inch man emerged from within it and, laughing all the while, asked Jack to remember when he and his son had last paid a visit. Jack, telling his story at last, now recounts his "earliest memory."

He was three years old, and because his parents were dead he lived with his grandmother, "a widow who belonged to the upper middle class." (Jack's description of her flat and of how the furniture and the nighttime shadows and sounds affected his imagination coincides exactly with Bergman's recollections of his own grandmother's home in Uppsala.) As he was trying to sleep one evening, he found a tiny girl, only five inches tall, crying at the foot of the bed because her father had left her.

> I felt wild with joy at being able to protect her and caress her [with my forefinger]. I whispered to her that she should try to sleep a little. She smiled at me and shut her eyes and rolled herself up on the pillow and lay there looking as if she were asleep. I was completely still and looked at that little, little person who suddenly had come into my life and made it so rich with new possibilities. I was going to play with her every day. I was going to build a little house for her in my toybox. . . . I felt so soft inside, as if I were going to melt and flow out of myself, as if my very young heart would burst with gratitude and joy. Instinctively, I took off my nightshirt and lay there, naked, and stared at the tiny, miniature person. I felt a little ashamed about that, but then nobody was going to find out.

When Jack awoke, the girl had left the bed and was running through the deep carpet nap with a man exactly twice her size. As Jack seized the girl, the little man began pleading, "Please let him go. . . . He is my only son . . . dressed up like a girl—we just wanted to have some fun." Jack suddenly felt "disgusted with myself, at my nakedness, at my softness and my recent make-believe. Everything came over me like a howling wind and a horrible nauseous smell." While the tiny boy poured tears of terror and his long hair tickled Jack's finger, Jack squeezed until the little heart beat madly and a cracked rib, like a white fishbone, pierced his blouse, staining it dark red. When Jack realized the mangled creature was still alive, he started to caress him again, but the dwarf-child screamed and bit his hand. Infuriated, Jack sliced his head off with a fruit knife, then calmly wiped the spilled blood from the carpet with some writing paper, stuffed the body into a pencase, went to sleep, and, the next day, buried the pencase in the garden.

Jack's story now returns to the flat which he shared with Marie. The memory of what had happened when he was three so enraged him that he threw a knife at the ten-inch man, who then dodged back into the clock and disappeared within its mechanism. When Jack reached for him, the clock weights fell on his right hand and cut it. This so upset him that he went to bed with Marie and cried himself to sleep in the cleavage between her breasts. But the anguish would not stop; despite Jack's pawning the clock and moving from one hotel to another, the little father kept reappearing. Finally, Jack came to believe he could stop these visits only by killing Marie. He murdered her, he says, "in the usual way" (presumably with a knife) and stored the body in her own trunk until she was discovered and properly buried. "I was quite fond of her," Jack adds nonchalantly in ending his narrative.

When Theobald, who knows his friend is incapable of hurting a fly, accuses him of lying, Jack merely shrugs: it was a "good story," and besides, "it doesn't mean a thing." Elin Gangster then enters bearing a tray with, among other things, the unlikely combination of anchovies and vanilla sauce. As they all help themselves, Theobald casually remarks in a non sequitur that he has probably inherited his own poetic gifts from his grandfather. The concluding paragraph that follows is short but cryptic. A new name, "Punch," is introduced, the pronouns become ambiguous, and the verbs shift from third to first person and from past to present tense: "He knew Punch's father very well. And he often used to talk about him when he was hanged. Punch took part in the execution. That's why I feel so sorry for Punch: he was only a little boy at the time."

In not explicitly explaining how Jack/Theobald/Punch, alias Bergman, became a "poet," this "good story" implicitly explains a great deal. The obvious key to the story (and its teller) rests in the relationship between child and parents. The circumstances of the telling suggest that Jack means it to be both a confession and a justification to Theobald—in this instance, the first of two father figures;* that the story cannot begin without the assurance of Elin's attention suggests even more forcefully that what needs to be confessed and justified concerns mother. This secret is linked with a clock—a common symbol of woman's complex interior sexual mystery—and, moreover, a clock which Jack *owned* when he was *rich* (implying the bond of mother to child either in the son's fetal state or in his early childhood).

In time, Marie, the third of the mother figures, enters the story, representing the dawning awareness of the mother as a potential sexual partner. A curiously chaste mistress, she sleeps in a different bedroom—as though in obedience to the incest taboo. Significantly, it is her bedroom that has the clock. Furthermore, Jack insists on the arrangement (thus at once acknowledging the taboo and protecting against discovery of his sexual incapacity). But then, typical of the fantasies of sons (and consonant with Bergman's view of his mother as victimized by his father), one particularly vibrant night, she calls on her champion for deliverance from that other male, who, unlike Jack, "inhabits" her "clock." Jack responds by seizing a knife invested with instinctive male knowledge—i.e., he wishes to castrate the rival, his father. Jack fails the test, however. The father (whose "officiousness" ties him to the Royal Chaplain, Bergman's own father) simply laughs at the boyish Jack's presumption—as well he can, for he possesses an unmanning knowledge about his antagonist.

Here the story jumps to a masturbation fantasy (note the attention to the stroking, followed by sensations of softening, melting, flowing; then shame and sleep), but the import is much more complex. The episode's setting seems to indicate Ingmar's stay with his grandmother while his mother lay in childbed for the birth of Margareta (within a month of Ingmar's fourth birthday); thus, in addition to personifying the penis (which is at once the self and an infantilized version of the mother whom he would wish to engage in such tender play), the dwarf-child who has emerged from the clock represents the baby. This accounts for Jack's ambivalence toward his newfound playmate: Margareta and Ingmar would become inseparable, forming a bond abnormally close even for a brother and sister (and especially unusual for siblings four years apart), but among the "earliest childhood memories" of the extremely possessive, jealous boy must also have been a deep resentment of the infant who invaded his domain.

*His name indicates one link to Erik Bergman: *Theo*bald points to the latter's theological career and his God-like image to his son. In *Jack Among the Actors*, written shortly before this story, Bergman signaled a similar link in the name Theodor Sharp.

The crux of this innermost section in Jack's story, however, involves the dwarf-father's laughter that evokes the memory. Curiously, despite the fact that he is confronting his son's killer, the father is neither vengeful nor recriminating; instead, his laugh shows scorn, for the real issue here is a question of masculinity, not murder, and the father is gloating over the easy access he enjoys to the clock. (When Jack later sticks his hand into the clock, a weight cuts it. In one respect, this is a punishment for masturbation, but in another, it illustrates the peril of the *vagina dentata*, here enacting the boy's fear that his presuming to enter the forbidden territory of the taboo will earn him castration by the mother.)

The memory itself gives the father an additional reason to sneer. Jack's feelings on discovering the dwarf-child are feminine, passive, and maternal. Moreover, in this fantasy within a fantasy, the sexually ambivalent dwarf-child is also, rather obviously, Jack's projected self. (Bergman recalls that, as a child, he sometimes wished he were a girl, like mother, and could wear girls' clothes.) When the father appears, Jack's sense of guilt causes him to reverse their relationship. Reacting against his shameful identification with mother, he now seeks to assert masculinity, first by shifting blame for the transvestism onto the father, then by reducing him to impotent pleading, and finally (after Jack's momentary relapse into tenderness earns him a "castrating" bite) by cruelly killing the dwarf-child—a doubly symbolic act in that it is simultaneously an aggressive, sadistic "proof" of his maleness and a punishment visited on a surrogate self for the very sin (sexual ambiguity) which his sadism is meant to disclaim.

Most significantly (since the *full* story would reveal "why Gangster writes poetry"), this episode ends with Jack's attempt to hide his crime. Expunging the traces is one way of pretending that neither the "disgusting" revelation of his feminine nature nor the sadism prompted by the need to refute its implications ever occurred. Behind this motive, however, lurks another. Given the Oedipal elements that ultimately drive the entire tale, his wiping the blood from the deep-napped carpet suggests an effort to deny his desire for a sexual violation of the mother ("virginal" because the boy could not accept the fact of her liaison with her husband) and thereby achieve a reconciliation with his father. But these endeavors, Jack admits, are "without complete success." The writing paper with which he tried to remove the telltale blood from the carpet only spreads the stain, and his "planting" of the pencase in the garden indicates that his guilt will sprout, grow, and eventually flower into literature.

The tale's next phase iterates the meaning of the preceding events in a modified form. Although cohabiting with a mistress advertises his masculinity, the father's reappearance destroys the illusion. Jack flings his knife at him—i.e., tries to castrate the castrator—but the father's escape into the clock serves to taunt Jack all the more with the truth of his inadequacy. Going to bed with Marie is an attempt to restore the illusion, but his regression to an infantile (or even fetal) state at (or between) her breasts only confirms his impotence, and despite attempts to rid himself of the clock and to change locales for his erotic ventures, the father continues to haunt him.

At last, Jack concludes that he must murder Marie. Thus, beyond avoiding the conditions that prove his lack of manliness, he will also eliminate the mother who has brought on his problem and, thereby, slip free of the father's accusations. Even more telling than the murder itself is its virtual replication of his slaying the dwarf-child. Once again, Jack is trying "in the usual way" to establish his masculinity through a willful sadistic act—which is now more overt in its implications because it is directed against the maternal Marie: the "mother" ultimately responsible for all the disturbances that underlay the first murder. Once again, presumably, his buried guilt will lie dormant until its inevitable sprouting.

In altered form, the concluding section reflects exactly the same concerns as the story's two interior rings. Through his narration, Jack has in effect become the poet his account of the past foretold, yet the story ends by focusing on *Theobald* as poet. This apparent inconsistency has two explanations, both of which are grounded in Bergman's relationships with his parents. First: from earliest childhood, Bergman "identified" with his mother, and his displays of imagination were attempts to imitate her and win her favor. As the story demonstrates, this identification was profoundly troubling to the adolescent trying to assert his maleness; thus, for Jack to acknowledge openly that he is a poet would be to defeat his psychological purpose in telling the story. Second: Bergman saw his father as the personification of conscience in his meting out punishment; moreover, Bergman's own avowed "earliest memories" fasten on his inveterate lying as the cause of these punishments, the worst part of which involved being locked in the wardrobe where, in his vivid fantasy, the homunculus would gnaw at his body.

The two father figures in "A Shorter Tale" project both of these features: the dwarf-father who can turn little boys into girls* and who haunts

---

*Equally threatening, at another level, is the dwarf-father's insistence that the little girl Jack clasps to his bosom is a boy. One recalls, here, Bergman's childhood confusion over being forced to behave "like a man" when he would have preferred to act like a girl.

Jack for his disguised sexual sin is an extension of the castrating homunculus; Theobald, who recognizes Jack's elaborate tale as a lie, plays the role of Erik Bergman at the inception of what his son would later call "these grim rituals." In order to dispel the accusations of conscience (which is one reason for telling the tale), the story-maker inverts the traits of son and father—just as, to stress his maleness in the story's middle sections, Jack had exchanged his vulnerability with the dwarf-father's power. Thus, the tough Theobald Gangster not only becomes the poet but also is made to admit that his poetic nature is a congenital legacy from his paternal grandfather (a neat reversal, this, of Karin Bergman's excusing Ingmar's frail constitution and dreaminess as her genetic curse on her son.)

Making up stories, however, serves as more than a defense against guilt; it also functions as a means of fulfilling wishes. Set against the clangorous Oedipal conflicts in the early phases of "A Shorter Tale," the familial triad in the conclusion suddenly strikes a happy chord. Jack has made his terrible confession and received, if not absolution, at least acceptance. In contrast to the scornful dwarf-father, "Father" Theobald does not press his advantage; instead he falls into the role of congenial dupe. And Elin, detached from the menacing aspect of woman as *vagina dentata*, not only functions as the bountiful mother by bearing in the food but also—given the milky, egg-white-like vanilla sauce's resemblance to semen and the olfactory and gustative association of anchovies with the vagina—transforms what seems merely a social event into a love feast for a wonderfully harmonious ménage à trois. Even so, having constructed a happy ending in which a literary magic dissolves the tensions at the core of the tale, the author cannot quite surrender his illicit desires. Jack, the headnote states, "will eventually have a decisive influence" on the Gangsters' marriage—presumably by bedding the "mother"/wife. (A similar set of relationships in *Jack Among the Actors* leads to Jack's becoming the lover of the character who corresponds to Elin.) As examination of other stories will show, the use of fiction for these ambivalent purposes is typical of Bergman.

Central as they are to explaining "why Gangster [or Jack/Bergman] writes poetry," however, the rather conventional Oedipal manifestations do not go far enough in telling "the full story"; given the emphasis it receives, the sadistic content of "A Shorter Tale" is obviously an important part of the cipher's secret message. A penetrating insight into this element in the tale is offered by Risto Fried, a Finnish psychoanalyst.

Although I know virtually nothing of Bergman's biography, the frequency in so many of his films of conflicts between compassionate tenderness and impassioned cruelty, reality and fantasy, and the true self and the social mask would seem to warrant the presumption that he and Jack are *to some extent* interchangeable. The relationship between the protagonists of stories similar to "A Shorter Tale" and the personal histories of their authors also leads to this hypothesis. Poe's tales offer one example, but I prefer to cite instead a story, analogous to Bergman's, written by one of my patients, based on a recurrent dream that disturbed him.

In this story, a group of young boys finds a litter of abandoned kittens in a vacant lot. The children take home a kitten each, but their mothers refuse to let them keep the pets. So the children line some crates with soft material, hide them in the lot, and feed and play with them. The lonely boy who is the story's hero caresses the kittens tenderly. But then, while mothers stroll by pushing their prams, he begins to torture and kill the animals one after another, squeezing, bludgeoning, and burning them in an excruciatingly sadistic manner. The story ends with the child sticking his own arms into the pyre until only charred bits of bone remain.

Of the several correspondences between this story and Bergman's, three are crucial: (1) the sudden and apparently motiveless alternation between tenderness and brutality toward a helpless creature; (2) the protagonist's self-projection onto his victim; and (3) the witnessing of a sadistic act by a parental figure who is either unwilling or powerless to interfere. Significantly, in regard to the last, surrogates for the mother are prominent in both stories.

Fried proceeds to link the caressing of the kitten and the five-inch "girl" as masturbation fantasies to the creation of an imaginary sibling self in response to the birth of a real sibling. "The penis or clitoris," he states, "functions as the magic wand that brings this other self into corporeal existence and thus relieves the perceived insufficiency of the parents' love." On the one hand, the imaginary being provides a means for the lonely child to act the role of the loving mother, and thus feel her inattention less keenly; on the other, it allows the child to identify with the object of her attention and vicariously receive the fondling he misses. The displays of tenderness deriving from what is, in effect, a regression to his own infancy, however, do not remove the aggressive wish that the [real] rival might die or disappear back into the mother. The more affectionate the display, the greater the likelihood that it is an overcompensation for, a reaction-formation against, hostile feelings. It must be stressed that the primary aim is not to do something bad but to attract the mother's attention. Generally stated, sadists want to give and receive love, and they resort to cruelty only because they feel so impotent, so unsuccessful merely by being kind and loving in eliciting a strong reaction from the one they want to impress. The child who grows into a real, criminally violent sadist is invariably one in whom this quest for love has not been understood, and whose attention-seeking behavior has been ignored or brutally punished.

The artist who treats sadistic themes may have started out with much the same motives and fantasies, but is able to express them in behavior that does no direct physical harm. To return to my patient: his father was a cool, distant man whom the boy admired and whose love he craved, but who never let him come very close. The mother was a warm but moody and inconsistent woman; periods of intense affection for the child alternated with periods in which he was left alone or ignored, and he spent a great deal of time with his grandmother. Because of these circumstances, and the child's unusual sensitivity, when a brother was born, he experienced heightened degrees of tenderness and jealousy which were manifested in sadistic fantasies. My patient did not become a sadist in the normal meaning of the term—to the contrary, in his behavior he developed a protective attitude toward children and animals. Instead, his sadistic tendencies were directed into a career in the performing arts, where he has sublimated them into a desire to manipulate and move audiences emotionally.[1]

Remarkably, Fried's notation of the basic similarities in the two stories (and the implicit speculation as to the tie between sadistic impulses and Bergman's art) leads him to describe a patient whose biographical circumstances—even in the closeness to his grandmother—virtually replicate Bergman's own.

Torment

Although no Bergman filmscript of the 'forties is as revealing of its author's psyche as the dreamlike "A Shorter Tale," *Torment* expresses much the same roil in a realistic form. Again, and most significantly, sadism is a prominent feature. But before embarking on an inquiry into the intimate relationship between the story and its creator, one should be alert to the distinction between the film and the script.

Despite the tendency of critics to minimize Sjöberg's contribution to *Torment* while enlarging Bergman's, the film's impact owes principally to the director's composition. Sjöberg was the most serious (and eclectic) student of cinematic art among the Swedish directors of his generation; the lessons absorbed from the Russian and German masters, principally Eisenstein and Lang, are unmistakable here. The opening sequences constitute a montage of oppression. The ponderous architecture of the high school's exterior and the cavernous spaces within overwhelm not only the human figure but the human spirit as well. From a distance, a tardy pupil races to the school; once inside, like an animal being scared into a pen, he is chased to his classroom by a teacher. A sonorous pipe organ in a vaulted assembly hall contrasts with the reedy voices of the boys as they are isolated by the camera; close-ups of the furtive cramming shielded by music books intensify the sense of their subjugation. Minutes later, these same boys cringe in their Latin class as the teacher they have nicknamed Caligula strides through the aisles, using his pointer like a lash. Thus, before the story's action has even begun, Sjöberg has pinned the viewer to the emotional center of his film; although the idea conveyed lies in Bergman's script, the energy behind its development is Sjöberg's.

So, too, is the film's atmosphere of menace. Soon after Jan-Erik, Caligula's noblest pupil, meets Bertha and accompanies the drunken, terrified woman to her flat, the viewer has guessed that the sadistic man holding her in bondage as his mistress is the Latin teacher; since there is no plausible reason for her to keep his identity secret from her young lover, the suspense on which the plot depends is transparently artificial. But Sjöberg's use of ominous shadows, combined with shots at skewed camera angles, generates a fear that transcends the contrivance of the plot by evoking childhood memories of the bogeyman. In addition, Sjöberg's Caligula is more starkly villainous than Bergman's. Whereas the script oscillates uncertainly between a sick, pitiable Caligula and one who is a monster, the director creates a Swedish Nazi who reads a fascist newspaper and looks like Himmler in his physical manner and clipped mustache.* Although Sjöberg has been criticized for giving Bergman's story too melodramatic an interpretation, the melodrama helps to define aspects otherwise blurred by the author's subjectivity.

That *Torment* was drawn from life seems to have been taken for granted by everyone almost immediately. Reformers seized upon it as a muckraking exposé of an autocratic, degrading school system unsuited to a democratic nation; defensive teachers sought either to distinguish themselves from their sterner colleagues or to dismiss the film as a malcontent youth's petty revenge. Bergman himself became a focus of controversy. The rector at Palmgrenska Gymnasium (which Sjöberg as well as Bergman had attended) publicly expressed chagrin that this good pupil who had enjoyed amicable relations with his teachers should attack his old school; in any case, he told reporters, schools had to be tailored to the needs of normal, rational students, not to the whims of dreamy bohemians. Bergman parried in the press with an open letter deriding the assumption that students who did not fit some arbitrary prescription of worthiness deserved the system's cruel neglect and also rejecting, as wholly unfounded and unworthy of a gentleman, the rector's charge that he had sensationalized his subject in a bid for notoriety.**[9] The degree of verisimilitude in the film's depiction of Palmgrenska (or of any other Swedish school), however, is quite irrelevant to the central issue of the story's autobiographical nature. That core reflects a psychological distress, not a social quarrel.

The author's evident persona is Jan-Erik Widgren—who, like Bergman at the same age, lives in Östermalm, bows under the parental pressure to earn good grades and to respect bourgeois values, and eventually rebels. But these features constitute only a superficial resemblance; the deepest ties occur in Jan-Erik's relationship with the other main characters, Bertha and Caligula.

*Because of German pressure on the Swedish motion picture industry to avoid subjects dealing with the war or portraying the Third Reich in an unfavorable light, filmmakers masked their anti-Nazi biases (usually by choosing stories set in a distant past with obvious parallels to current events). Sjöberg himself had resorted to the practice. *Torment*, however, is not a political allegory, even though it makes an anti-Nazi statement.

**Despite Bergman's splenetic self-defense at the time, he later regretted the hurt he had caused the actual Latin teacher at Palmgrenska who, it was generally assumed, was the model for Caligula. When Bergman was to be feted by a Swedish television version of "This Is Your Life," he wrote to the teacher and offered to pay his expenses so he could appear on the program and be publicly exonerated. The teacher, by then in poor health, politely refused.

Bertha, the tobacco shop clerk who introduces Jan-Erik to the world's injustice, is a cross between two stock characters: the sensual, lower-class woman often encountered in Naturalistic fiction who wakens the middle-class male protagonist to his animal being, and a related figure (a type found in Swedish films of the 'thirties as well as in the general run of pulp fiction), the fallen woman with a pure heart awaiting rescue by a decent man. But, given the class-bound nature of Swedish society at the time, Jan-Erik's virtual engagement to Bertha seems highly improbable on its face, and the author makes no effort to render it plausible in terms of the story. One is left to wonder what there is about Bertha that could cause Jan-Erik to sacrifice everything for her sake. Sexual attraction would appear to be an obvious justification, but, as several critics have remarked, Bertha radiates a curious asexuality. Fright, not lust, motivates her seduction of Jan-Erik during their first night, and their subsequent association exhibits no signs of passion.

A key to the puzzle surfaces midway through the film. Exhausted by the effort to keep up his studies while spending nights with Bertha, Jan-Erik falls ill. His worried parents sit at his bedside, but when he opens his eyes, he sees Bertha and Caligula in their place.* Although this is the most obvious sign of the real significance of Bertha's relationship with Jan-Erik, the rest of the film leads to the same inference. Like Marie's ambiguous arrangement with Jack in "A Shorter Tale," the ostensibly sexual bond between this mistress and her young lover is actually that of a mother and son. On the one hand, the male child, knowing he is weak and inadequate (especially in comparison to his rival, the father), regresses to infancy to gain the mother's attention and reassuring comfort; on the other, he builds an image of his mother as the father's victim and fantasizes that he will be her champion. (In the latter regard, Bertha's dread of her tormentor and her clinging to Jan-Erik for security correspond to Marie's terrified scream that causes Jack to spring to her rescue when the dwarf-father first appears in "A Shorter Tale.") This Oedipal element, though more intricately wound in Jack's story, resounds with even greater force in *Torment*. Both the dwarf-father and Caligula haunt the protagonist and his mistress in their love nest, but in *Torment*, Jan-Erik's discovery of the tormentor's identity becomes the crucial event, for it is an acknowledgment, simultaneously, of the secret knowledge concerning the sexual relationship between his parents and of the son's wrong in trying to steal his father's woman.

*This shot has unfortunately been cut from some U.S. prints.

That the discovery occurs immediately after Jan-Erik finds Bertha dead in her flat is particularly significant in the light of its consequences. First, the student encounters Caligula cowering behind the coats in Bertha's hall wardrobe and turns him over to the police. The presumption that Caligula has murdered her is supported by his fright and incoherent babbling, but after his overnight detention at the station, an autopsy clears him of the charge by fixing the cause of death as alcoholism in combination with a weak heart. Next, reverting to his previous viciousness, Caligula reports Jan-Erik's liaison with the "immoral" Bertha to the school's headmaster. When he visited the tramp to ask her to stay away from his student, he says, she erupted in foul language, then clutched her heart and died. The outrageous lie and the teacher's triumphant sneer rob Jan-Erik of the ability to reply; instead, he strikes Caligula, thus ensuring his expulsion from school.

Clearly, the plot at this point seems to have escaped beyond Bergman's control. Not only does it produce confusion by giving several false signals, but it also becomes much more elaborate than the melodramatic purpose requires. Bertha's unanticipated death is a wholly unnecessary bolt from heaven (Caligula's informing the headmaster about Jan-Erik's illicit affair would have been sufficient motive for the assault and expulsion), and the circular detour into the question of Caligula's culpability dissipates the story's thematic momentum at just the point where it should accelerate. Only the psychological underside of the fiction explains this peculiar catenation.

Bertha's demise functions in the same way as Marie's murder: it represents a wish to escape from the complex effects of Oedipal guilt by eliminating its cause and, thereby, removing the impediment to development toward a "normal" manhood. In this instance, of course, Jan-Erik does not actually kill Bertha, but in the realm of dream beneath the refracted image on the realistic surface, the events subsequent to her death indicate that just such a wish has occurred. The presumption of Caligula's direct or indirect responsibility for her death should be seen as an attempt to deny guilt by shifting the blame to the accusing father/conscience; Caligula's terrified reaction and incarceration by the police authorities are a projection of the son's notion of his own deserved punishment and impotence onto the father.

But when the autopsy exculpates the "father," Caligula resumes his role as the authoritarian parent castigating a guilty son, because the "lie" he tells masks a psychological truth. The hidden nature of the relationship between Bertha and Jan-Erik would call for just such a warning as Caligula says he delivered. Even more central to the matter is his claim that Bertha rejected his honorable request with dirty words: if the obverse of the response to Oedipal guilt is to limn the mother-figure as the pure Madonna who is above sexual thoughts, the reverse side of the portrait depicts her as the whore who has stimulated and (in the son's fantasies) permitted the worst of sexual sins. Dumbstruck by this "truth," and by the recognition of his culpability for what lies behind Bertha's death, Jan-Erik hits the truthsayer and thus elicts the appropriate sentence for himself: exile from the community.

The argument for looking through the apparent issues and design to a level of psychodrama with a quite different meaning gathers greater force when one realizes that the confrontations between Jan-Erik and Caligula are essentially rearranged bits of Bergman's personal history. Most obviously, the designation of Caligula as a Latin teacher (despite the fact that the original tyrannical pedagogue at Palmgrenska taught a different subject) and Jan-Erik's failure in the preliminary examination recall Bergman's failure in the Latin preliminary—the first shot fired in his rebellion against his father. It is in the film's most highly charged moments, however, that the truly intriguing similarities emerge. In hitting Caligula, Jan-Erik repeats the blow in which Bergman's long-smoldering antagonism against his father finally exploded. (The circumstances of that decisive quarrel resulting in Bergman's "exile" from his parents' home parallel those of Jan-Erik's arraignment before the headmaster: like Jan-Erik, Bergman had neglected his studies to pursue what his father had called a dissolute life.) More arresting still: the inquiry before the headmaster that elicits Caligula's lie is also a mirror image of the sessions in which young Ingmar faced his father's wrath for lying; and Jan-Erik's discovery of Caligula, quaking with fear in Bertha's hall wardrobe, almost exactly reflects Bergman's account of his own ritualized punishment.

The fictional reversal of father and son in these climactic scenes underscores the disguised fantasy of emergence into manhood that drives the story. The conclusion is pure wish fulfillment. If Bergman were governed solely by his overt theme—the injustice and hypocrisy of society—the film would end with the graduation ceremonies in which Caligula stands in honor on the podium while Jan-Erik watches from below. A deeper current, however, dictates an additional scene. Now openly installed in Bertha's flat, Jan-Erik is visited by the headmaster, who feebly tries to make amends. Next, Jan-Erik encounters Caligula on the stairs, bleating about the darkness of his loneliness; as the timed hall-light switch, common in Swedish apartment houses, snaps off, he begs Jan-Erik to "turn on the light." Although the disgraced student has reason to savor this moment of revenge, a combination of serenity and moral superiority allows him to walk away from his triumph.

Each of these four elements has the emphasis of an exclamation point. The protagonist's confident stride into the new summer day after the struggles of his troubled spring is a complementary contrast to the story's opening scene. The other three parts of the conclusion supply the warrants for this implicit claim of adulthood. Residence in Bertha's rooms is virtually a marriage announcement, an advertisement that he is a man—and yet, given her death, she poses no threat to gainsay his masculinity. Moreover, in another respect, her death as the symbolic mother serves both his need to erase the cause of his psychic guilt and his wish to carry on his life as her heir and champion. The call paid by the headmaster pins a second badge of manhood on the protagonist: although Jan-Erik has been wronged, he accepts his sentence without whimpering. Also, since the headmaster's role embodies aspects of the father, his confession of fecklessness acts as a capitulation, offering the prospect of some future reconciliation between peers.

Clearly the most resonant event—and the one which least obeys the logic of the plot—is Caligula's abjection. Played, in effect, before the mother (Bertha's flat looks down from the top of the stairs), the scene inverts the roles of the strong father and powerless son: suddenly, control rests in Jan-Erik's hands, and Caligula, pleading for the light to be turned on, assumes the role of the child who is terrified of being alone in the dark. (The psychological motivation for the sequence stands out in greater relief when one considers its silliness as realism. Given the bright daylight outside, the stairway could not be *that* dark, but even if it were, Caligula is only a few steps from the light switch on the landing.)

This "happy ending," however, is patently contrived fantasy leaping from the dream nexus that precedes it; the disturbance it leaves behind, unresolved, casts the longer shadow over Bergman's work. Once more, "A Shorter Tale" provides a useful gloss.

Although Jack and Jan-Erik seem very different, their names signal that they are creatures of the same impulse. "Jack" and "Jan," of course, are nicknames for "Johan" (or "John")—all three of which Bergman repeatedly employs for his persona.* But the more significant marker is

---

*Several explanations for the variants comprising this signature are possible. Since "Johan" was the name of the maternal grandfather who built the house in Dalarna, Bergman may have chosen it as an emblem both of his preference for the mother's side of the family and

the author's affixing "Erik," his father's name, to "Jan." Just as Jack acts
sadistically in his strained assertion of masculinity (and in his effort to
free himself from his feminine identification with the mother), the name
"Jan-Erik" reflects the notion that, to become a man, the son must
incorporate the father's hateful "male" aggression. The surface content
of *Torment*, of course, will not allow its protagonist to manifest Jack's
behavior; nevertheless, sadism is an interwoven part of Jan-Erik's story.

For all that Caligula enacts the father's role in that story's Oedipal
conflict, he also represents an extension of the son himself, who, in
fashioning an image of the father from very limited experience, projects
an exaggerated version of his own feelings. (The phenomenon may
explain why Bergman's memories of punishment by his father clash
with Margareta's recollections.) Once this is understood, the strange
alternation between loathing and pity in the script's attitude toward
Caligula—an ambivalence which Sjöberg wisely sought to cut through
—becomes much less puzzling: despite his villainy, Caligula is fundamentally a bewildered child crying for love. When that appeal is rejected,
he tries to assert control through the opposite means.* Bergman illustrates the mechanism quite clearly in a dreamlike memory Caligula
relates; it is the most vivid passage in a script fraught with trite dialogue:

> A big cat was sitting in front of a house, sunning itself. I went up
> and talked kindly to it. It rubbed against me and purred. I stooped

---

of his emotional ties to the Dalarna retreat. Also: his great idol Strindberg calls himself "Johan" in his novelized autobiography. "Jan" may have been suggested by "Little
Jan's Wood," the forested park that adjoined Sophiahemmet. The jarringly un-Swedish
name "Jack" was used by Hjalmar Bergman in one of his best-known works of fiction,
Jack the Clown, and thus could have been regarded as a cipher for "Bergman"; or,
as is hinted in "A Shorter Tale," Bergman may have identified himself with Jack the
Ripper.

*Another eccentricity of the script derives from the same cause. Although the audience
may infer sexual intercourse between Caligula and Bertha, and although some confirmation of his forcing his way into her bed would add to the portrait of his iniquity,
Bergman's presentation stops at Caligula's compulsion to inflict pain. Caligula's tyranny
and evil are necessary features, but that they be seated in a specifically sadistic personality is not. Why, then, does Bergman introduce a disorienting element that is never
resolved? The answer, apparently, lies not in the dynamics of the artifice itself but
in the submerged record in the author's psyche that the artifice expresses. Caligula
is the child who behaves "sadistically" because of frustration; physically and emotionally
too immature to command the desired response from someone he loves, he will provoke
a display of emotion which, though different from what he desires, furnishes assurance
of some power over that person.

down and stroked its back. Suddenly it bit my hand. It seemed to tie itself into a knot. It dug all its twenty claws into my hand, hanging on savagely and boring in with its teeth. I shall never forget my panic. I think I screamed. What do you think I did then? I plunged the cat, the hand, and the arm into a near-by water barrel. The cat stiffened convulsively. It drowned but didn't release its hold. ... That's the way to be. Bite and hold on. Don't let go. If I don't bite, you will, and so I bite first.

In its similarity to Jack's tale about the little "girl" who bit his hand after he tenderly stroked "her" (and, by-the-by, to the recurring dream of Fried's patient), Caligula's grim anecdote suggests that both of these sadists spring from the same precinct in Bergman's imagination. (The fact that both also demonstrate an emotional attachment to their pen-knives strengthens the case.) Taking a roundabout route, one could then argue—given the parallel motifs of "A Shorter Tale" and *Torment*, and the equation Jack = Jan-Erik + Caligula—that the antagonists here reflect complementary aspects of a single personality which, ultimately, is Bergman's own. But the evidence for such an assertion is closer at hand. Even though Sandman, one of the students, has no involvement in the plot, he is prominent in the story as Jan-Erik's friend, confidant, and counterpart. Virtual alter egos, one is the idealist, the other, the self-proclaimed realist. Moreover, to the extent that Jan-Erik is the author's noble self-portrait, Sandman affects the haughty cynicism that Bergman advertised through his satanic association. Beyond Sandman's relation-ship to Jan-Erik, however, looms the more curious correspondence to Caligula. Only the gap between practice and principle separates the mentally sick, morally opprobrious teacher from this student who quotes Nietzsche and Strindberg to justify his misogynist views, and who parades his toughness while claiming disdain for the weakness of ordinary human beings.

Crisis

Played by the same actor (Stig Olin), Sandman, now resuming his earlier guise as Jack, turns up once again as the main male figure in *Crisis*. Since the character had not even been present in the play upon which the film was based, that prominence is especially noteworthy.

When Bergman had scheduled a Danish comedy, *The Mother Animal* (retitled *My Child Is Mine* in Sweden), for the 1944–45 season in Hälsingborg, he was looking at its commercial value. Leck Fischer's sentimental subject, the struggle for an adolescent girl between the woman who had raised her and the biological mother who had abandoned her in infancy, seemed sure to entice the unsophisticated whom Bergman wanted to introduce to theater; in addition, the playwrght's nationality promised an audience of Danes from across the strait. But, wary of investing his own reputation in the production, he had assigned it to another director and, in a public letter, sought to defuse the scorn he anticipated from critics. *My Child Is Mine*, he conceded, was nothing grand, and its theme deserved more serious treatment, yet he praised its "warmth, heart, understanding, and, most of all, humor and feeling"; the theater had an obligation to "help worried people forget their problems for a while and make Monday morning less horrible."[1] Less than two years later, when Dymling forced this orphan on him for his debut as a film director, he was less inclined to defend its homely virtues.

Combing the play for salvage, Bergman discarded Fischer's humor and fixed instead on the fairy-tale quality of its two major strands: the rescue of a girl from her ordinary circumstances by a secret real parent, and her discovery in a perilous moment that simple values are better than worldly temptations. Almost as though incanting "once upon a time," Bergman's off-camera voice describes the rural Northern town in which the film's opening scenes are set as "bathing its feet in the river and sinking quietly to sleep in the lush vegetation." Here Nelly has spent most of her eighteen years with her foster mother, Ingeborg; her apparent fate is to wait for Ulf, their boarder, to muster the courage to propose marriage and then spend the rest of her life tracing the town's pattern of existence. This dull serenity, however, is suddenly threatened by the arrival of Jenny, her natural mother, whose fears of loneliness past middle age have stimulated the idea of reclaiming her daughter.

Nelly's choice becomes the pivot on which the plot swings. Lured by Jenny's glamour, she elects to move to Stockholm, but when Ingeborg rises from her deathbed some months later and travels to the capital to see her beloved daughter for the last time, Nelly's disillusionment is apparent. Eventually, after the girl is shocked into admitting her mistake, she puts the morally dark forest of Stockholm behind her and returns to the radiant goodness of her hometown. Ingeborg now approaches death with a sense of fulfillment, and as Nelly is shown strolling with Ulf, Bergman says this now wiser child will live happily ever after.

What makes the play's restyling so intriguing is Bergman's need to associate the fable with himself. The extent of a parent's claim on a child's future was a question with which he had wrestled in his own life, but even after establishing common ground with the heroine, Bergman still found her interaction with the rest of Fischer's characters too "pleasant." He felt, he said, "nastier and more hopeless" than Fischer. To inject this malevolence, he summoned his demonic alter ego:

> The point was to find a seducer. And it was here that I began to get interested. He existed, not in the play but in my earlier unpublished production, and I knew that if anybody could be the seducer of a girl like Nelly it was Jack. He was asked and declared himself willing. . . . The idyl became vulnerable to evil and wickedness. Sacrifice and mother-love were set in hopeless battle against forces with different values.[2]

Although at one stage Bergman had intended to call the film *Play About Nelly*, in knitting a new thread into what was left of Fischer's fabric, he pulled the design completely awry: if the plot continues to revolve around Nelly, the motive for telling the story is to pursue Jack —and *not* in his putatively wicked role as Nelly's seducer. The daughter's position between two mothers anchors the film's formal scheme, but just as in "A Shorter Tale," it is Jack's Oedipal relationship to the split figure of the mother that excites its meaning. (The association of the two mothers is specifically indicated when Jenny looks into a mirror and states that, beneath her makeup, she and Ingeborg are the same woman.)

Jack's present "tale" crosses the central fable at four points. The first, a very brief cut at the beginning that shows Jack reveling in Jenny's bed, signals the immorality of Stockholm (in contrast with the simple goodness of the countryside). Anyone familiar with the psychological implications of the fiction from which Bergman "summoned" Jack will, of course, recognize a more important, ulterior purpose in establishing the young man as the lover of an older woman characterized, thus far, only as a mother.

A few scenes later, the connection between this Jack and his earlier manifestation becomes a bit more explicit. Having accompanied Jenny on her mission north, he invades the town's annual summer ball and quickly reduces the tedious rite to chaos after mixing and drinking a "Jack the Ripper cocktail." This "magic potion" seems to imbue him with satanic power: in a foyer off the ballroom, he plays an "infernal" boogie-woogie that lures all the town's young people to his piano; then, retreating to a balcony to look down on the brawl that ensues, he gloats,

"Have you ever seen such crazy marionettes! And do you know who set them going? I did." Bergman ties the scene to the plot by concluding it with a scuffle between Jack and Ulf that causes Nelly to forsake her oafish suitor and go to Stockholm, but it is a rather flimsy justification concealing the author's private reasons. (Nelly has obviously already made up he mind, and besides, what is at issue in her decision has little to do with Ulf—or, for that matter, with Jack.) Self-described as "a crea-ture of the moonlight," Jack is the juvenile Bergman's fantasy self: a marionette master controlling the strings of those who, in reality, con-trolled him; an adept at the very jazz he had regarded as the mark of his exclusion by his peers; a rebel who can, with amazing ease, destroy the social order that had subjugated him. Capping this dream of power, he breaks up the "family" by fighting with Ulf (who, in this instance, seems less a jealous beau than an ineffectual father).

Jack's third entrance shows an inverted image of the obstreperous child who had wreaked havoc in the ballroom. After Ingeborg, having discovered she can do nothing to relieve Nelly's unhappiness, decides to leave Stockholm, Jack volunteers to take her to the train station, presents one gift after another to comfort her on the journey home, and then pours out his heart to her. The episode dangles from the rest of the film and distracts the viewer's sympathy away from Nelly and Ingeborg, where the plot line should direct it. (The tender farewells ought to be exchanged between the girl and the woman who nurtured her, yet Jack, an outsider in every sense, not only displaces Nelly but also eclipses Ingeborg.)

Once it is understood that Bergman treats the plot as a vehicle to ferry Jack, however, the inner logic of the scene begins to shine through. Among the first declarations in "A Shorter Tale" is that Jack is an orphan; the combination of anarchy and dominance of will in the ballroom scene expresses the same fantasy: in wishing the parents dead (particularly, in the case of a male child, the mother), the child really wants freedom from their control and from the guilt he feels when he does not conform to their expectations. But after stating the wish—and, especially, after acting as though it were granted—the child's contrition becomes overwhelming. It is precisely this contrition that the scene at the train station dramatizes.

Significantly, Ingeborg is mortally ill, and Jack behaves as though he were responsible. The Oedipal anxieties illustrated by his sexual liaison with that other maternal aspect, Jenny, are one source of guilt. (In this respect, there is a parallel to Jack's symbolic killing of the mother to gain absolution in "A Shorter Tale.") Also, according to the primitive logic of post hoc ergo propter hoc, her dying is a consequence of Nelly's having left her—which, in Jack's mind, he caused. The gifts Jack bestows on her thus serve as earnests of atonement; he acts like the child who screams "I wish you were dead" or "I'm going to kill you," and then makes a sacrifice or harms himself to "take it back." In a similar effort to restore the balance upset by Jack's rampant egotism, the scene belabors the unalloyed goodness of the Madonnalike Ingeborg ("You've given without expecting anything in return," Jack says reverentially) while stressing Jack's remorse as he laments his inability to love anyone but himself. Clearly, these are a tortured son's confessions to his mother.

The final act of Jack's psychological drama is also the film's emotional culmination. On meeting Nelly in the beauty salon which Jenny owns, Jack confesses to having murdered a woman. Although he has become repentant and plans to surrender himself to the police, he says, she must first give him the strength to follow through with his decision by committing herself to him in a gesture of love. The girl disrobes, but suddenly Jenny steps out from a file of dummy heads to reveal that Jack has deceived Nelly with a well-rehearsed lie.

Despite Bergman's announced intention to cast Jack as Nelly's villain-ous arch-seducer in a metaphysical confrontation between good and evil, the failed seduction inherently concerns the same struggle to assert manhood that preoccupies Bergman in other works of this period. Its beauty salon setting connotes the mysterious sanctum of Woman and recalls Bergman's vibrant memories of being granted privileged access to his mother's bedroom and, on rare occasions of sheer delight, of being allowed to comb her hair. Nelly, the object of the seduction, may represent a younger image of mother (a beauty salon, after all, is a place where women seek to shed their age), but if so, in a more important respect she is also a female peer, the mother's heir as the focus of erotic interest. Winning her would prove his masculine maturity; the precon-dition, however, is his murder of a woman—i.e., the mother on whom he is Oedipally fixated. (The parallel to Jack's murder of Marie in "A Shorter Tale" and to Jan-Erik/Caligula's "murder" of Bertha in *Torment* is self-evident.) If Nelly will guarantee her love, Jack is willing to suffer the pain of breaking with that earlier phase of his life and to accept punishment for his sins by confessing to the police (figures of authority corresponding to the father). But at the decisive moment, Jenny, sound-ing more like a mother than a betrayed mistress, emerges from what seems a charnel row of skulls—in effect, refuting the claim of murder with the evidence that she, the implied victim, remains very much alive.

From this point on, Nelly is virtually forgotten; the question of his masculinity must be settled with Jenny. Playing on the fact that Jack is an unemployed actor (and thus not a "real" man), she mocks his theatrical pose: "I suppose you will shoot yourself now. You have your little revolver, and it's loaded with blanks." The sexual implications in the taunting reference to the size of his gun and its impotent ammunition are, of course, unmistakable, and Jack, exposed as only a histrionic child, seems to accept this truth. "You are so right" he says as he exits, "People like me don't commit suicide—it would be out of character." But seconds after he has reached the street, the gun fires and he lies dead—appropriately, under a theater marquee. In a sense, the actor—or artist, or child—has finally created his own "reality." By firing a real bullet into his brain, he has asserted his potency, gained revenge on the mother who holds him captive in childhood, and, ironically, executed sentence on himself for the Oedipal sin he has succeeded in committing only in his imagination. In varying forms, these impulses recur obsessively in Bergman's early fictions; nowhere, however, is the identification with his persona quite as explicit as here. The last image of Jack in *Crisis* shows a newspaper covering his face. Its banner headline announces the death of the town's theater director; beneath the headline is Bergman's photograph.

Woman Without a Face

Bergman's screenplays in the mid-'forties seem designed to recover the success of *Torment* by reproducing it. Set in the same period of his life, *Woman Without a Face*, like *Torment*, was first cast in the form of an autobiographical novella (entitled *The Puzzle Represents Eros*) and tells a similar story employing similar characters. The tension between the order of family and adult society on the one hand and adolescent rebellion on the other is once again uppermost. Here, Martin Grandé, a "mama's boy" only three years older than Jan-Erik Widgren, has been trapped into marriage by the pregnancy of his genteel girlfriend. When he subsequently falls under the spell of an erotic demimondaine, it is his wife and child who press the claims of a middle-class conscience (rather than the parents, as in Widgren's case), but the nature of the conflict within the protagonist remains fundamentally unchanged. Furthermore, Rut Köhler, who lures Martin from his family and his university studies, is essentially as much a victim as Bertha Olsson

—even though, superficially, the voluptuous, aggressive Rut appears quite different from the submissive Bertha.

Having looked on while Sjöberg interpreted his script for *Torment*, Bergman was keen on being given the chance to show what he could do with this closely related variation, but Dymling, stunned by the director's transformation of *Crisis* into a film so contrary to his expectation, was not about to reward a betrayal of trust. Nevertheless, the prospect of following *Torment*'s golden vein could not be ignored; the studio bought the script for *Woman Without a Face* and tried to reconstitute the elements of his first success. Alf Kjellin and Stig Olin, who had played Jan-Erik and Sandman, were assigned the parallel roles of Martin and his friend Ragnar, and since Alf Sjöberg was not available, Gustaf Molander, another seasoned director, was installed in his place.

Although, unlike Sjöberg, Molander made no basic changes in Bergman's conception, he did persuade the author to rearrange the sequence of events just before shooting started. The practice of beginning with the climax and then "explaining" what had led to it through an extended flashback had emanated from Hollywood and spread to most of Europe in the mid-'forties; Swedish film, its sense of idiosyncratic tradition lost, was especially prone to imitation of cinematic fads. But Molander also had good reason for insisting on the alteration: the revision created a dramatic focus missing from the original screenplay's narrative chain. Thus, the film opens with Martin slashing his wrists after a visit from Rut, then retreats to their first meeting and proceeds to trace their affair from the perspective of its consequences.

As in a Naturalistic tract, Martin's surrender to his animal instincts causes his steady deterioration. After shuttling between his wife's respectable cold bed and Rut's incendiary pleasures, he is called up for military service. This forces him to make a choice: unable to bear separation from Rut, he deserts, and thereby cuts himself off from his family. But life on the run with his mistress creates stresses that soon cause them to attack each other. One night, realizing he is doomed unless she can arrange for his escape from Sweden, she slips away to extort the necessary funds from her mother's lover. Although the mission is successful, Martin falsely accuses her of having earned the money by whorishly selling herself to the older man; rather than stoop to the level of a pimp, he leaves her. But Rut, too, has her pride. Later, she pretends to want a reconciliation, and when Martin has humbled himself, she takes her revenge by so destroying his dignity that he attempts suicide. (A coda then supplies an improbable happy ending: a period of rustication in America is to repair the ravages of the affair with Rut. Martin's wife bids him a smiling farewell as Rut, having somehow come to repent her sins, observes tearfully from a distance.)

Bergman declared that his intent was

> to demonstrate the general activity of evil, the precept that the least and most obscure act can propagate like independent living matter, like bacteria or something of the kind, in a boundless chain of causes and events. I wanted to capture what seems to me to be the most horrible, the most meaningless of all things: the power of evil over innocence.[1]

The burden of that demonstration, however, rests only on two brief interior flashbacks to Rut's past. The first reveals that she was sexually abused at the age of twelve by her mother's lover. In addition to providing the basis for Rut's blackmailing him, the molestation presumably explains her amorality, which is illustrated in the second flashback by her libertinism as a grown woman. (In fact, this sequence, in which she entices a chimney sweep into bed after he has entered her flat by mistake, portrays her as lustful, not evil. Moreover, the bawdy encounter has a comic air that defeats its serious purpose.) But even if one grants their validity as elucidations of the character's past, these biographical parentheses alternately depicting the "cuddly puma" as victim and predator fail to establish either how the two aspects join in one woman or what her position in evil's "boundless chain" finally signifies.

Such incoherence reflects a general confusion in the composition. Structurally, despite the commanding curiosity about Rut, Martin functions as the story's central consciousness. However, there is no intimation that he is grappling with the puzzle which Rut presents, or that, at the conclusion, he resolves it. Like Jan-Erik, and like Tomas in *Prison*, he operates on a two-dimensional plane. Bergman's more complex and consequently more vibrant self-projections during the early period are the Jacks and Caligulas who well from deep within the psyche; by labeling them "satanic," Bergman allows his imagination greater licence, and even though the fiction hides in the very act of revealing, the interplay between these opposing impulses raises the story's energy level. Here, the "Jack" character, Ragnar, remains detached. Taking over the function Bergman had reserved to himself in *Crisis*, Ragnar narrates the film's opening. Appropriately, since Ragnar is Bergman's mask, he introduces himself as a writer whose recent first novel has scored a great popular success (an obvious allusion to *Torment*). The story he is about to tell is his by virtue of his role as narrator, but it is also "his" in the sense that he represents Bergman, for whom the story is personal metaphor. Once past this introduction, however, Ragnar fades from view and is superseded by Martin, the "good," respectable, middle-class persona who must be insulated from the actual signification of the fiction. As a result, this inner meaning is conveyed by Rut, not as an independent character but as a reflection of "Martin's" mind.

That the immediate model for Rut was the woman with whom he lived before his first marriage has been generally recognized; *Woman Without a Face*, however, involves more than a fictionalized modification of that experience. Underlying the contest between unfettered hedonism and the values inculcated by a bourgeois upbringing is an ambiguous image of woman generated by the same psychological exigencies at work in other Bergman fictions. The puzzle indeed "represents Eros," but it concerns the erotic tangle in Bergman, not the misassembled picture of extramarital passions it purports to offer.

Although Rut is supposed to radiate an irresistible sexuality, she becomes quite childlike once her affair with Martin is under way; indeed, their flight from punishment by social authority resembles a children's fantasy of pretending to be husband and wife while running away from the strictures of home. Yet, if Martin deals with her as a playmate with whom he can share secrets, he also brands her as a whore who has sold herself to the man who had violated her as a child. These contrary images, so similar to the dual aspects of Bertha, also point toward the recurrence of the triad around which the private drama of *Torment* revolved.

The suggestion of sadism in the older man's attack recalls Caligula, and his identifying tag as mother's lover associates him with Caligula's symbolic role as father. According to the same paradigm, Rut stands for the mother (which, given Bergman's inability to confront his problem openly, may explain—as the script does not—why she is a "woman without a face.") In effect, Martin (or, more precisely, the child he represents) has reduced this "mother" to his own juvenile level and regarded their relationship as a league against both the "father" and the demands of male adulthood (as evidenced by his desertion not only from the army but also from his responsibilities as husband and father). When Rut delivers the money obtained because of a sexual tie with the "father," however, the illusion of her as a peer is destroyed. (Thus, there is a double sense in which Rut the child has been sexually violated.) That the scene echoes a mother's claims of self-sacrifice for her son further emphasizes her "prostitution" in Martin's eyes: regardless of her motive, she has been "father's" whore, performing with him the very act that is beyond a boy's capability, though not beyond his repressed desires.

In *Torment* the imagination had sought to resolve Oedipal guilt and anxiety through Bertha's death and a happy ending implicitly asserting Jan-Erik's arrival at maturity; here, invention expresses the same forces in a different form. The accusatory figure of the mother, whom Martin has been unable to dismiss from his life, leads him to slash his wrists—a punishment that is symbolically an emasculation. Following this grim settling of accounts, Bergman produces another ending, a remedial fantasy. Although Martin's leaving for America to recuperate from the effects of Rut is nonsensically gratuitous in terms of the story, the presumption that he will have outgrown his adolescence and return a whole man, ready at last to play his socially prescribed role as husband and father, responds to the psychological needs dictating the story's design.

Perception of the personal motives that govern the creative process, of course, neither increases nor diminishes a work's artistic merit, but it can offer insight into the reasons for the artist's success or failure. That *Woman Without a Face* reworks the same subject matter and retraces the same psychological pathways does not, in itself, explain why it is shallow and trite. None of Bergman's screenplays during the 'forties rises above the level of the cliché. But the repetitiveness of his pattern is significant in that it reveals the extent to which it imprisoned him. Later, when he at last began developing his creative powers, Bergman would learn to trust his imagination and translate his compulsions into metaphoric constructions that generate an intrinsic interest. In place of the mere dreamer who restates received, stereotypical notions of story would emerge the true artist. His next script to be made into a film indicates the direction he wished to take, but it also demonstrates that, as yet, he was unable to break loose from his tether.

Prison

The most complicated—and jumbled—of his early screenplays, *Prison* consists of several nested story ideas. The framing "story" (probably the last written, since it seems to allude to Dymling's rejection of the script) opens with Paul, a retired mathematics professor, walking onto a motion picture set to look for Martin Grandé, his former pupil.* The old man has just been released from a mental hospital, where he conceived an idea for a film he wants Grandé to direct. "Having assumed power over all the peoples and nations of the world," Satan would state at the film's beginning, "I hereby issue the following decree: I command that everything shall continue as before"—especially "religion and the church, which have labored long and hard for the Devil's success." Although humanity will be spared nuclear war, it is only because universal destruction would be too merciful a deliverance.

Grandé is convinced that no film based on such a "mad" premise could succeed. Art, he reasons, implies form—not just a beginning but also an end that vests the drama with meaning; the professor's story, predicated upon the endless, unalterable, and utterly purposeless horror of human existence, would seem to exclude the possibility of a conclusion. Also, as the romantic scene Grandé is shooting with back projection suggests (and as Bergman has repeatedly noted), cinema is an illusionist's art based upon deceiving the public into accepting the fantasies it wants to believe; the professor's film would require an uncompromised realism, exposing the destructive truth from which the audience tries to hide. Even so, the proposal intrigues Grandé, and after Paul states that he will return for a decision that evening, the director discusses the question with his friend Tomas, a 'Forties-ist writer. Tomas does not provide a direct answer. Instead, he relates a recent experience that, like Paul's "impossible" scenario, illustrates a world under the Devil's reign. Presented as a long flashback (it occupies most of the film), this account is central to any discussion of *Prison*, but preparation for its analysis first requires a closer examination of the framing story.

The philosophical issues raised by the professor's entrance into the studio generally correspond to the questions Bergman poses in the program notes for the premiere: "Is earth a hell? Does God nevertheless exist? Where is he? And where are the dead? Why must one mistrust one's innermost convictions, and why is it so hard to be faithful to oneself? I wanted to make a film about all this. I didn't want to end my film with an explanation or with 'something positive,' as the producers say."[1] And yet, despite his attraction to such speculation (perhaps as a way of elevating his claims as an artist), he scarcely pursues the metaphysical inquiry he promises. Whatever Bergman may have thought he

---

*Although he, too, is a Bergman persona, this Martin Grandé is not the same person as the protagonist of *Woman Without a Face*.

was doing, the film is spun from personal anxieties, not from concern with transcendental riddles.

The frame presents three potential tellers—and versions—of that personal story. Paul, the first, has unmistakable affinities with that earlier persona who espoused a "satanic" cause, Jack the Ripper. Although cast here in the guise of an old man (perhaps because Bergman was trying to void the indictment that his films showed an "adolescent" perspective), Paul, like Jack, is toying with a fantasy of power that fundamentally reflects a hurt, isolated child. Grandé, to whom he turns as his instrument, is the second teller. He is attracted by Paul's idea (just as the director of *Crisis* betrayed his sympathy for Jack), but is unwilling to risk veering too far from well-tested, commercial formulas and is thus ruled out as the interpreter of such a shocking "truth."

Consequently, the role of storyteller falls to a third persona, Tomas, an ostensibly normal adult who has no reason to distort his account of reality. In fact, however, this is only presumptively the case; closer inspection reveals that Tomas's story is an ambivalent combination of the stories that Paul and Grandé would tell. On the surface, it resembles an article in a "true confession" magazine: after claiming to be "fact" (Tomas speaks as a journalist who has been gathering information about Stockholm after dark), it develops into a sentimental account of his extramarital involvement with a prostitute, followed by their painful separation and the inevitable happy ending when he returns to his wife's bosom. Grandé could easily have cranked such pap through his camera. But beneath that conventionally lachrymose tale, a different drama is being expressed: Tomas, who moonlights as a screenwriter and—like Paul (and Jack and Bergman)—hopes someday to win acclaim as an author, is also a "poet" preoccupied with a subjective reality that scarcely conforms with the reassuring conclusion to his story.

Two strands lead into the flashback. One, grimly Naturalistic, synopsizes the sordid conditions of Birgitta-Carolina's life as a prostitute. After the birth of her baby brings a moment of happiness, Peter, her fiancé and pimp (in league with a monstrous, apparently lesbic sister), persuades her to let them murder the troublesome infant in exchange for Peter's promise of marriage. The second strand, apparently intended as ironic counterpoint to Birgitta-Carolina's illusion that marriage will improve her lot, switches the scene to the apartment of a middle-class couple, Tomas and Sofi. Their distress, in contrast to the prostitute's, plays as farce. When the drunken husband threatens to kill his wife unless she voluntarily signs a suicide pact, she smashes a bottle over his head; before collapsing, he staggers about like a silent-film comedian. Unable to locate Sofi after he regains consciousness, he becomes convinced he has murdered his wife and stuffed her body into the closet. He summons the police, but when they search the closet and find it empty, the abashed "killer" apologizes for having troubled them without cause.

Excessively elaborate and disjointed in its alternation between pathos and low comedy, this split prelude is ill-adapted to the film-within-the-film it introduces, yet it should not be dismissed merely as the product of ineptness; as elsewhere in his early screenplays, the crudity discloses psychological exigencies within the "poet" that overpower considerations of artistic discipline. Both Bergman, whose off-camera voice introduces the flashback as though it were a separate film, and Tomas, who is presumably recounting the events visualized on the screen, insist that what follows is "a film [or story] about Birgitta-Carolina." Its shape and meaning, however, actually refer to the single mind of its double narrator.

The first sign of a refracted autobiographical association occurs in the shot of a street in Stockholm's Old Town while Bergman reads the lead to the film-within-the-film. Although the location—a few steps from the Mäster Olofsgården mission—establishes nothing in particular about Birgitta-Carolina, it is linked not only with the start of Bergman's career but also with his break from his mother's dominating influence. This evocation of the filmmaker's struggle for manhood becomes more pronounced in the domestic burletta: the husband is an ineffectual, clownish child; the wife, a cool, superior, self-possessed adult. To be sure, the scene provides no specific information that identifies Tomas's past as Bergman's, but his evident insecurity about his masculinity is consistent with the effects of psychosexual ties between mother and son around which so many of Bergman's fictions revolve.

Tomas's urge to punish Sofi—so overwhelming that he cannot distinguish wish from deed—is even more revealing. His belief that he has murdered his wife and stuffed her body into a closet recalls "A Shorter Tale," where another would-be poet claims to have killed a sexually remote mistress and disposed of her corpse in similar fashion. In both instances, a double motivation underlies the hostility: on the one hand, it is an aggressively masculine assertion of power over a woman with whom he cannot function sexually; on the other, it is a retaliation against a surrogate for the mother he holds responsible for that sexual ineffectiveness.*

Birgitta-Carolina, the other female on whom the prelude focuses, is an equally significant figure in this psychological rebus. Besides contributing to the story's dolorous Naturalism, the exploitation of her economic and emotional weakness by her tyrannical partner veils a son's rationalization of his mother's dependency on his father. But the excuse that she is a victim cannot completely exonerate her: in agreeing to sacrifice her child as the price for conjugality with Peter, she is also a traitor who must be punished. By placing the teller at the center of the tale, this observation both alters the film's meaning and discloses a radical coherence. If one accepts Bergman's assertion that this is a "film about *Birgitta-Carolina*," the plot simply will not support the weight given to the infanticide; at most, it only serves to illustrate the extent of the world's hellishness. On the other hand, this emphasis on the "sacrificed" child is fully warranted once the story is seen as a psychologically complex reconstruction of a *son's* conflicted relationship with his mother. Viewed in this context, the rejection figured as infanticide underlies both Tomas's ambiguous attitude toward Sofi and the curious affair with Birgitta-Carolina following his flight from home. In effect, to grapple with the problem reflected in his fumbling behavior with his wife, Tomas (or Bergman) must regress to its childhood origin.

The plot of this central episode contains very few actions: soon after the writer and the prostitute accidentally meet, they forge an alliance against their loneliness, rent a room in a boardinghouse, and enjoy an idyll until Birgitta-Carolina has a dream in which she symbolically reviews her life; somehow, the shock destroys the illusion of happiness and sends her back to Peter. Contrary to the prefatory statement that this report would defy art by rendering the truth about life, the story here seems to leave the real world. That Tomas (like Jan-Erik in *Torment*) would so casually take up with a woman so alien to his middle-class experience is quite improbable—and Bergman neither supplies credible motivation nor exploits the improbability. At the other end of these events, Birgitta-Carolina's reasons for abandoning Tomas are even more

---

*Jack's tale resembles Tomas's in several other details as well. Jack uses his writing paper and pencase as shroud and coffin for the sexually ambiguous alter ego he has slain; Tomas, in effect, is "writing" about his attempt to overcome his sexual incapacity—which he first tries to deal with by proposing a double suicide or a murder and suicide.

Furthermore, the guilt manifested by the reappearances of the dwarf-father after the first murder in "A Shorter Tale" parallels Tomas's surrender to the authorities, and Jack's acknowledgment that (except in his fantasy) he was not really man enough to commit the second murder corresponds to the discovery that Tomas hallucinated his killing of Sofi.

puzzling, not only because her captivity with the pimp has been depicted as an unrelieved horror but also because the viewer never quite grasps what there is in the dream that should precipitate such a desperate act. Moreover, the details and activities that fill the outline of their affair seem pointless, creating the impression that Bergman, having determined that his plot requires the pair to become lovers, is just inventing "business" to give the event substance. Once more, however, the maladroit aspect of the story yields the clues to its hidden agenda.

The episode's fairy-tale quality becomes appropriate, quite apart from the content's romantic nature, if one recognizes that the actual setting is the subconscious and that Birgitta-Carolina represents the mother to whom Tomas is returning. The narrow plank over which the lovers walk to their attic room is a magic bridge. Crossing it wondrously transforms Birgitta-Carolina: as though Tomas had lifted a terrible spell cast by "father" Peter, she seems to have shed all traces of her whoring and lost the memory of her murdered baby. Curiously, despite the supposition of a love affair, the presumable lovers evince no sexual attraction; "mother," having been "revirginized," has become a playmate. Indeed, their moments of greatest intimacy stem from their discoveries of a music box and an old, hand-operated movie projector—"toys" that someone had outgrown, stored away, and forgotten. From this childhood perspective, reality assumes the aspect of unreality: viewing a reel of silent film in which a man in a nightshirt, a thief, and a policeman scurry between a horned devil and a skeleton, they respond with an innocent delight that protects them from recognizing the comedy as a masque about life's terrors.*

---

*Although the film itself offers no key to the allegory, similar figures in Bergman's other writings enable one to venture a rough translation. The thief and policeman who trouble the nightshirted man in his desire to sleep represent guilt and punitive authority. (Given the symbolic meaning of the context in which the reel is being projected, one might also speculate that the guilt involves the "theft" of the mother's love from the father, who, in the guise of policeman, is seeking retribution.) Almost literally bracketing this chase, the demon and skeleton—images of psychological self-destruction and of the fear of death—press from the boundaries of the mind.

Bergman's own explanation of how he came to insert the silent comedy may be worth noting, especially in light of his relationship to Tomas and of the regression symbolized in the surrounding episode. A Pathé reel he had bought as a boy, he claims, contained just such a chase, involving the same figures. But when he searched the archives for a print to splice into *Prison* and found no evidence of its ever having existed, he recreated it "from memory." It is tempting to conjecture that what he remembered as a movie was really a recurring childhood nightmare; certainly, the pains he took for this *apparently* unimportant sequence indicate something deeper than a merely nostalgic quotation from his youth.

But the innocence is a delusion—a wish reflected in a magic mirror, not a reconstitution of a real past. That reality, presented as a nightmare, eventually invades their make-believe when Birgitta-Carolina, in a dream, descends into her subconscious. A cellar trapdoor opens onto a path where the rebuffs and frustrations leading her into shame are symbolically recapitulated. At the end of her walk, she meets Tomas, leaning against a wrecked car with a damaged rocking horse in his arms, but this comforting vision of another hurt child in an adult shape suddenly changes into Alf, one of her sadistic customers. Next, she sees a doll in a bathtub; when Peter picks it up, it turns into a fish, which he then decapitates. The sight of the fish in the bloody water—a reminder of her dead baby—sends her running back to the trapdoor, where she beats her fists in panic until she awakens. The dream's apparent meaning, which she seems instantly to understand, is that the truth rediscovered through the self-encounter forces her to wake from Tomas's benign enchantment and accept the fate dictated by her experiences.

If Bergman's sole purpose was to engineer a means to separate the lovers, however, the dream is perplexing in its cluttering, often opaque details and odd twists and turns. (Why, at this point, allude to Birgitta-Carolina's earlier life when the reasons for her drift into prostitution have not previously been incorporated into the dramatic scheme? Why does Tomas merge into Alf—so minor a character, moreover, that the average viewer probably cannot identify him. And strangest of all, why should it be precisely the reenactment of the baby's murder that draws her back into cohabitation with the murderer?) But if one perceives her dream as an extension of *Tomas's* subconscious, and thereby as his confrontation with a "truth" about "mother" *and* himself that belies the previous happy (and conspicuously asexual) fantasy, then there is an explanation to most of the difficulties.

Peter's killing of the fish is obviously the key to the dream—and its most complex symbol. In referring to the infanticide committed to preserve the relationship between the parental figures, it forces Tomas to acknowledge that "mother" is not the innocent child-sweetheart but a perfidious creature. (Thus, in a sense, it is not Birgitta-Carolina who decides to leave Tomas but he who drives her away to be punished.) At the same time, underlying the innocence of their playing house was his immature—and not quite so innocent—sexual attraction to the mother; Peter, as "father," recognizes the doll as the fanciful issue of this desire and destroys it with gleeful brutality. That the doll is at once also a phallic fish gives an even more crushing turn to the father's vanquishment of the son—and to the mother's complicity.* Indeed, Tomas's only appearance in the dream stresses his sexual impairment. The wrecked car and the rocking horse with a broken leg that he clutches are damaged symbols of masculinity, and his transformation into the sadistic Alf that immediately follows implies not only a perverse attempt to assert potency but also (as the next scene will show) an urge for retribution against the mother.

Having pronounced judgment, the flashback proceeds to the execution. Put back to work by Peter, Birgitta-Carolina receives a customer's call from Alf, who prepares to torture her with a lighted cigarette. She recoils from the attack and manages to escape to the tenement's cellar, but this is a flight to accept her fate, not to elude it. In this setting that so clearly refers to the dream and the "crimes" for which it tried her, she retrieves a knife she had earlier seen hidden away by a young boy and commits suicide. Thus, Tomas figuratively exacts punishment through both of his doubles: Alf and the sacrificed child who reappears as the boy. (It is also a telling fact that the knife used here is the same weapon, vested with almost fetishistic powers, with which Jack dispatched "mother" Marie.)

Even if enacted in fantasy and veiled by symbols, however, matricide evokes a guilt so overwhelming that the mind tries to evade its acknowledgment. Peter's apparent repentance after finding Birgitta-Carolina's body, though obtrusively anticlimactic and inconsistent with everything the character has represented, shifts blame away from Tomas while simultaneously mitigating the force of the "false" accusation. The desire for exculpation takes another form in the halo that surrounds the body while Peter bears it away—a strained effort to deny the anger motivating her punishment that practically deifies Birgitta-Carolina. (The same instinct is evident in Bergman's retaining, until almost the last moment, the option of "saving" the prostitute at the film's end by having her join the Salvation Army.) Meanwhile, Tomas is shown wandering along the waterfront, disconsolate and completely mystified by her departure. And yet, despite these strenuous denials, the hidden mission into the past has accomplished its therapeutic purpose. In the next scene, Tomas and Sofi have reconciled (although there is still no hint of

---

*The equation of fish to phallus occurs several times in Bergman's fictions. In this early period it is most prominent in "The Fish" and most obvious in a scene in *Women's Waiting* where the camera fixes on swimming fish while Kaj is seducing Rakel. In the later films it appears in *Hour of the Wolf* and (indirectly but most significantly) in *Not to Speak of All These Women*.

what had caused their ostensible troubles.) Tomas, in astonishing contradiction to the previous scenes, declares that he never loved Birgitta-Carolina, but that knowing her has somehow changed his life. What is unstated is nonetheless clear: having settled accounts in his past, he no longer has to make Sofi the target of his aggression; the psychological impediment to his manhood having (presumably) been removed, the marriage can now succeed.

Given the happy ending—indeed, precisely the "positive note" Bergman claims the producers insisted upon—how is this story equatable to the proposed film about the Devil's reign, and why should it prove that the professor's scenario is not feasible?* The answers are implicit in *Prison*. Even though Bergman, boiling with literary ambitions, wanted to engage in the kind of metaphysical speculation he found in the writers he most admired, his view of earth as a hell was rooted in private ground. In itself, of course, this was not necessarily a hindrance: other writers (notably Strindberg, his favorite) had fed on their tortured personal lives. But Bergman could not bring himself to deal overtly with his inner strife, and as yet he lacked the skill and distance to convert it artistically.

His immaturity hobbled him in another respect as well. At thirty, he still depended on models. In writing for the theater, he could rely on a rich body of philosophical drama drenched in the despair to which he felt drawn. But cinema, especially in Sweden during the 'thirties and 'forties, aimed at an unsophisticated taste for romantic escapism. Moreover, part of the reason the movies had captivated Bergman in his youth was the comforting happy endings with which the Martin Grandés surmounted reality's trials. To have made a film, at this stage of his career, that proclaimed the everlasting triumph of evil would have affronted his vestigial faith in the screen's special magic. The alternative was to use the trappings of a quite conventional film (i.e., the flashback) as ciphers in a personal code about the "evil" within himself. At the end of *Prison*, however, the coy admission that Tomas's story is no more workable as a film than the professor's indicates that Bergman sensed the need for greater originality than he could conjure from the motion picture industry's bins of clichés.

---

*Grandé's reason for rejecting the professor's idea at the end of the day—"If God exists, there is no [dramatic] problem; if not, there is no solution"—curiously confuses theology and aesthetics to produce what much of the world's great literature attests is patent nonsense.

Eva

If mentioned at all, *Eva* is granted hasty notice from Bergman critics as the less interesting of the pair of scripts directed by Molander; absent Bergman's subsequent fame, it would long since have slipped easily into oblivion. That it is a minor work in the Bergman canon is beyond dispute, yet it marks the beginning of a transition that merits closer attention than it has received.

According to Bergman, its genesis was a premonition of danger that "fell out of some dark corner of the wardrobe of my subconscious: an executioner, a headsman, a black shadow behind my back.... Who? Death ..., not an unusual guest in my thoughts." Suddenly, the vehicle he was driving swerved off the road. When he regained his composure, he heard Handel over the car radio; the music seemed to accompany an epiphany. "Of one thing I was sure: life had never before been so real and shining. [I realized that] death was a part of life and that its waves were unkind and tireless as the ocean's." A new attitude was born: "It is better to be nonaggressive, to get out from the trenches, to stop baring my teeth. It may work."[1] The fact that the incident is supposed to have occurred a year before he gave *Prison* its final form may make its mystical revelation less credible; nonetheless, one does find in *Eva* a movement from personal resentment toward discovery of a liberating joy in being human.

Apparently not just a figure of speech, the "dark corner of the wardrobe of my subconscious" he cited as the film's source is manifested even more distinctly here than in other elaborations of his childhood guilt for which the tale of the parsonage wardrobe became an emblem. A flashback to Bo Fredriksson's boyhood shows him running away from home after he hears his father abuse his mother. Among a group of vagabonds, he meets a blind girl, who becomes his playmate. The friendship quickly leads to horror when Bo, in playing with the controls of an idle locomotive, sends it off the rails and kills the girl. Returned to his home, the boy receives a savage beating from his father; thereafter, the adult Bo states, death assumed the aspect of "a terrifying executioner, a headsman. I vowed to hate God."

First made evident in *Eva*, this transformation of guilt into hatred of the father and, in turn, the substitution of God for the father serves as a Rosetta stone for deciphering the "religious quarrel" that, misread, would eventually occupy a central place in Bergman criticism. But the flashback's more immediate significance is that, as another allotrope of

"A Shorter Tale," it illustrates the tenacity with which Bergman's Oedipal conflict gripped his imagination.

Clearly, what prompts this fantasy of escape is Bo's inability to challenge his father's might and thus act as his mother's champion. The vagabonds he joins, an unworldly crew who seem to subsist on the tunes they play with their simple instruments, are children projected as adults; unlike his father and mother, each of whom rouses a different reason for fear, these idealized parental figures impose neither claims nor strictures. As their "daughter," the little girl represents an extension of Bo, an imaginary self that takes female form because, given the son's inference of his father's jealousy, it is "safer." (Set against this context, Bergman's report that dressing in girls' clothes as a young boy gave him a feeling of security acquires a special pertinence.) But, since the male child's image of his feminine complement is his mother, the girl also assumes the role of that forbidden sweetheart.*

It is the resonance of the latter association that brings on the "accident" (much as Tomas's retreat from reality with Birgitta-Carolina and Jack's innocent games with the dwarf-child and Marie end in violence). If Bo's virtual adoption by these phantasmal beings represents a dream of release from sexual complexities, a confrontation with truth within the dream (similar to the nightmare in *Prison*) soon destroys the illusion. By leading the girl onto the locomotive and manipulating the levers of this symbol of masculinity, Bo is surrendering to his repressed desires. The resulting calamity, in a sense, dramatizes his fear of loosing an impulse he cannot control and of daring what is beyond his capacity to accomplish. But the girl's death, confirming a pattern in Bergman's previous filmscripts, also indicates both a veiled sadism that issues from an attempt to deny sexual inadequacy and a shifting of punishment (and, by implication, of responsibility) for his illicit erotic wish. Seen in this light, the brutal beating that follows—at once a masochistic fantasy (sadism inverted by a mirror of guilt) and the father's retribution for the son's Oedipal act—serves as payment for this double dissimulation.**

*The otherwise gratuitous fact of the girl's blindness—a common symbol of castration—suits both aspects. Not to be confused with the male's terror of actual castration, the "blinded" self reflects Bo's yearning to avoid the guilt and anxiety stirred by thoughts of his sexuality. Correlatively, a "castrated" mother—i.e., one reduced to the child's sexual level—insures both that she will make no impossible erotic demands on him and that the father, the more powerful rival, will not steal her away.

**Another, related explanation for the beating as an appropriate ending to this "story" may be found in the strappings Bergman claims his father administered for his lies, which his fantasy had convinced him were truth.

Adrift in "the nothingness of life" fifteen years later, Bo ventures into a second perilous experience; though ostensibly designed to show him still under death's shadow, the more significant link, moored in Bergman's own subconscious, is to the underlying content of the boyhood incident. Bo now earns his living as a jazz trumpeter in Stockholm, where he shares an apartment with a fellow musician and his wife. The Oedipal currents in this arrangement are soon apparent: one night, while the three members of this "family" are drinking and congratulating themselves on being unencumbered by antiquated notions, the husband tries to argue his wife and Bo into having an affair. (As in the case of the vagabonds, the life of a musician—or artist—seems to offer freedom beyond the pale of conventional morality.) Proving rather less liberated than he thought, the husband fights his friend when the proposal is put to the test; fortunately, the drunken blows do no damage and the consumption of brandy resumes, but later that night, with the husband passed out on the kitchen floor, the sexually incited antagonism takes a virulent turn. Egged on by the woman, Bo slashes the gas hose and seals the husband in the windowless room.

At this pivotal moment approximately halfway through the film, Bergman launches the story in a new direction. Eva, a young woman from Bo's hometown, arrives in Stockholm the morning after the incident and, like a ray of sunlight, awakens Bo to the happy discovery that the murder was only a dream. The spiritual health she exudes seems to cleanse him—of his original sin, one is tempted to say— and a year later, amid the paradisical surroundings of the Stockholm archipelago, they are a married couple awaiting the birth of their child. Then, one day, the pure joy they have found in their isolation from the rest of the world, and from his past, is tested when the body of a German soldier washes up on shore. For Bo, the corpse represents the blind girl he killed and the victim of the dream murder, buried guilt floating up to the surface of consciousness; for Eva—more obviously—this evidence of the war raging elsewhere in Europe proves the senselessness of bringing a child into a world without hope. Suddenly, however, an unreasoning Life Force responds to death by stimulating Eva's labor pains (just as, earlier, the couple had first become erotically aware of each other while an old man was dying in an adjoining room). Forced from their island home, Bo rows against a storm to ferry his wife to a medical station, where the baby is born. The film's final shot—of Bo holding his son aloft against the background of the sea—proclaims a personal triumph, not only over nature's hostility but also over the inner turbulence for which the storm operates as metaphor.

Such a romantic comfit invites scorn, of course, and one could easily assume that Bergman's interest in concocting it was chiefly monetary. But his declaration in a headnote to the script, "I have written this as a protest against myself," indicates a most serious intent: nothing less than a determination to effect a change in himself through his art. If the first half of the film reveals a mind and creative imagination imprisoned in a labyrinth, the second, starting with Bo's waking from the nightmare that transparently enacts parricide and incest, is a vault for freedom. Significantly, the woman who awakens the "murderer" bears no resemblance either to his blind playmate or to the musician's treacherous, sexually alluring wife (which is to say that she wears neither of the mother's masks and, therefore, is unlike any major female character in a previous Bergman filmscript). That Eva is too much an ideal who expresses too little of an interior life to generate drama weakens the film, but it attests her essential role as a good "anima" conjured to banish the bad; like Dante's Beatrice, her identity consists in her mission to lead the sinner up from the depths of his anguish.

Perhaps even more important than the appearance of this new character is the new respect for structural integrity evinced in the film's conclusion. As in earlier scripts, the ending coincides with an assertion of psychological deliverance, but here, instead of being lashed on, it is the logical terminus of a sustained thematic development. Moreover, in reaching beyond his personal psychological tangle to resolve the story's meaning, Bergman takes his first step in film into the "philosophical" dimension that *Prison* rather disingenuously claims as its locus. (Indeed, the design *Eva* traces—despair, arising from preoccupation with death, overcome through the hope manifested by an infant—would recur in *Wild Strawberries* and in his operatically philosophical statement of the 'fifties, *The Seventh Seal*.)

To be sure, neither the imaginative leap *Eva* represents nor Bergman's greater regard for formal unity makes this script a major aesthetic achievement: its characters are shallowly conceived beings defined almost entirely by events, and the plot housing the film's three episodes is a rather obvious contraption that depends upon clichés at crucial points. Still less does either development signal Bergman's readiness to emerge as one of the principal cultural figures of his generation. Like the rest of his 'forties filmscripts, *Eva* remains the product of an immature sensibility as yet unequipped to uncover the complexities inherent in its subject. In addition, Bergman's depressed mental state scarcely stimulated a fresh start: the "protest against myself" trumpeted in the headnote was a strained cry of optimism, directed not only at his past but also at "the new influences I feel within me"—and, as his labors with *Joakim Naked* were to prove, he would soon yield to the corrosive effects of these influences, old and new. Even so, in pushing the perimeter of his attention beyond an involuted preoccupation with the self, *Eva* established a range within which he could grow as an artist.

To Joy

"Something began to stir in my head," Bergman has said of his direction in *To Joy*, "I started to find my own routes."[1] Perhaps the most noticeable indication of self-confidence is an apparent spontaneity in the performances of his cast that, aside from their talent, bespeaks the director's appreciation of the collusion between camera and actor. In part, of course, this increasing sophistication reflects half a decade of practical experience with the medium, but it also rests upon a different "literary" approach. Here, for the first time in any of his films, the characters are the primary element and the story's dramatic energy derives from the unfolding of their personalities. Although Bergman has heaped praise on Maj-Britt Nilsson for unveiling a human being in her role as Marta, the precondition for her "magic"—as well as for the equally vital characters created by Stig Olin (Stig Eriksson) and Victor Sjöström (Sönderby)—was already in his script.

The chief significance of *To Joy*, however, concerns the relationship between the filmmaker and his fiction. Resuming the assault on egoism Bergman had introduced in *Eva*, the film pulses toward the protagonist's eventual recognition that his selfish interests count for very little in the larger scheme of life's meaning. Clearly, in telling the story of Stig Eriksson (virtually his own patronym), Bergman was making this fictional self's circumstances a portmanteau of details from his marriage to Else Fisher and from the years in Hälsingborg and Gothenburg with Ellen Lundström; Bergman's cockiness in his mid-twenties had been dealt some humbling blows by the time he reached thirty. And yet, though the film's content treats resignation to mediocrity, it anticipates the artistic successes he would achieve in the new decade. The previous filmscripts had been flawed by his inability to gear the story at its surface to the private fantasies concealed within it. *To Joy* also rides atop a layer of dream (as do all his fictions), but by openly confronting the story's personal core, he gained firmer control over his materials—and thereby avoided the more egregious effects of dissociation that had been especially evident in his peremptory endings.

A second result, related to the first, was to have even greater consequence. Although Bergman's writing for the stage during this same period consisted of "moralities" fraught with metaphysical implications, his early filmscripts had manifested no such ambition. As adaptations of the stock stuff of popular fiction, they had aimed at nothing much beyond the sensations created by alternating emphases on melodrama and sentiment; as more complex manipulations of private symbols, their meaning coiled inward toward the author himself. Despite Bergman's fondness for sententious description of each new script as a parable about evil in one form or other, the notion that a film's story could develop metaphorically as a statement of transcendent values was not given dramatic expression before *Eva*, and it was not until *To Joy* that the "philosophical" purpose of the fiction became implicit throughout. In this respect, *To Joy* foreshadows all his major films of the next decade.

Critics have tended to distinguish *To Joy* as the first of his works to deal with the "problem of the artist," yet, even though its autobiographical base lends added weight to the fact that the protagonist is a musician, Bergman here skirts the question of art's problematical nature that he would later address in such films as *The Face*, *The Rite*, and *Not to Speak of All These Women*. Actually, it has a stronger affinity with *Wild Strawberries* (where art is not a subject) in that the body of the story consists of a long, uninterrupted flashback through which an egoist evaluates his life. At the start, Stig is called to the telephone in the midst of an orchestra rehearsal and notified that his wife and child have died in a kerosene stove explosion. After the present is held in suspension to allow the retracing of the couple's courtship, marriage, estrangement, and reconciliation—the four movements, as it were, of their "symphony" —the film ends with Stig's rejoining the orchestra as it plays the entire "Ode to Joy," the last movement of Beethoven's last symphony. But the music is more than an envelope for the film's contents: Bergman intends that its glory contrast with the foibles Stig has displayed and, at the same time, that his human struggle inform the music's meaning.

Stig's story resembles that of every other protagonist in Bergman's scripts of the 'forties in that it describes a difficult passage toward adulthood. That he is twenty-five and thus, like the others, physically long past adolescence does not alter the case; unwilling to accept reality's terms, he is emotionally and psychologically drawn back toward the comforting illusion of childhood. Once again, this retreat from reality is expressed through a woman (or, more accurately, a woman mentally transformed by the protagonist into a girl), but *To Joy* treats this recurring motif in a different way. Although the source of the psychological problem is in Bergman, he successfully objectifies the problem in Stig; having emerged from fiction's underside, it here dominates the visible design.

At the outset of their romance, when they meet as lonely, newly arrived violinists with the Hälsingborg orchestra, Stig wants to see Marta as a female extension of his innocent self—which is to say that she is another embodied dream-playmate in the line that stretches from *Torment*'s Bertha. Given the nature of this attraction to Marta, it is appropriate that the first crisis should erupt on the occasion of her birthday. A few hours before the celebration, Marcel, a fellow musician, boasts of previously having enjoyed her erotic favors; to erase the implications of this disclosure (among which may be the prospect of her sexual demands on him), Stig gets thoroughly drunk. Events at the party further accentuate his callowness: he acts like a child in bidding to be the center of attention while the guests, in their jaded, debauched behavior, present a nightmarish image of what lies ahead in life. The next morning, he steels himself to be a man and crudely attempts to bed Marta—which, of course, exposes him as an even greater fool. Just as the prospects for their future together seem dashed, however, he belatedly hands her his birthday gift: a teddy bear.* With this symbolic restoration of the innocence on which their association had been based, they reconcile.

A second crisis, at the flashback's midpoint, confirms the significance of the first. After several months of cohabitation (which, like similar situations in Bergman's previous films, he indicates without showing the least sign of sensuality), the couple have drifted toward marriage. But when Marta, while dressing for their wedding, casually informs the groom not only that she is pregnant but also that she had had four abortions during liaisons with other men, Stig instinctively tries to bolt.

---

*At the time he was filming *To Joy*, Bergman was also using a teddy bear as an emblem of nostalgia for childhood in his play *The City*. It recurs, with the same function, as late as *From the Life of the Marionettes* and *Fanny and Alexander*. Another, more narrowly autobiographical reference ties to the first days of Bergman's marriage with Else Fisher, when the newlyweds would entertain themselves by reading Winnie-the-Pooh aloud.

In addition to being emotionally unprepared for fatherhood, he apparently fears unfavorable comparison with her former lovers. Although the angry quarrel ignited by his fright subsides and the wedding ceremony proceeds on schedule, this time no equivalent to the gift of the teddy bear reconstructs the illusion of innocence. Stig has crossed a dividing line—and he cannot chase the suspicion that, in doing so, he has stepped into a trap.

Once it has sprung, however, it turns out to be a different trap from the one he had instinctively feared. That he resents the obligations marriage loads on him is obvious, but the stronger motive for his recalcitrance seems to be that he has thrust Marta—now neither an asexual playmate nor a challenging temptress—into the role of a demanding, smothering mother surrogate. Ironically, on finding he has cast himself as the child he had earlier wished to be, he fights to establish his manhood. Because of his sexual insecurity, however, this drive to assure himself of his potency takes the form of an obsessive quest for fame as an artist. (One cannot help recalling, here, not only Bergman's difficult battle to free himself of his mother's tenacious hold but also his frequent confessions of inadequacy in the ways boys manifest their prowess. Dreaming of becoming a new Strindberg provided a compensating sense of power.)

A bid to perform as a soloist during a national radio concert offers Stig his golden chance, but when a violin string loosens in the midst of his playing, he panics and ruins all his hopes. Blaming Marta—he accuses her of wanting him to fail so that she would not lose him—he turns to "artistic friends," Mikael and Nelly Bro, for solace. Significantly, it was this weary old actor and his licentious wife who had presented such a repugnant specter of "sophistication" at the birthday party; having fled from Marta's maternal embrace, Stig looks to them for acceptance as an adult.

It should be obvious to Stig that this initiation involves sexual intercourse with Nelly, but he is curiously slow to understand—or perhaps it would be more correct to say that he understands but, fearful of the risk it implies, he tries not to. When, at last, he is at the brink of succumbing to Nelly's persistence, duty sends him back to Marta, just as she is about to give birth to twins; in a sense, shrinking from the test, he returns to "mother." Four years later, however, while Mikael is dying, Nelly finally does succeed in luring him into an affair—not, it should be noted, through directly erotic means but by shrewdly baiting her hook with the promise of arranging for a renowned violinist to make Stig his protégé.

Enticed into what is effectively a satanic pact, Stig revels for a while in his sinfulness. One day, however, while at Mikael's deathbed, he glimpses Nelly fondling Marcel in the next room and is suddenly repelled by this mirror of his own lust. He has been played for a fool and, worse, he realizes he has been using his dedication to art as camouflage for his vanity and insecurity. Shortly after this cathartic revelation, he mends relations with Marta and sets their marriage on a new basis, but as he begins to savor life's riches, the flashback ends with death's snatching them away.

That the fiction about Stig's maturation draws on Bergman's emotional turmoil in the rebellion against his parents is apparent—and scarcely worth more than its notation in passing. On the plane of the obvious, such translation of experience furnishes the matter of most literary creation. But, as the preceding analysis of his stories has revealed, Bergman's reliance on the personal operates more vitally at a sunken level where the imagination expresses itself through a code that transcends the normal processes of metaphor—that, while germinal in the fiction's evolution, contains a meaning hidden from what metaphor reveals. In *To Joy*, this encryption is concentrated in the events gathered around the climactic scene: the disastrous radio concert.

If, in Stig's eyes, Marta is a mother who wishes him to fail in order to keep him her child, Sönderby, the stern old orchestra conductor, is a father who, in warning the young violinist prior to the broadcast not to accept an assignment beyond the level of his maturity, is jealously guarding his position of power against what amounts to a challenge from his son. (Stig's assumption that they have formed a repressive conspiracy further indicates their association in his mind as parental figures.) The actual anxieties at play in what is ostensibly a test of artistic competence may be seen in the nature of the fiasco: the ridicule that comes of "exposing" himself to a national audience resembles the universal dream in which the dreamer, on noticing the laughter of people around him, discovers his nakedness. Moreover, a parable of sexual inadequacy is described by the failure of his "masculine" bow to produce the right notes in stroking the patently "feminine" violin.

Thwarted in the attempt to prove himself before one set of "parents," Stig proceeds to exchange them for a second in which the qualities of the first are inverted: Mikael Bro—once an established principal actor who must now content himself with an occasional character role—is an enfeebled version of Sönderby; his many-years-younger wife Nelly is a sultry temptress who, in contrast to Marta, constantly dares Stig to be a man. Once again, Stig faces a "test," this time one with distinctly Oedipal implications. After he has cuckolded Mikael, however, and symbolically confronted what he has done at the dying "father's" bedside, guilt causes him to "undo" his act by returning to his previous "parents."

The indicated path toward manhood calls for Stig to live with Marta as wife rather than as mother, but the anxieties being figured here are too strong to permit more than a token of that development. Instead, death conveniently eliminates Marta. Moreover, the same accident kills his twin daughter—who, given the child-mother relationship between Stig and Marta, represents the feminine (or, at least, nonmasculine) component within himself that has frustrated a normal maturation. With the sexual tangle that had bound him thus "magically" removed, Stig is free to accept his mentor-"father's" guidance. Playing under the wise, masterful direction of Conductor Sönderby while his son, the surviving twin, gazes in wonder from among the hall's empty seats, Stig seems serene; although Bergman's lingering on this moving scene suggests multiple interpretations, the radical implication is that Stig, elevated through Sönderby, has finally passed beyond his emotional childhood.

In Bergman's earlier scripts, analysis of the machinery driving the imagination explains major anomalies and often reveals a quite different pattern of meaning. Deciphering the code in *To Joy* confirms the centrality of Bergman's troubled psyche in his fiction-making, yet aside from accounting for a few apparently gratuitous elements (such as the birth of twins and the fact that the girl is later killed), it does not basically alter one's understanding of the film. Indeed, in the one section where overt story and dream contradict each other (while pointing to the same result), the tragic elevation attending Stig's reaction to the death of his wife and daughter overwhelms its meaning as wish fulfillment. Bergman the artist was gaining ascendancy over Bergman the dreamer.

This is not to say, of course, that dream ceased to be the font from which he composed his films, or that, henceforth, his fictions' private significations and public statements would coalesce. Rather, *To Joy* signals his readiness to use film deliberately as a vehicle for serious themes in which he felt an emotional stake. Though by no measure his first great film, it is the first that convincingly shows great ambition.

Playwright Bergman

Throughout the 'forties, Bergman's drive for fame was divided among three contending careers: as theatrical director, filmmaker, and writer. As the new decade began, only the first seemed still to offer a bright future —although a succession of disappointments over the next two years would soon shake his confidence in that area as well. In film, the industry stood on such an uncertain financial footing that it was about to begin a strike against the government over the issue of the entertainment tax; moreover, the failure of *Prison* at the box office and the sarcastic scorn *To Joy* met upon its release in 1950 caused him to wonder how much longer the studios might be willing to indulge him. But his ambitions had fixed least on the cinema; far more painful to contemplate was his dwindling hope of becoming another Strindberg or Hjalmar Bergman.

On numerous occasions after achieving international renown—especially in speaking to foreign interviewers who knew nothing of his past —Bergman has denied ever having had literary aspirations. In fact, that longing had been enormous. When, during his early twenties, the 'Forties-ists excluded him from their circle, he felt deeply humiliated.* "I never belonged to the 'Forties-ist group," he recalled years after his reputation

---

*In *The City*, Bergman would vent his anger in a scene in which Joakim (Bergman's persona) meets Poet, obviously a younger "self" from a time when he dared to have ambitions, and lectures him sardonically on how to succeed: show disdain for ordinary people by aping the language of the Parnassians; ingratiate yourself with a clique; avoid writing anything which might warrant more than one edition; mouth the cant of the critics; and if all else fails, have the printer set the poems backward.

had eclipsed theirs, "I wasn't allowed to play in their yard, and that often made me very bitter."[1] So bitter, indeed, that despite his instinctive preference for drama, he set his sights on the novel to prove his worth to a literary establishment that "deeply disdained the theater."[2]

Even after he had passed the age of thirty, that yearning remained unappeased. During a visit to Paris in the fall of 1949, Vilgot Sjöman noticed that Bergman had not taken a holiday from his writing. Asked what he was trying to accomplish, he replied he was following a regimen to train his prose "so my instrument will be ready should the day come when I want to write a book." To Sjöman, the effort verged on the pathetic: "Bergman could not take hold of a lyrical image without thinking of it as a parable; and so he would expand his metaphor until it cracked in all its joints. [His first handicap] lay in a need for explicitness that drove him towards lifelessness . . . ; his second, in a predilection for the overwhelming, awesome word."[3] How taxing this labor was for Bergman may be inferred from a curious scene in *To Joy* in which Sönderby—who, for all that the film reveals, never tried to write a novel or even read one—offers thanks that he is an interpreter of music. Just think, he says, what it must be like for an author faced with the anguish of "filling page after page in a book with the events of the day, of the hour; of fixing the meaning of a thousand intonations; of trying to translate the complex secret language which two lovers create and use to shield their most secret, keenest perceptions." For all his persistence, however, Bergman had published only "A Shorter Tale" by 1949—and that slim story scarcely represents the sort of literature Sönderby describes.

His efforts as a dramatist over this same period were far more productive. From his debut in amateur theater with *The Death of Punch* to the presentation of *The Murder in Barjärna* in Malmö in 1952, ten Bergman plays (including the dramatization of *Torment*) were presented either on the stage or over national radio, and several appeared in print. Even if the reckoning were limited to his five premieres at Swedish city theaters, the record is impressive. No living Swede had more new plays produced during those six and a half years, and although none of the five established him as a major figure, most critics at the start were convinced they were witnessing the budding of an important dramatist.

That early promise, however, never matured, and as the critics gradually showed their impatience, Bergman grew more resentful of anything short of exuberant praise. He even felt jealous of himself as director. "Every time I directed one of my own plays," he later complained, "I had

to read that I was a good director who bailed out a poor author. Naturally,
I finally tired of hearing this."[4] Actually, a majority of the critics throughout the 'forties gave his plays favorable (if increasingly temperate) reviews;
the fact that he exaggerated the extent of their attack indicates not only
his prickly sensibilities but also a defensive response to his self-doubt.
His difficulty with writing stage dialogue that sounded natural had been
apparent from the start, and it gave no sign of easing with practice.
Worse, despite his aggressive self-promotion, he believed himself an
unoriginal writer, dependent on other dramatists; forgivable in a beginner,
such imitation was inexcusable for one with his pretensions.

The crisis came to a head in 1950. Two years earlier, he had begun to
think about a play set in a circus or variety show to be called *Joakim
Naked*, and, upon completing *Prison* and *Thirst* in 1949, he publicly
announced he was setting some time aside for this major work in which
he expected to speak in his own voice. Before and after *To Joy* interrupted the project, he wrote several rather different drafts, but none
measured up to his aspirations. When, at year's end, he finally submitted a collection of plays to his publisher with *Joakim Naked* as the
centerpiece and it was rejected, he felt crushed by what he regarded as
"the official verdict on his ineptitude as a writer."[5] Although the *Joakim
Naked* material was reworked for *The City*, a radio play broadcast in
1951, this provided faint compensation for his wrecked hopes. Indeed,
to the extent that it was more than a salvage operation, *The City* served
as a calculated symbolic public suicide of the once-heralded young
playwright.

Thereafter, Bergman presented only one more full-length play to the
public: *The Murder in Barjärna*, in February 1952.* Although one reviewer,
while noting its diffusiveness, managed to praise "the frenzy and flaming
talent," the rest hurled abuse at this "heedless stride into pretentious
drivel [that leaves one] not knowing whether to laugh or cry." The most
prestigious newspaper inflicted the deepest wound: "That Ingmar Bergman is a rare theatrical talent need not be restated. But is he growing or
developing? Or is he deceiving himself by trying to make a virtue of his
limitations? Is he thinking of remaining what he is, a reckless and intense
illusionist with a trace of half-decanted genius?" Three years later, *Painting
on Wood*, a one-act that emerged almost by accident from his acting
class, enjoyed an astonishing success. Bergman began to dream of a

*It was not, however, his last composition of a full-length work for the theater. For a 1954
production at the Malmö City Theater, he collaborated with C. G. Kruuse on a ballet
entitled *Twilight Games*.

new start as playwright, and to prepare the way he pronounced "my early plays dead, passé, gone. I have withdrawn them from further production."[6] The notion quickly faded, however. When he chose to expand this short morality play, it took the form of a filmscript for *The Seventh Seal*. What might have been the prologue for a second procession of Bergman dramas instead became the playwright's epilogue.

Studies of Bergman have either ignored his noncinematic writing or treated it lightly; strangely, much more attention has been paid to *Port of Call*, based on another writer's material, or to *Music in the Dark*, for which he did not even write the screenplay. Underlying this bias is the assumption that Bergman's artistic development proceeded along a single, unbroken line from *Torment* to his international successes of the mid-'fifties and beyond, and that anything he wrote which was not meant for the screen had little or no bearing on his career in cinema. This view is grossly mistaken. The early films were a training ground where he slowly learned how to tell a story visually. Also, scrutiny of the 'forties scripts reveals the preoccupations that would continue to steer his imagination, though along different routes. But the adolescent concerns addressed in their substance stand at a distant remove from the issues he would later confront. In contrast, the plays, even when naive in their postulations, directly engage the Great Questions: the contest between God and the Devil, despair, the testing of life by the consciousness of death. Evidently, having perceived the stage as loftier than the screen, Bergman segregated his areas of discourse accordingly. But with *To Joy* (where his borrowing of characters from his play *Jack Among the Actors* represents an important signal), the distinction begins to blur. Over the course of the next decade, the playwright incorporates the filmmaker to write for a celluloid stage. The filmscripts, with few exceptions, are constructed as plays and they elaborate ideas that he previously reserved for "literary" use.

That he would be able to achieve in film what had been beyond the reach of his pen as a writer seems paradoxical—until one considers the means film afforded of circumventing his major problems. One scene in *To Joy* is most instructive in this regard—especially in the light of Sönderby's remarks about the writer's frustrations. Stig and Marta are making up after a quarrel when Sönderby approaches the door to their room, sees that they are oblivious to his presence, turns to the camera and reflects for a moment, then walks away. This sequence, which Bergman would later replicate in *Wild Strawberries*, wordlessly conveys a central motif: the wisdom and sense of loss that comes with age, brought to relief through juxtaposition with the folly and unwitting richness of youth. Without the camera to frame the image, to control the perspective, and to focus on the old man's face, the same scene on stage would have a fraction of the force. And if Bergman had tried to depict it in a novel, he could not have commanded its nuances with words.

Equally important, transferring his literary ambitions to film relieved the "anxiety of influence" he felt writing within the tradition of the dramatists he most admired; if his derivations lent strength to his plays, they also inhibited separate development. His attraction to Expressionism illustrates one facet of this difficulty: although it at first seemed evidence that the young playwright was among the avant-garde, it was actually the avant-garde of an earlier generation beyond which he never evolved. Furthermore, in staging and interpreting the works of eminent dramatists, Bergman was constantly in the position of having to compare his own plays to these formidable "rivals." Film presented no such daunting competition. Once he learned to exploit its idiosyncratic properties, it gave him the means to "write" in a new way. New problems required new methods and new solutions that pushed his "rare theatrical talent" beyond his old "limitations," even when he was recasting material from his plays.

Although it became rather fashionable in the late 'fifties and early 'sixties to link Bergman's films with any number of literary sources, their reliance upon conceits previously rehearsed in his noncinematic writing overshadows all other indebtedness. The fact that he had created no revolutionary approach to theater through his plays does not mean he had nothing of his own to express, nor should the crudity of his composition be mistaken for superficiality and absence of a personal vision. The Bergman the world would come to recognize was already present in the early 'forties—and, in terms of the contours of his art, retrospectively more distinguishable in *The Death of Punch* and *Jack Among the Actors* than in *Torment* or *Prison*. In a sense, it was not Bergman the dramatist and author who was left behind in the 'fifties but the Bergman of the early films.

The Death of Punch, Tivoli, Jack Among the Actors

All written when he was twenty-four, the first three plays Bergman presented to the public gush from the disenchantment of a young man who believes he has discovered the nasty secret of existence. Each depicts the world as a stage for tragicomedy. But underlying this device, itself foreshadowing a motif in his later films, is his persistent conception of life as a cruel prison from which there are no reprieves and beyond which there is only the void.

Like the *Kaspernoveller* cycle of short tales Bergman was writing in his early twenties, *The Death of Punch* uses a puppet theater conceit to portray the struggle against despair. An anti-fairy tale—in a sense, the reverse side of *Beppo the Clown*—it assumes that no one lives happily ever after in real life. Oppressed by the boredom of his role as husband, Kasper (the Swedish name for Punch) leaves his Kasperina to carouse with gangsters and their loose women at a tavern. But Kasper makes too much of his liberty. His companions bully the swaggerer onto a table and force him to dance until he drops dead of exhaustion, whereupon Death arrives and leads his body away in a large black coffin. When his wife and friends eulogize the dead man as a person with good qualities who swore and boasted only to hide his fear, Kasper's soul angrily protests. Yet, despite his claim that he deserves to be remembered as a valiant rogue rather than to be pitied for his weakness, he soon confirms their assessment: he sings to allay his terror of the unknown while sitting in his grave, and when he is summoned before the Council of the Lord for judgment, he blames all his misdeeds on others. At the last, however, Kasper discovers he is braver than he suspected; offered heaven by the Lord, he recoils from the vision of an eternity governed by the pallid morality he found intolerable in living with Kasperina and pleads for the exciting torments of hell. Marriage, far from representing felicity attained, here symbolizes the anguish of consciousness without freedom.*

Reviewers had little difficulty in perceiving the influence of some of the young playwright's favorite writers: to judge from their reports, *The Death of Punch* gave the impression of being a play on which the authors of *With Higher Right* (Strindberg), *Death's Harlequin* (Hjalmar Bergman), and *The Difficult Hour* (Pär Lagerkvist) collaborated after a night's immersion in the underworld celebrated by Sweden's great eighteenth-century balladeer, Carl Mikael Bellman. Were the play to have been revived fifteen years later, however, the question of influence would surely have been displaced by comment on its anticipation of *The Seventh Seal*. More than in the parallel of the two tavern ordeals, or in the kinship of Skat,

---

*No copy of either *The Death of Punch* or *Tivoli* is available; their contents have been reconstructed from the reviews in *Svenska Dagbladet*, *Dagens Nyheter*, *Stockholms-Tidningen*, and *Bonniers Litterära Magasin*.

Jöns, Jof, and Plog to Kasper; the film is thematically an extension of the play in its preoccupation with death as the test of the value of existence.

In this regard, an "interview" between Kasper and Bergman in the play's program is almost as revealing as the play itself. Just as, early in *The Seventh Seal*, Skat and Jof discuss their reluctance to act the roles of Death and the Soul of Man while plague is ravaging the countryside, Kasper complains that five hundred years of cheating death in the Punch and Judy show have frazzled his nerves. He has begun to believe that the play is not just theater but reality, and he is afraid that one day, instead of deceiving his adversary into the noose, the trick will fail and he will himself be hanged; thus, he is particularly worried about taking part in Bergman's play about the "immortal Kasper's death." Like Jöns, who refuses to surrender to Death, Kasper closes the interview by insisting that, if *The Death of Punch* were reality, he would "kick those pallbearers in the pants and continue with my party. And then, when my wife came home, I'd beat her; and then I'd roll around with the molls, and then I'd pull God's beard and tickle the soles of his feet. Maybe I'd murder him too. Then I'd rape some angels—yes, that would be some play!"

Tivoli, presented the next year, also probes the psychological terror in the consciousness of life's futility. (One reviewer, taken aback by such gloom in a young playwright, questioned whether Bergman was drawn to "dark subjects" because they coincided with his philosophical views or simply because they lent themselves to stunning theatrical effects.) Described in Bergman's program notes as "four true stories" based on his observations at Stockholm's Gröna Lund amusement park, the play seeks to capture the "strange mood" generated by people with failed dreams who are in the business of selling gaiety to others. The most effective of the four seems to have been one in which a whore reveals the horrifying childhood experience that has led to her amorality—an idea Bergman would use again in *Women Without a Face*—but the central image for the entire play could be found in the distorting mirrors of the funhouse which, over the years, have blinded its custodian with their reflections. Illusion blinds and permits one to dream. The carnival people, the park attendant states, "are happier than most because they have something to look forward to—[even if it is only] Tivoli's opening in the spring."

Jack Among the Actors, arguably the best of Bergman's plays even though it has never been produced on stage, crystalizes a number of concepts that would still be flashing in such late and diverse films as *Persona*, *A Passion*, *The Serpent's Egg*, and *From the Life of the*

Marionettes. Among these, in addition to its controling metaphor of life as a theater and to its *Huis Clos*-like view of humanity as forming a roundabout of mutually inflicted tortures, is Bergman's first explicit rendering of his paradoxical notion of God as both absent and tyrannically manipulative.

Whereas *The Death of Punch* humanized the stock characters of the puppet theater, here human beings are presented as though they were marionettes. The simile is immediately evident in the chance encounter between Corporal Jack Kaspersson and Mikael Bro, an old actor looking for a place to drink his brandy and quiet his nerves before opening night in the provincial town. One is governed by orders that, in passing down through the ranks, lose all logical justification; the other must obey the dictates of an arbitrary theater director who, though he writes the plays and assigns the roles, has never shown himself.

Visiting backstage that evening on Bro's invitation, Jack stumbles through a complex of tensions in the company. Because *Trio*, the new play they are to perform, matches the actors' real-life domestic triangle, there is some concern over the possibility of reality's intruding upon art. For a while after the curtain rises, the actors manage to keep to the script, but when Bro, as the husband, shoots his wife's paramour, he suddenly breaks character and screams at the audience:

> No, I won't have anything to do with this. Do you hear, you who are sitting out there? We haven't much time. Soon we won't be able to do anything. Haven't you caught on that we're people? We are created to live, to love and help each other. . . . Don't sit there goggle-eyed like idiots. Get out of here, go home and begin at the beginning. Pray to God. That's all we have left. That is the only . . . that is the only. . . . We must love each other.

In the excitement, Bro suffers a fatal stroke, but before he dies, he warns Jack against joining the troupe and becoming his wife Nelly's lover, even though he knows this is inevitable. And indeed, Bro's body has not cooled in the grave before the mourners are toasting Jack's success as the lover in *Trio*, Nelly is enticing this new leading man to her bed, and Bernhard, the former lover who has been shifted to Bro's role as the husband, is relying on brandy to assuage his jealousy.

Some time later, as *Trio* is closing, the director announces by letter that the building has been condemned. Rather than spend the money for repairs, he has decided to abandon the theater; all personnel—except Nelly, whom he has placed in a Stockholm company—are to be discharged. The company's technician, a believer in God, gracefully accepts the pronouncement and prepares to enter a home for retired theater people, but the male actors panic: Bernhard attempts suicide by hanging, and Jack begs in vain for Nelly to intercede with the director so that he, too, might go to Stockholm.

Left alone in the darkened theater, Jack searches frantically for an exit from his "terrible dream," then concedes defeat. Suddenly, an arch laugh alerts him to the presence of the director, Teodor Skarp, "a small, crooked man with an ugly, disfigured face." This creature, at once diabolical and Godlike *(Skarp* is Swedish for "harsh" or "sharp"; *Teodor* suggests "God"), explains that, "knowing everything" and "having seen it from its inner side," he had created "a little cosmos for a few characters" to alleviate his boredom. Now, bored by his "fine plaything," he has decided to cast it aside.

> I've been sitting here, pulling my strings. Pull, pull. And the charac-
> ters have obeyed me. They have jumped and danced, and leaped,
> and spun around, and I have had my entertainment. Isn't that true?
> Yes. All their pride, their squalor, baseness, envy, egotism, screech-
> ing and squalling—they have wounded each other, killed each other,
> slept with each other. The whole spectrum of repulsiveness, they
> have shown me.... [But then] I grew tired of it. I saw everything
> from the inside one more time and it was exactly the same. Nothing
> changes, nothing. And now that I am going to die, I have no desire
> to sustain a gang of half-alive puppets.

Then he, too, vanishes. As the curtain descends, Jack's appeal to the "good God . . . who must be somewhere" is answered only by deafening thunder.

Although such despair haunts Bergman's films throughout the fifties, there he consistently contrives life-affirming resolutions. In contrast, the plays (with only one feeble exception) grind down toward a final obliteration of hope. The vision of nothingness as all-encompassing in *Jack Among the Actors,* however, stands out as especially bleak, even in this disconsoling gallery. More than spiritual desolation, it enunciates a philosophical nihilism that Bergman would not again expose until *Persona.*

Like *Persona,* the play postulates the absence of any residual self behind the mask. Its characters do not represent human beings but roles—moreover, roles that are interchangeable. When, early in the first act, Nelly maintains that life is all playacting, she furnishes the key to all the relationships that follow: not only do the characters posture for each other, but they also replicate in their own lives the characters in *Trio*, who in turn cast themselves as Red Ridinghood and the Wolf.* No one manifests free will or an abiding identity. Not even Skarp, the *artifex* of this spiral of reflecting mirrors, exists apart from his role. Although he derides God as not only a figment but also a criminal who "took his own life when He saw what a damnable creation he had brought into being," Skarp is at that very moment assuming that God's role by preparing to depart from the world of "loathsome, mean creatures" he has fashioned.

Still more devastating, the drama that defines the role has neither an author nor a moral, and when it is played out, it gives no evidence of having existed except in the actor's delusional mind. Consciousness, under these circumstances, is illusion stepping out from itself and trying to discern meaning in a fiction to which there is no plot. Bro, the play's one conscious character, says he suffers from *paranoia senilis*, a malady he describes as the knowledge one is about to die without having seen a purpose to either life or death.

The theology that accounts for this theater of nightmare is conjured from the abyss. Bro calls the director "the Devil and God the Father in one person," Manichean opposites meeting in their indifference to earthly suffering. But this is only figurative language: as Skarp explains at the end, neither God nor the Devil exists other than as the invention of a human mind refusing to accept eternal nothingness. The proper image of that nothingness (drawn first by Bro, then by Jack when he has assumed Bro's place) is a spider who, after watching a fly spend itself fighting the web, kills his prey and reduces it to a featureless "little gray clump" twirled in his thread, then retracts with it into the darkness from which he came.

A Kronos who eats his children as well as a God the Father fused with the Devil, the spider-God seems psychologically tied to the forbidding aspects of Bergman's own father—as the monstrous deity's reappearance in *Through a Glass Darkly* would more clearly indicate. And just as in that film, Bergman sets an act of love against the vacuity of paternal lovelessness. The plea with which Bro breaks out of his determined role in *Trio* suggests the Sermon on the Mount, and his death alludes to the Crucifixion that, according to Christian doctrine, represents divine

---

*In this first instance of the fairy tale in a Bergman work, the old husband makes a game of playing the Wolf while addressing his wife as Red Ridinghood. Although the analogy is not precisely indicated, the game suggests the interplay of death and innocence. A similar "mythic" use of the fairy tale occurs in *Dreams* and *Face to Face*.

love made human. In contrast to *Through a Glass Darkly*, however, here love fails. No new God comes into being as the result of a new relationship between "father" and "son." Bro is finally a Christ manqué; instead of bringing the promise of rebirth into eternal life, his death confirms the terror of nothingness.

The osmosis of psychological fantasy into metaphysical metaphor also accounts for another conceit that, though only inconspicuously present in *Jack Among the Actors*, would operate more prominently in Bergman's next play—and in numerous subsequent recurrences. If the father's stern, impersonal authority serves as paradigm for a merciless God presiding over a reality of pain and death, mother, as life-giving Woman, offers the illusion of escape—or, at least, of retreat to pre-consciousness in the womb and, ultimately, to the unthreatening nothingness before conception. Thus: the wife in *Trio*, refusing to accept her lover's death, addresses the corpse as her "little baby"; and after Bernhard (who had played the lover) is rescued from suicide, his pregnant wife vows to remove his fears by making him *totally* dependent—in effect, by transforming him into her fetus. But it is mainly through Nelly, the central female figure, that the conceit develops a thematic function. Bro's tired joke in repeatedly introducing her as "the woman towards whose womb all masculine interests converge," though overtly a reference to her eroticism, suggests the appeal of her womb as a refuge. And indeed, when she seduces Jack after Bro's death, he feels numbness gripping his brain, hears "crystal-clear swirling sounds," and notes with pleasure that Nelly has suddenly become maternal. On her part, she admits that it "amuses" her "to play mother" to this "little and frail and funny" creature with "no hair on [its] body"; alternately treating him as an infant and as a fetus, she feeds him with a spoon, calls him her "darling little boy," and promises him sleep, forgetfulness, and freedom from pain.

Under similar circumstances in later works, the beleaguered male realizes his fantastic desire to reenter the womb, either figuratively or, in one case, literally. Especially in Bergman's comedies, Woman can mystically repair what truth destroys. Here, however, Nelly finally proves as indifferent as Skarp to Jack's plea for "a chance to begin anew"; the tantalizing hope she has implicitly promised leads only to disillusionment. And without illusions, *Jack Among the Actors* declares, the universe dissolves into darkness.

Rakel and the Cinema Doorman

In September 1946, the same year *Jack Among the Actors* had its premiere on national radio, Bergman made his debut as a playwright for
the professional theater by directing *Rakel and the Cinema Doorman* in
a guest appearance at Malmö. By next October, he had staged two more
of his plays, *The Day Ends Early* and *To My Terror . . .* , as part of his
duties at Gothenburg. These three texts, collected under the title
Moralities, were published in 1948, and at year's end his successor in
Hälsingborg directed his comedy, *Kamma Noll.* Yet, while this flurry
made Bergman an obligatory subject in any discussion of the rising
generation of postwar dramatists in Sweden, each premiere added to
doubts about his future importance. The plays boiled with energy, but
the author gave no evidence of forward movement.

With *Rakel*, Bergman exchanged the Expressionism of his first plays
for a realistic mode strongly influenced by Ibsen. (Even the characters
seem lifted from Ibsen's dramas.) Yet, despite its bourgeois ambience,
the play makes its way to the same motifs presented in *Jack Among the
Actors*: the web of the spider-God, the fantasy of escape to the womb,
and the anguish of consciousness. What is realistic on first encounter
gradually yields to the contention that reality is the shell of nightmare.
The interior of this haunted world is unmistakably Bergman's own mind.

The island on which Eugen and Rakel Lobelius have been living for six
years provides a sanctuary from life. He masquerades as a scholar; she
justifies her existence by mothering him and protecting his pretenses.
As in Bergman's other sanctuaries, sex has been banished: the couple
have not slept together since she had a miscarriage three years before.
But one day her former boyfriend, Kaj Hesster, intrudes upon their
game. After seducing Rakel by daring her to deny her secret lust, he
humiliates Eugen as a weakling who, in swaddling himself in lies, is
beneath contempt. These successive shock waves of truth having demolished the Lobelius "nursery," Rakel argues for rebuilding the marriage
on a base of reality, but Eugen, trying to escape into another game,
insists that his wounded honor requires a divorce.

At this point, Kaj's victory over the illusions he professes to hate
seems complete, but when his pregnant wife Mia arrives on the island,
his own self-deceit is exposed. She confides to Rakel that he is an
emotionally tender child, repeatedly hurt by society's refusal to take
him seriously; even while he boasts to her of his vengeful acts of cruelty,
he lays his head on her lap and sobs. Her sole duty as wife and woman,

she says, is to comfort him. That he has made a conquest of Rakel is as unimportant to Mia as his blague about being the scourge of God.

The disclosure that this rogue is no more a man than the childish husband he has cuckolded, however, forms only one diagonal in the play's chiastic pattern; the other emerges when Eugen tries to emulate the masculine toughness he has seen his rival display. Earlier, while trouncing Eugen at targetshooting, Kaj bragged that he became an expert marksman in the army to overcome the shame of aiming his first rifle at his lieutenant. Now, Eugen points a rifle at *his* humiliators; having debated killing everyone, including himself, he first wants to perform a "mental experiment" in the immediacy of death. But Eugen has tempted fate too far. When the family servant grabs the gun barrel, the rifle fires and Mia falls dead—even though, Eugen insists, the weapon was unloaded. Just as Kaj's "experiment" in seducing Rakel had destroyed one set of pretenses, Eugen's has destroyed another.

Despite the obvious symmetry, all the reviewers seemed puzzled by the ending. Most attributed the confusion to the accidental gunshot as an arbitrary "violation" of realistic expectations—a puff of smoke, one said, to enable the author to escape committing himself on the issues he himself raised. The only two critics of Bergman's films who have paid attention to his stage dramas also miss the point.* Yet, contrary to what this befuddled commentary would suggest, the ending's meaning is not nearly so opaque—especially if it is held against the background of the rest of Bergman's production in the 'forties.

More than rivals, the two husbands represent a divided self. Eugen, another mental adolescent hiding from manhood's encroachment, is the "mama's boy" Bergman fought to overcome in himself. Kaj, a would-be writer who delights in fantasies of evil as a way of avenging his cheated innocence, is the alter ego, poured from the same mold as the "Jack" characters (indeed, "Kaj" is virtually "Jack" backward). Though Kaj's sadistic aggressiveness masks a dependence upon "mother" that is as entangling as Eugen's, it also expresses anger at a forbidding, unloving father. In this respect, psychological conflict once again takes on a theological shape.

When Kaj secretly enters the Lobelius house, the family's strangely

---

*To Vernon Young, the ending illogically manifests "poetic injustice . . . dealt by the Devil, who sacrifices an innocent female bystander and her incubus[!] apparently to demonstrate that the scheme of things is under universally perverted control." Birgitta Steene also perceives a sacrifice—in her view, of Woman for a man: "In dying, Mia releases Kaj from his evil intentions."[1]

canny servant is singing a hymn, "Behold the Savior Comes Here." Later,
she again signals that he is more than he appears to be, but this time by
remarking that he emits the strange odor of "the Devil's folk" who "lead
souls to hell." This apparent contradiction is soon explained by Kaj
himself. In his "fear and trembling," he had written a novel portraying
mankind as marionettes; believing that exposure of this most profound
secret of existence would purge people of their terror, he thought he
would become humanity's savior. Instead, his literary ineptness transformed the novel into grotesque comedy. In despair, he then surrendered to religious faith, only to discover that, against his will and
conscience, he had been made into an agent of torture by Father God.
Thus, he now ironically imitates Christ, not as Savior but as the paradigmatic sufferer: his life has become a constant crucifixion, relieved only
in those moments when he comes down from his "cross" into Mia's
(= Maria's) arms.

But it is not solely her arms that provide a refuge. At one point, Kaj
tells of a play—inferentially one he has written (or tried to write)—in
which all the characters are fetuses: "One of them was to take a great
sack of evil with him to earth and spread it out. The poor unborn soul
protested, but it didn't help a bit. The soul was born bearing its evil."
Transparently that soul who wished not to be born, Kaj finds a respite
from fate with Mia, for, in some mystical sense, the fetus he has conceived in her is himself. In this respect, too, Kaj is Eugen's twin. When
Rakel tells her lover about her miscarriage, the "truth-sayer" quickly
blames her husband's jealousy of the fetus. And when she further reveals
that Eugen has avoided conjugal relations ever since, Kaj, recognizing
his own fantasy at work in another's mind, attributes it to fear of conceiving a threat to his sole possession of her womb.

Therefore, the gunshot that brings the play to its conclusion does
more than kill Mia. For Kaj, the pregnant woman's death removes the
fear of being born into the horrible domain of Father God he has been
"dreaming" for twenty-seven years.

Now, today, the last stone in my prison is set in place. Yesterday
there was still a chink through which I could see Mia's face, but it
also let in the daylight and worry and other people's voices. Now
nothing more enters. I hear only the masons laying down their
trowels and carrying off the leftover bricks. And then it is quiet. I am
within the darkness in my little black cubicle and believe that it is
sailing forth through pitch-black nothingness and I am completely

calm and almost happy. Because now nothing more can happen to me.

Symbolically at least, fetus-Kaj "dies," not into the terrifying nothingness of the spider-God but into the tranquil nothingness of never having been or having to be. For his psychological twin self, however, the fatal shot has the opposite significance: it marks a birth, an expulsion from his egocentric universe. Both literally and figuratively, Eugen has been forced to murder this emblematic mother in order to destroy his escapist illusions. But the very act that offers liberation also imposes guilt. The agony Kaj had equated with consciousness of what it means to be human is now Eugen's legacy. At thirty-three, traditionally Christ's age at the Crucifixion, he is about to begin his own passion.

Clearly, the untwining of these identities issues from the author's need to solve the psychic tangle within himself. Like Marie's murder in "A Shorter Tale" and the deaths dealt to a series of maternal figures in his other works of the period, the killing of Mia is a violent translation of Bergman's effort to assert psychological independence from his mother. But here, in contrast to previous instances of this dominant motif, the matricide is overshadowed by the peculiar extinction of Kaj, the failed novelist whose literary ambitions—and subject matter—so obviously resemble the playwright's own, and whose age exactly matches Bergman's at the time he wrote the play.*

An immediate reason for this "suicide" is suggested by the title's focusing on the "cinema doorman." In itself, the fact that Kaj works at a movie theater seems a marginal detail, too slight to warrant such prominence. If, however, one recalls that the debacle of *Crisis* the previous year had been blamed on Bergman's revision to incorporate Jack, a Kaj-like character, then both Kaj's degradation to the lowest position in the film industry and his dismissal at the end of the play acquire special resonances. Jack's suicide in *Crisis* had already signalled Bergman's awareness that this "satanic" adolescent figure's power over his imagination was impeding his artistic growth; Bergman's banishment from SF following the film's release served as confirmation.

That Eugen's initiation into adulthood coincides with Kaj's "immurement" in nothingness represents a kind of sympathetic magic through

---

*The symbolic import of the ages of the two main male characters is underscored not only by Bergman's troubling to inject this otherwise irrelevant information but also by their incongruity. Since Rakel, Eugen, and Kaj were fellow university students, there is no evident reason why Kaj should be six years Eugen's junior.

which Bergman hoped to expunge a dangerous component of himself
—not only from his life but from his art as well. As the plays following
Rakel and the Cinema Doorman would demonstrate, however, the
struggle between the artist and the anxieties that impelled his fantasies
could not be so easily set aside.

*The Day Ends Early, To My Terror . . . , Kamma Noll**

Had Bergman addressed himself to dealing explicitly with the conflicts
of a divided self, his theatrical development might have eventuated in a
genuinely psychological drama; instead, he disguised his anxieties as
metaphysical propositions. At a time when Social Democracy was agitat-
ing Swedish literary currents, this apparent preoccupation with the
transcendent forces of Good and Evil seemed a quaint anachronism
—the product of a medieval mentality operating in nineteenth-century
terms. Bergman sensed the public's impatience. Pleading for time and
understanding in his introduction to *Moralities*, he conceded that all
his plays

> present one and the same situation: the Devil and God; a God who
> has perhaps forsaken the world and its human beings; the Devil's
> rule; Death as an executioner and headsman; the ambivalence and
> pitifulness that are part of man's condition; the means at our dis-
> posal to lessen our suffering and that of others. This is the elemen-
> tary matter of my intentions, which I have been trying to recast
> again and again with different nuances, tones, and combinations of
> actions. Up to now, I cannot say that I have succeeded.

Even so, he immodestly maintained, his repetitiveness indicated potential strength, not weakness. Citing the great painters and dramatists
whose genius produced crude early efforts, he vowed to rework the
same theme until he could refine it to artistic perfection.[1]
    The results of this determination, however, led in the opposite
direction. *Rakel and the Cinema Doorman* suffers from stilted, prolix
dialogue, yet its basic design is clearly conceived and pinned to an
organizing idea; in contrast, the patterns of meaning made available to
the audience in the subsequent plays tend to lapse toward incoherence.

Att kamma noll is a gambling term literally meaning "to draw zero"—or, more loosely, "to
gain nothing." Since no English equivalent felicitously conveys the conceit Bergman
intended, the original title has been retained.

Kamma Noll, essentially a reformulation of *Rakel*, illustrates the disintegration. Most obviously, its veneer of distressed comedy is incompatible with the play's substance, but the fundamental problem arises from the artistic failure to bind its overt thematic scheme to the psychological exigencies that remain hidden beneath the surface.

Like Eugen and Rakel, Jan and Ingeborg Karlberg have sought refuge from time and the world by living on an island. An extramarital affair between Jan and one of his music students a decade earlier had ended abruptly when Ingeborg gave birth to a severely retarded son. Ever since, convinced that this was God's punishment, Jan has been pretending the sin never happened by hiding the "knot of cells" in an institution. To force her husband to confront reality so that they might get on with their lives, Ingeborg invites the former mistress to visit the island. Gertrud's motives in agreeing to the plan, however, are anything but therapeutic; like Kaj Hesster, she arrives bent on using truth as a weapon of destruction.

The means to revenge against the lover who abandoned her is through his intense love for his daughter Susanne—an innocent engaged to a doltish music student. By awakening the fiancé's erotic desire and then coaxing the sexually starved Ingeborg into acknowledging a secret lust for the young man, Gertrud sets the stage for an incident that would embitter the girl (and cuckold Jan in the bargain). For some undisclosed reason, however, this elaborate plan is sidetracked in favor of one that is simpler and more direct. Shrewdly manipulating the instinctive Lutheranism that has caused Susanne to show her strength by resisting the temptation of sexual pleasure, Gertrud tells the inquisitive girl about the pain she suffered as a consequence of surrendering her maidenhood to Jan. Whereupon Susanne rushes to her fiancé's room to be deflowered.

As Gertrud had calculated, Susanne's sacrifice of her virginity to prove her love results in disillusionment: the final scene finds the deranged girl sitting in a tree, where, she hopes, a drenching rain will wash away her confusion. Like Kaj after he has made a shambles of the Lobelius marriage, Gertrud appears to have triumphed. But then, inspired by some force greater than Gertrud's dark powers, Susanne descends from her perch to ask why people do not trust in the simplicity of their love for each other. No one offers an answer, yet the fact that she can pose the question somehow supplies the courage with which to face life, and as the play closes, she and her fiancé affirm the power of love by running off to marry.

In patently spelling a moral from the contrast between Gertrud's dedication to hatred and Susanne's faith in love, the playwright presents a conclusion that is more expedient than satisfying—and not only because of its facile reliance on a platitude delivered by a deus ex machina (or *dea ex arbore*) to decide the contest of good and evil. Launched by Gertrud's malice toward Jan, the dramatic argument shifts to her antagonism toward his daughter by the play's end, but without resolving the antecedent issues in the process. Jan's insularity, for example, is unaffected by Susanne's experience, and the "knot of cells" packed away in an institution is still an unacknowledged son when the curtain falls. Also, given Ingeborg's recognition that she would betray Jan to gratify her concupiscence, one can only wonder about the future of the Karlbergs' marriage. More important than as evidence of slovenly dramaturgy, the fact that so much of the play is left unberthed indicates that the plot and Bergman's imagination were not traveling the same course.

The first clue that this comic morality play's "elementary matter" describes private conflicts rather than "man's condition" within a cosmic theater is the name Bergman gives to the principal male character: "Jan" (along with its variants) is a frequently used tag associating a character with himself; "Karlberg" is virtually "Bergman" reversed (*karl* and *man* being practically interchangeable in Swedish). Perhaps more striking to anyone well acquainted with Bergman's early writings is the initial stress on Jan's sexual guilt—the circumstances of which suggest another instance of the Oedipal complex at work. Ingeborg fusses over her childish husband like a mother, and (as is shown by her erotic interest in her daughter's fiancé—nearly a son) she has a lustful nature. As though to avoid this inflammable combination, Jan, like other Bergman personae in the same situation, flees to a figure of mother-as-playmate:young, innocent Gertrud, who finds sex distasteful. But despite the repression of Jan's desire, it surfaces, symbolically, in the birth of a child—a monster son embodying his monstrous sin. Horrified by this manifestation of the truth about himself, Jan tries to withdraw from life on his island, much as other Bergman characters seek to retreat from psychological and moral complexity through fantasies of uterine return.

All these events belong to the play's past, yet their meaning is reiterated in the dramatic present, where, in an inversion of genders not uncommon in Bergman's works, Gertrud displaces Jan as protagonist in an Oedipal triangle in which Jan assumes the mother's role and Ingeborg the father's. (The implications of Gertrud's liaison with a mentor her father's age are apparent enough, and Jan's desertion of her to return to his wife mirrors a familiar pattern, most conspicuous in *Prison*, in which the "mother" betrays the "son" by proving her loyalty to the "father" at a critical moment.) The sinful affair at the play's core thus retains essentially the same significance, even though there is a variation in the terms of the relationships. To be sure, the parallel reactions to the truth revealed in this sin seem to take opposite directions: whereas, in the first instance, Jan isolates himself from the world, in the second, Gertrud responds in the defiant, vengeful manner of the Jack prototype. In both cases, however, the motivation arises from a self-contempt that is rooted in Bergman.

Immediately following her shattering experience with Jan, Gertrud had entered into a strangely sexless marriage with another older man, Robert von Hijn. Transparently the Devil *(hijn* — or, in its modern spelling, *hin* — is Swedish for "the Fiend"), he conferred upon her the "gift" to see through all of life's lies, and thereby cheated her of the self-deception that sustains belief in love; as a result, she has dedicated herself to universal hate. This ostensibly explains her mission to destroy Jan. By causing his daughter to lose the virginity Jan obsessively tries to protect, Gertrud means to deprive him of his illusion that Susanne, at least, is free of evil. But the actual object of her need to punish is herself, not Jan. In contriving Susanne's joyless sacrifice of innocence — with her father's pupil, no less — Gertrud clearly reenacts her own condemnation to unhappiness (just as Bergman repeatedly recreates his Oedipal guilt).

Seen in this light, the concluding scene reflects an ulterior meaning, with Bergman as the reference point, that is only incidentally related to its proclamation of love's triumph over hate. Like *Rakel and the Cinema Doorman*, *Kamma Noll* performs a ritual of self-purgation as the condition for regeneration. Gertrud's rapid transformation from a seemingly invincible demon into a wasted, impotent being is a kind of suicide (or exorcism), analogous to Kaj's extinction. With the dissolution of this unworthy, sin-tormented "self," its alter ego is suddenly released to the future. Just as Eugen was thrust into adulthood and a new relationship with Rakel as wife instead of as surrogate mother, Susanne begins her new life as a woman by leaving her parents' house — and the psychological conflicts it represents.

But if the recognition that *Rakel* and *Kamma Noll* follow the same psychological blueprint helps explain the latter's otherwise disjointed structure, the comparison also underscores its inferiority. In the case of *Rakel*, Kaj's transition from villain to victim is the axis of the dramatic

action; to solve the character's complexity is to understand the necessity of his escape into the amnion of nonbeing. In contrast, the reversed
change from victim to villain in Gertrud, the corresponding character in
Kamma Noll, happens offstage. She is already the evil antagonist upon
making her entrance, and although she elicits sympathy in describing
the reason for her conversion to the Devil, the ambiguity this introduces
is not thereafter engaged. Bergman appears torn by contrary impulses.
On the one hand, Gertrud manifests a radical component of his psychic
being; her grim assessment of the human condition conveys the emotional authority of the playwright's own conviction. On the other, she
represents the self-accusing, self-destructive instincts he was fighting to
overcome for both his personal and artistic well-being.

Unwilling to have the play confirm Gertrud's despair, yet unable to
generate a counterargument through dramatic means, Bergman followed a strategy of evasion. One ploy was to trivialize his subject through
buffoonery: whereas his subsequent triumph as a comic filmmaker would
rest on suggesting the essential tragedy of life while evoking laughter at
his characters' efforts to deny it, here the comedy seems calculated to
undermine the potentially tragic.* Only Gertrud is exempt from ridicule
—apparently because what she projects from within Bergman was too
tender to be laughed at. To skirt that problem, he chose another route:
transposition of psychological anguish into religious allegory. But just as
Bergman fails to ground the jokes in a conception of what makes the
dramatic situation comic, he fails to establish the basis of a theological
conflict. Although love (or God) finally defeats hate (or the Devil), nothing contravenes Gertrud's reason for embracing the Devil. The protest
earlier hurled against God's cruelty (or against the evidence of God's
absence) remains unanswered by a simple declaration of faith in love,
and in that silence, the Devil must represent a heroic refusal to accept
the evil of injustice, not (as the last scene requires) an embodiment of
evil itself.

Bergman's reliance on the trappings of metaphysical allegory to
camouflage dramatic shortcomings becomes even more pronounced in
The Day Ends Early, the second-staged of the Moralities. Loosely taking
Everyman as its model, the core of the play consists of a simple tale. An

---

*E.g.: Jan is reduced to a burlesque comedian in his pedagogical method of beating music
lessons into his pupils' heads with his fists and in his constant sniffing about for signs that
his daughter has compromised her virginity; Susanne's innocence is exaggerated into
simplemindedness (of which her roosting in the tree is only one example); and Ingeborg
—who, as the loving mother of a deformed child, should elicit compassion—becomes a
middle-aged fool panting for romance.

old woman calls on Jenny Sjuberg, a middle-aged artist, with a message from God that they will die on the morrow. Jenny dismisses the warning as a tasteless joke, yet, at a Midsummer Eve party that night, it begins to steer her thoughts and behavior. Hiding in the garden as though she were already a ghost, she spies on the intrigues of the randy guests. At first, Jenny feels calmly superior to this exhibition of folly, but when her friend, a homosexual hairdresser, discloses that his death also has been foretold, she panics and frantically tries to join the hedonistic gambol before her time runs out. The next morning, the preternatural spell seems broken by the news that the old woman was only an escaped mental patient. But then a message arrives that the hairdresser has been crushed under a trolley, and, soon after, the old woman drops dead at the hospital of no explicable cause. With the prophecy thus confirmed, the play ends in a Dance of Death, led by Fate's messenger, into the "dark regions."

It requires only a moment's reflection to realize that the *Totentanz* serves as an exclamation point to a central irony that is thematically without meaning. Three of the six dancers have not previously appeared on stage, and only Jenny among the others has been portrayed within a context of actions warranting God's judgment—and, at that, what she is being condemned for, or even whether death actually *is* a judgment, remains unclear. But it is not just the temptation to write a grandiose finale that wobbles the play. Numerous signals, such as the emphasis on the hairdresser's homosexuality, ultimately point nowhere, and substantial portions of the plot lead toward a climax that never develops. Apparently, once Bergman had decided to base the drama outside the psychological sources of his imagination by imitating *Everyman*, he could not devise an integrating idea for his adaptation of the paradigm.

Attempting to fill that hollow, Bergman once more dragged in the Devil—even though neither the allegory nor the story easily accommodates a diabolical antagonist. Robert van Hijn, Jenny's former husband, plays essentially the same role as his virtual namesake in *Kamma Noll*. Here, too, psychosexual implications seem to underlie the character (Jenny refers to having "cuckolded" her second husband with van Hijn in some strange manner that did not involve sexual intercourse—an odd, gratuitously offered detail with distinctly Oedipal resonances). In *The Day Ends Early*, however, these implications do not extend beyond some private meaning the character holds for the playwright; in the play itself, van Hijn is an impersonal figure of abstract evil, incapable of generating genuine conflict. Only in the concluding scene, and then indirectly, is he implicated in the drama. Bergman ushers in a minister to describe the universe as a battleground upon which God is about to be slain by the Devil because of human failings; presumably, this signals van Hijn's imminent victory. But how and why will he have won? And in what does his victory consist? Jenny's death? If so, why does van Hijn know nothing about either its prediction or its occurrence, and why should it be God's voice that has prophesied her death through the old woman?

Muddling the play's allegorical meaning still more is Bergman's intro-duction of Peter, a puppeteer who, prior to selling his marionettes to Jenny, performs *Everyman* at the Midsummer Eve party. Reminiscent at first of Teodor Skarp, he seems to be the Godlike, weary adversary to van Hijn's Devil. Midway through the play, however, the symbolic cues shift: from the moment he perceives in Jenny an artist like himself—"a poor actor" who has played "five hundred unsuccessful roles [and] doesn't care enough to portray another in private life"—he becomes her male counterpart. Although he does not know about Jenny's prophesied death, a sense of futility that is somehow intensified by her presence precipi-tates a decision to commit suicide (and thus unwittingly embrace the nothingness that menaces her). But then, as Jenny is being led off at the end of the play, Peter recants. Pouring out the poison he had prepared, he declares that, after all, life is too sweet to be sacrificed for the sake of a Romantic gesture. (Or, in terms of the fatalism inherent in the mecha-nism of the prophecy: Peter cannot choose to die because he is not on the old woman's list.)

Whatever is gained schematically by this shallow irony is more than offset by the dislocations it causes. The comic effect of Peter's rejecting suicide ill-consorts with the somberness of the *Totentanz* and makes everything else the play has so solemnly intoned seem silly. Furthermore, neither the dramatic action nor the several monologues have concen-trated the argument on the fatalism "proved" by the ending. Since Bergman's previous writing for the stage shows consistently sound archi-tecture (whatever its other faults), this rude construction is puzzling. Is the clumsiness simply an instance of sudden failure in his analytical judgment, or did some necessity expressed through Peter override aes-thetic considerations?

The search for an answer has to begin with the observation that, although the puppet master clearly substitutes for the playwright, *The Day Ends Early* avoids the psychological problems at the hub of the earlier plays. Only once—when Jenny tries to seduce Peter—is this surrogate self brought close to actual engagement with the plot. But the fact that this curious scene leads nowhere and is never referred to again is significant, especially if one recognizes that it has the same ring as Jack's encounters with the two mothers in *Crisis*. It is as though Bergman felt compelled to dramatize first the temptation of once more orienting his imagination toward the Oedipal thicket and then his rejection of the possibility. By concentrating his attention on the play strictly as a morality, he evidently hoped to lever his art out of its solipsism and boost his pretension as a serious writer.

Stepping clear of one snare, however, he stepped into another. Bergman's God and Devil had been tropes for a conflict within himself, not genuinely theological antagonists. Despite the often morbid subject matter of his previous plays, they express his search for redemptive values (an Existentialist protest against fate in *The Death of Punch*; Christian love in *Jack Among the Actors*; reconciliation with adult reality in *Rakel and the Cinema Doorman*). When he excluded his psychic demons from the center of *The Day Ends Early*, it left an exposition of nihilism that was not only dramatically static but also personally intolerable. Consequently, he rigged the play to self-destruct. Peter's intention to commit suicide is the author's logical response to the despair the play has equated with existence; his decision to live then gainsays the very analysis on which the play rests.*

But the "anti-drama" that operates through Peter is not just a means of exploding the unsatisfying contrivance in one particular play; it also evinces Bergman's growing concern over his failure to progress as an artist. Years later, in *Through a Glass Darkly*, he would portray a callow playwright who writes moralities (one of which, performed in the film, concludes with the hero's rejecting the poetic appeal of death in order to obey the instinct in his bowels—an expedient rather similar to Peter's simple choice of life as an escape from a metaphysical quandary at the end of *The Day Ends Early*); Minus knows that his plays are overwrought and bombastic in their immaturity (using Bergman's favorite expletive, he pronounces them "shit"), yet literary ambition and emotional turmoil drive him to keep writing. The same awareness taxed Bergman in

---

*The Seventh Seal, although written almost a decade later, presents virtually the same donnée as *The Day Ends Early*: an announcement of death's imminence brings confrontation with apparent purposelessness, which is then followed by an act affirming life set against a procession of the dead. In the 'fifties, however, he had come to realize that the negation of futility had to arise from the dramatic argument itself. (Similar juxtapositions of hope and despair occur in most films before *Persona*, where Bergman would finally steel himself to accept futility as an ineluctable fact of existence.)

the late 'forties. Just as Peter, tired of mouthing the black letter lines of the *Everyman* morality through his puppets, wishes to rid himself of his theater of despondency, Bergman longed for a reprieve from obsessions that both haunted his mind and frustrated his effort at artistic achievement. Unlike the puppet master, however, he could not simply walk away from the trap; he had to write his way through it.

The troubled consciousness implicitly responsible for *The Day Ends Early* becomes the explicit subject in *To My Terror* . . . . Spanning thirty years in six discrete scenes, the play depicts the moral disintegration of a writer, Paul, who is as close to a self-portrait as any character Bergman would ever create. In light of this unrelenting self-accusation, the title, a shortening of the infamous motto "To my terror and as a warning to others" once placed over the steps to the gallows, strikes an appropriate keynote.

The one set that serves for all six scenes replicates the flat in Uppsala that so powerfully affected Bergman's imagination as a boy. Its primary occupants, a maternal grandmother and her servant Mean, correspond to Anna Åkerblom and her housekeeper; its furnishings, a stage note states, have been kept exactly as they were when Paul's grandmother became a young widow—just as time seemed to have stopped in the Uppsala flat with the death of Bergman's grandfather. Cathedral bells ring from the next block, student singing carries from the social hall across the way, and street light shining through the blinds casts magical patterns on the parlor draperies—all sounds and sights Bergman has repeatedly associated with his visits to Grandmother Åkerblom. The evocation of childhood memory is so strong that once, in a stage direction, Bergman lapses into the first person: "[Grandmother's false] teeth lie in a waterglass, *as well I know*." One also detects in this reconstruction of the past a child's propensity for enlarging unusual people into mythic figures. Isak, a cabalistic toy shop owner who passes judgment on Paul late in the play, derives from the old Jewish storekeeper in Uppsala who sold strips of film and other playthings to young Ingmar. And a peculiar reference to a man more than a hundred years old identified only as *Dassgubben* ("the old privy-emptier") seems to spring from infantile fantasies: in his periodic collection of decomposing excrement, he suggests a personification of death.

Upon this backdrop of early memories, Bergman superimposes a story that is half confessional commentary, half projection of his fears and self-recriminations into a vision of a damned future.

Although Paul seems destined for great things in any of several fields, he devotes himself to literature as the noblest use of his talents. A parallel with Bergman is quickly established: Paul's first novel, written soon after his marriage, concerns a protagonist (Joakim) who discovers that "the earth is hell," that

> all human life is a failure. All striving is in vain, all desire is indifference, all joy just relief from sorrow and pain. We must be crushed and obliterated, and our self-sufficiency razed, for it is of the devil. Then will come the moment when we can choose between God and annihilation. It is only through accepting God that we can find this world tolerable.

Like Kaj in *Rakel and the Cinema Doorman*, Paul claims his novel's purpose is to move unbelievers to faith, but when his publisher objects to its religious conclusion, the ambitious young author wavers. His wife urges him not to compromise: inartistic though the ending may be, she argues, its profession of faith in God is crucial to his mission as a writer; without it, he would be a mere wordsmith, inferior in talent to many others. The fact that the publisher subsequently relents moots the question, yet Paul knows in his heart he would have been willing to sacrifice belief to his lust for fame. Ironically, publication of the novel with its vindication of God intact becomes the seal on a diabolical contract.

The "note" eventually falls due: citing debts from unearned advances and the critics' view that the author "is hanging himself in his own spaghetti" of tangled religious sentiments, the publisher forces him into the hack work of rewriting a chemistry textbook (apparently a reference to Bergman's duties in films like *Music in the Dark*). Forced to recognize the wreckage of his literary career, Paul begins to lead a secret life with a mistress who mirrors the depravity he now acknowledges in himself. Years later, at his forty-fifth birthday party, the false conviviality of the guests is interrupted by Isak, a vaguely supernatural figure. First drawing a circle, then rubbing it out, the ancient Jew asserts that, although the sum of no life is ever more than zero, Paul's existence is a negative number: whereas others go blindly to their fate, he has "entered the void with open eyes" and thus become "not a man but an abstraction."

In illustration of this pronouncement, the final scene shows Paul as a teacher of the abstract science of mathematics. Life has cured him of his illusions, but at the expense of all his vitality: indeed, so thoroughly has he become an "abstraction" that even the ability to dream in his sleep has left him. When two students who have submitted the identical wrong answer on an examination appear before him, Paul quickly obtains a confession from the cheater, an aspiring dramatist. But instead of reproving the student, Paul asks about his ambitions: "No doubt you write about things students concern themselves with—the soul and the body and life and Satan and God. Think anything will come of it? Are you sure it isn't just a kind of exhibitionism? Something you'll get over?" In effect an encounter between Paul and his younger self—who, in a sense, had also cheated—the interview closes the circle of Paul's existence.

The manner in which Paul's damnation unfolds more closely resembles the conventions of the morality than Bergman's approach in his previous plays, yet the religious allegory of *To My Terror* ... is more trompe l'oeil than genuine. At the start, the opposition between the sinister grandmother and Mean, whose "volcanic" laughter "proves" God's existence, foreshadows a challenge by Evil against Good, but the following scenes define no such conflict; similarly, the play marks the publisher as Satan and Isak as an Old Testament God without establishing the allegorical context for their actions. Even Paul's ironic descent into the very hell from which he once sought to save unbelievers is curiously devoid of religious implications. The real reason for his torment seems to lie in his psychological makeup. The playwright comments that the grandmother's spying on the young couple's lovemaking at the conclusion of the first scene signals the eventual corrosion of their happiness; still more suggestive is Paul's subsequent rejection of his wife for a mistress who radiates perverseness—clearly an act of self-hatred rooted in sexual disturbance. Yet, though compelled to inject these elements, Bergman kept them beneath the dramatic surface.

Between the specious allegory that never quite touches ground and the subterranean psychological rumbling is the play's actual subject: not a writer's bad faith with God but his loss of faith in his genius. Though Paul tries to defend himself against critical attack by claiming that "to talk of God is not always artistic," the truth is that he talks of God to hide the limitations of his talent; finally, despite his resentment of the literary establishment's sneering at his work as "garrulous estheticizing ... [and, at that,] a bit too clichéd," he is forced to concede that all his artistic pretensions amount to nothing more than exhibitionism. In 1947, disparagement of Bergman was on the rise—as the reaction to *To My Terror* ... itself would show. Although a corps of his admirers wrote very flattering reviews, Olof Lagercrantz, Sweden's most distinguished theater critic, delivered an excoriating judgment in *Svenska Dagbladet*.

But even Lagercrantz's harshest words about the play were not as devastating as the self-indictment within it. *To My Terror . . .* is an obituary for illusions. Remarkably, however, Bergman was not yet ready to quit the drama; somehow, he hoped, a rebirth as a writer was still possible.

Joakim Naked: *The City,* "The Story of the Eiffel Tower," "The Fish"

Instead of trying to shake himself out of the trajectory described in *To My Terror . . .*, Bergman seemed determined to follow it. For almost four years, he worked at *Joakim Naked*, the major drama corresponding to Paul's major novel about another Joakim who "goes to hell," and fought the same battle as Paul against his growing conviction that he had overestimated his talent. Whatever his conception of *Joakim Naked* may have been at the start, by the time it evolved into the radio play *The City*, he had also reproduced much the same self-indictment. *The City*, however, is a dream play: the autobiographical elements that had been pieced together in *To My Terror . . .* to form an objectified portrait of failure here reveal a mind's disintegration. If *To My Terror . . .* can be compared to an obituary, *The City* is an act of psychological suicide itself.*

The setting, a "city of memory" that blends Uppsala and Falun (the

---

*Ever the exhibitionist, Bergman was so eager to have listeners identify Joakim as himself that he published his notes for the play immediately prior to its broadcast. The first records his hypersensitivity to the biological sounds of his body and his visions of jagged images set vibrating by "the pressure of the future"—sensations that eventually coalesced into "extraordinary concrete situations." The second describes one of these "situations," which became the initial scene of the play: "I see myself as an unendingly diminishing person standing in this knot of consciousness that has suddenly assumed the aspect of a busy street crossing. . . . I decide to go for a stroll. But to avoid the danger of being killed, since I have many enemies among the inhabitants, I've called myself Joakim Naked. Clad in the protection of this alias, I experience strange events from the past, present, and future." The history of these feelings of persecution is suggested by the third note. In childhood, "Joakim" had no illusions about himself or the figures of authority who ruled mercilessly over him, yet he accepted the condition of fear without panic; his only difficulty was "a terror of the dark which could come over him in the middle of the day in bright sunlight. But after he reached the age of eight, a tumult began which has continued for twenty-three years." The final note, presumably written after the play, looks back on this period of crisis as a struggle for sanity that he has apparently either won or, at least, brought to a moment of truce: "something has been accomplished and a great deal has been destroyed, and on such occasions a need arises to count the bodies and the supplies, one's own and others' rebuffs, betrayals, and truths." Even so, Bergman reminds himself, "Joakim" must guard against overconfidence: his belief that "the battle has subsided may be the greatest self-deception of his life."[1]

mining center close by the Åkerblom summer house), reflects a mind teetering over the abyss: winding, uncharted mine shafts beneath the city collapse; shifting stresses craze house walls as they settle into the yawing earth; water pumps run incessantly to keep the swell of underground water from flooding the city; above, the atmosphere is heavy and sheet lightning flashes. In addition, a recitation of the city's history implicitly associates it with Bergman's wasted talent. Founded to exploit abundant mineral resources thirty-two years before (coincident with Bergman's birth), it seemed destined to become one of the world's richest cities: "Harbor and mines, right next to each other; no transportation problems, fine golden days." But then greedy "profit sharks" opened too many shafts. The mines filled with water and the profiteers abandoned the enterprise, leaving the city "a poor, damned hole of no importance." Now that the city lies in ruin, nature has turned monstrous: talking fish have appeared; an old hag has given birth to birds; severed hands copulate in the water; a dead horse has floated up from deep in the earth. Apocalypse is near—signifying the imminent death or insanity of the mind dreaming the play.

Two encounters dramatize Joakim's metaphysical dilemma. In an argument with a minister (who rather obviously represents Bergman's father), Joakim blames religion for transforming the paradise of earth into a "house of correction," yet he also is forced to concede that, without God, the universe would have no moral coordinates. Shortly thereafter, an actress with whom he had once had an affair illustrates the implications of such total relativism: daring God by refusing to mourn the death of an "ugly, unaesthetic" daughter has liberated Marie from guilt and turned her into a hedonist for whom existence is nothing more than a cosmic masquerade. Joakim's mind spins as he tries to fix reality under these conditions:

> Marie is theater, and theater is reality on skates and Marie is reality in theater. But is theater reality to Marie and is Marie real to me even though I am theater? If, now, this reality on skates is not real to me except in theater, despite the fact that I am theater, then Marie becomes a reality seen through mirrors reflecting each other—that is, a sliding reality, infinitely manifold.

As if in response, Oliver Mortis presents himself as the personification of the one incontestable fact through which one knows one exists: the death everyone carries in his "bowels and soul." In Joakim's case, that knowledge is insistent: he is terminally ill, says Mortis, with the "disease" of suicide. Joakim makes no protest. His life has been a "fiasco," and he would prefer to kill himself rather than to destroy his fantasies or to keep patching them "until my disgust has consumed itself."

This discussion carries them to a cellblock where Joakim's wife, Anne Schalter, awaits execution for the murder of three of their four children. Here Bergman lets fly not only the self-recriminations brought on by the failure of his marriage with Ellen Lundström but also his Strindbergian wrath against the hypocrisies on which the coupling of men and women rests. Although Anne has received the sentence, the responsibility for her crimes is Joakim's: his inability to love her, he acknowledges, drove her to kill the children "born in hatred and pity." Anne and Joakim had come to know each other too well. As a result, they could no longer believe that their love was more than lust, their tenderness more than pity, their moments of happiness more than chances to regroup in a never-ending war. Finally, the "magic formula" of forgiveness lost its efficacy. Seeking the mercy of illusions, Joakim took mistresses, but eventually the game of "pretending to be" filled him with disgust.

> I don't know what is a lie and what is truth anymore. Therefore, I prefer to be silent as long as I'm not asked directly. Then I say what I think, but by no means do I regard it as true, because the truth is always somewhere other than where I am. "I am truth and the life," saith Our Lord; but the Lord is not among mankind, at least He is not with me, and so there is only one thing which really is true: namely, that I shall die. Even the fact that I live is doubtful, but death is certain.

When Joakim arrives at his grandmother's residence on Garden Street (which corresponds exactly to Anna Åkerblom's flat in Uppsala), he is relieved to discover that the suffocating heat and the turbulence have vanished. Here it is early spring, and instead of the din of pneumatic drills and squeaking pumps, he hears the delicate sound of a music box. Inside this house of delectable memory are the relics of Joakim's (and Bergman's) boyhood: a toy train, the tin soldiers who live in a cigar box, the magic lantern with its wondrous visions. Yet Joakim senses accusation in the scene. When his teddy bear chides him for betraying the stuffed toy's loyalty and for not joining the circus as he had sworn to do, Joakim shudders and confesses, "I have buried myself in women, religious ecstasy, and in my faith in so-called artistic work—but it has all been for nothing. The tension has only increased, and now I give it all up and await the executioner."

Like Paul at the end of *To My Terror . . .*, Joakim is expressing Bergman's own despair. Unlike the earlier play, however, *The City* concludes by looking to the future; having, in a sense, pronounced himself dead, Bergman goes on to incorporate the possibility of rebirth. Thus, like a good angel, Joakim's grandmother insists he exaggerates his troubles by dwelling on them. If he can learn to be content with life's humbler delights — "playing with children, listening to music, eating good food, reading books, sleeping" — his spiritual disease, she says, will prove no worse than the measles he suffered as a boy. "You love your guilt feelings because they make you look a bit better in your own eyes by keeping you from perceiving clearly that you are a small (very small) cog in a rather great machine of causes and effects. It's your insignificance that scares you, my boy, not the twisted shadow-game of reality or the pricks of your bad conscience." Suddenly, the various characters Joakim has encountered in the city convene in Grandmother's parlor, and he realizes that they strikingly resemble the dolls with which he used to stage his plays — even Oliver Mortis, the most frightening of them, is only the doll he dressed as the villain. Next, Anne Schalter comes to pick up their children. The murders, the trial, and her condemnation to death were all a dream, she says, and although she remains bitter over Joakim's infidelities and bids him a final farewell, she relieves the oppressive guilt he had felt.

Bergman's psychic turmoil, however, had been (and would continue to be) chronic; the acute concern during this period of crisis was the artistic frustration that explodes in the play's final scene. Joakim's younger alter ego, named Poet, steps forward to read a proclamation: the few valuables are to be moved to Garden Street to await the building of a new city; everything else will be demolished and the ruins left to the rising waters. Joakim then orders his tin soldiers to blow horns and bang drums "over the wretched death train of illusions" as the city raised "by the carpentry of carelessness and slovenliness" sinks from sight. Suddenly, the apocalyptic din gives way to a serenity that is "like the morning of the first day," and Joakim's final words stress anticipation: "I'm standing on my little island in the swift, black water, outside time, empty-handed and a little cold, and turn my face to the dawn. . . . I notice that I am waiting. I wait."

As to the question of which values or new vision should justify the artist's rebirth from that womblike island, the play is silent. For the moment, the more pressing business was to reject what encouragement he might still have drawn from friendly critics and openly acknowledge that his half-decade-long career had been a failure at a deeper level than attacks from his most hostile critics had reached. Although *The City* is no better constructed than the least successful of the plays it figuratively destroys, it cleared the way for renewal. The "city of memory" it repudiates is not only the vexing experience of thirty years of life but also, more painfully, the quarrel within himself that, wrapped in theological fustian, he had made the focus of his literary activity. To be sure, the psychic self would never be far removed from Bergman's writing, and the autobiographical sources of his material would often be transparently evident, but, for the next ten years, he would liberate the artist in himself to exploit the aesthetic distance between the personal and the fictive—not, as had been his practice, use the devices of art as primarily a vehicle for his ruminations. After *The City*, Bergman seems to open his imagination to let in the world and respond to it, and although his characters would often continue to project his thoughts, their voices would become more distinctly their own.

The two stories he published as by-products of his work on the Joakim Naked drama are very much part of the same process, but they already signal new energy. Both portray Joakim as a movie director, not as a writer—an indication that Bergman had put his literary ambitions to the side and was looking to film as the main avenue of his career in the future. The more striking change, however, is in the nature of the author's performance. In contrast to the weariness he had begun to show in *The Day Ends Early*, these stories are almost giddily inventive. Bergman evidently enjoyed writing them (perhaps because he expected little), and with that rediscovery of playfulness, he was able to disengage himself sufficiently from his persona to depict this Joakim with ironically humorous detachment. Even so, this ease in writing should not be confused with ease of mind. This other version of Joakim is every bit as haunted by anxieties as the protagonist of *The City*.

In "The Story of the Eiffel Tower," Joakim has exchanged identities with another person and taken refuge in Lyon in order to escape from unspecified "personal and artistic difficulties." Chatting with his landlady's daughter, he reveals that he makes movies, but since this is just after the turn of the century and the girl is an unsophisticated provincial, he must explain what a movie is. When she asks whether a motion picture could be made about a stationary object like the Eiffel Tower, he invents a scenario in which the Paris landmark decides to move.

On a hot afternoon a week before Bastille Day, the Tower, in torment

from the itching caused by the people scampering around his body,
concludes that "the meaninglessness of this ridiculous life of duty is all
too apparent" and surrenders to a "secret desire" to stroll into the
deepest part of the English Channel. While the Tower luxuriates in the
bliss of submersion up to his iron cap, consternation in the National
Assembly brings down three governments in quick succession. A delegation of prominent officials begs the Tower to return, but to no avail. In
desperation, the deputies adopt a plan suggested by an inconspicuous
cardinal. When the Tower began his fateful walk, five of the hundreds of
people shaken from the stairways were killed; the cardinal proposes to
gather the survivors into boats and lead them into the Channel, where
they will encircle the Tower and stare at him.

Here Joakim stops the story, unable to choose between the only two
alternatives in which it could end: the Tower must either resume his
post in Paris or drown himself in the Atlantic. The landlady's daughter,
annoyed by Joakim's refusal to supply a conclusion, huffily pronounces
the Eiffel Tower's dilemma a silly story and leaves, even though Joakim,
starving for company, offers to tell a more amusing tale. The scene closes
with the lonely filmmaker playing the cello while he rehearses the Eiffel
Tower's adventures in his mind:

> Now comes the question: should this motion picture end happily
> or tragically? Does he go back to the exact place where he was on
> July 14 [presumably Paris], or does he go out and sink down into
> the Atlantic's deepest water? I can hear the board of directors:
> "Let's have something light at the end! Have you seen the box office
> reports? Don't saw off the branch you're sitting on, Monsieur!"
>
> *Aha!* I know: the Eiffel Tower does none of these things! He takes
> off to New York and marries the Statue of Liberty and they live
> happily ever after. Well now, Mr. Member of the Board, wasn't that a
> happy ending?
>
> "You've become completely fantastic, Monsieur Joakim! We can't
> follow you!"

Like the landlady's daughter, most readers surely did not catch the
sinister implications behind the whimsy. That the Eiffel Tower is Joakim
is fairly obvious, but few were sufficiently familiar with Bergman's biography to realize that the Tower is also the author who was born on Bastille
Day, that the cardinal who oppresses the Tower with guilt is patently
Royal Chaplain Erik Bergman, and that the five victims of the Tower's
decision to abandon his "duty" correspond to the daughter born in his

first marriage and the four children sired in a second (from which, in 1950, he was taking his own walk). The most disturbing part of this veiled confession, however, is revealed by the Tower's unresolvable dilemma. The images of the soft Channel bottom and the lambent delight of this watery world strongly suggest the womb. But soon after the Tower has satisfied his "irrepressible yearning" to settle into the Channel, he becomes aware of the dark, boundless sea—the symbol of death —and is "astonished" and "shaken." Suddenly realizing that the currents sweeping through the Channel lead to the sea, the Tower is unable to think or act.

Significantly, Joakim refuses at this point to follow "the interior logic in this story" to its necessary conclusion: either the horror of the Tower's suicide in the cold Atlantic or resumption of a life of suffering. But the story must have an ending, and so, finally, instead of choosing between repugnant resolutions, he evades the issue through a trick. Marrying the Tower to the Statue of Liberty no more solves the problem hidden behind the allegory than running off to Hollywood (where the board members "can't follow") would free the filmmaker from the anxiety of his "personal and artistic difficulties," but, like the distraction the magician employs in order to confound logic, the ending's cleverness has allowed the storyteller to dodge the implications of his tale. In this respect, "The Story of the Eiffel Tower" furnishes an important lesson in understanding most of the films Bergman made before the 'sixties. Throughout the 'forties, he had resorted to specious happy endings to cover up the unresolved psychological conflicts stirring the stories. In the next decade, when Bergman would offer his films as wise commentaries on life, the difficulty of devising reassuring conclusions to arguments in which the "interior logic" led to an unacceptable truth called for even greater ingenuity. Repeatedly, he would use the same strategy as Joakim to deal with the problem.

"The Fish," which *BLM*, Sweden's leading literary quarterly, serialized in 1950 and 1951, is the most elaborate piece in the Joakim cycle and, aside from his better filmscripts, his most interesting work of fiction. In its clues to the nature of the "tumult" from which the other Joakims are trying to flee, it may also reveal more about the inner Bergman than anything he had written after "A Shorter Tale." Its headnote advises the reader to regard this "diary" spanning the last four months of Joakim's life as a document representing the human condition, but, several lines on, the author hints that it points specifically toward himself: "The setting for the events is said to be the silk city of Lyon," yet some would insist "it all occurred in Stockholm."

A silent film Joakim is directing at the story's beginning foreshadows the sexual insecurity that will goad him into a series of bizarre acts. A husband, arriving home early, greets his wife with professions of his devotion while her lover is hiding under the bed. Susanne and Peter play their roles as the wife and the lover without a hitch, but Albert, Joakim's closest friend (and alter ego), keeps bungling his part as the husband. The actor protests that he is too young and too handsome to be cast as a cuckold, but the real reason is his inability to concentrate on his lines while imagining Peter laughing at him from under the bed. Curiously, this provokes Joakim to spout ardent professions of love for his wife Anne—and thus, unwittingly, to establish the parallel between himself and the cuckolded husband. Later, the director learns that a mechanically defective camera, by accelerating the action, has transformed what Joakim had conceived (rather improbably) as a serious romantic drama into a very funny farce. The anguish he is about to record in his diary will seem ridiculous in much the same way.

That night, a senseless but furious quarrel with Anne sends Joakim into exile at his studio office. To assuage his anger, he fishes through a trapdoor in the office, which is built over an old canal. One evening, he lands a great, wart-covered fish which, to his amazement, begins to speak and offers to grant its captor three wishes in exchange for freedom. Joakim quickly cuts the line. Convinced he has been working too hard, he tries to forget the "insane dream" about this "nauseating creature."

Upon returning to Anne, however, he finds another reason to wonder about his hold on reality. "Evidence" of his wife's infidelity seems everywhere—and her plausible explanations for all of it only inflame his suspicions. Finally, he notes in the diary, "a repulsive decision ripened in my heart." Summoning the fish, he uses his first wish to demand proof of Anne's infidelity. "And if she hasn't betrayed you, do you want her to do so?" asks the fish. "You've understood correctly," Joakim answers.

A few days later, Susanne is lamenting that her fiancé, Peter, has left her for an older woman. Of course, the "old hag" turns out to be Anne, who confesses she has betrayed Joakim because of a recent feeling that he wished it. Husband and lover agree to meet in a duel, but like everything else in Joakim's life of late, this ceremonious confrontation for the sake of honor rapidly develops into farce: as the men stand ready with loaded pistols, gangsters run across the field, chased by police wildly firing their guns. "I sat down," Joakim writes, "thinking that, for me, reality is a parody of parody—to the extent that I completely forgot what the parody once parodied."

Blaming himself for his wife's behavior, he becomes her devoted protector. When Anne departs for a rendezvous with her lover at a hotel, Joakim arranges to observe their caresses through the aid of a bellhop, a "researcher into the human condition" who has installed transparent mirrors in the rooms. What he sees provokes deep anger—but not for the reason one would expect under such circumstances. As Anne pleads for her lover's affection, Peter insults her: "You disgust and bore me, you have wrinkles, you are messy in your love. Try to age with dignity." Infuriated by this rejection of his beloved, Joakim wishes Peter dead. The fish, apparently responding from the deep, instantly places a knife in Anne's hand, which she plunges into Peter's throat. Joakim now leaps into the room, calls the police, and confesses to the murder.

The diary ends a month later with Joakim in his death cell, but an "editor," impelled "to describe one of the most peculiar, most fantastic events ever to occur in history," continues the story. At the guillotine, Joakim called out to the fish, and the blade screeched to a stop ten centimeters from his neck. A psychiatrist attending the execution took advantage of the mechanical failure to satisfy a professional interest by placing his own head in the contraption. Suddenly, the blade hurtled down, severing his head and producing a recoil that shot the prison warden up to the roof. In the confusion, Joakim walked out of the execution chamber and found his way to Susanne's apartment. While the police gathered on the street below, he made a desperate request of his loyal friend: "I hereby respectfully ask permission to crawl into your belly and remain there for at least nine months, after which I shall be reborn into another life." The police then burst through the door and demanded to know the condemned man's whereabouts. Susanne pointed to her abdomen.

After having repeatedly been implied and disguised in earlier works, the conceit of flight to the womb had finally breached the surface and become the most prominent feature of the story's design. What motivates this dream of escape is also more fully and consistently developed.

From the outset, where he reacts emotionally to Albert's problems with the husband's role, Joakim's fears of sexual inadequacy spread through the diary's pages. His fidelity through many years of marriage, he confesses, is not the result of virtue but of the fact that "deep down I lack an interest in women (other women, that is.)" Even the saving qualification of the parenthesis, however, is undermined in the very next entry by Anne's accusation that he is frightened of her, and later, observing Anne's passion toward Peter, the bellhop speaks of her as "a dry tree stretching her branches toward the rain." Joakim's films also attest his sexual insecurity. In one example, a man played by Joakim is laughed at repeatedly for no apparent reason, chased and beaten by a policeman and a gang of young hooligans (symbols of the masculine authority and aggressiveness he lacks), and, finally, regarded with contempt by two matrons (one of whom crashes a flower vase on his head).

Set against this background, the figure of the fish strongly implies an autoerotic fantasy through which Joakim gains a sense of potency in a world that renders him impotent. "I'd rather fish than be with interesting people," Joakim writes. "That may be because I'm always taken aback when some trick is played on me." On the night he catches the talking fish, he is in retreat from Anne's explicitly sexual rebuff; his resort to fishing, after sitting "in the lonely silence, unable to sleep," plainly substitutes for the conjugal relationship he cannot establish with his wife. Joakim's description of capturing the wart-covered creature —emphasizing pulling, jerking, sliding on his buttocks, rolling on the floor, and labored breathing—unmistakably suggests masturbation. Furthermore, the fish later deprecates the "primitive," distasteful nature of sexual intercourse with women, who are all "unfaithful, deceitful, and treacherous."

That Joakim's problems are rooted in an Oedipal conflict is amply evident—so much so, in fact, that the author, as though to defend or retaliate against the reader who would peer too closely, has the psychiatrist pay for his curiosity with the loss of his head.* Anne's role as maternal surrogate—at one point, she openly charges him with having treated her like a mother rather than a wife—is central to Joakim's confusion. She is two women in one, the idealized playmate he loves and the mature sexual creature he hates "with every fiber in my body." At the start of the story, he adoringly pores over photographs of his wife as a girl—images of an innocence that makes no demands on him that he cannot satisfy (or that will cause him to feel guilt). Yet, although she

---

*Other than for the purpose of this grim joke, there is no reason to introduce the psychiatrist into the story. Clearly, the presence of a psychiatrist at an execution *in 1891*, the year of Joakim's diary, is a glaring anachronism.

Also anachronistic is the fact that films such as Joakim's would not be made until more than a decade later. (Edwin Porter's *The Life of the American Fireman* and *The Great Train Robbery*, the first films to tell a story, appeared in 1902 and 1903.) Why, then, did Bergman push his setting into the nineteenth century? Given Joakim's Oedipal complex, the psychiatrist would have found a ready answer: Karin Åkerblom Bergman was born in 1891.

cannot be much past her mid-thirties, he is obsessed by the thought that she is old—and thus in some way vitiated by a sophistication greater than his. Ultimately, the urge to resolve the intolerable contradiction precipitates all his actions.

But this ambivalent fascination with "mother" necessarily also makes his relationship with the father figure, represented by Peter, a primary complication. In the serious drama turned farce being shot as the diary begins, the ineffective, cuckolded husband (Joakim's stand-in as the jealous son) eventually kills his wife's lover (the "father") and then surrenders to the police. Almost exactly the same "scenario" is replayed after Joakim, like a boy observing (or imagining) his parents' lovemaking, stations himself behind the transparent mirror to watch Peter live the role he had acted in the film. That Joakim should accept the blame for his rival's murder is not quite the altruistic sacrifice he would have the reader believe. Earlier, he had come close to killing Peter in the duel; this time, the secret wish for his "father's" death has been granted.*

Significantly, although forces behind his control and understanding have made Peter an adversary, Joakim wants to like him—and be liked by him; consistently, the diary speaks of him as a friend. This ambivalence toward the father figure emerges as the crucial element in *The Bomb*, another of Joakim's films. A man—Joakim assigns the role to himself—decides to kill his neighbor (played by Peter) with a bomb inserted in a beer bottle. But after the bomb has been placed among the neighbor's stores, the would-be killer, feeling guilty, strikes up a friendship with his intended victim. The neighbor's wife invites him to dinner and they spend a pleasant evening together—just like a happy family. Horrified now by the thought of their death, he reenters their apartment in the middle of the night and, unable to distinguish the bomb from the other bottles, carries off their entire supply of beer. Brimming with feelings of virtue, he slips into their bedroom to "watch the two sleeping people [i.e., his parents] I have so wondrously saved from certain death," then returns to his quarters and opens a beer. It explodes.

The deep-seated yearning for punishment dramatized by *The Bomb* subtends the entire diary, and although it originates in a libidinous desire for the mother that underlies Joakim's fears of sexual incapacity, its more immediate cause is guilt for wanting to steal the woman who rightfully belongs to the father. The thieves, gangsters, and hooligans

---

*Joakim is also guilty in another sense. Peter's "disgust" over Anne's age and her "messy" eroticism articulates the very thoughts Joakim has tried to suppress. Thus, in stabbing her lover, Anne is merely the instrument through which Joakim punishes himself.

who pop up at various times for no particular reason emanate from this sense of criminality; the frequent appearances of policemen manifest just retribution. Finally, in prison for Peter's murder, Joakim must face the officials of the law (including a minister who addresses him as "my son") who are to mete out a punishment that is as much a castration as an execution.

Although, to be sure, Joakim escapes the guillotine's blade, the manner in which this is accomplished confirms the hidden nature of his crime. In fleeing to Susanne, he deliberately chooses "the one woman whose greatest ambition is to be a mother," but in requesting permission to crawl into her belly, he fastidiously assures her (and himself) that it will not involve the taint of intercourse. Moreover, although he claims the ability to enter her against her will through the power of the talking fish (apparently forgetting that he has used up the three wishes), he eschews the aid of this magic symbolic penis. Thus, when Susanne relents and, in some mysterious way, admits him into her uterus, it is a guiltless, "immaculate" conception. Not only does this reentry into the womb place him beyond the reach of the police (the avenging father), but it also removes the offense that would warrant punishment.

Two important similarities mark the Joakim fictions as a dividing line. First, all three are fantastical versions of intensely psychosexual matters. Bergman's realistic translation of the same psychological subjects in his films had been compromised: if the rudder of his imagination found purchase in his psyche, the steering wheel had to be turned to meet what he and the studio bosses believed were the public's expectations. The theater posed comparable demands: instead of romantic plots to satisfy the masses, lofty philosophical arguments to justify his notions of what great drama should entail. The radio play and the two short stories, however, were deliberately confessional in intent, and by imitating the dream (as he had in "A Shorter Tale"), he could dive as far into the interior of consciousness as he dared.

The second common feature, that Joakim is in a fetal state at the end of each story, derives principally from those deeper layers, but it is also a more apparent symbol of his determination to make a new beginning on his career—like Stig Eriksson in *To Joy*, to begin devoting himself to his craft rather than to the cravings of his ego. Although the self-preoccupation of the Joakim cycle might seem contrary to that objective, it served as a catharsis that would make it possible.

The Murder in Barjärna

Clearly, the new start on which Bergman set his hopes as a creative artist would lie in film; even so, his last full-length play shows some interesting changes. In contrast to the moralities, it maintains a frenzied pace, and despite a sudden shift from bawdy comedy to *drame noir* (itself a new development), there is not a moment of slack in the tension the playwright generates: horror seems imminent throughout. Much of Bergman's previous writing for the stage is vulnerable to the criticism that the dramatic argument tends to be used as a mounting for explanation; here, action and dialogue are indivisible. (Especially in respect to this theatricality, *The Murder in Barjärna* differs from *The City*, where the story is minimally dramatic and Bergman liberally indulges his penchant for soliloquies.) Perhaps the most notable change, however, is the playwright's detachment. Jonas, the oafish protagonist, is scarcely a Bergman persona, and although this randy, God-possessed minister's struggle to free himself from his mother's domination is a means of defining the character, whatever Oedipal elements may be implied in that struggle do not constitute a polar conceit.

Set in a remote district of Dalarna at the turn of the century, the play opens with Jonas entertaining a company of actors he has rescued from the bitter cold when their carriage overturned on the road. Brandy and the presence of beautiful women inspire him to describe his terrifying visions, unaware that the guests' expressions of fascination barely conceal their ridicule. This lumpishness encourages the troupe's leader to propose duping the minister. Mari, the ingénue, has been jilted by a handsome young noble who had made her pregnant; if, while pretending to be a virgin, she were to entice Jonas into "seducing" her, the leader explains, the actors could then insist on a marriage to restore her honor. Mari, in no position to object, agrees to the scheme, and soon her friends are vying for the bedroom keyhole to watch Jonas perform prodigious sexual feats.

Some months past this initial joke, Mari, realizing that the trap devised for Jonas has shut on her, aborts "his" child in an attempt to regain her freedom. But Jonas is obdurate. Threatening prosecution for murder under an ancient law, he coerces her into staying to conceive a replacement for the son she has killed. Through necromancy, however, Mari uses this second pregnancy as her means of revenge. After baptism of the fetus in the Devil's name, she mocks her husband by revealing she carried another man's child when they married, then by claiming to have cuckolded him repeatedly with the hired man. When Jonas finally curses both her and his issue, Mari gives birth to the fragmented body of his son.

Eight years later, they have slipped into a hell in which only their mutual hatred sustains them: Jonas confesses his life would be strangely empty without Mari to torture him, and she recognizes that there would be no meaning to her existence without him as the object of her vengeance. At last exhausted by the futility of their rites of cruelty, Mari tacitly consents to being strangled by Jonas. When the sheriff arrives to arrest him, the two old friends try to solve a chess problem—an overt symbol of fate's dominion; upon being checkmated, the minister goes to the woodshed, where he plucks out his eyes and severs his testicles and right hand with an axe.

Although a strain of Strindbergian misogyny had frequently appeared in Bergman's writing, none of his previous depictions of conjugality had been steeped in so corrosive an acid, and although he had often favored shocking effects, none approached the horror of this murder and self-mutilation. Understandably, audiences squirmed (or laughed in the wrong places to hide their discomfit), and even reviewers who had been generous toward the playwright in the past expressed uneasiness over the "excess" into which he had fallen. That the play *is* shocking is beyond dispute; even critics who found fault with the dramaturgy conceded that Bergman's direction had successfully exploited its theatricality to stimulate emotion. Yet to respond only viscerally to *The Murder in Barjärna* is to miss half of it—and to misconstrue the other half. Subtitled *A Passion Play*, it unfolds a religious theme—indeed, it is his first genuinely religious drama since *Jack Among the Actors*. Although radically unlike traditional retellings of Christ's agony and resurrection, it concerns the hope for victory over death symbolized by Good Friday and Easter.

Medieval iconographers used Jonah as an Old Testament emblem of the risen Christ; this Jonas (a Swedish variant of the same name) is a Christ-manqué who, early in the opening scene, boasts of having raised the dead. This "miracle" actually consisted of nothing more than reviving a parishioner from snakebite, but the minister's obsession with overcoming the death he finds in all nature causes him to base his faith on such fantasies. The miraculous Christ must exist, even if Jonas has to invent him in himself; otherwise, man is but a contemptible insect struggling in life's "web of suffering" until the spider-God digests him into nothingness.

To this minister in a community of the old and dying who, moreover, is prepared to read divine will in every occurrence, Mari's sudden entrance is a sign that his "tree of life" will at last begin to blossom. The name Mari, of course, suggests the Virgin Mary, and while the minister is out of the room, her fellow actors, hatching their scheme, sarcastically call her pregnancy an "immaculate conception," but what they propose in raillery Jonas has already accepted in earnest.* If he cannot be Christ, he will conceive Christ in her.

Up to this point, the Christology has chiefly been the product of Jonas's own fixation on escape from the meaninglessness inherent in mortality, but for the rest of the play, it is Bergman's broader interpretation of the Christ myth that informs the action. Thus, the abortion of the first child, sired by the mysterious noble, implies a rejection (or loss) of Jesus, God the Father's sign of his love for mankind. Mari (the fallen woman, not the Virgin Jonas sees) believes this will bring freedom—i.e., in the absence of God and salvation, all is permissible—but Jonas shatters her illusions with his command (which one can almost read "commandment") that she compensate for the destroyed babe by conceiving another child—implicitly representing human love for one another. When the second child is dedicated to the Devil, however, the instinctual basis of love is cursed, and the fetus—the possibility of solidarity against the fears that menace life—is expelled from the womb in pieces. Suddenly, Jonas sees not only Mari transformed from a Madonna into a cess of bestiality but also the processes of regeneration as

> a dance of death: first comes Mari—who dances at the head—then we others, all we others, a long dance line; we are everlastingly linked, each penis indissolubly stuck to another. We have all died through you. You have harvested our seed. You have extinguished us like flickering candles. We are all dead: the only one alive is Death himself, swollen with his booty, bearing immortality in his bowels; a new dance begins, winding through the forest from night till dawn.

Jonas first responds to this despair with revolt. The man who had believed he carried Christ within him becomes an Antichrist, preaching a new Gospel of negation that urges his congregation to cheat Death of the future by abstaining from procreation and killing their children. But

*The Immaculate Conception refers to the birth of Mary, not Jesus, but Bergman uses the term as it is commonly misunderstood.

then, when the elders ask him to leave the village because he has demolished their familiar belief and replaced it with another "in which we can
neither live nor die," he begs their forgiveness. All versions of reality, he
now realizes, are solipsistic: "I have acted badly by exchanging an old
defective world for a new frightening one, just as false. For who is to say
that one world is more true or illusory or false than any other? Everything is finally specters of the brain and ideas in a God's tired head."
Unable to go on living with the terrible God he perceives, he decides "to
mutilate him, perhaps kill him" by destroying in himself those
"foundations on which man builds his world: the membranes of the
eye, the work of the hands, and last, the mad and concupiscent stones
between his legs."

Ironically, by renouncing Christ, Jonas has retraced the path to Calvary:
just as Jesus was repudiated by his followers, Jonas relives the solitude
of the Passion when the congregation banishes him for disturbing their
lives; and just as Jesus cried out, "My God, my God, why hast thou
forsaken me?" Jonas, without faith, feels the dread of abandonment. But
the central irony—and paradox—is that, in attempting to "kill" the God
within him, the minister reenacts the Crucifixion and becomes, finally,
that Christ he professed to be at the play's start. His last words to his
fellow villagers, "I invite you to a feast where a dying god gives his body
for food and reconciliation," hold no promise of resurrection, but in
devoting the culmination of his human Passion to them, Jonas has
made that gift of love manifesting all man can express of divinity.

Although *The Murder in Barjärna* deserved greater understanding
than it received from reviewers, much of the blame falls on Bergman.
The complex weave of the unorthodox Passion motif is difficult to
follow—as witnessed by the fact that not a single critic, then or since,
pursued the implications of the subtitle. Also contributing to the opac-
ity of meaning is the conflict between Jonas and his mother that runs
throughout the play without either affecting the main thesis or developing as a subordinate plot. Despite the inescapable suggestion that this
ancient, tyrannical matriarch in some way represents a diabolical God,
Bergman fails to relate her actions to the evil against which Jonas con-
tends or to his quest for a Redeemer. In addition, the playwright clutters
the stage with the entrances and exits of far too many minor characters:
a simpleminded member of the household, the hired man with whom
Mari claims to have been intimate, the midwife who teaches the spells
for abortion, a "chorus" of church elders, the sheriff who comes to
arrest Jonas, etc. Some of these characters do add marginal value, but

each distracts attention from the central contest of wills. Yet, for all its imperfection, the play is conceptually the most dramatic to appear after his professional debut with *Rakel and the Cinema Doorman* in the same Malmö theater. Considering the fervor of his ambitions as a playwright, one would think he would quickly have begun another, more disciplined play; instead, he abandoned those ambitions.

Certainly, one reason was the daunting attack by the critics—as Bergman himself has admitted—but there were also others. Eight months after *The Murder in Barjärna*, he mounted a production of Strindberg's *The Crown-Bride* as guest director at the Malmö City Theater. The two plays have much in common—not only in their Dalarna settings and in their folk ballad flavor but also in their themes; moreover, almost as though he were uniquely privileged to revise Strindberg, Bergman stripped *The Crown-Bride* of much of its picturesqueness and supernaturalism and altered the text to bring Strindberg's concern with evil and redemption into sharper relief. If, as one reviewer noted, Bergman had partially transformed *The Crown-Bride* into *Barjärna*, he had also leaned on Strindberg in writing his own play the previous year. Given the premium he placed on originality—and the guilt over "plagiarism" he would later confess—he seems to have concluded from this reliance that, since he possessed no genius of his own, his future as a dramatist would be limited to purveying inferior imitations.

The Crown-Bride also turned Bergman away from writing for the theater in another respect. In Sweden as in every European country, the test of a director's greatness is the ability to renew the glory of its national playwright. With his rendering of the most Swedish of Strindberg's plays, Bergman emphatically established his credentials as the preeminent interpreter of Strindberg for his generation. Moreover, he accomplished the feat in "the Big Boo," the main theater in the Malmö complex that, with its cavernous expanse, had intimidated directors ever since the building's erection in 1944; revealing for the first time "the unique combination of intimacy and space the stage's construction makes possible," he transformed an expensive architectural embarrassment into a national theatrical treasure.[1] Rewarded with a staff appointment as ranking director and artistic adviser, the next fall he began a six-year association with the City Theater that made Malmö the focal point of theater in Sweden. Having raised himself to this peak, Bergman could ill-afford to make that reputation hostage to scrutiny of another attempt at playwriting. It was far more politic to channel his dramatic writing into film.

But if *The Murder in Barjärna* extended no link to a playwright's future, it was to prove an important link in the development of the filmmaker. Although the notion of the human drama as essentially a Passion had occurred earlier, most notably in *Jack Among the Actors*, with this play Bergman first explored the manifold complexities of a trope that would become a cardinal feature not only of the specific content of his films but also of his imagination.

The Lengthening Shadows of Summer

The first five years of the 'fifties brought a drastic change in Bergman's fortunes. In 1955, halfway through his tenure at Malmö, he had assembled the outstanding acting company in Sweden, and each of his productions was feeding his growing reputation as one of Europe's most brilliant young directors. Especially gratifying were the cheers still ringing from the previous season, when he lavishly staged *The Merry Widow* to celebrate the City Theater's tenth anniversary. Frequently compared with Max Reinhardt's production of *Die Fledermaus*, his fresh, subtly ironic rendition of Lehar's operetta was the centerpiece of a national feast. In film, too, despite the critics' savaging of *Evening of the Jesters* two years earlier, Bergman had become a major force—albeit in an industry fighting to survive. This ascendancy had mainly been the result of an enormous success as a director—and writer—of comedy, and in the summer of 1955, because his comic touch seemed to guarantee profits, SF allowed him to make one of the most expensive films ever produced in Sweden.* That investment, however, would yield an astonishing return. When *Smiles of the Summer Night* won a special award at the next Cannes Festival, it ushered in a new era for Swedish film and launched Bergman into international prominence.

At the decade's start, such attainments would have been beyond dreaming. His venture with Lorens Marmstedt in founding the Intimate

---

*SF's figures place the cost at around $150,000; Bergman's, at half that amount.

Theater in 1950 collapsed after only two productions, and there was no prospect of affiliation with a major city theater. Worse, in his struggle with *Joakim Naked*, he was being forced to acknowledge that his hope of one day emerging as an important dramatist had been nurtured by years of self-deception. The instability of the Swedish film industry compounded his worries — and increased his concern over meeting the bills for child support after the recent dissolution of his second marriage. Bergman made two films in 1950 as the studios were building an inventory to carry them through a shutdown of production to force the government to rescind its tax policy; how long the strike would last, or even whether the studios would ever reopen, was most uncertain. What sort of future he might have in cinema if an accord were reached also troubled him. The promise of *Torment* had come to very little. Even the modest role the once-presumptuous young filmmaker had projected for himself in *To Joy* as a humble "soldier in the infantry" was imperiled by the scathing reviews that film received. "Everything went to hell in this period," he later said. "There was only one thing that mattered, and that was to make something the public liked."[1]

One of that pair of 1950 films, *Summergame*, would prove to be the artistic turning point of his career, but its premiere was postponed to October 1951, when its impact on the public was much softened by its comparison with another "summer film," Arne Mattsson's *One Summer of Happiness*. (Mattsson's film, made after Bergman's, packed the theaters in Sweden and caused a sensation abroad, where its nude bathing scene helped foster an image of Sweden as a sexual fairyland. When *Summergame* was exported, critics tended to dismiss it, unfairly, as an exploitation of Mattsson's success.) Bergman's second 1950 film, *Such Things Don't Happen Here*, was much more typical of his employments during this two-year period — and a discouraging omen. An adaptation of a Danish espionage novel (in which Herbert Grevenius assisted), it was strictly work done on commission. In the West's mounting fears of further Soviet predations in Europe, SF saw an opportunity for profit with a quickly made, inexpensive package of clichés about a man who escapes from a Baltic Soviet republic with compromising documents and is hunted down by its secret agents. Two versions were planned — one in Swedish for the domestic market, another in English for export; for the starring role, SF called home Signe Hasso, a Swedish actress who had been making films in Hollywood. Although Bergman's direction was more than competent, he later felt deep shame for having undertaken a film that he knew from the start would be "rubbish."*

Financial pressures also pushed Bergman into two other scripts at this time, neither of which he directed. *While the City Sleeps*, from a novel by Per Anders Fogelström, may be the worst film with which he was ever associated. Among its many faults is a risible confusion about the main character, a juvenile delinquent who impregnates a decent working-class girl, briefly settles into a job, then resumes his criminal habits and is eventually killed by the police: apparently, Bergman and his collaborator on the script could not agree on whether he should be a thorough knave or a victim of society's callousness toward the young and poor. *Divorced*, written with Grevenius, focuses on the loneliness of a middle-aged woman following the breakup of her marriage and on the uncertainties raised by her subsequent romance with a much younger man. Despite the sensitive performance Gustaf Molander elicited from Inga Tidblad in the lead role, the film falls below the level of the two earlier products of the Molander-Bergman partnership. Perhaps, if Bergman had written *While the City Sleeps* and *Divorced* in the mid-'forties, the former might have become, like *Crisis*, a vehicle for Jack; the latter, another outlet for the complex mother motif. But in 1950, he treated them as hackwork. Both are listless, anonymous articles assembled for sale in a backstreet market.

Fortunately for Bergman, he brought far more verve to the nine advertisements for Bris, a deodorant soap, that he made during the studios' strike. In European movie theaters, a series of commercials precedes the previews. In Sweden, prior to 1951, these were loud but lifeless announcements generally limited to showing the product while extolling its virtues. More than any other individual, Bergman was responsible for revolutionizing the practice. The public's enthusiastic response to his ingenious one-minute skits—in which exaggeratedly unrealistic problems are wittily and wondrously solved by use of the product —forced other advertisers to try to be as entertaining. (Well into the

---

*Most of the attention drawn by the film came by way of attacks on Bergman by the left for contributing to anti-Soviet hysteria. References to his having lent support to Cold War attitudes with this film still occasionally appear in the Swedish press.

Bergman himself later suppressed the film—but for a very different reason. Through his fourth wife, an Estonian émigré, he met some of those who had luckily survived Russian oppression of the Baltic nations and felt remorseful over having treated their national agony so naively.

'sixties, Swedish moviegoers were still hurrying to the theater so as not
to miss the *reklam*.) Of far greater consequence to Bergman than their
influence on the future of Swedish advertising, however, these skits
triggered his rise to international celebrity. Dymling quickly spotted this
new, and potentially very profitable, facet of Bergman, and when the
strike ended, coaxed him into making a comedy. The remarkable popularity of that film, *Women's Waiting*, would lead to another comedy, *A
Lesson in Love*, and then to still another, *Smiles of the Summer Night*
—which would in turn enable him to make *The Seventh Seal*, the film
that was not only to transform his career but also to establish him as
one of the great lions on the world's cultural scene. In retrospect, it
appears Bris did indeed have wondrous powers.

Largely because Bergman's success during the first half of the decade
is dominated by his comedies, these years have customarily been labeled
his "rose period." The anger that, in his 'forties films, had earned him a
sobriquet as the laureate of puberty suddenly dissipated; the filmmaker
in whom critics (and much of the public) would later find a mid-
twentieth-century Kierkegaard had yet to flush speculation that film
had become the heir to the philosophical novel. As generally presented,
the "rose" Bergman is a knowing gentleman who shows no malice in
exposing the humorous side of quarrels between husband and wife,
parent and child; who, even when he is not making comedies, affirms
the fundamental goodness of life and teaches the wisdom of accepting
the world as it is. Much in these films warrants such description, yet to
group them as a "rose" interlude would be a distortion ignoring not
only such dark hues as the surrender of innocence in *Summergame*,
the visitation of bleak reality at the conclusion of *The Summer with
Monika* and *Dreams*, and the resignation to existential suffering in
Evening of the Jesters but also the fears that wind the comedies
themselves. Ironically identified with Bergman's comic genius, the period
actually shows the maturation of a tragic sensibility, grounded in the
recognition of life as a process of loss.

As the overarching metaphor through which this tragic view is
expressed, what has been called "the summer theme" suddenly becomes
conspicuous (of the seven films, three even include "summer" in their
titles). Contrary to what foreign viewers tend to assume, there is nothing
idiosyncratic about Bergman's reliance on summer and such emotion-
laden signs of the season as the wild strawberry patch. (Ask any native
who has gone through gymnasium for an explanation of Swedish

character, and he will probably quote Montesquieu's theory that climate molds a people's soul. Certainly, the rhythmic alternation between the bewitching, nearly nightless days of late June and that latitude's long, cold, dark winter enters the marrow—one can almost gauge the national consciousness of a writer or artist by his attention to the mystical aspects of the natural year.) Nor is conscious use of the summer as metaphor a newly installed feature of the 'fifties. Beginning with *Torment*, several of the early films had closed with the protagonist looking toward summer's arrival—a trumpet flourish of hope and of trust in the future. In the 'fifties, however, summer is no longer the promise of ease beyond the troubled present; instead, it represents illusion all too briefly sustainable, illusion hostage to awareness of the approach of autumn and death. Although evidence of the shift had first appeared in *Eva* and *To Joy*, in both instances the summer motif was formally rather mechanical and thematically more like a grace note introduced in the final movement than a major chord. From *Summergame* through *Smiles of the Summer Night*, however, it becomes the shaping metaphor. Even when, as in *Evening of the Jesters*, summer itself is not involved in the story, the same pattern of ideas manifested through the summer theme in the adjacent films continues to rule meaning.

Summergame also inaugurates a period in which Bergman emerged as a master film director. For the first time, he has said, "I felt I was functioning independently, with a style of my own, making a film all my own, with a particular appearance of its own, which no one could ape."[2] To some extent, this newness grew out of the summer theme itself. The natural world that provides the "objective correlative" to the innocence of the film's young lovers is vividly, sensually captured in the images of the rocks, skies, and waters of the Stockholm skerries that recur in one splendidly composed sequence after another. But the sensitivity to the importance of cinematography is not limited by his responsiveness to the beauty of the Swedish summer: if anything, the virtuosity of some of the interior shots is even more arresting. One cannot but be reminded of Degas by the photography of the ballerinas, yet—as in the shot of a ballerina holding her sore foot while a cigarette dangles from her mouth —there is often a trenchancy that goes beyond the world of the paintings. And in his use of mirrors to unite multiple images, each contributing a different dramatic element, he created some of the classic frames of cinema history. Less obvious, but even more important as an indication that he at last understood the peculiar nature of the medium well enough to evolve an idiosyncratic style, is a new emphasis on the close-up, not only as a way to reveal the inner life of a character but also as a base in the rhythmic orchestration of shots. The six films that follow *Summergame*, apart from their thematic commonality, are a varied lot that can be sorted in several ways, but cinematically each owes something to it.

Summergame

Curiously, the film which launched the new phase of Bergman's career derived from one of his earliest attempts at writing fiction. Some weeks after graduating from gymnasium in 1937, he was confined to bed with a minor illness; to pass the time, he began writing a novella in the blank pages of his Latin notebook.

> There was going to be war, and fear of an emphatically uncertain future made me, within myself, gather all my faculties for an onslaught against uncertainty and a not-especially-bright future. It was to deal with the best imaginable: a summer vacation in the skerries and The First Great Love, two phenomena rather fresh in my mind yet which already seemed tremendously far removed —yes, experienced in another, happier life. I really don't want to assert that it resulted in a story which was original to any great degree; in fact, I wasn't writing a story at all but playing a game with shining pearls—a summer game.[1]

Marie, as he first called the story, remained close to his heart—indeed, he accepted the job offered by SF in 1942 partly for the opportunity to adapt it for the screen. Three years later, in his excitement over the upcoming premiere of *Crisis*, he confidently told an interviewer he would soon make a film of the story (now retitled *Sentimental Journey*). The banishment caused by the reaction to *Crisis* scotched those plans, but even after his reinstallation at SF, and several rewritings of the script, the project found no backers. Finally, he showed the much-revised *Marie* to his friend Grevenius.

> We removed the abused painting from its corner of shame. Cautiously yet directly, he washed off the layers of paint it had accumulated over the years. Gradually, the original image came to light. To my great astonishment, I saw how beautiful and uncluttered the first version was, and now it was only a matter of restoring it and piecing it together under Grevenius's strict supervision.[2]

Evidently, however, the process of "piecing it together" involved at least as much transformation as restoration. Bergman has claimed that he based the young man in the story on one of his best friends who had just died and that Marie had a real-life counterpart who became crippled by polio, but whatever the stimuli may have been, one can readily discern in the gawky Henrik the self-portrait of Bergman as a withdrawn, bookish teenager and, in the graceful ballerina who deigns to love him, a figure from that adolescent misfit's reveries. Since the same sort of fantasy was at the core of *Torment* and the variations that followed, one can assume that the *Sentimental Journey* planned for the mid-'forties would have been a similar film—centered on the young man and tangled by the filmmaker's own psychological urgencies.* The *Summergame* of 1950, even if it recovers the gist of the original, is art of a different order, disclosing "the presence of a great artist, not merely a gifted, or precocious, or ambitious one."[4]

For the first time in a Bergman film, the protagonist is not a masked extension of himself but a young woman—and, moreover, not an extrusion from his throbbing node of Oedipal complexity but a fully developed, independent being. With this step from his inner prison, he realized both a new freedom and a new obligation to form a character from the inside out. The major characters of his earlier films are all divisible into a few types, but even though Marie's story is essentially defined by the same initiation into knowledge of the world's evil that occurs in the previous films, Marie herself has no precedent.

Nor is any of the 'forties films as "literary" in its symbolic weave, or as elegant in its dramatic construction. Ironically, under Grevenius's "strict supervision," Bergman was exploiting the unique possibilities of cinema to prove his dramaturgic talent at the very time when his aspirations as a playwright were foundering. If the story of *Summergame* were told with chronological linearity, it would be a simple, rather commonplace narrative; broken up and reassembled through flashbacks, it develops a much more intriguing thematic geometry.

Bergman had initially used the long flashback in *Ship to India* and

---

*In 1951, Bergman himself noted that *Summergame* basically employs the formula of *Torment*: "both are elegies to youth's pure, irresponsible love and its struggle against the devil of its environment." Another comment in the same interview suggests that Henrik was the focus of the original story. Henrik's death, he said, was "a beautiful ending" to the affair. "Wouldn't it have been worse if, back in town later in the fall, the boy had found the girl less sweet and she had discovered that he wasn't at all charming?"[3] But Bergman's remark must have been colored by his memory of an earlier version, for this Romantic view is directly opposite to the point made by *Summergame*.

Woman Without a Face, influenced partly by the example of Marcel Carné, his idol during the 'forties, and partly by its postwar vogue in Hollywood. In both of these 1947 films, it was merely an arbitrary way to launch the story; then, with *To Joy* in 1949, it took on strategic significance in formulating the resolution. *Summergame* clearly shows its debt to *To Joy* (a rehearsal frames both), but its deployment of the flashback is more sophisticated. As a means of controlling the disclosure of information, it operates as a function of the plot. More important, the three time shifts divide the film's five "acts" so that Act V is the resumption of the action of I (time present); IV, of II (time past); and III (set in the present but explaining the past) serves as the linchpin locking the temporal pairs. Not just for the sake of symmetry, this formal arrangement apposes events of the past and present that implicitly inform Marie's decision at the film's conclusion.

Act I: As the Royal Opera Ballet Company is rehearsing *Swan Lake*, Marie, the prima ballerina, receives a mysterious package containing the diary of her long-dead first lover, Henrik. The sight of the black notebook troubles her, not only because it awakens dormant emotions but also because this "greeting from her lost youth" reminds her that she is aging. After an electrical problem forces postponement of the rehearsal to the evening, and this in turn has led to a quarrel with David, her current boyfriend, she impulsively boards the island ferry she used to ride as a ballet student. This dreamlike passage backward in time takes her to a child's gingerbread playhouse that, thirteen years before, had served as her bedroom.

Act II: Paralleling the start of Act I, the first flashback begins at a ballet school recital of *Swan Lake*; occupying David's place in the wings is Henrik—at this point, an unknown admirer. Although the university student is crestfallen when, at the end of the performance, Marie rushes past him into the arms of "Uncle" Erland, an old family friend and once her mother's beau, a meeting on the island ferry gives him a second chance. Happily, they are summer neighbors, and soon she is taking him to her secret wild strawberry patch; amid the natural beauty of the skerries, a romance begins.

At midsummer, Erland, lately arrived at his stately villa on the island, gives Marie a bracelet. The innocent girl treats his professions of his love for her as though they were offered in jest, and after playfully "encouraging" him, she bounds down the terrace to meet Henrik. That night, the young couple hear Erland, now drunk, playing Chopin's "Fantasie Impromptu" for the ghosts of his youth. As Marie leads Henrik upstairs to her studio, Erland's caustic words assault them. Later, safe behind the locked door, they endure one last pathetic protest by the embittered middle-aged man; then, eased by the magic of the Swedish summer night, they make love.

Act III: The aging Marie, back in the same studio, is startled by the sound of "Fantasie Impromptu" in what she had believed was an empty house. Downstairs, she finds Erland. One infers from their conversation that Erland had recovered from his humiliation and somehow succeeded in his suit for Marie; correctly assuming the diary would draw her to the island, he sent it to her with the hope of renewing that relationship. But Marie coldly rejects him.

Act IV: As the end of the young lovers' idyll approaches, frightening omens gather about them. These intimations culminate in Henrik's crashing against the rocks when he attempts to close the summer with a final dive into the sea. Upon his death that night, innocence fades from Marie's life. Sitting in Erland's apartment after the funeral, she reflects on what has happened.

> *Marie*: Is there nothing which means anything?
> *Erland*: No, my girl. In the long run, nothing means anything.
> *Marie*: I don't believe God exists. And if he does, I hate him. And I won't stop there. If he stood before me, I would spit in his face. I shall hate him as long as I live. . . .
> *Erland*: Look, Marie, there's only one thing to do. Protect yourself. Wall yourself in. Protect yourself so that all the devil's creation can't reach you. I shall help you. I shall help you build a wall around yourself. I shall teach you, Marie.

Here, Bergman's voice intrudes to tell the audience that, after a winter of intense work in the theater, Marie joined Erland on a long trip and became his mistress. (Besides explaining the affair to which Act III alludes and foreshadowing Marie's insularity at the start of Act V, this information serves as the counterpoint to the ending of Act III.)

Act V: Following the evening rehearsal of *Swan Lake*, Marie is removing her makeup before the mirror while the ballet master, costumed as Coppelius for another ballet, talks to her. With cruel objectivity, he estimates that, at best, she has eight years left in her career. He knows her terror precisely:

> Don't you think I understand, Marie? You don't dare remove your make-up. You don't dare leave it on. You don't dare leave. You don't

dare stay. Do you know that one sees one's life for what it is just once? That all the protective walls one has erected around oneself tumble down, and one stands naked and shivering . . . ?

Thought, desire, and hope, he cautions, are dangerous. "You dance. Period. That is your formula. Hold to it. Otherwise things will go badly for you."

At this moment, the alternative to the anesthesia of art enters in the person of David, who drives out "Coppelius" and offers to marry her. Fearing that her past has transformed her into something evil, capable of destroying David, she hands him the diary and tells him they can discuss marriage after he reads it—if he should choose to return.* The next day, David enters the wings at exactly the same moment in the performance of *Swan Lake* at which Henrik had entered her life thirteen years ago. Gliding into his embrace, she goes *en pointe* to kiss him, then, in continuation of the same motion, rejoins the dance.

The long, artfully photographed sequence devoted to the swan ballerinas in performance at the ending emphasizes the interrelatationship of the film's paired themes: one, the opposition of life and death; the other, the opposition of life and art. Similar to the Beethoven piece at the conclusion of *To Joy*, the passage from *Swan Lake* functions as a reprise, for, in large part, *Summergame* is a variation on the story of youth's defeat told in the ballet's second and third acts.** Marie, of course, corresponds to Odette: once she is chosen at the ballet school recital to open

---

*Twice in the plot, the mechanism of the diary misfires. Earlier, in the otherwise unnecessary scene in which Henrik dies in the hospital, Bergman shows Erland pocketing the diary; this explains how it came into his possession, but that the diary should have been brought to the hospital in the first place is annoyingly improbable. Here, the flaw in logic is more serious: Marie's concern over being debased, and thus unworthy of David, can only refer to her liaison with Erland—about which the diary can have nothing to relate —not to the affair with Henrik which, in the context of the film, is morally innocent. Nor is it likely that Marie, who is over thirty, thinks David would expect her to be a virgin, but if that were the case, he would not have to read the diary—she could just tell him.

**Pursuing a flock of swans to their lake, Prince Siegfrid discovers they are really enchanted maidens who nightly resume human shape. After falling in love with Odette, the swan princess, he decides to announce their betrothal at a ball celebrating his coming of age. This public declaration would break the spell and free Odette from her swan existence. But when the sorcerer von Rothbart learns of their plan, he transforms his wicked daughter Odile into Odette's double. Suspecting nothing, Siegfrid pledges his love to the impostor, whereupon she mocks him and leaves with her father. Having doomed Odette to her enchantment by making his vows to Odile, the prince returns to the lake, where he and the swan princess drown themselves.

the fall season in the role, the events of her life begin to parallel *Swan Lake*. Henrik and, later, David play Siegfrid, while Erland, who, in a sense, substitutes Odile for Odette by "corrupting" Marie, is the sinister von Rothbart. At the film's conclusion, however, the fairy tale's spell on Marie is broken. By offering to marry Marie—not the Odile she has imagined herself ever since she became Erland's mistress but the Odette who has been enthralled—David restores her to human life.

Bergman reinforces the point through the allusion to *Coppelia*, the ballet based on E. T. A. Hoffmann's tale. The ballet-master corresponds to the coldhearted dollmaker whose costume he wears; Marie, the "painted doll suspended from strings," to Olympia, Coppelius's soul-less automaton. Recognizing her yearning for a normal life, the balletmaster tells her it is futile to hope for escape from the career to which she has sacrificed her humanity; instead, she must take solace in the thought that, as a "marionette," she is spared the pain of conscious-ness.* But when David arrives, the "temptor" retreats, as though sensing he has already lost his Olympia.

In choosing David (or allowing him to choose her), however, Marie is not just escaping from the "artificiality" of her existence; she also acknowledges her "natural" vulnerability—that mutability which is cen-tral to the summer theme. Most immediately, she knows she is growing too old for the ballet and will soon need the emotional comfort and security David offers, but her choice also signifies recognition that, like her art, the summer with Henrik she has preserved in amber was an illusion.

In retrospect, one perceives death's hovering presence from the begin-ning of the young lovers' summer. In their first serious talk, Henrik mentions his fear of death (characteristically, Marie changes the subject by offering to show him her secret wild strawberry patch). Unlike her light-filled playhouse and studio, his house (Bergman notes in the script) is "enshrouded in half-dead fruit trees and . . . blighted grape vines." Henrik's guardian, the ancient Mrs. Callwagen, has breast cancer; her chess partner, a minister, admits to a "professional interest" in playing a

---

*The reference to Coppelius also invokes one of Bergman's favorite conceits: that life is a play written and directed by a God cruelly indifferent to the suffering of his actors. At the start of the conversation between the ballet-master and his tearful prima ballerina, he is a fellow victim of God's trap, but as he continues to speak, he gradually "becomes" the evil mechanician whose guise he wears. Like Teodor Skarp, the director in *Jack Among the Actors*, he gloats that he is an inventive artist who can go on creating forever, while she, a mere instrument of his designs, will enjoy the protection of art's illusion for only a few more years before being forced from the stage by her aging body.

match with Death.* The old woman's casual remark to Marie at their first meeting also has a dark implication: "*Henrik ska ärva mej*" can mean either "Henrik will be my heir," or "Henrik will inherit me [i.e., Death]." This suggestion recurs when young lovers take turns drawing a cartoon version of their "story." The stick figure Henrik extends a fistful of flowers to the stick figure Marie while Mrs. Callwagen sits on a money chest. The old lady's head is then lopped off, releasing a stream of money, and her ghost haunts the lovers. The minister steps into the drawing to observe, "purely out of professional interest," vanishes, and is replaced by a "horrid troll" (identified by his inflamed nose as the inebriated Erland). The troll then destroys Henrik, leaving Marie staring in amazement at his student cap, the only thing that survives him.** The lovers find great fun in drawing the cartoon, but in walking from the playhouse, they hear an owl hooting, a portent of death.

That all these things foreshadow Henrik's death is obvious, but in another sense, more fundamental to the film's theme, they also apply to Marie. By becoming a "doll" (or, in Erland's and the ballet master's metaphor, by walling herself in), she "died" as a human being because she could not accept death as a part of life. The question she faces thirteen years later is whether to continue her inanimation. In this respect, Bergman's description of *Summergame* as an elegy is quite accurate (perhaps more than he realized): just as in the traditional elegy, its subject is not the one who actually died but the admirer who, through a new understanding of nature, eventually overcomes the spiritual morbidity and alienation from the world caused by the bereavement.

Marie's elegiac process begins with her receipt of the diary (which, among other things, contains Henrik's broodings about death) and her subsequent ferry ride to the island of her dead youth. On the boat, she sees the minister who, long ago, had expressed his interest in observing the living dead; the first person she meets on landing is Mrs. Callwagen (who evidently survived her breast cancer). Both stir the embers of her

---

*Besides being another instance, along with *The Murder in Barjärna* and *The Seventh Seal*, of Bergman's linking chess with death and fate, this scene foreshadows Isak Borg's meeting with his mother in *Wild Strawberries*.

Curiously, Bergman gives the name of his grandmother's maiden name to Henrik's guardian (identified in the text as Henrik's paternal aunt). Bergman has always spoken of his grandmother with great affection and respect, yet here and elsewhere (e.g., *To My Terror* . . .) the grandmotherly guardian figure is a cold representation of death.

**This little play-within-the-play, presented as an animated cartoon, better serves Bergman's thematic point than the comparable injection of the silent movie sequence in *Prison*; even so, the transition from drawings to animation not only is too cute by half but it also works against the viewer's immersion in the film's realism.

resentment, but one can also see in these figure a reflection of her own detachment from life and her own emotional "breast cancer." Once she moves about the island and begins to recall the past, however, her mood begins to change. A widely held folk belief maintains that if a corpse can be made to bleed, life will return; the reopening of Marie's old wounds causes her to feel again.

This revitalization culminates in the marriage proposal. In analogy with the elegy, David represents the restoration of the dead lover to her, but in another form and as part of a different vision of life. Henrik was a dreamy boy, attracted to ballet (as well as the ballerina) because reality frightened him. In contrast, David, a hard-nosed journalist immersed in the world, looks upon the theater's make-believe with suspicion. The boy symbolizes a past youth and innocence to which Marie can never return; the man, a future in which they will fight, and love, and grow old. Bergman had superimposed the title and opening credits of *Summergame* on a shot of fall leaves scudding along the Strandvägen pavement adjacent to the Royal Dramatic Theater. Marie's acceptance of David at the film's conclusion is the seal on her acceptance of the autumn that awaits her.

The Early Comedies:
Women's Waiting and *A Lesson in Love*

Although *Summergame* was praised by reviewers and well enough received by the public to make money for SF, its success was relatively modest. In unlocking the possibilities of the summer theme, however, it led to the treasure room he would enter with the next film, *Women's Waiting*.

Eager to replenish the distributors' shelves after settlement of the film industry's strike had lifted months of uncertainty, producers looked for scripts that could be filmed quickly and inexpensively. Dymling, sensing better international prospects for Swedish films, was also in the market for multiple-story scripts that might provide a showcase for a cluster of Swedish actresses, and attentive to the preferences of the domestic audience, he was especially interested in comedies. Bergman fit the prescription: not only had the Bris commercials given evidence that he might have a flair for comedy, but he had also built a reputation for delivering a script swiftly and for making films on schedule and within tight budgets.

The film concocted in response consists of an odd mixture. The first element, a refurbished *Rakel and the Cinema Doorman*, retains the same characters (minus the servant and the lover's wife), basically the same plot, and even much of the original dialogue, yet here the motive is thoroughly comic. Formerly an "emissary of the Devil," the seducer in this more benign version is only a rapscallion bent on mischief that has the unexpected result of reuniting husband and wife. More significantly, the accidental murder arranged by Fate at the play's conclusion is replaced by farce in which the cuckolded husband attempts suicide but wounds only his pride. What had originally been metaphysical was thus transposed into a tale about male folly.

Behind the jokes, however, Bergman had also inserted a variation on the theme of *Summergame*. Rakel's dalliance with the lover from her youth occurs under the spell of summer's timelessness; eventually, she accepts reality and time's consequences. Her husband cannot: after clutching abstractions like honor and chastity instead of life itself, and then being exposed as a fool when they evaporate in his grasp, he takes refuge in his wife's recognition of him as a scared, confused boy in need of mothering. In this respect (as well as in the burlesque attempted suicide), the reworked *Rakel* is a bridge toward *Smiles of the Summer Night*.

The middle story casts a harsher light on the same theme. Divided into three parts, it begins in a maternity ward. Branches blown by the autumn wind appear in shadow against the wall; as they assume the shapes of a cancan line, they remind an unmarried, abandoned, and frightened woman of the Parisian adventure that has led to her predicament. This introduces the second segment, a flashback without dialogue: after shocking her companion (a prudish American soldier) by holding a franc between her thighs in public to win a magnum of champagne, the young woman returns to her hotel, where a Swedish art student ingeniously lures her to his bed. Reversion to dialogue marks the start of the third segment, set some time later, within the same flashback. The woman rushes to the apartment she now shares with her compatriot to tell him the happy news that she is pregnant. But the artist (who is subsequently revealed to be the younger brother of Rakel's husband) spoils the moment by first blurting out news of his own: summoned to join the family business in Sweden, he is quitting his bohemian existence and the suddenly inconvenient arrangement with his mistress. Too proud to reveal the pregnancy and force him into either marriage or a cash settlement, she resolves to have her baby in secret. At the end, the camera is again in the autumnal setting of the ward, focusing on her pain while giving birth.

Of the stories comprising *Women's Waiting*, Bergman felt this one achieved most. Describing himself as a cinematic dramatist-poet in an interview at the time of the film's release, he chose the passage without dialogue to illustrate what he meant: "There is absolutely nothing to that small Paris story. You can tell it in a few words—and in telling it, it sounds like one of those horrible short stories in the magazines. But it *is* film; film gives it its form. I think it is the best thing I've done in cinema because it is cinematographic all the way."[1]

Neither the public nor the critics, however, was much impressed by the experiment; instead, it was the third episode—to the purist, scarcely "filmic"—that captured their fancy and thereby had a major effect on his career.

This bedroom comedy without a bedroom concentrates on a middle-aged (i.e., "autumnal") couple trapped in an elevator while on their way home from the family firm's centenary dinner. (He is the elder brother of the husbands in the two previous stories.) The wife seizes upon the freak accident as an opportunity to refresh a marriage gone stale. By first confessing to affairs of her own, she coaxes him into talking about his mistresses, then—trading on the Stendhalian thesis that uncertainty is love's catalyst—she repudiates the confession. Her tactics are to rip down his pretensions as the conquering male in order to apply a poultice to his bruised ego; eventually, with the cramped quarters adding piquancy to the occasion, she seduces him. When morning brings rescue, the husband vows to be a changed man; he will cancel all appointments and spend the day in bed with his "wench." But on being reminded that an important foreign representative is arriving, he once again takes his post as a captain of commerce. As in the other two stories, the immediate moral is that although women are wise, the enjoyment of a foolish world's games is given to men.

With the exception of the Parisian story (and even there, the added information that the lovers later married removes its sting), these episodes reach smiling conclusions. But there is a dark underside to the reflecting surface—the summer theme's essence. The tales are "told" by three of the four Lobelius women while sitting in the kitchen of their summer cottage awaiting their husbands.* In discussing their lot, the

---

*Bergman has credited his third wife, Gun Grut, with giving him the idea for the frame and for supplying some of the dialogue. This contribution would soon acquire an ironic twist. Bergman had met Miss Grut in 1949, a bad time for him personally and professionally, and

eldest, Anita, speaks of the secret knowledge all wives hide, even from other women: that they are the preservers of an elaborate lie created by men for their own benefit. After a lifetime of cheating themselves, she concludes, women have no choice except to find consolation "either in Jesus or the grandchildren." Her sisters-in-law then narrate their experiences, which confirm the truth of Anita's view. But when it at last falls to Anita to tell her story, she refuses, thereby implying that this most knowing and disillusioned of the women could relate a tale certain to shatter the *faire-le-mieux* attitude on which the comedy depends. Consequently, her place as "teller" of the final "story" is taken by a younger sister of one of the wives. This innocent has heard the evening's secrets, yet, unwilling to believe their lesson applies to her love or her future, she proceeds to elope with another Lobelius brother. As the husbands return, they discover the lovers' boat gliding away from the cottage—and, in effect, from the "truth" that has just been revealed there. Her sister wants to stop them, but Anita's husband interrupts. "Let them enjoy their summer," he says, encapsulating the film's final meaning; "all too soon, they will come to know pain, wisdom, and the rest of life's silliness."

Following the premiere on November 3, 1952, the director of *Women's Waiting* was being talked about as the successor to Mauritz Stiller. In his eleventh film, the problem child of Swedish cinema in the 'forties finally had a hit—and with a film fundamentally unlike any of the other ten. Bergman could scarcely believe it. As though to reassure himself he was not dreaming, every so often he would drop in at the movie theater during the elevator episode to listen to the audience laughing.*

Neither *The Summer with Monika* (which he shot during the summer of 1952) nor *Evening of the Jesters* (made early the next summer) was in the vein of *Women's Waiting*, but its success had made a return to comedy all but inevitable. According to Bergman, this happened in a very casual way. He and Harriet Andersson had rented a tower overlook-

---

like the wise Lobelius wives, she nursed his wounds; shortly after making *Women's Waiting*, however, he began a romance with Harriet Andersson, who was then barely more than a teenager. This Lobelius-like fling soon caused the Bergmans to separate.

*With that episode, Gunnar Björnstrand and Eva Dahlbeck, who were appearing together for the first time, became associated as a comedy team in the public's mind. It was also the first appearance of either in a Bergman-directed film (although Björnstrand had had a minor role in *Torment*). Almost a decade earlier, when the Citizens' Theater production of *The Ghost Sonata* closed after only three performances, Bergman and Björnstrand had quarreled over the director's inability to pay the actor's wages. Bergman thought Björnstrand's demands unreasonable; Björnstrand accused Bergman of being unprofessional. The two men vowed never again to speak to one another.

ing the sea after completing *Evening of the Jesters*. While relaxing, he began composing short scenes about different phases of marriage, "just for the fun of it." As the scenes emerged, he recognized their resemblance to the elevator episode of *Women's Waiting*, and he began imagining the dialogue as lines spoken by Gunnar Björnstrand and Eva Dahlbeck. A week or so after he started, the script was finished.* "I submitted it to Sandrews [to whom he felt a debt of gratitude for producing *Evening of the Jesters*], but everyone there was on vacation, and so I left it at SF. Carl Anders Dymling, for some reason, wasn't on vacation. He read it quick as the devil and phoned to say that I should drop in. A fortnight later, the film was under way."[2]

This hastiness shows—*A Lesson in Love* has not weathered well—but in 1954 it enjoyed an enormous success, eclipsing that of *Women's Waiting*. Comedy in Swedish films, with few exceptions over the course of three decades, had tended to be oafish. *A Lesson in Love* seemed light-fingered by contrast: like the Dahlbeck-Björnstrand segment of *Women's Waiting*, it played on the audience's presumption of sophistication in its blend of naughtiness and aphoristic sagacity. It was also fresh in that, as Bergman noted shortly after its premiere, it presented an alternative to the "artless pornography" of most cinematic depictions of women. Although Sweden's economic and social development had given its women increasing independence, Swedish film, especially in its comedies, had been slow to recognize the change. The response to *Women's Waiting* had alerted Bergman to a neglected constituency; in *A Lesson in Love*, he made his bid to claim it with a bright, assertive, and completely feminine heroine who demands equal standing in questions of spousal privileges. Despite the film's faults, one can well understand the judgment of one critic that "it was superior to all previous Swedish comedies."[3]

"A comedy for grown-ups," according to its subtitle, *A Lesson in Love* takes as its point of departure the entry into middle age with which *Summergame* had concluded. Once a shy stripling (not unlike Henrik—or Bergman), David Erneman, a gynecologist, has been overcompensated for the sexual deprivation in his youth: as soon as he returns one mistress's key, another female presses her candidacy as successor. But when he learns that his wife Marianne, tired of his philandering, is leaving for Copenhagen to marry Carl-Adam, her former fiancé, he decides

---

*It has often been said that Bergman wrote *A Lesson in Love* after the calamitous failure of *Evening of the Jesters*, either to revive his spirits or to express his cynicism over public taste. In fact, he began and completed the script well before the premiere of the circus film in mid-September.

to put his juvenile amusements behind him; boarding the Copenhagen train, he launches his campaign to win her back.

Although Bergman makes much the same comic use of the couple's confinement to the train compartment as he had of the imprisonment in the elevator in *Women's Waiting*, the train trip serves mainly to string together the film's several flashbacks; nothing that occurs on the train itself is basic to the plot or necessary to the concluding scenes in Copenhagen. Nevertheless, the train assumes major significance as metaphor for the Ernemans' passage through life. This is accentuated by the flashbacks that, in a sense, the train carries. In the first, Nix, the Ernemans' teenage daughter, reveals her fear of leaving childhood and of having to deal with the sexual complexities that await her; in the last, David's parents portray what Wordsworth called the "abundant recompense" that comes when the "aching joys" and "dizzy raptures" have slipped into the past. The crisis that David and Marianne face is one of mid-life.

Like the summer theme that is its analogue, Bergman's journeys essentially express a tragic sense of marching toward death—and, indeed, the "lecturer" who delivers the Prologue alerts the audience to the fact that the "lesson" represented by the film could have been a tragedy except for the kindness of the gods. Since this is a comedy, Bergman goes out of his way to soften the darker implications of the metaphor—as in the last flashback, where Nix questions her "so very old" grandfather about death and is told that it is only the condition for new life. Conceptually, however, the "kindness" of the comic spirit is manifested through the "gods'" suspension of tragic reality to allow a reversal of the journey in time.

Arranged chronologically, the Ernemans' story begins at their wedding —which had been scheduled to be Marianne's wedding to a sculptor named Carl-Adam. When David, the best man, had found the bride about to hang herself, he learned in rescuing her that she loved him all along; after a wild battle with Carl-Adam at the wedding hall, he then replaced him as the groom. Sixteen years later, David understands that what is really motivating Marianne's return to Copenhagen to marry Carl-Adam is her desire to recapture her youth by erasing the intervening years. In a way, that impossible wish is granted: the meeting of wife, husband, and lover in a Copenhagen bar leads to a brawl that virtually replays the wedding scene and ends with David and Marianne—for the moment, young lovers again—in a hotel's newlyweds' suite.

Counter-motion in time obviously fascinated Bergman during this period. He had used it in *Summergame* and, less prominently, in *Evening of the Jesters*; upon finishing *A Lesson in Love*, he reassembled the idea as the basis for the contrapuntal structure of *Dreams* (where a train journey is again a central conceit), and, in 1956, he would give it its richest tonal expression in *Wild Strawberries*. Of all these variations, the one in *A Lesson in Love* is least dynamic. Once David reveals his strategy of regaining his middle-aged wife by behaving like a youth—of demonstrating his wisdom by acting in praise of folly—there is nothing much left to reveal; the problem with the ending is not that it is predictable but that it unfolds no new insight. Despite the fundamental importance Bergman assigns to illusion's mercy, he does very little to build a tension between illusion and reality and exploit its comic possibilities. Instead, the humor rests in jokes—some, dispatched in a single phrase; some, spread over a skit—that mostly fall outside the film's dramatic line. Perhaps this flaccidity simply bespeaks the leisurely manner in which Bergman began the script's composition and his rush to finish it. But, aside from this explanation, one can also speculate on another: by choosing to draw the thread of the elevator episode for *A Lesson in Love*, Bergman seems to have led himself back into the very labyrinth he had tried to explode in *The City*.

That Lobelius story had been based on an incident in which, after a night on the town in Copenhagen, Bergman and Gun Grut returned to a friends' apartment that had been turned over to them; as he tells it, he was a little drunk and looking forward to going to bed with his wife, but when the key broke in the lock, they were forced to spend a celibate night on the stairs. That, in fictionalizing the incident, he gave his mother's name to the wife is a minor curiosity, but its import enlarges when one realizes that, by introducing the question of Karin Lobelius's infidelity, he was surely joggling his painful memory of Karin Bergman's extramarital affair. However, except possibly in the unmasking of the boy in Fredrik Lobelius or in the cancellation of the couple's lovemaking at the end (a joke that may indicate avoidance of incest), the crossover of wife and mother seems to have had little or no consequence in terms of the tale's design. The sketch's intrinsically comic circumstances, coupled with its brevity, allowed Bergman to fix his attention elsewhere. Its extrapolation into the full-length *A Lesson in Love* was another matter.

Changing the name of the wife from "Karin" to "Marianne" would seem to set the association with Karin Bergman at a greater distance, but what is sent out one door reenters through another. Although Bergman uses "Marianne" for the first time here, both parts of the compound name recur in a number of earlier works—generally manifesting, in some respect, that ambivalence toward women so clearly traceable to his relationship with his mother. "Marie" appears six times: in "A Shorter Tale," *Rakel and the Cinema Doorman* (where it takes the short form "Mia"), *The City*, "The Story of the Eiffel Tower," *Summergame*, and *The Murder in Barjärna* (where the name is "Mari"). In half of these instances, the character explicitly reflects forbidden libidinous desires—she is "reality on skates"; in the others, implicitly.* Through the diminutive form, Mary the Virgin Mother shows her inverted aspect of concupiscence —and, as if in payment for that sin, the Marie character is violently killed in three of the fictions. "Anne," though the mistress in *Evening of the Jesters*, is the wife in *The City*, "The Fish," and (as Anita) *Women's Waiting*. If, as wife, she is aloof and strangely unerotic, "The Fish" makes it fairly obvious that the reason has to do with the perception of her as a mother—in this representation, the distant, mature adult who so over-whelms her son/husband that he is reduced to infantile impotence.

The key to the idea behind *A Lesson in Love* is, in a sense, the key that must be turned in the lock in Copenhagen to permit David to make love to "Marie-Anne." Other men may see Marianne as "Marie," but to David his strong-willed wife has been "Anne." Repeatedly, David says that "the con-jugal bed is the grave of love"—and though the aphorism strikes a comic note, it also suggests his inability to function conjugally. The cause of his failure is implied not only by David's words and deportment but also, more significantly, by the plot. Marianne is David's wife by virtue of his having "stolen" her from the "rightful" groom—the father figure (in David's, or Bergman's, mind) to whom she is now returning. The "happy ending" depends upon David's ability to repeat the "theft" and to make good his presumption in bed. The closing shot confirms this success, but first its precondition must be established. Thus: in the bar (situated in Nyhavn, Copenhagen's notorious red-light district), David approaches a

---

*In the Eiffel Tower story, Marie is the landlady's daughter to whom Joakim tells the tale. Although nothing sexual actually happens between them, the scent of its possibility is quite evident, and in Marie's angry exit, there is more than a hint of her frustration over Joakim's stupid insistence on telling stories when he has the opportunity for a rather more exciting activity.

In *Rakel and the Cinema Doorman*, though Mia is not herself an erotic figure, she uniquely understands her Jack-like consort.

Marie in *Summergame* seems furthest from what is connoted by the name in the other cases, but if one imagines Henrik as the story's central consciousness (as would almost certainly have been the case had the film been made in the 'forties), she emerges more clearly as an embodiment of his adolescent sexual fantasy. (In this respect, since the fantasy is ultimately tied to the mother, Erland's role as the father who sexually vitiates Marie becomes rather transparent.) Both Henrik's death (the punishment for his sexual guilt) and Marie's curious sense of her sinfulness are also referable to this fantasy element.

prostitute, announcing he will kiss "the most beautiful woman in Denmark." Marianne, who has dismissed all his other ploys, is suddenly inflamed by jealousy and begins the fight that culminates in their reunion. The fact that she gets the kiss signals her sexual acceptance by David.

But why should what lies behind the story make any difference? The answer is that, by again letting himself be drawn into his psychosexual tangle, Bergman produced a comedy radically divided against itself. Counter to the sermonizing that sex is a part of life is the latent wish that it were not. The only Ernemans who are at peace are David's mother and father, who have lost their passionate instincts; for the rest, sex spells trouble. Even while carousing, David speaks of the advantages of "the kindly indifferent log fire" of domesticity over the "entirely different kind of fire which is very, very dangerous because it consumes home, children, responsibility, and decency and leads to absolutely nothing." Nothing in his pursuit of Marianne should convince the audience that he longs to stir the home embers—not even the final "nuptial" scene, which, in terms of what the film has explicitly presented (whatever else may implicitly be at work), has to be seen as the triumph of David's efforts to restore a family for Nix's sake and to secure a companion for his old age. Nor is Marianne really an erotic animal. What was missed by the women who wrote to Swedish newspapers applauding Marianne's stance for equal privileges in extramarital affairs is that she wants no affairs at all. Moreover, in taking her husband back, she is more dupe than feminist champion: as lover, David seems to be feigning ardor he does not feel in order to appease a feminine foible.

Erotic comedy need not, of course, advocate eroticism: even the bawdy plots of the English Restoration stage took care to affirm the middle-class values of domesticity at the curtain. But, antierotic at its core, *A Lesson in Love* tries to overcome its nature by straining to make jokes that pretend a different sympathy. Furthermore, although what makes it schematically a comedy is the Ernemans' counter-motion toward their youth, that tide of pleasant illusion never quite overcomes the effect of another—one which has nothing to do with death or old age. Nix's trepidation over the onset of sexual maturity, for example, seems entirely in keeping with what the film is overtly about. A rutting fever has seized her once-sane world and driven it mad: her father has become an "erotic baboon" and her mother is "acting like a cow" in carrying on with Carl-Adam; worse (because it raises fears of what awaits her), her best friend has begun "painting her mouth, curling her hair, swinging her behind, and doing distasteful things with the damn fool she's in love with." But when Bergman has the miserable girl beg her father to transform her anatomically into a boy so that she might resume her happy childhood, he begins stepping toward the haunted precincts of "A Shorter Tale." (And, indeed, there may have been a connection in Bergman's mind: in the filmscript, besides her pidgin German nickname Nix, she also bears her given name, Jacqueline—the feminine form of Jack.) The same echo is heard in Sam, the elder Ernemans' family servant. A felon who murdered his girlfriend, Sam has enjoyed the serenity of life without passion ever since David's father surgically removed his libido by performing a lobotomy—symbolically a castration.

Less than two years later, Bergman would write *Smiles of the Summer Night*, another comedy for the Björnstrand-Dahlbeck team that derives from much the same psychological sources. In that film, too, Björnstrand plays a character who, for all his masculine swagger, has sexually failed with his Anne, and Eva Dahlbeck portrays a woman who, at the end, emerges as a maternal companion rather than a sexual partner; moreover, in Henrik, the son who tries suicide to escape from his sexual confusion, one can see a certain resemblance to Nix. But in *Smiles of the Summer Night*, the gears of comic fantasy smoothly transfer the energy supplied by Bergman's psyche; in *A Lesson in Love*, the comedy pulls against the drive of the machinery.

The Summer with Monika

Of the two very different films bracketed by the pair of comedies, *The Summer with Monika* must be rated the lesser, despite vigorous advocates who would have it among Bergman's best films. Certainly, judged strictly as a piece of fiction, it is a slight thing—in which, moreover, the extent of Bergman's contribution is difficult to determine.

According to Bergman, the origin of the film was a street meeting with Per Anders Fogelström shortly after their collaboration on *While the City Sleeps*. When Fogelström mentioned he was thinking of writing a story about a couple of adolescents who flee their jobs and families for the wild pleasures of life in the Stockholm archipelago, the idea immediately hit the filmmaker's fancy, and about a year later, they patched together a script which Fogelström then rewrote as a novel before the film was made. Others, equally authoritative, insist that Fogelström's novel preceded the script and that SF had brought it to the director's attention. But even if fact were completely on the side of the latter version, Bergman quickly took over the story; *The Summer with Monika* was never just an assignment.

Harriet Andersson was a major reason. A variety show entertainer who excited the interest of several males in the Stockholm film colony, she had had only a few bit parts (including one in *While the City Sleeps*) before her minor role in *Defiance*, released in early 1952, convinced Bergman she would be the perfect Monika. With the vision of a month in the skerries in the company of the young actress to spur him on, he began urging SF to make a commitment. It would be, he promised, "the world's cheapest film": nature had already provided most of the sets; he would use a silent camera for the outdoor scenes (and dub the soundtrack later); and only a small crew would be required. Dymling was enthusiastic: *One Summer of Happiness* was fast becoming the most profitable Swedish film ever, and he thought the love alfresco elements of the Fogelström-Bergman script would also appeal to a foreign market eager for confirmation of the myth of a sexual playground lit by the Midnight Sun. This same aspect, however, roused opposition from some SF board members who were unwilling to lay their moral scruples aside for the sake of profits. After long debate and even resignations from the board, Dymling prevailed, but Bergman had to consent not to go beyond the approved script. (Since the potential for sexual frankness depended on the director's judgment on what the camera should show, he still had great licence—which he took, and which caused some squabbling with SF. He won the arguments, but after the film was completed, the Swedish censor removed much of the "offensive" material.) In retrospect, it is hard to see what could have provoked such recalcitrance: the story basically preaches a rather conventional morality.

Monika Eriksson lives in a squalid flat, crowded by younger siblings and her parents' problems. Her job in a vegetable wholesale house intensifies the dreamy girl's frustration, making her convenient prey for sexual conquest by male co-workers, who then ridicule her. Harry's material circumstances are more comfortable, but he is just as lonely. His mother is dead; his father has been a silent, distant parent; the older employees in the glass and porcelain shop where he works as a stock boy harass him as an outlet for their resentment of their dull, routine labor. These two victims meet at the beginning of spring and dare believe it will bring a new season in their lives as well.

Blinded by their emotions, they fail to recognize differences in their characters: after a date watching a movie (suggestively entitled *Summer and Love*), Harry swells with manly pride over at last having a girlfriend, but to Monika the clumsy fellow by her side is a lover to be pressed into a mold of Hollywood-inspired fantasies. When Harry loses his job after spending the night with her, they set off for the skerries to live Monika's dream of escape from all restrictions.

For a while, their island is a domain of innocence where they forage, bathe in the sun, make love on the sand, and exult in their freedom with chest-beating and Tarzan yells. When evil intrudes on their paradise in the person of Lelle, Monika's former lover, they vanquish him. But on Midsummer Night, Monika announces she is pregnant, and suddenly everything changes. Dissatisfied with a diet of mushrooms, the manna of their first weeks in the wild, Monika begins scavenging among the summer cottages. Once, she snatches a roast from under the eyes of the family that has caught her and rips at her prize while on the run. Snarling at her mate for his timidity, she reveals the feral nature within her.

As summer ends, all illusion dies with it. Forced by their creature needs to return to Stockholm, the couple deliver themselves to Harry's aunt, who arranges a wedding and furnishes their flat. Harry accepts his fate, gets a job, and studies at night toward an engineering degree, but Monika is an angry, caged animal, contemptuous of Harry's diligence. Except for naming the newborn baby "June"—a name she cannot even pronounce but which evokes the Hollywood of her fantasies—she shows no interest in the child. Predictably, on returning early from work one day, Harry finds her in bed with Lelle. The film concludes with a shot of Harry's aunt haggling with a junk dealer over the sale of the furniture while Harry, holding his infant daughter, stares into a mirror outside his former employer's shop. He has been jarred out of youth, but one senses he will soon achieve that middle-class respectabilty to which he is temperamentally suited. A far different future awaits Monika. In the last shot of her, she is in a café with a prospective lover; as she turns and stares into the camera ("a forbidden practice at the time," Bergman later noted with satisfaction), she seems to defy the audience's judgment.

A publicity still, showing an obviously posed Harriet Andersson with a half-unbuttoned sweater pulled down over her shoulders and her legs tucked back to expose her thighs, expresses very little of the film but tells a great deal about how the film was marketed—and received. It turned a good profit at home and had a checkered success elsewhere in Europe. (It also attracted attention in various parts of the New World. Uruguay gave it much fanfare and a long run. In the United States, where pirated prints found their way into the sleazier big city theaters, it reached a larger audience than any previously exported Bergman picture.) Almost everywhere, interest centered on the erotic appeal of Harriet Andersson, not on the director. France was the exception.

To the young cinemaphiles clustered around André Bazin and the militant *Cahiers du Cinéma* he had founded in 1950, *The Summer with Monika* marked the arrival of an important filmmaker who validated their theoretical prejudices. Jean-Luc Godard (who would later recant his admiration for Bergman) ecstatically hailed it as "the most beautiful film of this most original of cinéastes." François Truffaut's respect transcended his critical praise: in *Les Quatre Cents Coups*, his first feature, he paid homage by giving prominent display to the Harriet Andersson poster outside the theater visited by his autobiographical hero. The reasons for this infatuation with *The Summer with Monika* are easily discerned. Like Monika herself, most of the *Cahiers* circle had grown up escaping the strictures of the real world through the fantasies on the screen, and in her sexual divagations and feisty rejection of an oppressive society, they saw a reflection of their own revolt. Monika is at once seductive and repugnant, innocent and corrupt, but beneath an implicit assertion of the filmmaker's neutrality, his sympathy for his subject is evident. Just such a fusion of sentimentality and antisentimentality would be a hallmark of these critics when, in a few years, they would become the directors of the *Nouvelle Vague*. In addition, in presenting a brutalized lower class, advancing a deterministic view of life, and—consistent with the tradition of the French Left—contrasting the unfettered *homme primitif* against the daunted *citadin-victime*, Fogelström's story (more than Bergman's treatment of it) suited their ideological predispositions.

The chief appeal, however, was not in what the film said but in how it said it. These theorists proposed a *cinema gratuit*, free of the restrictions of the set, free-flowing in form, and impromptu in expression; if *The Summer with Monika* was not the full realization of the theory, it at least pointed toward its possibility. Most important, it was a film in which the director's hand was conspicuous. This new generation of French cinema critics idolized directors of American B-movies who redeemed their trite plots by concentrating on image and style; *The Summer with Monika*, which, in terms of its story, could have been plucked from an American studio's script bins, heavily depends on those "nonliterary" means through which the cinematic auteur "writes." (E.g., to make the viewer feel the tension of Harry's inner anger, the camera shows him poking a decanter toward the edge of a shelf until it tips and shatters; to complement the thematic contrast of freedom in the skerries and oppression in the city, Bergman employs the sound of a power riveter—diminishing as the young lovers sail away from Stockholm and increasing when they return from their adventure.)

But what the French rejoiced over in the film had little to do with Bergman's own evolution. Although the portrait of Monika's sensuality is imbued with an energy completely missing in the supposedly sensual women of Bergman's 'forties films, no characters of Monika's stamp would recur in his subsequent films. Nor would he graft onto his own work the sociological concerns that emanated from Fogelström. Even as a manifestation of the summer theme, *The Summer with Monika* is an anomaly: despite its often being associated with *Summergame*, it is fundamentally unlike that film or the others of the period in that it does not locate the theme in the consciousness of its characters. More than any other factor, however, what isolates it from the rest of his production is the very *gratuit* quality the *Nouvelle Vague* prized most. Beginning with *Thirst*, Bergman made great strides in developing a visual expressiveness, and *The Summer with Monika* is evidence of his growing confidence in the camera as a narrative instrument, but his sense of what constitutes the story a film tells would still be disciplined by his theatrical background. To the extent that *The Summer with Monika* is "nonliterary," it is an aberration—as his next film would emphatically demonstrate.

Evening of the Jesters

The true successor to *Summergame* was not the hastily thrown together *Women's Waiting*, or *The Summer with Monika*, a detour which served to excuse a holiday with Harriet Andersson, but *Evening of the Jesters*. Before either of the other two films had their premieres, Bergman had worked out the story and submitted it to SF. Leery of another "dark" Bergman film that might prove as unremunerative as *Prison* and *To Joy*, however, SF peremptorily rejected it. Bergman next passed it to Sandrews, a smaller rival, where, except for Rune Waldekranz, the chief of production, it would have met the same fate. But Waldekranz (who would later become Sweden's first professor of cinema) had discerned an unusual talent in Bergman long before his name commanded respect in the industry, and he had faith enough in this script to fight for it until his judgment prevailed against that of the rest of the organization. In the meanwhile, *Women's Waiting* had its exhilarating success and *The Summer with Monika* exceeded Dymling's expectations; by the time Bergman had finished shooting the new film in the summer of 1953, he had every reason to believe "life was at last more than tolerable." Convinced *Evening of the Jesters* was an exceptional achievement, he was looking forward not just to the fourth profitable film in a row but, more important, to recognition for the kind of film he wanted to make. When it opened in mid-September, he read the reviews with incredulity. They were not disappointing; they were utterly devastating.

What seemed to have incensed the critics' genteel sensibilities was the film's remarkable evocation of the characters' wretchedness—one can almost feel the itch of the circus performers' fleabites and smell the sour, sweat-stained costumes. Neither the reviewers nor the public could accept such rude honesty or the film's trenchantly unromantic depiction of love. To them, this was "tastelessness," and the director who confronted them with it was "impudent." "I hardly dare examine the vomit Ingmar Bergman leaves behind him this time," snorted the critic for one of the two major tabloids, and although his attack was unusually hysterical, it reflected the general opinion.[1] *Evening of the Jesters* played to half-empty houses in Stockholm and completely collapsed elsewhere in the country. Bergman, disconsolate, worried aloud that a decade might pass before a producer reckless enough "to stake his gold on my talents" would permit him to make another serious film.[2] Fortunately for him, *A Lesson in Love* was already under way, and it would prove such a hit that he soon again would have a chance to be serious; even so, the impact of the blow should not be underestimated. *Evening of the Jesters* marked the transfer to cinema of the ambitions the playwright surrendered after *The Murder in Barjärna*; no previous Bergman film, not even *Summergame*, is as skillful in its dramaturgy—indeed, it is the best *play* he ever wrote. At the same time, it is cinematically a brilliant display of technique and innovative in its application of film theory.* Not

---

*In place of Gunnar Fischer, who had been his cinematographer in all his films for SF except *Crisis*, Bergman was to renew his collaboration with Göran Strindberg, who had photographed all the Marmstedt films. But just as shooting began, Strindberg departed for Hollywood to study Cinemascope, and Bergman was forced to accept a newcomer, Sven Nykvist. When Nykvist had to leave to fulfill a commitment to an Alf Sjöberg picture, Hilding Bladh took over for the outdoor scenes. Despite the shuffle, there are no seams in the visual unity; Bergman's imprint went deeper than the idiosyncrasies of any single cinematographer.

One of the noteworthy innovations concerned the use of music. For several years, Bergman had questioned the practice of superimposing music as a complement to the emotional values of a scene. In *To Joy* and *Summergame*, he had restricted himself to the music that is intrinsically part of the film. But in *Evening of the Jesters*, for the first time, he had the opportunity to work with a composer whose ideas coincided with his. Karl-Birger Blomdahl, a prominent Swedish composer, had long argued that film, as a modern art, should avail itself of modern music's freedom to employ any sound; furthermore, he had inveighed against recourse to orchestral music when the essence of a scene could be accented by a single sound effect isolated by silence. Given his head by Bergman, Blomdahl wrote a spare score dominated by just a few sounds: a hurdy-gurdy, cannons, military drums.

only was it Bergman's first masterpiece but also arguably the greatest sound film that had ever been made in Sweden. To have realized so much only then to have it scorned and called "vomit" was maddening.

One senses the filmmaker's assurance from the opening frames. A circus caravan, seen first as a silhouette against the dawn, then as a reflection on still water, moves in an absolute silence that, following the jangly organ-grinder music accompanying the title and credits, imbues each image with portent. As the distance between camera and circus shortens, the plodding hooves of the straining horses are heard. The rough movement over the road jostles a caged bear and, in the main wagon, the sleeping bodies of Albert the circus owner and Anne, his mistress. When Albert awakens, he solicitously kisses Anne's armpit and covers her, then exits into the gray chill. A conversation with his driver reveals that the circus is returning to the town where Albert left his family three years before. One assumes that the story's action is about to unfold, but these first lines of dialogue only briefly interrupt the extended "silent" prelude, which now flashes back seven years to an incident involving Frost the clown.

Processed to transform the grain of the image into chalky whites and flat blacks, this dumb-show prologue has the quality of a nightmare. Soldiers are firing cannons into the sea and gambling when Alma, Frost's wife, enters their camp. Responding to her garish dress and hoydenish manner, the soldiers pay her to bathe naked before them. The phallic cannons boom. An officer then decides to improve upon this spectacle of degradation by sending a messenger to Frost with news of the scandal. On his arrival at the beach, the clown's instinct to preserve what little dignity he still possesses momentarily prevents him from acting, but love and obligation prove the stronger force: stripping off his own clothes, he staggers over the sharp rocks, lifts his wife from the water, and, falling three times under her weight, bears his human "Cross" up the "Calvary" that leads back to the circus grounds. The crowd that had been mocking him stares in awe and follows in a train to the couple's tent, where Alma cradles her half-dead husband.

Judged by the usual meaning of the term, this episode from the past is not a flashback at all, for its purpose is not to explain the present through anterior events but to introduce, in parvo, the themes, imagery, and general scheme of the central drama. The association of clothes with the covering of one's vulnerability (which, besides its prominence in the action, is also manifest in the painted smiling face on Frost's costume over his genitals); the urge to humiliate others; the perversion of erotic desire through power; the susceptibilty to betrayal consequent to trust—all foreshadow the story of Albert and Anne. Chiefly, however, in a series of allusions that extend from the crowd's reviling of Frost, to Alma's holding his body at the end of his agony in a Pietà-like posture, to the last shot, in which the messenger boy lays the clown's costume at the entrance to the tent as though it were the Holy Shroud, the prologue serves to introduce the motif of crucifixion. In their theme of betrayed love, both the prologue and the main story resemble those melodramatic ballads, enormously popular at the turn of the century, indicated by Bergman's subtitle, "a *skillingtryck* [= penny print] on film."* The perfidy of lovers recounted in the *skillingtryck*, however, itself becomes a device for a secularized Passion play—much like *The Murder in Barjärna*. Several of Bergman's plays had reflected his view of Everyman as Christ; with *Evening of the Jesters*, it becomes a capital theme of his films.

As the first "act" begins, Albert and his hungry troupe are in desperate circumstances and fretting over their prospects for drawing an audience. If only they were in America where they honor artists, the owner of the Cirkus Alberti muses, they would parade grandly into town and customers would throng for tickets; instead, they are a despised tribe of flea-bitten paupers deprived by bad luck of even the glittering costumes to create the illusion on which the circus depends. But while they bemoan their misery, the mention of the missing clothes (the first echo from the Frost story) inspires the hope for a "miracle." Sjuberg's company of traveling actors has come to the same town; if these fellow entertainers would share their extra costumes, the circus might yet make that American entrance. With the overdressed Anne on his arm, he struts foppishly to the theater. "Let me do all the talking," he instructs her, "breathe deeply so your bosom sticks out, and if he wants to see your legs, go along. I won't desert you." As he stands at the entrance, the bill announces that the play being performed inside is *Betrayal*.

Two precisely parallel scenes in the next act illustrate one concept. Albert's carefully prepared pose of importance wilts before the elegantly bearded Sjuberg, who contemptuously sets the price for the costumes at "whatever you cannot afford to pay."

---

*Perhaps the most famous *skillingtryck* was "Elvira Madigan," which Bo Widerberg used as the basis for his film with the same title. The American "Frankie and Johnny" roughly corresponds to these Swedish ballads.

The evocation of the silent film by the prologue may, in part, reinforce the subtitle. As popular entertainment and as narrative reduced to its simplest components, the silent film was analogous to the *skillingtryck*.

> We despise you because you live in wagons and we in filthy hotel
> rooms, because we perform art and you perform stunts. The sim-
> plest and most untalented of us can spit on the best of you. Why?
> Because you risk your lives and we our vanity.... Why shouldn't I
> humiliate you?

Since, in submitting to humiliation, Albert has paid Sjuberg's price,
Sjuberg now disdainfully gives him the costumes—which are practically worthless to the acting company. Meanwhile, Anne has wandered
into a dressing room, where Frans, the company's romantic lead, pretends to be smitten by her beauty. Pridefully, she questions his masculinity and demands that he bang his head on the floor as a condition for
her kiss, but it is soon clear that she has overplayed the hand he has
dealt her. Having "risked his vanity," the actor now claims a greater prize
than her kiss: her humiliation. Not only is she a whore bartering for her
favors, he says, but the goods she sells are of inferior quality. Like the
archetypal fool in folktales, she has made a bad trade in paying the same
price as Albert—and Alma—for the illusion of being admired.

The motif of the fool continues in the act's closing scene.* Just as
Albert had hoped, the public turns out in large numbers for the parade
of his troupe in their borrowed costumes, but their march is swiftly
converted into a rout by the police, who charge them with disturbing
the peace and seize their horses. Forced to take up the harnesses themselves and drag the heavy circus wagons through the streets, the artists
(like Frost in the prologue) become the object of scornful laughter.

Act III repeats the structure of Act II: two scenes (here intercut) cli-
maxing in the separate humiliations of Albert and Anne are braced by a
third revealing both as fools. With hat in hand, Albert calls on Agda, the
wife he deserted in this very town when he decided to make the circus
his life. He concedes he made a mistake and he wants Agda to take him
back, but as soon as he crosses the threshold of the tobacco shop she
now keeps, he is aware of being an outsider. His son no longer recognizes him, and he uncomfortably observes the protocol of a guest in
speaking with his wife. Worst of all, he has none of the respectability this
petite bourgeois world equates with human dignity. Echoing Sjuberg,
Agda speaks of the "lice and disease" infesting his profession and notes

---

*Indefensibly, this scene has been clipped from the print distributed in the United States
—which has been butchered more than that of any other Bergman film. The sequence
upon which the title and credits are superimposed in the Swedish version—of a tethered
monkey and a hurdy-gurdy—has also been cut from the U.S. print.

the dickey he wears because he cannot afford a shirt; beyond the pity she shows by mending his coat and offering to lend him money, she can do nothing for this childlike bear of a man. As a clock chimes in the silence of the apartment, she remarks, "To me, it is fulfillment"; referring ambivalently to the sedate life he fled and to his moribund future, her husband replies, "To me, it is emptiness." Emphasizing the exchange Albert made three years before, a close-up of Agda's face dissolves into the face of his mistress.

While Albert is meeting defeat in his attempt to leave the circus (and to betray Anne), his mistress is at Sjuberg's theater, seeking to effect her own escape through a betrayal of Albert. Watching Frans rehearse a suicide scene from the wings, she is in awe of what she is too naive to recognize is egregiously bad acting. He is an artist; she, a lowly equestrienne who smells of the stables. Abasing herself, she begs to be allowed to join him: "You need not marry me. Just take care of me." Then, as though to recover her dignity, she challenges the slightly built actor to hand wrestle. When, to her astonishment, he pulls her to the floor, rape seems imminent, but Frans allays her fear. "How do you make the bear dance?" he asks, implying that it is not by trying to match his strength but by playing to his weakness. Her weakness is all too obvious: dangling a gem before her eyes, he offers to exchange it for her sexual favors. No one need ever know, he promises, and if she should choose to sell the jewel, she could quit the circus and buy respectability.

The braided scenes terminate in an ironic cut: from Anne stripping off her clothes for the promise of money and freedom to Albert donning his mended jacket, searching his empty purse to give his son a penny for the organ-grinder's monkey, and pleading one last time to be allowed to trade his shattered dream of freedom for the security of an old age spent in bourgeois confinement with Agda. After a bridging shot of the hurdy-gurdy being cranked, Albert, on leaving Agda's shop, sees Anne enter a jewelry store and immediately surmises her infidelity. But in cheating on Albert, Anne has herself been cheated: Frans's magnificent gem, she learns, is only glass. As though resonating from the prologue, a thunderous drumbeat marks the impact of truth striking them.

As Act IV begins, the two fools are back in their wagon when Frost enters, bursts into a bawdy song, and passes round his brandy flask —implying that resignation is the only response to being the butt of life's joke. But Albert will not accept victimization so placidly. Spurred, in Bergman's words, "to do something mean," he grabs his gun and asks, "Why not shoot the bear?" Misunderstanding his intent, Frost lends enthusiastic support, then adds that a coup de grace for the bear's keeper, his similarly aging and useless wife Alma, would also be an act of kindness. Suddenly struck by this new and obvious thought that death is a merciful end to suffering, Albert points the pistol at his own head.

Before pulling the trigger, however, Albert, like Eugen in *Rakel and the Cinema Doorman*, decides to experiment by aiming the pistol at Frost, his fellow fool. The clown's trembling as soon as he realizes the threat of death is real alerts Albert to a simple truth: although life's pain may have no meaning, the prospect of death holds greater terror. In an abrupt shift of pace and mood, as though the mystery of life had thrust them from its loins in a magical rebirth, the two men tumble from the circus wagon into the light of day. With Frost imitating his every gesture, Albert celebrates the fullness of the earth; drunkenly singing a *skillingtryck*, he seems to have gained a new perspective on his troubles with Anne, Agda, and the circus as so much sentimental self-indulgence.

Act V, a mirror image of Act IV, is also a reprise of all that has gone before. Just as though Bergman were starting from the beginning (while also reinforcing the analogy of life as a circus), the act is introduced by another dumb show—here a routine by the circus clowns at the start of the evening's performance in which sadism, frustration, and the stench of man's animality are transformed into buffoonery. With ringmaster Albert's announcement of the entrance of his equestrienne, however, the terrible counterpart to the comedy begins. Sjuberg's company, invited as guests in return for their lending the costumes, is in the tent, and Frans, losing no time in exacting interest, cries out that the equestrienne herself has been mounted and well-ridden. Exposed as a cuckold, Albert stands para-lyzed in mid-ring, but when a firecracker frightens Anne's horse and he bravely subdues the animal, pride surges back. His expertly lashed whip flicks off Frans's hat, forcing him into the ring to retrieve it. Now it is the actor's turn to play the clown: as he bends over to pick up the hat, Albert boots his rump—just as Frost had kicked his hapless partner in the clowns' skit. But the revenge is short-lived. As they fight, Frans kicks sawdust in his adversary's eyes, fells him with a vicious blow to the testicles, then cunningly exploits his ursine rage to beat him to a bloody heap. Frost, his voice a quavering echo of Albert's in opening the circus, tells the crowd (which includes some of the same soldiers who had watched his agony seven years before) to go home: "The show is over." Like the clown at the end of the prologue, the circus owner is carried to his quarters; like Alma, Anne succors the man she had betrayed.

In the final scene, retracing the first part of Act IV, Albert again raises the pistol to his head, then aims it at a symbolic self—this time his reflection in the mirror. The gun fires. The comic release that comes when Frost calls, "Are you dead?" and Albert bellows his denial is comparable to the previous "rebirth," but now, after the "scourging" he has experienced, he cannot facilely proclaim the joy of being alive. Something within him requires an act—and so, apparently not understanding why, he shoots Alma's bear. On the way back from the cage, he chats with Frost, who then breaks off the conversation with the simple statement that he must join Alma in their tent because "she can't sleep without me." Just as, in the morning, the tale of Frost's "crucifixion" foreshadowed Albert's day of torment, the clown's parting words at dusk point to Albert's future with Anne. After a moment's hesitation, the circus owner walks up to his mistress and takes her arm. In a sense, the Calvary that is life's journey resumes, with only the companionship of another imperfect human being as anodyne for the agony of consciousness.

In the main, *Evening of the Jesters* provides its own best commentary: to notice is to explain—and there is scarcely a detail that is not implicated in the design of meaning. Clothes, for example, besides figuring in the plot, also constitute an image chain in the process of discovery, from the false confidence in their finery with which Albert and Anne begin their mission to Sjuberg, to the sobering reflection of Albert's sorry pretension when Agda mends his coat, to revelation of the "naked" self when he strips to his underwear in the fight with Frans. A second strand dealing with imposture extends from the mazelike array of masks and mirrors Albert and Anne encounter upon entering Sjuberg's theater. After Anne is emotionally taken in by Frans rehearsing the suicide scene, the image of a theatrical mask fills the screen as she makes her way to his dressing room. The ensuing seduction leads to the corresponding scene at Albert's dressing table, where, in parallel to Frans's flowery monologue, he mutely considers suicide. First he studies his "mask" in the mirror, then he shoots it—in effect, protesting his role. But, ironically, the shattered mirror now gives an even more accurate image of the man whose illusions have been shattered. Yet another pattern of imagery emerges in the various references to horses. The analogy to man's difficult journey through life suggested by the straining movement of the horse-drawn caravan at the film's beginning and end becomes quite pointed when the circus people are forced to pull the wagons through the jeering town. But the horse also relates specifically to Albert's "journey" with his equestrienne mistress. By allowing herself to be "mounted and ridden" by Frans, Anne devastates Albert's pride. Bringing Anne's terrified horse under control that evening restores his sense of manhood, and he immediately becomes her champion, defending her against Frans's taunts. Later, pressing his tear-choked face against his favorite horse (an evident substitute for Anne) after he has killed the bear, he seems to realize that, just as she needs him, he needs her. Significantly, he then orders that the horse be reshod as the circus prepares to continue its itinerary.

In two instances, however, explication depends more upon a knowledge of Bergman than upon scrutiny of the film itself. One of these, a brief passage just before the film ends in which Frost tells Albert a dream he has had, strikes a familiar chord for anyone acquainted with Bergman's earlier plays and stories:

> I dreamed Alma came to me and said: "Poor Frost, you look tired and unhappy. Don't you need a little rest?" "Yes," I said. "Then I shall make you small as a penis," she said, "so that you can crawl into my belly where you may sleep properly." I did as she said and lay right in her belly, where I slept so beautifully, so sweetly, rocked to rest as in a cradle, until I grew smaller and smaller, and, at last, I was just a little seedcorn, and then I was gone.

Caught by the unusual conceit, critics have either quickly noted it in passing or interpreted the dream as the sign of Frost's reconciliation with Alma—and, thereby, of Albert's reconciliation with Anne. Reference to the fantasy of the womb in Bergman's previous works, however, indicates a different meaning. Frost's image of the womb is not only of a perfect sanctuary from anxiety (like Joakim's in "The Fish"), but also (like Kaj's in *Rakel and the Cinema Doorman*) of a place where time runs backward, to the moment of his conception and beyond, until he disappears. Bergman presents this retreat from the anguish of being as supremely appealing—and, of course, impossible. Since, like the prologue, Albert's drama builds toward his confrontation with truth —about his mate, about himself, about the condition of being human —the dream has to represent illusion surrendered. The journey moves forward in time toward death, and with his recognition that there is no escape from the agony of reality, Bergman is saying, man relives Christ's suffering. Albert has just begun his Passion. Like Frost in the prologue, he takes up his cross in taking the arm of the woman who has betrayed him; it is, finally, an act of love which invests suffering with meaning.

Given the unmistakable pattern of allusions to Calvary, misreading the function of Frost's dream does not seriously upset the general interpretation of the film. The second point which has caused confusion, however, is critical to the plot. From the conspicuous attention to the caged bear in the opening sequence and the suggestion, made at the very start of Albert's story, that the hungry circus troupe should kill and eat the bear, one senses that it somehow lies at heart of the symbolic action. But when Albert's gun (like Chekhov's famous loaded pistol) finally fires and the animal lies dead, what import does it carry?

The answer *seems* obvious. Albert looks like a bear; his mentioning killing the bear leads to his first "experiment" with suicide; and the actual deed immediately follows his firing at his image in the mirror. Clearly, all this would indicate the "suicide" of a surrogate self. But what aspect of himself is Albert killing, and why? Moreover, since he has already shot the mirror, what is gained by a second symbolic suicide? Bergman has dismissed the problem by denying there is anything symbolic in the act; according to him, Albert simply wants to retaliate against the world. But, although this may explain *Albert's* psychological motive, it still fails to account for *Bergman's* identification of Albert with the bear, or, more important, for the carefully laid dramatic preparation for the bear's death. Bergman has also stated that Albert wants to hurt Alma, and some critics, responding to this prompt, have argued that killing the chained bear avenges Frost's humiliation; yet the film provides no reason for Albert to have any ill feeling toward Alma (in fact, the two characters are not at all involved with each other), and one can scarcely find a message calling for vengeance in Frost's Christlike behavior in the prologue.

But if Bergman's explanations do not fit the film he has made, they suggest what led to its making. In an interview dealing with *Evening of the Jesters*, he restated the fundamental relationship between his films and his childhood:

> It is a recognized principle that artists—especially if they function as I do—retain a strong infantile impulse throughout life; or, more accurately, that the creative impulse is so deeply intermeshed with a kind of childishness, with a remnant of the child's attitude to his world, that much of the [child's mental] conduct on the margin [of reality] is also preserved. . . . If one examines the faces of many artists, they look like adult children, adult children full of secrets. . . . one can see that Beethoven has the wrathful face of a babe.[3]

The child-within-the-artist in this film is most evident in the prologue, which, significantly, Bergman has said was practically a transcription of a dream he had had. Once one perceives the clown as the child's picture of himself, and Alma as his ambivalent portrait of the mother, the episode acquires a meaning that, though not unrelated to the Passion motif, is different from it. Alma's traitorousness consists in the sexuality that attracts her to the ostentatiously masculine soldiers who fire their dangerous, phallic cannons for sport. Frost, his genitals covered by the smiling mask on his costume, is a figure of childish impotence in comparison. Indeed, stripping to his underwear to fetch Alma from the water makes him very self-conscious before this company of men, and he holds his hands over his penis; their laughter as he does so clearly implies his sexual inferiority. The only way he can compete with these rivals and save Alma from herself is to shame her by proving a love that is more filial than conjugal. Carrying her over the rocks makes no practical sense—both could walk with less pain—but by making himself physically ill through his exertion, Frost gains Alma's devoted, maternal attention as she nurses him in their tent—much as Bergman used illness in childhood to win reassurance of his mother's love.

In the main story, Albert replaces Frost as the author's persona: Anne is his Alma, Frans corresponds to the soldiers, and the battering the circus owner receives in the ring parallels Frost's Calvary. But the rudiments of the original dream are here made to serve a different psychological purpose. To understand that purpose, the film should be set in the greater context of Bergman's previous fiction. The protagonist's surname, "Johansson," points to his long line of Jans, Jacks, and Joakims (as well as the Johans in later films) who struggle with their Oedipal problem, and "Albert" recalls Joakim Naked's alter ego in "The Fish" who cannot "act" knowing his rival is under the bed. Equally pertinent, one remembers, from *The City*, Joakim's boyhood dream of running away with the circus and his guilt over abandoning Baloo, the teddy bear to whom he confided his secrets as a child, for a series of adult misadventures with women.

Unlike the prologue, which depicts a recovery of childhood, the main story expresses a difficult emergence into manhood. In a sense, it is Baloo, the symbol of childhood, that Albert (or Bergman) kills at the end of *Evening of the Jesters*. The chained bear, which is not only fussed over and protected by Alma as though it were her child but also always described as "sickly," represents an emotional dependence on the mother that must be destroyed if Albert is to achieve a different, sexually mature relationship with Anne. As Bergman himself has said, shooting the bear is an act of sheer meanness; like Jack's sadism, it represents a strained assertion of manliness. Furthermore, this "murder" is meant to hurt Alma; it is an act of painfully severing a bond. When

Albert next takes a few steps down the path to where Anne is waiting for him, he in effect steps out of childhood. Anne has reenacted Alma's betrayal of her "son," but through Albert's violent destruction of the emblem of psychological enchainment to the mother figure, he frees himself to forgive his mistress and to begin a new kind of relationship.

Of how much of this was Bergman conscious? In an interview, he spoke wearily of "that question I have been asked so many times—What do you mean with that damned bear? People have a feeling that I mean something. . . . For me, there's no symbolism in it."[4] No doubt, he was being sincere. Nevertheless, the bear does *mean* something, and from that something the film takes its form. That its meaning lies submerged, that it can be "felt" but not satisfactorily explained through the film itself, is a structural weakness, yet *Evening of the Jesters* remains a splendid achievement. Although it boils from the same area of the unconscious as far lesser earlier works, that energy is at last at the disposal of a master artist.

Dreams

The sparkling success of *A Lesson in Love* after the humiliating failure of *Evening of the Jesters* confirmed Dymling's opinion that Bergman should stick to comedy, but the filmmaker resisted committing himself to a future restricted to tickling audiences with the foibles of the sexes. With *Dreams*, he again turned to Sandrews and Rune Waldekranz, who again showed his faith in Bergman—and again lost money on a film that deserved better fortune. Like Dymling, the public had apparently fixed its mind as to what a Bergman film ought to be, and *Dreams* did not fit that preconception.

More surprising than its disappointing reception in 1955, however, has been its subsequent neglect. The tendency to regard the early 'fifties as Bergman's comic period proved so strong that, for the next two decades, the inclination was to adjudge it a comedy spoiled by the infusion of melancholy themes. And when there was no confusion as to its genre, it was overshadowed by *Evening of the Jesters*, which, from the mid-'fifties on, steadily climbed in critical esteem. *Dreams* is a subtle film of delicate patterns; instead of valuing that subtlety, critics have treated it as a pale print of previously stamped ideas. One critic disparages it by citing a similarity to *A Lesson in Love*:

in both, there is a train, bearing someone toward an unresolved relationship; in both, absurd male animals are at the mercy of their age or their women; in both there is a daughter as *deus ex machina* or as *memento mori*, and in both there is a kind of contrapuntal movement and structure.[1]

Another critic, invoking the curious logic that Bergman was "falling back" on an old "ground plan" because he wanted to work again with Eva Dahlbeck and Harriet Andersson, sees a tracing of *Evening of the Jesters*:

> If one removes the flesh from both films, the skeletons prove closely similar, as will be clear from the fact that the following synopsis would do for either: Two people, one verging on middle age, the other young, irresponsible, and played by Harriet Andersson, travel to a town where the older has links with the past. During their short stay, each tries to make real a personal dream: for the older, a dream of stability connected with the old acquaintance settled in the town; for the younger, a dream of romance and glitter, developed through a chance encounter with a man she has never met before. Both dreams prove illusory or incapable of fulfillment. The two people, reunited, leave the town together in a mood somewhere between resignation and acceptance.[2]

The resemblance to a third precursor, *Summergame*, could be argued at least as persuasively. Both examine career women, first in their public roles and then in the contrasting moods of their private lives; both conclude with the displacement of illusions by accommodations to an unexciting reality. More obviously, the protagonists in *Dreams*—Doris, a young model just beginning in the business, and Susanne, a former model who has reached the threshold of middle age—correspond to the younger and older Maries.

But what these similarities illustrate, quite simply, is the cluster of ideas variously expressing the "summer theme"—not, in Vernon Young's phrase, an "inventiveness ... out of breath." Pairings of other Bergman films (and of works by most artists) would also show correspondences; except when they result in flaccidity, no adverse conclusions need be drawn from recurrences of motifs, patterns, or character types. *Dreams* may be a minor film if ranked against Bergman's best, and it lacks the intensity of *Evening of the Jesters*; nevertheless, it is a well-wrought, significant part of his canon that attests his growth both as a filmmaker and as a writer of cinematic fiction. The experiment with purely visual narrative in the Paris episode of *Women's Waiting* continues here, with more sophistication and to much greater effect: in several long passages, the camera becomes an extension of the character's thoughts. In consort with this exploitation of the medium's idiosyncratic possibilities, Bergman composes his story in a different manner: except for *The Summer with Monika*, none of his films during the period is less derivative from a theatrical model. Although it has become a commonplace of Bergman criticism to draw analogies with musical forms, *Dreams*, which develops as a double fugue, warrants the comparison more than most of his works. In this respect, it anticipates the reorientation in his approach to cinema during the mid-'sixties.

The film begins where it will end—in a fashion photography studio. After a shot of a camera, one sees an enlarged photograph of lips emerging from a developing bath, followed by close-ups of those who trade in romantic illusions.* Susanne, the studio's proprietor, looks straight ahead in dispassionate assessment. An epicene makeup man yawns. Fashion director Magnus, a man of great girth, drums his fingers on the table. All eyes focus on the posed model, Doris. Her innocence seems prey to something as yet undefined but embodied in the fashion director. Although Magnus will be absent from the double story about to begin, his presence here implies an arch power over it. He recalls Teodor Skarp from *Jack Among the Actors*; a spider-God waiting in the middle of his web.** When Doris meets his stare, she flinches, as if reacting instinctively to an evil emanation.

Following this wordless introduction, Susanne invites Doris to Gothenburg, where the rest of the fashion collection is to be photographed. When her boyfriend forbids her to go, they quarrel; resentful of being treated as though she were already his wife, Doris asserts her independence by accepting the invitation. Susanne's motive in going to Gothenburg is just the opposite. Her successful fashion studio assures her the independence Doris wishes to have, but she would exchange her authority for marriage and motherhood. All the backstairs gossips know that her business trip is an excuse for a frantic mission to win back her erstwhile lover, a married executive in the port city.

---

*Bergman would use a very similar framing device in *Persona*, which also begins and ends in a studio and with a shot of a camera.

**Magnus also suggests the monstrously fat father mentioned in *The Silence* who implies a perverse God.

Of the two stories, Susanne's is much the weaker; despite Bergman's sympathy for the woman (and Eva Dahlbeck's sensitive portrayal), it never gets beyond the cliché of its premise. Having established her anguish, Bergman simply repeats its illustration. On the train, she thinks of how easily she could end her unhappiness by leaping to her death. Women strolling the streets of Gothenburg with baby carriages reflect the kind of life she dreams of having. The several humiliations to which she submits in attempting to arrange a rendezvous with Henrik Lobelius, who is obviously resisting a renewal of their affair, attest her desperation; even when he relents and comes to her hotel room, she must beg and scrape before the weak-willed man joins her in bed.

This redundant preparation finally leads to the scene that most interests Bergman. Like the curious spaces detached from the world in some of the 'forties films, the hotel room offers a temporary sanctuary for childish illusion. Henrik accepts his role as her "teddy bear," while Susanne, holding his "boyish fingers," wishes his wife and children were dead so that they might be young lovers unencumbered by what life has thrust on them. When Henrik accidentally rips his fingernail, however, the sting breaks the spell of their make-believe; soon after, his wife bursts in on these "two children who have played forbidden games and await their punishment" and flails them with truth. Henrik, she says, has passed beyond hope of "renewing himself"; he is an exhausted, beaten man, habituated to the luxuries her money provides and "helplessly bound" to his children and his sense of guilt. Susanne has been no less a victim of self-deception. Her eagerness to sacrifice herself for her lover shows only a woman's "brilliant talent for romanticizing her real motives"—not love but a selfish attempt to recapture youth. The wife then caps her triumph over their fantasies of escaping from their trap: "I have only said what you yourselves know but refuse to think about."

Doris's adventure during this same day also revolves around an illusion of dispensation from the effects of time. While she admires a splendid gown in a shop window, a dapper gentleman in late middle age draws up behind her. Like a fairy godfather, obedient to all her wishes, Consul Sönderby offers to make her a gift of the dress. Although Doris is enough a woman to be wary of this unsolicited generosity and to fear that the worldly gentleman may represent quite another fairy-tale figure —Little Red Ridinghood's wolf—Sönderby persuades her to trust the child in herself; in addition to the gown, he rewards her with elegant shoes fit for such a Cinderella and a fabulously expensive string of pearls. These gifts support his claims of being "a great sorcerer": the white gown symbolizes her reentry into the purity of a child's world; the shoes are magic slippers for the journey; and, most extraordinary of all, the "magic pearls" imply "wholeness," "unheard of power," and "absolute perfection." When, with "ritualistic appreciation," the merchant clasps the strand around her neck, the image reflected by the mirror "is Doris and yet not Doris"; and in the moment the pearls absorb warmth from her skin, the shop's clocks, which have been ticking throughout the scene, seem to stop as the hour very slowly begins to chime. Her recoil from Magnus has landed her in a wondrous kingdom, ruled by an indulgent potentate who shelters her from time.

Just as Cinderella's night at the ball ended in disenchantment when she forgot to note the hour, Doris loses her job by failing to appear on time for her modeling assignment. And like Cinderella, she is soon rescued from her unhappiness through the chance arrival of her "royal" benefactor. Emboldened by his delight in watching her eat a gooey treat, she asks for "the impossible": an amusement park all to herself. Sönderby does not disappoint her. Although the amusement park has closed for the season, its owner is a friend who owes him a favor.

As the couple ride through the tunnel of the "Terror Express," Doris laughs at the papier-mâché spider, wolf, and skeleton that spring at them from the tunnel's walls, but her companion (the script notes) "thinks he has arrived in hell"; when they emerge into the light, he faints and falls. Somehow, suddenly, the day's magic spell has been broken. Back at Sönderby's mansion, Doris works to revive it: reversing their roles, in a sense, she calls him by his childhood name and bandages the hand he had scraped in falling. When this fails, she hints that she would become his mistress if he would pay for capping her teeth, produce a film in which she would star, and buy her a sports car and a summer cottage. Shuddering, Sönderby asks her to leave.

With the collapse of the fairy tale, the "great sorcerer" begins to reveal his motive. Standing before his wife's portrait, he explains that she has been confined in a madhouse ever since she convinced herself her newborn daughter Marianne had the head of a wolf. From the evident resemblance between Doris and the woman in the painting, one infers that Sönderby has been indulging in a fanciful return to a happier time in his life, and that the Terror Express, by reminding him of his wife's madness, destroyed the illusion. But there is more to the mystery of Sönderby's behavior, and when Marianne unexpectedly enters the house, one begins to realize that Doris, after serving as stand-in for his young wife, blundered into acting like his daughter—who has indeed become the vulpine creature envisioned in her mother's insanity. Like Doris only a few minutes earlier, Marianne makes monetary demands on her father; and when she finds the model hiding in the bedroom, she denounces Sönderby for squandering on an "expensive playmate" the inheritance that is rightfully her own. The most obvious indication of their association, however, is a bracelet Doris had playfully slipped onto her wrist. Marianne recognizes it as hers and commands the "thief" to return it.

Marianne has misconstrued the evidence, of course, because she has read it "realistically"—just as Doris, in offering to become Sönderby's mistress, had assessed his motives according to her knowledge of the human marketplace. This eclipse of innocence by the "real world" is central to the wolf image's significance, but it is not the only significance, and the "wolves" are not just the two women.

As the story winds to a close, the metaphorical reference unmistakably turns toward Sönderby himself. In responding to his statement that her "wolfishness" may not have been just a figment of her mother's madness, Marianne counters that she inherited it from him, not from her mother. Sönderby agrees: "It's possible. You and I have great similarities." One of these similarities surfaces in the tightfisted daughter's charge that a stingy heart has been her father's "special perversity." When he does not demur, the broader purpose of the "fairy godfather's" explosive generosity to the model—and of his pointedly rejecting the role of wolf during their first encounter—comes into view: in reversing time for Doris, Sönderby also sought, for one day of fantasy, to reverse the course of his own life and to exorcise the wolf in his being. Now the day and the fantasy have come to an end. The clock strikes. Doris leaves, still unable to understand the meaning of what she has witnessed. The last shot of Sönderby shows him standing at the window of his palatial home, a prisoner of his emptiness.

Each story plays off the other's theme, structure, and symbolic detail, either in counterpoint or complement, and as they move toward their conclusions, the analogies become more pronounced. Henrik's torn fingernail corresponds to Sönderby's injured hand; Marta Lobelius's intrusion on one set of "playmates" parallels Marianne's assault on the other; Henrik's enslavement by money resonates against both Sönderby's lavish spending for Doris and Marianne's disclosure of his "special perversity." And, of course, the clocks ticking in the hotel room and the mansion represent time's ravaging of dreams—the film's principal theme that Bergman reiterates in a coda. Doris, rehired by her employer at the end of the day, cannot wait to report on her experience in the strangeness of the world. She has been through a "nightmare," she sighs, which has taught her that "people are terribly mean to each other." Yet her innocence spares her from the lesson. Reuniting with her fiancé, she believes there will never again be cause for their quarreling, and she whispers joyously, "Isn't life wonderful?" In contrast, reality has overtaken such dreams for Susanne. A few days later, back in Stockholm, she receives a note from Henrik offering a lovers' meeting in Oslo. Shredding it as "just another letter begging for charity," she then exchanges an "amiable" laugh with Magnus—implicitly an acknowledgment of the spider-God by his trapped prey.

Bergman's rather terse comments about *Dreams* foster the impression that it was an impersonal work, an intellectually elaborated idea that never came to life. To be sure, one does sense the notebook diagram behind it all, and the artificiality is one of its limitations, but what activated the fiction was the same nexus of personal conceits that operates elsewhere. That Magnus represents the spider-God, for example, is never defined within the film's context, yet anyone acquainted with the earlier works should recognize the emblem's significance to Bergman in framing the fiction's meaning. An even more idiosyncratic trope underlies the Doris/Sönderby story. Through the "sorcerer's" magic, she regresses from being the sleek mannequin seen in the opening sequence, to childhood, and finally, in the tunnel of the Terror Express, to uterine isolation from the world. Sönderby finds vicarious pleasure in this dream of journeying backward in time until they enter the Terror Express. What, for the innocent girl, are harmless fright figures are for him specters of the real terrors he faces in real time—an evocation of Bergman's crucifixion motif that may be suggested by Sönderby's fall and his wounded hand. Clearly, these things connote more than a literal meaning for Bergman—even though that meaning does not develop beyond serving as the mandrel for the fiction.*

But concealment of the dream machinery beneath the art it produces occurs almost everywhere in Bergman—and especially in *Evening of the Jesters* and the succession of celebrated films that would soon follow. The problem in *Dreams* is that the artistic structure is to the side of the creative stimulus: although its design is predicated upon contrast-

---

*It is hard to believe that Sönderby would be so shaken by an amusement park ride as to think he is in hell, and the injured hand seems no less gratuitous a detail for its correspondence with Henrik's fingernail.

ing the young model and her employer, it is Sönderby who engages
Bergman's imagination. Both the dramatic process of discovery in Doris's
story and the symbol of the wolf that reaches toward the film's metaphoric center relate to the aging "sorcerer," not to the girl. Yet, con-
stricted by the formal device he chose, Bergman does not exfoliate the
crucial elements of the Sönderby material. Buried somewhere within
the character is a secret that Bergman had first touched in *Kamma Noll*
(where Jan's wife became insane after the birth of her "monster" child)
and that would eventually erupt in *Hour of the Wolf*. Locked to the
secret is the figure of the daughter in whom, for some undefined reason,
Bergman joins the images of her mother and her father's innocent
"playmate"—and whose compound name evokes that ambivalent relationship with his mother reflected by Bergman's various Maries and
Annes. But this is not a mystery *Dreams* engages. The hateful scene
between Sönderby and Marianne seems to explode from another drama;
in introducing more than is relevant to Doris's tale, it raises more questions than it answers.

Ironically, the dark interior glimpsed through the Sönderby character
would be given much fuller expression in the comedy Bergman made
the same year.

Smiles of the Summer Night

When Dymling stipulated that Bergman would either supply a comedy
or be without employment at SF, the financially strapped filmmaker
reverted to an idea, which he had abandoned some years earlier, for a
serious drama about a young man in love with his father's second wife.*
In reworking this material, he went to the same well from which he was
simultaneously drawing his characters for his film for Sandrews: the
actors who play Susanne and Sönderby in *Dreams* would be called
upon to give essentially the same roles a comic turn in *Smiles of the
Summer Night*, and though Bergman substituted Ulla Jacobsson for
Harriet Andersson, there is more than a casual resemblance to Doris in
Anne. But the more obvious resource was *A Lesson in Love*. By this time,
for Bergman to think about writing comedy was to think in terms of

---

*Although, in its original conception, *An Ancient Chinese Proverb* had a contemporary
setting, almost the first step he took in recasting it as *Smiles of the Summer Night* was to
shift the time to the turn of the century—the period of his recently triumphant production of *The Merry Widow*.

characters defined by Björnstrand and Dahlbeck, who, in this third
round in their games of love, appear as Fredrik Egerman and Desirée
Armfeldt. *A Lesson in Love* also provided two ancillary characters, here
transsexed: wise old Father Erneman resurfaces as Desirée's mother,
and Nix, as though she had undergone the sex change operation she
begged of her father, bobs up as Fredrik's son Henrik. But more important than the transposition of characters, in refashioning *Dreams* and *A
Lesson in Love*—as well as in resurrecting the subject of the original
play—Bergman again dove deeply into his psyche. Of course, as he has
said, his task was to construct a comedy of manners, not "to ritualize a
heap of inner and outer tensions." "I thought of it as a technical challenge to write a comedy with a mathematical relationship: man—woman,
man—woman . . . four pairs. Scramble them and then solve the equation."[1] Nevertheless, both the complication and the solution are as much
functions of fantasy as of intellect.

At the start, three sets of mismatched lovers reflect a world out of
joint:

(1) Fredrik and Anne Egerman. The prominent middle-aged lawyer,
having married the sixteen-year-old Anne to please his vanity, basks in
the envy of his employees and carries her photographs as if they were a
private trophy.* But despite his pose as the virile conqueror, he has not
been able to consummate the marriage in the two years since their
wedding night. Anne had proposed to him out of pity for his loneliness,
and although she expected love to grow from charity, she is too much
ruled by notions of romance to behave like anything more than a dutiful
daughter toward a "terribly old" father. Secretly, she pines for Henrik, her
husband's son by his deceased first wife. Fredrik, who tells his son he
must learn to be bold with women (in love as in horseback riding, he
says, "if you are thrown, remount before you become frightened"), cannot summon the courage to act on his own advice. In part, this shyness
owes to Anne's childlike quality; in part, to the fact that, although he has
not admitted it to himself, he really loves Desirée, an actress with whom
he had had an affair years before.

(2) Desirée Armfeldt and Count Carl Magnus Malcolm. Flaunting her
liberties as an eminent lady of the theater, the cigar-smoking Desirée is

---

*Like *Smiles of the Summer Night*, "The Fish" begins with the husband lovingly poring
over photographs of his wife, who is also named Anne. Moreover, although Joakim's Anne
is starting to grow old, the photographs he treasures are of her as a girl the same age as
Fredrik's Anne. The parallel in this detail reflects the similarity in the underlying psychological patterns traced by the two stories.

currently amusing herself as the mistress of the strutting army officer, a mechanism of "unfailingly functional masculinity" who treats her like a battle ribbon. She pretends to be completely content with this arrangement, but when Fredrik calls on her for counsel in dealing with Anne's frigidity, the actress's irritation shows she has not dismissed their former affair as casually as she claims. And the interruption of their argument by the entrance of a four-year-old boy—named Fredrik—indicates that she has reason enough to remember it.

(3) Petra and Henrik. She is the free-spirited servant who serves best in the bedroom; he, the moralistic youth, a theology student who employs Luther's texts as a defense against Petra's wriggling hips. When, at last, temptation overcomes theology, Henrik sins—only to suffer remorse for having sinned ineptly.

The reshuffling that will occur is entirely predictable: Desirée wins Fredrik back; Anne gets Henrik; Malcolm is restored to his hard-edged wife Charlotte; and Petra, who really wants only a comfortable berth in life, finds a suitable mate in Frid, the Armfeldt family's coachman. Interest depends on the ingeniousness of the contrivance that will produce the inevitable outcome while seeming to impede it, and in this, Bergman proves himself a master artificer in the great tradition of the comic theater.

Desirée schemes with her mother, a superannuated courtesan, to arrange a dinner party at her elegant manor for the misaligned pairs. Something of a witch in touch with tellurian forces, Mrs. Armfeldt serves her guests a wine of "mysterious, stimulating power" said to contain stallion semen and drops of milk produced by a woman just after the birth of her first child. Its immediate effect is to reveal the painful complexity of love: to arouse Malcolm's jealousy, Charlotte wagers at the dinner table that she can seduce Fredrik within a quarter of an hour; Henrik, disturbed by his elders' discussion of love as though it were a matter of military strategy, obstreperously scolds them, then withdraws in shame; Anne's distraught reaction to her stepson's embarrassment opens Fredrik's eyes to the reason she has remained a virgin bride. As a contrast to the anguish of these lovers, Bergman presents the simple erotic appetites of the servants. Encouraged by Petra's giggling when he shows her a bedroom wall rigged to deliver a bed from the adjoining chamber, Frid chases her about the park "like a gay, giant Pan."

The resolution proceeds from the depths of Henrik's despair—and the marvelous bed. Watching the servants at their game from the bedroom window, Henrik decides to exit this world erupting with voluptuousness by hanging himself. But when the noose slips, he falls against the button that activates the trick bed; as if by magic, the wall opens and in rolls the sleeping Anne. Three hours later, Fredrik sees his son and wife eloping. Suddenly feeling the full weight of his years upon him, he walks to the park pavilion to keep his appointment with Charlotte —not for amorous excitement but to seek solace for his defeat. Malcolm, apprised of what is happening by Desirée, rushes to the pavilion and challenges his "rival" to a duel by Russian roulette. As Fredrik raises the pistol to his temple for the third round, the camera moves outside the pavilion and a shot rings in the silence. The conclusion that he is dead is inescapable; like Renoir with the final gunshot in *La Règle du jeu*, Bergman seems deliberately to have violated the rules of comedy by changing farce into horror. But then Fredrik, his face blackened with soot, emerges from the pavilion—unwilling to gamble his life with a "damned lawyer," Malcolm has used a blank cartridge. Desirée recovers her old lover by dressing his wounded pride. Charlotte, alleging she has won the bet by seducing Fredrik in half the time, claims a vow of fidelity from Malcolm as her prize. And in a haystack where she has made love to Frid, Petra holds him to his promise of marriage.

If all has come to an apparently benign end, it is because the Swedish summer night of the film's title, a night without darkness, signifies illusion; its three smiles—as interpreted by Frid—palliate the sting of truth. The night's first smile, he tells Petra after Anne and Henrik elope, is for young lovers. Petra feels cheated: "Why," she asks ruefully, "have I never been a young lover?" "Oh, my dear, don't be sorry," wise Frid answers. "There are only a few young lovers on this earth. Yes, one can almost count them. Love has smitten them both as a gift and *as a punishment.*" At dawn, the night smiles again. This time, he says, it is for them and the others who have just been joined with their proper mates: "for the clowns, the fools, the unredeemable . . . [who] invoke love, call out for it, beg for it, cry for it, try to imitate it, think [they] have it, lie about it." Although these couples have neither the gift nor the punishment, they are the lucky ones who discover that (in the words of one of Bergman's earliest films) "hell together is better than hell alone." The last smile, "for the sad, the depressed, the sleepless, the confused, the frightened, the lonely," is meant for the audience. In effect, the film slips aside its comic mask to say: Although you have had your amusement and momentarily forgotten your pain, the world you are about to reenter is not so forgiving. If the summer night is benign, the reality it smiles upon is not.

Perverse as it may sound, Bergman's best comedy reads the human condition as dismally as his most pessimistic films. Its motto could be the "one lesson" Mrs. Armfeldt says her many years have taught her: "You can never protect a single human being from suffering." Its implicit conceit surfaces in Charlotte's description of life as "a play, a ridiculous farce" in which they are all trapped, and of Fredrik as a "prisoner imprisoned, locked in, raging, hurt, wounded without reason or sense." Although the comedy revolves around Fredrik's self-delusion in marrying Anne, what makes him a fool, a victim, and a prisoner is only incidentally related to that romantic confusion. Time, not his wife's love for his son, is Fredrik's undoing, and more emphatically here than in the other summer theme films, time wears a tragic mask.

Underscoring time's antagonism, clocks mark the progress of the action. At the very start, the late afternoon hour strikes while Fredrik's employees hint behind his back that young Henrik may be "poaching on the old man's preserve." A few scenes later, this suggestion recurs. Soaking wet from a fall into a puddle while accompanying Desirée home from the theater, Fredrik changes into Malcolm's nightgown and a nightcap resembling the jester's horned hat of cuckoldry; as Desirée teasingly raises the possibility that Anne may have found Henrik more attractive than his father, the cry of a cuckoo clock reinforces the image. A third clock chimes when, just after Anne's quarrel with Henrik reveals her secret love to the audience, she sits like a young daughter in Fredrik's lap. In these three instances, Fredrik takes no notice of the monitory clocks, but when "the mighty hour beats" from the town clock as Anne and Henrik are eloping, he backs against a high stone wall as though truth were clapping him into prison. The fifth clock strikes in Fredrik's final scene, where, battered and stripped of his dignity, he accepts the solace of Desirée's love.

The most conspicuously symbolic clock, however, is one that has no fixed place in the film's setting. At the start of *A Lesson in Love*, a clock with spinning Meissen figurines implied the predetermined movements in life's dance. Here, Bergman twice cuts into the narrative a shot of another clock with a turning base that conveys a similar, but finally more sinister meaning. Marking midnight in their first appearance, the carved wooden figures—a priest (Henrik the theology student), a soldier (Malcolm the army officer), a man humped with age (Fredrik the father), and a queen (Woman)—encapsulate the film's action. But when the figures march again at 3 A.M. (which Bergman would later denominate "the hour of the wolf"), the scythe-bearing symbol of Death has somehow replaced the queen.

The difference between the two processions is emblematically the difference between Bergman's comic and tragic visions. In the first, which coincides with Henrik's decision to hang himself, the queen represents the magical overcoming of despair. Instead of death, the suicide attempt brings Henrik his heart's desire when the wall opens and admits Anne.* The second procession, which follows Anne's elopement, signals Fredrik's tragic awareness—and acceptance—of death. Minutes later, when Malcolm proposes Russian roulette, Fredrik is practically consenting to suicide. ("This is not courage, sir," he says in the middle of the duel.)

Unlike the son's wish to die, which springs from a misprision, the father's resignation gives the impression of being warranted. His defeat is real; even though he will have Desirée to console him, there is no sign of gaiety or of life's renewal for him. Yet, despite the dourness at its core, the film is formally a comedy—and thus, Bergman concludes with a palliating illusion.

> *Desirée*: Remember your saying, "You are my only friend, the only one to whom I can show myself as I really am"? I am so sorry for you. So terribly sorry. It's tragic. . . . Your fall was very great, Fredrik Egerman. But you are falling softly.
> *Fredrik*: Don't leave me.
> *Desirée*: I make no promises, Mr. Lawyer. You are a terribly dull and ordinary person, while I am a great artist.
> *Fredrik*: I must lie down a bit. I have a headache. What are you doing?
> *Desirée*: [Holding Anne's photographs.] I'm putting your love into my big pocket.
> *Fredrik*: Just don't leave me alone.
> *Desirée*: I'm here.
> *Fredrik*: That's good. That's really good. . . . Why did you call [your] son "Fredrik"?
> *Desirée*: Isn't that a good name—for a little boy?

Beneath the surface that suggests a mother comforting her hurt child lies the same fantasy that had provided Joakim Naked refuge in "The

---

*In contrast to this deliverance through Woman at the climax of the comedy, Karin's prayer for a miracle to free her from despair in *Through a Glass Darkly* brings the masculine spider-God from behind the wall.

Fish"—and the same dream denied at the end of *Evening of the Jesters*. Whereas Henrik has crossed the threshold of adulthood by absconding with his father's wife, Fredrik, falling asleep on motherly Desirée's lap, symbolically reverses this journey of life toward death by drawing into the role of his own little son. In one sense, by placing the photographs in her pocket (an image of the womb), Desirée, the "great artist" capable of dissimulating reality, restores to Fredrik the innocent Anne he has lost; in another, it is Fredrik's love itself that is being returned to its perfect relationship with the mother, who will shelter it from the world.

Bergman may very well have conceived of *Smiles of the Summer Night* as a "mathematical" problem intended solely for entertainment, but in the process of factoring, he arrived at the same basic equation found in his other films. Form is ultimately meaning, and what it "ritualizes" here are the tensions arising from his childhood attachment to Karin Bergman. Although the reversal of Ingmar and Erik Bergman in the rivalry between Fredrik and his theologian son is a sign of the fiction's personal reference, the psychological mechanism at work here does not directly involve antagonism between father and son. Fundamentally, both Fredrik and Henrik are projections of a struggle within Bergman himself, the object of which is the virginized mother represented by Anne.

Contrary to its air of sexual sophistication, *Smiles of the Summer Night*, like *A Lesson in Love*, betrays a deep-seated puritanical distaste for the "false smiles" and "loving whispers without meaning" of adults relieving their boredom. But the film's attitude is not just antierotic; it is also specifically antimasculine. Malcolm's sexual prowess is held up to derision. Petra and Anne discuss what having a penis would be like and find the idea of maleness so ludicrous they are overcome by giggling. The most telling indictment of the priapic male, however, is a rancorous explosion, utterly beyond comic purpose, in which Charlotte confesses to Anne that she despises herself for being sexually dependent on Malcolm: "I hate him! Men are beasts. They are foolish and vain. They have hair all over their bodies.... Love is a disgusting business." Were this only Charlotte's opinion, it could be dismissed as a wife's anger toward her womanizing husband, but, curiously, it also mirrors Fredrik's view of himself—or, more accurately, something within Bergman that is expressed through his central character.

Fredrik is repeatedly referred to by two bestial epithets.* As in English,

---

*Most of these references are lost to non-Swedish audiences because the film's subtitles either ignore them entirely or else translate them with other idiomatic expressions.

gamla bocken ("old billy goat") connotes randiness, but *bocken* is also the sign of the Devil in Swedish folklore—and the Devil, as his association with the various Jack figures attests, has Oedipal implications for Bergman. The second epithet, "big bad wolf," which Fredrik applies to himself while discussing the unconsummated marriage with Anne in their bedroom, obviously alludes to the tale of Little Red Ridinghood that was Bergman's childhood favorite. (One need not analyze that fairy tale's densely sexual content to appreciate its symbolic meaning for the filmmaker: his intricate reworking of it in *Dreams* should suffice.) But, interestingly, Fredrik's behavior is neither goatish nor wolfish; indeed, like Consul Sönderby with Doris, he seems to rely on Anne's innocence for reassurance that something evil, in himself and in the world, has been kept in check. Although the plot turns on his desire for Anne to surrender her virginity to him and he is shown once placing his hand on her breast, his motivation is to be the man he publicly pretends to be, not to satisfy a sexual longing.

Bergman openly suggests as much when Fredrik whispers Desirée's name in his sleep, not Anne's, but the story's contour reveals more than anything Fredrik says. To begin with, one has to wonder about a middle-aged man who weds a sixteen-year-old girl. Fredrik's visit to Desirée is also a bit suspicious. Although he seeks advice on how to thaw his icy wife, it is unclear what instructions he might expect from his former mistress. Could one not see the visit to the maternal Desirée as a subconscious attempt to confront the symbolic source of the psychological problem with women that caused him to marry the childlike Anne? The key factor, however, is the stress Bergman places on Anne's virginity. Nothing in the plot requires that she be a virgin (mere sexual indifference toward her husband would be sufficient), but once one perceives the concern about incest that underlies the story, it becomes a crucial element.

From Henrik's point of view, of course, the fact that his father has failed to consummate the marriage eases the guilt attached to making love to his "mother." The importance of Anne's purity to Fredrik is rather more complicated. Like most of Bergman's previous protagonists, he is emotionally a child, terribly insecure about his sexual capabilities. Despite his posturing in front of his son, he is just as inept with women; indeed, if one looks upon this story as a kind of dream, it is apparent that Fredrik and Henrik function as doubles. Just as Henrik feels daunted by Fredrik's pretensions of sexual mastery, Fredrik is daunted before Malcolm—that cartoon of masculinity who is an expert marksman, who can throw a knife with unerring accuracy, and who (most significantly) has laid claim to the maternal Desirée with his unfailing sexual proficiency. From this perspective, Anne emerges as another of Bergman's surrogates for the mother, transformed into a child by a male who seeks libidinous satisfaction and yet dares not risk humiliation by a woman, like mother, whose sexual expectations he cannot fulfill. Thus, when Anne loses her virginity, Fredrik loses the safety the "playmate mother" has provided; the little boy's masquerade of manhood is now vulnerable to exposure and ridicule —which is precisely what happens in the duel and its aftermath.

But Anne's deflowering also holds a second, related meaning. The son, as alter ego, has enacted Fredrik's most sinful, repressed desire. (On this point, it is worth noting that Fredrik's astonishment in the elopement scene focuses not on the sight of the fleeing couple—which represents the end of his marriage—but on the veil Anne has let flutter to the dirt in her flight—patently the symbol of her lost virginity.) As if to test the implications of what has happened by repeating it, he next goes to the pavilion, where he is to be seduced by Charlotte, the wife of father-figure Malcolm. The consequences dramatize his fears and his guilt. Even though the duel between this "father" and "son" ends with Fredrik's firing a blank cartridge—proof, as it were, of his impotence —symbolically, he is punished for his incestuous presumption with death.

Frid closes the film with his exultant cry, "There's no better life than this!" and the audience infers a happy ending, and a new beginning, from the reuniting of the humbled lawyer and his former mistress. But a very different drama has unfolded deep beneath this veneer. The "desire" Desirée represents for Fredrik is neither romantic nor hopeful; rather, it is a tantalizing dream—like Kaj's and Joakim's and Frost's—of escape from the terrors of consciousness and life itself through being unborn.

Quests

Curiously, while Dymling was restricting Bergman to comedy, SF elected to begin production of *Last Couple Out* (originally entitled *For the Sake of the Children*), a joyless piece of hackwork about rebellious adolescents that he had drafted before *Summergame* and sold to the studio at the end of the strike. In retrospect, this seems to have been an odd choice, but *The Summer with Monika* had turned a profit, and films about teenagers in revolt were now suddenly in vogue (the release of Nicholas Ray's *Rebel Without a Cause* in 1955 had just generated an international James Dean craze). The studio evidently sniffed an opportunity, and, hoping to re-create the success of the first of Bergman's "puberty crisis" films, assigned the script to Alf Sjöberg. This time, the combination failed, principally because of the material Bergman provided.

In *Torment*, Sjöberg had found a contest between good and evil, simplified the terms of the conflict, and used the camera to heighten the melodramatic effect, but in *Last Couple Out*, he confronted a loosely sewn patchwork without dramatically defined issues. On the surface, Bo Dahlin's difficulties concern his having to reconcile his juvenile ideals of what parents should be with his newly gained perspective on them as flawed human beings. The roots of his problem, however, are much more knotted. Bo obviously looks upon his mother as his sweetheart, held captive in a loveless marriage. Mainly for this reason, he contemns his father (as his dream of kicking in the father's face attests), yet he also finds their relationship reassuring: with this stolid, weak man as a "rival," he has no doubts about being first in his mother's affection. But then he learns that Mother has taken a psychiatrist named Ernst Farell as her lover. Unlike the father, the interloper poses a real threat; when Bo confronts him, the self-assured Farell invites the young man to do his best to wreck the affair.

Had Bergman confined himself to this set of tensions, he might have built a drama; instead, from the moment that Mrs. Dahlin, perplexed by the different claims on her, withdraws from the men in her life (and from the film) to sort her feelings, he forsakes the initial quadrangle to construct a different triangle. Anita, who would like to be Bo's girlfriend, takes advantage of her parents' absence to throw a party—which quickly turns into a melee. In the confusion, another girl, Kerstin, draws Bo to her house. After she tries, without success, to arouse him sexually, her parents arrive home unexpectedly and scold the young man for betraying their trust. The irony is too much for Bo, who lashes out at all parents for being too concerned with themselves to tend to their children's needs. Returning to Anita's house, he asks her forgiveness, and they part with the understanding that, sometime in the future, they will become lovers. This would seem an opportune note on which to end, but Bergman adds another scene. Appealing for guidance, Bo tells a teacher that he is torn between killing himself and severing all ties to his family and friends in the hope of beginning a new existence elsewhere. The teacher advises a third course: to contend with life as it is while recognizing that, in shaping his future, he will make mistakes similar to those of his parents.

That both strands of the film lead from a psychoautobiographical skein is beyond argument. The double aspect of Mr. Dahlin as weak and tyrannical clearly owes to Bergman's ambivalent view of his father, and Mrs. Dahlin's dilemma imitates that of Karin Bergman. Perhaps the most revealing of these figures is Ernst Farell. Besides representing the lover who threatened the stability of the Bergman household, he is also both a projection of the erotically competent suitor for mother that the child yearned to be (one notes that Bergman gave him his own first name) and of the father who, whatever else he lacked, could command the sexual privileges denied to the son (far is "father" in Swedish); in making Farell a psychiatrist, Bergman seems to have been alluding to the psychological matter the character reflects.

The second strand winds around the same Oedipal center as the first, even though the two barely touch on the story's surface. Bouncing from his mother to the two girls his own age, Bo meets his sexual problem in another form. Not only can he not rise to the occasion (so to speak) provided by Kerstin—a younger version of the mother as temptress —but he implicitly blames Kerstin's mother (who is specifically made the representative mother) for creating the conditions in which he has failed. Burdened with a guilt scarcely justified by the overt import of the action, he reverts to the sexually undemanding Anita, but this only grants him a temporary reprieve from the tests of adulthood—as the odd concluding scene indicates. Measured in terms of the antecedent events, Bo's consideration of suicide seems a very extreme (and inappropriate) response; in terms of their underlying meaning, however, it is at least understandable.

If it were only to supply another instance of Bergman's compulsive personal story, *Last Couple Out* would be worth no more than a mention, but, given its release in 1956, it affords an opportunity to look back on the progress he had made since he first set it to paper. In simple terms, the summer theme transposed the "life crisis" of the 'forties films from the threshold of adulthood to the threshold of life's later phases, and although his treatment of relations between men and women became more complex and acquired the sheen of sophistication, the controlling impulse continued to derive from the throbbing psychic wounds of his childhood. What changed was the role of art. Although close study of *Last Couple Out* will disclose basal similarities with *Smiles of the Summer Night*, with *A Lesson in Love*, and even with *Evening of the Jesters*, the latter films were conceptually more intricate and far better designed. The sources were still subjective, but their manipulation became far more objective; what the inner self had been driven to express, the artist now sought to compose. The fact that composition often involved deception only demonstrates the greater reliance on artistry. In contrast to *Last Couple Out*, which, like his 'forties films, ends without a resolution, *Smiles of the Summer Night* manages to generate a sense of aesthetic completeness—even though the ostensibly "happy ending" is fundamentally at odds with the vision at the film's core.

But in drawing attention to the common nucleus from which a dozen years of filmscripts derive, *Last Couple Out* also accentuates the shift that occurred halfway through the decade. Personal anxiety is no less evident as the stimulus for *The Seventh Seal*, *Wild Strawberries*, *The Face*, and *The Virgin Spring* than it was during the first two phases of his film career, but the focus of artistic concern veers toward philosophical deliberations. Bergman's notion that a great artist must address the most profound issues mankind faced had been manifest from the very beginning, of course. From *The Death of Punch* through *The Murder in Barjärna*, all his plays gave prominence to the question of God's relationship to his creation—indeed, one of his problems as a playwright had been a fatal tendency to assert, at a stentorian decibel, more than his dramas aesthetically supported. The same grand intentions were proclaimed by the first wholly Bergman film, but, again, the manifest promised more than was in the cargo: the link between the mathematics professor's conceit of a world ruled by Satan and Tomas's account of Birgitta-Carolina existed in the filmmaker's psyche—not, to any credible extent, in the film itself.

In the evolution of the summer theme, however, Bergman found his way toward philosophical inquiry through a more natural route. The disillusionment that attends the passage from youth in *Summergame* and *Women's Waiting* leads to implicit recognition of the ultimate reality of death signaled by the clocks that tick relentlessly for the older protagonists in *Dreams* and *Smiles of the Summer Night*. Bergman was now artistically prepared to address the "big questions": What is life's meaning? Where is the basis for faith? How can man's need for God be reconciled with the evidence of his absence? Whether the Swedish film industry and Swedish audiences would accommodate those ambitions, however, was another matter.

For all that he had scorned the Swedish literati in his early struggle to establish his credentials, and for all his protesting during the 'sixties and 'seventies that he did not care to be the darling of a cultural elite, Bergman in the mid-'fifties panted for appreciation as a serious artist. The fact that what success he had enjoyed in film had been won by catering to the appetites of a mass public obviously bothered the stunted playwright. As the commerical failure of *Evening of the Jesters* had demonstrated, deviation from popular tastes was risky, yet, he worried in a published dialogue with himself, to attempt only to please them would lock him to "ambitions limited to provoking an objectified, indifferent laughter." Two egos argue over his future in this dialogue. One acknowledges somewhat ruefully that making films is a luxury supported by a public interested only in entertainment. "I hate the audience—it scares me—and yet I love it. I have an irrepressible need to move, to charm, to frighten, to humiliate, to insult. My dependence on it is painful but stimulating, nauseating but rewarding. . . . In embittered affection, I give it what is mine or what I can steal or lie about." The other, impatient with such craven appeasement, yearns to create "immortal masterpieces in the eye of eternity" and bravely insists "cinema can be art." If the industry ignores the challenge, this second voice tells the first, "then I'll rewrite my rejected manuscript as a novel and leave you to your hopeless profession."[1]

That rejected "immortal masterpiece" was *The Seventh Seal*, but his more immediate concern was surviving *Smiles of the Summer Night*. From the start of shooting until its screening at the 1956 Cannes Film Festival, it seemed governed by an unlucky star. Temperatures in Sweden that summer hovered at record levels: equipment broke down and the actors and crew who had to suffer the heat without air-conditioning grew testy. But Bergman had more than the weather to worry him. Ulla Jacobsson, who played Anne, was pregnant; Bibi Andersson stood ready to take over the role in case the virgin bride's abdomen swelled too much in the course of the two months of shooting—which would require more time and expense. The studio, edgy about the film's high costs, was breathing down his neck; a quarrel erupted over his "extravagance" in reupholstering the furniture for the Armstedt manor scenes in white cloth. The director's temper flared with his crew. His digestion bothered him. Despite the profits earned by his previous two comedies for SF, he openly fretted that, if this expensive film flopped, he would be sent packing. When the rough cut was shown, his worst premonitions seemed confirmed: the studio executives told him the whole thing "had been a grave mistake. The film was not funny; it was too stylized, too lame, too long. They had also discovered that it was in costume, and costume films were doomed. Above all, they expressed a general pessimism."[2] The premiere did little to lift his spirits—afterward, he remarked that he had seldom seen such a grim audience—and the mixed reviews included some vituperative comments about his salacious, immature humor that were reminiscent of the attack on *Evening of the Jesters*.

SF did choose to send the film to Cannes, but this was something less than the vote of confidence it might appear. For years, Swedish films had been sheepishly entered in the festival as a way of rewarding one or another member of the industry with an expense-paid vacation on the Mediterranean. No one entertained any great hopes for *Smiles of the Summer Night*—least of all Bergman, whose *Ship to India* had been hooted at by a Cannes audience years before. Thus, when the news that the comedy had been awarded the Jury Prize reached him, he was stunned:

I sat in the shithouse reading the paper. I read "Swedish Film Awarded Prize in Cannes," "Swedish Film Causes Sensation," or something like that. What damn film is that? I thought; I didn't believe my eyes when I saw that it was *Smiles of the Summer Night*.

. . . Sandrews had let it be known that they were still counting their losses after *Dreams* and *Evening of the Jesters* and that they weren't very interested [in more of my films.] Therefore, I took a train to Carl Anders [Dymling, who was attending the Festival] . . . he was on the telephone selling *Smiles of the Summer Night* to all countries imaginable. . . . I said, "Now, Carl Anders, now or never." Then, laying *The Seventh Seal* on the table in front of him, I said, "Now you must make up your mind."[3]

A bit lightheaded over the unexpected acclaim, Dymling surrendered — though not unconditionally. More convinced than ever that Bergman's forte was comedy, he was willing to allow the director a measure of self-indulgence to protect SF's interest in Bergman's future, but as a conservative businessman he also insisted on keeping potential losses to a minimum: Bergman could proceed with *The Seventh Seal* only if he agreed to complete it within a shooting schedule of thirty-five days.

Bergman worked feverishly on the script, revising it, according to his account, five times before he was satisfied. Shooting began in July, only a month after the final revision. With meager resources, the director managed to create an utterly convincing illusion. Except for three days on Sweden's southwest coast, he re-created a medieval world on a site so close to downtown Stockholm that the reflection of sunlight off the glass of a modern apartment house showed in some frames. The discharge from a fire hose placed in a patch of trees served as a creek gurgling through a fourteenth-century forest. Extras recruited from nearby geriatric homes for their "interesting faces" suggested the terror and hardship of life in medieval society. Costumes were borrowed and props were kept simple. The usual cinematic version of the Middle Ages had been a gaudy display of the costumier's art, a Romantic reproduction of storybook figures moving in perfumed glory; Bergman's captured the pediculous reality.

What excited the world's admiration within the few months after its February 1957 premiere in Sweden, however, was its intellectual ambition. Not only was it received almost everywhere as a new film "classic," but it was treated with the kind of respect usually reserved for great works of literature. The latter 'fifties and early 'sixties were recognizing that cinema had finally come of age as a serious art form. Indeed, it was spoken of as the natural heir of the stage: henceforth, the vitality of drama would be found in the filmmakers. No film encouraged such talk more than *The Seventh Seal*. Ironically, the promising playwright who never matured had now realized his most grandiose dreams; the filmmaker who had been derided as an arrested adolescent, then cheered for his comic gift by his countrymen, now was being hailed internationally as a profound literary genius.

For the next three decades, Bergman's reputation as a master of the esoteric would continue to derive from the impact registered by *The Seventh Seal*, but his hold on the public's favor had as much to do with its successors. *Wild Strawberries*, issued ten months after *The Seventh Seal*, surpassed it in popularity (especially in Sweden, where it remains the most-loved of his films); the performance of Victor Sjöström won the audience's heart, while the symbolism of the surrealistic dream passages enticed its intellect. *Close to Life*, although a minor work by any reckoning, sustained the enthusiasm—at least in Europe, where critics praised its "classical" spareness and "intimate disclosures"; very well-received at the Cannes Festival, it won a special prize for the three actresses in the leading roles. With *The Face*, Bergmanomania continued virtually unabated, despite the fact that it disturbed critics in some quarters (mainly in Britain) with its mixture of comedy and mysticism; to admirers, it was a confession de profundis in parabolic form. *The Virgin Spring*—regarded not only as brilliant cinema but also, in its crying the power of faith over evil, as an almost vatic pronouncement —raised Bergman's standing to its zenith. When it won the 1960 Oscar as Best Foreign Film, the award sparked criticism of the Academy's provincialism in relegating recognition of its achievement to an implicitly subordinate category.

In these few years, public devotion to his films had come to resemble the adulation of a cult formed around a philosopher-poet of gnostic parables. Film by film, followers tracked his penetration of religious mysteries and interpreted the "answers" he sent back encoded in ambiguous metaphors. Yet, in looking back on the films of this period, one sees the seeker, not the savant. It is the intensity with which the questions are posed that gives these films their power. In comparison, the redemptive "truths" toward which the questions presumably lead ring false.

From the very beginning, Bergman approached story-making as a way of resolving problems: if that theater of puppets he controlled in his fiction could be made to enact the answers, then, in some magical way, the rite would undo the problem—reality would imitate art. The straining to perform this sympathetic magic is most evident in the early films, where "happy endings" are plucked from the air to dissipate a turbulence in the depths beneath the story's surface. When he recognized the insufficiency of his magic, he resorted to evasion—like M. Eiffel Tower. Briefly, with the "summer theme" that began forming in the late 'forties and early 'fifties, he adopted another strategy: art here works toward a moment of reconciliation with reality. But such resignation was fundamentally alien to an artistic instinct driven by the wish to transform rather than to accept.

The reorientation toward philosophical issues that begins with *The Seventh Seal* can be seen as an attempt to establish a different relationship between himself and his fictions. Instead of addressing a psychological conflict within himself that lay beyond the power of art to solve, he would substitute a philosophical one that he could resolve (and control) through his intellect. Bergman has often stated that making *The Seventh Seal* released him from his terror of death—as though, by extricating the knight from despair, he also liberated himself. But in fact, behind the putatively philosophical problem lies the same psychological urgency. Appearance to the contrary notwithstanding, the film is not radically about death at all; rather, it focuses on the terror of emptiness *in life*. What that emptiness implies for Bergman may be inferred from the vision of the virginal mother, the unmenacing father, and the child that he calls upon to countervail it. Moreover, the resolution is introduced from outside the boundaries of the dramatic argument he initially presents, and, as the differing responses to Death of knight and squire in their final scene illustrates, it does not dispose of the central philosophical question posed. Here as in *The Virgin Spring*, Bergman tries to overwhelm the anguish he portrays by invoking the hallelujahs of celestial choirs. Not until *Persona* would he confront the specter of emptiness without using art to produce a comforting self-deception.

The Seventh Seal

The unfinished script of *The Seventh Seal* that Bergman thrust at Dymling in Cannes had its genesis two years earlier. In an acting class he was teaching at the Malmö Theater, he asked the students to suggest roles they would like to play; after withdrawing into his office, he emerged with a few pages of dialogue. The exercise struck his fancy, and in late 1954, it emerged as "Painting on Wood," a one-act play he directed on a national radio broadcast. It was the first of three very successful productions. Six months later, he staged the play in Malmö; then, in September, Bengt Ekerot (who would assume the role of Death in the film) revived it at Dramaten. The play, however, reveals little more about the film that derives from it than would a writer's notebook entries.

Basically a morality, "Painting on Wood" consists of several declamatory tableaux. On returning from a crusade to the Holy Land, an unnamed knight and his squire, Jöns, meet a girl who tells them plague is ravaging the countryside. They next encounter the ghost of a witch burned that day. While she recounts the story of her execution, a smith enters looking for his wife, who has run off with an actor. Minutes later, the smith surprises the amorous couple behind some trees, but the actor averts the husband's wrath by feigning suicide. After the knight, the squire, and the reunited husband and wife leave, the girl who had greeted the crusaders appears before the resurrected "corpse" and reveals that she is Death's servant, come to lead the actor to her master. The following scene returns to the knight's party, now joined by Maria, a young woman trying to escape with her child from the plague-ridden forest. At the conclusion of a folk legend she relates about her namesake, the Virgin, the travelers have reached the knight's castle, where they are greeted by his wife Karin. Politely, she announces the presence of the Grave Gentleman (Death) and relays to her guests his instructions that they "take each other's hands and form a chain." As the curtain falls, they all move in a solemn dance to the music of the actor's lute.

As Bergman tells it, the elaboration of this simple outline began as he was shaving on a morning in January 1956. The phonograph, turned to full volume to drown out the noise of the electric razor, was playing one of his favorite pieces of music, *Carmina Burana*. Suddenly, mental pictures inspired by Orff's opera became associated with earlier impressions from Picasso's *Les Saltimbanques* and Dürer's copper engraving "Knight, Death, and Devil"; invading the morality and fusing themselves to its scenes, these images prompted the author to expand and redraw its contours.[1]

Other sources are either self-evident or probable. If the apocalyptic vision of the Book of Revelation influenced the orginal conception at all, the connection was tenuous, but its relationship to the film became quite pronounced—as not only the title he eventually settled on but also the provisional title of one of the drafts (*And the Name of the Star Is*

The Knight (Max von Sydow) unwittingly confesses to Death (Bengt Ekerot). Permission from Svenska Filmindustri.

Called Wormwood) indicate. Perhaps inspired by *Faust* (his 1958 production of the *Ur-Faust* in Malmö would often be compared to *The Seventh Seal*), he introduced the knight's compulsion for knowledge at any cost as a key element, and to accentuate the knight's intellectualism, he borrowed a convention from *Don Quixote* and made the squire an earthy sensualist. Camus's *The Plague*, which may have stimulated his writing the play, evidently supplied Father Paneloux as a model for the leader of the flagellants. Several classic films, too, almost surely guided his thoughts as he rewrote. Certain sequences in *The Seventh Seal* suggest counterparts in Carné's *The Evening Vistors* and Dreyer's *Day of Wrath*. A more important source, apparently, was one of the best-known products of the Swedish silent era. Victor Sjöström's *The Phantom Carriage*, to which Bergman had devoted careful study during his earliest days at SF, is the story of a man assessing the value of his life as he meets an appointment with Death; more than any of the other revisions, it was the incorporation of this conceit into *The Seventh Seal* that distinguishes it from "Painting on Wood."

The primary impulse for both the play and the film, however, came from within Bergman. As the hostess to Death in both versions, Karin, the knight's wife, plays a role so minor it is practically superfluous;

moreover, the story provides no dramatic justification for her dying or for the postponement of her husband's death until he meets her again in the castle. Yet her position at the terminus of the knight's journey suggests that, for some reason not manifested by the story, his struggle is tied to what she represents. That hidden significance is almost surely signaled by the fact that Bergman gave her his mother's name. Death is the extreme punishment for guilt, and although *The Seventh Seal* gives few clues as to what guilt it metaphorically treats, the succession of mother figures killed in Bergman's earlier writings (as well as the symbolic death of Fredrik after his alter ego has had intercourse with Anne) suggests the nature of the concealed sin. Indeed, one is tempted to see a connection between the implicit search for the source (or meaning) of the medieval plague that takes the knight back home to Karin, and Oedipus's search for the cause of the Theban plague that leads to the shattering knowledge of his incest with Jocasta.

The link between the film and Bergman's father is much less suppositious. Ingmar's trips around the Uppland countryside to the churches served by his father contained some of the tenderest moments in their usually stormy relationship, but each stop brought sudden alienation. When Pastor Bergman tended to the mysteries of the altar and preached, he became a remote figure, the embodiment of the austere, punitive God in his texts. To avoid thinking about the eerie transformation in his father (and about the guilt he felt toward him), the boy would surrender his mind to the naive religious illustrations from the fifteenth century that covered the church interiors: "There was everything my imagination could desire—angels, saints, dragons, prophets, devils, humans. All this was surrounded by a heavenly, earthly, subterranean landscape of a strange yet familiar beauty."[2] As the preface to "Painting on Wood" further reveals, this *Biblia pauperum* suggested not only the subject for his drama but also its message that faith, hope, and love can overcome despair. The memory of a particular church had an especially strong effect. In one of a pair of arches, Death was depicted playing chess, sawing the tree of life, and leading the final dance toward darkness, "but in the other arch, the Holy Virgin was walking in a rosegarden, supporting the Child's faltering steps."[3] That the juxtaposition should have so impressed Bergman is not surprising, for the panels icongraphically represented his favorite pairing of opposites: the severity of God the Father's rule and the mercy of the Virgin Mother.

As the filmscript evolved, the seminal importance of the church paintings increased. Maria's very brief scene in the play merely suggests that, though Death will overtake the travelers, the hope she personifies will live on; in the film (where she is called Mia), she acquires a husband Jof (=Joseph), and, together with their son Michael, they furnish the means for the knight's victory. Death as the sawyer of the tree of life, a favorite motif of the medieval painters, does not appear in the play, but in the film the image expands into a whole scene.* So, too, the chess game between Death and a knight—which supplies the film with its central conceit. Indeed, Bergman became so caught up in the paintings that, in the film, he identifies himself with Albertus Pictor, the most famous of the Uppland artists. When Jöns the squire meets Albertus in the act of painting a *Totentanz* on the church wall, their dialogue suggests that *The Seventh Seal* is Bergman's *Totentanz* and that, should it fail at the box office, he would be forced back into making comedies.

Jöns: What is this supposed to represent?
Albertus: The Dance of Death.
Jöns: It's not going to make people any happier.
Albertus: Why should I make people happy? It might not be a bad idea to frighten them a little every now and then.
Jöns: Then they'll close their eyes and refuse to look at your art.
Albertus: Oh, they will look. A skull is almost more interesting than a naked woman.
Jöns: And if you frighten them . . .
Albertus: They'll think. . . .
Jöns: You're only painting your Dance of Death.
Albertus: I'm only painting things as they are. Everyone else can do as he likes.
Jöns: Just think how some people will curse you.
Albertus: Perhaps. But then I'll paint something amusing for them to look at. I have to make a living. . . .

The "mural" Bergman developed from the "Painting on Wood" sketch begins with the knight Antonius Block and his squire Jöns, weary from ten years of Crusading, lying on a beach of their homeland. Block, an intellectual troubled by the futility of his errand to the Holy Land, stares with eyes "bloodshot from lack of sleep"; his first action on awakening is to pray. In contrast, Jöns, a man of the senses, snores, scratches his

---

*In the church at Tensta (a few miles from Uppsala), Johannes Rosenrod's sketch shows Death felling a youth's tree while the perched victim bemusedly counts his treasure. The Swedish word for "treasure" is *skatt*; the name Bergman gave to the traveling player who loses his life to Death's saw in the film is Skat.

stubbled head, belches, and sings a bawdy verse extolling the joys to be found between a strumpet's legs over obedience to a God "so very far away." Somewhere in the vicinity, a trio of juggler-actors are also waking to the new day. The parallel action implies the reversed, mirror images the two sets of characters present. Jof—who regularly plays "the Soul of Man" in the troupe's small repertoire—corresponds to Block. He is instinctive and innocent; the knight, pensive and burdened by his experience of the world. But both are on the side of faith: Jof believes completely in God; the knight desperately wants to justify believing. Jof's day begins with his seeing a vision of the Virgin; later in the day, the knight will, in a sense, have his own vision of the Virgin—and will base his faith upon it. The second pairing aligns Jonas Skat, the troupe's leader, with Jöns. Like the squire, Skat is a sensualist, but he lacks the squire's courage—as the contrast in their reactions to Death will illustrate. Finally, Bergman's arrangement suggests a relationship between Jof's wife Mia, to whom he sings of "great joy on high," and the strumpet in Jöns's song. They represent the two aspects of man's (or Bergman's) view of Woman: the latter, responding to his lustful nature; the former, a young mother who radiates a virginal purity, answering to his deeper needs.

The parallelism of the two sets of characters is extended in the reactions of each to a memento mori. Skat, holding the skull-mask with which he will play Death in their next performance at Elsinore, scoffs at the "nonsense" that scares people, but fear lurks beneath his nonchalance. Jof, momentarily taken aback by the sight of his partner in the mask, soon dismisses its suggestion: he is too much the celebrant of life to be affected by sham terror. Meanwhile, in contrast to Skat, Jöns is showing a genuine contempt for the real thing. Sent by his master to ask directions, he discovers that the recumbent figure he addresses is a rotting corpse; making an ironic joke of the grisly sight, he reports that the man was "rather eloquent" in pointing the way. But the most important of these confrontations, paralleling Jof's facing the masked Skat, is the knight's meeting with the cowled personification of Death. Typically, he challenges Death with his intellect by proposing a chess match. By virtue of his request to "live as long as I hold out against you," the match becomes a metaphor for life itself: though Block knows he must lose in the end, he hopes that contesting his fate may reveal something that will make the effort worthwhile.

Having established a correspondence between the troupe and the returning Crusaders, Bergman next emphasizes the contrast between the squire and his knight in parallel scenes. Declaring his indifference

to the plague's horrors as he watches Albertus paint the *Totentanz*, Jöns
draws his crude self-portrait and describes it as the picture of one who
"grins at Death, mocks the Lord, laughs at himself and leers at the girls.
His world is a Jöns-world, believable only to himself, ridiculous to all
including himself, meaningless to Heaven and of no interest to Hell."
Meanwhile, in another part of the church, the knight is preparing for his
test against Death by going to confession. He, too, presents a self-portrait.
"My heart is empty," he begins. "The emptiness is a mirror turned
toward my own face. I see myself in it, and I am filled with fear and
disgust. Through my indifference to my fellow men, I have isolated
myself from their company. Now I live in a world of phantoms. I am
imprisoned in my dreams and fantasies." Unlike the irreverent Jöns, he
is tormented by God's hiding "in a mist of half-spoken promises and
unseen miracles" and cruelly teased by his human inability "to grasp
God with the senses." In his anguish over a God who "remains silent" in
the darkness, he calls for "knowledge, not faith, not suppositions, but
knowledge. I want God to stretch out his hand toward me, reveal himself and speak to me." But in the darkness of the confessional that
corresponds to the spiritual darkness, there is only Death. Having tricked
his opponent by assuming the confessor's place, Death finally reveals
himself and echoes Block's terrifying thought that there may be no God
to answer. Whereupon the knight announces he will use the reprieve
afforded by the chess game to perform just "one meaningful deed."
Presumably, since to him the nonexistence of God would imply the
futility of life, such a deed would prove that God exists.*

After dedicating himself to his mission (in effect, the close of Act I), the
knight descends, like Faust, into the tumult of the world. The two episodes constituting the second act of the drama, however, seem to gainsay both the possibility for meaning and the validity of faith.

Outside a church, Tyan, a girl accused of causing the plague by having had sexual relations with the Devil, hangs limply from the stocks.
Although she has been tortured nearly to the point of death, the terror-
stricken inhabitants of the parish are not yet satisfied: to demonstrate
their faith in God, they have decided to burn her at the stake. In her own
terror, she has conceived a faith as resolute as theirs—not in God but in
the Devil, who, she is convinced, will save her from the flames. Her

---

*That Block is confessing to Death is appropriate, since it is the consciousness of his
mortality that prompts this *self*-examination. All the statements by Death in his role as
father confessor are either reflections of the knight's own utterances or fragments of
sentences that the knight completes.

professed intimacy with the Devil prompts the knight to ask for an introduction: "I want to question him about God. He, if anyone, must know." When the "witch" tells him he will find the Devil by looking in her eyes, Block, seeing only fear, is disappointed. And yet, in a sense, his question has found its answer. Fear generates not only Tyan's Devil but also the God of those who persecute her—and the greatest fear is that, beyond life, there is only the void.

It is this nothingness Tyan finally apprehends when, as the flames reach toward her, she realizes that the savior she has fashioned will not intercede. As Block studies her eyes, Jöns voices his master's thoughts: "Who watches over that child? Is it the angels, or God, or the Devil, or only the emptiness? Emptiness, my lord. Her poor brain has just made a discovery. Emptiness under the moon. We stand powerless . . . because we see what she sees, and our terror and hers are the same." "This cannot be," Block protests, but the words express the anger of forlorn desire, not conviction: Tyan's discovery directly reflects his confession to Death. Even more damaging to his attempt to prove that life, despite its suffering, has purpose, his only response to her painful death is to give her an anesthetizing potion to cut short her agony. Thus, his first significant act after leaving the confessional is not an affirmation of life's meaning but a concession to meaninglessness. If no God watches over Tyan (or the knight) then death, like the potion, is simply a merciful end to suffering—and playing chess with Death represents only an intellectual game.

The second episode also revolves around the implications of a world without God. While plundering a corpse of its jewels, Raval, a former seminarian, realizes that a young woman has witnessed his crime. "Each of us has to save his own skin," he tells her; then, taking the precept a step farther, he announces that he must murder her to protect himself and that there is no God to interfere. Jöns, entering the house at this point, saves the girl's life and discovers in subduing her assailant that he is the same man who "spewed out the holy venom" which had persuaded the squire's master to join the crusade. When Raval defends his rhetoric of ten years ago as having been issued in "good faith," Jöns retorts that now, "knowing better"—i.e., that without God, life dissolves into a moral chaos in which might makes right—the seminarian has become a thief. Jöns warns Raval that he will brand his face should they meet again, yet, when the squire tells the woman that only his weariness of "that dry kind of love" prevents him from raping her, he reveals an egocentric moral code no different from that of the seminarian he detests.

Curiously, the film's central section (its "third act") involves Block and Jöns very little; indeed, except for the squire's making good his threat against Raval and the knight's meeting with Mia in its final scene, the two are either absent or reduced to spectators. Nevertheless, what it depicts impinges directly on the questions raised by the knight's challenge to Death. Its several scenes portray human beings as lascivious, dishonest, and cruel—as exhibiting that propensity for humiliation Bergman has called the fundamental element in human experience—yet this is the creature the knight has chosen to champion. If there is a meaning to life, he must find it here.

Outside a tavern, suggestively named Embarrassment Inn, the knight joins an audience watching Skat's company perform a burletta—essentially the same "play within a play" found in *Jack Among the Actors* and "The Fish"—in which Mia plays the wife, Skat her lover, and Jof the jealous husband. Suddenly, this drama of man in his paradigmatic folly is interrupted by the Dies Irae chanted by a procession of flagellants (carrying the same crucifix seen earlier in the confessional scene). At the head of the procession, a monk, dressed like Death, shouts his warning to a humanity universally sentenced to death and asks that the "Lord have mercy on us in our humiliation."

Meanwhile, too busy with the sins of the flesh to worry about repentance, Skat is pursuing his adulterer's role offstage with Lisa, a voluptuous passerby. When Plog the smith discovers them walking hand in hand down a forest lane, he—like the husband in the skit—wants to kill his wife's lover. Lisa, switching her allegiance to the stronger man, goads the smith on, and Skat's fate seems sealed. But he is not an actor for nothing. Inventing a remorseful monologue that brings the gullible oaf to tears, he then caps his performance by committing "suicide" with a trick knife. When the others, deciding nothing is to be gained by mourning, have moved on, Skat hides in a tree, but just as he is congratulating himself on his cleverness, Death appears, announces that the actor's "contract" has been canceled, and saws through the base of the tree.

Despite its culmination in Skat's death, which itself is treated as trivial, the forest interlude is a comic exhibition of folly; in the next scene, back at Embarrassment Inn, the mood is ugly and something of far greater moment is at stake. Vending the booty he has snatched from the dead, Raval tries to sell Jof a bracelet. When the offer is politely refused, the seminarian brandishes a knife and forces the "Soul of Man" to dance like a bear.* The crowd jeers, lending its support to the humiliator, until

*The incident closely resembles a scene in *The Death of Punch*, where Kasper is forced to

Jöns, with righteous vengeance, puts a stop to Raval's mischief by slashing his face. Taking advantage of the distraction, Jof grabs the bracelet and runs away to his wagon, where Mia is entertaining the knight.

While Mia maternally nurses his bruises, her meek husband presents her with his trophy and invents an improbable tale of his brave deeds in obtaining it which brings knowing smiles from his listeners. But though the account is pure sham, the conveyance of the bracelet nevertheless represents an extraordinary victory. From his humiliation, Jof has wrested a token of his love; through love, the bracelet has passed from the dead to a woman who symbolizes the fount of new life. For the first time in the film, the mood is serene, and one senses that hope has been regenerated. As if in recognition of the moment's significance, Jof sings a poem in praise of spring while the couple's infant son Mikael, the embodiment of the future, plays nearby.

This display of simple joy has the quality of a religious revelation for the knight. It reminds him, as he contemplates his death, of the laughter when he was newly married and "the house was full of life." His mistake had been to turn from that fullness to the torment of serving the image of a God who stands beyond life: his devotion to that God was "like loving someone who is out there in the darkness but never appears, no matter how loudly you call." The ardor of that search, he says, "seems meaningless and unreal while I sit here with you and your husband. How unimportant it all becomes suddenly." Sharing in the family's meal of wild strawberries and milk (recurring symbols of innocence in Bergman's films), the Crusader who had quested in distant lands for the Holy Grail ironically finds the Grail's meaning in a tranquil manifestation of human love within walking distance of his own home.

> I shall remember this moment. The silence, the twilight, the bowls of strawberries and milk, your faces in the evening light. Mikael sleeping, Jof with his lyre. I'll try to remember what we have talked about. I'll carry this memory between my hands as carefully as if it were a bowl filled to the brim with fresh milk. And it will be an adequate sign—it will be enough for me.

Armed with this sign, Block is prepared to resume his match with Death (which now enters the endgame phase), and, at last, to perform his "meaningful deed." The opportunity for this redemptive act arises when Death, chatting idly at the chessboard, lets slip his intention of

dance on the tavern table. Reminiscent, too, of Albert's fight with Frans in *Evening of the Jesters*, it is one of several echoes from that film.

claiming the juggler family the next day. The knight knocks over the chess pieces. Misperceiving the calculated clumsiness as Block's desperate attempt to save himself, Death resets the board from memory and gloats that he will mate his opponent on the next move. But in securing this victory, Death has been cheated of another—exactly as the knight planned. Jof has observed the two at their game; correctly inferring its significance, he takes advantage of Death's concentration on the knight to gather his family into their wagon and escape into the forest.

On the other side of the forest, the knight is about to pay the forfeit for his unselfish act. Accompanied by Jöns, Lisa, Plog, and the girl the squire had rescued from Raval, he is greeted at Block Castle by his wife, who, following a meager, dry breakfast (evidently a symbolic "Last Supper"), reads from the eighth chapter of the Book of Revelation. Suddenly, three knocks are heard at the door. Jöns, investigating, reports he saw no one. A moment later, however, Death stands before them. Jöns's girl, acknowledging the end of their life's journey, quotes Christ's last words on the Cross: "It is finished." Meanwhile, after a night-long battle through a storm, Jof, Mia, and Mikael have emerged into the calm dawn of a new day. Pointing to the horizon, Jof describes the vision he sees of Death leading Plog, Lisa, Raval, Skat, the knight and Jöns on their "solemn dance toward the dark lands."

There is nothing particularly abstruse about *The Seventh Seal*—its Gothic letter intentions are discernible in virtually every scene. Yet, from the time of its release, it has been regarded as the quintessentially recondite Bergman product, and in that guise it has probably attracted more fanciful interpretations than any of the rest of his films. Influenced by the Existentialist vogue that was cresting in the late 'fifties, many commentators presumed that Bergman was Albert Camus translated to the screen. To be sure, the film exhibits many of the Existentialist code words—"emptiness," the "meaningful act" performed in the consciousness of death, Jöns's "protest" against his fate, the knight's implicit solidarity with mankind's future—but the connection is more apparent than real; examining the film through an Existentialist lens does not clarify its meaning. Another nudge sending the exegetes in the wrong direction was supplied by the promotional release quoting Bergman's statement that the Black Plague was comparable to the threat of atomic war. This offhand comment quickly became a warrant for a fruitless search of the film as a parable of the Dilemma of Modern Man.

The greatest encouragement to misinterpretation, however, lies in the film itself. In posing as a grandiose allegory, it invites attention to every detail as a constituent of an overarching meaning; thus, when the author lapses into inconsistencies, the tendency to treat them as signs of intent can lead far off course. The most obvious example of the problem is the *Totentanz* at the close. Perhaps for aesthetic reasons, Bergman omitted three of those who have died during the previous day from Death's party; as a result, some commentators have labored to derive a theological statement from the absence of Tyan, Block's wife, and the girl who has followed Jöns after he saved her from Raval.

Normally, the double rails of literal and figurative action on which allegory rides are tied firmly enough to restrict such interpretive divagations, but, in elaborating "Painting on Wood" into a much more complex filmscript, Bergman allowed structural considerations to distort the allegory's meaning. His material presented two major problems: first, it was episodic; second, to avoid a precipitous ending, he had to devise some means of separating the knight's discovery of life's meaning in the company of Mia and her family from his meaningful act in rescuing them from Death. His solution was to arrange the film so that each of the early episodes involving Death is interrupted by the beginning of the next and left uncompleted until after the knight's climactic meeting with the family, thereby cross-weaving the various strands and creating a crescendo of deaths as a contrast to the family's escape. But in gaining these advantages, Bergman weakened and confused the thematic development.

The comedy of Skat's death—which, chronologically, has had to have occurred before Raval's humiliation of Jof at the inn—is of a piece with his comical dalliance with Lisa. By delaying its presentation until after the climax, Bergman not only regresses from the epiphany toward which the film has been moving but also makes Death a less menacing antagonist. Similarly, Raval's lonely, horrible death from the plague he has exploited for profit would have made an ironic ending to his story had it immediately followed the scene at the inn. Placed in the latter portion of the film, where it seems superfluous, it conflicts with the spirit of the love the knight has just witnessed. When the squire's girl, touched by pity for her former oppressor, is about to offer the expiring man a drink of water, Jöns stops her, saying that such charity would be "totally meaningless." Strangely, the knight acquiesces—implying a qualification to the value of *caritas* that Bergman does not explain. Perhaps the greatest confusion of all is produced by the postponement of Tyan's execution. Since her torment is the most devastating evidence of the very forlornness of mankind that the milk-and-strawberries "communion" has just dispelled, and since nothing subsequently occurs to gainsay the futility of her agony, the force of the knight's meaningful deed is somewhat compromised.

A sampling of critical discussions of *The Seventh Seal* illustrates the variety of erroneous inferences this arrangement of events can produce. One critic assumes that the film ends on a "pessimistic note" because the knight, compelled by the cruelty of Tyan's fate to resume his self-destructive questioning, has forgotten the lesson of love and thus earned a "horribly negative death."[4] Another, missing the point of both the communion scene and the knight's tricking Death, argues that Block finally fails because he lacks Jof's artistic vision and is therefore incapable of leaping beyond ordinary reality.[5] A third, drawing the opposite conclusion from the same tangled signals, sees the knight achieving an ironic success by making possible the emergence of the Messiah through the flight of the Holy Family.[6] Most understandable of all is the bewilderment of an English critic who asks what has been accomplished by the rescue of the family: "Are they now immortal, or what?"[7]

But even though the thematic confusion in the film's second half has given license to some rather peculiar readings, the blame is not entirely Bergman's. More fundamental misprisions arise from loose assumptions as to what the allegory concerns. Clearly, what is at stake in the chess game is not personal immortality, and the escape of the "Soul of Man" and his family is not a last-minute mitigation of the knight's defeat. Nor does the film dramatize a debate over God's existence. Finally, although the pattern of Christological imagery—the obvious association of Jof, Mia, and Mikael with Joseph, Mary, and Jesus, the prominence of the crucifix in the confessional and in the procession of flagellants, the visual and textual allusions to the Passion in the execution of Tyan, and the quotation of Christ's words from the Cross at the end—has major importance, it implies neither the manifestation of God's love for man nor the promise of it.

Block always knows that his death is inevitable, and Death knows that he knows—which is why Death is puzzled by the request to play chess. In contracting to "live as long as I hold out against you," the knight is simply gaining a delay; the "release" that is to be his prize if he wins means release from his sense of futility through an act that will prove his life has served a meaningful purpose. Whether God exists and is remote, silent, and indifferent to man, or, as the knight himself says, God is only a name we give to an idol we make of our fears, bears on the possibility of obtaining answers as to life's purpose, but it is finally irrelevant to the despair the knight feels as he contemplates his own existence. What will eventually bring him the release he seeks is not faith in God but faith in man.

As this suggests, the allusions to Christ scarcely invoke traditional Christian belief. Here as elsewhere in his writings, Bergman's Jesus recalls the words from the Cross, "My God, my God, why has Thou forsaken me?" Describing the crucifix that hangs outside the confessional where Block speaks of his emptiness, the script stresses the fact that "Christ's face is turned upward, His mouth open as if in a cry of anguish." Again, when the crucifix swings over the heads of the self-flagellating Slaves of Sin, the script calls attention to the human aspect of Jesus: "It is not Christ triumphant, but the suffering Jesus with the sores, the blood, the hammered nails, and the face in convulsive pain. The Son of God, nailed on the wood of the Cross, suffering scorn and shame." And, of course, the suffering, scorn, and shame Tyan endures in her "crucifixion" underscore her having been forsaken by both God and the Devil she has taken as her god. All these signs reflect the knight's own Calvary in his consciousness of utter solitude and emptiness. Then he meets the "Soul of Man" and his family—"holy" in that they signify human love and the simple joy of life—and through his act of love for them, he finds release from his crucifixion.

In a sense, the innocence embodied by the family, and especially by the infant Mikael, corresponds to Bergman's recurrent fantasy of reversing time and escaping from the oppression of guilt by returning to the womb. Significantly, after the knight's death, the film's last frames are of Mikael being held aloft. But even though that paradigm undoubtedly operated at some level of Bergman's imagination, the concluding emphasis on Mikael also serves a carefully prepared, overt resolution of the problem announced at the beginning. Through his commitment to the family, the knight has overcome his egocentricity, the prison of "dreams and fantasies" created by "indifference to my fellow men." The import of his meaningful deed is that something other than "emptiness under the moon" lies beyond his death as an individual: Mikael, the emblem of the human community's future, will be his heir—in a manner of speaking, his "reincarnation."

That, like Block, Mikael will contend against Death is indicated by his name: in Revelation 12, the Archangel Michael is the adversary of Satan, the old serpent who brought death to paradise. In the very first scene in which Mikael appears, Jof states his dream that the boy will become the supreme juggler, achieving "the one impossible trick" for a human being:

making one of the balls "stand absolutely still in the air" (i.e., a mastery over natural forces tantamount to mastery over the power of death.) Further establishing this link to Block, Mia remarks in the communion scene that her son may become a knight. In time, of course, death will overtake Mikael just as it is soon to overcome the knight; what matters is that love for the infant, creating a chain of renewal stretching into the unseen reaches of the future, represents a hope that defeats the despair arising from the apparent finality of death.

In broad terms, the transition from Block's initial encounter with Death to the final shot of the infant describes the turning of the wheel of life, a favorite motif in medieval art. It also resembles the pattern traced by the various Grail legends and the vegetation myths. The script begins with the words, "The night has brought little relief from the heat, and at dawn a hot gust of wind blows across the sea," and thereafter refers repeatedly to drought and the life-sapping sun. This wasteland corresponds to the knight's spiritual paralysis, cured when the love and hope demonstrated by the family regenerate his faith and enable him to perform a meaningful act. With the protagonist's spiritual rebirth—ironically at the hour of his death—the land is revivified by the drenching rain that falls as the family escapes bearing the seed of the future.

And yet, finally, this scheme does not fully account for the film's action. Even though the knight eventually goes beyond the limits of intellect in finding the value of life in the emotions of the family, it is a solution that, one feels, is intellectually imposed by an author who is playing his own chess game with Death—and who mistrusts his ingenuity. Bergman himself has admitted that in Block, the protagonist around whom the dramatic argument revolves, he was expressing only one side of his personality; the other is featured in Jöns.[8] Not only does the squire respond to Death in a way that contradicts the knight's faith, but he is also the more commanding character.

Almost as though Bergman could not restrain himself, Jöns steadily grows in stature. When he first appears, he is a scurrilous fellow mocking his master behind his back; by the closing scene, without any of the intervening events having effected a noticeable change in him, he has become a noble exponent of man's pride. His last words are the essence of Romantic defiance to a God he refuses to acknowledge:

In the darkness where You are supposed to be, where all of us probably are.... In the darkness You will find no one to listen to

Your cries or be touched by Your sufferings. Wash Your tears and mirror Yourself in Your indifference.... [To the knight:] Feel the immense triumph of this last minute when you can still roll your eyes and move your toes. I shall be silent, but under protest.

Heroic as the speech is, it lies outside the drama Bergman has constructed. If the knight controls the film's statement, the squire's words are irrelevant. On the other hand, if, as some critics, moved by his courage, have assumed, Jöns is really the protagonist, then the focus of the preceding action has been misplaced. However much Bergman tried to employ his art as an act of will transforming himself and the conditions of his world to bring about acceptance, an inner rebelliousness remained. Jöns is not all that far removed from Jack.

That Bergman would emphasize his ambivalence by juxtaposing Jöns's stirring credo to the knight's serene prayer in Death's presence is characteristic of his films of this period. Underlying all of them is an urgent need to believe that life has a transcendent purpose, that it is not a moral chaos. Yet the artifice could not wholly absorb the artificer.

Wild Strawberries

Despite obvious differences in its setting, in the dramatic conventions it observes, and in its emotional tone, *Wild Strawberries* is so closely related to *The Seventh Seal* that, once the story is reduced to a simple outline, it seems almost its twin. After years of indifference to his fellow man which have left him emotionally isolated, the protagonist embarks on a journey that begins with a premonition of death and ends with its imminence. The journey thus becomes the occasion for retrospect on the value of his life. He comes to realize that, in making his way in the world, he lost sight of virtues near at hand in his youth. A scene involving wild strawberries sharpens this awareness by reminding him of the celebration of life from which he has been deflected by his intellectual pursuits. At one point, he meets a party of fellow travelers whose joy contrasts not only with the emptiness of his own existence but also with the evidence, encountered during the journey, of man's capacity for cruelty. Finally, he reaches his destination, but the other travelers, representing the persistence of hope, continue. Although the protagonist's life is over, the experience of the journey and the survival of good in a select few he has met along its route have in some way produced a sacramental moment in which he finds redemption.

Behind the similar schemes lies the filmmaker's impulse to resolve his personal conflicts by projecting them in fictive form. But unlike the spiritual allegory of the self presented by *The Seventh Seal*, the autobiographical element in *Wild Strawberries* comes directly from memory.

The idea for the new film originated during a predawn drive from Stockholm. Bergman was heading north to Dalarna on Highway E 4, but when he reached Uppsala, he yielded to a sudden desire to see his grandmother's house again.

> The sun was just rising over the cathedral and the bell struck five. I entered the little cobblestoned yard and went into the house. I grabbed the knob to the kitchen door, which still had the same colored glass design. It was like touching a raw nerve. What if I were to open the door and Lalla, the old cook, were to be standing there in her big kitchen apron preparing the breakfast porridge as she used to when I was little? What if I could suddenly walk into my childhood? Not so much now, but then I was terribly nostalgic. I think it was Maria Wine who said somewhere that we sleep in the shoes of our childhood. That was just how it hit me. I thought: suppose I were to make a film, completely realistically, about suddenly opening a door, emerging in reality, then turning a corner and entering another period of one's existence, and all the time the past is going on, alive.
>
> It was in the fall of 1956 that I made the trip. I began to write the manuscript in the spring, as I remember. . . . Because one of my best friends is a doctor, I thought it practical to make the central character a doctor. Then I somehow thought that this old man should be an old, tired egoist who had cut himself off from everything around—as I myself had done.[1]

From this emotional confrontation with his past, Bergman spun a story of "the events, dreams, and thoughts" of June 1, 1957, a day Isak Borg spends traveling along E 4 to the commencement ceremony at the University of Lund, where the seventy-six year-old doctor is to be feted on the fiftieth anniversary of his having received his degree.*

Isak's day begins before dawn when he awakes from a nightmare. The

---

*American accounts of the film invariably refer to the "Jubilee Doctor" degree he is to receive as honorary, but the translation is misleading. The granting of the Jubilee Doctor occurs on the fiftieth anniversary of the person's graduation from the university.

dreamscape is identical to the street where Isak takes his customary morning stroll, except that it is strangely deserted, the sun gives no warmth, a clock against which he habitually checks the accuracy of his timepiece has a blank dial, and the giant eyeglasses suspended from this clock (an optician's sign) have been smashed, causing the painted eyes to look like "watery, infected sores." His pocket watch, too, is without hands, and when he places it to his ear, he hears his heart beating. A man who wears a soft felt hat like Isak's turns around, revealing he has no face, then melts away. As a bell tolls, a hearse advances toward the frightened Isak, loses a wheel that almost hits him, bangs repeatedly into a lamppost, disgorges its coffin, and then rolls on. Isak peers at the corpse and discovers it is himself dressed in the very frock coat he is to wear for the Lund ceremony.*

Besides introducing death as the keynote to the day, the dream, like the Frost episode at the start of *Evening of the Jesters*, functions as a prologue. Virtually every one of its strange occurrences has a parallel in the events to follow, but the most important of them is the eerie creaking of springs, like an infant's wail, as the hearse ejects the coffin. This image of spiritual stillbirth strikes to the film's thematic core. Isak, whose dreams tell him that all his life he has been "dead although alive," has fostered a replica of himself in his son, and at the old man's side during the trip sits his daughter-in-law Marianne, pregnant with the heir of these lifeless generations.

Some miles south of Stockholm, Isak, on an impulse, turns his automobile onto an old country road. This detour to the house where he spent the first twenty summers of his life becomes the initial station of a mental journey into the past as real to him as his physical journey to Lund. Approaching the abandoned house, he seems to reexperience his sensations at the start of his morning dream. Suddenly, he sees Sara, the cousin to whom he was engaged in his youth, as a young girl picking wild strawberries. His brother Sigfrid surprises the girl and steals a kiss. Though conscience-stricken by her infidelity to her fiancé, she passionately returns it, spilling the berries and spotting her frock in the process. When the breakfast gong rings, old Isak follows the gathering family into the dining room where they celebrate Uncle Aron's name day. The scene teems with life, and although the gifts

---

*Like the ride on E 4, this dream derived from Bergman's own experience: "It was an obsessing dream. That it was I myself who lay in the casket was something I invented, but the part about a hearse hitting a lamppost and the coffin falling out and dumping its corpse I had dreamt many times."[2]

to Uncle Aron are absurdly inappropriate trifles, they express genuine affection.*

Young Isak and his parents reside in the same house, yet all three are conspicuous by their absence from the family occasion—as though their presence would violate the gaiety and the outpouring of love. The dream thus serves to remind old Isak of what he missed in life, of the early loneliness that has remained with him over his many years. In the middle of the festivities, he hears Sara describe his younger self as "extremely intellectual and aloof"; the charge coincides with Marianne's indictment of her father-in-law, at the start of the ride to Lund, as a completely inconsiderate egoist.

Past and present appear to join seamlessly when a girl's voice awakens the dreamer. Her name is also Sara (Bibi Andersson plays both roles), and it is her father who now owns the Borg family's summer house. Rather cheekily, she announces that she is hitchhiking to Italy with two male companions—one, a candidate in theology, is "masculine and warm" like Sigfrid; the other, a self-centered medical student, is reminiscent of young Isak. When Isak offers to take them as far as Lund, the trio respond enthusiastically.

After the journey resumes, a Volkswagen swerves toward the Borg automobile, then goes off the road—a near-collision corresponding to Isak's dream encounter with the hearse. Although the man who clambers out of the disabled vehicle, Sten Alman, is not as immediately recognizable a mirror-self as the corpse, he clearly resembles Isak in his lack of

---

*The extent to which this scene, which revolves around the deaf paternal uncle and a bustling, disciplinarian maternal aunt, was drawn from Bergman's memories of family occasions is revealed by a Christmas memoir he wrote for a magazine printed by his father's old church:

"Here were we now gathered in the narrow sunlight of Christmas morning: Father and Mother still young and beautiful, my elder brother and I (in a sailor suit and clean itchy wool stockings), my little sister with a colossal bow in her thin baby hair.

"Grandmother had just come from Uppsala (she hadn't yet removed her hat—a great black millwheel); there were also several cousins. And fat paternal Uncle Kalle who was deaf but had such a lovely voice, and maternal Aunt Emma, a dignified lady who came each Christmas from Gävle and furnished the presents, the remonstrances on behavior, and the overall regimentation. There sat old Lalla who ruled the kitchen to such a degree that Mother sometimes did not dare show herself there. And there was the children's nurse, Maj, lame and freckled and always happy (until her fiancé abandoned her a few years later), and the maid, Siri, big and warm and with a respect-inspiring humor."[3]

Here and there in the film, Bergman insinuates other details from his childhood. E.g., in the last of Isak's dreams, he describes an old yacht as "an ancient relic from the days of my parents' childhood; a mad impulse of our grandfather, the Admiral." Bergman's Grandfather Åkerblom was called "Admiral" in the town of Mora because of the yacht he had bought.

compassion. Not only does the name "Sten" (Swedish for "stone") point to Marianne's reproof of her father-in-law as inhumanly hard, but also, as Isak later admits, Sten Alman's merciless badgering of his wife all the time they are in the car reminds him of his own marriage.

Beyond its connection to the morning dream, the Alman episode also illustrates one of Bergman's recurring theses: that beneath the masks people use to negotiate their way in society lie aggressive, selfish needs; the closer the relationship between human beings, the less effective are the disguises. Neither of the Almans allows the other refuge in a role: the husband belittles his wife's tears as the stage tricks of a former actress; she, in turn, undermines his masculinity and the piety he professes as a Roman Catholic. Yet, for all their vicious bickering, they are bound together. "We need each other's company," Sten confesses. "It's only out of pure selfishness that we haven't murdered each other by now."

This disclosure of what may be "the terrible truth" finally prompts Marianne to order the Almans out of the car, ostensibly to shield the "three children" from further exposure to their ghastly conduct. Later in the day, however, she will reveal that she is going through her own marital crisis. Since Sten, to the extent that he resembles Isak, also resembles her husband, the spectacle presented by the Alman marriage obviously hits too uncomfortably near to home for toleration.

In contrast to the starkness of the Almans' scene, the next nestles in the radiance of a past warmly remembered. The Borg car stops for refueling just outside of Gränna, where Isak practiced medicine for fifteen years after receiving his medical degree.* The gas station owner, Henrik Åkerman, at whose birth Isak attended, lavishly praises the old man's reputation for generosity and, calling forth his pregnant wife to see "the world's best doctor," announces that the new baby will be named Isak Åkerman (literally, "Isak the traveler") in his honor. Later, it will become apparent that the happiness of Isak's Gränna years is an illusion, but for the moment the old doctor basks in sentiment and mutters, "Perhaps I should have stayed here."

This mood carries over to their lunch on the terrace of the Golden Otter, a gracious, famous old inn overlooking Lake Vättern. Sara's boyfriends, arguing over science and religion, try to draw in Isak, but the old man only smiles indulgently at their callow earnestness. Then Isak starts to recite a hymn, and, abruptly, amusement gives way to an uncom-

---

*A picturesque village on the shore of Lake Vättern, Gränna has a fairy-tale glow for children as the fabled candy cane capital of Sweden.

fortable solemnity: the hymn, one of the most familiar selections in the *Swedish Hymnal*, is from the section marked "The Last Judgment" under the heading "The Christian Hope Before Death."

The juxtaposition of the coming birth of a "new Isak" in Gränna and the meditation on death at the inn reflects the image of the hearse's stillbirth in the morning dream, and thereby foreshadows Isak's visit to his ninety-six-year-old mother. Bergman intended the mother to be a "practically mythical" character.

> She says: "I feel so cold — what accounts for it — especially here in my belly." The image I had in mind was to show children born from a cold womb. Small fetuses lying there, shaking with cold — it's a terrifying thought. It was that line of dialogue which brought the mother into being. She should have been long dead.[4]

As Mother Borg pokes about in a box of old toys, she remarks that, except for Isak, all her children who played with them are dead. Her voice betrays no emotion; indeed, she takes perverse comfort in having outlived "the smart young people" who had counted on her inheritance. Her only legacy seems to be her inner deadness — a suggestion underscored when she pulls out her father's gold watch and announces she is thinking of giving it to her grandson. Like the watch in Isak's dream, it has lost its hands.

Letting Marianne take the wheel when they resume their journey, Isak soon falls asleep and again dreams of the strawberry patch. This time, the Sara of long ago speaks directly to him as he is now. Holding a mirror to his face, she directs him to examine himself while she tells him that he is an anxious old man at death's threshold, that he can't bear the truth, that he really knows nothing — least of all why he is in pain. She then flings the mirror aside and, despite Isak's entreaties, leaves him to the shrieks of the encircling black birds while she comforts her cousin Sigbritt's baby boy.

Sara has obviously changed since her first appearance. The loss of innocence that had been symbolized by the spilling of the strawberries seems to have invested her with a sense of suffering; as she soothes the crying child, "her voice [is] sorrowful and tears [run] down her cheeks without end." Isak's aloofness has spared him such sadness, but it has also deprived him of the contentment he next sees through the window of the summer house: a laughing, "womanly" Sara celebrating some family event with her husband Sigfrid. Figuratively and literally walled out from this intimacy, Isak feels abandoned. In the film's one explicit reference to the Crucifixion motif, the old man presses his hand against a nail in the window frame until it rips into his flesh.

Strangely, the door to the house opens, and Sten Alman, in the role of an examining professor, politely ushers Isak into the amphitheater where the old doctor used to lecture. Sitting in the audience are the latter-day Sara and her boyfriends, ready, as in the waking-life experience of the day, to draw a lesson from their observation of the old man. Alman calls for Isak's *tentamensbok* (the booklet in which all university grades are recorded), flips through it, and shows he is unimpressed. He then starts the examination by directing Isak to look into a microscope, where the shaken professor emeritus can detect only his own eye staring back at him "in an absurd enlargement." The humiliation continues when Isak, called upon to decipher a foreign phrase on the blackboard, protests, "I'm a doctor, not a linguist." Even after Alman coaches him that the words spell out the first duty of a doctor, Isak still cannot respond. At last he has to be told what the text means: "*a doctor's first duty is to ask forgiveness.*" For the final question, Alman orders him to diagnose a patient. Isak pronounces her dead, at which point the patient, Mrs. Alman, erupts with mocking laughter. The examiner reaches for the *tentamensbok* and inscribes his conclusion: "Incompetent."*

Mrs. Alman's appearance in the dream evidently signals Isak's guilt over his relationship with his wife Karin, dead for thirty years. Alman next conducts Isak over a snake-infested swamp to a clearing where, just as he had forty years ago, he passively watches Karin copulate with a stranger. The horror of the incident, as Karin describes it to her seducer, is Isak's inhuman disengagement:

> Now I will go home and tell this to Isak and I know exactly what he'll say: . . . . You shouldn't ask forgiveness from me. I have nothing to forgive. But he doesn't mean a word of it, because he's completely cold. And then he'll suddenly be very tender and I'll yell at him that he's not really sane and that such hypocritical nobility is sickening. And he'll say that he'll bring me a sedative and that he understands everything. And then I'll say that it's his fault that I'm the way that I am, and then he'll look very sad and will say that he

---

*The verdict has a special meaning in Sweden, where academics must compete for professorial appointments. To be ranked below first carries no stigma—the candidate is free to apply again the next time a vacancy appears—but the verdict "Incompetent," which means "not worthy of any ranking at all," disqualifies the candidate from all future competitions. It is the severest professional blow imaginable.

is to blame. But he doesn't care about anything because he's completely cold.

Karin laughs (recalling Mrs. Alman's laughter at Isak's diagnosis), then disappears, and Alman—the self as examiner—pronounces judgment on the old man's life. "She is gone. Everyone is gone. Can't you hear how quiet it is? Everything has been dissected, Professor Borg. A surgical masterpiece. There is no pain, no bleeding, no quivering." But the price of this "perfect achievement of its kind," Alman says, is loneliness.

When Isak awakes, the car has been parked to allow the "children" to take a walk in the rain. He begins to relate his dream to Marianne, as if to search out its meaning, but she interrupts him with her own story (presented as a flashback). A few months before, she had informed her husband she was pregnant. Evald responded with an ultimatum: abortion or divorce. Since he was himself an unwelcome child in a hellish marriage (his name suggests *ej vald* = not chosen), he has vowed not to be responsible for another generation: "It's absurd to live in this world, but it's even more ridiculous to populate it with new victims and it's most absurd of all to believe that they will have it any better than we." In its revelation of spiritual and emotional sterility, the flashback is the equivalent of Isak's dream. Evald is another Isak: the son's ambition to be "absolutely, totally dead" and thus free of suffering matches what Alman, in the dream, has called the father's "perfect achievement." (Bergman accentuates the parallel by setting the flashback, like its frame, in a rain-washed car, and by placing Evald in Isak's seat.)

Ever since being given that harsh choice, Marianne has weighed the alternatives, but now, she tells her father-in-law, she has come to a decision. Haunted by the thought of three generations of "coldness and death, and death and loneliness" during the visit with Mother Borg, she made up her mind to try to break the cycle. Even at the cost of her marriage, she is resolved to have the baby. This commitment to life in the face of the despair engendered in Evald by his father figuratively concludes the journey. What follows is an anticlimactic extension of what the journey has metaphorically implied.

The ceremonies honoring the public Professor Borg upon his arrival in Lund, a mandatory scene, serves mainly as contrast to his private failures.* That evening, he timidly asks his son about the future

---

*Bergman had originally intended to make more of this scene. In the published script, Isak chats with two former schoolmates (who are also to be made Jubilee Doctors) about death soon settling their youthful disputes over "metaphysical questions"; and in an earlier draft, the academic procession was to have met a funeral.[5] Both sequences were

of his marriage. Evald indicates that he hopes for a reconciliation with Marianne, not because his heart has softened toward the pregnancy but because he cannot be without her. Unable to offer counsel, Isak changes the subject to a loan he had made his son. He obviously intends either to cancel the debt or to relax its terms, but Evald misunderstands and grimly reassures his father he intends to repay the loan according to the letter of their agreement. It is too late for new starts.

The clock strikes, and Isak, listening to his heart and old watch beat away what little time remains in his life, sinks into the film's final dream. The Sara of long ago, after telling him there are no wild strawberries left, leads him to his father, who, surrounded by other members of the family, is fishing from the far bank of an inlet. Thus, the day ends with Isak figuratively about to cross to the land of the dead. He shouts to the "shades," but when he realizes that the breeze has carried off his cries, he feels lighthearted. The effort of life, like the striving for meaning that has characterized Isak's extraordinary day, will soon be over.

The sentimental ending is patently contrived to confer a final blessing on the old man: the modern-day Sara calls after the doctoral ceremony to say it is really him she loves, "today, tomorrow, and forever"; Marianne, in her exit line, expresses fondness for him and kisses his cheek; even the housekeeper—who, after quarreling with him that morning, has flown to Lund for the ceremony—bids him good-night with an affectionate smile, as if to say that his worst is no meaner than a schoolboy's pigheadedness. Only Evald's brusque dismissal of his father mars the general beneficence of the leave-takings—but because Isak has tried to make a generous gesture, the weight of blame *seems* to shift from the offending father to the unforgiving son. Most sentimental of all is the last dream, photographed in soft focus and accompanied by a harp on the soundtrack: Life, it suggests, finally smiles mercifully on the old sinner.

Wild Strawberries enjoys a privileged position among Bergman's films in that it is lauded by both his admirers and, very often, by his detractors as well. To those who find him too austere, too intellectual, too bloodlessly Nordic, it is the glowing exception: a film with a heart.* And

eliminated as unnecessary. By referring to the first dream of the day, the tolling bells at the ceremony and the frock coat Isak wears are sufficient to make the point that Isak's death is near.

*The only objections regularly raised concern the present-day Sara. No personality resides beneath her surface of mincing innocence, and her presence in the film appears contrived. (The parallel with the earlier Sara would have been evident enough without the use of the

yet, despite its beguiling emotional appeal, the more one thinks about the film, the clearer it becomes that the response it elicits does not quite match the drama Bergman wrote.

Since all the dreams and events of June 1, 1957, are presented as a recollection, Isak's remarks that begin the film are actually his final words, spoken some time after the fateful day.

> At the age of seventy-six, I feel that I'm much too old to lie to myself. But of course I can't be too sure. My complacent attitude toward my own truthfulness could be dishonesty in disguise, although I don't quite know what I might want to hide.... But if I should be asked to express an opinion about someone else, I would be considerably more cautious. There is the greatest danger in passing such judgment. In all probability one is guilty of errors, exaggerations, even tremendous lies. Rather than commit such follies, I remain silent.
>
> As a result, I have of my own free will withdrawn almost completely from society, because one's relations with other people consist mainly of discussing and evaluating one's neighbor's conduct. Therefore I have found myself rather alone in my old age. This is not a regret but a statement of fact. All I ask of life is to be left alone and to have the opportunity to devote myself to the few things which continue to interest me, however superficial they may be.

This emphasis on withdrawal and on his refusal to regret his egocentrism contrasts sharply with the appearance of absolution fostered by the closing scene. The vision at the water's edge is of a world remade by the imagination, not of the world in which Isak lives. For Isak, life is beset by the most extreme moral and metaphysical uncertainty—greater, Bergman implies, than even he is willing to admit. Toward the end of this initial statement, Isak lists "all the things I have to say about myself." What he offers is a series of predicates, pronounced with a scientific objectivity that allows for no trace of emotion or valuative distinction. The subject in which the predicates reside, however, is elusive. If, as Isak says, the most truthful statement may only be "dishonesty in disguise," the truth-seeker is constrained to silence, not just in regard to others

---

same name and the assignment of the role to the same actress.) Her two boyfriends further diminish her believability, for they are caricatures, poorly drawn by the author and amateurishly portrayed by the actors. Even Bergman has admitted that the scenes in which the young people appear are "stone dead."[6]

but also in regard to himself. (One discerns here the kernel of Elisabet's silence in *Persona*.)

To be sure, Isak does undergo a transition from his morning gruffness to a misty-eyed sweetness in the late afternoon and evening, and presumably this signals a conversion. But to what? At no time does he acknowledge his past faults or embrace a new faith. The closest he comes is when he offers to help first Marianne, then Evald. The import of both occasions, however, is not regeneration but the futility of the attempted penance. After Marianne tells him she will have her baby, he asks, "Can I help you?" But she replies, "We are too old, Isak. It has gone too far"—and he tacitly agrees. A similar failure greets his gesture toward his son. Evald remarks that the rupture in relations cannot be mended because it, too, has "gone too far"; once again, Isak is evidently forced to agree, for he does not press beyond his son's rebuff.

The reason the resolution is so murky is that Bergman has shaped no conflict from the long review of Isak's life. The old man calls this his "day of decision," yet the only decision is made by his daughter-in-law. Riding in the wake of her affirmation of life's value, the concluding scenes seem carried by grace. But this is manifestly discordant. The putative protagonist has performed no act to bring her decision about, and when it comes, it in no way redeems or changes Isak (indeed, Marianne's choice is determined by a desire to repudiate the sum of his life).

Clearly, Bergman wanted an ending that would countervail the hopelessness he felt in unfolding Isak's life: what Mikael is to *The Seventh Seal*, Marianne's vow to continue the pregnancy is meant to be to *Wild Strawberries*. The portrait of emptiness he painted here, however, is too gloom-ridden in its realism to permit a credible illumination in his final strokes. Marianne and Evald may weather their own storms, but they are no Holy Family, and Isak's isolation is too profound for the film to be lifted to a yea-saying finale by the prospective birth of a grandchild. Bergman himself concedes as much: at the end of the day, Marianne promises Evald that she will "think over" her rejection of an abortion —thereby compromising the very affirmation she had supplied. Despite the film's being aimed at an assertion of life's value, the most Bergman can muster is ambivalence.

But there is another "Mikael" in *Wild Strawberries*—the baby son of Isak's sister Sigbritt. Unlike Marianne's fetus, which the filmmaker seems to have imposed on the film as a way out of a dramatic problem, this child expresses something lodged far deeper in the story's psychological meaning for Bergman.

First introduced casually as one of the family gathered at the summer house, the baby takes on a special importance in the second dream with Sara. Isak says there is "something fateful" in the babe's crying, and after Sara has comforted the infant by singing and holding him close, the old man confesses, "I wanted to scream until my lungs were bloody." Exactly what causes this extreme reaction is unstated, but the fact that the baby's presence is disclosed by his cry at the moment Sara shatters the mirror reflecting the old man's face implies the link between the vital infant and the "worried old man who will soon die." Not only is Isak near death, but, as Sara has just told him, his life has been a horrifying waste. Seen in this light, the infant represents Bergman's fantasy of regression from guilt and the pain of consciousness to the mother's all-providing love.* When Sara enters the house, she carries the baby with her, while Isak, presumably barred from the joyous scene by his corruption, watches from without. Later, during Isak's visit to his mother, the suggestion of an alter ego recurs—although now this "self" no longer represents innocence. By having Mother Borg consider giving the damaged pocket watch—a direct reference to Isak's morning dream—to Sigbritt's son on his upcoming fiftieth birthday, Bergman associates her grandson's lifetime with her son's fifty sterile years as a doctor.** The third time this child enters the film is in the final scene. Looking across the inlet, Isak sees, along with his parents, Sara holding Sigbritt's son aloft (just as Mikael is held up at the end of *The Seventh Seal*). Although it is too late for Isak to regenerate himself in reality, Isak escapes the nightmare of his existence through fantasy.

The source of guilt within Bergman that motivates this ultimate dream (in more than one sense) is more transparent in *Wild Strawberries* than in most of his films. Of all the recriminations dredged up by Isak's dreams, the harshest has to do with his wife's infidelity. Since Karin Borg rather patently represents Karin Bergman, Isak, it would seem, deputizes for the cold husband from whom that woman of impacted passions wanted release.

---

*Although Sara acts like the boy's mother and the rest of the scene suggests that she and Sigfrid are his parents, she is, of course, his aunt. Since no purpose is served by making the child Sigbritt's, one has to wonder why Bergman complicated the relationship. The answer may lie in his predilection for imaging the ideal mother as either a virgin (vide "The Fish") or as virginal (vide *The Seventh Seal*). The present-day Sara makes a great deal of her virginity.

**In fact, Sigbritt's son is approaching his sixtieth, not his fiftieth, birthday. (He is a baby in the summer house scene when Isak's brother, one year older than Isak, was "eighteen or nineteen"; Isak is now seventy-six.) Either the mistake is deliberate, to show that Mother Borg has confused the birthday with Isak's Jubilee year, or Bergman nodded.

But if the analogy indicates the father, the circumstances point to the son.

Immediately prior to being ushered into the woods to observe the tryst between Karin and her lover, Isak has failed his examination. First, in looking into the microscope, he cannot see beyond the reflection of his own eye—i.e., the pathology is in himself. Next, when he is unable to translate the foreign text's reference to the need to ask forgiveness, Alman pronounces him "guilty of guilt." What guilt needs to be forgiven is contained in the encrypted words, which have a distinctly Oedipal resonance.* Alman, who, as a superego figure, also represents the father, then asks Isak to examine Mrs. Alman. As though to protest his innocence (or to assert that the question of his guilt is no longer a vital issue), this "son" claims he cannot do so because she is dead—whereupon she lets out a chilling laugh that is at once belittling and accusatory. Finally, in perhaps the dream's most baldly Freudian moment, "Father" Alman not only declares Isak "Incompetent" but also drives the point

*The words on the board are: INKE TAN MAGROV / STAK FARSIN LOS / KRET FAJNE KASERTE / MJOTRON PRESETE. If one assumes a metathesis (such as a child would make) of the *k* and *t* in the first two words, the substitution of variants in some inflected endings, and recombinations of syllables, the text could be restored to read: INTE KAN MAGROV / STAKA FARS INLÖS / KR. ET FAN (JE) KASSERADE / OTRON PRESSADE MEJ. This is still pidgin Swedish, but its meaning is inferrable.

MAGROV, the key word in the first line, consists of two words: *mage* (in the combining form, *mag-*) is "stomach" or "womb"; *rov*, "plunder" or "rapine." (Bergman will use *magrov* again in *The Communicants* as a word in the artificial Timokan language. There he translates it as "anxiety." Whose womb has, in a sense, been plundered—and by whom—so as to engender anxiety should be fairly clear.) The words preceding MAGROV are "can not."

In the second line, STAKA is "punt," "push away, as with a pole." FARS is "father's." INLÖS is, roughly, "reservation" (in the sense of a booking), or "submission of a claim for payment."

Thus, the first half of the coded statement, translated across two languages, suggests something like: [My] illicit desire for mother cannot free itself of father's claims [on her].

The third line is more problematical. "Christ" is commonly abbreviated *Kr.* in Swedish. *ET* could be either the Swedish noun marker or the often-used Latin for "and." FAJNE may be a portmanteau of the word for "devil" *(fan)* and the French first person singular (one recalls Bergman's incorporation of the diabolus in his signature). KASSERADE is "rejected" (as in the case of PRESSADE, Bergman apparently exchanged one preterite verb form for another). Given Bergman's childhood jealousy of Jesus and his association of himself with Satan, the line could refer to viewing oneself as the devil as a consequence of rejecting Christ—or, alternatively, to the equation of "devil" to the abandoned Son on the Cross. In the last line, OTRON is "lack of faith" or "disbelief"; PRESSADE, "oppressed"; and MEJ, "me."

The Oedipal indications in this text and in the entire scene have been foreshadowed by the first meeting between Isak and the present-day Sara—who, as the reincarnation of the first Sara, represents the sexually pure mother. When Isak introduces himself, Sara asks, "Weren't they [the Biblical Isaac and Sarah] married?" The old man replies, "Unfortunately not. It was Abraham and Sara."

home by requiring him to observe impotently while another man makes love to Karin.*

That Isak in this crucial scene is psychologically a son projected into the role of Bergman's father reflects the essential duality of the character. Although the guilt permeating this film originates from Bergman's emotional tie to his mother, what motivates the fiction is the effect of that guilt on the son's view of his father. (Both the relationship between Isak and his son and that between Isak and his mother refer to matters "so colossally personal," Bergman has said, that they almost could not be explicated.)[8]

At the time Bergman wrote *Wild Strawberries*, Erik Bergman had just retired as Royal Chaplain and pastor of Hedvig Eleonora. After having maintained a distance for almost two decades, Bergman was trying to mend relations. He had been most eager for his father to see *The Seventh Seal*, and when the "old man" said he liked it very much, the son beamed. In *Wild Strawberries*, he was employing the language of his art as another effort at reconciliation.

> During practically all of my father's lifetime, I felt a deep alienation towards him. Understand, it was not [sic] because of his senseless upbringing of me with its prohibitions and beatings and different varieties of torture for body and soul, so that finally I conceived a hatred for my father which I've only recently gotten over. Only after overcoming it could I, without forcing myself to, talk with him and see that he was a poor old man whom I could take pity on and feel sympathy for.[9]

Like the elder Bergman, Isak, at the end of an illustrious career, is a man whose public honor contrasts with his family's antipathy toward him.** Significantly, Evald (at thirty-eight, exactly Bergman's age on June 1,

---

*Bergman, who had been dipping into psychoanalytical literature, has stated that he planned to have snakes surround the lovers in order to play up to the critics—"the *Cahiers du Cinema* gang that had just started to discover me."[7] Actually, since the *Cahiers* "gang" had discovered him several years earlier and, in 1957, would not have been particularly interested in Freudian allusions anyway, the admission may have been calculated to mislead more than to reveal.

As it happened, not a single snake would appear in the scene. Before the cameras were ready, the "hundreds" that had been assembled for the film disappeared through a hole in the enclosure built to hold them.

**Åkerman's praise for Isak's virtually pastoral solicitousness toward his patients during his early years in Gränna echoes the general esteem for Erik Bergman, who would be eulogized at his funeral as "the true family minister."[10]

1957) cannot overcome his "deep alienation" toward his father—and thus the film is cheated of the happy ending toward which it has been heading.* And yet, despite the residual bitterness Bergman felt impelled to register in this final scene between father and son, the longing for his father's love remains the most powerful force behind the film.

Bergman claims he chose the name "Isak" for his protagonist because of the chill in its first syllable, and that he was unaware until "a good while" after completing the script of the "pure coincidence" in the initials of Emanuel Isak Borg matching those of Ernst Ingmar Bergman.[11] But if he is to be taken at his word, one must assume that his subconscious baptized the character. "Borg" is of course approximately half of "Bergman," but the choice of the first names is more telling. "Emanuel," Isaiah's prophetic designation for Jesus, ties him to the long line of Bergman figures identified with the crucified Christ forsaken by his heavenly father. "Isak" makes the point of parental betrayal more emphatically; given the experiences of Bergman's youth, the story of Abraham leading Isaac to Moriah must have seemed a terrifying illustration of a father's readiness to sacrifice his son, not an example of wondrous faith. But there is another betrayal concealed beneath the surface of *Wild Strawberries*: the Oedipal betrayal of the father by the son. The fact that Isak is at once father and son reflects the impulse for reconciliation.

This impulse accounts for the film's basic design: Isak's journey is not only a metaphor for the advance of his life toward death and, simultaneously, a fantasy retreat from life's guilt back toward infancy but also a quest for the father. In a sense, the hymn Isak recites at the Golden Otter mirrors the course and significance of his "day of decision." It begins: "Where is the friend whom everywhere I seek? When day breaks, my longing grows; at dusk, I still don't find him, although my heart is burning." It ends: "Be comforted, my soul. Hope, pray, try. Your friend waves to you. You shall see and taste how sweet he is and sink into his arms which are merciful. Soon to that shore where the water neither billows nor heaves, like the Ark's tired dove, you shall glide to the shepherd's embrace; like the saved lamb hasten there and find rest." As

*The "philosophical" premise Evald cites as governing his conduct—"There is nothing which can be called right or wrong. One functions according to one's needs: you can read that in a school text"—also identifies him with Bergman. In the preface to *Four Screenplays*, he, too, cites this "school text": "Philosophically, there is a book which was a tremendous experience for me: Eiono Kaila's *Psychology of the Personality*. His thesis that man lives strictly according to his needs—negative and positive—was shattering to me, but terribly true. And I built upon this ground."

in English, *herden*—"shepherd" or "pastor"—is also synonymous with "minister"; thus, the closing lines of the Wallin hymn not only fore-shadow the film's final frames but also suggest whose "merciful arms" lie at the end of this quest.

Except at the very end of the film, young Isak and his parents are pointedly missing in all the old man's dreams of the strawberry patch. In the first reversion to the past, Isak's twin sisters state that young Isak is off with his father; old Isak, attaching great importance to the fact, comments: "Oh, yes, Father and I were out fishing together. I felt a secret and completely inexplicable happiness at this message, and I stood for a long while wondering what I should do in this new old world which I had suddenly been given the opportunity to visit." The next direct men-tion of the father immediately follows the reenactment of Karin's infidelity and the declaration of Isak's incompetence. Condemned to loneliness, Isak asks Alman, "Is there no grace?" Suddenly, the lecture hall is trans-formed into the yard of the summer house and Sara appears in the place of the vanished Alman. Her first words, "Weren't you supposed to go with them to get your father?" serve as an oblique answer to Isak's question. Finally, in the concluding dream, Sara again implies a special meaning in the paternal quest.

> *Sara*: Dear Isak, there are no wild strawberries left. Aunt wants you to search for your father. . . .
> *Isak*: I have already searched for him, but I can't find either Father or Mother.
> *Sara*: Your mother was supposed to go with him.
> *Isak*: Yes, but I can't find them.
> *Sara*: I will help you.

She leads him to the water's edge and points to his parents on the other side; then, as if her mission has been completed, she disappears. Through the dream, Isak achieves a kind of grace in the wordless recognition by his parents: the "new old world" yields up the happiness denied him in the old world of reality.

Bergman has occasionally referred to *Wild Strawberries* as a dream which happens to contain other dreams. More than to this film, however, the description applies generally to his artistic creativity—and particu-larly to his works in this period. The fundamental ambivalence of *Wild Strawberries* is not the product of a careless artist but of an artist torn between two objectives. On the one hand, Bergman was impelled to render life as he knew it from painful experience—and to obey that imperative meant drawing a portrait of despair. On the other, constructing stories from personal materials tempted him to escape from the punishments of reality into a dream where the impossible could be made real. The warm, happy film almost everyone finds in *Wild Strawberries* is that illusion Bergman magically creates. But, finally, it is only an illusion.

Close to Life

Every once in a while, a critic on either side of the Atlantic has postulated that Bergman would be a better director if he were less personally involved in his subject matter. *Close to Life* indicates the contrary. A Bergman film without Bergman, it is one of his least engaging works.

In the early 'fifties, Bergman had agreed to film his version of *The Crown-Bride* for Nordisk Tonefilm. The project was eventually abandoned, yet, even though no contract had been signed, he felt an obligation to NT. Four years later, he discharged it with *Close to Life*. The idea for the film itself arose from his reading Ulla Isaksson's short story collection, *Death's Aunt*. One of the group, "The Kind Solemnity," especially appealed to him, and he advised the author to think about refashioning it as a film; since she had never written for the screen before, he offered to guide her hand in the work.*

From the results of their collaboration, it appears that Bergman's initial attraction to the story had more to do with the subject matter than with Isaksson's presentation of it. The original consists of an interior monologue in which Cecilia interprets her miscarried pregnancy as the sign of her failure as a human being. The film not only changes that experience phenomenologically by examining it from an exterior point of view but also alters its significance by making Cecilia's story just one of three segments in what is essentially an anthology film. What had been of psychological interest was thus transformed into material for a study of three types of women who happen to be in an obstetrical ward at the same time.

Unlike her counterpart in Isaksson's story, the Cecilia of the film evokes

---

*In playing Grevenius to her Bergman, he may have been looking beyond the film for NT to *The Virgin Spring*. Isaksson had sent him *Death's Aunt* in response to his praise of *Dit du icke vill*, her novel about witchcraft in seventeenth-century Sweden; quite possibly, Bergman was already considering collaboration on the filmscript of his medieval tale and was using *Close to Life* as a test of their compatibility.

little sympathy. An official with the state board of education, the character is the Professional Woman—and the bias of the script makes clear that this is not a healthy thing to be. Cecilia apparently believes her intelligence entitles her to be a mother, but her body, as though sensing that the fetus really belongs to her mind, refuses to nourish it. The hostility to the unborn child is compounded by the attitude of the father, an intellectual journalist, who resents the competition for his wife's attention. Predictably, the pregnancy ends in her losing the fetus.

Stina, a laborer's wife described by the script as "one of our Lord's best creations," is as vibrant as Cecilia is morose. Childbirth would appear to be the natural expression of this maternal woman's body, yet, when she finally gives birth a month late, the baby is dead. As in the case of Cecilia's miscarriage, a precept is implicit. Stina would accept motherhood in the same mindlessly enthusiastic way that she has clung to her role as wife; in her eagerness to please others, she has resigned herself to passivity. Life, the film proposes, must come from the will for life.

In contrast to these two women who desperately want children in order to compensate for their meaningless existences, Hjördis has come to the hospital because of an unsuccessful abortion. A hedonistic, spiritually rudderless product of the same welfare-state society that frustrates Cecilia's ambitions and snugly accommodates Stina's docility, this unmarried nineteen year old shrinks from the responsibility of motherhood and hides the medication prescribed to save the life of her baby. Yet, as is connoted by her name (*hjord* is "earth"), the girl's animal vitality will not be denied. Despite all her efforts to destroy it, her fetus clings to life, and Hjördis finally decides to keep her child. This triumph of the élan vital serves as the culmination of the film's argument.

Although it has since become the most easily forgotten of Bergman's 'fifties films, *Close to Life* briefly excited Europeans—especially the British. Perhaps, after two "difficult" Bergman films, it was merely a case of audiences rejoicing in its simple, unmistakable message, but the critics, reaching for a more sophisticated judgment, acclaimed it for its "naturalism." Although, over the years, Gunnar Fischer's photography had become almost inseparable from what one thought of as a Bergman picture, for this film he used Max Wilén, who produced a strikingly different effect by restricting the camera to an area only a few feet from the actors and by fixing on objects in their immediate surroundings. Today, accustomed to television studio drama and to the intimate style many cinema directors have adopted, audiences would find nothing unusual in this technique, but for Europeans in 1958 it was rather novel. Arresting as this "naturalistic" technique may be, however, it is at odds with the film's theme. The studied attention to the obstetrical instruments and the pervasive, antiseptic whiteness of the hospital setting make the intimations of a mystical entelechy choosing the right mother look silly.

The pseudo-documentary approach that governs most of the film also conflicts with an all too neatly arranged ending. What has pretended to be a recording of life as found suddenly implies the intricacy of a plot: Cecilia draws the strength to accept her husband's egocentricity from her observation of Stina's suffering; Stina overcomes her sorrow through Hjördis's decision to have her baby; and Hjördis learns unselfishness from the other two. Yet, despite the presumptive importance of one woman's experience in changing another's attitudes, the women have actually played very minor roles in each other's stories. The various dramatic lines touch, but there is no resonance at the points of contact.

The Face

Beyond any question, *The Face* derives from G. K. Chesterton's *Magic*, a mild comedy Bergman had directed at Gothenburg in 1947. The play concerns a conjurer's disquieting effect on the guests at a ducal estate: when all his magical acts, save one, can be explained as tricks, that single exception becomes the test of their absolute faith in their "religion" of materialistic rationalism. The only guest willing to listen when the conjurer swears that all the "tricks" were the work of true magic is a liberal clergyman, and when he cannot overcome his skepticism, the conjurer seizes on the minister's inherent hypocrisy:

> I want you to be martyred. I want you to bear witness to your own creed. I say these things are supernatural.... [W]hat the devil are you for, if you don't believe in a miracle? What does your coat mean, if it doesn't mean that there is such a thing as the supernatural?

"I wish I *could* believe," the clergyman confesses; "I wish I could disbelieve," the conjurer replies.

Aside from its premise, Chesterton's play is rather pedestrian—indeed, the author finally turns his back on his own argument to embrace a cliché (after saving one of the guests from insanity by inventing a natural explanation for an actually supernatural feat, the conjurer is rewarded with marriage to the man's sister). Even so, it is easy to see why Bergman chose to stage the play and why, a decade later, he reverted to it as the basis for a film. Not only does it strike directly at the problem of faith that had been one of his abiding concerns but also, in the figure of the magician, it presented him with a perfect metaphor for himself as an artist.*

The immediate motive for the film, Bergman has said, was to protect the quality of his company at the Malmö Theater. To avoid the usual dispersion of actors after the end of the 1957–58 contract year, Bergman promised to write a filmscript calling for a cast large enough to provide summer employment for much of his ensemble. As is suggested by the film's subtitle, *A Comedy*, he apparently meant to write something along the lines of *The Murder at Barjärna*, but with the ribaldry a more sustained element. "Unfortunately," he later commented,

> it wasn't as funny as it was conceived to be. . . . The actor who plays the chief comic role was so drunk the whole time he couldn't remember what he should have said or done, so I had to cut away a third of his part, which resulted in its becoming much too weighted toward seriousness. . . . [And the old witch, too,] became perhaps a little more doleful than I had imagined, a bit more brutal than I had planned.[1]

That, in his mind's eye, Bergman had seen a funnier film than the one his cameras recorded is entirely possible, yet from the moment he began exploring the grounds of faith and associating faith with art, a disturbance of the intended balance between low comedy and high seriousness was inevitable.

Certainly, nothing in the opening scene hints at a comic development. It is 1846 and the carriage of Vogler's Magnetic Health Theater is rumbling toward Stockholm. Tubal, the glib impresario, and "Grandmother," a crone whose potions and incantations provide the troupe with its meager but steady income, are continuing a long-standing argument over their relative importance to the troupe, which has fallen on hard

---

*The first instances of Bergman's frequent references to himself as a conjurer when discussing the filmmaker's craft coincide with the date of his working with *Magic*. The association of cinema with magic, of course, also has a firm historical basis. Magicians, such as Méliès, were pioneers in experimenting with the motion picture. Cinema was introduced into Sweden by a Danish magician named Jansson, who built the country's first movie houses.

days. But something more serious is troubling Vogler, the ostensibly mute magician, and his assistant Aman—who, it subsequently transpires, is his wife Manda disguised as a young man. Along the way, they pick up Spegel, a drink-rotted actor; before he falls into a coma (which the troupe mistakes for death), the newcomer notes the magician's false beard and dyed hair and asks, "Are you a swindler who must hide his real face?" As the film's original title, *The Charlatans*, suggests, Spegel's question strikes at a central issue.

Bergman's debt to *Magic* first becomes evident after the company is stopped by Constable Starbeck on the pretext that they will need a licence to perform in the capital. Actually, it is Councilor Egerman who, intrigued by the claims of occult powers in the bills Tubal has circulated, has arranged their detention at his house and invited Royal Physician Vergérus to conduct a scientific examination. When Vogler fails the tests, the nonbelievers show relief: ironically, the licence will be granted, for, as a certified fraud, the magician poses no threat to the established order. Grasping a chance to extort some free entertainment, however, Starbeck demands a private performance the next morning as a final condition.

The film's major comic interlude occurs that night in the servants' quarters of the Egerman house. Grandmother briskly sells her love potions; Tubal tends the deeply banked libidinous fire in the matronly cook; and while Spegel, having recovered consciousness, synergistically adds to the ruttishness by stumbling about in search of brandy, one of the young maids seduces the Voglers' inexperienced coachman in a laundry basket. But upstairs, the erotic maneuvering is ominous. Moved by passion that is sexual as well as religious, Mrs. Egerman unsuccessfully seeks an assignation with Vogler, whom she believes to be either the Messiah himself or someone sent by God to explain why her daughter died. At the same moment, Vergérus, on discovering that Aman is actually the magician's wife, tries to seduce her into becoming his mistress.

The morning's required performance begins disastrously when Starbeck takes childish delight in exposing the apparatus for the tricks, but the magician quickly turns the tables by hypnotizing Mrs. Starbeck and eliciting the information that her husband farts through dinner, patronizes the local whorehouse, and probably has not fathered all their children. This is good fun; Starbeck deserves his comeuppance. But when Vogler next "binds" Antonsson, the Egermans' coachman, with an "invisible chain" that renders him helpless, the mood changes radically. More than a mesmerist's power over his subject is at stake as Antonsson struggles; at last, he frees his hand and clutches his oppressor's throat. The magician drops to the floor and is pronounced dead.

Social authority quickly asserts control as Starbeck writes an official report absolving the coachman, and Vergérus dissects the victim "for scientific purposes." Even so, the script speaks of "something ominous in the silence." Soon, Antonsson is found hanging in the laundry, a suicide. And after the Royal Physician has completed the autopsy in the attic, weird occurrences shatter his confidence in his senses: an eyeball appears in his inkwell; a stopped clock chimes; a severed hand seems empowered with volition; his eyeglasses are mysteriously snatched away and crushed. Finally abandoning himself to fear, he careens down the steps and huddles at the door whimpering like an animal. At this moment of devastation for scientific truth, Vogler strides into view wearing Spegel's rags. Suddenly, the explanation for the ghostly phenomena is obvious. Spegel had died during the night, and the magician placed the corpse in a trick coffin: then, after feigning his own death, he "resurrected" himself by switching the actor's body with his.

To gain his vengeance, however, Vogler has had to pay a price. Once he has shed the supernatural suggestion of his costume and his muteness, Mrs. Egerman treats him with haughty disdain. And when he demands payment for having provided thrilling entertainment, Vergérus contemptuously tosses a coin on the ground. So complete is his humiliation that even Grandmother scorns him for being "careless and stupid" and "not knowing [his] limits." But then, in a stunning reversal, a delegation arrives bearing a letter from the King that summons the Magnetic Health Theater to perform at court. The nightmare has acquired a fairy-tale ending: a torrential rain stops abruptly, the sun bursts through black clouds, and the Vogler carriage climbs a glistening road toward "triumphant entrance into the Royal Palace."*

On release of *The Face*, discordant voices were audible for the first time since the paean to Bergman had begun to swell in 1956. Only in the United States was it received with enthusiasm. English critics, objecting to the mixture of comedy and horror, greeted it sarcastically, and the French—perhaps goaded by Bergman's spurning an offer to direct in

---

*As has often been noted, the ending closely resembles the queen's rescue of Macheath at the conclusion of *The Threepenny Opera*, a play Bergman had directed in 1950. Although he denied any debt to Brecht in an interview with John Simon, on other occasions, he has readily acknowledged it. To a group of Swedish interviewers, he stated that, while he owed "a little bit" to Brecht, the principal inspiration for the message from the king was his receipt of a royal grant at a time when his spirits were low.[2]

their country—retreated from their recent delirious praise. Elsewhere, although reactions tended to be more moderate and more varied, the critics' restraint signaled their disappointment. On one count, however, there was international agreement: *The Face* was Bergman's most cryptic film until that time.

Nothing dispels the clouds about a difficult work so effectively as more difficult subsequent productions by the artist or his fellows. After Bergman's "Silence of God" trilogy and *Persona, A Passion,* and *Cries and Whispers,* after the abstruse films of the 'sixties by Antonioni, Fellini, Godard, and Resnais, *The Face* no longer seemed particularly puzzling. Indeed, most commentary since the 'seventies has implied, in the words of one critic, that once the Gothic trappings, the backstairs ribaldry, and the debate between science and faith have been set aside as irrelevant, "only a simple effort is required to divine what [*The Face*] is all about."[3] What this "simple effort" supposedly reveals is an examination of artistic conscience. Obviously, Vogler's attitude toward his vocation *is* a major element, but it is scarcely what the film is *all* about.

Far from being irrelevant, religious imagery is the loom on which the film is woven. Vogler's fake beard and makeup, the repeated references to the mysterious allure of his face, and the title itself all indicate the face of Jesus; the confrontation with secular authority in the Egerman parlor evokes the trial of Jesus before Pilate; the agony of Vogler's humiliation begins on a Friday and ends in glory on a Sunday.* Most explicitly, Mrs. Egerman "instantly" recognizes the magician as Christ. "You must forgive these people," she says, as though asking him to accept her restatement of Jesus' dying words, "I mean, for humiliating you. They cannot understand you, that's why they hate you." Bergman drives the point home in the stage directions: Vogler "lowers his head and looks at his hands. Then he clenches his fist so that his nails puncture his skin and drops of blood emerge." More certain than ever of his "true" identity, she "falls on her knees" and, with concupiscent religiosity, "presses her mouth" to his Christlike wound.

At the hub of this imagery is the paradoxical meaning of Christ. As magician, Vogler suggests the miraculous Christ who transcends human limits. Almost the first question Vergérus asks is, "Does Mr. Vogler heal the sick?" Later, the doctor argues it would be "catastrophic" to believe in the "intangible and inexplicable forces" the magician supposedly commands, for to do so would mean having to conceive a God. To

---

*Through allusion to Veronica's Veil, the connection of Jesus to the name Vogler will recur in *Hour of the Wolf.*

reassure themselves, the materialists obsessively search Vogler's body
for "abnormalities," first in the Friday night inquiry, then in the autopsy;
finding nothing that makes him more than an ordinary man, they righ-
teously "crucify" him. But this is not the "crucifixion" Vogler experiences,
even though it owes to the same cause. Once, belief in his supernatural
ability gave him power: in Ascona, he "invented seven new miracles and
cured pilgrims for three weeks." Now, that memory rebukes him; he
suffers, Christlike, because he is not Christ, and because, without proof
that God is manifest in him, he cannot believe in God. The resurrection
of the "dead" magician is therefore a key moment in the film. Apparently,
it is the miracle of miracles, the victory over death through which Vogler
would be Christ—and, thereby, "resurrect" his faith. But when Vogler
reveals to his enemies that the magic is sham—and confronts that fact
himself—he concedes not only his own failure but also the emptiness
of God's promise to mankind. Thus, ironically, Vogler re-creates the
forsakenness of man that, in all of Bergman's variations on the Passion
theme, is the essence of Christ's agony.

Although Vogler's torment is personal, it reflects and is reflected by
the anguish of those he encounters. Among these mirror selves, Spegel
is the most conspicuous (his name is the Swedish word for "mirror").
The first time he "dies," Spegel brands the assumption of "some great
general thing called truth somewhere upstage" an "illusion" that mankind pursues with "beautiful passion." Later, when death actually does
come, the actor iterates his discovery that any utterable statement is
necessarily a lie: "One walks step by step into the darkness. The motion
itself is the only truth." (At the same moment in another room of the
Egerman house, Manda is echoing Spegel: *"Nothing is true."*) That, finally,
there is only illusion in this "darkness" is precisely what Vogler fears
—and what he desperately wants not to admit to himself. Similarly,
Spegel's last words—"I have prayed just one prayer in my life. Use me.
Handle me. But God never understood what a strong and devoted slave
I had become"—speak to the sense of purposelessness that has haunted
Vogler since he ceased to believe himself an instrument of a higher
power. Although Vogler desperately wishes to redeem Spegel's futile life,
and his own, through the substitution of the actor's corpse on the
autopsy table, the fact that it is finally only a trick has precisely the
opposite result.

The Egermans also mirror the emptiness of Vogler's belief. When the
husband calls upon Vogler to perform a supernatural feat, he echoes the
magician's own demand of God; both men long for evidence that will

restore their faith. The wife's dealings with Vogler demonstrate the same irony. Believing that, as Christ, he can furnish an explanation of God's purpose in the death of her child, Mrs. Egerman claims to be his disciple. But the words she uses, "I have lived your life," carry a more puissant meaning for Vogler: that her questioning and pain reflect his.

Even though he has fewer than half a dozen lines in the film, Antonsson, the dim-witted coachman, is the most complex of Vogler's doubles. The moment Grandmother sets eyes on him, she sees that he is marked for hanging, even though this "Goliath" who has "never offended anyone" wants only to be left in peace. Something about Vogler —which he cannot identify but which apparently relates to his Christ-like aspect—deeply threatens him. When one of the other servants says there is a quality in the troupe's faces that incites a desire to destroy them, he absorbs the thought; later, at the close of the "invisible chain" demonstration, it is the sight of Vogler's face as it leans toward him that seems to trigger his urge to murder—in effect, to play Judas to Vogler's Christ. This suggestion is reinforced by the fulfillment of Grandmother's prophecy: like Judas, Antonsson hangs himself. But Antonsson's exertions against the invisible chain that binds him also reflect Vogler's own effort of will to go beyond his human limitations, to be, like Christ, a true miracle worker. (Antonsson's anguished frustration in trying to break his "chain" directly recalls Vogler's when he failed Vergérus's first test.) Unable to convince himself that he performs real magic, Vogler has become a Judas of sorts to the Christ mask he wears by resorting to charlatanism —for which, in the end, he demands his "pieces of silver."

The most important of the reflecting selves, however, is the magician's main adversary—and his reversed image: when Vergérus looks into the mirror during the autopsy scene and sees "his own image, strongly lit by the sunlight," the mirror blurs and then clarifies to reveal Vogler's "glaring face, lit from inside." Seemingly as ardent a proponent of what Grandmother calls "the new faith" as Vogler is of the old, the Royal Physician persecutes his opponent with the fervor of a convert trying to extirpate the stain of heresy in himself—just as, conversely, the magician strains to overcome his religious doubt. Vergérus admits to "a strange feeling of sympathy" for the Voglers, yet he cannot leave them in peace because they "represent something I most abhor—the unexplainable"; Vogler "hates" Vergérus because he makes him feel afraid and powerless.

That Vogler should try to vanquish Vergérus in the film's climax is inevitable, not because the two men represent, in simple terms, faith and science, but because the physician embodies the disbelief in the magician's own mind. "Miracles don't happen," Vergérus says to Manda. "It's always the apparatus and the spiel which have to do the work. The clergy have the same experience. God is silent and the people chatter." After Vogler displaces Vergérus in the bedroom at the end of this scene, he expresses despair for exactly the same reason. Although he subsequently brings the physician to his knees, the victory belongs immediately to the charlatan who has skillfully used his apparatus and ultimately to the Vergérus within Vogler himself.

But if the dramatic argument concludes with the magician's failure, why does Bergman then turn the fiction on its head by having the King summon the Magnetic Health Theater to the palace in triumph? No element in *The Face* has generated more contorted readings. In terms of the religious question the film raises, this "happy ending" makes no sense—either from the point of view of Bergman's conception of Christ or that of Lutheran teaching. A second avenue of interpretation is suggested by the parallel between *The Face* and *The Rite*, where the conflict between social authority and the artists implies a fertility rite that also ends with the artists' liberation.* Yet, although *The Face* unquestionably does concern barrenness (both within the artist and in the world he inhabits), the issue is not joined in such a way as to be resolved by the King's intervention. What the 1968 television film would unambiguously define remains undeveloped here. The fact is, no matter how one construes the drama in the Egerman house, the ending is as incongruous as the ending of *Magic*. Unlike Chesterton's last-minute conversion of his play into a love story, however, this incongruity is what the film is finally about.

Behind Vogler, who tries to invoke "psychic" power by means of mesmerism, projects visions through a *laterna magica*, and creates illusions with the aid of apparatus, one can readily discern Bergman, the frightened boy who discovered there was power in being able to manipulate fantasy through his toy projectors and who went on to become one of the principal "conjurers" of his time. That much, virtually everyone who has commented on the film has noted. What has generally been deduced from that observation, however, is a misperception. Vogler's

---

*In *The Face*, the mask the artist wears in the sacrificial rite is that of Christ; in *The Rite*, the masks are Dionysian. The fertility aspect of the rites is underscored by the fact that both films begin in the electric atmosphere of summer heat and eventually discharge their accumulated tension during a storm. In *The Face*, the artist's role as archetypal scapegoat is foreshadowed at the film's start when Grandmother, on the site of a gallows, digs for mandrake root, an herb anciently presumed to grow from the ejaculate of hanged men; later, Tubal characterizes Vogler's "murder" as an execution by society.

magic patently corresponds to Bergman's art, but the crisis portrayed in *The Face* does not concern the relationship between the artist and his public. Rather, it arises from the artist's confrontation with his art.

Like most Bergman films, *The Face* vibrates with echoes of earlier works. The filmmaker himself has repeatedly stated that *The Face* "corrects" *Evening of the Jesters*, although he has left unsaid what he corrected and how. Obviously, Albert Emanuel Vogler resembles Albert Johansson in his humiliation, but the deeper connection—reflected by another Albert, Joakim's "impotent" alter ego in "The Fish"—seems bedded in the circus film's previously described psychological under-layers. The same buried source is indicated by similarities between *The Face* and *Wild Strawberries*. Not only does the magician's middle name link him to Emanuel Isak Borg but key scenes in the two films also rise from common foundations.* Alman's finding Isak incompetent corresponds to the judgment passed on Vogler. Both "trials" humiliate the protagonists, and, in at least that respect, recreate Bergman's childhood ordeals before his parents. (The examiner, in each instance, is at once the protagonist's double and a father figure. In *The Face*, Vergérus, as Royal Physician, suggests Royal Chaplain Bergman. Moreover, he acts at the behest of Councilor Egerman, who also suggests Bergman's father through his office and—again showing the ties between *The Face* and *Wild Strawberries*—through his first name, Abraham.)

Of even greater significance is what the incompetence implies. Just as, immediately after the verdict against Isak is pronounced, its hidden meaning emerges in Karin Borg's meeting with her lover, there is an underlying connection between Vogler's impotence as a real magician and his encounter with Mrs. Egerman. On the surface, nothing in the film satisfactorily accounts for Vogler's anguish when this woman he has just met offers herself to him. He might regard her concupiscence as silly, or pathetic, or disgusting, but none of these possibilities would justify a reaction so intense that he inflicts a Christlike wound on himself. If, however, one sees beneath the surface another instance of a "son" challenged by a mother figure to act on the thought he has repressed in guilt and fear, Vogler's strange response becomes understandable.

Several bits of circumstantial evidence are consistent with such a reading. First, Mrs. Egerman's dead child—like the dead, destroyed, or

---

*In addition to sharing the name "Emanuel," Vogler is also tied to Isak Borg through his alter ego Spegel, identified as a member of the Stenborg acting company—a combination of the names of that other pair of doubles, *Sten* Alman and Isak *Borg*. (It is also worth noting that Spegel's first name, Johan, invariably associates a character with Bergman.)

monstrous babes in other Bergman plays and films—reflects Oedipal sin in two ways: on the one hand, as punishment; on the other, as the rejection the son feels in the mother's continuing to sleep with father. (Significantly, after the shattering possibility of "incest" has arisen, Bergman detours from his plot to undo its effect and restore relations between the "parents." Egerman takes Vogler's place in the sexual appointment his wife has arranged for the magician, and after accusing her of having feigned grief to avoid his bed, they are reconciled.)* Second, the erotic revels among the servants—which are otherwise an irrelevant comic intrusion upon very serious themes—operate as counterpoint to the tortured eroticism expressed in the upstairs bedrooms. The former, which implies an arc of life extending from the callow young lovers, through the middle-aged Tubal and the plump cook, to wise old Grandmother reassuring the youngest servant that she will experience the fullness of womanhood in her turn, is natural, uncomplicated, and joyous; the latter exhibits the suffering of sexually twisted lives. (A similar contrast, springing from the same psychological source, can be found in *Smiles of the Summer Night*.) Third, although the ambiguous gender of Vogler's mate is scarcely an essential element of the film's design, it suggests a psychosexual emanation from the story's core. (One recalls the sexual transformation of Jack's playmate in "A Shorter Tale," where the protagonist tries to deny his Oedipal guilt.) That Aman is revealed as Manda at the same moment Mrs. Egerman is trying to entice the magician reinforces the suggestion. Finally, the guilt lodged in Vogler is mirrored by Spegel's dying wish to have the "uncleanness" deep within him cut out with a knife. In a sense, the Royal Physican's dissection of Vogler/Spegel represents an attempt to fulfill this wish for a therapeutic "castration." (Cf. Jack's knife in "A Shorter Tale" that reaches the secret within men, and the even more telling parallel to the elder Dr. Erneman's surgical cure of Sam, the chauffeur who had killed his girlfriend in *A Lesson in Love*.)

Once one perceives the inner similarity of Vogler's ordeal to Isak Borg's, the similarity of the "happy endings" Bergman imposes on the two films becomes apparent. Just as Isak's search for father, and forgiveness, ends in a dream of reconciliation, the guilt that underlies Vogler's humiliation is providentially absolved by the summons from the king—clearly a

*Mrs. Egerman's uncommon first name, Ottilia, further hints at an Oedipal connection between her dead child and Mrs. Sönderby's belief that she gave birth to a wolflike monster in *Dreams*. Among Consul Sönderby's "many names" is Otto, the one he was called by his mother.

father figure. Moreover, the regeneration symbolized by the conjunction of the approaching death of Isak, who is "guilty of guilt," with the vision of Sigbritt's baby, Isak's innocent other self, also marks the ending of *The Face*: Vergérus's autopsy report and the king's letter bear the same date —July 14, Bergman's own birthday.

The very similarity of the two conclusions, however, calls attention to a most significant difference. Although the serenity visited on Isak conflicts with the import of the dramatic action that leads up to it, Bergman fogs the inconsistency in a sentimental cloud. In contrast, *The Face* flaunts the artificiality of the magician's deliverance; it is as "utterly fantastic" an ending as (in another story tied to his birth date) the Eiffel Tower's marriage to the Statue of Liberty—and for basically the same reason. In "The Story of the Eiffel Tower," filmmaker Joakim draws on his inner torment to concoct a comedy—much as Bergman began *The Face* intending that the audience receive it as a comedy. When Joakim's audience of one, "unamused," abandons him because, seeing no solution to his personal dilemma, he cannot bring his fiction to a satisfactory close, he invents a preposterous happy ending that mocks his despair as a man and his failure as an artist.

Commentators on *The Face* almost invariably cite a statement Bergman first published in 1956 and later used again in the preface to *Four Screenplays*: "I am either an impostor or, when the audience is willing to be taken in, a conjurer. I perform conjuring tricks with apparatus so expensive and so wonderful that any entertainer in history would have given anything to have it." Linked with the magician's deception of Vergérus in the attic, the quotation is presumed to show Bergman's "bad conscience" as an artist or a combination of contempt for his audience and fear of its power to destroy him. Certainly, not only *The Face* but also numerous films and public statements he has made over the years lend themselves to such interpretation, yet tricking the public is not the central issue here. Vogler suffers profoundly, not because he is out of favor with the audience but because he wants to perform *real* miracles —just as, for Bergman, the magic of art lay in its promise of changing reality. The magician who reveals that his resurrection was only an illusion is finally Bergman himself, confessing that Frid's exultant cry at the end of *Smiles of the Summer Night*, the "meaningful deed" insuring continuance of hope in *The Seventh Seal*, and the absolution Isak seems to attain with his last vision in *Wild Strawberries* were, after all, only tricks. That he then ends this film with another Voglerian trick is anything but an expression of confidence in his artistic magic. Ironically, at the moment Bergman was being hailed as the one true genius the cinema had produced, he was entering a crisis as deep as the one he had experienced a decade earlier, when his frustration over the Joakim Naked material culminated in the destructive finale of *The City*.

The Virgin Spring

"I was in a state of confusion," Bergman has said of the next couple of years, "mostly because I had left the Malmö City Theater—I was no longer securely moored in theater, I was shifted about, I had broken off. I had to contend with relocation in Djursholm [an upper-class section of Stockholm] and an entirely new style of life—I didn't rightly know whether I was fish or fowl or where I belonged."[1] All these changes, however, had been of his own choosing, and they were as much effect as cause. In the summer of 1958, Bergman had turned forty—an especially momentous occasion in Swedish culture. Gnawed by doubt about the value of his accomplishments and haunted by a sense of emptiness in his life, he was apparently afflicted by what a recent fashion has identified as the mid-life crisis. Change was necessary for regeneration.

The most important change in his personal life was his marriage in September 1959 to Käbi Laretei, an Estonian refugee who had built a successful career as a concert pianist. They had met the previous fall and quickly became copy for the gossip journalists. She was then married and had a young daughter; he, thrice divorced, had had successive, very public affairs with his leading actresses, Harriet Andersson and Bibi Andersson.* In the press, it seemed that Bergman was once again playing Lothario, but his own description of their courtship presents a quite different picture of two wounded souls finding solace in each other: "She had her time as a refugee behind her. And I, I felt myself to be dying."[2] Both had fathers who were ministers, both had spent their early years in an aristocratic ambience, both had a passsionate interest in music.** Probably the most vital attraction, however, was that Bergman

---

*Bergman had first met Bibi Andersson during his shooting of the Bris commercials, when she was half his age; their affair began in the mid-'fifties. Like his affair with the young Harriet Andersson—reflected by her roles in *The Summer With Monika*, *Evening of the Jesters*, and *Dreams*, and, less directly, by *Smiles of the Summer Night*—the liaison with Bibi Andersson focused his creative imagination on her as a type. As Mia in *The Seventh Seal* (which Bergman dedicated to her) and Sara in *Wild Strawberries*, she represents a virginal Madonna, a spiritual beacon for the protagonist in his darkness.
**Coincidentally, they also shared the same birthday.

appears to have found qualities like his mother's in her. She read to him, fussed over his taste in clothes (the beret he had worn since the 'forties soon disappeared), got him to shave every day, introduced him to a new circle of friends, and nudged him back into the ambit of the haute bourgeoisie. In a sense, setting up a home in Djursholm was a bit like returning to the world of Östermalm he fled when he had moved into the bohemian Old Town. She offered him stability. To friends, Bergman spoke admiringly of his wife as a survivor, a woman of enormous inner strength.

This leaning on others for strength also became evident in his professional life. Toward the end of the decade, his partnership with Gunnar Fischer, his regular cinematographer, had begun to deteriorate, ostensibly because of artistic differences, but in fact because Bergman's uncertainties prodded him into increasingly aggressive behavior. By his own account, he "became more and more domineering, more and more tyrannical, and more and more aware that I was humiliating [Fischer]." When Fischer had to tend to other commitments while Bergman was planning *The Virgin Spring*, the director, not entirely unhappy, turned to Sven Nykvist, with whom he had previously worked only on *Evening of the Jesters*. Although Bergman would reengage Fischer for *The Devil's Eye* out of loyalty, their relations were tense; thereafter, Nykvist became his steady cinematographer. "Collaboration with Fischer," Bergman confessed, "always made me unsure of myself." In contrast, Nykvist presented "a much tougher personality," a sense of command that gave the director "no reason to be nasty with him."[3]

Besides a new hand on the camera, Bergman also sought a fresh start through a different style. A decade earlier, while groping for a cinematic technique to imitate, he had experimented with Italian neorealism; now, at a time when he had his own imitators, he fell under the sway of the Japanese. Bergman studied Kurosawa intensely—*Rashomon* alone, he viewed dozens of times. That he absorbed the influence is apparent: one need only imagine the actors in *The Virgin Spring* as Japanese to appreciate how thoroughly he applied the model.*

Perhaps the clearest indication that he was grasping for a way out of his malaise was his decision to enlist Ulla Isaksson as collaborator on the script of *The Virgin Spring*. He had, of course, worked with a collabo-

*When the film was released, Bergman thought this new style had liberated him to do his best work, but a few years later he would look back on it with embarrassment. "I want to say now that *The Virgin Spring* was a misadventure, a wretched imitation of Kurosawa. It was a period in which I surrendered so completely to the Japanese film that I almost became a bit of a samurai myself."[4]

rator before—in the 'forties, when he was still learning the craft of screenwriting, and again in 1957, when he first engaged Isaksson for *Close to Life*—but these were aberrations; his contentions with Dymling during the mid-'fifties testify to the fact that Bergman regarded cinema as a very personal instrument. Why, after his unprecedented success, did he relinquish sole control over that instrument?

One factor may have been mistrust of his language. After *The Seventh Seal*, foreigners cheered Bergman for bringing a literary quality to the cinema, but some Swedes, even those who liked the film, had noted his old weakness for overblown rhetoric—and as another questioning of God, *The Virgin Spring* invited grandiloquence. A second collaboration with Isaksson, whose novel set in the Middle Ages had been praised for its realistic manner, may have seemed an expedient means of circumventing the problem.

A more compelling reason can be inferred from the contrast between the collapse of faith in *The Face*, where the miracle is false, and faith's resurrection in *The Virgin Spring*, where the miracle is real. The impetus for making *The Virgin Spring* was to cry hosanna at the end, to displace wrath over God's unfathomable purpose with acceptance of divine mystery—and that called for firmer belief than Bergman could summon. Isaksson's staunch Christianity offered a bridge over the difficulty. Moreover, like the "religious spaghetti" ensnarling Paul in *To My Terror . . .*, the metaphysical perplexity his fictions could not slice through ultimately derived from psychological sources. Collaboration seemed an enticingly simple means of creating distance between himself and his material. As he explained just before the film's premiere, "I didn't want it to be another projection of my inner drama but a free, objective presentation."[5]

The basic story in *The Virgin Spring* had teased his imagination for twenty years. During his student days, he had chanced across a medieval ballad about the seven daughters of Herr Töre and their seven rapists. The material begged for some sort of adaptation: at one time, he suggested its presentation as a ballet to the chief choreographer of the Royal Opera; at another, he considered developing it as a play. Not until he was shooting *Wild Strawberries* did he finally hit upon what should have been an obvious choice for Bergman all along: "it was, of course, a film! I went home, re-read the ballad, and saw it materialize in scenes."[6]

The version of "Töres dottrar i Vänge" Bergman eventually selected from among a score of extant variations is the simplest.* Comprising the events of a single day, the ballad begins by relating that Karin, Herr Töre's much-indulged daughter, has overslept. Her mother, Lady Märeta, awakens her and tenderly urges her to hurry to mass, but the girl's vanity (four stanzas detail her toilet and the luxury of her apparel) is stronger than her sense of religious duty. When Karin at last sets out on her journey, she meets three herdsmen, who rape and behead her. A spring gushes from the spot where the body lies, and the murderers strip off her clothes and flee. That night they stop for food and shelter, by chance, at the home of their victim's parents. As Töre and his wife, worried by their daughter's absence, uneasily prepare for bed, one of the herdsmen offers to sell Karin's shift to Märeta. Immediately understanding what has happened, she tells her husband, who slays the three with his sword; then, asking God to look with mercy on his act of vengeance, he vows to build a church of lime and stone in penance.

Some of the differences between the ballad and *The Virgin Spring* evolved in the course of expanding a seventy-two-line poem into a "realistic, comprehensive, coherent [film], convincing in psychology and milieu."[6] Others, extending well beyond what was necessary to meet these requirements, reflect the separate interests of the collaborators in refashioning the material. Isaksson's special concern lay in developing a drama about Christian faith in conflict with pagan thought; Bergman's, in excavating guilt.

Both interests were served by the introduction of Ingeri into the original story. The opening scene signals her thematic prominence. Swollen by her advanced pregnancy and tired as a result of a sleepless night, she stumbles about the hearth in the performance of her morning tasks; despite her obvious physical strength, she has the look of a frightened, feral child, only half domesticated. In her desperation, she grabs the pole attached to the vent in the roof (the *vind öga*, or wind's eye) and summons Odin to aid her. Meanwhile, before a crucifix in the main house, Töre says his prayers perfunctorily as Märeta almost perversely feeds on the image of Christ's agony and mortifies her flesh with hot candle wax.

The entrance of Karin, a pretty child at the threshhold of womanhood, briefly relieves the dark tones of the opening diptych, but intimations of

---

*After his initial discovery of the ballad, Bergman states, he found twenty-six more versions, but Bengt Jonsson, in *Svenska Medeltidsballader* (Stockholm, 1962), counts twenty, not including Danish, Norwegian, and Faeroese examples.

a struggle between opposing religious values quickly reemerge. Acting as her parents' delegate, Karin, attended by Ingeri, is to take the Holy Virgin's candles to church. As the girls ride into the forest, the proud daughter sits sidesaddle on her steed, high above the servant girl whose legs, astraddle a swaybacked mare, reach to the ground. Corrupted, bedraggled, swarth, and raven-haired, Ingeri is a creature of the night who smolders with secret passions; from the film's first frames, in which she blows on the embers in the hearth, she is associated with earthly fire. In contrast, the resplendently garbed virgin is a heavenly vision, a personification of light: the appointed bearer of holy candles, blonde, her skin unusually white in order (she says) to set off the gold of her trinkets, she is called the Queen of the Sun.

Yet, beneath the differences in their circumstances and in what they represent symbolically, the two girls are not all that dissimilar. At a dance the night before, they had been rivals for the attentions of the same man. When Ingeri accuses Karin of having stolen into the barn with Simon of Smollsta, a goatherd, the virgin protests that she did so only to urge him to help the servant-girl, pregnant with Simon's child. But Ingeri will not be put off, for she sat hidden in the barn and watched as they kissed and tossed in the hay. Clearly, Karin's boast of moral superiority pretends to too much, and Ingeri wants to pull down her vanity.

> *Ingeri*: We'll see what happens to your honor when a man takes you around the waist or strokes your neck.
> *Karin* (violently): A man will never get me into bed without marriage.
> *Ingeri*: And if you meet one in a pasture at night and he forces you behind a bush . . .?
> *Karin*: Then I shall struggle free!

Ingeri knows—and wishes—otherwise. Forced to prepare Karin's lunch for the journey, she had spat into her sister's sandwich, and after furtively eating the innards of the white bread reserved for her social betters, had made a magical appeal for the virgin's defilement by inserting a live toad, an ancient symbol of the penis, into the hollow.

Ingeri's private quarrel with her favored sister is once again invested with religious meaning at the entrance to the forest. After the girls encounter a one-eyed old man whose house sits over a stream, Karin soon resumes her journey, but Ingeri, as if drawn by a preternatural force, follows him to his hearth. A narrow shaft of light from the *vind öga* recalls her dawn prayer, and when the old man produces grisly relics of human sacrifice to Odin and then interprets a roar heard from outside the house as the sound of three dead men riding north, she senses a forecast of Karin's death. Even as her hands clutch the heads of Odin and Thor carved on her chair, Ingeri tries to renounce the power she had prayed for. Finally, she flees the house, but remorse has come too late: what she set in motion that morning cannot be stopped.

Meanwhile, proceeding alone, Karin has come to a clearing. She pauses to look at the sun, her emblem, but its blinding light—a correlate of horror for Bergman—now announces danger, not the solicitude of a protective deity. Suddenly, three brothers emerge from the forest. The youngest of these goatherds, a boy of twelve or thirteen, appears harmless, but his adult brothers are ominous figures: one has lost his tongue, presumably as a punishment for a crime; the other, a thin, Panlike man twanging a Jew's harp, suggests the amoral sexuality of nature. Karin, as innocent of what the song of the "funny flute" implies as she is of the mating calls of the birds or the chase of the squirrels, invites them to share her lunch. Pretending to be a fairy-tale princess from a majestic palace, she then tempts fate by raising her skirt to show them the pearl-stitched hem of her undergarment.

In the same fearful moment that Karin realizes that the goats they tend carry Simon of Smollsta's markings, the two adult brothers lunge for her. Startled by this eruption of lust, the boy drops the sandwich Karin has shared with him, releasing the toad Ingeri had imprisoned in the bread. When Karin tries to run, the boy trips her and she is raped by his brothers. The tongueless one then beats her to death with a tree limb.

The horror of this brutal scene is intensified by the fact that Ingeri, hidden behind a streambank, has been a silent witness. Before Karin had become aware of her peril, Ingeri, preparing to spring to her defense, had reached for the knife in her belt only to find that, as though transported by some supernatural power, it lay beyond reach on the field below. Then, when the herdsmen began their attack, Ingeri grabbed a stone to use as a weapon, but, again as if a greater force were intervening, the stone dropped from her hand and rolled into the stream—significantly, the same stream flowing under the house of Odin's servant. Despite her intentions, she then watched the rape with "wild pleasure."

This fulfillment of Ingeri's morning prayer concludes the first part of the film; in the second, devoted to retribution, the moral focus shifts to Töre. As in the ballad, the murderers unwittingly retrace Karin's path to her home. Except for the boy's vomiting his gruel at the dinner table, nothing in their behavior arouses suspicion. But when the boy's scream in the middle of the night draws Märeta down from her bedroom, and the thin brother, taking advantage of their unexpected meeting, offers to sell his "dead sister's" dress, Märeta knows her daughter's fate. After Töre is told of her discovery and then has it confirmed by the terrified Ingeri, he sheds his Christian principles and dedicates himself to vengeance. He uproots a birch, strips its branches for a flail, and enters the sauna for a purifying cleansing. That done, he strides into the hall with the slaughter knife, stabs the tongueless brother, snaps the thin one's neck and drops him onto the fiery hearth, and kills the boy by hurling him against the wall.

Along the march to recover Karin's body at dawn, the parents ponder God's design. Märeta blames herself for inciting heaven: "I loved her too much, Töre, more than God himself. And when I saw that she turned more to you than to me, I began to hate you. It is I whom he punishes with this, Töre." Her husband implies that the guilt may be his. By the time they have found the fly-covered corpse, however, the question of responsibility has given way to Töre's need for reconciliation with a God he does not understand who has permitted both "the death of the innocent child and my vengeance." Asking forgiveness, he promises to build a church "of lime and stone and *with these two hands of mine*" on the spot where his child's body lies. A spring immediately gushes from beneath the girl's head—God's response to Töre's vow. Then, joining the first part of the film to the conclusion of the second, the camera tracks the spring's flow toward Ingeri, who washes her brow (the mind in which she conceived her sin) and her eyes (which enjoyed the sight of Karin's ravishment); finally, taking the absolution into her soul, she drinks the water.

The transposition of the spring's appearance from the moment of Karin's murder in the ballad to the ending in the film—where, dissociated from the virgin herself, it manifests God's forgiveness of Töre and Ingeri—is the most radical of the alterations in the story's adaptation. In Scandinavia, as in other parts of the world, folk worship often associated virgins and water in fertility rites. Although the text of the ballad Bergman chose is from the thirteenth century, the conjunction of a virgin's violent death and the emergence of a life-giving spring indicates an origin in the sacrifices of pagan times. (The recurrence of a birch, a Nordic symbol of fertility, as an execution block in other versions of the ballad also points to this source.) As Christianity began spreading through Sweden in the first centuries of the second millenium, the ballad took on a new metaphoric function; thus: the names "Töre" and "Märeta" (i.e., Thor and Mary) suggest the clash between two systems of belief that, when the father vows to raise a church on the same spot where the virgin was killed, ends in the victory of Christianity.* Neither Isaksson nor Bergman, it seems, understood the story they appropriated. At one point in her introduction to the published screenplay, Isaksson infers that the ballad meant the flow of pure water to be taken as proof of the girl's innocence—which is surely not at issue. At another, she half apologizes for introducing "a line of tension which does not appear in the song" by providing Karin with a stepsister who worships the Norse gods.**[7] More than a dramatization, the adaptation gave the story a new axis, reflected in the change of emphasis in the title from the daughters in all the ballad variants to the spring in the film.

The collaborators were under no obligation to remain faithful to the original material, of course, but in their reinterpretation they created thematic confusion. *The Virgin Spring* consists of two separate strands. The first, concerning Ingeri's malevolence toward Karin, pretends to be about Christianity in conflict with Odin worship, yet the vain "Queen of the Sun" scarcely manifests any Christian principle, and the allusions to Odin never penetrate the mumbo jumbo to suggest the power of pagan religion. Ingeri's sin is nothing more than envy, seen from a Christian perspective, and Odin becomes merely another name for the Devil. The second component, focused on the father's vengeance against the evil that has destroyed his child, is wholly unrelated to the presumption of Odin's complicity in her death and takes almost no cognizance of Ingeri's guilt. The miracle of the spring directly responds to Töre's vow, an acceptance of God despite the mystery of his purpose, but the force of this divine forgiveness for his having put retribution before piety is attenuated by its extension to Ingeri. Why, one wonders, should his

*Medieval ballads provide rich evidence of this commingling, principally in the manifold variations of a story about the rape and murder of a virgin (or virgins) during the course of a devotional duty. Vestiges of the connection between the ballads and folk religion have continued to exist up to modern times in at least one location. Parishioners in Kärna, a remote village in Östergötland, have gathered about a spring in the churchyard each Midsummer Day since the thirteenth century to sing "Per Tyrssons dottrar" in celebration of the leafing of the forest.

**Although the script uses the specific word for stepsister, the girl must be Karin's foster sister since, at different times, both Töre and Märeta say she is no daughter of theirs. The addition of a stepsister to the plot may have been suggested by one of the ballad variants in which two daughters ride into the wood.

consecration of his hands to God result in her absolution for an entirely
different sin?

Apart from its specious yoking of two disparate story lines, the conclusion is also unsatisfactory on other counts. One problem is dramaturgic:
whatever one's moral position on vengeance may be, the construction
of the film has aligned the audience on Töre's side during his slaughter
of the herdsmen, and since no subsequent dramatic action alters that
emotional commitment, one is unprepared to give full assent to his
remorse. A second problem, partly the result of the first, is more serious
in that it affects meaning. In her preface to the screenplay, Isaksson
insists that all three brothers are equally guilty (and, according to the
New Testament theology she espouses, equally deserving of forgiveness).[8]
As published, the script is consistent with that view, but the film is
not. Despite Ingeri's description of the rape to Töre, "They flung
her down and held her and they took her—*all three*," the camera
implicates the youngest brother only to the extent of his tripping
the victim. Moments later, obviously moved by contrition, the boy
scoops handfuls of dirt on the corpse, and when he gives up the
task as too great for him to accomplish, snow begins to fall—
as though God has taken it over. The two versions also differ markedly in their treatment of what happens that night. Whereas the
script explains the boy's vomiting during dinner as "anger" at the
dead girl for turning the food he has just eaten to "dust in his
mouth," the film unmistakably indicates it is caused by revulsion over
his brothers' deeds. And when Töre looses his wrath on the murderers, Isaksson shows him reluctant to attack the boy (perhaps because it would be unequal combat) until Märeta demands his
death; in the film, Töre snatches the boy from his wife's protective
embrace.

Coupled with the suddenness of Töre's penitence and the absence of
an explicit statement about what he is repenting, Bergman's exculpation of the boy—or, at least, mitigation of his guilt—has fostered the
view that the father's sin is his *excess* of vengeance in killing this
"innocent."[9] Indeed, no other interpretation would account for the
emphasis given to the boy's special claim to mercy. Such a construction,
however, nullifies the Christian precept the film is ostensibly meant to
illustrate. If Töre's atonement signifies acceptance of a Christian God,
the film should stress his forgiveness of the most evil of the brothers; by
implying that his offense against God wholly or mainly rests in killing
the least evil of them, Bergman reduces that act to a mere error in

judgment and gives Töre's vow to build a church an overtone of dealing in indulgences.

Ironically, Bergman's strategem of relying on Isaksson to furnish the unambiguous religious statement he felt incapable of formulating had just the opposite effect. Despite the international acclamation won by *The Virgin Spring*, Bergman began having second thoughts before the cheering had subsided: the film had falsified his original inspiration; its theology was suspect; and the raw beauty of the ballad had been transformed into a "touristy" display. Everything impressive about it, he realized, was on its exterior; inside, it was hollow. He and Isaksson had "influenced one another in the wrong way, and it was rather unfortunate."[10]

But the failure of the collaboration involved more than confusion in the film's theological pronouncement or in the dramatic means to substantiate it. As in the rest of Bergman's fictions that wrestle with God, the religious questions are only the superstructure; the molten core of the work is the same "inner drama" he had hoped to put behind him by working with Isaksson. Instead of achieving the benefit of an aesthetic distance, however, the division of responsibility only created a wider separation between the film's inner and outer layers.

As in the preceding films, guilt permeates the inner *The Virgin Spring*. One sign of this interior emerges through an incidental detail in an early scene in which a wandering beggar speaks of having been to lands where the churches were "high as heaven itself, and vast! Not made of wood, but of limestone and granite.... And ['*significantly*,' the script adds] with a dozen confessionals." Though patently introduced to foreshadow the ending, something else may also be at work: the stress here implies the universality and depth of man's sin—not, as in Töre's vow, acknowledgment of the greatness of God in his mystery. (The implicit connection between sin and the erection of great churches invites noting Bergman's frequent comparison of himself as a filmmaker to the artisans who raised medieval cathedrals.)

Closer to the locus of guilt, however, is what the tale itself "confesses." If, superficially, the opening scenes portray a clash between Odin and Christ, the energy revealed by their pairing derives from currents that stir below. Märeta's sexual repression is evident: she shrinks from her husband's touch; she drips fiery wax on her skin to burn away the evil dreams she says have been troubling her nights. In contrast, Ingeri's erotic nature seems to bring the embers to life as she blows into the hearth. But the correspondence between the two women whose opposite attitudes toward the senses are mirrored in their equally intense prayers to different gods also has darker, more complex intimations. Ingeri, too, has been kept awake by dreams, stimulated by envy of Karin. Given Märeta's subsequent confession of her own jealousy toward Karin, the fact that Ingeri here calls on Odin to strike the girl down suggests that the mother's dreams have sprung from a similar secret wish.*

This initial implication of an Oedipal triangle is reinforced by Karin's flirtation with her father and his response in kind. Each is obviously the center of the other's world—and Karin, as though sensing a rivalry with her mother, vaunts that special bond in front of Märeta. For Töre, the daughter's effusive affection compensates for his wife's emotional retreat from him: even as Karin embraces him, whispers in his ear, and evokes memories of what it was like to be young, Märeta scratches the sores of her mortified flesh. At least one critic has made the apparent connection between the behavior of father and daughter in this early scene and the events that follow in its train: since the herdsmen have acted out Töre's incestual fantasies, the exorbitance of his revenge and consequent contrition expresses the profound sense of his own guilt.[11]

Even if the fact that the virgin in the ballad bore his mother's name played no part in Bergman's twenty-year fascination with the story, it seems likely that that coincidence, coupled with the inveterate tendencies of his imagination, affected the elaboration of the original material. But the Oedipal conflicts so readily observable in Bergman's personal history have not been schematically overlaid on the ballad. Though, like several of the women in his 'forties stories, Karin meets a violent death, the circumstances here do not fit quite the same pattern or lead to quite the same inferences. Nor has Märeta anything in common with Karin Bergman. And surely Töre is not a fictional version of Erik Bergman. To see any analogy at all between Bergman's parents and the stern mother and indulgent father in the film, one has to reverse their roles—and though that would lend an autobiographical base to the early scenes, it would be psychoanalytically inconsistent with the later ones. Nevertheless, childhood sexual guilt is deeply etched on the film's underside, and it is manifested through Karin—not as a figure of the sexually desired mother but as a projection of the son who identified himself with her.

*Significantly, the clearing where the girl will be raped and murdered is described in the script as seeming to have been "scorched by fire"—an apparent allusion not only to the hearth where Ingeri prayed for Karin's destruction but also to Märeta's self-"scorching" and the jealousy that, at least in part, she attempts to cauterize.

An understanding of how this operates follows from the perception of *The Virgin Spring* as similar to one type of fairy tale. Karin, who tempts misfortune through her pride, corresponds to the pampered princess (a role to which she literally pretends in her meeting with the herdsmen). Her virginity is crucial both to that pride and to her special status at home; indeed, one could get the impression her parents' love depends upon her innocence—and it is her purity that qualifies her for the honor of carrying the Virgin's candles. But, as so often occurs in fairy tales, there is a bad side of the good child, embodied in a counter-self. If Karin represents a child's fantasy of the self admired and loved by the parents, Ingeri, the despised foundling who is her "sister," is the dirty, foul, sinful person unworthy of love that the child fears is the true self. Significantly, Märeta scorns her by contrasting her with Karin: "I'm not afraid that my daughter will follow in your rotten footsteps. You have never resembled each other any more than the rose resembles the thorn. . . . we should drive you from our door, especially now that you've made a mess of yourself." Yet, the evening before her holy errand, Karin rolled in the hay with the very man who made Ingeri pregnant. To punish the sister self for her hypocrisy—and thereby reveal that she is no better than herself—Ingeri conceals the toad in her bread and (presumably) wishes her rape. (That the "sinfulness" the good sister masks from her parents concerns her sexuality is also reflected by Karin's dream during the night of dancing with "three swains"—a fore-shadowing of the three herdsmen who will later respond to her hidden desires with punitive violence.)

Although the conflicts within the self metaphorically depicted by this tale are probably universal, the tensions they engendered in Bergman as a boy were exacerbated by the wild swings in his parents' behavior toward him. As the favored child, he shouldered an especially heavy burden in having to justify that privilege, and when he disappointed their expectations, the pain in the rituals of shame he was made to endure far exceeded that of any physical punishment he received. Suddenly, the love and security this sensitive child required were with-drawn as his parents treated him with prolonged silence. Still worse, he quickly came to believe that he merited rejection, that his sexual impulses, compounded with his intense attraction to his mother, proved he was evil. The condition for reinstatement was confession, but genu-ine confession would only confirm his unworthiness.

An intriguing sign of the personal guilt motivating this tale is the fact that Karin's mission through the forest is to take her to the village's confessor—whose name, most suggestively, is *Father Erik*. But the chief expression of Bergman's ambiguous self-image as a child consists in Ingeri's role as Karin's alter ego. Here, too, the name he chose for his character says a great deal: "Ingeri" is a feminine form of "Ingmar." And in her worship of Odin (who, in early Christian Sweden, became confused with Satan), one can see a parallel to Bergman's pretentious affiliation with the devil during the 'forties. Ingeri steps from the same corner of his mind as that other sympathetically drawn acolyte of evil, Jack the Ripper. Perhaps the most telling use of Ingeri, however, involves the ending. When the camera leaves Töre to follow the flow of the spring's water toward her and then concentrates on her absolution in the last frames, the film finally reveals its inner purpose—not a parent's resolution of a question concerning obedience to a Christian God but a child's relief of psychological guilt.

No sudden lapse, this incongruency accentuates the disparity between what Bergman's unbidden fantasy dictated and what the film purports to be about that has been present throughout. The strained emotional relationship between the parents, to cite one example, has no bearing on either the plot or the ostensible theme. Another: Karin's pride and the intimation that she feels the same sexual itch as her sister provide a warrant for Ingeri's jealousy, but nothing ties these features to what is overtly the central, theological issue—in fact, to the extent that they blemish her image, they lessen the sense of God's injustice in permitting the desecration of perfect innocence. More troublesome still, neither Ingeri's spitefulness toward her foster sister nor her feelings of remorse really touches on the questions of vengeance or of the necessity to accept the mystery of God's ways; indeed, nothing she does affects Töre's actions. And, finally, whether Märeta and Töre are in some way to blame for Karin's fate is ultimately irrelevant to their presumed moral culpability in the killing of her murderers.

In the judgment of Vernon Young, the most encomiastic of its admirers, *The Virgin Spring* is Bergman's masterpiece, the work in which he surmounted a "besetting [religious] dualism, which was largely a histrionic convenience," and surrendered wholly to artistic inspiration: "If you do not feel the power and truth of such a film as this one, no argument can persuade you.... I cannot impose, by intellectual urgency, an emotion you cannot share."[12] The extravagant praise seems justified on first encounter with the film. The acting is utterly convincing; the mise-en-scène, flawless; and the emotional impact, as overwhelming as Young insists. But the art of drama involves more than theatrical brilliance or, even, aesthetic effect. At some point, intellect engages emotion as one tries to understand what one feels—and at that moment in the response to *The Virgin Spring*, it reveals its imposture.

The Devil's Eye

In order to gain SF's approval to make *The Virgin Spring*—which the studio believed would not have much public appeal—Bergman had had to agree to supply a comedy. That the internationally celebrated filmmaker who had been principally responsible for the renaissance of the Swedish cinema should have capitulated to such extortion seems very odd, but he had ready no other idea for a film, and, as he later confessed, he felt artistically "insecure and unproductive."[1] Besides, he thought a bit of "enforced playfulness" might be a useful "weapon against the unreality of fame."[2]

The germ of the new script came from *The Return of Don Juan*, a Danish radio drama by Oluf Bang that SF had bought and packed away in its archives. Thanks largely to the astonishing success of staged readings of the "Don Juan in Hell" section from *Man and Superman*, Juan had recently been much in vogue in the international theater, and although Bang's play was undistinguished, Bergman, who had himself directed Moliere's version of the story in 1956 at Malmö, was attracted by the notion of the legendary Spanish lover's reappearance in contemporary Scandinavia. He began rewriting the play in Dalarna, where he and Isaksson had sequestered themselves for their collaboration on *The Virgin Spring*; then, in the interval between completion of the screenplay for the medieval film and the start of shooting, he thoroughly revised the manuscript, retaining only a few sections from the first draft. By the time *The Devil's Eye* was ready for the cameras, it had become almost entirely Bergman's own work.

Although, in its mixture of fantasy and naughty innocence, the film recalls several comedies popular in the 'fifties—especially Peter Ustinov's *The Loves of Four Colonels*—the presentation is familiarly Bergman's.* A narrator (Gunnar Björnstrand) "tells" the story—which, like a previous Bergman comedy "narrated" by Björnstrand, concerns a lesson in love.

---

*As Ustinov had adapted *Torment* for the London stage in 1947, Bergman had probably read his comedy, which had successful runs in London (1951) and New York (1953).

Satan has a sty, caused by the fact that a lovely girl, about to be married, is still a virgin; if this "monstrous challenge to Hell" is not met, "Heaven will exult, the archangels will blow their trumpets, and there will be an unholy row" as others will follow her unprecedented example.* Thus, attended by his servant Pablo, Don Juan is dispatched to Earth to wage battle against the virgin, a vicar's daughter named Britt-Marie.

The immediate consequences of Hell's offensive are triumphs for Heaven. Although Britt-Marie offers herself to Juan, he suppresses his lust because he has fallen in love with her. The virgin's mother, described by Satan as "an unusually competent woman, well-qualified for Hell," is bedded by Pablo, but this causes her to "awaken to self-knowledge, be seized with pity for her husband, and, perhaps, even become a good wife." And as a further result of her seduction, the cuckolded vicar "acquires seeing eyes" for the sins hidden in the heart, yet retains the grace to forgive. Satan is enraged, and to punish the infamous lover for bungling so simple a mission, he forces Juan to listen from Hell as his inamorta is deflowered on her wedding night. But the final triumph quite unexpectedly falls to Satan when the girl, still bearing the mark of Juan's passion on her lips, tells her groom that she has never kissed another man. Miraculously, Satan's sty disappears; the lie has restored Hell to continue its contention with Heaven.

Bergman had earlier shown his adeptness at just this type of sage comedy in which erotic sport tempers recognition of life's futility, but these same elements remain inert in *The Devil's Eye*. If, in summary form, the plot seems to warrant the film's description in the opening titles as a *rondo capriccioso*, in the actual playing, the tempo slows to *largo*. Even the intermittent use of fast cuts and the sprightly score from Scarlatti—obviously meant to quicken the piece—betray the filmmaker by calling attention to the contrasting slow pace of the scenes.

Much of the problem stems from Bergman's insistence that the audience is watching a play. (It is almost as though he had decided to do penance for "stealing" from Kurosawa in *The Virgin Spring* by purging this film of cinematic style.) His theatrical training had been evident throughout his films of the 'forties and 'fifties, of course, but here the stage becomes, more than an influence, a physical part of the performance. The Narrator (or Prologue and Epilogue) not only frames the action, he also interrupts it by, in effect, striding onto the apron to

*A motto, "A woman's chastity is a sty in the Devil's eye," appears on the screen just after the title. Although it carries the ascription "Old Irish Proverb," it is of Bergman's own coinage.

inform the audience when one act is over and the next about to begin. Entrances and exits accommodate the requirements of a phantom stage. Scenic effects, such as the eighteenth-century wigs worn by Satan's councilors and the flares outside the windows in Hell, stress theatrical artifice rather than the "realism" of film. The most damaging reliance on stage conventions, however—as Bergman himself later realized—is in his approach to dialogue.

> Because I have long worked with theater and because I once wrote plays, I sometimes have a longing to write plays, real plays. By "plays" in this sense I mean something that moves forward through the word, in which the word has priority. It is of course extremely difficult to delimit what theater is—so I fell quite naturally into that category. I wrote a play to which I gave an inappropriate cinematic form. It is very defective because the play is actually a stage play, and unfortunately, not even a very good stage play.[3]

One would be hard put to name another of his films in which language is quite so independent of its visual complement. A lover of words despite his difficulties with style, Bergman suddenly surrendered to the pleasure of chiseling Shavian epigrams; the comic intrigues and, even, the story itself become mere mountings for the verbal gems. The technique suits the theater, where the audience's reaction to the actor's lines is a dynamic part of the performance, not film, where the epigrammatic periods jerk the action to a halt, as though awaiting an appreciation of wit the medium cannot supply.

But the fundamental weakness of *The Devil's Eye* lies deeper than the inappropriateness of the "form." In the filmscript's opening monologue, the Narrator apologizes for his presence: "I must beg you to excuse me—the idea is not mine. But I have my duty as an actor; I also have to support myself and—why not?—sustain my ambitions. What is of the utmost importance is that, despite everything, the assignment be well-executed." The lines, transparently Bergman's own confession, were cut from the final version, yet their apologetic tone remains imbedded in the film. If, "despite everything," he felt impelled to go on, he could bring no conviction to the assignment. Consequently, his characters track along the design of the story's premise without generating drama from within themselves. Britt-Marie's virginity is expressed by merely a country cousin naiveté that scarcely qualifies as a casus belli between Heaven and Hell. Her mother's infidelity seems to have interested Bergman more than the issue of the girl's chastity, but whether she is moved by

compassion for Pablo, by curiosity about a lover who has been "storing
[his] substance for three hundred years," or by her own half a lifetime of
unrequited lust is unclear—and surely it makes a difference in understanding the woman. The males are equally shallow. Satan projects no
idea of evil; he just seems bored. Pablo's mentality is all in his genitals.
Even the figure of the most famous lover in history failed to stimulate
Bergman's imagination: his Don Juan is only a jaded sophisticate whose
infatuation with innocence suggests no experience of passion.*

But even though *The Devil's Eye* is among Bergman's feeblest efforts, it
is nonetheless a revealing personal document. With *The Virgin Spring*,
he had tried to use an assertion of religious faith to overcome the artistic
crisis dramatized in *The Face*; with *The Devil's Eye*, he seems to have
been issuing a retraction. Point by point, the second film about a virgin
virtually cancels the first. Here the plot rotates around a mission from
Hell instead of a holy errand, and in place of the horrible rape, there is a
comic campaign aimed at seduction. In contrast to the ascetic Märeta,
this mother is a sexually avid woman who welcomes an infernal lover in
her bed, and the virile Töre who wrathfully disobeys God is replaced by
a meek vicar who is God's gullible fool. In both films, the virgin's parents
offer the hospitality of their home to the agents of evil, but the discovery
which follows produces destructive fury in one and the reconstruction
of love in the other. Whereas *The Virgin Spring* ends with God triumphant and the sinners redeemed, the last-minute reversal concluding
the comedy shows the Devil victorious and the worm of sin sweetly
ensconced in the human heart. And, most conspicuous of all, in contrast to Töre's testimony of reconciliation, Don Juan, in the one moment
of the film in which the character comes alive, hurls a final vow of
Jöns-like defiance against the lords of both Heaven and Hell:

> If it gives you pleasure, I am suffering. But I shall not collapse and
> I'm not complaining. I find you ridiculous with your punishment
> —you, Satan, and Him up there—and I despise you. Never in all
> eternity will Don Juan give in, even if you lay upon him worse
> horrors than those now tearing at his vitals. I shall remain Don
> Juan, the despiser of God and the devil.

---

*Although Jarl Kulle, the comic actor who plays the role, is usually blamed for the stolid
characterization, the principal fault was Bergman's. When Kulle tried to decline the part
because it called for an older man who could convey Juan's tragic stature, the director
argued that that was not the interpretation he wanted. Unfortunately, as Bergman later
acknowledged, Kulle was right.[4]

If one can read a personal significance in this speech and in *The Devil's Eye* generally as an inversion of *The Virgin Spring*, its implications are more artistic than religious. The attempt to transmute private anguish into films about a quest for faith had only exacerbated his sense of bad faith as an artist. His films had won most of the major prizes and had been principally responsible for elevating the intellectual status of cinema; he had become an international luminary, featured on the covers of the world's leading newsmagazines. But, like Vogler, he feared that his effects were only concealed tricks, that whatever real powers he had possessed were spent. In an open letter to his "dear frightening public" in 1960, he confessed to feeling "as though I were already dead, stuffed, filed away in the cinema archives."[5] If *The Devil's Eye* testifies to an exhaustion of creativity, it also forced Bergman to begin the self-examination that would produce a fresh start.

God's Silence

The renewal Bergman began in 1961 drew inspiration from several directions. Marriage to a pianist heightened a lifelong love of music and focused an interest in chamber music and the works of modern composers. Fascinated by Bartók, he conceived of constructing a film in a similar manner. The film-as-symphony, he told reporters, no longer interested him; noting, by way of analogy, that there was as much intensity in the string quartets of Beethoven or Bartók as in the forced efforts of Wagner or Richard Strauss, he announced that he had abandoned his former "orchestration" to explore "the chamber music format."

Another stimulus for change was the new cinema from France and Italy that had swiftly become the intellectual rage in Sweden while he, suddenly, was treated as old hat. Discussion of these new directors, he grumbled, occupied the culture section of Swedish newspapers; accounts of his own work were assigned to the entertainment pages. Yet, much as he contemned the "slovenliness" of the New Wave and sneered at the adulation accorded Antonioni, he also recognized in their approaches a revolutionary vision of film that owed very little to the traditions of theater; to have ignored the challenge would have been tantamount to choosing to work in an anachronistic mode.* Although he proceeded

---

*The subsequent designation of *Through a Glass Darkly* as "Certainty Achieved," of *The Communicants* as "Certainty Unmasked," and of *The Silence* as "God's Silence—The Negative Impression" implies that, from the very beginning, Bergman had planned a trilogy to illustrate a quasi-Hegelian argument of philosophical necessity. Apparently, however, the

with no fixed program before him, he realized, finally, that he would have to discard the conventional notion of the screen as a substitute proscenium arch of a perfectly naturalistic, infinitely mobile stage and concentrate on treating its patterns of light and shadow as a plane of dream.

Ironically, part of the foundation for this revised film aesthetic derived from two playwrights. Although his January 1961 production of *The Sea Gull* at Dramaten was criticized as listless, his first professional encounter with Chekhov proved something of a revelation for Bergman. The fabric of the Russian's drama was woven of reality, yet the experience had the fluid quality of the dream. Bergman had sought to achieve just such an ambivalence in *Wild Strawberries*, where, as he said, the dream sequences were meant to foster an impression of the surrounding reality as itself a kind of dream; now he believed he had discovered a model for a purer means to that goal. But Chekhov also had a more important lesson to teach. Throughout his films—and especially in the later 'fifties —Bergman had struggled over endings that, he felt, had to produce the answer to the problem expressed in the dramatic conflict. Since the real problem, however he might disguise it, lay unresolved within himself, he resorted either to sleight of hand or, hoping to overwhelm his uncertainty, to a loud flourish. In Chekhov, he saw a different strategy: instead of advancing toward a resolution that illustrates some external truth, the play takes its form from the exposure of the truth about the relationships of its characters.

The second playwright was Strindberg. Given Bergman's almost mystical kinship with the towering figure of Swedish drama, his choosing a Strindberg play for his directorial debut on television in 1960 was perhaps inevitable. That the play should be *Storm*, however, gave the event an almost talismanic significance.

Written in 1907 for the Intimate, *Storm* was the first of the four Chamber Plays which, in the words of Martin Lamm (a principal Strindberg scholar and Bergman's teacher at the University of Stockholm), "more than any other of his works secured his reputation as a theatrical revolutionary."[1] A decade earlier, Strindberg had emerged from the psychotic turmoil of his Inferno Period prepared, while assuming Jacob's

idea of linking three films under a loosely unifying rubric was a riposte to the fuss being made over Antonioni's trilogy, and it did not occur to him until after *Through a Glass Darkly*. Initially, he thought of announcing that *The Virgin Spring* should be regarded as the first unit of the trilogy; only after he had begun work on *The Communicants* did the scheme become fixed.

role in wrestling with God, to examine the inner sources of his monstrous guilt. The plays that gushed from his pen in the next few years are among his most imposing—and among his most difficult to produce. Then, suddenly, he changed course. Odd as it may seem, for most of his life Strindberg had had only superficial contact with the working theater; drama for him had been either essentially literary or suited to an imaginary stage unencumbered by practical considerations. But once launched on planning a theater devoted to his plays with August Falck, he immersed himself in the details of production and, in anticipation of the Intimate's opening, began to apply his study to a new dramaturgy. At about the same time, too, he revised *A Dream Play* while finishing his naturalistic novel, *Black Banners*—an experience which apparently led him to think about reconciling their diverse modes. The confluence of these activities produced a drama in which dialogue and the nuances in its delivery rather than action or elaborate sets established character; in which he would strike even more boldly than in the past against the conventional dramatic constructions (which Strindberg called "old machines") by "exhaustively" depicting the details of observed human behavior; in which the ambience of the dream showed through the realistic surface. "Intimate in form" and limited to "few characters [expressing] great points of view," the Chamber Play would demonstrate "the idea of chamber music transferred to drama."[2]

Although Bergman's circumstances at the start of the 'sixties were not precisely congruent with Strindberg's in 1906, there are some obvious parallels. In one sense, television was his new theater, forcing him to rethink his camerawork, to work even closer than before to the faces of his actors, to consider the effect of the proximity of the viewer to the "stage" in that most intimate theater, the living room. What he learned would soon have an impact on his films: from *Through a Glass Darkly* on, television would have a growing influence on his technique. But that other new theater—the cinema itself—for which he sought to reject his own "old machines" and write a new kind of drama also drew directly on Strindberg's example. On the eve of the first day's shooting of *The Communicants* (at the same press conference where he spoke of a new "orchestration"), Bergman underscored his intention "to create human beings, write human beings . . . , in a manner of speaking, to move away from mechanical drawing and to try to draw a human hand. . . . In this era of strange non-art, it is important that the human not fall from the center, that we constantly strive to express a human image—a personal form of human image."[3] The import was clear: the trilogy he had begun marked the founding of an Intimate Theater of his own, where, instead of Chamber Plays, he would present "Chamber Films."

But more than radical transformations in form and technique distinguish the first of the Chamber Films from those of the earlier periods. In making a new start artistically, Bergman seemed compelled toward a personal purgation, not unlike what he had done at the start of the previous decade with *The City*.

Inspired by the success of *Cahiers du Cinema* in elevating the power of a determined group of young film critics, Swedish cinema enthusiasts launched their own journal, *Chaplin*, in 1960. Its ideological orientation was apparent in the November issue, its second, which has become known as the "anti-Bergman" number. Three of the articles bear the names of well-known Swedish film critics; while conceding the filmmaker's "technical brilliance" and superb handling of actors, they censure him for being a "totally empty person spiritually," guilty, moreover, of a long list of artistic sins including "mechanical repetitiveness," "negativism," "parasitic dependence on the films of others," "rambling constructions," inability to breathe life into his "artificial dolls," and an annoying fascination with puzzles. The fourth attack, carrying the byline of a Frenchman, Ernest Riffe, resembles the other three except that its knife has a sharper edge and plunges farther into the man himself. Riffe charges that Bergman is less a creator than an impostor, forced to borrow material because his "deep misanthropy" and "lack of contact with his surroundings" deprive him of the sources of originality; he is arrogantly egocentric, and yet, behind the haughty facade, he "mistrusts his intentions" and suspects that his inspirations are "blanched and stale." Most scathing was Riffe's claim that Bergman hides his derivativeness and incompetence as a poetic dramatist behind the trickery of film. "Never having been well-regarded as a writer in his homeland," Riffe adds, "he has certainly suffered under the contempt from his literary colleagues," yet in practicing his fraud, he confirms the verdict his critics have brought against him. By the time the next issue of *Chaplin* was out, curiosity about Riffe, who was unknown to even the most assiduous readers of the French journals, had been generally satisfied: he was, in fact, Ingmar Bergman. Bergman later justified the hoax as an amusing self-indulgence: "I experienced a special freedom in collecting my innermost self-criticism (which, to some extent, matched the criticism directed at me from outside), verbalizing it, tricking it out to seem a bad Swedish translation from the French, and then opening *Expressen* to read: 'This is the best statement about Ingmar Bergman in recent years.'"[4]

But a man who, under whatever guise, arranges for his public crucifixion has more on his mind than humor. On one level, the ruse was a defensive maneuver—a preemptive strike at detractors among his own generation and among the younger crowd of Swedish cinema enthusiasts who dressed their views according to the mode set by *Cahiers du Cinema*. (The New Wave, which had lauded Bergman earlier in the 'fifties, had shifted position and condemned *The Face* and *The Virgin Spring* rather roundly.) Aware of his vulnerability, he sought to disarm his critics by turning the worst they might say into a joke. At a deeper level, however, the essay was motivated not by a need for protection but by an aggressive impulse against disturbing elements within himself.

All of "Riffe's" points, save one, are variations on criticisms either found elsewhere in the anti-Bergman issue or generally raised in the press, but the exception, the derogation of Bergman as a writer (or, as the more expressive Swedish word *diktare* also denotes, poet), is significantly the most severe indictment. The failure to realize his literary aspirations evidently still rankled. Shortly after publication of the Riffe article, he and actor, director, and longtime friend Erland Josephson secretly collaborated under the name Buntel Eriksson on a film called *The Garden of Eden.** David, the protagonist of this comedy (for which Bergman supplied the story and Josephson the dialogue), is a small-town schoolteacher who fears his neighbors' ridicule and discovery of personal secrets when he pseudononymously publishes verses from his youth that voice beliefs he no longer holds. At about the same time, Bergman was also writing *Through a Glass Darkly*, in which another David, an author being mentioned for the Nobel Prize, knows that his novels are vapid performances without conviction. Although one film is fluff and the other is grave drama, the opposing images of David the poet and David the posturer reflect the same Bergman. Instead of insuring confidence in his achievement, the astonishing heights he had reached intensified his insecurity. What did success in cinema mean if it could be won by someone who was unable to write a competent short story or novel and whose promise as a dramatist had never matured?

The Garden of Eden was written, cast, and shot rather hurriedly in 1961 to fill a void in production caused when cancer forced studio head Dymling from his post. As the major figure in Swedish cinema, Bergman took the lead in forming an "interim government" at SF and, in addition, became a producer. These extra duties brought few rewards, but his experience with *The Garden of Eden* was especially bitter. A critical fiasco, it subsequently furnished an easy target for Bo Widerberg's condemnation of Bergman in his book *Visionen i Svensk Film*.

Yet artistic frustration alone does not account for "Riffe's" tremulous undertone; the fascination with deception and pathetic ineptitude far exceeds the purposes of real or parodic criticism. What guilt prompts this self-castigation is implied in the pseudonym chosen for the attack.

Making light of the article, Bergman claimed he borrowed the name "Riffe" from a fashionable hairdresser who had affronted him by shearing the "very beautiful, long, and thick" hair of a woman with whom he had traveled to France in 1949; "I vowed bloody revenge, and thus I christened my antagonist 'Ernest Riffe.'"* But the anecdote raises questions more interesting than the one it purports to answer. How would applying the hairdresser's name to a devastating "antagonist" serve revenge? The vengeance is flowing the wrong way. And why incubate such a trivial incident for almost a dozen years? The essential clue surfaces in Bergman's parenthetical comment that Riffe "was surely a pederast."[5] In *Hour of the Wolf*, six years after the *Chaplin* article, he would again associate "Ernest" with homosexuality: there, the "worst" of the demons who escape from the artist-protagonist's tortured psyche and acquire physical form is named Ernst von Merkens. The only previous instance where Bergman uses "Ernst" contributes another piece to the puzzle: in *Last Couple Out*, the psychiatrist who has an affair with the confused young protagonist's mother is Ernest Farell. When one adds the fact that Bergman's own baptismal name is Ernst to the rebus and then recalls his confession of the rare "secret pleasure" he felt as a child in being allowed into his mother's bedroom while she combed her "long, dark brown hair," the composite meaning becomes rather evident. In cutting the girlfriend's hair, the hairdresser in effect punished him both by taking away the object Bergman associated with his sexual attraction to his mother and, in reminding him of that illicit desire, by spoiling his fun with the girlfriend. Another form of punishment is involved in Bergman's denigration of Riffe as a pederast: if being a hairdresser suggests homosexuality, then the exquisite delight Bergman had derived from watching his mother at her toilet would make him vulnerable to the same taunt. But the most revealing aspect of the Riffe hoax is the link it implicitly forges between the sexual complexity of his relationship with his mother and his "failure" as an artist. The interior conflicts that had both impelled and hobbled his films were rising to the threshold of con-

---

*The woman was probably Gun Grut, who accompanied him to Paris after the completion of *To Joy*. They married a little more than a year later.

sciousness; in a peculiar, left-handed way, "Riffe's" attack represented an attempt to deal with the problem.

Another manifestation of Bergman's self-examination during this period is recorded in Vilgot Sjöman's *L136*, a diary he kept in 1961 tracing the evolution of *The Communicants* from idea into finished film. Although, in the past, Bergman had disparaged psychoanalytic theory, Sjöman noted that he now showed a sudden interest in it as a tool for self-therapy. When the subject of Freudian slips led to a discussion of dream interpretation, Bergman described a pair of dreams that "battled" him:

> "In the first dream, I was with a woman I once knew. And the room we were in—yes, it was both the children's room in the Sophiahem parsonage and my present home in Djursholm. I heard mama's voice and became angry. Why, just now, couldn't she leave me in peace?"' [Here Sjöman summarizes the rest of the dream.] He runs down the stairs, then back up again and embraces the woman [with whom he was about to have intercourse in the bedroom] around her knees. But in one instant, that woman becomes his wife Käbi; in the next, his mother. Then she is Käbi again. And then his mother again.

The confusion of the three women in the dream—mother, wife, and lover—clearly restates the conflict, most transparent in *Prison*, that kept recurring in his films. The self is simultaneously an adult and a child. The adult resents his mother's power to prevent successful coitus with the female partner, but the child, erotically dependent on the mother, welcomes her intrusion for two reasons: it saves him from being "unfaithful" to her, and it rescues him from having to prove his virility —about which, he has some doubts. (Presumably there is relief as well as anxiety in his discovery, while embracing the lover, that the mother is not downstairs, where he expected her to be, but upstairs, where she has replaced the sexually demanding woman and merged with his wife.) In his own interpretation, Bergman arrived at a somewhat similar conclusion: the dream was forcing him, as it were, to

> separate my mother and my wife—a substitution, an interblending which has been constant with me. I now recognize the probable un-conscious reason why, during a certain period, I was attracted only by younger women: just to make the possibility of that substitution as remote as possible. . . . I've always been damnably afraid of women, though my enthusiasm has always taken precedence over the fear.

(Perhaps as revealing as this textbook expression of the Oedipus complex is a remark that followed in which he acknowledged, as a feminine component in his nature, his need to "exchange souls" with a woman in order to be sexually aroused.)[6]

In the second dream, Bergman finds himself locked in a prison — "for some idealistic reason."

> I am in that prison. I am to be there three days. When I entered the cell . . . oh, I forgot to mention that there is a purling fountain in the corridor. But in the cell there are three women: Bertha Sånell [a wardrobe mistress at SF], someone who resembles Käbi, and someone who resembles my mother. I decide to vanquish all three in this singular way: by remaining silent. No matter what, they won't get one sound out of me.[7]

The three-day sentence suggests Christ's three days in the tomb before Resurrection — a sexual pun indicating a longing for potency (*uppståndelse* [literally, "the standing up"] = resurrection; stånd = erection). The more explicit symbol of this desire is the phallic fountain; after "forgetting" to mention it, he goes on to mention it twice in his account, stressing the wonderfully "free-flowing water" that the women — jailers, not fellow prisoners — keep him from reaching. Two of the women form the same composite of wife and mother that infantilize the self in the first dream. The third represents the threat to his masculinity in another guise: as the wardrobe mistress, she is associated with Bergman's often-recited account of his punishment in the parsonage wardrobe in which he believed a "castrating" imp dwelt; also, as a dispenser of women's clothes, she can "transform" his sex.

As in the Riffe article, however, fear of sexual impotence is related to fear of artistic impotence. Bergman's own interpretation was that it dramatized a wish for freedom from the authority of the studio, his wife, and his mother, but this does not go far enough. More than "freedom of action," "freedom from authority" implies potency, and the Sånell figure in the dream, whom he identifies as the studio, more forcefully suggests his product for the studio. At this level, the dream reflects his sense of artistic failure. Confinement in the cell corresponds to his practice of completely isolating himself in a room for long periods while writing his scripts, but, in recalling the underlying meaning of that inaugural work, *Prison*, it also indicates the Oedipal problems that have "imprisoned" his imagination; significantly, the three jailers, who associate the constraining of imagination with the problematical linkage of wife and mother, are all women. (Note, too, that the women *resemble*, but are not identical with, Käbi, Karin, and Bertha Sånell—just as fictive characters are altered representations of real life.) The prospect of release from this prison equates to the artistic "resurrection" Bergman hoped to achieve. The more telling symbol of the dreamer's yearning, however, is the tantalizing fountain in the corridor which the jailers keep the prisoner from reaching. Rather obviously, its easy, constant, clear flow contrasts with the embottled nature of Bergman's work, but the fact that there is one word for "fountain" and "spring" in Swedish *(källa)* points to a further meaning: the absolution figured in the flow of water toward Ingeri at the conclusion of *The Virgin Spring*.

Both levels of the dream's meaning coalesce in the prisoner's silence at its culmination. Unmistakably, this scene refers to his ritualized child-hood punishment in which, according to his account, silence played a major role—first as his response to his father's accusation; then, after he had confessed and received a beating, as an extension of his parents' discipline. Given the father's role as castigator and the embrace of for-giveness by the mother which ended the ritual, that the child would confuse his offense with his sexually inspired feelings toward his par-ents was understandable, especially since he often did not know what specific sin he had committed to incur their displeasure. In the dream, this combination of innocence and guilt is quite emphatic: he has been imprisoned for his "idealism" (which also implies sexual repression), yet, when the women confront him, his defiant silence clearly bespeaks his guilt. In addition, the boast to use silence as a means of vanquishing them plainly represents an inversion of the powerless child's role in the parsonage drama of humiliation.

Some time after relating his dreams to Sjöman, Bergman described the horror he felt over the methodical nature of the punishment ritual and the emotional detachment with which it was administered. Obliquely acknowledging its psychosexual impact, he told Sjöman, "It's a wonder that I didn't turn out a homosexual or a masochist"; then, reflecting on the interval of absolute silence between the physical punishment and the obligatory begging of parental forgiveness, he added, "That, that was truly God's silence."[8] Sjöman duly noted in the diary that this was Bergman's first use of the phrase that would become the trilogy's title. In a sense, all three films are set in that interval of overwhelming anxiety: each represents Bergman's struggle as a son to discover and affirm his own identity.

What the dreams express, and what Bergman was attempting to do by analyzing them, is essentially reflected by *The Silence of God*. With the possible exception of *The City*, none of his previous works had been quite so radically motivated by self-examination (one is struck by the appropriateness of the allusion to a mirror in the title of the film that begins the trilogy); none had a greater effect on the filmmaker's relationship to his work. From 1956 through 1960, three characters named Karin had signified a buried agenda; with a fourth Karin in *Through a Glass Darkly*, incest is released from his psychic prison, and a new ease and spareness in Bergman's treatment of profoundly personal material immediately becomes evident. In factoring a complex psychological equation, Bergman finally developed a lucid, completely integrated dramatic statement; the internal contradictions and the imposed, false resolutions that had marred such films as *The Seventh Seal*, *Wild Strawberries*, and *The Virgin Spring* suddenly vanish from his scripts.

Through a Glass Darkly

Having, like Vogler, come to mistrust his craft because of its temptation to engage in "trickery," Bergman began working on his new film by thinking of it not as cinema but as a three-act play: "I felt it was important to put aside all artificial devices and just concentrate on the human drama. Thus, it became . . . a veiled stage play with distinct scenes laid side by side."[1] Arranged within each act like mirror panels, these scenes reflect the same image from different angles. Accordingly, I Corinthians 13, which supplied the film's title—"For now we see through a glass, darkly; but then face to face; now I know in part; but then I shall know even as I am known"— not only points toward the faith, hope, and love at the end of the passage as the film's theme but also implies its structure. In the course of twenty-four hours, the characters progress from self-delusion to self-recognition, a process in which each character first sees himself as he is seen by others and then sees in others a mirror of himself.*

Act I introduces the failure of love. The opening image of a happy family, swimming and joking together at their island summer cottage, dissolves as quickly as their reflections on the water. David, a famous novelist who has just returned from one of his long trips abroad, passes

---

*The Swedish title, *Såsom i en spegel*—literally, *As in a Mirror*—connotes this more clearly than the English translation which, by picking up the word "darkly" from the King James phrasing, tends to mislead.

David (Gunnar Björnstrand) works on his manuscript in the dim light of midsummer. Permission from Svenska Filmindustri.

out gifts to appease his bad conscience, but their inappropriateness proves he has given no thought to their selection. For all his show of affection, he is unwilling to accept his obligations at home—as his announcement that he will soon go abroad again with a cultural delegation attests. The illusion of family solidarity is briefly restored when Minus, his sister Karin, and her husband Martin mount a makeshift stage to perform a play the boy has written for his father, but David quickly understands that the play is a mirror of his insincerity.

As the family withdraws for the night, they also withdraw into themselves. Karin coldly shuns her husband's erotic overtures; then, as dawn ends the short Swedish summer night, she steals upstairs to an empty room and masturbates. Here the camera cuts from her hands rising up her thighs to David's hands turning the pages of his manuscript —suggesting the equation of her autoeroticism to his isolating himself in "the wandering sentences, the hateful words, the situational banalities, and the uni-dimensional poverty of his characters." Shortly thereafter, this mirroring relationship between father and daughter assumes a second, ghastly aspect when she reads in his notebook (figuratively, his mirror—which becomes hers): "Her illness is hopeless. . . . To my horror, I note my own curiosity. The impulse to register its course, to note concisely her gradual dissolution. To make use of her." Frightened as much by her father's exploitation of her struggle against insanity as by the diagnosis itself, she runs to her husband for reassurance. But—in another manifestation of Bergman's mirror technique—Martin (who is approximately her father's age) only reflects David's egocentricity. When she pleads, "Anyone who really loves always does right by the person he loves," he turns the plea back on herself to reproach her for denying him his conjugal rights.

Throughout Act I, the sound of a brewing storm accompanies each moment showing the hypocrisy behind the avowals of love: stage thunder accentuates the climax of Minus's play, and the distant rumble of the real thing punctuates each of the film's first three scenes. Corresponding to the storm, the pressures of emotional turbulence within the characters are building. When Karin lures her brother to the upstairs room at the start of Act II, an explosion seems imminent. In the musty stillness, she reveals her secret: "One day someone called to me from behind the wallpaper. . . . The voice went on calling me, so I pressed myself against the wall and it opened up like a lot of leaves *and I was there inside!* . . . I believe God is going to reveal himself to us. And he'll come in to us through that door. Everyone's so calm—and so gentle. And they're waiting. And their love. LOVE." Though shaken by the sudden realization that his sister is insane, Minus loyally promises not to "betray" her to the others.

As with the masturbation scene in Act I, Karin's escape into fantasy is followed by demonstrations of David's and Martin's insufficient love for her. Seated face to face in a rowboat, Martin accuses David of trying to fill his emptiness with Karin's extinction; David intuits that his son-in-law has selfishly wished his wife's death. Each recognizes himself in the other. When the father speaks of deceiving oneself with belief in good intentions, of the importance of going through the correct motions because "activity stimulates self-confidence and hinders reflection," the husband, acknowledging that these are indeed his thoughts, assumes he is being reproached. But David insists that the criticism was really directed against himself—or, rather, against the man he has been.

Just recently, he explains, he tried to commit suicide, but the car in which he intended to plunge to his death stalled with two wheels over the edge of the cliff; at that moment, a love for his family was conceived. Here again, the film's dramatic structure shows a parallel between father and daughter. In his automobile's tottering above the void, David has perceived a symbol of his existence, suspended over the emptiness created by his refusal to love. Karin has become aware of a similar emptiness—caused, in her case, by lack of love. Both now await a kind of rebirth—and with the torrential downpour that marks the start of the third scene of Act II, these new "selves" begin to emerge. In a sense, the storm corresponds to the rupture of the amnion which initiates the painful birth process.

Worried when Karin fails to answer his calls, Minus runs to the wreck of an old schooner, where he finds her lying in the hull. She appears to be unconscious, but as he kneels beside her, she claps him in a sudden, passionate embrace. The next scene leaves no doubt that incest has occurred: frightened and horrified, Minus confesses to his father and leads him to Karin. The David who now accepts responsibility for the guilt his children will bear and asks his daughter's forgiveness is no longer the remote, self-centered figure he had seemed only a few hours earlier. For Karin, however, his loving concern has come too late.* Rather than try to go on "living in two worlds," she says, she has decided to surrender to her illness.

As Act III begins, a helicopter ambulance has been summoned, and Karin is packing her clothes. Although at first she seems placidly resigned to spending the rest of her life in a mental hospital, after a few minutes she enters the wallpapered room to pray for God to show himself—and when vibrations from the arriving helicopter cause the wallpapered door to open, she believes her prayer is being answered. Suddenly, however, anticipation of joy gives way to a frenzied defense of her body—as though she were being sexually attacked. Once she has been sedated, she explains that God did indeed appear to her, but instead of being the God of love she expected, he was an ugly spider.

In the wake of Karin's departure, a perplexed Minus tests the new relationship with his father. The psychological burden of incest and the shock of his sister's mental collapse have robbed him of belief in God, yet he is unable "to live with this new thing" without evidence of some guiding value to life. Against the absence of faith and the confounding of hope, David offers love. God, he proposes, is neither an invisible potentate in the distant dark nor Karin's spider-God: "God is love and love is

---

*David's penitence is made more explicit in the script: there, he retreats to his study, weighs his manuscript as if to calculate what his pursuit of fame has cost, and then feeds the pages into the stove.

In recognizing the error of sacrificing his familial obligations in order to pursue egotistical ends, this David is not unlike David Erneman in *A Lesson in Love* (especially in regard to his daughter Nix) and Stig Eriksson in *To Joy*.

God"—the two concepts "are one and the same phenomenon." What makes belief tenable for Minus is not the formulation itself but David's manifestation of the love he preaches. The two characters who have been furthest apart in understanding have now met "face to face"; astonished and uplifted, as though visited by divine revelation, Minus says, "Papa spoke to me."

In the controlled power of its dialogue, the economy of its plot, the formal balance and interrelationship of its constituent parts, and the density of thematic suggestion, *Through a Glass Darkly* attests Bergman's recovery from his disorientation of the late 'fifties; with the possible exception of *Evening of the Jesters*, no script he wrote before 1960 better displays his skill as a dramatist. As a realized film, too, it attains a new level of excellence: Gunnar Björnstrand, Harriet Andersson, Lars Passgård, and Max von Sydow give perfect performances; Sven Nykvist's cinematography is flawless; and the director's use of natural sounds to imply the dimensions of the silence the characters inhabit (the cello music after the incest is the sole non-naturalistic intrusion) demonstrates an unusual appreciation of cinema's synaesthetic possibilities.

Yet, even while recognizing these merits, critics tend to consign the film to the second rank, generally citing the ending as their reason. To be sure, the closing scene is relatively weak: the reactions to losing a daughter and sister to madness are too calmly composed, and the benediction equating love to God seems pale beside the dark hues of the drama's contents; furthermore, the rapid shift of emotional concentration from Karin in the preceding scene to Minus in the final minutes creates the impression of a rush to conclusion. These are not the arguments the critics raise, however. Ironically, Bergman had repeatedly resorted to sleight of hand to conceal flaws in the conclusions of his 'fifties films without anyone being the least disturbed—or even noticing. But in *Through a Glass Darkly*, where, though imperfectly executed, the ending is not only consistent with the thematic structure but also its necessary complement, it is criticized for being artificial and "arbitrary."[2]

Underlying this misjudgment is the assumption that the film is Karin's story; given that premise, it is reasonable to state—as does one critic —that Minus, "a mere shadowy presence," is a distraction, or even that "Bergman's great error . . . was to make Karin insane" since her vision of reality is the director's own.[3] But Karin's slide into insanity is central only in the respect that it forces her father, husband, and brother to confront themselves; their experiences, not her illness, shape the film. (Bergman's account of how he wrote *Through a Glass Darkly* underscores the point: it was a relatively easy task, he said, to create three male characters who are self-portraits and then have them reveal themselves by their reactions to a horrifying situation.)[4]

As the son in this reworking of Bergman's recurrent family dama, Minus is the pivotal figure: it is his consciousness that organizes the film. And the key to Minus lies in his play, which, like similar interpolated material in previous Bergman films, stands as an emblem for the entire work.* Set in Saint Teresa's Chapel (possibly representing the "interior castle," Teresa's metaphor for the soul), it features two characters: the Princess of Castile (acted by Karin), who has been deserted by her husband, and her suitor, the Artist (Minus). When the Princess, asking for proof of his devotion, invites him to follow her "into the realm of death," the Artist readily agrees: "I am standing on the threshold of an

---

*While Bergman was writing *Through a Glass Darkly*, he was also preparing *The Sea Gull* for Dramaten. Chekhov's imprint is unmistakable, not only in the general composition of the film as drama but also in one particular detail: the circumstances in which Minus's "tragedy" is performed for his father virtually replicate those of Konstantin's staging his ludicrously bad play. In one instance, the young playwright is bidding for his neglectful, famous father's attention; in the other, for the mother's. Just such borrowings had led to the criticism printed in *Chaplin* that Bergman was "unoriginal," yet, here as elsewhere, what he borrowed had deeply personal resonances. Through Minus, an adolescent playwright who boasts of having written a slew of plays in a summer, Bergman was certainly remembering his own prodigious output of eight plays (including *The Death of Punch* and *Tivoli*) in 1942.

Bergman's debts for various other elements of *Through a Glass Darkly* have also been cited. Eleonora in Strindberg's *Easter* could serve as a model for Karin (both women totter between madness and sanity after returning from a mental asylum). And several critics have proposed the wallpapered door in *The Ghost Sonata* as the basis for Karin's mad belief that she can enter a spirit world through her room's wallpaper—though Swedish film scholar Torsten Jungstedt insists on another source: Charlotte Perkins Gilman's "The Yellow Wall-Paper," a short story about a doctor's mentally ill young wife who passes back and forth through the "florid arabesques" that decorate her prisonlike room. (Jungstedt, who had compiled an anthology of Gothic tales which included a translation of this nineteenth-century American story, claims that, after he personally brought it to Bergman's attention, the filmmaker used it as the basis for *The Wallpaper*. Scheduled to be SF's first color film, *The Wallpaper* was aborted soon after Bergman shot tests for it.)

Bergman gives a different accounting for these same elements, however. According to him, the model for Karin was a woman he lived with in his youth who suffered from spells in which she received instructions from voices;[5] his interest in making a film about a schizophrenic can be dated to an interview at the time *Crisis* was about to have its premiere. The idea of a spirit world beyond a wallpapered wall is almost as old: in a scene written for *Prison* (but never filmed because of technical problems and a tight shooting schedule), Birgitta-Carolina, beckoned into an artist's room after sleeping with a poet, hears whispering from the tormented, laughing faces behind the wallpaper. That scene, in turn, may have derived from his memory of the parsonage nursery, where designs on the window shade assumed grotesque shapes at night and made horrifying sounds.

ultimate consummation! I tremble with excitement. Oblivion shall possess me and only death shall love me. So—I go. Nothing can restrain me." But, at the decisive moment, he changes his mind. To sacrifice his life, he says, would be insane, and besides, he is having stomach trouble and it would be improper to enter eternity with diarrhea. The final rationalization, however, is his obligation to art: "I could write a poem about my meeting with the princess. Or paint a picture, or compose an opera—though the end, of course, must be given a more heroic twist. Let me see: 'Oblivion shall claim me and only death shall love me.' That's not bad." Satisfied with himself, he goes home to sleep.

Minus has written "The Artistic Haunting; or, The Funeral Vault of Illusions" as a "morality play, intended only for poets and authors"; underlying its Gothic nonsense is the boy's attempt to open his father's eyes to the truth (significantly, the performance begins with the removal of a blindfold put on David as he entered the "theater.") The Artist's trite sententiousness reflects the fact that David, despite his fame, has never been more than a second-rate writer who lacks the genius to be original; still worse, the Artist's use of art to rationalize the falseness of his love points to David's use of his literary career to excuse his abandoning Karin—just as, many years earlier, he had abandoned his dying, schizophrenic wife to write his first successful novel.

But the Artist is not only a parodic version of the father; he is also Minus himself, grappling with the conflicting emotions aroused by his sister. Karin—the Princess forsaken by a husband whose "thoughts have turned to other women"—feels betrayed by the two most important men in her life. David, frightened by his daughter's needs, has turned away from her (and compounded the rejection by chasing a succession of mistresses).* Evidently, in marrying a man her father's age, she sought a substitute for him, but Martin, too, has failed her. (At one point, she dares him to deny that he wishes he were free of his sick wife and wedded instead to a matronly, simple woman who would bear his children and serve him coffee in bed.) Thus, when the Artist at first assures the Princess that his love, unlike her husband's, will be constant, it is quite obvious that this is Minus pledging loyalty to his sister.

As her flirtatious teasing about his interest in pictures of nude women suggests, however, Minus's feelings toward Karin involve more than fraternal love—and, in terms of Bergman's imagination, imply an enormity

---

*The similarity between this David and David Erneman in *A Lesson in Love*—and between Karin and Nix—is not coincidental. The fact that the same pairs of actors appear in these roles points to the common psychological elements in the two stories.

beyond even that of sibling incest. Given that Karin's husband represents a doubling of her father (who, of course, is also Minus's father), "sister" becomes virtually interchangeable with "mother"; hence, the thought of sexual intercourse with Karin also carries with it the greater burden of Oedipal guilt.* Furthermore, consummation of his dangerous desires would deepen the estrangement from the father from whom he craves approval and affection. All these factors bear on the Artist's reneging on his vow to the Princess at the play's conclusion. Most immediately, it expresses Minus's psychological need to void the charge of incest, but, by symbolically reenacting David's abandonment of Karin and his wife, it also manifests one of the film's central motifs: the son's effort to create a bond with his father.

The next day, Minus confronts the same choice faced by his persona on stage. When Karin reveals her insanity by telling him of her intention to pass through the wallpaper and leave reality behind, she is in effect posing the same test of love as the Princess when she asks her suitor to walk with her through the door leading into the realm of the dead. But unlike the Artist, who refuses to sacrifice himself, Minus soon risks everything. Committing incest is a step into an insane unreality, a kind of spiritual death. Yet taking that step because of love for his sister will lead Minus to a new, redeeming perception of life. And, ironically, instead of destroying the possibility of winning his father's love, the incest will result in its expression.

Immediately after the act, however, Minus is too overwhelmed to understand its implications. As Bergman's description in the filmscript metaphorically suggests, he is like a baby who has just experienced the trauma of birth:

> Minus is sitting somewhere in eternity with his sick sister in his arms. He is empty, exhausted, frozen. Reality, as he has known it until now, has been shattered, ceased to exist. Neither in his dreams nor in his fantasies has he known anything to correspond to this moment of weightlessness and grief. His mind has forced its way through the membrane of merciful ignorance. From this moment on his senses will change and harden, his receptivity will become sharpened, as he goes from the make-believe world of innocence to the torment of insight.

*The equation of sister to mother is reinforced not only by Bergman's use of his mother's name for Karin but also by his making Karin and *her* mother virtual doubles (both are schizophrenics; both have been shunned in the same way and for the same reasons by David).

This "newborn" is, of course, an adult Minus, and although it is the incest that finally expels him into a world of terrible knowledge, his passage toward a new self is already evident at the film's beginning. The previous summer his agility made walking on his hands easy; now, he says, "I've grown so tall I can't keep my balance any more."* This adolescent physical awkwardness accompanies a loss of psychological equilibrium as consciousness of sex causes his "make-believe world of innocence" to disintegrate. Everyone except himself seems in on some secret joke; women, he complains, "smell and stick out their stomachs and make special sorts of movements and comb their hair and gossip —till you feel like a skinned rabbit." Worse than this insecurity is a new sense of sin—especially in regard to his sister. In an early scene, he watches as she unselfconsciously towels her naked body; as soon as she nods to him, he skitters away guiltily through the bushes. When they next meet, an overturned milk jug is nearby—a symbol of lost innocence that recurs minutes later. Minus holds the jug, now filled with milk, while he talks to his sister; when she snuggles up to him, "as to a baby," he spills the milk. That he reacts by saying, "Think, if just once in my life I could talk to Papa" is significant: the spilling of the milk foreshadows the incest, which then becomes, at the film's end, the basis for communication between father and son.

Unlike the Artist (and unlike David, that other artist who has used his writing to escape from Karin's sickness), Minus has met terror with love, but he is too shamed by his sin to understand the redemptive power of this response until it is explained to him by his father. David, who has himself had a "rebirth" after his suicide attempt failed, speaks of "*every sort of love*" as evincing God's presence: "The highest and the lowest, the poorest and the richest, the most ridiculous and the most sublime. The obsessive and the banal." Like the Knight in *The Seventh Seal*, he has discovered a basis for faith and hope in the one "meaningful act" of love. "Suddenly the emptiness turns into wealth, and hopelessness into life," he tells his son. "It's like a pardon, Minus. From sentence of death." There is, of course, an implicitly Christian message here. In the fact that "Papa *spoke* to me," Minus finds absolution; having "regained" the father he thought had abandoned him, he has also regained a sustaining belief in God. The selfless act in the wreck, not the selfish rejection of the Princess in the play, has proved to be "The Funeral Vault of Illusions," and out of it has come a kind of resurrection.

---

*In the script, Minus is fifteen, but Bergman aged him two years in the film.

Karin's role in the film, however, extends well beyond serving as the instrument through which Minus "finds" his father and completes a rite of passage. If her brother is the protagonist who emerges from emptiness and hopelessness, she is, in the strictest sense of the term, the antagonist whose retreat represents the counter-motion against which he strives.

Adulthood frightens Karin no less than it does Minus, and her actions plainly indicate a desire to regress to her younger self. When she visits David in his workroom, she sits on his knee, and when he tucks her into bed as though she were a child being comforted after awakening from a nightmare, she says with satisfaction, "Just like when I was little." But the key in her wish to regress is her schizophrenia. She evidently recognizes the connection: noticing that David and Martin persist in calling her "Kajsa," her nickname as a girl, she asks, "Am I so little or is it that my illness has turned me into a child?" More revealing still, she uses her illness to explain the loss of sexual desire for her husband; insanity, she later implies, offers a way of recapturing innocence: "I must choose between [Martin] and the other thing. And I've decided. I've given up Martin." Significantly, the wallpapered room into which she withdraws had apparently been her nursery.

Karin compares her "real" existence to being "exposed in the desert at night"; among the fantasied animals who stalk her in that desert, the worst is the wolf, Bergman's symbol of degeneracy and death. Other images of death also threaten her. At the film's beginning, she hears a cuckoo (the same bird that presaged death in *Summergame*); as tensions intensify, the cuckoo's cries become shriller and more numerous. The house that symbolically contains her life is described as "dying" in the filmscript, and a grandfather clock prominently situated in its central hall measures time's erosion. Similarly, the waves' metronomic action is tearing apart the wreck in which she takes refuge from the storm.

In contrast to Minus, reborn when "his mind has forced its way through the membrane of merciful ignorance," Karin tries to force her way in the opposite direction through the nursery's membranelike wallpaper. On its outer aspect, time is turning its pattern of green leaves sere, and death, figured as a phantasmagoric "laughing moon-face with one dud eye, a gaping mouth and a huge potato nose," leers at her, but beyond this terrifying surface she imagines a "still and silent" universe of timeless innocence that suggests the womb. A slit in the wallpaper resembles a vagina, and when Karin describes her movement from reality to her world of voices, her language unmistakably implies a reversal of birth: "I pressed myself against the wall and it opened up like a lot of leaves and *there I was inside!*"

As Bergman's comments in the script indicate, these regression fantasies are linked to the incest. Just before Karin masturbates, the light reflected onto the wallpaper from the sea creates an erotic image of "small flames . . . in the heavy petals"; simultaneously, "a convulsive puff of wind comes from the sea [causing] the house [to] sigh like an old ship." If, like her madness, her autoeroticism represents a narcissistic withdrawal from reality, what happens in the schooner goes a step beyond to the extreme of negating being itself. In a sense, given the parallel identities of Karin and her mother in this dreamlike film and the implicit role of Minus (who also mirrors David in other respects) as substitute for the father in her Oedipal fantasies, the incest symbolically reenacts her conception, the zero hour of her life. Her first words after copulating with her brother reinforce the suggestion. "What's the time?" she asks Martin; ten lines later, as though she has been incapable of grasping the answer, she repeats the same question to her father.

The incest that leads Minus to the courage to accept life through a new vision of his father and the revelation of God as love has entirely the opposite implications for Karin, however. By retreating into herself, she is following the same course as the "old" David who isolated himself from his family; consequently, the "God" she meets in her last visit to the nursery is the apotheosis of that father's emptiness. As Karin waits for her God of love to appear through the half-open closet door, David, whose failure to love has stimulated the religious fantasy, stands in the room's doorway. The parallel's meaning is unmistakable.

Although the spider-God who observes the exertions of those caught in his universal web is one of Bergman's earliest conceits, nowhere is its symbolization of the father quite so patent as here. The monstrous "deity" who emerges climbs her thighs and tries to force his way inside her clearly alludes to the incest (in which she had made Minus the substitute for her father), but the spider's effort to penetrate her and suck her being into itself for nourishment is also a nightmare version of the cold author recording his study of his daughter in his notebook. To avoid the "rape," Karin presses against the wallpaper, hoping for sanctuary among the "feminine" spirits; when she realizes it will not admit her, she tries to wriggle free from the "spider"—i.e., David, who pins her down, and Martin, who, much like a spider paralyzing its victim, finally sedates her by inserting a hypodermic needle into her thigh. Once her "convulsive jerks" subside (another suggestion of the incest), the helicopter, "a gigantic dark insect" dangling from the sky, takes her to a hospital on the mainland where she will presumably spend the rest of her life. Thus, ironically, in this failure of love she attains the "nothingness" she has sought in her regression.

In several respects, *Through a Glass Darkly* is a pivotal film. Resumption of the collaboration with Sven Nykvist introduced a new cinematographic style that would become a distinctive feature of Bergman's films from this point on. Spare, highly disciplined, and marked by minimal camera movement, it was the visual complement to Bergman's attempt at transposing the principles of chamber music and the chamber play to cinema. Also, this was the first of his films to be shot on Fårö—that remote, bleak island where he would settle five years later and where, from *Persona* through the end of the decade, all his films would be set. Its register on his work was not just a matter of scenery. Bergman had been attracted to island settings ever since the 'forties (vide *Rakel and the Cinema Doorman* and *Kamma Noll*), but after his discovery of Fårö, the island reflects a state of mind and takes on metaphysical implications; even *The Communicants* and *The Silence*, where no physical island occurs, portray characters in figuratively insular settings. The most important evidence of change, however, rests in the shifting values assigned to those recurring, underlying metaphors that have shaped meaning and form.

In general, Bergman's fictions had previously traveled along an axis with the Cross at one pole, signifying the tragic realization of abandonment by God the Father, and the womb at the other as a symbol of maternal love, illusion, and release from pain. But here the father, after having abandoned his children, undergoes a conversion, teaches the power of love, and gives his son courage to meet his future, while the mother (in the figure of Karin) is associated with a resignation from life that, for the first time, is tantamount to death. Regression to the womb, which had represented a dream of refuge, now represents a dangerous delusion, a surrender to the spider-God. Similarly, the notion of salvation through the ideal of woman as Virgin is set aside. Before the incest, Minus condemns women for their sexuality—and himself for being aroused by it—but at the conclusion, he begins to accept sex as an essential human expression. In a sense, in having committed the gravest of sexual sins, he has met the most terrible thing in himself, and through that confrontation, broken its power over him. Besides whatever else the filmmaker sought to depict by contraposing Karin and Minus, she encapsulates an attitude toward life he was trying to discard, while her -

brother, who comes closest to being a self-portrait, represents Bergman's determination to put his guilt behind him. "When I was younger,
I had illusions about how things should be," he said on completing
the trilogy. "Now I see things as they are. No longer any questions of
'God, why?' or 'Mother, why?' One has to settle for suicide or acceptance.
Either destroy oneself (which is romantic) or accept life. I choose now
to accept it."[6]

But it is not only because of what it initiates that *Through a Glass
Darkly* marks a turning point; equally important, it is the last of his films
to employ a "closed" structure of meaning. *Certainty Achieved*, the subtitle it acquired when Bergman assembled the trilogy, refers as much to
certainty as a component of form as to the certainty that is revealed by
the content. From the very beginning, Bergman had regarded dramatic
conflict as a means of solving riddles: more than completing the film's
design, a conclusion had to answer a question that stood for life's dis-
maying complexity. *Through a Glass Darkly* holds to the same concep-
tual pattern. Minus's final utterance, "Papa spoke to me," is analogous to
Stig's playing the "Ode to Joy" for his son at the end of *To Joy*, the
close-up of Mikael in *The Seventh Seal*, Isak's vision of his parents in
Wild Strawberries, Töre's uplifted hands and Ingeri's absolution in *The
Virgin Spring*. But during the course of filming *Through a Glass Darkly*,
Bergman came to reject this kind of schematization as false and
presumptuous; using a dramatic fiction to establish grounds for belief,
he now realized, had been an expression of his insecurity, an extension
of his need for certainty that was not a legitimate artistic concern, a
"fierce effort of will" that sent him "groping backwards into the bourgeois world I'd grown up in and which I'd been trying to recreate."[7]
Although he chose not to tamper with the ending during production
for fear that the unity of the original script would be destroyed, he
was already thinking about a different kind of film. *Through a Glass
Darkly* had been a major breakthrough, but it was still, he said, the
product of

> an inclination to fly from reality and a great self-deception . . . , a
> kind of desperation for security, an attempt to present a solution, a
> kind of weariness with approaching the real question and, instead
> of giving an answer, continuing to pose the question — like a circus
> artist who goes through the preparations for a *salto mortale* and
> then makes an ironic sign of the cross and climbs down without
> having performed the death leap.[8]

Philosophically, he would finally make that "death leap" in *Persona*, but already in *The Communicants* and *The Silence* (subsequently subtitled *Certainty Unmasked* and *God's Silence—The Negative Print*), the dramatic equation omits belief in "solutions."

The Communicants

During the year after the shooting for *Through a Glass Darkly* had ended, Bergman conceived at least three separate ideas for his next script. His much-acclaimed staging of Stravinsky's *The Rake's Progress* at the Royal Opera in the early spring of 1961 apparently inspired the notion of a film, set in Sweden during the same period, about an aristocrat who "cannot accept love": after spending his lust with a succession of women, the rake would realize how helplessly dependent he was on his wife's devotion and return to her. Although Bergman quickly tired of the story—he had, he said, already written it too many times before—the next idea he took up, based on the *mariage devant Dieu seul* between the eighteenth-century Swedish artist J. T. Sergel and his Anna-Rella, dealt with a similar struggle between flesh and soul.[1] But interest in this second possibility proved equally ephemeral. Given the course of uncompromising self-examination on which Bergman had recently embarked, it seems unlikely that thoughts of dressing his fictive self in a powered wig for a costume film were ever more than a playful recreation. Furthermore, the retreat to feminine solace with which both stories were to end represented the same dangerous illusion he had just sought to dispel.

Even so, the psychological confusion of mother, wife, and mistress discernible behind these aborted scripts recurred in a third outline, about a minister who has lost his faith. As the film was originally conceived, the minister's wife was to be the instrument for resolving the crisis, but after almost four frustrating months in which the character thwarted the story's development, Bergman replaced her with a mistress. The block to his creativity suddenly gave way. Yet this wife had been too closely tied to the initial idea to disappear. Four years dead in the new draft, she lingers in the minister's mind as a saintly image more suggestive of a maternal spirit than of a corporeal wife.

But, just as in *Through a Glass Darkly*, if the psychological energy in *The Communicants* derives from a conflicted response to women traceable to the author's mother; its motive reflects desire for reconciliation with the father. Bergman has said the germ of the story came to him while listening to Stravinsky's *Symphony of Psalms*: "A minister locks himself in his church. And says to God: 'Now I shall wait here until you reveal yourself. Take as much time as you want.'"[2] That the idea arose at Eastertime is significant, for, in a figurative sense, the film is set in the interval between Good Friday and Easter—or, in Bergman's sense of the Christian myth, between God the Father's abandonment of his son on the Cross and the resurrecting proof of his love. But, even apart from these overtones, Bergman's minister obviously represented an attempt to see the world through his father's eyes. Before beginning to write, he asked Erik Bergman to join him on a tour of Uppland churches. This re-creation of the parish rounds the son remembered from childhood disclosed nothing unexpected: "spiritual misery, the lack of public interest, the ministers' lamentable spiritual state, the sermons' meagerness, the sloppiness and nonchalance of the ritual."[3] The object of Bergman's study, however, was not the decay in contemporary Sweden's established church; rather, it was the reactions of a man confronting the apparent futility of his life's work.

From the start, Bergman had wanted to smash the "security-God" raised in the "coda" of *Through a Glass Darkly*, but he was still groping for a suitable conclusion when one of the day-trips to the countryside supplied the answer. As father and son sat in a church, empty except for a few old women, the local minister stated that illness forced him to abbreviate the service by omitting the liturgy. Erik Bergman rose from his seat and marched into the sacristy. After a few minutes, the warden called new instructions to the organist and announced there would be a complete service after all—the Royal Chaplain would perform the liturgy. The moral the son drew—"that, whatever happens, one should do one's duty, especially in spiritual matters, even if it might seem meaningless"—was exactly the ending he was seeking.[4] Although Bergman had never before discussed his films with his father prior to their release, this time he made a point of showing him the manuscript. "The old man has read [it] *three* times," he proudly told his colleagues on the set. "Can you imagine that? And he understands the ending precisely right."[5] In a sense, *The Communicants* corresponds in its purpose to "The Artistic Haunting": what Erik Bergman was meant to understand was that his son understood him—and was appealing to be understood in turn.

As the name "Tomas Eriksson" indicates, however, the crisis of the

Suffering from fever and loss of faith, Tomas (Gunnar Björnstrand) rests after the mass in Mittsunda while the verger (Kolbjörn Knudsen) counts the meager collection. Permission from Svenska Filmindustri.

fictional minister beset by despair is fundamentally not that of the father but of the son: underlying God's silence is the remoteness of Tomas's father (and of Erik Bergman). At one point in the script, when the ache of his spiritual emptiness is especially acute, he speaks of awakening with terror one night in his boyhood:

> I got out of bed, ran round all the rooms looking for Father. But the house was empty. I shouted and screamed, but no one answered. So I dressed as well as I could and ran down to the shore, all the time screaming and crying for Father.* I'd been left without Father and Mother in a completely dead world. I was sick with terror. Father sat up and watched over me all night. Father and Mother wanted me to become a minister—and I did as they wished.

Elsewhere, he intimates that he had entered the priesthood not only to settle a doubt as to whether he truly loved his parents but also to find a God who would fill the need his father had failed to meet:

> Please you *must* understand. I'm no good as a clergyman. I chose my calling because my mother and father were religious, pious, in a

---

*Cf. the final vision in *Wild Strawberries*, in which Isak rushes to the shore crying after his father.

deep, natural way. Maybe I didn't really love them, but I wanted to please them. So I became a clergyman and believed in God. An improbable, entirely private, fatherly god. Who loved mankind, of course, but most of all me. A god who guaranteed me every imaginable security. Against fear of death. Against fear of life. A god I'd suggested myself into believing in, a god I'd borrowed from various quarters, fabricated with my own hands.

As a result of yearning for a God who would supply a father's love, Tomas has brooded a sibling rivalry toward Jesus—a rivalry that Bergman admits he felt as a boy while accompanying his father on his circuit of Uppland churches.

This minister has a hatred of Christ which he will not admit to anyone. He is envious of Christ. Yes, and jealous, He feels something like the hate the son who stayed at home felt towards the prodigal son, the one who gets all the attention when he finally comes home: the fatted calf, etc. I decided, quite simply, that I would confess my own envy and jealousy of the Christ-image.[6]

Paradoxically, in the service of a Jesus he jealously hates, Tomas reenacts Christ's suffering. More explicitly than any of Bergman's previous films, *The Communicants* is a Passion play—according to his own description, a journey between two stations of the Cross.

The first quarter hour of the film consists of Tomas's officiating at a mass in a small, medieval country church.* Just seven people have turned out for the service. Four incidental characters represent the usual attendance: a mother who responds perfunctorily while her bored little girl falls asleep; an elderly gentleman given to loud singing as a show of piety; an old woman who seems a relic from an earlier century. The other three are there for special reasons: Märta Lundberg, the homely schoolteacher Tomas has taken as a mistress, is grasping for some way to change her lover's heart; Jonas Persson and his pregnant wife Karin have come because of her hope that pastoral counsel may alleviate her husband's despondency. As the camera moves down the row of those receiving communion, the miracle of Christ's Real Pres-

---

*Bergman originally conceived of the whole film as being played in front of the altar—like an early church drama. Even after the story assumed its final form, he planned to begin by presenting the mass in its entirety, but when he started shooting, he realized this would unbalance the film. Pared down to the communion, however, the mass still functions as a prelude—a play-before-the-play that encapsulates the meaning of what will follow.

ence at the Last Supper appears very distant from their lives—and furthest of all from the priest.

The first words Tomas recites, "Our Lord Jesus Christ in the night when he was betrayed . . . ," point to his own "crucifixion" by life—as do repeated shots of the altarpiece (sculpted to Bergman's precise specifi- cations), which shows Christ nailed to a Cross suspended between the knees of God the Father. His head aches and he is running a fever; more than his body, however, it is his spirit that is being scourged. In this desolate Dalarna parish of Mittsunda (i.e., "middle strait"), the middle- aged minister sees a mirror of the blight that has afflicted him ever since the death of his wife robbed him of illusions and left him without ambitions. At the conclusion of the mass, he feels mocked by the collec- tion spread on the vestry table that amounts to less than a dollar; the frugal meal he makes of biscuits and coffee nourishes his body as poorly as the bread and wine of the Eucharist sustain his soul.

Although, as is underscored by the repeated shots of the crucifix on the vestry wall, the film's central irony rests in Tomas's Christ- like suffering, its construction relates to the priest's role as a descen- dant of the apostles. Tomas represents not only the doubting disciple Thomas but also Peter, who thrice denied his master on the eve of the Crucifixion. The first person to approach the minister in the vestry is the sexton, Algot Frövik. Afflicted with a painful disease that, as though it were a cross he carries, has humped his back, Frövik wants to ask about faith, but before he can pose the question, Tomas wearily puts him off. Next, the Perssons enter. Jonas, his wife explains, has read that the Chinese, "brought up to hate," would soon have atomic bombs; since then, this pensive man who divides his time between fishing and carpentry has been convinced that there is no purpose in continuing to live. When Karin pleads for a word of hope that might counteract his sense of futility, Tomas advises "trust in God"; then, seeing the meaninglessness of such hypocritical cant reflected in Jonas's expression, he stalls for time to think of a better answer by making his parishioner promise to return in half an hour. Märta, the third visitor to the vestry, is the most clearly marked of these Christ figures: she is thirty-three years old and is afflicted with eczema that appears at the same spots on her body as Christ's stigmata.* Her

*Although Bergman associated Märta with Christ almost from the moment he conceived the character, he has claimed that the specific connection between the eczema and the stigmata was fortuitous. In his diary, Vilgot Sjöman records Bergman's "discovery" as occurring on November 21, 1961, seven weeks after shooting had begun, yet, at some level

appeal is for love. In her artless, self-deprecatory manner, she begs Tomas to marry her. To emerge from "the very bottom of the vale of tears," she says, he must put aside his maundering about God's silence and "learn to love." But the minister scoffs at her presuming she is the one to teach him that lesson.

Bergman states that he laid out the screenplay in three "movements." The first — designated as smashing the coda of the "auto-suggested God" of love presented at the conclusion of *Through a Glass Darkly* — reaches its climax as Tomas, waiting in solitude for Jonas to return, "experiences for the first time how it must have been for Christ when he felt abandoned on the Cross."[8] As in other films, Bergman associates crucifixion with consciousness of time and mortality: while a grandfather clock ticks "its own secret life" and a death's head on a coat of arms watches mutely, Tomas takes photographic proofs of his dead wife from his pocket and studies them. Suddenly, he is seized by the thought that her death and his misery have been cast down on him as punishment. The idea brings a strange comfort: if he is being punished, he seems to reason, then a personal God — a God of judgment — really exists. At that instant, Bergman comments in the text, "all doubt is silenced and his uncertainty dissolves itself in a triumphant cry: 'God has stricken me!' " This cry begins the film's second movement — "the emptiness that results [from the destruction of the God of love.]" Once again, though in reverse order, the development is through the three characters who had approached the minister after the mass.

First, Tomas reads a letter from Märta he has been carrying unopened since it arrived the previous day.* Having grown up an atheist in a non-Christian home filled with joy, she writes, she is perplexed by his neurotic, otherworldly preoccupation with God and his "indifference to the gospels and to Jesus Christ," the only parts of his professed religion she can comprehend. To make her point, she refers to her request for his prayers the previous summer when she was tormented by her

---

of consciousness, he surely must have been aware of the symbolism previously. On November 1, three weeks before he supposedly first noticed the "coincidence," he spoke of the eczema to Ingrid Thulin (who plays Märta) as "a nail through the hands."[7]

*For a full five minutes, Märta's face appears in close-up as she speaks the words Tomas is reading; only once does the camera shift, and then in a very brief flashback. Like Bergman's use of the mass at the opening, this sequence was a bold stroke; nothing quite like it had ever been tried in cinema before. Mindful of the risk, the director kept some alternate shots as a hedge until the very last moment of editing, but in the end he decided to gamble on showing "the movements of the soul" in "as naked a way as possible."[9]

eczema. Jesus touched the leper and healed him, but Tomas, disgusted by her sores, avoided her. Yet, despite this "incontrovertible proof we didn't love each other," the atheist pledges her love to the minister as an instrument of God's will:

> God . . . why have you created me so eternally dissatisfied, so frightened, so bitter? Why must I understand how wretched I am, why have I got to suffer as in the hell of my own indifference? If there is a purpose in my suffering, then tell me what it is! And I'll bear my pain without complaining. I'm strong. You've made me so terribly strong, both in body and soul, but you give me nothing to do with my strength. Give me a meaning to my life, and I'll be your obedient slave! . . . This autumn, I've realized my prayer has been heard. . . . I realized I love you. I prayed for a task to apply my strength to, and got it, too. It's you.

When Tomas looks up, he sees Jonas standing before him—as though this fisherman who can find no purpose in life and who believes hatred has overcome love were a mirror image. Too frightened to address the philosophical issue Jonas has honestly confronted, the minister almost comically takes the approach of a social worker. Does Jonas have financial worries? Are his marital relations satisfactory? Is it actually the problem of the Chinese that oppresses him?—if so, then "those of us who can see the danger mustn't sit and wait for the catastrophe to happen. We must fight it, tooth and nail, do everything we can to support the forces of peace." When Tomas at last accepts the fact that this Jonah who has sailed beyond the Lord will not be berthed by such homilies, he launches his own renunciation of God.

From childhood, the minister confesses, his mother kept him in ignorance of "everything evil, everything ugly, everything dangerous"; even after he had grown up and gone to Lisbon during the Spanish Civil War, he continued to inhabit a "specially arranged world where everything made sense."* Eventually, the existence of evil intruded upon his consciousness, and when Tomas confronted God with this new vision of reality, God "became ugly, revolting, a spider god—a monster. That's why I hid him away from the light, from life."** But now, face to face with

---

*This detail in Tomas's life probably alludes to Bergman's stay in Hitler's Germany during his gymnasium studies. Long afterward, Bergman was to marvel at how oblivious he had been to the horrors being perpetrated around him.

**The blending of mother and wife so often found in Bergman's films is also evident here. The only person to whom Tomas dared show the spider-God was his wife, who "plugged

this fellow subject of the spider-God, Tomas summons the courage to shed his burden of childhood delusions. God does not exist; "suffering is incomprehensible, so it needn't be explained. The stars out in space, worlds, heavens, all have given birth to themselves and to each other. There isn't any creator, no one who holds it all together, no immeasurable thought to make one's head spin." Immediately testing this discovery, he adopts the stance of Satan tempting Jesus to reject Gethsemane by offering Jonas (and, in effect, himself) the kingdom of earth: "You must live, Jonas. Summer's on the way. After all, the darkness won't last forever. You've got your strawberry beds, haven't you, and your flowering jasmine? What perfume! Long hot days. It's the earthly paradise, Jonas." Turning his face toward the wall, Tomas speaks of the "gifts" they have exchanged: "You have given me your fear and I've given you a god I've killed." But when he turns his head back, Jonas has vanished, and Tomas is once more alone with "Christ's twisted face" in "God's silence."

Having gone much further than he thought he could in repudiating God, the minister now vacillates. First, like the crucified Jesus, he moans, "My God, why have you abandoned me?" (In the film, the line is shortened to, simply, "God.") Then, again insisting that there is no God, he giddily declares, "I'm free now. At last, free." But when Märta, who has been outside the vestry the whole time, tells him she has not seen Jonas, Tomas realizes that he has imagined the visit. Suddenly the possibility of liberation from the Christ nexus dissipates like the mirage which inspired it. As though surrendering to his fate, the minister sinks into Märta's lap in a pose that suggests the Pietà.

Moments later, the news arrives that Jonas has shot himself to death.* As Tomas stands beside the rapids where the body was found, the personal God he had constructed in his youth and the promise of freedom in an earthly paradise without God seem equally absurd. The perfunctory manner of the police in dealing with the corpse emphasizes the swiftness with which death degrades a person into an object,

---

up all the holes." The wife thus took the place of the mother who protected him from the threatening knowledge of the world.

*Obviously—as Bergman himself pointed out in conversation with Sjöman—the second meeting with Jonas could have occurred only in the minister's feverish mind. Not only had Märta not seen him, but it would have been impossible for the fisherman to leave the church, fetch his gun, and walk to the suicide site; for the body to be found and reported to the police; for the police to arrive; and, finally, for the old woman who brings the news to climb the long hill to the church —all within the two minutes after his departure from the vestry.[10]

an "it," and the roar of the water, blotting up speech and overwhelming the human presence on the site, attests Nature's indifference to man. In talking to Jonas's apparition in the vestry, Tomas had argued that "life becomes something understandable" once God is expunged from human consciousness, that death loses its terror and becomes mere extinction, "a dissolution of body and soul." But this encounter with death produces neither understanding nor relief—only a profound feeling of emptiness.

The next scene, which has no bearing on the plot, exists to provide a buffer between the film's two most emotionally charged passages, but Bergman converts dramatic necessity into an opportunity to extend the dimensions of the minister's futility. While Tomas and Märta stop at her schoolhouse to get medicine for his cold, Johan, a ten-year-old boy who has come to the classroom to retrieve a comic book, tells the minister he will no longer be attending confirmation classes; like his elder brother, he has found religious instruction boring and irrelevant. "What are you going to be when you grow up?" Tomas asks. "Astronaut," Johan answers. The boy represents the new man the minister had described to Jonas—a mentality freed from the anxieties engendered by Tomas's own religious upbringing. Johan's ambition to become a *rymdfarare*—literally, "space voyager"—suggests a future predicated upon Tomas's vision of self-generating stars in heavens void of purpose. But if the boy's answers remind Tomas that he has wasted his life on a foolish vocation, they also imply a spiritual emptiness that seems to discomfit him even more.

Perhaps to vent the exasperation Johan has stirred, Tomas tells Märta the time has come to quiet gossip in the congregation by putting an end to their affair. When she suggests that marriage would be a better way of disposing of the problem, Tomas admits that gossip was only an excuse he had invented to be "kind"; the truth—which Bergman came to call an "orgasm of hate" on the set—is simply that he wants to be rid of her.

I'm tired of your loving care, your fussing over me, your good advice, your little candlesticks and table-runners. I'm fed up with your myopia and your clumsy hands, your eagerness for love-making and your reserve when we make love. You force on me your physical condition, your stomach problems, your eczema, your menstruation, your chilblained cheek. Once and for all I must quit this rubbish, this junkheap of idiotic circumstances. I am sick and tired of the whole thing, of everything to do with you.

Worst of all, he says, she behaves like "an ugly parody" of his beloved dead wife—whom Märta never even met.*

Once the vicious outburst against his "idiotic circumstances" subsides, Tomas settles into resignation—as though accepting his role in the drama of Calvary. It is the turning point of the film. Earlier, in the vestry at Mittsunda, he had ignored Märta's request to join him at mass in the Frostnäs church which shares his pastorate (the second of the film's "two stations of the Cross"); now, in an exchange that recalls the ending of *Evening of the Jesters*, he asks for her company, and she, acknowledging her own fate, replies, "Of course, naturally I'll come. I haven't any choice, have I?"**

Along the route, the couple pause for Tomas to notify Karin Persson of her husband's suicide. Though the scene follows the logic of events since the noon mass, it is scarcely instrumental to the plot; even so, it functions as an integral part of the film's design. Structurally, it presents the contrasting complement to the interview between Tomas and Jonas in the vestry; thematically, it illustrates the central contradiction embraced in Bergman's metaphor of the Way of the Cross: man's need for hope and the ravaging certainty of death.

Karin and her three children have just sat down to their Sunday dinner when the minister arrives. She knows Jonas has been intending to kill himself, and since the family has evidently delayed beginning the meal to wait for their husband and father, she must suspect the worst. But when Tomas blurts out the purpose of his errand, her response, "So

---

*Märta's remarkable resemblance to the wife is made apparent for the viewer through the photographs Tomas carries with him: the face is Ingrid Thulin's. Bergman also uses the photographs to imply that Tomas's love for his wife is based on illusion. Stamped across the face is the word *råkopia* (= "proofs" or, literally, "raw copy"); from the raw, imperfect materials of life, Tomas has constructed a suprahuman ideal who makes no demands. (In light of the connotations of the name "Anna" in earlier works—and the similar use of photographs of a wife named "Anne" in "The Fish" and *Smiles of the Summer Night*—it is interesting to note that here the wife's name is Anna Magdalena.)

**At the end of this sequence, the pair walk to the road, where an old man leading a black horse touches his cap to salute the minister. That several critics have expressed mystification at this minor detail may justify more comment than it might otherwise warrant.

The figure of Death leading a horse or driving a horse-drawn cart on his rounds for souls, a motif in Swedish folklore, enters cinema in Sjöström's *The Phantom Chariot*. Bergman often alludes to the conceit, particularly in the later films. In *The Communicants*, it occurs twice. A wall painting of a horse and cart led by Death dominates the background to the Pietà scene. (Imitative of the Albertus frescoes in Uppland churches, it was painted for the film according to Bergman's instructions.) In the second instance, the appearance of the horse immediately following the couple's conciliation again accents Märta's role as comforter during Tomas's "crucifixion."

I'm alone then," implies a gritty appraisal of her situation, not grief for the dead. Similarly, she refuses his offer to read from the Bible, not because of bitterness over the loss of her husband but because she is too engrossed in thinking about her responsibilities to seek comfort in a "security God." Troubled by his conscience, he protests that he did his best to persuade Jonas to live, but she has cast no blame. "I'm sure you did what you could, sir," she says, then returns to the kitchen. Ironically, his attempts to console the widow have revealed his own need for consolation—just as, earlier, he had revealed his inadequacy and lack of faith in trying to minister to Jonas.

On his exit into the chilly outdoors, Tomas glances back into the warm house through a porch window and sees Karin, braced against the table, breaking the news to her children. Despite her plight, he seems to realize that he is more alone and more oppressed by death than she. This moroseness surfaces a few minutes later when Tomas's car is forced to stop at a railroad crossing: as he watches the train's coffin-shaped tank cars pass by on their way to Frostnäs, his own destination, he remembers the terror of abandonment he had felt as a child and confesses his unsuitability for the priesthood.*

The wintry, barren connotations of Frostnäs (= Frost Cape)—linked with death, darkness, and fear of abandonment—extend into the final scene, in which Bergman closes the film's second movement, "emptiness," and then sets out the opening bars of the third, "the outburst of a new creed." On greeting Tomas and Märta inside the church, Algot Frövik apologizes for having let the bells ring twenty seconds too long while he was preoccupied with trying to light defective candles. Like the minister's meeting his obligations in Frostnäs despite his illness, this punctilio becomes comic when one realizes that all the pews are vacant.

---

*Despite obvious differences in attitude as well as in scale and tone, the basic pattern of *The Communicants* resembles that of the Knight's quest in *The Seventh Seal*. The similarity between Tomas's call on Mrs. Persson and the Knight's visit with the "Holy Family" is especially revealing. In both instances, a man in the grip of despair encounters a vital woman who, in preparing a meal for her family, transforms the commonplace into a sacrament of life. Like Mia, Karin is free of the tangles of the intellect (both women describe themselves as "unimaginative"), and much like Mia's devotion to Baby Mikael, her advanced pregnancy symbolizes life's continuity.

The Communicants, however, has none of the forced optimism of *The Seventh Seal*. The bond of familial love evident when Karin withdraws to tell her children of their father's death is forged in sorrow, not joy, and her virtue is not in innocence but in her strength. Most significantly, in contrast to the Knight, enabled to outwit Death with a meaningful deed because of what he has experienced with the family, Tomas is rendered helpless, not only by Jonas's death but also by the contemplation of his own.

Perhaps to pass time while waiting for a few straggling churchgoers to arrive, Tomas now indicates his willingness to discuss whatever was troubling Frövik earlier in the day— whereupon the humpbacked sexton presents his theory of the Crucifixion.

He took up the Gospels, he says, because Tomas had advised reading as a distraction from his constant pain. At first, they were "as good as sleeping pills," but then Christ's Passion began to stimulate his thoughts. The actual torture, he is certain, has been exaggerated: he himself has suffered "at least as much as ever Christ did," and besides, the agony on the Cross was over in a matter of hours. Christ's awareness that the Last Supper had meant nothing to the disciples, he surmises, caused greater anguish. And then Peter denied Jesus. "That must have been a terrible suffering! To understand that no one has understood you. To be abandoned when one really needs someone to rely on." But the worst, he concludes, was Christ's thought that God had abandoned him in his torment on the Cross: "The moment before he died, Christ was seized with a great doubt. Surely that must have been his most monstrous suffering of all? I mean God's silence. Isn't that true, Vicar?" With this exposition, the film's implicit metaphor becomes almost too obtrusively explicit. Convinced that no one other than his dead wife has ever understood him, oppressed by the evidence that he has been forsaken by God, and paralyzed by doubt, Tomas is literally the vicar of the Jesus the sexton describes.

As in *The Seventh Seal* and *Through a Glass Darkly*, resolution of the spiritual crisis depends upon overcoming egocentricity through faith, hope, and love. Here, however, that resolution is still beyond the protagonist's grasp at the conclusion. In Karin, Jonas's heir, Tomas has witnessed the embodiment of hope, but even though he admires her fortitude, his state of mind as he leaves her continues to reflect the despair that has driven her husband to suicide. Algot Frövik (whose name suggests "all good harbor of life") exemplifies faith—not because of his office in the church or because he reads the Gospels but because, instead of cursing God for crippling him, he goes on performing his menial tasks in devotion to God's unfathomable purpose.* While the

---

*The model for Frövik was K. A. Bergman (no kin to Ingmar), a victim of Bechterev's disease whom Bergman had employed as an aide ever since *Wild Strawberries*. Sjöman notes in his diary that "Ingmar speaks of K. A. with warmth and fascination and with a fearsome empathy for his suffering." A subsequent entry records the director's enthusiastic response to K. A.'s "shining presence" in a taped TV interview: "When *he* says that *it is wrong for someone to lie down when he is sick* . . . a thousand old men and women will jump out of their beds on hearing that and realizing how pampered they are." This same "holy"

minister listens to his interpretation of Christ's agony, polite patience gives way to the recognition that this account of Gethesemane and Calvary applies to himself. Even so, he misses the point. The sexton does not presume to compare his suffering to Christ's—indeed, in claiming to have endured greater physical torment than was involved in the actual Crucifixion, he belittles his own ordeal; in contrast, when Tomas says, "Yes, yes," and turns his head away on hearing the words "God's silence," he reveals that he still feels God's indifference as a personal humiliation.

His most damning failure, however, lies in repelling the love offered by Märta—"the nonbeliever" who, Bergman has commented, "bears in herself the seed of a new image of god."[12] ("New," that is, to the minister.) The irony of this failure is the foundation of the concluding scene, in which, while Tomas is pondering the significance of the Crucifixion in terms of the silence of his "auto-suggested God," Märta demonstrates its meaning as a sacrifice offered in love.

Echoing Tomas's temptation of Jonas with an earthly paradise, Blom the organist urges Märta to quit her lover and leave the environs of Mittsunda and Frostnäs, where everything "is in the grip of death and decay." When she ignores the advice, Blom poses a more compelling argument. Tomas's wife was "a real woodlouse," he says, "who hadn't a genuine feeling in her whole body, not an honest thought"; for Märta to continue pursuing the self-deluding fool who has enshrined such a fraud while preaching the twaddle of "God is love and love is God" would be to waste her life. But Blom only fortifies her dedication to lead the frightened minister out from the treacherous illusions into which he has withdrawn. Just as, at the end of *Through a Glass Darkly*, David tells his son that their love will help Karin, betrayed by the God of her fantasies, Märta renews her vow of devotion to Tomas. "If I could only lead him out of his emptiness, away from his lie-god," she prays after Blom has retreated. "If we could dare to show each other tenderness. If we could believe in a truth. . . . If we could believe. . . . "

The recurrence of the conditional in her prayer reflects the tentative nature of the film's ending: there is no truth to believe in except the truth created by belief—and Tomas is still riddled by doubt, still immured by the lies he has erected as a shield against life. In terms of the seminal

---

quality is evident in the sexton, described by Bergman as "truly, literally, an angel" in whom there is "fifty times more religion" than in the self-absorbed minister. K. A. was so closely tied to Frövik in Bergman's mind that he used the aide as the stand-in and instructed Allan Edwall, who plays the sexton, to study and imitate K. A.'s physical manner.[11]

image from which the idea for the film emerged, the minister remains locked in his church, awaiting God's response to his challenge. And yet, Bergman has often insisted, the final note is not entirely bleak. When the sexton, forced to concede that his ringing of the bells has gone unheeded by the Frostnäs population, asks whether there will be a service, the minister nods. Like Erik Bergman in filling in for the ailing clergyman, Tomas bows to duty, "even if it might seem meaningless"—and although the performance of duty does not constitute belief, it staves off surrender to despair. But symbolically more important is the incipient celebration of the mass itself, the "love feast" in re-creation of the Last Supper to which the title finally refers. Although the minister remains "in the grip of death and decay," a resurrection of the spirit is possible. "Through communion," Bergman has explained, "we can accept the appalling fact of total aloneness."[13]

This conclusion is near to being a paraphrase of the "God and love are one and the same phenomenon" formulation at the close of *Through a Glass Darkly*. Despite the fact that the protagonist himself finds no deliverance, Bergman construes an answer to his problem. The film had begun with Tomas looking toward the altar; it ends with his turning his "pale and anxiety-filled face" toward his "congregation" of fellow sufferers.* Similarly, whereas an austere Father God had dominated the Mittsunda altar and the first words spoken had referred to the night of Christ's betrayal, the altarpiece at Frostnäs shows Mary with the Infant in her arms and the last words Tomas recites are "Holy, holy, holy, Lord God Almighty. All the earth is full of his glory...." If the priest could forget the resentment bred by his yearning for a privileged relationship with a God above and accept instead the consolations available within humanity, the words he has been rattling about God being love would become flesh and the earth would indeed reveal God's glory.

Given the subject matter of the story, the ironic figure of the minister who lacks faith, the allusive interplay with the Passion, and, moreover, the film's position as the second part of a trilogy called "The Silence of God," the presumption that Bergman was working his way through a crisis brought on by a questioning of his Christianity seems inescapable.

---

*In a sense, the action between Mittsunda and Frostnäs is a parenthesis set within the mass that begins and ends the film. While he was editing *The Communicants*, Bergman cited Cocteau's *Blood of a Poet* as an example of the almost infinite elasticity of time in cinema: "It begins with a chimney beginning to fall and ends with its fall. Thus, during the moment of fall—which is perhaps a second long—the whole drama is played."[14] Clearly, he was aiming for the same effect in his own film.

And indeed, ever since the premiere of *The Communicants* in Sweden, critical interpretation has examined it in that light. But the film is religious in the sense that religion concerns fundamental values, not in any narrowly theological respect; although the Gospels and Paul's First Epistle to the Corinthians provide a frame of reference, the nature of a Christian God is not what is at issue. To the contrary, the film rejects theology as an answer to the humanistic question it poses about life's purpose—a question which takes form in the context of a specifically psychological problem.

In middle age, Tomas still suffers guilt for not having measured up to his parents' expectations; at the same time, he tries to conceal the anger he felt when they withheld their love (or failed to love him enough) because he disappointed them. The "security-God" he subsequently erected was to substitute for father; the illusions he has invested in his wife were to compensate for insecurity in the relationship with mother. That the anxieties fixed in childhood have sexual origins is rather apparent. He berates Märta for not being the wife/mother he idealizes —and for being too much like her; she disgusts him because she is a woman and because he hates himself for sleeping with her. In short, Tomas's problem replicates the conflicts embedded in almost all of Bergman's fictions.

But between the figure of the minister tortured by God's silence and Bergman's recurring interior drama, something else is at work that would radically affect his aesthetic principles for the rest of his career. In the protagonist who has lost belief in the rituals he performs and who confronts a vision of life without sureties, there is at least an analogy to the filmmaker who was rebelling against the falsity that entered his films through the imposition of his wishes. Perhaps, instead of focusing on the trilogy as three stages of an inquiry into the existence of God, one should regard the shift from "certainty achieved" to "certainty unmasked" to "the negative print" as a transition in the artist's assumptions about art. From this point of view, the question of certainty itself as a function of form overshadows that of what the certainty is about. Whereas, like his previous films, *Through a Glass Darkly* had been predicated upon a clear resolution in which the author unriddles the world he has presented, *The Communicants* departs from that obligation. To be sure, Bergman points the way toward a "new faith" that holds the possibility of redemption, but the structure is left open: Tomas's pain and confusion are as great at the end as at the beginning, and whether he can

break through his egoism is a question that falls outside the drama.*
The Silence would take a step beyond: in that "negative print," form no
longer reflects even the possibility of resolving meaning. And in *Persona*,
Bergman would pitch art against itself in a nihilistic explosion of reality.

The Silence

At some point in the fall of 1961, Bergman began sporting with the idea
of a burlesque fairy tale about the devil and a princess who is overtaken
by old age while she waits for her suitors. Shooting on *The Communicants*
was to finish by the end of the year; in January, he planned to retreat to
Dalarna to work on the script of the new film, for which he had already
discussed possible locations with Sven Nykvist. But then, in mid-
December, a severe throat infection forced a three-week suspension in
the filming of *The Communicants*, and during his illness he began to
fashion a story, set in the dreamscape of a strange foreign city, about a
boy and two women, one driven by her eroticism and the other dying of
consumption. By the time he returned to the set, the comedy had been
dismissed. His next film would be the third panel in his Silence of God
trilogy.

The Silence fed on more than Bergman's fever and his difficulty in
drawing breath, however. Two of its working titles, *The City* and *Timoka*
(Estonian for "pertaining to the executioner"), imply some connection
with *The City*, his hallucinatory 1951 radio play in which the executioner stalks the protagonist. A pair of his discarded film ideas contributed more directly. One, which had sprung from the horror Bergman
felt while passing through the bombed ruins of Hamburg in 1946, revolved
around tensions between an aging, sick acrobat and his younger partner that develop when they are trapped in a German city by the war.**
The other was the project that, before the fairy tale jostled it aside, was
intended to follow *The Communicants*. Conceived as a three-hour
"kaleidoscope" with scenes spinning backward through the stages of

---

*The fact that the published script carries the initials S.D.G. (for *Soli Deo Gloria*—To God
Alone the Glory) next to the date of its completion has prompted various critics to assert
that Bergman was offering the film as a token of restored religious belief. Actually, in
imitation of Bach, he had made a practice of inscribing the abbreviation at the bottom of
manuscripts ever since *The Seventh Seal*.
**Bergman would again draw on this idea in writing *The Serpent's Egg*. A fainter image of
its contours is also discernible in *Shame*.

life, *The Big Picture Book* would have consisted of "only pictures, *pictures*, *pictures* . . . long reams of pictures. As in a dream. Not an ordinary time progression, but dream time."[1] This expressionistic mode carried over to *The Silence*, which, though less obtrusively, also encapsulates the Ages of Man.* But the major link between the abandoned film and the one he made lies in the premise that God is dead—an expression, in turn, of a wish to be free of the psychologically crippling effects of the father and mother who are fused with the image of God. *The Big Picture Book* was to have begun with the death of a shriveled androgynous figure in a wheelchair, immediately followed by a boy's discovery of a toy representing that figure in his dollhouse. A sequence originally incorporated in *The Silence* showing the dying androgyne was cut because Bergman thought it would be "too obviously symbolic," but a no less obvious symbol of God—the dead, four-hundred-pound father of the two women in the film—conveys much the same significance.

In a manner reminiscent of *Evening of the Jesters* and *The Face*, *The Silence* begins with a journey in progress. Two women, separated by a boy, occupy opposite corners of a train compartment that "floats onward in the silence of dawn." Bergman indicates at the very start that these sisters, like a split self, represent body and mind: Anna, Johan's mother, sits in a crumpled summer dress "with sweating thighs far apart"; Ester, in contrast, seems so far removed from her own flesh that she is "apparently unaffected by the heat." (That the filmmaker conceives of them as the physical and mental aspects of the self later becomes quite clear. To Anna's plea for a severance of their relationship, Ester replies, "How do you want us to live, then? After all, we own everything in common.")

When a racking cough brings blood from Ester's lungs, they decide to get off the train so that Ester may rest, but once they have registered at the hotel, Anna shows no concern for her sister. She draws a bath, invites her son to scrub her back, naps, then takes a walk into Timoka, a completely alien city (the language is some form of Finno-Ugric). At a bar, a waiter brushes his chin against her leg; though she gives no sign of annoyance, she quickly leaves. Entering a theater, she sees a troupe of dwarfs on stage who have interlocked themselves in imitation of a millipede (or perhaps—given that this is a Bergman film—a spider).** Proba-

---

The Dream was another working title of *The Silence*.
**In the published script, the theater is a movie house, and instead of the dwarfs, Anna sees a film in which "a comedian wholly devoid of comedy" plays a ruined piano while a buxom woman tries to seduce him. Both figures vanish from view behind a great cloud of

bly because the figure is erotically suggestive and Anna, already aroused, is trying to control herself, she turns her head. But down her row of seats, she notices a couple copulating. This sends her hurrying from the theater into the crowded street (where, as if in projection of her sexual thoughts, there are only men). Returning to the bar, she signals the waiter.

Meanwhile, Ester has been reading, smoking, drinking brandy, listening to the radio, and intermittently working at her trade as a translator. Her only human contact is with Johan and an aged bellhop (the counterpart to Anna's waiter) who brings her the brandy and teaches her the words for hand and music, *kasi* and *musike*.* At one point, she flops backward on the bed and masturbates. This would seem inconsistent with the mental signification of the character, yet, despite the intensity of her orgasm, the onanism seems only a casual physical function; as pleasure, it means at most just a short respite from boredom.

Anna's return to the hotel brings the sisters' antagonism into the open. On discovering that, while she was bathing, Ester has been scrutinizing her clothes for evidence of sexual activity, she flares out at her for presuming to be her conscience. Later, this same quarrel erupts again. Ester, she says, is trying to act in place of their father, a huge man who enforced his commandments with fearsome authority, but Anna insists she will enjoy the freedom his death brought. Moreover, she adds, Ester's moral professions are a sham. Once, when they were younger, Ester had demanded that she confess the intimate details of an affair; Anna, overcome by guilt, complied. But now she realizes that her sister's interest was nothing more than voyeurism, and to lash her with her hypocrisy, she proceeds to describe her adventure with the waiter, taking particular delight in telling her that they had copulated in a church.

As though erotically stimulated by the quarrel, Anna meets her lover in the hotel corridor and dashes with him into the nearest room. But for all her claims of being free to relish her sensuality, this second lust-driven encounter exudes pain and loneliness. After they have had

---

dust emitted by a powder puff; when the dust settles, the comedian is alone, playing a cello. (The skit not only is reminiscent of "The Fish" but also anticipates *Not to Speak of All These Women*.)

*Bergman: "*Through a Glass Darkly* concerns God and love. Then comes *The Communicants*, which criticizes this and ends stripped down to the bottom layer with a prayer to an unnamed God. A god beyond formulas, the living religion represented by Frövik [and, Bergman notes elsewhere, Märta]. And then *The Silence*—everything is even more stripped down, a world totally without God. Only the hand—fellowship—is left. And music."[2]

intercourse, neither seems cognizant of the other's presence; the faint metalic sound produced by the waiter's tapping of her bracelet rings accentuates the emotional emptiness in the room. "How wonderful that we can't understand each other," she says; then, blaming Ester for her unhappiness, she wishes her sister were dead. Meanwhile, Johan has told his aunt of having seen his mother and the stranger enter the room. When Anna realizes that Ester is peeking through the door, she resumes her coupling with the waiter. In the angry confrontation that follows, Anna accuses her sister of intellectual arrogance, of being full of hate while always talking about love, of insisting that life must be "meaningful" and yet spending her days to no purpose. "When Father died you said, 'Now I don't want to live any longer.' Well, why do you live, then? For my sake? For Johan? For your work, perhaps? Or for nothing in particular?" But after this screaming attack has driven Ester away, Anna's own life appears no less futile. As she kneels, weeping and holding the bedstead's iron posts as though they were the bars to her prison, the waiter pene-trates her from behind; when she kicks a bedside lamp, an explosion of stark, blinding light symbolizes the nightmare she calls liberation.

The next afternoon, Anna and Johan begin their return trip to Sweden; Ester will remain in Timoka with only the old bellhop, like a tender angel of death, to minister to her. Although Ester does not, in any narrow sense, represent Christ, the allusion of her agony to crucifixion is unmis-takable as fluid fills her lungs and as she grasps the bars of the bedstead behind her, calling to her mother for pity in what are presumably her last hours. Like Christ, too, she has left a testament. In her farewell to Johan, she had given him a letter—a bequest of sorts summing up her experience of life: "It's *important*, do you understand? You must read it carefully. It's all. . . . You'll understand." When Johan opens the letter on the train, he finds a list of words Ester has learned in the language of Timoka: *hadjek* = spirit; *magrov* = anxiety; *krasqt* = joy. . . .

To Anna, the "secret message" is only more of Ester's prattle—after taking the letter from Johan, she returns it with a shrug—yet the eman-cipation she believed would result from her sister's death still eludes her. In the film's closing seconds, rain begins to fall, and Anna, exposing herself to the train's open window, rubs the moisture over her skin. Rain at the end of *The Seventh Seal*, *Wild Strawberries*, and *The Face*—like the springwater in *The Virgin Spring*—implied regeneration or absolu-tion; here, too, Anna seems to wish for revival or cleansing, but the look on her face bespeaks a terror that the water will not wash away.

Approached as allegory, *The Silence* can be read as a rather simple morality. Timoka is yet another of this century's fictional mindscapes registering alienation, anxiety, purposelessness, and an ever-present threat of violence. The dying Ester represents the entropic state of Western intellectual and religious traditions; Anna, the joyless hedonism incited by desperation. But if the terms of the allegory are obvious, the argument they are meant to describe is not—as the confused, overboiled interpretations of the film ever since its release attest. The sisters are essentially static characters, fixed symbols which, though elaborated upon as the story advances, do not themselves advance the story toward a denouement of the conflict they portray. It could hardly be said that any value is affirmed in Anna's frantic effort to find satisfaction through the senses. Nor, clearly, does Bergman intend Ester to be seen as something more than a pitiable creature. The despotic father whose memory she venerates prescribed rules that fostered an illusion of security (rather like Tomas's "security-God"); now that he is dead, she tries to anesthetize the pain of reality with brandy and Bach. (Significantly, the music she listens to over the radio is *The Goldberg Variations*, written to lull the pain-racked Count Keyserlingk to sleep.) Once that reality, reflected by her diseased body, overtakes her in a final death agony, her suffering is as meaningless as Tyan's in the "emptiness under the moon" in *The Seventh Seal*.

But even though the plot rests in the sisters' actions, to confine analysis of *The Silence* to them is to miss the way the film operates as a dream. God's silence has no direct bearing on this dream; rather, it describes Bergman's recurrent psychological anxieties, here seated in Johan. The boy's actions during the twenty-eight hours covered by the film trace no coherent story and only affect the plot at one critical juncture, but it is his consciousness that determines the viewer's perspective on events, even in the scenes from which he is absent. He is, in effect, the "dreamer."

Intimations that the train (like the train in *The Communicants*) is a metaphor for life's journey come to the surface soon after the film's start. Wandering into the corridor, Johan sees an old man so deeply asleep that he looks dead and a conductor who ominously points to a figure in his timetable, shakes his head, and shows his wristwatch. But the prepubescent boy's death is still a long way off; the more immediate fear—of the aggressions he associates with sex—is represented by the railroad cars laden with military vehicles he watches pass before his window. Once he is in Timoka, the first sounds "that disturb the oppressive silence" are of the newsboys crying the headlines about the war that is threatening the city; at the same moment, significantly, he sees "garish mountains of womanhood" on the movie theater advertisements.

The interplay of sex and violence becomes more elaborate in the first scene within the hotel room. While his mother paces, half-naked, in front of him, Johan winds his watch (as though to hasten his sexual maturation by hurrying time). The "magic" seems to work: Anna summons him to the bathtub to scrub her back. But when he sputters (apparently an oral substitute for ejaculation) and then drifts into an evidently erotic reverie, she dismisses him from the room. Reflecting what has just happened, Johan flops onto the bed's bolster, pretends his forefinger is a jet plane, then punishes this phallic symbol by shooting it down. (Subsequently, Ester will be seen masturbating on the bolster from the same camera angle. The two acts are also linked by the sound of an air-raid siren in the background.)* Minutes later, having symbolically destroyed the sexual threat to his relationship to his mother, Johan is allowed to sleep at Anna's side. But the screech of a low-flying fighter plane soon ends this respite. After tucking a toy pistol in his pants (the Freudian meaning of which is obvious) and again winding his watch, he begins to explore the hotel's corridors—a maze of passages into the world of adults.

A circle in the carpet where the hallways intersect takes on a special import throughout these forays. The pattern of rosettes at its edge resemble markings on a gnomon-less sundial or a clockface without hands; for the boy who is probing the scary effects of growing up, it is a magic ring where time stands at zero. This sanctuary is immediately invaded, however, by a workman who raises a stepladder on it to replace a light bulb in the chandelier. The ladder suggests both a gnomon and the spread legs of the giant—i.e., the dual menace of time and sexuality. Johan, standing within the dial, fires his pistol into the ladder's crotch, then sputters (just as he had when his mother bathed). As the workman looks down quizzically on this impertinence, the boy walks away, satisfied that he has defeated his foe.

The sight of the hotel's aged bellhop at the foot of the hall, however, quickly dispels his sense of triumph and starts the boy's pulse "beating madly." Johan flees from the old man—whom he evidently perceives as Death—by running, through the dial, down another corridor, where he stops before a Rubens painting of a satyr and a "fat, very pink, entirely

---

*On neither occasion—nor at any other time—does anyone pay any heed to the sirens. Besides implying an acceptance of danger as an ordinary state, this curious behavior further contributes to the dreamlike unreality of Timoka.

naked lady." Johan's first impression is that the two figures are fighting, but on closer inspection, Bergman notes, he discovers something far from displeasure in her "stupid smile." While he is engrossed in the mystery, the cadaverous old man seizes him. Clearly, the bellhop means no harm—he is simply playing his part in the "game" he infers from the boy's actions—but Johan is genuinely afraid. As though to protest that his interest in the painting has been misinterpreted, that he is really a sexual innocent and thus not eligible prey for Death, he shakes his head and pulls free of the bellhop's grasp.

In an extension of this logic, Johan meets a dwarf passing through the hall; then, after a series of cuts—to Anna as she prepares for her lover, to Johan casting a monstrous shadow in front of him, and to another shot of the Rubens—he enters the dwarf's room. The meaning is apparent: were he able to arrest his development (i.e., become a dwarf), the sexual threat that looms over him would be disarmed. Initially, the experiment seems a great success. Five dwarfs (the same troupe Anna had watched on stage) laugh, do tricks, and don animal masks, all for the boy's amusement; better still, among these stunted, childlike men Johan is no longer a puny, hunted figure but a dominant presence. Testing his new-found power, he takes aim with his pistol; the dwarfs comply by falling down, then—as if to prove the unreality of death within their privileged world—bouncing back to life.

But the game takes a sinister turn when, after another cut to Anna dressing for her tryst, the dwarfs slip a dress on Johan. Implicitly, the alternative to becoming a male adult is to be female (or a homosexual). Although everyone treats Johan's transformation into a girl as harmless fun, the pretense of innocence evaporates upon the entrance of the troupe's leader. He chastises his fellow dwarfs, orders removal of the dress, and ushers Johan from the room (just as Anna had expelled him from the bathroom). The boy instantly feels shame and accepts his banishment as just punishment:

> Johan goes wordlessly out into the corridor. As the door closes behind him, he hears a sharp, dark voice speaking within.
>
> Once again he is standing beneath the picture of the pink lady and the fellow in hairy long pants; in the distance he hears the howling of air raid sirens, only suppressed, in a world remote.
>
> In a new and frightened way the solitude closes in around him and he finds he urgently needs to pee.... [He walks through the dial.]

Quickly he sets off for his own room, but soon realizes that he
has lost his way among the corridors.

Resigned, he stands and relieves himself in a corner. It turns into
quite a river, with many little streams, dividing, all running toward
the red carpet.

When he has finished he stuffs his hand into his trouser pockets
and whistles. [Returns through the dial.]

But it doesn't help much.

Without Johan's understanding exactly how, the interlude with the dwarfs
has in some manner changed him. The Rubens and the air raid siren
now affect him strangely, producing loneliness, guilt, and dread that he
senses derive from his having crossed a sexual divide. Urinating against
the wall reasserts his maleness, but it is also confirms his "naughtiness"
while, simultaneously, he tries to purge himself of it.[3] Sadly, the magical
effort "doesn't help much": the "many little streams" all flow toward the
red carpet, the symbol of time, the arch force that now controls him.
(The screenplay makes the point even more emphatically: as he stands
within the carpet's dial pattern, Johan sees the bellhop—Death—"baring
his big horse-teeth" at the end of the corridor.)

Ester notices his sadness when he returns to his room, and she tries
to console him with the thought that he will soon be with his grandmother in the country where he can play with horses. Johan's reply,
"I'm scared of horses," alludes not only to another little Hans's fear of
horses in Freud's classic case of castration anxiety but also to Bergman's
association of the horse with death.* To chase his gloom (and hers,
since he senses both her own fear of sex and her nearness to death), he
offers to draw a "lovely picture" for his aunt, but his changed consciousness will not allow it: the crayon line, Bergman says, "forms itself" into a
picture of a demon.

Before his banishment from the dwarfs' room, Johan had fled from
the bellhop; now, as if realizing that his loss of innocence militates
acquaintance with Death, he seeks him out. The bellhop seems almost
aware of his allegorical role. Enclosing a phallic sausage in a vaginal

---

*A scraggy horse drawing a heavily loaded cart appears twice in *The Silence*. When,
immediately prior to the bellhop's first entrance, it stops outside the hotel while Johan is
sleeping beside Anna, it suggests a juxtaposition of death to the image of fetal repose. The
second time, at twilight, Ester sees the horse at the point where the screenplay notes: "In
the shadow of annihilation her awareness quivers." The linkage of "horse" to "death" is
further indicated by Bergman's reference to the bellhop as having "horse-teeth."

lettuce leaf and bun, he makes it bow to Johan (just as Johan, at the start of their "interview," had bowed to him); then, with a sudden swoop, he bites it in two.* Although the old man laughs, the boy is frightened, not only by the association of sex with punishment by castration but also by the message that his emergence from childhood will lead to death. Confirming this insight with a kind of initiation ritual, the bellhop next drains his cup of brandy and shakes the last drops over Johan's head. Finally, he pulls some old photographs from his wallet and points to himself as a boy standing by the corpse of a woman in a coffin. Johan is shaken by the evidence that this ancient man was once his own age, and that, at the bellhop's side, he is standing as close to death as did the boy in the photograph. But at the height of his apprehension, he hears his mother in the hall, runs through the dial, and throws his arms around her. Drawing comfort from the thought that he is still a child —and, perhaps, that his mother is alive, he then slips the photographs under the carpet.

The reassurance provided by his mother's embrace quickly fades, however, when he observes her stealing into the room across the hall with her lover. "Swallowing his grief and fury," Johan backs away from the door and lingers in the center of the rosette dial before retreating to his own room. But the tremors that are rocking his world are unremitting. A rumbling noise from the street causes a glass to vibrate against a water carafe (though more rapid, the sound is nearly identical to that produced by the waiter's striking Anna's bracelet during the pause in their lovemaking.) When Johan looks out the window, he sees a tank squeeze into a narrow passage and stop. As though the reason for his anxiety had taken concrete form, the tank's erect gun protrudes from a camouflaged turret that has a distinctly vaginal appearance.

Betrayed by his mother, Johan now turns in fellowship to Ester (who also regards Anna's eroticism as treachery). To lift her spirits (and his own), he stages Kasper and Kasperina (Punch and Judy) at the foot of her bed, but, like the "lovely picture" he had earlier tried to draw, the improvised puppet play becomes demonic. In a rage, Kasper beats Kasperina to death with a stick, then weeps because, now that she is dead, he does not know what to do. The meaning of this violent drama

---

*Bergman insists that this was a bit of "business" invented by the actor when he could not remember his lines, not contrived symbolism.[4] If so, it was an inspired accident. But Bergman is least trustworthy when he is asked to discuss the intentions that underlie his symbolism. What he denies in one interview may be confirmed in another, only to be denied again later. (Sjöman's diary supplies several examples of such shifts.)

is transparent: Kasper is giving sadistic expression to the boy's hurt over his mother's "infidelity" with the waiter. Significantly, when Ester asks for a translation of what Kasper is saying, Johan replies, "How should I know? He's talking in a funny language. Because he's frightened." (Kasper's speech, apparently meant to be in the language of Timoka, contains several repetitions of the syllable "piss"—an echo of Johan's urinating in the hall to reassure himself of his masculinity.) Prevented by his own tears from continuing the performance, Johan creeps into bed with Ester. While he lies in her embrace, the tank, as though reflecting his wishes, clatters away from the hotel.

Although Johan launched his investigation of the hotel's corridors by winding his outsized watch, his reaction to everything the adventure has disclosed has been to deny reality by trying to stop, or even reverse, time's advance. Once he confronts the fact of his mother's sexual perfidy, however, this psychological effort ceases—indeed, time seems to accelerate through the remainder of the film. When, at the end of the puppet drama scene, Bergman cuts to the room occupied by Anna and her lover, the first sound heard is of a clock ticking loudly. This association of sex with time becomes even more pronounced while Ester is dying. Now it is the bellhop who winds his big pocket watch. As its "fast hard ticking" fills the silence, Ester explains the erotic sensation brought on by the morbidity of her disease as "all a matter of fluids and erectile tissue. It's because the blood vessels are overflowing, and [because of] all the mucous."* Johan is not a witness to this monologue—nor, of course, is he present while his mother and the waiter are in bed—yet one senses that the magnified sounds of the timepieces are being refracted · through his troubled consciousness.

The conclusion of the intervening scene carries the same implication. As Ester stands in the hall while the waiter copulates *a tergo* with her sister, the dwarf troupe, swigging liquor as they walk, file by dressed in a variety of costumes. Cyrano leads the march; Death tails behind. They salute Ester (who has been drinking heavily ever since she arrived in Timoka); after Death has passed, she faints—patently foreshadowing her death throes in the next scene. But even though the note struck by this procession relates to Ester, its deeper symbolic resonances are keyed to her nephew. It is in terms of Johan's perceptions that the

---

*The rest of the line, in elaborating her aversion to sex, continues to associate it with death: "Before extreme unction [i.e., death's 'orgasm'—as well as the Christian last rites], a confession. I think semen smells nasty. You see, I've a sensitive nose. I found I stank like a rotten fish after being fructified."

labyrinthian corridor has signified time; moreover, the child-sized men have reflected his wish to stop his biological "clock." Now, as though anticipating the discovery that awaits Johan, the corridor spills its secret: like the figures of the musical clock in *Smiles of the Summer Night*, the parade of dwarfs depicts life as a succession of roles culminating inevitably in death. Even Ester's reaction to the dwarfs leads ultimately to Johan. In the next scene, verbalizing what the parade has illustrated, she describes human existence as a drama: "We try [the roles] out, one attitude after another, and find them all meaningless. The powers are too strong for us, I mean the *monstrous* powers." At the scene's end, "the agonizing scream" of the air-raid siren coincides with a close-up of Ester as she slips toward death, the "wretched part" that is the sum of meaninglessness. The film's last frames are another close-up, this time of Johan, and the last sound, another terrifying, inhuman scream that drowns out his recitation of the words in his aunt's secret message.

Mostly because of the notoriety it quickly acquired in Sweden and then abroad for its "pornographic" sequences, *The Silence* achieved an unexpected financial success, but the critical response, if generally respectful toward the director, was decidedly cool toward the film. Evidently comparing it to the Bergman films of the 'fifties which were still fresh memories, reviewers found it slow-moving, depressing, and excessively cerebral; the most frequent complaint was that, in making his characters serve an abstruse symbolism, Bergman had occluded their humanity.* Once it had run the gauntlet of reviewers, however, the film gradually rose in reputation, not only because critics developed a more sophisticated appreciation of a cinematic narrative mode that owed

---

*Two typical samples from American reviews illustrate the irritation born of confusion that critics had begun to express after the release of *The Communicants*. "There are, of course, a hundred ambiguities inside the narrow compass of *The Silence*," Brendan Gill told readers of *The New Yorker*, "many of which I look forward to unravelling out at odd hours for the rest of the winter; meanwhile, let me assure you that while you will not enjoy the picture—it is one of the least *enjoyable* pictures I ever sat through—you will find plenty of rewards along the way, among them the high pictorial interest (unlike its predecessor, with its cold dessication of landscape and bleak architecture, *The Silence* is all stifling heat and pillowy opulence). . . . " In the *New York Times*, Bosley Crowther wrote: "The grapplings of Ingmar Bergman with loneliness, lust and loss of faith, so weirdly displayed in his two last pictures, *Through a Glass Darkly* and *Winter Light* [the American title of *The Communicants*], have plunged him at last into a tangle of brooding confusions and despairs. . . . Whether this strange amalgam of various states of loneliness and lust articulates a message may be questionable, but it does, at least, resolve into a vaguely affecting experience that moves one like a vagrant symphony. . . . But, unfortunately, Mr. Bergman has not given us enough to draw on, to find the underlying meaning or emotional satisfaction in this film."[5]

relatively little to literary and dramatic conventions but also because the symbolic content began to seem less opaque. By 1971, even Vernon Young, who had lost his taste for Bergman after *The Virgin Spring*, would pronounce *The Silence* "an extraordinary achievement in its way." Looking back on earlier disfavor, Young avowed his sympathy with "critics who do not care for art as cryptology," yet he felt forced to concede that *"The Silence* rewards effort; at its core, there is a rancid integrity which compels one's recognition, if not one's affection."[6]

Other revisionists have been less sensitive to its "rancid" temper; curiously, as the film has assumed a more honored place in the Bergman canon, there has been a tendency to sweeten its acerbity—partly because of a disposition to seek thematic uniformity in the trilogy; partly because the later films would seem to plunge much deeper into despair. E.g.: writing in 1968, Birgitta Steene saw a final convergence toward hope: Ester's letter to her nephew "has finally established contact with someone outside herself"; Anna "leads [Johan] into a world of comforting sensuality"; and the old bellhop (a "modern version of [God] as a benevolent Parent," in her view) "helps Johan attain the freedom that is reflected in the boy's face at the end of the film." Fifteen years later, Peter Cowie would invent a similar deliverance: after construing Anna's exposing herself to the rain as a ritualistic cleansing to "rid her body of its hatred for Ester," he declares that "hope for the future lies with Johan."[7]

Neither freedom nor hope is writ in a single line or image of the film's conclusion, of course, and to infer that Bergman meant to beam a ray of optimism into this hell of writhing souls is not only to distort the fundamental matter of *The Silence* but also to misread the trilogy's significance. In *Through a Glass Darkly* and *The Communicants*, Bergman had proposed that love is God—or, more accurately, that since "God" is a construct answering to the human need for love, expressing love is tantamount to creating God. The crucial difference between those two films lay in the fact that, whereas Minus is saved by loving and accepting love, Tomas is incapable of either. In *The Silence*, however, love is dead—or, to the extent to which Ester professes to love Anna and both sisters claim to love the boy, rendered powerless. Bergman's acknowledgment of this personal "truth" at exactly the middle of his career would echo in every film he would write hereafter. But the trilogy does more than mark the point where redemption through love ceases; like shifting patterns of iron filings spread on paper, the three films also chart the moving psychological magnet underneath. In the first, incest—at last actually committed—leads to absolution by the father. The second, rejecting this wish fulfillment as a self-deceiving contrivance, sprang from the image of a minister waiting for God the Father to appear, and although that conceit never directly enters the film, the psychological dynamics behind the emblem are evident. Tomas's guilt traces back to his parents. A fear buried in his childhood makes him feel unworthy, and Märta's claims on him as a woman fill him with self-disgust. Unable to forgive himself, he believes he cannot be forgiven; thus, Father-God never comes. In *The Silence*, the Oedipal motif again surfaces, but forgiveness is no longer the issue, and the father, in any guise, is conspicuous by his absence. The sisters' father is dead; Johan's father—at least by implication a cuckold—is far away in Sweden; and God seems to have been banished from the Timoka-world. The tension in this dream-as-film derives from Johan's disquieting encounter with the consequences of growing up, but Bergman offers no prospect of eventual relief from the anxieties that churn the nightmare; to be conscious is already to be condemned. From this point on, the quest for father that had taken the guise of a quest for God disappears from Bergman's films.

Not to Speak of All These Women

Neither the lukewarm reviews *The Communicants* received in 1963 nor its failure to attract the public dismayed Bergman; he had known from the start that its subject matter would have little appeal, and while making the film, he was determined not to compromise its integrity. *The Silence*, too, was meant to satisfy himself—indeed, after completing the picture, he warned the new head of SF that they should consider themselves lucky if it sold a hundred thousand tickets worldwide. Thus, months in advance of the premiere of *The Silence*, he decided that the time had come to recover his popular audience with a comedy—and to have a bit of fun in the bargain.

His interest in the burlesque fairy tale he had considered the previous year having faded, he turned instead to an idea he got from Käbi Laretei's tales about her former music teacher, whose husband, a prominent violinist with a roving eye, expected her to "direct traffic" to his bed.[1] Bergman developed the story and enlisted Erland Josephson, with whom he had collaborated on *The Garden of Eden*, to write the dialogue. (Once again, the two assigned script credit to "Buntel Eriksson.") The weekly sessions at Bergman's house had a sportive air for these old friends, and the script seemed to write itself. Bergman grew confident the film would be a hit. Unlike his earlier comedies, *Not to Speak of All These Women* would be straight farce, a blend of Jacques Tati and American slapstick comedy that he thought would have universal appeal—and that the U.S. market on which Bergman had come to depend would find irresistible. SF, sharing his expectations, designated it to be its first feature film in color and invested in training personnel for the switch.

Ironically, benefiting from a brisk public debate over the government's initial decision to censor its sex scenes, *The Silence* drew a hundred thousand Swedes a week during its first run and went on to great financial success abroad; *Not to Speak of All These Women* was an immediate and unmitigated disaster. For once, the critics' ill-tempered thrusts at Bergman were entirely justified. The dialogue is flat; the humor is snickeringly juvenile; Bergman's notion of using color as "a contrapuntal element" is so ostentatiously clever it becomes a constant distraction; the plot revolves tediously around one joke; the actors seem not to know what to do with their parts. Three days before the film's premiere, his production of Harry Martinson's *Three Knives from Wei* at Dramaten had been roundly panned; with this second drubbing, he said, he could claim the rare distinction of "two fiascos in one week!" But even though he felt the film critics had been laying for him and had slashed with an unseemly glee, he blamed himself for presenting them with such an easy target. Five years would pass before he could bear to view the comedy again.

Without notable exception, the great body of Bergman criticism reflects his embarrassment and dismisses this botched work within a few paragraphs. None of his post-1950 films has been found less interesting, even in its failure. And yet, if one sets artistic evaluation aside and examines it as a document of Bergman's imagination, it is as revealing as any film he made during this period. What at first glance appears to be a rowdy holiday from the trilogy's themes is actually an antic rendering of the same vision.

The film opens at the bier of master cellist Felix: after an improbable popinjay of a critic named Cornelius lays the manuscript of his biography of the great man in the coffin, each of seven "widows"—Felix's wife and mistresses—steps forward to pay her last respects. It ends with a resumption of the same scene. Cornelius, moved to read aloud from his book, discovers that someone has absconded with the crucial chapter, about "the essence of the personal." But the commotion caused by the theft is brief. As soon as a handsome, poor young man carrying a cello case enters and asks for Felix's patroness, the critic and the dead man's women desert the bier to flock to the new master of the instrument.

The hour-long flashback between—spanning the four days from Cornelius's arrival at Villa Tremolo, Felix's grand mansion, to the cellist's death— traces the critic-biographer's misadventures while seeking the great man's intimate secret. Clues abound. Felix's valet, said to be so like the master that he is virtually an alter ego, was once his rival as a musician; surely the scent of sadomasochism emanating from the valet's humiliation would be worth investigating. Similarly dark hints surround the eldest mistress, whom Felix cruelly betrayed with other women after her patronage opened his door to fame. But Cornelius fails to pursue such intriguing evidence. Eager to prove he is the master's equal as a lover, he chases the master's women instead. Yet, despite his pretensions, he succeeds in bedding only Bumble Bee, the "official mistress," an easy conquest who gives the critic a bad review for his performance. And when another mistress, mistaking him for Felix, fires a shot at him, Cornelius shows he lacks the master's nerve for amorous sport. An even more ludicrous presumption—that he is a gifted composer—also deflects him from his avowed purpose. Believing his fame will be assured if he can persuade Felix to play his "Song of the Fish: Abstraction Number 14" in the cellist's upcoming international radio concert, he tries to obtain an audience with the master through a number of ruses, including masquerading in a dress to attract the notorious womanizer's interest. All these outrageous efforts are self-defeating, of course, and Cornelius never does meet Felix. (Nor does the viewer: throughout the film, the cellist's face remains absent from the screen.)

All the while the critic strains to advance his petty cause, the mansion is astir over a more urgent matter: although the hour of the concert is fast approaching, Felix still has not announced his program. The reason for this strange reluctance is unstated, but there are strong hints that the cellist is in the grip of an artistic crisis arising from either loss of confidence in his preeminence or doubt about the value of his art. Years earlier, Felix had instructed his wife Adelaide to kill him if he should ever "abase my art or prove unfaithful to it"; ominously, Adelaide is now taking target practice. Thus, when he finally makes public his selection of the wretched "Song of the Fish," it is tantamount to suicide. True to their pact, Adelaide enters the studio as the concert is about to start and raises her pistol, but, perhaps because he has already "died" as an artist, Felix collapses before the gun is fired. The illusion of his integrity is preserved, even though the artist has become faithless. The next day, to insure that his secret will remain safe, Adelaide steals the chapter on the "personal" from Cornelius's manuscript.

Virtually everyone who saw the film, however, believed the secret was quite transparent: Bergman—whose romantic involvements had often been advertised in the gossip magazines, and who, moreover, had not only compared his films to music but also had just completed a trilogy in which the cello was the sole musical instrument heard—had made a *film à clef* in which Felix embodied his grandiose fantasies. But that aspect, though noted, drew little comment; instead, critics reacted to the ridiculous Cornelius with a stentorian defense against what they perceived to be a contemptuous attack on themselves. Bergman, according to their reading, was seeking revenge by asserting the artist's superiority over the parasitic critic—a silly argument that betrayed his misprision of the critic's function. To be sure, Bergman has always held critics in low regard—not without justification—and some of that ill-temper does seep into *Not to Speak of All These Women*, yet its real subject is the master artist's insecurity, not the critic's crassness. Ironically, had the critics not behaved like Cornelius, they might have discovered, if not a better film, a more interesting one.

The year before he and Josephson began writing *Not to Speak of All These Women*, Bergman had seen 8½ and been so profoundly moved by it he said he felt as if Fellini had made the film just for him. Whether consciously or not, Bergman obviously fell under its influence. Felix corresponds to Guido, Fellini's persona, and the harem at Villa Tremolo recalls Guido's fantasy mansion of women who answer to his every mood and need. Just as Guido's women straddle the line between his art and his life, so, too, do Felix's (or Bergman's). If, as is often assumed, the cellist's retinue consists of counterparts to women in Bergman's biography, it also assembles various types of women characters in his films. The chambermaid called Isolde, for example, is reminiscent of Petra, the maid in *Smiles of the Summer Night* also played by Harriet Andersson; Gertrud Fridh's Traviata is similar to Ottilia Egerman, whom she portrayed in *The Face*; and though Bibi Andersson's role as Felix's "official mistress" suggests her affair with Bergman, Bumble Bee's hoydenish innocence points toward the flirtatious second Sara in *Wild Strawberries* and Britt-Marie, the virgin in *The Devil's Eye*. Like Guido, Felix apparently regards all his women except one as mere complements of his sexual fantasies; for each of the filmmaker's personae, the exception is the complex figure of the wife-mother he has betrayed with all the rest. In Bergman's film, the wife-mother once more reflects the paradigm he introduced in the early plays and then exploited with such success in the Eva Dahlbeck characters of the 'fifties comedies. Adelaide —the only woman Felix calls by her true name and the only one who sees through the unreality of Villa Tremolo—is both his protectress and, rather like the mothers whose wombs offer escape, a merciful "executioner" who stands ready to deliver him from the mess he has made of his life. When Adelaide removes the chapter on "the essence of the personal" from Cornelius's manuscript to keep it safe with her, she acts like Desireé, who shields Fredrik from the world at the end of *Smiles of the Summer Night*.

But more than just affinities in respect to women link *Not to Speak of All These Women* to *8½*. Fellini's film revolves around the impossibility of his making a film. While Guido's public and co-workers wait impatiently for his genius to produce, he delays, beset by personal anxieties that have destroyed his belief in art's capacity to resolve meaning; finally, he conjures an escape through suicide, whereupon the young Guido is reborn to relive the fantasies from which he wove his art. Bergman's comedy shows a parallel pattern. Felix's concert corresponds to Guido's film: reporters besiege the villa, hoping to be first with news of the program the entire world is eager to hear, and his impresario warns him that time for indulging his artistic temperament has run out, but the cellist has not even begun to select his program, and in the end, there is no performance. His raising the bow to play "The Song of the Fish" signals his suicide—which, through the unmistakable allusion to "The Fish," carries an implication of a magical escape into the womb that is further supported by the final scene. Although the entrance of the handsome young cellist manifestly comments on the ephemerality of the artist and the immortality of the art, it also suggests a dream of rebirth.

Overshadowing any particular similarity between *8½* and *Not to Speak of All These Women* as fictive constructions is what they express of the filmmakers' own sense of creative paralysis. In this regard, Bergman's is the more disturbing—and disturbed—work, partly because, whereas Fellini transcends the crisis he describes by creating a masterpiece, Bergman's flaccid invention confirms the very exhaustion of the artist he makes his subject. But the problem extends well beyond imaginative fatigue. Although Guido's *bella confusione* (along with *The Labyrinth*, one of the working titles for *8½*) is reflected by layer upon layer of complex symbolism, Fellini's analysis of his protagonist is frank and uninhibited. In contrast, the strained laughter of Bergman's comedy conceals a paranoiac game.

The critic may be a boob, yet, for all the jokes at his expense, he holds the artist hostage. Artists die, technique improves, new virtuosi spring up, values change, Cornelius reminds Felix. "You will completely disappear, except from the minds of a few specialists, and then as something passé. . . . Who will point out what is significant about you? . . . And who, for that matter, will trust your fame when your decline begins and there is not a single slim volume about you to consult in all the world's libraries?" Felix affects indifference—"the playing is all that counts," one of the mistresses reports him saying—but the more the film insists upon the ignobility of the fame the critic offers, the more reason one has to infer that oblivion, the silent "song of the fish," obsesses him.

Much as Felix/Bergman contemns the ignorance and pretensions of the critic on whom his reputation depends, however, he also has a psychologically vital stake in that stupidity. Appropriately named, Villa Tremolo (i.e., chez Bergman) trembles at the edge of catastrophe—rather like the House of Usher, that mansion of the haunted self depicted by one of Bergman's favorite authors. Only Cornelius's Inspector Clouseau-esque bumbling in this "house of secrets where nothing is secret" prevents discovery of the "essence of the personal"; were the critic-biographer to blunder across the obvious and pronounce the secret of secrets at the core of Felix's anxiety—and art—the entire edifice of fantasies would explode. (And indeed, as a sign of this menacing possibility, Bergman has Cornelius misplace a lit cigar, which then ignites a store of fireworks that shoot through the house and out its chimneys and windows. Teasing, or daring, the audience to recognize what this symbolizes in respect to his films, Bergman here interjects, "These fireworks should not be taken symbolically.")

Although *Not to Speak of All These Women* never reveals the "essence of the personal" or why it should be so threatening to Felix, there is a real secret, and what it concerns is imprinted on the film's underside. The first of two clues rests in the illogical turn in the plot at the end. Somehow, the devastating information that is the object of Cornelius's errand is transcribed in his manuscript, yet no scene has shown him stumbling upon the answer to the mystery, nor does this boastful fool blurt out a word of the findings that would certify his acumen. As in a dream, the secret is both known and hidden. What could be more fitting, therefore, than that the crucial chapter fall into the possession of the maternal Adelaide—the one person besides Felix who, it seems, already knows the dreadful secret, presumably because she has been a party in it?

The second clue, which ultimately leads in the same direction as the first, is rather more obvious. Cornelius is not the first critic Bergman had conjured who engages in a destructive campaign to expose the secret of the artist: three years earlier, Bergman had "exposed" himself in the Ernest Riffe hoax. Like Riffe, Cornelius is maladroit in his language —one of the major faults with which Swedish critics lashed Bergman during the 'fifties. More important, like Riffe, Cornelius is reduced to risibility by insinuations of homosexuality: the film's theme song, heard when Cornelius appears on screen, is "Yes, We Have No Bananas"—an aspersion on his masculinity echoed by his failure with the harem and his humiliation when he is caught in female disguise. But if the joke plays on homosexuality, its meaning indicates a fear of impotence that, though sexual in its origin, concerns the artistic in its operation. From "Riffe's" Oedipal roots sprang the "revelation" of Bergman's bankruptcy as a filmmaker. So, too, here. Whether, as one may deduce, Cornelius has coerced Felix into agreeing to perform "Song of the Fish" by threatening to publish the "essence of the personal," or the cellist, feeling strangled as an artist by the tentacles of that secret, has decided to concede the absurdity of his struggle, the import is virtually the same.

Significantly, while examining his manuscript, Cornelius reads: "The boundary between the subjectively personal and the objectively musical is extremely hard to draw and involves a choice between discretion and silence. [But] complete silence under these circumstances would convey a skewed portrait of the Master, and that [too] would be deceptive and morally abominable." On one level, this is gibberish—even Cornelius asks, between sentences, "What the devil do I mean by that?" But behind its humorous intent, the passage encapsulates the predicament faced by Felix—and Bergman. Whatever else the cellist's seclusion and indecision before the grand concert might suggest, it cogently implies a conflict between his realization that art had become a meaningless exercise and his instinctive need and moral obligation to continue. As the Erasmus address would soon disclose more directly, the filmmaker was wrestling with the same issue.

A Twilight World

In mid-1963, nineteen years after his departure for Hälsingborg as a brash young man on a rescue mission, Bergman was installed as chief executive at the Royal Dramatic Theater. Since its founding in the eighteenth century, Dramaten had been the most prestigious theater in Sweden, though not consistently the best; during much of its recent history, it had grown stodgy and self-contented. The new theater chief meant to change that. Taking a direct interest in every level of its operation, he soon bruised the sensibilities of some co-workers through radical policy changes. With the same zeal, he campaigned for greater recognition from the state of the stage's importance to the nation's cultural life—and succeeded to the extent of more than doubling Dramaten's subsidy. And, of course, he also excited attention through his own work as a director. Beginning in the fall of his first year with a daring *Who's Afraid of Virginia Woolf* stripped of its realistic trappings, he mounted seven plays. Not all were well received, but his willingness to take risks resulted in some remarkable productions, including a *Hedda Gabler* which has become one of that play's classic interpretations.

Halfway through what had been projected as a six-year term, however, Bergman quit. "These people thought I should have been grateful for the post, that it was the highest happiness," he complained to a Stockholm reporter after the resignation. "That, it was not. It was the worst agony of my life." At the time of his appointment, he had said he looked forward to the challenge of solving managerial problems, but as fifteen-hour workdays became more rule than exception, he found the routine increasingly nettlesome. If only to protect his freedom as a creative artist—or, as he put it, to allow his demons to visit—a withdrawal was necessary. "Why should I sit suffering at Dramaten," he asked, "when I have the whole world before me and can do what I will?"[1]

But it was to Fårö, not to the "world," that he turned. During the shooting of *Persona* on that remote Baltic island, rumors began to circulate of an affair between the director and Liv Ullmann, the Norwegian actress who was appearing in her first Bergman film. Soon after, he moved out of the Djursholm villa he had occupied since his marriage to Käbi Laretei and built a simple house for himself and Liv amid the stony desolation where they would live as virtually husband and wife for the next five years. Fårö offered more than a retreat for lovers who wanted privacy, however; to Bergman, it represented at once a stable reality and that unreal island in the flow of time so many of his characters had yearned to inhabit.

> [E]ver since I was a child and felt a strong sense of home at my grandmother's in Dalarna, I never had an abiding feeling of security or home that I could associate with a geographical place. Nowhere. Not before Fårö.... The whole cycle of life there, of people and animals, has an enormously calming effect on an hysterical personality like mine because, there, no purpose is served by any form of hysteria. Whether I cry or shriek or I am angry or anxious or upset or whatever, nature remains exactly the same, life goes on in the exact same way. In Stockholm, I have my public. I can always change matters with an outburst which, temporarily at least, can satisfy my vanity, or an urge for freedom, the need to start a ruckus. On Fårö, the same behavior would have no effect at all.... Fårö is still as it was when it poked up from a Silurian sea; there is something primeval about this island.[2]

Bergman's films for the remainder of the decade would demonstrate the importance of the island, not just as setting but also as symbol. Contrary to what his description of Fårö as a pastoral haven suggests, however, that symbol refers to a nightmare in which the self is threatened with extinction from all sides. The very concept of identity is crumbling, the values that have sustained life's moral conduct shimmer, and the universe stands revealed as a violent, incomprehensible chaos. "I could suddenly see the world, and that is a terrifying experience," Bergman told his interviewers. "We're quite definitely living in a twilight world. But I don't know when the darkness will descend."[3]

The extent of this pessimism can be seen in his acceptance speech for Holland's Erasmus Prize. Established in 1958, the prize had first recognized the Austrian people for their struggle "to preserve their European character and culture" during the postwar occupation; subsequently, the committee had honored Karl Jaspers, Robert Schumann, Romano Guardini, and Martin Buber for exceptional contributions to European culture. In 1965 the judges chose to acknowledge the importance of cinema by selecting Chaplin and Bergman as the outstanding figures of its two most exciting periods. The award would seem to have called for a flourish of trumpets; instead, Bergman, who sent a substitute to receive the prize and deliver his remarks, responded with Spenglerian gloom.

Several times in the past, he had compared his films to the work of the antlike procession of artisans who built Chartres Cathedral. By binding a community together while materializing its inner hopes and fears, Chartres expressed art's public function; as an artist, he had said, his intention was to help rebuild a cathedral for our time in which art and worship joined.[4] Now, though he again analogized the artist to an ant, the metaphor took on an entirely different meaning: the ants fill the sloughed-off snakeskin art has become and give it the illusion of life, but this apparent vitality is aimless, an epiphenomenal result of each individual ant's pushing and shoving *only* because, in its "unruly curiosity," it "completely substitutes hunger for the future for communion with the past." Like religion, the humanistic art the Erasmus jury meant to celebrate was only being "kept alive for sentimental reasons, as a conventional politeness." The artist, he maintained, could no longer affect his audience because art had lost the capacity to imitate and contain the reality of their experience.

> Today people can reject the theater because they live in the middle of a drama that is constantly exploding in local tragedies. They don't need music because every minute their hearing is bombarded with a powerful torrent of sound reaching and surpassing the threshold of pain. They don't need poetry because the new world situation has changed them into functional animals concerned with interesting—but, from a poet's point of view, useless—problems of metabolism.

While contemporary life erupts, the arts, unable to contend with the tumult, have turned in upon themselves: the serious cinema (including his own) he described as less stimulating than Westerns; the new music, as "so attenuated by its mathematical precision that it leaves us choking for air"; painting and sculpture, as "sterile and moribund in their paralyzing freedom"; and literature, as "a rockpile of words without message or danger." Bergman had always sneered at the pretensions of the artist who "considers his isolation, his subjectivity, his individualism almost holy."[5] Now, he was emphasizing alienation as a rudimentary fact of contemporary life; the breakdown of art was an inescapable consequence of "this sad situation." The only remnant of hope in these circumstances, he concluded, lay in recognition that "the artist shares his condition with every other living being who also exists for his own sake. In concert, there is the possibility that we may become a rather large brotherhood existing in this manner in selfish fellowship on this warm, dirty earth under a cold and empty sky."

Significantly, when the script of *Persona* was issued as a book, the Erasmus address served as preface. Even though nothing in the address comments specifically on the film, its appraisal of the terms under which an artist labors becomes, in effect, an apologia for the paradox of art undermining itself that is central to *Persona*. Bergman had occasionally taken risks in the course of evolving a personal cinematic syntax, but *Persona* is the first of his films to break ranks with the past and step toward the avant-garde. One can see this development as part of the new cinema that emerged in the 'sixties—and no doubt he was looking over his shoulder at the revolution led by the *Nouvelle Vague*. Bergman, however, espoused no new theory of cinema, nor could anyone accuse him of imitating a fashion. *Persona* repeatedly questions the means by which it exists because its creator was questioning the assumptions of existence itself. In this regard, one should recognize that the doleful cadence of the Erasmus address owes less to the state of art and civilization than to a personal malaise. As with the references to contemporary history that occasionally crop up in Bergman's films—e.g., Jonas's concern over the atomic bomb in *The Communicants*; Timoka's war jitters in *The Silence*; the news program about Vietnam in *Persona*—the entropic world he describes is fundamentally a metaphor for a self confronted by its ultimate meaninglessness.

Even more clearly than in the trilogy or in *Not to Speak of All These Women*, this plunge toward despair is evident in *The Deception*, an unfilmed screenplay published in a Swedish popular magazine in 1967 but apparently written several years earlier—perhaps while he was making the comedy.

Physically and emotionally exhausted, Axel Andersson, a prominent comic actor, hopes that a meeting with his estranged wife Elsa will produce a new start. (Surely, there is more than coincidence in the fact that Elsa, like Bergman's first wife Else Fisher, is a dancer.) When they embrace, it is "like a weld," created by their common desire "to extinguish their miserable selves," but as "the old antipathy, fear, and bitterness begin to enter the room like smoke," it quickly becomes apparent that the weld will not hold. Desperation, not love, has motivated this attempt at reconciliation, and in their pain, each tries to hurt the other. Nevertheless, they agree to defer a decision on whether to resume their marriage until after Axel has finished that evening's shooting for a film comedy.

The intermediate scenes elaborate Axel's anguish. In retake after retake of the comic sequence being filmed, the actor strains to be funny while his insides writhe with dread. The director calls a recess, but Axel's ordeal continues when Anne, a young actress who has come to the studio for a screen test, seeks to further her ambitions by offering to sleep with him. Besides being lashed by the irony in Anne's eagerness to prostitute herself in pursuit of a career that, in his case, has led to a life of torture, Axel is reminded of the grim conclusion to an earlier affair with his co-star Nelly. In a flashback to their final quarrel, Nelly flaunts her promiscuity in order to humiliate him, then demands that he look past her naked body to the suffering human being he has ignored while sharing her bed.

The inability to love at the core of that egoism is precisely what had destroyed Axel's marriage—and, Elsa finally realizes, would doom any attempt to restore it; when she returns to the studio that night, she announces that she is leaving him again, this time forever. At the end, while Elsa and Anne (who has failed her screen test) wait for their train at the station, Axel is once more in front of the camera as the clapperboard snaps to the director's command, "Begin." Ironically, what "begins" is not the new life the middle-aged actor had dared think possible only a few hours before but a sentence to hell from which he has no hope for pardon.

The Deception bears a close resemblance to *The Communicants*, not just in its two main characters but also in the religious argument they represent. Sounding much like Märta, Elsa in the first scene explains she has come back to Axel because they both "suffer rather severely and in a deeply personal way from fear, from lack of tenderness, lack of contact. From the terror of death." Through her mistakes, she says, she has found a new faith: "at the end, nothing means anything; one feels disgust for one's self and the world. One can't stand it any longer. Suddenly there are only two paths to follow. Suicide or God. Everything else is anaesthesia . . . to put off the decision." And for her, that decision to accept God implies a commitment to love. Axel responds like Tomas, the faithless minister locked within himself:

> Please don't pity me. I was born and I shall die. In between there are damnably many defeats and a smaller number of minor successes. I've seen through myself and seen my absurdity and my complete lack of meaning in the universe. I think it is comforting to know that one is only a mass of cells put together at random which, during a short moment, can perform a number of mechanical movements. The ache in my soul weighs exactly as much as my hangnail, or stomach ache, or the pain in my tooth. In the final analysis, they are trifling imperfections in a great sophisticated imperfection.

With *The Deception*, however, Bergman slid into a deeper despondency. In *The Communicants*, spiritual blight is concentrated in one man, and though the personal implications in the portrait of the oppressed minister are not to be discounted, Bergman nonetheless presents Märta's unconditional, potentially redemptive love as an alternative to Tomas's cramping egoism. In *The Deception*, the surrender to nihilism is unqualified. Like Tomas, Axel is lost from the start; the failure to win his wife back only confirms the impossibility of escape from the pit he has dug for himself. Elsa, on the other hand, begins where Bergman had left Märta: with the conviction that God (i.e., the belief in a value beyond mere physical existence) has given purpose to her life. But by the end of the day, she has come to understand that the faith which had produced "a feeling of happiness, a kind of certainty," is a monstrous self-deception. "We are powerless," she says, and in that realization the possibility of hope and love die: "What had become of all my vows, all my tenderness. Where could God be found? He was silent in any case. And it was dark and empty."

The Deception may be seen as another example of what Bergman called the "dematerialization of the whole religious superstructure [that occurred] in *The Communicants* and *The Silence*"; after the trilogy, the question of God's existence virtually disappears from his films.[6] But entirely too much has been made of his search for God. Ever since *The Seventh Seal*, each new film had been regarded as a report from the mountaintop Bergman periodically ascended to scan the heavens. In fact, none of his films had really been about man's relationship to God. Religion furnished a superstructure of metaphor, but the foundation, resting on pilings driven deep into his psyche, reflected his need to assert that life had meaning—and whether God existed or not finally had no bearing on those culminative moments of affirmation. The radical shift marked by *The Silence*, *The Deception*, and the Erasmus address lay in Bergman's concession, at last, to his sense of futility. Not surprisingly, in a discussion on Swedish television in 1966, Bergman admitted that, before embarking on *Persona*, he had considered giving up his profession.[7]

To the obvious question—Why go on making films or even living if neither art nor life has meaning?—Bergman had already given an answer in the Erasmus address:

> a boundless, insatiable, constantly reviving, intolerable curiosity unceasingly drives me on—a curiosity that has wholly displaced my old hunger for fellowship. I feel like a freed prisoner suddenly tumbled forth into the world, the crashing, howling, snorting world. That unruly curiosity grips me: I note, observe, stay alert. . . . I snatch a flying speck of dust. Maybe it's a film—what does it mean? Nothing at all, perhaps, but it interests *me*.

But he faced a more difficult question. Now that he had abandoned the quest for meaning around which his fiction had arranged itself, what form could the investigations of his curiosity describe? Having concluded that the silence—or absence—of God had "dematerialized" as a useful issue, he turned to the dematerialization of the self, to the void within.

Persona

Shooting on *The Cannibals*, a four-hour, wide-screen film in two parts, was to begin in mid-1965, just after Bergman's return from directing *The Magic Flute* in Hamburg. But then a respiratory infection during the winter developed very serious complications, incapacitating him for months. He withdrew from the opera; later, following a short postponement, the film was scuttled and the crew that had been assembled disbanded.* Around Midsummer Day, however, the call went out to

---

*One often reads that *The Cannibals* refloated as *Hour of the Wolf*, yet it should be evident that the two scripts were far apart. *Hour of the Wolf* runs eighty-nine minutes, much less than half the length of the abandoned film. Moreover, since Bergman writes his scripts

Visual representation of the crossing identities of Alma (Bibi Andersson) and Elisabet (Liv Ullmann). Note the sprocket holes at the right, included in the still at Bergman's insistence. Permission from Svenska Filmindustri.

reconvene. There would be a 1965 Bergman film after all: a "sonata for two instruments" he finished writing on June 17.

According to one account Bergman has given, the origins of *Persona* trace to an accidental meeting on a Stockholm street corner in which Bibi Andersson introduced him to Liv Ullmann. When the conversation turned to *The Cannibals*, for which Andersson was already under contract, he impulsively offered to add a small part for the Norwegian actress; despite the subsequent cancellation, his mental association of the women guided the idea for the new film into place. In another account, not altogether inconsistent with the first, he states that its seminal image—of two women "wearing big hats and laying their hands alongside each other"—derived from the "uncanny resemblance" he noticed in a slide he was shown of Andersson and Ullmann sunbathing.[1] But whatever the "speck of dust" may have been or exactly when it caught his eye, the "curiosity" that pounded the script into being led from personal desperation. *Persona*, he has said, was nothing less than "a creation that saved its creator."

> I was ill, having twice had pneumonia and antibiotic poisoning. I [literally] lost my balance for three months. . . . I remember sitting

with specific actors in mind, it is significant that neither Anders Ek nor Bibi Andersson, who were to have leading roles in *The Cannibals*, appears in *Hour of the Wolf*.

in my hospital bed, looking directly in front of me at a black spot
—because if I turned my head at all, the whole room began to spin.
I thought to myself that I would never create anything anymore. I
was completely empty, almost dead. . . .

Suddenly, one day I started thinking of two women sitting next to
each other and comparing hands. This was a single scene, which,
after an enormous effort, I was able to write down. Then, I thought
that if I could make a very small picture—perhaps in 16mm—about
two women, one talking, the other not, it would not be too hard for
me. Every day I wrote a little bit. I had as yet no idea about making a
regular film, because I was so sick, but I trained myself for it. Each
morning at ten I moved from the bed to the writing table, sat down,
and sometimes wrote and at other times couldn't. After I left the
hospital, I went to the seaside, where I finished the script, although
I was still sick. Nevertheless, we decided to go ahead. The producer
was very, very understanding. He kept telling me to go on, that we
could throw it away if it was bad because it wasn't an expensive
project. In the middle of July, I started shooting, still so sick that
when I stood up I became dizzy.[2]

What impelled this heroic effort, he later told a Swedish television
audience, was "a sort of truth-crisis that made me feel suddenly that I
had to take a stand. What is true and when does one tell the truth? It
became so difficult that I thought the only form of truth is silence. And
in the end, going a step further, I discovered that it, too, was a kind of
role, also a kind of mask. The need is to find a step beyond."[3]

The story in which Bergman wraps his meditation on truth is more
donneé than plot. Elisabet Vogler, a celebrated actress, suddenly stops
speaking midway through a performance of *Electra*, and, rejecting her
real-life "roles" as wife and mother as well, continues her self-imposed
muteness offstage.* The woman psychiatrist at the hospital, finding no

---

*The fact that Bergman not only cites a specific play but also states that the actress fell
mute in the second act implies some correspondence between the play and Elisabet's
decision. What it might be, however, is difficult to determine—especially since Bergman
does not indicate which role she played. Presumably, she would have had the lead. Yet, if
Bergman intended to draw a parallel, subsequent developments in *Persona* point to
Clytemnestra, the wife and mother who, in the second episode of the Sophocles drama,
lies about her motive in killing Agamemnon and then rejoices at the report of her son's
death. Then again, if one sees *Persona* emanating from a troubled relationship between
son and mother, Electra's denunciation of her mother's lust for Aegisthus and her vow to
kill him become most suggestive—not in terms of Elisabet but in respect to Bergman's

physical or mental illness that would explain her condition, is confident the actress will in time decide to function normally again. She assigns the case to a young nurse, Alma, and sends both to spend the summer at her own house by the sea. There, flattered by the great actress's attention as she chirps away, Alma pours out her private life, including details about an abortion she underwent. But when she discovers that the actress has been coldly studying her, trust is replaced by resentment. Then, without Alma's being fully cognizant of what is happening, Elisabet's perception slowly begins to infiltrate her mind. This psychic transfer culminates in a long, complex dream in which the nurse becomes her patient, then "cures" her (and thus herself) by forcing acknowledgment that the mask of identity is a lie—even when the mask is rendered mute by a commitment to truth—and that, beyond the lie, there is only nothingness.

Obviously, the chase after a will-o'-the-wisp Truth dancing over the void had fascinated Bergman long before *Persona*. Most of his plays were about an encounter with nothingness—indeed, an image in *The Day Ends Early* vividly foreshadows the cycle *Persona* introduces. "Now I am naked in front of you," Jenny tells the actor Peter, "and the same thing has happened to me as to a person I saw in a film. When he undressed and unwound the bandages around his face and hands, there was neither body nor hands. There was only nothing." Manifested in various permutations, this terror of nothingness repeatedly surfaces in the films, from *Not to Speak of All These Women* back to *Crisis* (where Jack, confronted by another Jenny, stands amid a gallery of dummy heads just before committing suicide).* *The Face*, particularly, seems almost a preliminary exercise for *Persona*: like Elisabet Vogler, the magician who bears the same surname withdraws behind a mute mask, then casts it aside when it proves inadequate.

Yet, if the theme itself is not new, its treatment marks a significant departure from past films. Up to *The Communicants* (and, in a sense, including that pivotal film as well), Bergman had raised the dread of

psyche. (Cf. Bergman's incorporation of Hamlet—who resembles Electra in this episode—in *Fanny and Alexander*.)

Curiously, a mimeographed description of *Persona* distributed by SF, perhaps based on material Bergman had furnished, referred to the play as *Phaedra*, not *Electra*. Bergman then made the same mistake during an interview in 1969.[4] Might it have been this other play that Elisabet was performing in some earlier draft of *Persona*? If so, what lies in the film's depths has dark psychological implications.

*Virtually the same image found in *The Day Ends Early* recurs in *Wild Strawberries*, where the self Isak meets in his first dream dissolves before his eyes.

life's barrenness only to counter it at the end, either by invoking a kind of salvation through illusion (e.g., in *Women's Waiting* and *Smiles of the Summer Night*) or by an outright refutation (e.g., *The Seventh Seal* and *Through a Glass Darkly*). This changed with *The Silence* and *Not to Speak of All These Women*, but *Persona* goes well beyond these films: whereas, previously, he had exfoliated the anxiety of confronting meaninglessness, here the discovery that nothingness is all-encompassing, that the only truth is that everything is a lie, becomes the burden of the film's argument. One can misconstrue the significance of the final scenes in *The Silence* and *Not to Speak of All These Women* and the rest will still hold together; were one to misread the conclusion of *Persona* (or of the films that follow), the entire fiction would become incoherent.*

The thesis that reality exists only as the surface of the void—i.e., as the mask of nothingness—is also inherent in Bergman's use of the film to call attention to its own unreality. In this respect, too, *Persona* is not without antecedents; never before, however, had he invoked the conceit in such spectacular fashion or incorporated it so fundamentally into the presentation of the fiction.** Like much modern drama and literature —and particularly like *Six Characters in Search of an Author*, which Bergman had staged at Malmö in 1953 and would stage again in 1967 for the National Theater in *Oslo*—*Persona* insists on the illusory quality of art in making its statement about the illusory nature of truth; the dilemma of the artist has become not merely a metaphor for the human dilemma (as in *The Face*) but the phenomenological condition of the art itself.

Before it becomes anything else, the film is the medium between artist and audience—the illusionist's mask (analogous to the *persona*,

---

*In its argument, as well as in some aspects of the story, *The Deception* is quite close to *Persona*. Like Elisabet, Axel is paralyzed by the realization that everything he might say or do is false, that life is a role he "playacts." (Bergman stresses that asking or granting forgiveness under these conditions can never be more than recitation of lines on cue —hence the infernal atmosphere of both works. Existential guilt seems implicitly the only absolute this side of an ultimate nothingness.) Accentuating life's inauthenticity, *The Deception* begins with Axel in the dressing room, preparing for his "performance" (not only in the comedy being shot but also with Elsa); in the final scenes, he returns to the dressing room to hear Elsa's decision, then stands before the cameras as the next day's agony in filming the comedy begins. Similarly, *Persona* is bracketed by shots of Elisabet performing *Electra*, outside of which, moreover, is another frame calling attention to the fact that this is a film being made.

**Perhaps the clearest example of the fiction's "self-consciousness" occurs in *Prison*, where the studio scenes that frame the story of Birgitta-Carolina—the film that cannot be made—pose art against life.

or character mask, used in the ancient theater).* In the original script, the film was to begin with a clear strip of celluloid clattering through the projector accompanied by the noise of dust particles traveling over the sound head. Next, word fragments were to drop to the screen from the ceiling and walls, followed by indistinct contours which, in the whiteness of backlighting, would appear to be first a cloud, then a water glass, again a cloud, then a tree, and then a moonscape before finally assuming the shape of Nurse Alma's face peering directly into the camera.

Somewhat modified, this representation of the infinitely plastic possibilities of the cinematic image as it forms ex nihilo is retained in the actual film, but Bergman greatly expanded the concept to encompass a brief autobiography of the film itself. Thus, the first frames show the carbon arc lamp lighting—producing the light on which the film's images depend for their existence—and the film's leader as it winds over the spool. A cartoon of a woman bathing, inverted as if not yet righted by the lens, is followed by the picture of the projector ostensibly producing the image, then by the slow movements of a child's hands. Through these allusions to Bergman's boyhood interest in motion pictures as a means to "seek contact" with the world outside his "fantasy-ridden self," the film's beginnings have now merged with the filmmaker's.[5] Next, a fragment of the silent farce sequence from *Prison* shows a skeleton popping up from a chest—a reference to the fear of death that has haunted Bergman. In similar fashion, a spider evokes the spider-God, and shots of a lamb being killed (presumably in a sacrifice) and of a hand being pierced by a spike reflect his recurrent use of the Crucifixion motif. This progression of images illustrates the desire to make a film which, as yet, has not found its subject—as Bergman later commented, "there were only old, dull ideas" rattling in his head.[6]

A change in the character of the images indicates the start of another phase. Shots of a wall, a wooded park, an iron fence, and dirty snow piled before a building situate the film's gestation at the Sophiahem hospital, where the filmmaker grew up and where he was undergoing treatment during the early spring when he began writing the film. From these views of the grounds, Bergman moves to the hospital's morgue, in which an old man, an old woman, and a boy are lying on slabs. (Bergman: "My existence [at the hospital] consisted of dead people and tiled walls.")[7] Suddenly, the old woman's eyes pop open. Perhaps this signs the persistence of another "old idea": the "impossible trick" of defeating death. Or,

---

*The working title of *Persona* was *Cinematograph*.

given the startled look on the dead woman's face, it may refer to Bergman's examination of a naked female corpse when, as a boy, he stole into the Sophiahem morgue. Or it may represent the beginning of the new idea (later, both Alma and Elisabet will be seen in the same position as the old woman).

In any case, the camera's attention now shifts to the boy, awakened by a ringing telephone. (While thinking about *Persona*, Bergman has explained, "I pretended I was a little boy who was dead but really shouldn't be dead because Dramaten is constantly waking him with telephone calls.")[8] Ignoring the ringing, he pulls his sheet over him and assumes a fetal tuck, but he cannot get back to sleep (or return to the unconscious state of the womb). The boy then puts on a pair or wire-rimmed glasses and begins to read a page-marked copy of *A Hero of Our Time*. Although, in itself, Lermontov's novel about an emotionally dead protagonist who is filled with nothingness would be an appropriate epigraph for *Persona*, its more important symbolic function rests in its being the same book which Johan, played by the same actor wearing the same glasses, had been reading in *The Silence*. Besides bringing the recapitulation of Bergman's past films up to the edge of the new film, the unmistakable reference to *The Silence* also links Johan's study of Anna and Ester to the study of Alma and Elisabet about to begin.

As the camera moves toward the boy, he stretches his hand toward it (i.e., toward the screen and the audience with which the screen interfaces); then, with the camera behind him so that the audience assumes his perspective, he feels the screen (now shown within the frame) on which is projected a woman's face (Bibi Andersson's) that changes into another face (Liv Ullmann's) while he is probing its features. This curious sequence prompts several related interpretations. First, the boy (who both represents the filmmaker and is a surrogate for the viewer being addressed) is apparently seeking to understand something through art (the screened images that deputize for the film). Second, the effect of the reverse shots associating the viewer with both the boy and the screen is to suggest that, in a sense, the film is about himself. Third, given that *Persona* grew out of the resemblance between Andersson and Ullmann, their faces (which are not yet the faces of the Alma and Elisabet) mark the point of conception in this ontogeny. Fourth, the interchanging faces (or *personae*) foreshadow the film's scheme: the transfer of two women's "identity masks" through a recognition of their common relationship to a child. This last signification seems to trigger a new and much more rapid sequence of images: indicating what Bergman called "the film's impatience to get started," the title and credits flash by, interspersed with proleptic quotations of ideas to be developed—a Vietnamese monk's self-immolation; a negative print of a pair of lips, turned vertically to suggest a vagina; a seacoast; the faces of the two principal characters; a much-magnified, quivering eyelid; and, again, this time anticipating a subsequent insertion, a few frames of the silent farce from *Prison*.[9] The dominant image, however, is of the boy's face, which reappears nine times within half a minute.*

Like an image becoming visible in a bath of developing solution—or as though it were being summoned by the boy's concentration—faint outlines of a door and wall emerge from a completely white screen; the film proper has at last materialized. Alma opens the door, enters, and listens while the psychiatrist, off camera, describes the case to which she is being assigned. The nurse then visits Elisabet in her hospital room, awkwardly chats about herself, and leaves. On returning to the psychiatrist, she reports her impression that the actress's great mental strength may call for a nurse with more experience, but the same diffidence that makes her wish the case were reassigned prevents her from refusing it.

After this *mise en jeu*, Bergman presents a complex set of four discontinuous scenes. Alma and Elisabet are alone in the second and third; together in the first and fourth. Another symmetry balances illusion in the initial pair against reality in the latter. Still another counterposes the theatricality of what is heard over the radio in the first and the horrifying reality of what is seen on television in the third; the comfort of established personal relationships in the second and their rejection in the fourth. One begins to suspect that the psychiatrist, like God conducting an experiment, has a special purpose in matching this nurse and this patient.

Scene One. Alma performs her evening chores in Elisabet's room while listening to a romantic radio melodrama. To the actress, the dialogue is ridiculous, and when one of the voices speaks sententiously of mercy, she giggles, but to the unsophisticated nurse, this sort of maudlin fare is "enormously important, especially for people with problems."

---

*In *Styles of Radical Will* (New York, 1968), Susan Sontag reports the presence of an erect penis among these images; after the essay's appearance, several critics have either relied on her account or assumed that these frames were later cut by the American distributor. I also cannot recall having seen any such image when I attended the Swedish premiere of *Persona* or in two later viewings in Sweden. Having examined the U.S. print on a viewer, I can vouch that there was no penis to shock American audiences.

Offended by Elisabet's persistent smile, Alma angrily switches the dial to a program of Bach and leaves; in their first skirmish, she has been made to feel like a fool. And yet it is not at all certain that the other woman has won. As darkness envelopes Elisabet, her smile fades, and the abstract aesthetic perfection of the music seems to intensify the isolation into which she has cast herself.

Scene Two. In contrast to Elisabet, who passively accepts the darkness, Alma nervously flicks the light on and off while trying to sleep that night. Something about the actress disconcerts her, and to calm herself, she creams her skin and mutters reassuringly about her fiancé, the family they will one day have, the satisfaction she derives from meeting people's needs in her job—the very consolations Elisabet has repudiated. Life, she trusts, will be good to her: "There's nothing to worry about." But her restlessness will not subside; in a tone halfway between fear and awe, almost as though she were wondering what it would be like to be the other woman, she speaks the name "Elisabet Vogler."

Scene Three. Perhaps at the same hour, Elisabet, watching the late night news on television, recoils with horror at the sight of a Vietnamese monk setting fire to his gasoline-soaked body. The viewer may see this grisly act of political protest as undercutting Alma's smug belief in life's goodness, but what drives Elisabet cowering into a corner of the room is not the threat to Swedish placidity. Rather, it is the monk's terrible silence while enduring extreme pain in dying for his conviction—in contrast to her silence because she can find no basis for belief in anything. Set against the monk's agony, her renunciation seems intellectually pretentious self-indulgence.

Scene Four. Again the friendly, helpful nurse, Alma volunteers to read aloud Mr. Vogler's letter to his wife. (In a sense, she has taken the first step toward "becoming" Elisabet.) Indirectly asking his wife to return, the letter recalls the sentiments expressed in the radio play, but Elisabet no longer finds such pleading funny: agitated by her husband's reminiscence about a more innocent period in their lives, she snatches the letter from the nurse's hands. Alma then gives her a snapshot of the Voglers' son that the husband had enclosed in the letter—a tacit appeal to motherliness (another echo from the radio play) which produces an even stronger reaction than his words.* After staring at it for a moment, Elisabet tears the photograph in two.

*In the film, the only line of the radio play that is clearly heard is "What do you know of mercy?" But in the published screenplay, that line continues " . . . what do you know of a mother's suffering, a woman's bleeding pain?" Interestingly, this apparently quite personal

This emphasis on her rejection of her child (foreshadowing the discovery at the film's conclusion) is followed by a scene that complements the introductory interview between Alma and the psychiatrist. Now it is Elisabet who looks into the doctor's penetrating eyes and hears a precise analysis of her muteness.

> Don't you think I understand? The hopeless dream to *be*. Not seem but be. Conscious and watchful every second. And at the same time the abyss between what you are to others and what you are to yourself. The feeling of dizziness and the constant hunger to be unmasked. At last to be seen through, reduced, perhaps extinguished. Each accent a lie and a betrayal. Each gesture a falsification. Each smile a grimace.

Reconstructing the actress' thought process, the doctor says that, oppressed by disgust and an unrelenting demand for truth, she had considered suicide before rejecting it as too horrible; then she decided to disengage from life's deceitfulness by immuring herself in silence.

> But reality is fiendish. Your hiding place isn't tight enough and life seeps in everywhere. You are forced to react. . . . Elisabet, I understand your refusal to speak, your immobility, your making willlessness into a fantastic system. I understand and I admire. I believe you will hold onto this role until you find it uninteresting, played out, and you can [then] drop it as, one by one, you've dropped all your others.

Here, in the script's printed version, the filmmaker's "voice" "speaks" to the "viewer," telling him that his emotional and intellectual involvement with these women is nothing less than magic—an effect produced by a ribbon of film rattling inexorably through a projector at twenty-four frames a second. Confident that the illusion has taken hold, the voice virtually dares the viewer to "turn off the switch, extinguish the hissing arc, rewind the film, lay it in its case and forget it." In the actual film, the reassertion of the relationship between filmmaker and film is much less obtrusive: Bergman's voice simply tells the audience that nurse and patient have become easy companions in the weeks since they left the hospital to live at the psychiatrist's cottage. Although

allusion to the quarrel that separated Bergman from his mother is followed (in the published version) by a line that echoes several of his plays and films: "Oh God, you who are out there, somewhere in the darkness surrounding us all, have pity on me. You who are love. . . . "

this is scarcely necessary information, the supervention serves to bridge the first grouping of short, sharply chiseled scenes and the more fluid action that follows; in effect, it is the transition between the first and second acts (or, given Bergman's comparison of the film to a sonata, between the first and second movements).

Just as the first part of the Alma-Elisabet story had been preceded by an account of its ontogeny, the second begins with a reference to the image of the women "wearing big hats and laying their hands alongside each other" from which the film hatched. Shielded from the sun by straw hats, the nurse and the actress sort mushrooms they have gathered and check for poisonous varieties by consulting pictures in a field guide; comparing mushrooms then leads Alma to infer that Elisabet wants to compare hands.* But Bergman is not just making a private allusion to the film's conception. The mushrooms suggest the theme of parasitism; the fact that Alma, afraid comparing hands would bring bad luck, draws back from the intimate game she believes the other woman has proposed foreshadows the elaboration of that theme.

At the start of the next scene, Alma reads aloud a passage she finds in a book: "The cries of our faith and doubt into the darkness are the most terrible proofs of our forlornness and our frightened, unspoken knowledge." When Elisabet nods in agreement, Alma meekly protests that the axiom is unacceptable; shortly thereafter, she speaks of the retired nurses who will die in the modest little rooms of the old age home, a secular convent adjacent to the hospital where they served.** Her goal, she says, is to be like them. "To believe in something so strongly that one devotes his whole life to it. . . . thinking your life has meaning. That appeals to me."*** One soon perceives, however, that this attraction to altruism is a romantic self-deception concealing her sense of personal worthlessness.

---

*Ever since Stig Ahlgren wrote in his review that the women's hats resemble those worn by Vietnamese peasants, most critics have offered the same observation and tried to tie this scene to the clip of the monk's suicide.[10] But the monk, of course, wears no such hat; moreover, beyond being made of straw, the women's hats in fact bear no resemblance at all to the Vietnamese variety.

**Just such a retirement home for nurses existed on the Sophiahem grounds in Bergman's youth. Its inhabitants were routinely included in the coffee and cakes receptions at the parsonage following the hospital chapel services conducted by Pastor Bergman.

***Given Bergman's interest in depicting Alma and Elisabet as opposites at this point, one can assume that the similarity between the nurse's aspiration and the dedication to a cause implicit in the Vietnamese monk's suicide is intentional. What the nurse naively professes to admire corresponds to the extreme form of self-abnegation from which the actress had recoiled in horror.

A bit under the influence of alcohol, Alma recalls her affair with a married man—the first and only man she ever loved—who deserted her after five years; significantly, she implies that he was justified in tiring of her. Then, Bergman notes, "becom[ing] increasingly unself-conscious, heedless, fascinated and confused that someone (for the first time in her life) should find her interesting," Alma risks a second confidence. The previous summer, she and a girlfriend were sunbathing nude when they noticed two teenage boys watching from the rocks above. Summoning first one, then the other, they engaged in various sexual acts, including fellatio and switching partners in mid-intercourse. Twice Alma felt orgasm as she never had before. That night, she experienced the same ecstasy with her fiancé Karl-Henrik. Alma relives every sensual detail in telling the story, yet her face and voice express sadness, not pleasure, and she seems dimly aware that these extraordinary sexual moments were encounters between carnal objects, not persons.* As though confirming her reduction to "thingness," when she discovered she was pregnant, Karl-Henrik casually arranged for an abortion. This admission—which, in effect, belies the noble sentiments she had earlier expressed—is most painful of all. Breaking into sobs, she asks, "What comes of everything one believes in? Doesn't it matter at all?"

That Alma lacks a firm sense of ego is further indicated by a number of remarks that patter through her confessions. She would like to change: "there's a lot about myself I don't like." Karl-Henrik "says I live like a sleepwalker." "I was never quite real to him [the married man she loved]." "A lot of people have said I'm a good listener. That's funny, isn't it? I mean, no one has ever bothered to listen to me." Obviously envious of Elisabet's strength, she speaks of wishing they could trade selves:

> That evening when I had been to see your film, I stood in front of the mirror and thought, "We're rather alike."** Oh, don't misunderstand. You are much more beautiful. But we're alike in some way. And I should probably be able to turn myself into you. If I strained myself. I mean inside me. Don't you think so? And for you, it wouldn't be any trick at all to turn into me. You could do it just like that. Of

---

*When she asks herself, "Can one be completely different human beings, exactly alongside one another, at the same time?" the word she uses for "one another" is the neuter *vartannat*, not the *varandra* called for by the reference to persons.

**She is referring to the evening following the reading of Mr. Vogler's letter and Elisabet's tearing the photograph of her son, but the context makes it seem Alma means to indicate the day of her abortion, about which she has just been talking. The ambivalence may be deliberate: the film will later show the two incidents to be related.

course, your soul would stick out a bit everywhere because it's too big to be inside me.

Alma smiles at her own girlish chatter, but it is quite revealing. The child she surrendered was far more important to her than she allows herself to believe: almost literally, a child would have filled her with meaning as a mother and a wife. Thus, in her fantasy, Elisabet would substitute for the aborted fetus, swelling within her until the actress entirely fills her being—or, put another way, until the nurse captures the stronger ego within her own vacuous shell. Indeed, her desire to become Elisabet is so strong she "hears" the other woman tell her to go to bed lest she fall asleep at the table—the very words Alma herself is about to speak. And sometime during the night, she imagines Elisabet coming to her room, smoothing Alma's hair back from her forehead (just as Alma, in a characteristic gesture, has repeatedly done), and tenderly kissing her neck as though she were a lover about to enter her. (Bergman suggests a merging of identities by having Elisabet's hair enclose both women.)*

Structurally, this first dream of coalescence, midway through the film, corresponds to the dream at the end. Whereas the movement culminating in the first traces Alma's surrendering her "self" to Elisabet, however, the second half of the film deals with the nurse's struggle for dignity as a separate individual—ironically, while she becomes increasingly aware that the actress's views have infiltrated her mind. The pivotal moment occurs during Alma's drive into town to post some letters, including one from Elisabet to the psychiatrist. (One might well wonder what principle in the actress's code of silence allows her to discriminate the written from the spoken word. Apparently, Bergman bowed to a necessary inconsistency.) Noticing that Elisabet has left her letter unsealed, Alma feebly battles temptation, then pulls off the road to read it. One violation of privacy reveals another. After commenting on the "new health, a sort of barbaric cheerfulness" the letter-writer has gained by immersing herself in "elementary sensations," the letter becomes a report filed on Alma:

> [S]he is attached to me to the extent that she is a bit infatuated in an unconscious and charming way. All in all, it's very amusing to study

---

*That Alma has dreamed this intimate encounter is indicated by her asking the actress the next morning whether she had visited the bedroom during the night; puzzled by the question, Elisabet shakes her head. Although several critics have raised the possibility that Elisabet is lying, such an interpretation would be radically at odds with her reason for remaining mute: to avoid all lies, all hypocrisy, no matter how great the cost.

her. . . . I encourage her to talk, it's truly educational. Sometimes she cries over past sins (some sort of episodic orgy with a wild teen age stranger and a subsequent abortion). She complains that her concepts about life don't accord with what she encounters. In any case, I have her trust and she relates the important and trivial about herself. As you can see, I stuff myself with everything I come across, and as long as she doesn't suspect anything, it doesn't matter.

Nurse and patient have switched positions. Elisabet's familiar tone with the psychiatrist implies that they are the associates in a study of "our dear Alma." The watcher has become the watched. Feeling utterly betrayed, Alma pulls herself in; her features harden. Confronting her humiliation and the deceptions inherent in human relations, she has made a discovery similar to the one that led Elisabet into muteness.

At the first opportunity, Alma acts to repay her hurt. One can almost see the seed of a cruel thought germinate after she accidentally breaks a water glass; setting a jagged piece of glass in front of the cottage door and then waiting for Elisabet's bare foot to come down on it, she seems to be testing her capacity for malice. When her victim winces in pain and stares at her unbelievingly, Alma's icy composure indicates triumph, not only over her betrayer but also over the pliant ninny she has been. At this moment, the frame showing Alma peering at her victim through a gauze curtain "cracks" and "burns." A few fragments of the "old ideas" from the prelude—the sequence from *Prison*, the spiked hand, the close-up of the eye—flash by as the film strains to recompose itself. Then a blurry image of a woman looking though the curtain appears; when it pops back into focus, however, one sees the woman is not Alma but Elisabet. If the film's "break down" initially implies hatred too intense for the celluloid to support, the virtual substitution of the actress for the nurse at its resumption implies something even more insupportable than hatred has been responsible—a horror that will be represented by the fusion of the women's identities at the film's conclusion.

Shying from the "truth" about Elisabet and about herself that has surfaced in the previous two scenes, Alma seeks to repair communication with her patient. First she invites comment on a pair of dark sunglasses she has bought (a new mask, as it were). When Elisabet, showing no interest, starts reading a play, Alma falls back into the role of solicitous nurse—and thereby tries to restore the line of authority subverted by the letter. "I'll tell the doctor. It's a good sign," she says. "Perhaps we can leave this place soon." But Elisabet barely takes notice. Finally, not as a nurse assisting in therapy now but as one who is herself in desperate need, she openly begs for "just a couple of words" in recognition of her human existence—yet, paradoxically, her appeal acknowledges the very falsity of language that has led Elisabet to renounce speech.

> It's not easy to live with someone who just says nothing, I tell you. It ruins everything. I can't bear hearing Karl-Henrik's voice on the telephone. He sounds so false and histrionic. I can't talk with him anymore. It's unnatural. You hear your own voice, too, and *no one else*. You think: how phony I sound. All these words I use. Look, I'm talking a streak now, but it pains me to talk because I still say nothing. No, I must try not to get angry. You say nothing and, strictly speaking, that's your affair. But now *I need* you to talk to me. Please, can't you talk to me just a bit? It's almost intolerable.

Exasperated by Elisabet's third refusal to be drawn into conversation, Alma accuses her of artistic bad faith and personal immorality in withholding compassion. Here, again, however, language mocks her need for confirmation that she exists, not just as a biological phenomenon or as a reflection in someone else's eye but in herself, as *Alma*. What attests that genuine self when even her anger, she says, sounds artificial, like lines spoken by a character in a melodrama?

While the nurse's frustration mounts, she repeatedly removes and replaces her sunglasses—vacillating, as it were, between shielding and exposing her naked, vulnerable being—until, finally, she flings the glasses to the ground, grabs Elisabet, and vows to force her to speak. A nasty scuffle ensues in which Alma's nose is bloodied. Bent on retaliation, she snatches a pot of boiling water from the stove, whereupon Elisabet suddenly cries out, "No, don't do it!" Terror has brought Alma an unexpected victory. Lowering her arm, she gloats over having at last breeched the actress's "fantastic system" of silence.* But the enigmatic smile that appears on Elisabet's face soon belies that victory. Possibly, one begins to suspect, the letter had deliberately been left unsealed to demonstrate the insidious power of words—in which case, Alma's hateful reaction would justify the principle behind Elisabet's muteness. At the very least, even if no trap had been laid, the eruption of the nurse's will to hurt has blasted whatever remained of her meek, benign facade and exposed a core of primitive instincts. Elisabet's outcry, her smile implies, came

---

*That Elisabet's discipline cracks when she is threatened by the scalding water presents an obvious contrast to the Vietnamese monk's controlled acceptance of the flames.

from that core; everything else is a layered mask of hypocrisies from which she has retreated into silence.

When Alma returns from washing her wound, Elisabet offers a sip from her own cup of coffee (probably made with the same hot water that has just been aimed at her). The mood suggests a perception of futility rather than a truce. Alma asks, "Must it be this way? Is it *important* that one not lie, that one speak the truth, and in a truthful tone of voice? Is it necessary? Can one live at all without just chatter? Without flattering, without self-excuses, lies, evasions? . . . Isn't it better to let yourself be just what you are?" But what does it mean to "be just what you are?"

The frenetic pace of the scene that follows this languid interlude accentuates Alma's disorientation. Chasing after Elisabet, she rants about the actress's rottenness, then asks forgiveness, then calls her cruelly proud. Her words, however, have little more meaning than the squawks of the seabirds. Finally surrendering to her frustration, she sits, dreadfully silent and alone, among the rocks rimming the sea. Meanwhile, Elisabet, having gone into the house to read, removes a photograph from between the pages of her book. The viewer can only guess at her thoughts as she studies this often-reproduced photograph of a Jewish boy, arms raised in surrender, being led at gunpoint from his home in the Warsaw ghetto. The child may remind her of her son, who has suffered the loss of his mother because of her uncompromising stance; he may suggest Alma, surrendering her illusions; or he may simply illustrate the fear and vulnerability always present beneath the mask—an equation of existence with terror that makes Elisabet's dedication to "truth" an irrelevant abstraction.

At this point, the conflict between the women has been played out without resolution; although no clear boundary marks the transition from reality (evidently because Bergman means to imply that the suppositions on which the concept of reality rests are themselves unreal), the rest of the film, except for the closing minutes, consists of a long nightmare. Thrashing in her sleep that night, Alma dreams of awakening. (For some reason, the shot of Alma in bed and of her eyes popping open exactly corresponds to the shot of the old woman in the morgue.) Voices on the radio—the same ones earlier heard in the radio drama—gurgle through the static. In broken sentences, they seem to be expressing Alma's frustration: " . . . doesn't talk, doesn't listen, can't understand. . . . What means will . . . use to get to listen. Practically . . . played out. These constant cries. . . . "

Just then, one of these "constant cries," Mr. Vogler calling for his wife, comes from afar. Alma enters Elisabet's bedroom and stares at the sleeping woman's "corpse-like" form. As though she were examining herself in a mirror, the nurse comments on the signs of aging in Elisabet's face, the ugliness it reveals seen close up. When Mr. Vogler calls again, Alma joins him in the garden. Wearing dark glasses (like the ones Alma cast off), he takes her for Elisabet, but even after she says she is not his wife, he persists in treating her as though she were. Eerily, Elisabet, who has been standing unnoticed at their side, places Alma's hand on his face, as if instructing her in the role she is to play.

The locale now shifts to Alma's room, where, with Elisabet standing at bedside, the nurse and Vogler have been making love as husband and wife. Most of their conversation initially consists of rephrased material gleaned from her reading of his letter to Elisabet, but then Alma starts improvising concern for "her" son and reassurance for "her" husband that he is a "wonderful lover."* The deceptions necessary to their intimacy, however, eventually prove too much to bear. "Drug me, beat me to death, I can't, I can't take it any more. You mustn't touch me, it's a sham, a complete sham, it's just counterfeit, a lie. Let me be, I'm poisonous, bad, I am cold and rotten. Why can't I be permitted to cease to be, I don't have the courage." The sham, of course, is not the impersonation but the "seeming" that conflicts with "being." In this dream fulfillment of her earlier wish to "become" Elisabet, the nurse has reenacted the patient's revolt against the role of wife.

The dream's next phase examines an even more shocking element of that revolt. While the actress sits holding her hands over the photograph of her son, Alma, like a prosecutor reconstructing the circumstances of a crime, gives an account of how Elisabet became a mother. Taunted by a remark that, despite having realized her ambitions to be a wife and artist, she still lacked fulfillment as a woman, the actress allowed herself to become pregnant. Once the child began growing within her, however, she found the experience distasteful and tried unsuccessfully to induce abortion. After the birth, she nursed the baby with disgust; his incessant demands so invaded her independence that she wished him dead. (Underscoring the enormity of that desire, Alma speaks the phrase twice.) She sought to rid herself of the burden by leaving him with relatives, and when that failed, she escaped the child by returning to the

---

*Alma is apparently well-practiced in playing substitute. The first sentence she speaks as Elisabet, "I love you as much as before," ties her role in this instance to her affair with the only man she ever loved—also married to another woman. (In addition, her sexual activity in Elisabet's presence recalls the orgy on the beach, in which her partner penetrated her after beginning copulation with the other woman.)

stage. But the more she repelled him, the more the boy showed his love for her. Afraid and haunted by a bad conscience, she hid behind principle and retreated into silence.

This long monologue is delivered twice, first with the camera on Elisabet's face; then, in exactly the same words (although slightly abridged), with the camera on Alma. At the conclusion of the second telling, a look of astonishment comes over Alma's face—as though she has just been hit by the discovery that the horrible selfishness she has been condemning in the other woman is her own.* Suddenly manifesting the thought, the screen shows a face that is half Alma's, half Elisabet's. Alma protests: "No, I'm not like you. I am Nurse Alma, here to help you. I am not Elisabet Vogler. I. . . . " But the recognition of oneness is irrepressible: again the screen displays the two faces merged.

Unwilling to accept this terrifying discovery, Alma now tries to assert a separate self. She snatches at Elisabet's face, as though to twist off a mask. "I'll never be like you, never," she says with a sudden hardness in her voice; then, banging the table, she pours forth a series of sentence fragments in an effort to exorcise the other woman's spirit: "The colors, that quick cast, the inconceivable nausea of the pain, and also the many words. I, me, us, no, what is it called, where is the nearest, where shall I apply leverage for the pushing off." Alma then rips her nails along the inside of her forearm and pulls Elisabet's head down to suck her blood (forcing her, as it were, to repossess the incubus that had invaded the nurse). Finally, Alma repeatedly slaps the "demon's" face, and the screen turns black.**

The dream's last segment returns to the hospital setting where the women's relationship began. Alma, once more in her position as healer, instructs her patient, "Repeat after me: Nothing," and Elisabet, drained of her strength, weakly says, "Nothing." "That's right," Alma responds,

---

*In the published version, the account is given just once, but Bergman achieves the same effect by having Alma oscillate between "I" and "Fru Vogler" in her account.

**The printed version assigns the incoherent phrases to Elisabet (Bergman comments, however, that the voice is neither Elisabet's nor Alma's—an indication of the degree to which the two women have fused). It also makes the exorcism more explicit and extends it over a longer period. The process begins with Elisabet clad in Alma's uniform (thus emphasizing the interchange). Once her blood has been sucked, Alma puffs her cheeks "like a child blowing air into a balloon," letting the breath hiss out (as if literally expelling a spirit). At the same time, after shaking her head violently as if refusing to be exorcised, Elisabet "extends her tongue with a scornful, cruel expression." The actress then says: "Perhaps a violation of what is one's own, a despairing carnation [sic]. Or the other, prevailing, collects one's self. No, not internally. It ought to happen, but I can stand there by myself."

"that's how it will be." In retrospect, one realizes that the dream (or series of dreams) has recapitulated the course of events which precede it. Alma's discovery of the "Elisabet" in herself, punctuated by the startling image joining the halves of their faces, parallels the scene in which she sits among the rocks, bereaved of illusions—the first of the pair of scenes immediately anterior to the dream's start. Now, corresponding to the second of that pair—Elisabet's contemplation of the Jewish boy's surrender—the actress's concession to nothingness announces her discovery, in turn, of the "Alma" within her. Elisabet's silence, her testimony to the truth that there is no truth, has been clearly exposed as a role no less based on self-deception than the ones she abandoned—or the ones Alma had adopted to justify herself. Moreover, as the psychiatrist had warned, the distinction Elisabet has tried to draw between "being" and "seeming" is ultimately untenable, for the instant "being" becomes self-conscious it is transformed into "seeming." In token of this complex awareness, at the very end of the dream, Elisabet stands directly behind Alma and brushes an imaginary lock back from the nurse's brow with her hand—a nervous gesture Alma had repeatedly made during the confessions culminating in the disclosure of her abortion. Once again, Elisabet, who initially had sought to pursue pure "being," and Alma, whose life had been all "seeming," meld into one woman, or one mind—just as in the image fusing the women's faces. And just as Alma's exorcism of Elisabet had followed that moment of recognition, Elisabet now dissociates herself from Alma: one body crosses the other in a balletic movement of separation. Each woman will resume the persona she had before this shadow show of identities began, but conscious of the nothingness that invalidates all hope of meaningful action. The screen flashes white—a reverse image of the black in which the previous sequence ended. Proceeding from opposite positions, both women have arrived at the same blankness.

Alma had "wakened" *into* her dream; now she wakes *from* the dream into a return to her "sleepwalking." Without exchanging a word or even a glance, the women prepare to leave the cottage. For a moment, Alma looks into a mirror and repeats the hand-across-the-brow gesture Elisabet had performed at the dream's close; then she quickly turns away and walks to the bus that will carry her back to her job and her fiancé. A shot of Elisabet dressed as Electra indicates that she, too, is returning, has returned, or will return to the role(s) she interrupted. Having played itself out, the film surrenders its hold on the story it has been and devolves into the elements from which it was composed. Cinematographer Sven Nykvist is shown filming Liv Ullmann-as-Electra in the supine posture of the old woman in the morgue; in turn, this yields to quotation of a couple of the other ideas involved in the film's evolution—a shot of the pebbly beach (which one now recognizes as the ground outside the cottage), and another of the boy from the prelude still groping the screen with the image of Andersson/Ullmann. Finally, the film is seen winding off the projector's sprockets, and the arc lamp is extinguished. All that remains is for the film to be rewound and replaced in its cannister, and for the members of the audience—like Alma and Elisabet—to resume their lives.*

Even if *Persona* is not, as John Simon has suggested, "the most difficult film ever made," it does make uncommon demands on the viewer.[11] Bergman had been notorious for the supposedly abstruse content of his films ever since the mid-'fifties, but here the manner of presentation added another dimension of complexity. Although the film easily recovered its very modest cost, it did not draw a large audience. Nor was it a succès d'estime. Some critics, venting an exasperation that had been building since *The Communicants*, condemned it as "unseeable," merely an "exhibition of outré technical virtuosity," "emotional self-indulgence," "a riddle without a sphinx, an infinitely portentous mystery, lying inert, without intellect, or art, to make it reverberate." Others were respectful but obviously bewildered. Among the various interpretations, one could read that *Persona* was a horror film refurbished in Swedish Modern, an investigation of schizophrenia, a story about lesbian attraction, or a parable about the artist. Very few seemed ready to see what the film reveals as it rides on its own melting. In the two decades since its premiere, *Persona* has steadily grown in reputation, yet it continues to

---

*Given the frequency with which critics have found either an affirmation of hope or an ambivalence in the ending, it should be noted that the printed version unequivocally points to despair. There, Alma is left in a setting of "gray crepuscular days, a dark turbulent sea and a quiet snowfall." The arrival of an old man who has come with his horse and ax to fell trees (iconographic representations of mortality that recur in Bergman's works) reinforces the suggestion of a moribund existence for Alma. Amid these omens, she speaks of having tried, in her loneliness, to formulate a letter to Elisabet. But once she discovered the Warsaw ghetto photograph in Elisabet's desk, she says, she realized that she could never write the letter. Finally, after looking at the dusk and the old man, she repeats her credo: "I'm terribly fond of people. Mostly when they're sick and I can help them. I'll marry and have children. I believe that is what life has in store for me in this world."

Elisabet's fate is no better. The doctor, in a sort of epilogue, reports that the actress returned to her home and the theater, "warmly welcomed in both places." But then, in ironic juxtaposition to news of the "cure," the "screen" shows Elisabet's "howling, wide-open face, twisted by dread, with wildly distended eyes and furrows of sweat running through the theatrical make-up."

baffle even those who regard it as Bergman's most nearly perfect film. None of his works has met with greater disagreement about its meaning. Recently, Peter Cowie has written: "Everything one says about *Persona* may be contradicted; the opposite will also be true."[12] The claim is, of course, patent nonsense, but it reflects the state of critical disarray.

Much of the confusion arises because the failure to discern when the dream begins and ends has caused interpreters to approach the film as an allegorical riddle. Among the theories this has produced, one finds such views as that Mr. Vogler stands for the theater, calling Elisabet/Bergman to return; or that the two women represent the artist and the public, the image and the word, or God's silence and man's yearning for communion with the divine. The more ingenious the interpretation, however, the less it accords with what happens in the film. Actually, *Persona* unfolds the conflict between seeming and being that is enunciated by the psychiatrist at the end of this "sonata's" first "movement"; except for the symbolic values in the professions of the main characters—"actress" represents the accretion of roles constituting the elusive concept of self; "nurse," the ideal of unselfish service to others—the argument proceeds without allegorical embellishment. What makes Bergman's development of this simple premise appear difficult is the intricate weave of thematic variations shuttling between Alma and Elisabet.

The second major difficulty over which interpreters have stumbled concerns the framing sections and the "break" midway through the film. If, as many of the reviewers maintained, Bergman was simply trying to join the the ranks of a trendy modernism by calling attention to the artificiality of the illusion he was purveying, their irritation would have been entirely justified. On the other hand, if the self-referential device is not a gratuitous comment on the conditions of art but an integral part of the film's statement, then its relationship to the story of Alma and Elisabet has to be explained. As Susan Sontag quite correctly states, "Any account which leaves out or dismisses as incidental how *Persona* begins and ends hasn't been talking about the film that Bergman made."*

---

*Sontag's own account—that the "self-reflexiveness" of the encasing segments is related to the doubling manifested through the nurse and patient—is unconvincingly presented, however. Moreover, it begs the question.[13]

Other explanations have been equally inadequate. Birgitta Steene, for example, maintains that, by incorporating an awareness of the medium's artificiality, Bergman justifies his "merely let[ting] the film come to an end" and, thereby, destroying the fictive illusion without satisfying the spectator's expectations of a "definite answer."[14] But surely there is

Solving the problem requires, at the outset, recognition of three elementary facts about the prelude. First, it concerns not art or even cinema in general but this particular film. Second, in tracing the evolution toward and of *Persona*, it points specifically to the man who lay in Sophiahemmet thinking about the career behind him while wondering whether he would ever make another film. Third, the progression of fragments culminates in the appearance of the boy (Bergman himself) in circumstances evoking that crucial, recurrent coupling of death and rebirth in this filmmaker's imagination (e.g., in *Eva*, *The Seventh Seal*, *Wild Strawberries*). Here, plainly, death is associated with the exhaustion of creative vitality (the old, dead ideas); rebirth, with the awaited new film. But what will quicken that rebirth? In the Erasmus address, Bergman compared art to a dead, empty snakeskin, and the personal curiosity of the artist to the appetite of the ants which fill the snakeskin and give it the semblance of vitality. Significantly, the "new film" begins when the boy's curiosity causes him to explore the projected image that suddenly confronts him—projected, as it were, from within his mind.

Most immediately, the strangely seductive image toward which the boy reaches represents the mystery of Woman. Never very far below the surface of the artist in Bergman is the child simultaneously intrigued and revulsed by the sexual enigma that challenges him from every quarter. By identifying the boy in the prelude with Johan in *The Silence*, Bergman directly ties *Persona* to the disconcerting encounter with sexuality—and its associated terrors—that lay at the heart of the earlier film. Here, the boy is "outside" the drama, yet he is not wholly detached from it. Bergman wants the audience to sense, even if only subliminally, that the boy is witnessing the women's intimate disclosures. In addition to coloring the audience's emotional response to what it sees, this relationship of the "outside" to the "inside" film focuses on the primary tension between the artist and his art. Like the one-way transparent mirror in "The Fish," the screen presenting the female face that leads into the Alma-Elisabet story mediates between the filmmaker's curiosity (represented by the boy) and the frightening "truth" his curiosity has conjured into being.*

----

a fundamental difference between Bergman's refusal to supply an upbeat, affirmative resolution and what Steene perceives as arbitrary incompleteness; between a despairing assessment of life's possibilities and a confession of artistic failure.

*In "The Fish," Joakim is a filmmaker whose films and dreams reflect his sexual anxieties. The wife's betrayal that he sees through the mirror corresponds to those fantasies; moreover, it has occurred because he has (literally) wished it to happen. Psychologically, he "knows"

More particularly, of course, given that Bergman makes himself the point of reference, the "boy's" curiosity about Woman refines into a fiction about Mother. Among the initial wave of commentaries on *Persona*, several identified the boy as Elisabet's son. In the literal sense in which this explanation was offered, this is a mistake—as comparison of the boy in the morgue with young Vogler's photograph clearly shows. Metaphorically, however, the first boy does represent the child who responds to his mother's abhorrence with a desperate love—and, as well, the child Alma aborted. Understanding how these three children are connected crucially affects the film's interpretation.

To a greater extent than any critic has recognized, *Persona* relies on a double-threaded process of discovery involving motherhood. The principal thread concerns Elisabet. In diagnosing the actress's muteness as a retreat into utter subjectivity—a resolve to be "what you are to yourself" rather than "what you are to others"—the psychiatrist lists the roles that tortured her. "Which is the worst?" she asks, then adds, as if answering the question herself by posing another, "Where did it break apart? . . . Was it the role of mother that finally did it?" Although the psychiatrist is only guessing at this point, Alma later confirms the hypothesis at the end of the dream in which she has become Elisabet. Motherhood, she explains, was the one role the actress could not slough off; frightened when her efforts to shed her son made him more tenacious, she returned his love with hate and withdrew into silence. But, in some radical way, the whim that led Elisabet to conceive the child created a new reality, and by defining her through obligations to someone outside herself, that reality has made her hope of escape into pure being a monstrous illusion.

Alma, however, is not just the means by which Elisabet arrives at recognition of despair. In recounting the history of the actress's motherhood, the nurse also realizes, suddenly, that she has done precisely what Elisabet tried and failed to do: erase a child from her life. Significantly, the woman who "was never quite real" to anyone else and who, in her fiancé's phrase, "lives like a sleepwalker," had become pregnant as a result of a unique day when, on the beach with the boys and again with Karl-Henrik, she felt the true thunder of orgasm. For once in her life, she transcended mere *seeming* into *being*, and with her maternity, she became "real." But then, by aborting the fetus, Alma destroyed that

---

she is unfaithful—even before she has thought of cuckolding him—and he wants evidence of her infidelity to confirm that truth.

vital spark of reality. Ironically, the mirror she holds up to Elisabet shows the reversed image of herself.

The boy outside the fiction surely foreshadows this revelation, which in turn loops the story's end back onto its beginning. Interior joins exterior in a continuous, single plane—like that of a Möbius strip. Bergman evidently conceived this arrangement quite late in the process of making *Persona*—perhaps not until after all the scenes with Ullmann and Andersson had been shot. Yet, even though the script mentions no boy in its very brief "prologue," the metamorphosing image with which the film was to have begun does imply the creating mind of the filmmaker. By giving that implied presence concrete form in the actual film and associating the child in the morgue with Alma's unborn child and the child Elisabet wished dead, Bergman establishes the story of the two mothers as the product of an imagination stirred by the childhood memory of maternal rejection. In the final analysis, *Persona* focuses as much on that imagination as on the fiction it has spawned.*

During the press conference at the start of production on *Persona*, Bergman had announced that the new film would have no connection with the trilogy. But if he had a discriminating principle in mind, it is hard to guess what that may have been, for *Persona* is so clearly an extension of the trilogy it virtually converts it into a tetralogy. The Chamber Film concept launched in 1961 here reaches its apogee: not until *Cries and Whispers* would Bergman approach the similarity to chamber music of this "sonata for two instruments"—or, for that matter, to the "drama of souls" Strindberg composed for his Intimate Theater. More pertinently, if, as Bergman has stated, the trilogy is bound together by the fact that it demonstrates "a reduction—in the metaphysical sense," then *Persona* takes that descent toward nothingness a step beyond. The personal "truth crisis" it expresses marks the culmination of a struggle for absolute honesty. *Through a Glass Darkly* had begun that process, only to fail, he thought, in its coda. *The Communicants* showed him

---

*Of course, as observer as well as creator, the boy also represents the audience, but Bergman virtually fuses the two guises by leading the viewer through a recollection of earlier films to the start of the new conception—in effect, summoning the viewer to engage the story as though it were his own. The preface Bergman added to the script explicitly invites such participation: "I have not produced a filmscript in the usual sense. . . . On many points I am uncertain, and at one place at least, I know nothing at all. I discovered, in fact, that the subject I chose was very large and that what I wrote or carried over into the final film (horrid thought!) had to be extremely arbitrary. Therefore, I invite the reader's or spectator's imagination to take free command over this material which I have placed at his command."

resolute in resisting "the Willed," and in *The Silence* he excluded even
the possibility of hope. But in *Persona*—where, as if to seal off the
temptation of surrendering to "the Willed," he stations his symbolic self
"outside" the film—the analysis plunges to a still deeper level of despair
at which absolute honesty confronts the paradoxical truth that self-
deception is an absolute condition of life.

Significantly, in driving to this discovery, Bergman repudiates the two
major conceits through which "the Willed" had escaped accepting the
reality of man's abandonment. Elisabet's attempt to retreat into silence
and thereby achieve a persona-less state of pure being represents another
version of regression to the womb. (In the script, the notion becomes
rather explicit. "I am blank and simple minded as though floating in a
soft half-sleep," Elisabet writes in her letter to the psychiatrist. "I feel a
new health, a barbaric cheer. I am surrounded by the sea and I rock like a
fetus in the womb.") But, in contrast to the "comic" pattern in which
Bergman proffered this illusion as a deliverance from anguish at the
fiction's conclusion, here it is the premise that the drama tests—and
proves ultimately untenable. Life "seeps in," destroying the (literally)
"fantastic system" she has tried to create for herself. Elisabet and, through
her, Alma, are finally condemned to endure within the consciousness of
their essential hypocrisy.

With equally devastating impact, the second repudiation strikes at the
life-affirming resolutions manifested through children in a variety of films
from the late 'forties to the start of the trilogy. To cite only the clearest
instances: in *Eva* and *Close to Life*, birth confirms the renewal of hope,
and in *Wild Strawberries*, Marianne's pregnancy at least holds out the
possibility that the Borgs' cycle of death-in-life might be broken; in *To Joy*,
the music Stig plays for his son after Marta's death celebrates life's value;
and, of course, in *The Seventh Seal*, the meaningful act that redeems
not only the Knight's life but life itself saves the "holy family" from
Death. In *Persona*, however, the abortion of the one child and the rejection of the other become testimony to life's emptiness, to the evanescence
of the mirage of hope. For the next sixteen years, Bergman's films would
thrash in a sterile meaninglessness; until *Fanny and Alexander*, no birth
would occur, no child would signify confidence in the future.

Hour of the Wolf

Persona crowns the remarkable period initiated by *Through a Glass
Darkly* in which he remade himself as an artist: if not his best film, it

certainly ranks among his best—which is to say that it stands alongside the most distinguished works in the history of cinema. *Hour of the Wolf* is nothing short of an embarrassment. A story of an artist's disintegration, it documents Bergman's own unraveling.

The contrast in the quality of the two films becomes all the more arresting in light of their similarities. *Persona*, even though it derived from a separate impulse, took a great deal from *The Cannibals*—which, pared to a quarter of the original length and thoroughly rewrittten, Bergman then developed into *Hour of the Wolf*. Both films lead from reality to an interior region of nightmare where the masks of the self dissolve; both play upon a motif of vampirism to illustrate a threat to identity. In *Hour of the Wolf*, however, Johan's descent toward extinction reflects a surrender to insanity that involves neither a dramatic conflict nor a metaphoric significance; Bergman may be fascinated by the spectacle, but he creates no reason beyond voyeuristic curiosity for the audience to share his interest. Worse, the demons meant to be seen as terrors projected from Johan's mind are cut from the cardboard of 'thirties and 'forties horror movies; just when the sense of menace should be at its height, one is more likely to giggle than gasp. Moreover, because none of the demons is sufficiently realized as an antagonist, the potential for tension between Johan and the incarnations of his anxieties quickly dissipates.

Like *Persona*, too, *Hour of the Wolf* is set within an advertisement of its "artificiality" and interrupted in the middle (here by the reappearance of the title). But, unlike *Persona*, where incorporation of the perspective on its fictiveness affects how it is to be understood, the reason for the frame in *Hour of the Wolf* is entirely private. Originally much more elaborate, the prelude and postlude were cut by more than a thousand feet when, during editing, Bergman recognized that he had been "guilty of self-deception. It was better not to play aesthetic games to set myself off from the film." Only half-intelligible phrases spoken in darkness by the film crew at the beginning and end remain. Yet, if he saw his mistake, why retain even this vestige? Bergman's answer offers perhaps the most revealing clue to what went wrong in *Hour of the Wolf*: the film was so "terribly personal," he said, he felt he could not entirely eliminate a reference to the "games" that had allowed him to be "playful" with his material.[1] Clearly, that measure of playfulness—or artistic distance—was not enough. Johan, Bergman's surrogate who is the puzzled observer in *The Silence* and who reappears in *Persona* to peer at the story of Alma and Elisabet and ponder its implications, here becomes the protagonist in a drama essentially without an agon. The boy in the other two films determines their structure: what he registers leads to the discovery of hopelessness. In *Hour of the Wolf*, Johan's despair is manifest from the start, and since nothing more is at issue, the film becomes only an exposition of his doom.*

The plot for this tale of dementia is minimal. Following Bergman's statement that Johan Borg, a painter, had vanished, his widow Alma picks up the account of his final days. The details are scattered, almost impressionistic. They had arrived at their Frisian island cottage in spring, shortly after she learned that she was pregnant. The apple tree was in bloom. They were happy and looking forward to the long days of summer.** But then mysterious footprints appeared in the flower bed. Johan had trouble working; he could not sleep; they hardly spoke to each other; his fear of people and of the dark grew worse. As Alma goes on talking, the rest of her story is dramatized in flashback.

Like Karin in *Through a Glass Darkly*, Johan has reached the point where he must choose between two worlds. Alma represents the attraction of a healthy reality; if, as he says, he were to draw her, day after day, her influence might heal him. But his twisted fantasies exert the stronger pull: instead of Alma, he draws the members of the von Merkens clan, an array of demons who haunt him. When he shows his wife the sketchbook, the demons become as real to her as they are to him. Indeed, so real that the Borgs accept their invitation to dinner at Merkens castle.

At the party, the nattering, incohesive conversations about degradation, fetishistic sex, and the vanity of art obviously allude to Johan's sense of guilt. The key topic is Veronica Vogler, Johan's former mistress. The demons indicate that they all know about the perverse fascination she holds for Johan; in fact, Baroness von Merkens has hung his portrait of Veronica in her bedroom to rouse a jaded sexual appetite. Later that evening, a puppet theater performance of a scene from *The Magic Flute*

---

*Bergman himself was aware of the problem: realizing that "to see a man who is already mad become crazier is boring," he tried to give the story a further import by relating it to the madman's wife.[2] Thus, he presents the film as a visualization of her "narrative," based on what she has read in her husband's diary. The apparent reason for establishing this point of view is to warrant the return to the wife in an epilogue, where she asks two questions: Was the fact that she saw the demons who destroyed Johan proof of her love for him? or, Did he fall victim to the demons because she did not love him enough? The intended effect of the questions, of course, is to shift the focus from the tale to the teller, but since the degree of her love—or sanity, or guilt—neither would have altered events nor now impinges on their interpretation, the manuever merely produces confusion.

**Although Alma's pregnancy accords with the other signs of vitality, it owes more to the fact that Liv Ullmann was herself visibly pregnant with Bergman's child than to any metaphoric purpose.

(with homunculi instead of puppets) serves as another sharply pointed reminder of Johan's obsession for Veronica. Mozart's "naive text," comments the demon who stages the opera, represents "the highest manifestation of art." The implication is unmistakable: having surrendered his naiveté to morbid fantasies, Johan has ruined himself as an artist. But, as the staged passage further suggests, Johan is on the brink of sacrificing much more. Tamino, brought outside the Temple of Wisdom, asks when his "eternal night" will end. The chorus answers, "Soon, soon, youth, or never." Tamino's next question, "Is Pamina still alive?" insures that it will be soon: his fidelity to her perfect love will raise him to the light of wisdom. Johan, of course, corresponds to Tamino; Alma, to Pamina. But this "Tamino" is about to abandon his life-bearing "Pamina"; submitting instead to Veronica (his "Queen of the Night"), he will sink into darkness and madness.

During a sleepless night at the cottage, Johan remembers a terrifying punishment inflicted on him by his parents; then, encouraged by Alma's patient interest, he recounts a bizarre incident in which, only a few days before, he crushed a young boy to death. (This was surely a hallucination, but Johan can no longer distinguish dream from reality.) Suddenly, even though the cottage door has been bolted shut, one of the demons appears in the room. His errand is to summon Johan to an intimate party for Veronica—and to give him a pistol so he can "defend" himself "against all the small game on the island." When Alma tries to keep her husband in the house, Johan fires three shots at her.

The film presents two versions of what happens next. In the first, Johan hurries past his dead wife to the castle, where the demons impose degrading conditions as the price for meeting Veronica. Mother von Merkens forces him to admire and kiss her foot; another member of the clan paints a blue cupid's bow on Johan's lips, dresses him in feminine silk pajamas, and sprays him with perfume. At last prepared for the consummation of his perverted desire, he enters the bedchamber and finds Veronica laid out under a sheet, like a corpse awaiting burial. As they kiss passionately, all the von Merkens demons reveal their presence in the room by cackling in triumph.

In Alma's own report of these same hours, spoken at the film's end, Johan only nicked her arm. After pacing the house wildly, he wrote in his diary for several hours, then packed a bag and headed into the woods. Alma followed him, but the shrill song of a nightingale caused her to fall asleep. When she awoke, Johan was standing in his bloody, torn clothes, surrounded by dancing, birdlike shadows. A large figure

—half human, half pheasant—struck him in the neck and (according to the script) chanted a list of Johan's destroyed organs: tongue, ears, eyes, penis, and anus. Finally, she saw her huband sink into the boggy ground, leaving not so much as a spot of blood behind.

Even more pointedly than the birdlike cackling demons who exult in Johan's capitulation to madness in the first version, the pheasant-man who destroys him in the second emphasizes Bergman's ironic inversion of *The Magic Flute*. At the film's beginning, Johan tells Alma that the worst of the demons, the Birdman, is kin to Papageno; at the end, it is this same "Pagageno" who pecks him to death. Mozart's part-man, part-bird child of nature anticipated a Romantic age in which children and nature symbolize purity and benevolence; Bergman's Birdman personifies corruptive self-knowledge and a "natural" evil seated in childhood psychosexuality. Mozart's forest is a naive realm of magic; Bergman's, the thicket of a crazed mind. Similarly, the tests Tamino passes to gain admission to the Temple of Wisdom and confirmation of his manhood by father-figure Sarastro here become a degrading ordeal of passage to the castle's inner sanctum, where, after acknowledging his perverted effeminateness, Johan embraces the "dead" Veronica. But the most telling irony lies in the implicit parallel between the composer and the film-maker. At the culmination of his lecture on s-1Mozart, the demon who stages what Bergman himself has called the pivotal scene in *The Magic Flute* states that the mortally ill composer felt "a secret closeness" both to Tamino's appeal for an end to darkness and to his profession of faith in Pamina: "With these lines as a foundation, Mozart has written his credo in fifty bars. So completely naked, so deeply, impenetrably personal, and yet so clearly self-evident and unencumbered." In contrast to this "fairy tale play," a grand symbol of heroic artistic progress from confusion to lucidity, Bergman's own "impenetrably personal" tale records inexorable decline.

Bergman has been remarkably frank in avowing the confessional nature of *Hour of the Wolf*, which he called an open display of "the sore on my soul."*[4] During "long periods in my life," he told a startled interviewer, *real* "demons and bad wolf-hours" had plagued him.[5] Writing the screenplay revived the dread: in keeping with his usual practice of cloistering himself until he finished a draft, he intended to sleep and work in the same room, but this time he had to change the arrangement because, at night, "the demons wouldn't get out."[6]

*Besides its allusions to Mozart (and his librettist Schikaneder), *Hour of the Wolf* also points to the Gothic, psychologically convoluted fiction of E. T. A. Hoffmann—one of Bergman's favorite writers. In the unfinished novel *Kater Murr*, Hoffmann's literary alter

Some of the demons—Bergman has specifically mentioned the old lady who removes her face and the creature who walks on the ceiling —entered the film directly from his recurring dreams.[7] Others appear to have been deliberately shaped out of self-reproach. Lindhorst, the authority on Mozart, analyzes *The Magic Flute* in precisely the same terms Bergman himself has employed in talking about his favorite opera. He is the self-mocking consciousness, the artist's persecuting intellect. (For no evident reason, Lindhorst states that he is forty-six—Bergman's own age while he was writing *The Cannibals*. "Life sparkles all around me in its greatest richness," he continues, "but I rush ever deeper into the labyrinth.") Even more sinister implications attach to Ernst, the "commonest specimen" among the demons. This contemptible figure on whom Bergman bestows his own first name is not only a thief —given the extent to which *Hour of the Wolf* relies on Hoffmann and Mozart, one should recall "Ernest Riffe's" indictment of Bergman for plagiarism and artistic bankruptcy—but he is also presumed to be a homosexual and a traitor to his family who has shamefully embezzled its funds. Although Ernst's role in Johan's insanity is never quite defined,

ego Johannes Kreisler was to devolve into utter madness; in the film, Johan hears a demon named Kreisler playing the violin within the castle just as he is about to enter and, as another demon says, "meet himself." Also, a digression on *Don Juan* in the midst of *Kater Murr* corresponds to the lecture on *The Magic Flute*, and Bergman himself has indicated that he let the film end in the middle of a phrase as a gesture toward Hoffmann's uncompleted novel.[3]

The greater obligation, however, is to Hoffmann's first full-length tale, *The Golden Pot*. Again, Bergman signals the debt by assigning the same names to corresponding characters. Lindhorst the archivist (in *Hour of the Wolf*, the demon who discourses on Mozart) plays a similar role in both. And although Hoffmann's Heerbrand may appear less noxious than Bergman's demon who invites Johan to the rendezvous with Veronica and gives him the gun to kill Alma, from the point of view of the German tale's mentally diseased protagonist, he, too, "turns souls inside out." Veronica, a sweet bourgeoise in *The Golden Pot*, seems quite unlike the depraved former mistress in the film (who more closely resembles Serpentina); yet Hoffmann clearly implies that Veronica and Serpentina constitute a double image of Woman—just as Bergman's Veronica is Alma inverted. One can also see an analogy between Johan and Hoffmann's Anselmus (whose name is the latinized form of "Hansel," a variant of "Johan"): the demons take control of Johan and lead him to the tryst that seals his insanity; Anselmus is drawn into a mad relationship with Serpentina by copying Lindhorst's texts while repressing his desire for Veronica.

The "hour of the wolf" is defined in both the screenplay's epigraph and within the text as "the hour between night and dawn . . . when most people die, sleep is deepest, nightmares are most real. It is the hour when the sleepless are haunted by their worst anguish, when ghosts and demons are most powerful. The hour of the wolf is also the hour when most babies are born." Before the film's premiere, Bergman said the phrase came from a Latin text he remembered reading in his student days, but researchers at SF could not find the source. Like the proverbs about the devil's eye and the smiles of the summer night, the "hour of the wolf" was undoubtedly invented by the filmmaker.

he typifies the corrosive psychological forces embodied by the von Merkens tribe: "Born in childhood experiences," Bergman said, "they reside below the level of consciousness. Their task is to separate the artist from life's opportunities and step by step to destroy him and themselves."[8] On another occasion, he made their autobiographical origin still more explicit: after reciting once again his story of the punishment ritual at the parsonage, he told his interviewer that "the demons in *Hour of the Wolf* are born and have sprung out of the wardrobe."[9]

It is precisely that memory which Johan recounts to Alma at the start of Act II.* (Bergman had originally intended to show it in flashback, but the emotional hurt was still too tender: "it choked me so much that I gave it up pretty damned quickly. I couldn't do it any other way than through oral description.")[10] During Act I, the audience has been in Alma's position, entering Johan's deranged mind from the outside and trying to understand the pathology. But from this point—where, in effect, the film starts again—the implicit point of view shifts to her husband: it is his diseased imagination, driven to admit his depravity and to seek punishment for it, that governs. Like the dreams of another autobiographical figure named Borg—Isak in *Wild Strawberries*—Johan's hallucinations derive from the past; his painful recollection of the wardrobe torture points directly to an anxiety involving his parents.

I was thrown in, furious, screaming and frightened. . . . I had been told that a little man lived in that very wardrobe—something between a troll and an elf. He could gnaw away a wrong-doer's toes. When I held my panting breath, I heard rustling in a corner. I knew my number was up. In silent panic . . . I hit wildly in all directions to defend myself against that little creature. At the same time, howling with dread, I prayed for forgiveness. My surrender was accepted. The door opened and I was permitted to emerge into daylight.

My father said: "I hear from your mother that you beg forgiveness." "Yes," I answered. "I beg so terribly much for forgiveness." . . . Then I fetched the switch, pulled down my pants, and lay prostrate over the green pillows. "How many strokes do you deserve?" my father asked. "As many strokes as possible," I answered. Then the strokes hit rather hard, but it was not insufferable. When the punishment was finished, I pulled up my pants and returned the switch to the corner behind the bookcase. Then I turned to my mother and said: "Do you forgive me now, Mother?" She replied: "Of course I forgive

Hour of the Wolf consists of two acts, plus a prologue and an epilogue. As in most of his scripts, Bergman here keeps to the theatrical convention of marking act and scene divisions.

you." She reached her hand out to me and I kissed it. Next I turned to my father. "Can you forgive me now, Father?" "Now I forgive you," he answered and put forth his hand, which I kissed.

The psychosexual associations of this memory become more obtrusive in the tale he next tells about murdering the boy. As the episode begins, Johan, clad only in swim briefs, has interrupted his sketching to fish. When the boy comes into view, Johan notes his effeminate body —especially his "well-developed mouth"; yet, despite this onlooker's appearance (or because of it), Johan feels threatened: "I got an uneasy feeling that he was thinking of pushing me [over the cliff] into the water." The boy disdainfully inspects his sketches, then sneers at the small number of fish he has caught. Unnerved, Johan hurriedly puts on his clothes to escape, but when he realizes that his watch is missing, he confronts the boy, who responds by curling himself on the ground. This so enrages Johan that he hurls him against the rocks. As he stands over his dying victim's rhythmically convulsing body, however, the boy bites his attacker's foot—whereupon Johan rolls the body over the ledge and watches it plummet into the sea's depths.

Like Jack and the dwarf-child of ambiguous sex in "A Shorter Tale" (which this episode strongly resembles), Johan and the boy are twin figures in a complex relationship. Johan's jerking pole, held in a phallic position, and his frenetic effort to reel in the line as soon as he senses he is being watched unmistakably indicate masturbation. The boy seems to materialize in response to guilt—significantly, Johan's first thought is that the boy means to harm (i.e., punish) him. The sketches apparently betray some secret weakness, and the disparagement of the catch clearly reflects the artist's anxiety about his manhood. Feeling "exposed," Johan rushes for his clothes. But the fact that, like Johan, the boy is naked except for his swim briefs also points to another reason for this reaction. By dressing, Johan tries to set himself apart from the boy—who, besides denoting conscience, images the illicit libidinous desires Johan has been repressing. The same impulse is responsible for his suddenly remembering his watch and placing such importance on its recovery—as though possession of this symbol of time (or age) would affirm that he is not this epicene youth. But the boy ignores the question about the watch; instead, with a knowing expression on his face, he assumes a submissive, sexual posture.

Once violence explodes, the similarity to the memory of the wardrobe becomes increasingly apparent. The fury of Johan's attack in attempting to deny what the patently homosexual invitation implies suggests the intense sexual guilt bound up in that childhood experience; in a sense, Johan is punishing himself by assuming his father's role as the righteous castigator. The bite on the foot further indicates the connection to that guilt: the boy does just what Johan's wild blows had sought to prevent the creature in the wardrobe from doing. Of course, in symbolically elaborating the meaning of the wardrobe drama, the dream also serves as preamble to the degradation and destruction that occupy the rest of the film. When Johan drops the bleeding corpse into the water —which is exactly what he expected the boy would do to him—it foreshadows the sinking of his own bloodied body beneath the surface of the bog; the buried guilt manifested by one act of implicit self-punishment informs the other.

But why, if the dream expresses Johan's fear that he is homosexual, should it be Veronica's eroticism—scarcely a homosexual interest—that draws him back to the castle? His perversity manifests itself in transvestism, masochism, and necrophilia, yet none of these necessarily indicates homosexuality. Moreover, given the series of mirrors Bergman erects to reflect the past, how is the death that results from the rendez-vous with Veronica specifically related to the punishment Johan had received from his father?

Before these questions can be answered, one has to step back and consider the homosexual motif in the broader context of Bergman's various writings, from "A Shorter Tale" to *Fanny and Alexander*. On cursory examination, homosexuality might seem a nasty secret he tried to hide from his audiences and from himself until it breached the surface in *Hour of the Wolf*—from which point, as though he had finally gathered the courage to confront the truth, it begins to recur in quite overt form. And yet, all public indications of his private life have been vigorously and unstintingly heterosexual; furthermore, the dreamlike patterns of his fictions afford no evidence of being the products of a homoerotic imagination. What one finds instead is an *anxiety* about homosexuality which radiates from an uneasiness about his masculinity—and below that epicenter, as the greater mass of his works attests, lie the sexual conflicts traceable to his mother. The confusion of homosexuality with Oedipal guilt would become most apparent in *From the Life of the Marionettes*, but it also operates in *Hour of the Wolf*.

Had Bergman not cut a monologue which was to have bridged the wardrobe memory and the dream, the further link to the meeting with Veronica would have been more obvious. In that missing passage, Johan recalls a hospital park—his favorite playfield, he tells Alma—and the small chapel where the newly dead were stored. One Sunday afternoon, he and a friend entered the chapel to look at the corpses. When the door slammed and he realized that the other boy had fled, Johan, though terrified, seized the opportunity for his first sexual experience with a naked woman.* After pulling the sheet off a female corpse, he remembers, "I raised my hand and touched her face, her ears, her shoulders, her breasts; I let my fingers glide over her hips' roundness, over the reddish-gold tuft of hair on her sex, over the long, powerful thighs."

Most significantly, Johan's diary entry about the tryst in the castle's inner sanctum later uses exactly the same words to describe his caressing the "dead" Veronica. Yet Johan's pathological guilt and compulsion toward punishment in this "terribly personal" film suggest that Veronica represents someone more deeply immersed in the filmmaker's psyche than a corpse he may once have fondled. Could it be only a bizarre coincidence that Karin Bergman, after suffering her third heart attack, died in early March of 1966 (and that Bergman sat beside his niece Veronica during the funeral services)?

That Bergman was projecting his tortured Oedipal fantasies through Johan is demonstrated in several ways by the film itself. One indication emerges from the inverse parallelism to *The Magic Flute*. In discussing the opera in the mid-'seventies, Bergman would contend that the Queen of the Night represents the crippling maternal influence which tries to keep Tamino from attaining manhood. If Johan is a Tamino who fails, Veronica is certainly the Queen who reigns over the dark center of his dreams, the source of his demons.** The counterface to this psychologically destructive "former mistress" is Alma—woman stamped in the image of the selfless, nurturing "good mother." Any interpretation of the film hinges on recognizing that these two characters are doubles reflecting an ambivalence Johan is driven to resolve by choosing between them. (Thus, "killing" Alma becomes the price for admission to Veronica's bedchamber.) Several lines Bergman removed from the film's first scene

---

*Given the unmistakable reference to the Sophiahem park and chapel, Johan's acount also sheds light on the significance of the morgue sequence in *Persona*—especially those frames in which the dead old woman's eyes pop open.

**The demons' family name, von Merkens, tempts speculation that Bergman had somewhere come across the English word "merkin" (or some Scandinavian cognate) referring to a woman's pudendum or pubic hair, or to a theatrical pubic wig. Given the nature of the demons, such an allusion would certainly be appropriate.

make this divided image of mother even more emphatic. The cottage that symbolizes his life with Alma, Johan says, seems "a great, calm creature. A mother-animal, Alma. And every evening we creep into the mother-animal's belly." In contrast to the calm, womblike cottage, the castle on the other side of the island that is Johan's mind pulses with the turbid morbidity emanating from Veronica.

The most persuasive evidence that Veronica is a grotesque portrait of Bergman's Oedipal attachment to his mother, however, arises from Johan's memory of the wardrobe ordeal—a memory which matches in every detail Bergman's own often recited account of what happened in the parsonage. Although the father administers the punishment, the fact that the boy's release from his prison depends upon the mother's acknowledging his plea for forgiveness implies she is the one whom he has offended. That this unnamed offense involves sexual desire is corroborated not only by the penalty Johan fears the toe-gnawing creature in the wardrobe will impose—a symbolic castration (or loss of the penis)—but also by his reaction to the thrashing he actually receives. Painful as the punishment is, Johan invites it and even seems to derive a peculiar satisfaction from its severity. Why? Partly, it seems, because he recognizes the foulness of the sin he has committed in deed or thought, partly because the beating will prove that his father is a bully and thereby elicit the mother's sympathy for himself, but mostly because the boy has come to confuse the suffering and humiliation with the pleasure of kissing his mother's hand it will bring. (Whether or not Bergman ever received the chastisement he claims was regularly inflicted on him, there seems to be no question that his older brother was often caned. On these occasions, Bergman has said, their mother would bathe the welts that covered Dag's buttocks and soothe her son's anger with soft words. To Ingmar, this tender treatment "proved" that their mother loved Dag more than him, and he was extremely jealous.)

What had festered just beneath the surface in the wardrobe memory erupts in the fantasy assignation with Veronica. In introducing himself to Johan early in the film, Baron von Merkens had suggestively remarked that the castle is "famous for its salmon fishing"; the sexual meaning of that allusion—repeated in the dream—now becomes quite plain. Three sinister mother figures—the grandmotherly old lady, Mother von Merkens, and the Baron's wife—seem to exercise a strange power over the castle, itself a uterine labyrinth leading to Veronica. Significantly, to gain entry to Veronica's chamber, Johan must first kiss Mother von Merkens's foot—an act of abasement and an admission of perversity

which obviously refer to Johan's kissing his mother's hand at the finale
of the wardrobe ritual. The incestuous undertones in that memory are
further amplified when the Baron divulges that he, too, has been
Veronica's sexual partner; manifestly a father figure, the Baron states
that he will stand at the bedside, observing every movement while Johan
makes love to his former mistress. Veronica's curious greeting to Johan, a
reminder that she had worn green the last time they had met, also
suggests the incestuous associations in the childhood punishment: both
the sofa and the pillows on which the boy lay as the blows fell were
green. But the most conclusive testimony to the nature of the guilt at the
film's center emerges after the diseased Oedipal fantasy is played out.
Among the torments inflicted by the Pheasant-man is the very one
Johan had expected to receive in the wardrobe: "He can't piss," this
"worst" demon gloats, "because I have bitten off a piece there and for
certain he is a little swollen."

A far cry from the quests for redemption in the 'fifties films, *Hour of
the Wolf* is a journey of damnation—like *Not to Speak of All These
Women*, a suicidal expedition into the "essence of the personal." The
self-accusation, however, involves the artist as much as the man. Apparently referring to the decline in Bergman's popularity since the mid-
'fifties, one of the demons speaks of the castle grounds, "a showplace for
tourists" only a decade earlier, as an overgrown, neglected tangle. With
mocking flattery, another demon tells Johan, "You know the human
heart. Who has not seen your facial studies, to say nothing of your
self-portraits?" And Lindhorst, commenting on the major motif in Johan's
paintings (and Bergman's films), scoffs, "Salvation through a woman.
How original!" The artist's only defense against this chorus of what is
really self-doubt echoes the Erasmus address. He harbors no pretensions to immortality, Johan protests; he became an artist only because
he is a misfit, a "calf with five legs": "Oh yes, I have felt megalomania
waft about my brow, but I think I am immune. I have only to think of the
utter unimportance of art in the world of men to cool off. But the
compulsion is still there all the same."

Clearly, however, Bergman's artistic crisis concerned something much
mre debilitating than frustrated ambitions, public indifference, or even
self-doubt. Before the trilogy, art had served as a magic mirror, curved by
his will to dissimulate what it reflected—as though, by altering its picture of life, the artist could change life itself. With *Through a Glass
Darkly*, where the mirror indicated by the title is expressly trained to
reveal truth, Bergman began a concerted effort to eliminate such

distortions. That reductive process culminated in the nihilistic meta-physics of *Persona*, where the possibility that the mirror of art could compose an image of meaning is negated by the meaninglessness of the existential conditions it reflects. In *Hour of the Wolf*, he no longer even pretends to hold the mirror up to the world; instead, it is turned inward to the inflamed, diseased tissue of the artist's mind.

After lying on the bed which displays the awful secret of Merkens castle, Johan cries out, "The limit has at last been reached. The mirror is shattered, but what do the splinters reflect? Can you tell me that?" Bergman was obviously asking himself the question. Having exposed the source of his "artistic haunting," he released the pressure that had driven his imagination. Bergman would continue to make films for almost two decades, and at various moments during those years he would regain both popular and critical success, yet he would never recover the energy with which he had once polished the "essence of the personal" to artistic brilliance. The self he had sought to redeem, he now conceded, was corrupt beyond hope. Johan's closing statement in *Hour of the Wolf* was to have been: "The void has finally sprung through its thin shell, and it meets—the void? Just so. What a triumph for the void." Bergman cut the line, but the pronouncement would reverberate in every subse-quent work.

Shame

Despite having pushed his curiosity to "the limit" in *Hour of the Wolf*, Bergman generated three new scripts in 1967. While in Oslo preparing *Six Characters in Search of an Author* for its April opening, he began writing a film about a couple subjected to psychological stress in a scientific experiment. The premise fascinated him—a decade later, it would reemerge in *The Serpent's Egg*—but in this initial attempt, he found the story too difficult to develop. The second script, written dur-ing the spring, pursued the same theme of psychological deterioration, even though he changed the story and substituted a war setting for the couple's confinement in a laboratory. But whether *War*, later retitled *Shame*, would become a film was less than certain. Because staging credible battle scenes called for a larger budget than a Swedish com-pany could support, SF sought American investment; negotiations for a co-production broke down, however, when Bergman backed away from the American demand that the film be shot in color.[1] Reacting against the financial complexity of filmmaking, he wrote a third script in July—a simple play, shorn of all cinematic considerations, that required virtually no sets. But as soon as *The Rite* was finished, Bergman put it aside to prepare for *Shame*, which, with its budget pared to Swedish proportions, SF had decided to finance on its own.

Upon its premiere the following September, *Shame* stirred almost as much debate in the Swedish press as *The Silence* had five years earlier. This time, the issue was entirely political. Anti-American sentiment over the Vietnam War, though still two years from reaching its peak, had been growing steadily louder since the Tet Offensive. Then, in late August, the Soviet Union toppled the Dubcek government in Prague. Although the average Swede did not quite equate Washington and Moscow, the nation paraded its fraternal sympathy for both Vietnam and Czechoslovakia as victims of superpower arrogance and felt duty-bound to break from its traditional "blue-eyed" reticence. Given the backdrop of world events and the volatility of the country's mood, it was inevitable that *Shame*, depicting an invasion of Sweden set one year in the future (1969), would be judged in political terms. Whereas one camp praised Bergman for having forsaken his egocentric preoccupations to declare his solidarity with a humanity trembling at the verge of catastrophe, however, another accused him of moral dereliction in failing to take an explicitly ideological stance.*

Although Bergman scoffed at the arguments of his detractors, he soon looked back on *Shame* as a bungled work. "When one undertakes such a serious subject," he said in February 1969, "the aesthetic demands become much stricter"; instead of obeying those imperatives, he lapsed into "dramaturgic tricks." His only defense was that he wrote the script before the escalation of the Vietnam War and the occupation of Czechoslovakia: "The film would have had a different aspect if those

---

*Sara Lidman, the irascible harpy of the Swedish Left, led the assault with an article in *Aftonbladet*, the tabloid affiliated with the ruling Social Democratic party. In her view, *Shame* was a vile masquerade, an evasion typifying not only Bergman's effeteness but also the paralysis of Western intellectuals in the face of evil. To be sure, this was a denunciation from the fringe of the political establishment. (Lidman's notion of political morality should be weighed against her remarks, a few years later, about the boat people who were dying at sea in their exodus from Vietnam: refusing to be moved by their plight, she dismissed these refugees as vermin unworthy of mercy.) But the critique of *Shame* in *Dagens Nyheter*, the country's most respected Liberal newspaper, sounded very much the same theme in deprecating Bergman's political disengagement as worse than the actions of the quislings. Sweden's intellectual life was listing toward a Marxist position. Within a short time, journalists for *Dagens Nyheter* would proclaim that the press should abandon the pretense of objectivity for direct advocacy.

two events had already occurred."[2] And yet, whatever Bergman may have thought he was writing about, *Shame* is not fundamentally a political film, nor, except in an incidental way, is war its subject. Instead of marking a departure from *Hour of the Wolf*, it expresses the very same concerns. The island that is invaded in *Shame* is no less an extension of a haunted mind than the island infested with demons.

Jan and Eva Rosenberg, violinists in an orchestra disbanded because of war, have retreated to a place much like Fårö. Despite hardship—they barely sustain themselves with what they grow and can earn by selling their small surplus to neighbors—life still has definition. Meeting bills, going to the dentist, laying flowers on a relative's grave—these quotidian rituals of continuity offer reassurance that there is reason to hope. Jan thinks about returning to the orchestra when the war ends; Eva, about learning Italian and someday having a baby. But then the long-expected invasion finally occurs, and suddenly all coordinates become meaningless.

The radios of the opposing armies issue contradictory reports; to act on the basis of one version of the "truth" instead of another, equally likely, is to risk death. The Rosenbergs flee, but because the battle is everywhere and nowhere, they return home. When the enemy's television reporter tries to elicit gratitude for their "liberation," they plead that their broken radio has left them uninformed. "You do care, don't you?" the interviewer asks. "You've decided, then?" They answer "Yes" to both questions, but what they care about or have decided is not pursued. When Jan collapses, the reporter turns not to him but to the crew, yelling, "Hold the camera! Keep in the faint!" The defending army proves just as callous. After repelling the invaders, they herd the Rosenbergs into a schoolroom along with others they accuse of collaboration. Producing a captured copy of the television interview, clumsily doctored to make the Rosenbergs appear enthusiastic supporters of the invasion, they warn the couple to admit the "truth" or face severe punishment. The real purpose of the interrogation, however, is not to discover the truth (the captors have known from the start that the Rosenbergs are innocent) but to "set an example" by humiliating their prisoners.

What ideological difference distinguishes invaders from defenders—if indeed there is any—never transpires. Bergman implies that the opposing causes have their true believers, but in the main the functionaries serve because of fear and self-interest, not principle. Jacobi, formerly the town's mayor and now a colonel in charge of interrogation and torture, is the prime example. He admits to having accepted the "distasteful" job to avoid the dangers of battle, and he appeases his conscience by arguing that he can palliate the excesses of his superiors. Yet, in reprieving the Rosenbergs, he is motivated less by the memory of the pleasant evenings when they were guests in each other's homes or even by a residual sense of decency than by his sexual desire for Eva.

While Jacobi enjoys the upper hand, Jan plays the sycophant; although Eva tells her husband she dislikes and mistrusts the official, Jan depends too much on the Colonel's protection and gifts to discourage his visits. Even after Jan's behavior drives his wife into a liaison with Jacobi, he chooses to be a wittol, and when Jacobi presses his life's savings on Eva, saying he wants to make her his heir, Jan finds the money and stuffs it into his pocket. But shortly thereafter, the tables are turned. Jacobi, accused of treason by his own forces, wants to borrow his savings back from Eva so that he may buy his life. Once the theft of the money is discovered, it is obvious to everyone that Jan has stolen it, yet he professes ignorance while the soldiers ransack the house and then blow it up. Finally, given the choice of admitting he has the money or shooting Jacobi, the timid musician who earlier did not have the stomach to kill his chickens for food now performs the execution in cold blood.

If an element of vengeance in this murder mitigates Jan's guilt, nothing excuses him for killing again in the very next scene. When a young soldier surprises the Rosenbergs, Jan fears he will be shot, but the hungry, exhausted boy—a deserter who is as frightened as they are —only wants a temporary sanctuary. Nevertheless, Jan snatches the machine gun from the sleeping soldier's arms and shoots him. Then, after stealing the dead boy's boots, he persuades Eva that they should meet the boat on which the deserter and a confederate had planned to escape and take their places. Significantly, when they arrive at the boat, they discover that the operation is being run by Filip—the same man who, as an officer in the home guard, had forced Jan to shoot Jacobi; Jan now uses Jacobi's money to pay for their passage.

Because the real price for a seat on this boat is the loss of moral dignity, the voyage leads only toward greater despair. Food and water are soon exhausted, and the floating, bloated corpses of soldiers clog the boat's oars. When Filip, recognizing the futility of the struggle to survive, commits suicide by quietly lowering himself over the side, Jan merely turns his head. In the film's final lines, Eva describes a dream she had in which an attacking airplane set fire to a wall of roses while she held her infant daughter—the child she had always wanted to have who will now never be born. Even if the drifting refugees should be rescued, Bergman implies, life would have neither value nor purpose.

Like a number of the earlier scenes, the conclusion has an undeniable affective force. While jolting the emotions, however, *Shame* offends the intellect. The problem is not that an aesthetic medium makes a poor forum in which to expound political and philosophical theses, especially if those theses run athwart the viewer's convictions; rather, it is the muddled, inconsistent terms of the fiction as a metaphoric statement.

Bergman has said that the film led from his asking himself how he would have behaved if the Nazis had occupied Sweden—and from his "panicky" realization that, as "both a physical and psychological coward," he might have shown something less than courage.[3] The protagonist of the film he wrote, however, never confronts that moral question; he simply wants to be left alone. Moreover, if either side in its war were tied to such crimes as those perpetrated by the Nazis in the concentration camps (or by the Soviets in the Gulag), the Rosenbergs' indifference would take on a different hue. These armies are simply evil because the filmmaker wants to illustrate the horror of war. Yet, even at that, *Shame* is not quite the protest Bergman claimed he was making on behalf of "the frightened and terrified people who sense the twilight."[4] If it were, one should expect the film to champion some good in humanity; instead, it displays a fundamental misanthropy while pretending the opposite. Although Jan is a victim, he deserves his fate as surely as Jacobi and Filip deserve theirs. Only Eva remains a sympathetic character, but the film defines no dramatic argument through her.

Bergman's emphasis on music as a symbol further confuses the issue—to the extent that some critics inferred a pleading of special privilege for art and the artist. Although *Shame* advances no such claim, it does equate music with "the small holy part of the human being" that has been overcome by bestiality, with the possibility of "believing in something, in hope and dreams" that has receded before the horror of reality.[5] Thus: a Meissen musical ornament in an antique shop the Rosenbergs visit on the day of the invasion recalls an age in which art could naively affirm the universe's inherent order and goodness. A first edition of a Dvořák piece which Jacobi gives to Jan similarly nods to a shattered grace of civilization; although Jacobi says he hopes they might one day perform quartets as they did in the past, the baseness the two men have already shown to each other makes that impossible. "The only artist who tells us about some sort of god," Bergman has stated, "is the musician," and in *Shame*, "music is dead."[6] One might even say that he depicts its "murder": during the furious destruction accompanying Jacobi's execution, the soldiers crush Eva's violin (made by a contemporary of Beethoven in the same year as the Congress of Vienna) and beat a piano to pieces in a yard strewn with decapitated chickens and rubble. The more blatant the symbolism becomes, however, the more one realizes how superfluous it is. If Jan and Eva were bureaucrats instead of violinists, if their evenings with the Jacobis had been spent playing bridge instead of Bach, if, indeed, every reference to music were expunged, the film would remain essentially unchanged. The barbarism exposed by the war would be no less ugly; Jan's dishonor, no less repugnant. Nor would the deletion affect how the characters are perceived. For all the talk about music, there is not a single gesture in which the Rosenbergs convey a sense of what the "death" of music has meant to their lives or one moment in which Bergman convinces us that they have even been musicians.*

But if the music-is-dead refrain has little bearing on what *Shame* purports to be about, it has a great deal to do with the personal story it conceals. In the Erasmus speech, Bergman had vaguely blamed the demise of art on the conditions of contemporary life, but the suicide of the artist in *Not to Speak of All These Women* was wholly unrelated to the state of the world, and the "breakdown" of art in *Persona* scarcely reflected an insupportably horrified response to a Vietnamese monk's suicide or to the suppression of the Warsaw ghetto more than two decades before. *Hour of the Wolf* garishly demonstrated the real reason art had become "a snakeskin filled with ants." *Shame*, like its immediate predecessors and like *The Rite*, the other script he wrote in 1967, twists and turns in the same psychosexual pit.

During an interview on Swedish television in February 1968, Bergman was asked why his films so often dealt with humiliation. The subject, he answered, was "of surpassing importance" for the artist because it treats "one of mankind's worst attendant ills." From "mankind," the focus then quickly narrowed to "me."

> Our whole social system, to an awfully high degree, is built on humiliation. Think of laws, the theory of legal punishments, which

---

*Bergman's contention that appreciation of music reflects human nobility scarcely accords with historical experience. If *Shame* is an outgrowth of his wondering how he would have conducted himself during a Nazi occupation of Sweden, he should have remembered the high place given to music in the Third Reich and the orchestras of Jewish inmates forced to play for the concentration camp officers.

are nothing other than humiliations. The schooling I lived through
was a form of humiliation. The religion that we publicly profess is a
terrible series of inherent humiliations.... Every form of humiliation rouses in me a powerful aggressiveness and a dangerous desire
to reciprocate in kind—forces I myself often can't control.[7]

Were anyone else speaking, the latter part of the statement might mean
nothing more than that humiliation incites a desire for vengeance. For
Bergman, however, the word "humiliation" is virtually bound to
"childhood" and conjures not only the punishments he physically
endured but also the psychological pain of guilt and desires that went
far beyond his actual transgressions. Whatever it may seem to be saying
about mankind, *Shame*—the very sound of the word evokes the accusation of a child—is another return to the early world of the self.

Jan, around whose shame the film revolves, is conspicuously childlike in
his petty fears, his fumbling ineptitude, his egocentricity (Eva, while reminding him of his infidelity with a singer, says she has forgiven him because he loves only himself), his confusion and sense of powerlessness in
responding to authority. Eva's motherliness, manifest in almost every scene,
clearly identifies her role in this psychic drama. The third member of the
"family" is Jacobi—marked as "father" not only by being an authority figure (first as mayor of the town, then as colonel of the home guard), a protector (who also threatens to send the Rosenbergs to a labor camp if they
are not properly appreciative), and a provider, but also, more pointedly, by
his giving Eva a ring that is a family heirloom and becoming her lover.*

---

*These three characters closely correspond to the triangle in *Torment*. Although Jan's
behavior sharply contrasts with Jan-Erik's nobility (not only in confronting Caligula but
also in standing firm before the school authorities), the virtue of the earlier "self-portrait"
may be seen as a romanticized compensation for the moral flaw Bergman would later
magnify. The two women, besides having similar longings—Bertha dreams of being a
bride and settling into domesticity; Eva, of becoming a mother and enjoying a normal
family life—are also cast in similar relationships with Caligula and Jacobi. The most
interesting resemblance, however, lies in the psychological features of the two oppressors
who, in addition to being father figures, are mirror images of Jan and Jan-Erik. Jacobi's
account of two scenes from his past—one of looking on while his son put his grandchild to
bed, the other of sitting with his mother's corpse—expresses the loneliness of a man
whose fear of human contact has caused him to restrain his emotions; his confession that
he has "only known human intimacy a very few times, always in connection with pain"
suggests a latent sadism. Like Caligula, too, he imposes himself on Eva not because of
passion but because he hungers for maternal tenderness in a world where "there is
nowhere to hide, no excuses, no evasions, only a great guilt, a great pain, and a great fear."
Huddling by the schoolroom's heater during the interrogation of the "collaborators" or
complaining of the cold outdoors while he lingers in the warmth of the Rosenbergs'
cottage, he recalls the cowering, isolated Caligula, terrified of the dark.

Once one perceives the nature of this triad, the events immediately prior to Jacobi's execution take on a new meaning. This highly contrived scene seems implausible on its face, even if the presumption that currency could still have value at this stage of the war were granted. After Jan finds the money and surmises that Jacobi has given it to Eva, what motive can he have for stealing it—not from Jacobi but from his wife? And if he means to keep it for himself, why would he show it to her after the execution? Certainly, revenge cannot be on his mind when he decides to take it: that possibility only arises after Jacobi is offered the chance to buy his life. But what appears implausible as realism becomes quite plausible if the money is understood to symbolize a son's desire for sexual potency. Jan stuffs the great wad of bills into his pocket at the very moment Eva and Jacobi are having intercourse in the greenhouse. Then, significantly, he refuses to surrender his prize back to the "father," even though it means that the house—the symbol of the family—will be destroyed. (Curiously, the soldiers never think of searching his person; even more curiously, Jan, despite his cowardice, stakes his life on the supposition that the bulge created by 23,000 crowns will not be noticed. Might the covert reason for this odd behavior be that, as a "child," he would not be suspected of having the sexual capability symbolized by the money?) The Oedipal rivalry becomes still more obvious when, as the price for having kept the money, Jan must kill Jacobi: although Filip orders the first shot, Jan acts on his own in firing twice more at the father figure. (That Jan later uses Jacobi's money to pay for his and Eva's places on Filip's boat has a double symbolic meaning. To the extent to which the boat represents an escape, the payment expresses Jan's attempt to undo his sin. But the "escape" is effectively a banishment, and in this respect, the payment constitutes an admission of guilt, not only of murder but also of what killing the "father" represents.)

The second murder elaborates the Oedipal implications of the first. When the deserter appears, the Rosenbergs have taken up residence in the very greenhouse where Eva and Jacobi made love. Immediately, with his submachine gun pointed at Jan (and knowing that he should shoot in order to save himself), the young soldier is in Jan's position vis-à-vis Jacobi in the previous scene. This mirroring and exchange of identities operates at a deeper level as well. The soldier's Christian name, "Johan," is, of course, the root of "Jan." That he bears the surname "Egerman" is also significant. Near the film's beginning, the Rosenbergs visit the grave of Eva's grandfather, whose name, curiously, is David Fredrik Egerman. Like "Johan" and "Jan," "David," "Fredrik," and "Egerman" have all been used by Bergman for characters associated in some nuclear, personal way with himself ("David" in *A Lesson in Love* and, more obviously, *Through a Glass Darkly*; "Fredrik Egerman" in *Smiles of the Summer Night*). Thus, one may deduce not only that the soldier represents Jan's alter ego but also that, in the psychological machinery behind the fiction, Johan (i.e., Bergman) and Eva are familially linked. What that relationship is soon becomes evident when Eva feeds the boy, dresses his wound, and cradles his head on her lap—a figurative parallel to the symbolic mother-son relationship between Eva and Jan. But why should Jan kill this other "self" (and then literally put himself in Johan's shoes and take his place in the boat)? From an artistic point of view, the murder is a melodramatic climax to an unnecessary scene. Jan's moral failure has already been established; showing him as a monster only diffuses the power of the previous episode. Psychologically, however, the murder serves as the "son's" self-punishment for Oedipal guilt—a guilt which nonetheless continues to haunt him in the form of the floating corpses (Johan multiplied many times over).*

Interpretation of *Shame* as though it were a dream is quite consistent with the way in which the film is presented. A dream, Bergman has often observed, is always perceived as real while it is happening, even though the dreamer is disconcertingly aware of the strangeness in its circumstances. *Shame* produces this effect by joining a vivid realism (enhanced by Bergman's use, for the first time, of a hand-held camera to give portions of the film the look of a documentary) and a background that verges on the expressionistic. The setting is neither quite the present nor quite the future (it is 1969, yet the war has been going on for years); the elapsed time between scenes could be months or hours (the shifts in the fortunes of the contending armies not only occur offscreen but also seem timed by a much faster clock than the one governing the action shown); and some glaring inconsistencies occur in the course of the story's development.** But the stronger argument for treating the film as a dream comes from the characters themselves. Jan, in the very

---

*In a closely related sense, these bodies also suggest the reemergence from *Hour of the Wolf* of that other alter ego murdered by Johan Borg in his dream.

**The most conspicuous of these concerns Mrs. Jacobi. The first time Jacobi appears, he and his wife converse with the Rosenbergs aboard a ferry. In the script, the only subsequent mention of the fact that Jacobi is married is a reference to her having fled to Switzerland. In the film, even that minimal explanation of her disappearance is omitted, yet she turns up as one of the passengers on Filip's boat; strangely, neither the Rosenbergs nor anyone else on the boat gives the least sign of knowing who she is.

first line of dialogue, tells Eva he dreamt they were playing a Bach concerto back on the mainland and "all this was behind us, like a nightmare." Midway through the film, the simile recurs more forcefully: "At times," Eva says, "everything is like a dream. It's not my dream. It's someone else's that I've become part of. What will happen when that person wakes up and is ashamed?" Then, in the film's last lines, Eva recites her dream about holding her daughter and trying "to remember something someone had said, though I'd forgotten what it was."

Like pieces of a code—or like fragments of a dream—these three references to dreams spell out a message when fitted together. In a sense, it is of course Bergman who has made Eva part of the dream that is *Shame*, and its Oedipal implications that are "shameful." This recognition helps explain the significance of the first dream. The memory of playing Bach, before music "died," relates to Bergman's ideal of art before he pronounced it dead in the Erasmus address; the "nightmare" from which Jan cannot awaken corresponds to the films after *The Communicants*. The final dream, prominently mounted as an emblem of the film itself, identifies what gives rise to the nightmare.

Asked to comment on Eva's dream, Bergman replied that it was one he himself had had, "a pure visual experience of something beautiful and pleasurable which is gone, something unattainable, wasted through carelessness. No doubt, [what Eva has forgotten] has to do with love."[8] Although critics often cite this dream as an indictment of war's terror, Eva's narration (like Bergman's gloss) scarcely supports such an interpretation. "I came to a high wall overgrown with roses," she says. "Then an airplane came with great force and set the roses afire. They burned with a clear flame, *and it wasn't particularly terrible because it was so beautiful*." What should make this experience "beautiful" and, in Bergman's odd syntax, at once "pleasurable" and "unattainable"? The answer lies in the dream's symbolic language: the plane is unmistakably phallic (cf. Johan's make-believe plane in *The Silence*); the sexually ignited roses that cover the high wall (forming a "hill," or *berg*, of roses) patently represent Eva.*

---

*The infant girl who presses her moist open mouth to Eva's cheek during this conflagration not only emphasizes Eva's significance as mother but also contrasts the innocence of the pre-Oedipal, oral phase in the mother-child relationship to the consuming passion figured by the burning roses.

  The association between mother and roses was impressed upon Bergman in childhood by the church painting showing the Virgin and Child in a rose garden—the memory of which, he said, inspired his portrait of Mia in *The Seventh Seal*.

One of the script's most telling passages, cut from the film, also focuses on this guilt. Just before Filip's boat pushes off into the Baltic, a voice amplified by a loudspeaker calls out the names of the refugees and heaps scorn on their "shame": they have forsaken all right to their "fosterland"; they are so polluted, not even their dead bodies should remain; the air will be cleaner once they have gone. The Rosenbergs' names are not mentioned, of course, since they are taking the places of Johan and his dead partner. Even so, Jan is enraged. In a protest that sounds strangely like a confession, he screams: "What about us, then? Have you forgotten us? Jan and Eva Rosenberg. Why not call out our names? Don't we exist any more? Why won't you answer? What is the offense we have committed?" Leading the roll of those "beneath disgust" among whom Jan demands to be included is the name of a "traitor," former Advocate (i.e., lawyer) Ernst Bergman.

The Rite

When, in the spring of 1968, Bergman returned to the script he had laid aside in mid-August, he immediately realized that, though written as a play, *The Rite* required the intimacy of the camera.* The solution he hit upon was a television production on a spartan budget. "Damn it, I thought to myself, I'll gather four of my good friends, rehearse four weeks, and shoot it. I figured I could shoot it in nine days."**[1]

On March 25 of the following year, curious Swedes switched on their sets to see what the filmmaker had concocted for his television debut as playwright. Bergman's introductory remarks promised them a different experience. Many years earlier, when he was the "youngest theater director in Europe," he had asked the citizens of Hälsingborg to look upon their theater as a bathhouse for the spirit, as a combination temple and brothel uniting the sacred and the profane. Now, to a playhouse elec-

---

*When the script was published, Bergman added *An Exercise for Camera and Four Entertainers* as a subtitle.

**Cinematograph, the corporation Bergman organized to make *The Rite*, would produce or co-produce all his films except *The Magic Flute* for the next seven years.

Bergman indicated the pivotal importance of *Persona* in his career not only through the company's name (a reference to that film's original title) but also through its logo, the figurehead of a woman that had stood outside the cottage occupied by Elisabet and Alma. (The same figurehead also appears in *Shame* and *A Passion*.) After Cinematograph was dissolved as a result of his 1976 tax dispute with the Swedish government, Bergman named the new corporation he formed to succeed it Personafilm.

tronically enlarged to include living rooms all over Sweden, he was presenting a play that reached into the purgation and renewal rituals of drama's primitive origins. Any viewer offended by its shocking subject matter, Bergman advised, should read a book instead, or peruse the banal gossip of a weekly magazine, or hurry to the nine o'clock show at the local movie house.

Before the telecast ended, much of the audience apparently wished it had taken his advice—not because it was shocked but because it was bored. The next day, the critics were as unimpressed as the general public. Although some alluded to a depth of meaning, none dove eagerly to explore it; a typical review, in *Dagens Nyheter*, called the slow-moving drama an opaque, lifeless allegory fashioned by a half-medieval mind. Later, distributed as a theatrical film outside Scandinavia, it went almost unnoticed. The reaction was quite understandable. The play relies almost entirely on exposition rather than on action to bind its nine scenes, and as cinema *The Rite* is threadbare and visually without interest. Yet, though a flawed work, it is among Bergman's most searching self-appraisals.

The play's framework consists of two symmetrical series of encounters, set in motion by obscenity charges against a trio of cabaret performers who call themselves Les Riens. After the whole group appears before Judge Ernst Abramsson in the first scene, he interviews them singly in the third, fifth, and seventh. Sebastian Fisher spits out his contempt; Hans Winkelmann, the group's leader, tries appeasement by offering a bribe; Thea, Hans's wife and Sebastian's mistress, loses control of herself when the Judge insults her and then responds to his sexual attack with nymphomaniacal hysteria. The adjacent even-numbered scenes turn from the conflict between the artists and the law to the mounting sense of hopelessness within the two opposed sides. Thus, different pairings of Les Riens in the second, sixth, and eighth scenes reveal tensions that seem certain to split the group apart; in the fourth, the atheistic Abramsson seeks out a priest to confess his fear of death and loneliness, his disgust for his decaying body, his daunting vision of the ferocity rampant beyond "the thin ring of human warmth." The ninth scene parallels the first, but with the power relationship reversed. Reconvening in the Judge's office, Les Riens start to perform their version of a religious ritual—the "obscene" act which has precipitated their troubles with the law. Abramsson pleads for mercy, but the artists laugh scornfully and Sebastian slaps his face. At the ritual's conclusion, the Judge dies of heart failure. The last frames of the filmed play display a text: "The three artists were later sentenced in connection with the mimed number they called 'The Rite.' They paid their fines, gave several interviews, and at the end of the summer went away on holiday. They never returned to this country."

Reminiscent of the arrival of the King's letter at the end of *The Face*, this deliverance of the artists underscores the basic similarity of the two works. Les Riens are citizens of Ascona, the Swiss town where Albert Emanuel Vogler's Magnetic Theater once worked "genuine miracles," and like the magician, they have become tired of their profession, conscious of the public's disaffection, and riddled by self-doubt. The fact that Sebastian's full name is Albert Emanuel Sebastian Fisher makes the link quite explicit (although Bergman has said that he reflects an increasingly pessimistic view: "Vogler still possessed vitality and spiritual strength; Sebastian is starting to crumble").[2] Furthermore, as several critics have noted, both stories show almost the same outline: Arrival in a new city brings a troupe of touring entertainers into difficulties with the law. The city's officers assert their moral and social superiority by humiliating the artists, yet, despite their show of disdain, they are intrigued by the mystical element in the artists' routines and erotically drawn to the performers. (Abramsson bears some resemblance to the similarly named Consul Abraham Egerman, and his rapelike assault on Thea is reminiscent of the sexual overtures to Amanda by Starbeck and Vergérus.) Finally, after a long, degrading inquiry by the authorities, the artists gain vengeance through a performance of their art. (Abramsson's abasement during the ritual, culminating in his death, parallels Antonsson's reaction to the Invisible Chain trick and Vergérus's terror in the attic.) But the crucial similarity lies still deeper, in the conflict within Bergman that underlies both fictions. The essential struggle in *The Face*, one should recall, was not between Vogler and Vergérus as representatives of the artist and society but between Vogler and that part of his consciousness Vergérus reflects. *The Rite* retraces that same *drame intérieur*.

Not only does Ernst Abramsson share Bergman's own first name but, as nominally "Abraham's son," he is also tied to two of Bergman's most transparent masks: Isak Borg and, proleptically, Jenny Isaksson (the protagonist of *Face to Face*). Like them, and most of the other Isak figures, Abramsson is forced to confront a spiritual emptiness which has its origin in his childhood. This intimate association between the Judge and Bergman becomes most apparent in the church scene. Consisting of one long speech, it requires no second actor to appear, yet

Bergman cast himself as the priest who hears the confession—which is essentially an internal monologue. At the end of the scene (interestingly, by Bergman's own admission, a cross-reference to the Knight's confession to Death in *The Seventh Seal*), Abramsson speaks "with the weak and changed voice" of a frightened child: "It is evening and dark and I am afraid. My mother has left and closed the door. I know that no one would hear if I called. I don't dare walk onto the floor because of all the animals; I must stay in my bed. If I start to cry in anguish, I'll be even more afraid." Later, groping in the final scene for the "key to myself" that will enable the artists to understand his life, the Judge again admits, "I have always been afraid. My first memories are of fear." Virtually the same recitation recurs in many of Bergman's films—and in his descriptions of his own earliest years.*

In part, Bergman suggests, Abramsson has surrendered his life to the law to compensate for that radical fear. By wrapping himself in the law, he has found strength, security, an illusion of purpose. "I have my superiors and my subordinates," he explains. "I obey instructions and I give orders. . . . I am just an instrument. And we live under the law and the law is necessary. " But guilt, another aspect of the terror he—and Bergman—knew in childhood, seems to have furnished an even more powerful psychological reason. Abramsson concedes that the law (like a punishing father) "rebukes, humiliates, judges," that it satisfies "the lust of cruelty." Yet he defends its tyranny: "What else is possible? Yes, you

*Abramsson's memories point most directly back to *The Communicants*, where Tomas Eriksson confesses that, despite having had no aptitude for the ministry, he became a clergyman to please his parents, and that he willed himself into believing in a fatherly God who ordered the world just for him. With the loss of his faith in that father-God, he has become "a bankrupt wretch," overcome by the same terror he had experienced when he awoke in an empty house as a child and "ran down to the shore, all the time screaming and crying for Father." The father's influence has also shaped the Judge's life. In what he himself calls the "preface" to his humiliation in the ritual, he states: "It was my father who wanted me to be a lawyer. He was himself an outstanding attorney, and his father—[but] I had no talent for it." Significantly, at the start of the play the Judge has just returned from his father's funeral. Without this "father-God" whose commandments have ruled his life, the Judge faces a crisis that is analogous to Tomas's.

The similarity, however, also serves to demonstrate a major shift in Bergman's thinking since the early 'sixties. In *The Communicants*, the filmmaker held out the possiblity of redemption through love; in *The Rite*, love is no longer a factor. Indeed, Bergman seems to mock the catechism of the trilogy. In an evident allusion to the assertion at the end of *Through a Glass Darkly* that "God is love, love is God," Hans speaks of loving his sexually insatiable wife "in the spirit of the Epistle to the Corinthians"—in other words, of copulating with her "face to face." Also: like Märta in *The Communicants*, Thea has eczema, but what had symbolized stigmata on the loving, Christlike Märta has a different ironic meaning in *The Rite*.

artists, I ask you that." The license of Les Riens, allowing expression of every uncensored impulse, appalls him. "I don't envy you," he tells them. "It is a horrible freedom."

What he has suppressed in himself, Les Riens give overt symbolic form through the ritual, a kind of pagan mass in which the killing of God is intertwined with the liberation of the profoundly sexual. Thea stands barebreasted; Hans and Sebastian strap on great phalluses and cover their faces with bird beaks. (One should recall, at this point, the psycho-sexual implications of the bird-demon in *Hour of the Wolf.*) A knife stab into a wine-filled bladder (representing God's body) produces a flow that is caught in a chalice. Hans holds the chalice to the sun to capture its reflection on the liquid's surface ("This is taken from the cult of Dionysius," Bergman has explained, "in which the priest held the bowl of blood above his head to mirror the face of the god behind his back in order to drive the god away.")[3] Sebastian then lifts Thea so that the "wine or blood" will reflect her image, which Hans drinks off. Finally, after replying "I understand" to the ritual's last three steps, Abramsson dies of shock at the "horror" of what he has understood.

To the extent to which Abramsson, *as judge*, represents a despotic superego, Les Riens represent ego and id. Bergman seems to have had some such schematization in mind when he categorized them as func-tions of a single entity. Hans, he said, is the "ordering, organizing, planning" center, "the anchor" of the artist's personality who is "deeply bourgeois in his demeanor."[4] The mediator for his partners, both to the outside world and to the superego, he roughly corresponds to the ego. (Not only does he try to "reason" with the Judge—by offering him a bribe—but also, Bergman states, he is the only one who really speaks the Judge's language.)[5] Just as clearly, Bergman's descriptions of the other two are idinal: "Sebastian Fisher is the creative force, the execut-ing element, the active shaping factor, the manifestations of which are kept in check—partly by certain social considerations, partly by human feelings, and partly by a sense of how human beings should conduct themselves." Thea signifies "that which is most dangerous, most irrational, most instinctual in this conglomerate—that which is most easily hurt but also that which is most necessary."[6]

Though Hans and his partners are interdependent, a constant ten-sion between them represents an even greater threat to the survival of the self-as-artist than that posed by the Judge. Ominously, the contract that binds the members of the trio to each other is about to expire. Hans, emotionally exhausted by the petulance of Thea and Sebastian, wishes he were a farmer with a nice, mothering wife, while they itch from having to be grateful for his sufferance. Furthermore, they realize that "they are artists on the way out, and that between their profession and death they possess nothing."[7] As *Hour of the Wolf* demonstrates most emphatically, Bergman's central concern after the trilogy had become the terror of disintegration—the shattering of the mirror which is at once art and the artist. It is this Nothingness which menaces the three aspects of Bergman fragilely united in Les Riens.

"Hans," of course, is a variant of "Johan," that recurring mark of the Bergman persona, and as the only member of the trio who reflects on his condition as artist, Hans echoes the dismal appraisal the filmmaker had first delivered in the Erasmus address. "Service to an artistic ideal was once an ennobling ambition," he says bitterly, "but I've grown tired of our so-called artistry. I no longer believe in what we're doing. I think we're meaningless, disgusting, absurd. We're not relevant any more." (The public seems to have come to the same conclusion: booking Les Riens in Europe has become increasingly difficult, and "a blasted obscenity fuss" has endangered plans for an American tour.)* But more than art's sterile response to contemporary reality prompts this outburst. After *Through a Glass Darkly*, where David is saved from suicide by his discovery of a faith in love, Bergman's artists repeatedly succumb to guilt. Hans further illustrates the propensity for self-flagellation. Comparison with a scene in *Hour of the Wolf* is especially illuminating. There, Lindhorst taunts Johan Borg, a disintegrating artist fatally attracted to humiliation, with a performance of the masterpiece through which the dying Mozart achieved personal transcendence. Here, Hans begins a rambling apology before the Judge by stating, "I have learnt almost everything about humiliation. I don't know why, but something in me seems to invite humiliations. Perhaps an unbounded arrogance. The truly great artists are immune, profoundly unwoundable. I am not one of them."

---

*Les Riens' problems suggest Bergman's own declining popularity during the 'sixties, not only in Sweden and on the Continent but also in America, where enthusiasm for his films had been most fervid. In addition, Hans's remark that "the war" has forced cancellation of their trip to the Far East may allude to the warrant the Swedish intelligentsia found in the Vietnam War for their assertions that art must be politically engaged; as the controversy raised by *Shame* had demonstrated, Bergman was looked upon as a bourgeois artist whose vision of the world had become irrelevant.

The "obscenity fuss" perhaps refers to the two squabbles with the censors over *The Virgin Spring* and *The Silence*. Although "the fuss" had actually boosted attendance everywhere, the sexual scenes in both films were trimmed down in most countries, including the United States.

That arrogance and susceptibility to humiliation, however, reside in a deeper layer of the self than that manifested by Hans. Proud and rebellious, Sebastian freely insults the Judge and boasts of acknowledging no authority—not civil, and especially not divine: "I have never needed any God, or salvation, or eternal life. I am my own god, I supply my own angels and demons. I live on a stony shore which sinks in the waves into a protective sea. . . . *You can never frighten me again.*" But, as with the Jack figures in Bergman's early fictions, the swagger is transparent. The true Sebastian is revealed by a dream he relates in which he is a boy, frightened by the discovery that he has unwittingly been truant; instead of asking forgiveness, he tells his mother he no longer has to endure the ordeal of school as he is really an adult with a three-quarter million crown annual income. The need to bend reality to his will that motivates the boy's lie motivates the adult's art as well.*

As the hurt, willful child who survives in Bergman, Sebastian personifies the reckless aggression the filmmaker has identified as his own *vis vitae*. "There is a constant tension within me between my urge to destroy and my will to live," he admitted while discussing Sebastian. "It's one of my most elementary tensions, both in the way I create and in my material existence."[8] Later, he added, "I have no inhibitions for my aggressions. . . . no threshold at all. I've got an awfully short fuse."[9] Striking one match after another, Sebastian seems literally always ready to light that fuse, and when he deliberately sets his bed afire, he stands in the middle of the blaze, fascinated by the flames that express his rage. Like the image of himself as a bird in one of Sebastian's poems, this evocation of the phoenix implies the artist's renewal through the same energy that consumes him. But the psychological association of pyromania with bed-wetting may indicate another, more private meaning as well: the shame young Ingmar endured when he was forced to wear a red shirt for the sin of incontinence—and, thereby, the childhood steeped in humiliation which has continued to agitate Bergman's imagination.

The third facet of this prismatic self-portrait also reflects Bergman's

*Rebellion against God's paternal authority takes the form of a child's oral fantasy in Sebastian's description of a cabaret act he has written: "A man comes into a police station, looking for the superintendent. He has something odd to report. What must he report? This. He has been seized with a colossal and fateful appetite. He has eaten up his wife, the shop assistant, his two children, his dried-up old grandmother. Towards afternoon, a bearded man entered the shop. It was God himself. The man cut a fillet from God's inner thigh and ate it. Then he felt a pressing need to shit. When he was through, he went to the police, as I said. . . . [There] he lifts his skull, which he had sawn through at ear level, and shows the amazed commissioner the empty interior. His head was completely empty. Deep down by the cervical vertebrae sat a drawstring for the eyelids, but that was all."

painful early memories. A delicate child who developed a hypersensitivity to unusually strong light, sounds, and odors, Thea has always suffered from an anxious awareness of being utterly vulnerable. Her childhood was a suffocating ordeal in which strict religious parents tolerated no opposition to their regimen. Harsh punishments afflicted the spirit as well as the flesh: one in particular, involving a piece of clothing (apparently Bergman's red shirt) haunted her "like a waking nightmare" during a two-year period. Still bearing the effect of her subjugation, Thea stammers when confronted by authority—just as Bergman claims he did as a boy.

Strangely, however, all the information about Thea's childhood is contained in a letter written for her by Hans and read aloud by the Judge. Why should Bergman employ this roundabout device, emphasizing that these are Hans's words, not Thea's? Apparently, to imply that Hans (i.e., Bergman) is describing his own experience and, more important, that the psychological stresses of that childhood have led him to create a fictive Thea—a name which not only points to her theatrical (or ritualistic) role as goddess but also associates her with Bergman's symbolic Virgins, with motherly pity, Christlike sacrifice, and love. A paragraph toward the end of the letter connotes just such an imaginary leap:

> I make believe that I am a saint or a martyr. That's why I call myself Thea [i.e., why Hans calls her Thea]. I can sit at the big table in the hall for hours looking at the palms of my hands. Once, a red spot arose on my left hand. But no blood came out. I make believe I sacrifice myself to save Hans or Sebastian. I make up ecstasy and conversations with the Holy Virgin, faith and disbelief, defiance and doubt. I am a poor sinner with unbearable guilt. And so I repudiate faith and forgive myself. Everything is a game. At the core of the game, I am always the same, sometimes utterly tragic, sometimes incredibly exhilarated.

At this point, Thea interrupts the Judge's reading. "That is not at all what I mean," she says, indicating that Hans's dissimulation of her has become insupportable. The Judge, who now realizes she has not written the letter, soon forces her to disclose her true identity—not "Thea" but "Claudia Monteverdi."* Immediately, he calls her a two-bit whore—whereupon she begs for a kiss, lifts her skirt, and rolls on the floor. His lust provoked beyond all restraint, he then falls viciously on top of her. Thea's "real

---

*The name obviously alludes to Claudio Monteverdi, but why Bergman should refer to the composer who helped lay the foundations of opera is unclear.

self" radiates madness; weak, sluttish, foul in the very fact of being female, "Claudia" incites demonic instincts to erupt with destructive fury.

Thea's double identity patently mirrors the ambivalent image of Woman which troubles the "dreams" that are Bergman's fictions—an ambivalence rooted in his conflicting images of mother. Certainly, at the level on which the play revolves around Thea, Les Riens' ménage à trois constitutes another of his Oedipal triangles. Hans—"so gentle, so thoughtful, so wise, so dignified, so devilish"—stands in the position of father. Sebastian, who is said to bear "a family resemblance" to Thea (and who, moreover, wears his actual father's wedding ring), is the jealous son.* A curious account of Les Riens' history seems to have been inserted by Bergman to underscore the psycho-mythic nature of the triangle. Before Hans, Thea had another husband, whom Sebastian stabbed to death in a knife fight. Sebastian then expected to succeed to his "rightful" place in Thea's bed, but while the law kept him jailed, Thea instead married Hans (in effect, the first husband—or father—who has survived the "murder" the son has fantasied). Even if Bergman had omitted this gloss, however, the Oedipal rivalry between Thea's two men would still be evident. Hans's sexual prowess with his wife is unerring. Sebastian, in contrast, has yet to bring Thea to orgasm—despite their putatively licentious relationship. Significantly, "Mother Earth's own sister" Thea keeps her inept lover's desires in check by praising Hans's skill, then, humiliating him even more "meanly," by raking up a homosexual affair in Sebastian's past.**

But *The Rite* is not just another Bergman fiction in which the Oedipal mother appears; more specifically, it shows him grappling with the problem posed by this "most dangerous" and yet "most necessary"

---

*One indication of Sebastian's symbolic role may lie in the fact that his first name—not common in Sweden—is also the middle name of Bergman's son with Käbi Laretei, and that he has the same surname as Bergman's first wife; hence, "Sebastian Fisher" implies one who is both son and mate. Perhaps another personal reference accounts for Sebastian's gratuitous revelation that his mother was related to the Vaalendorffs (a name suggesting "Walloon village"): Karin Bergman's family was of Walloon stock.

**Oedipal conflict is expressed in various ways throughout *The Rite*. A particularly revealing instance occurs in the penultimate scene, where Sebastian tells Hans he is going to run away with Thea. "Father" quickly dashes the plan by reminding this "son" that his financial insolvency makes him incapable of supporting himself, much less Thea. But then, as if to prove the love he professes for Sebastian by enabling him to become a man, Hans passes on the secret of his sexual success: "Don't try love or tenderness, that just makes her nervous. Shove your left hand in as far as it will go and squeeze the right hard against the clitoris, so that it causes pain. She'll have several orgasms within two minutes. Then you can fuck her in any way for as long as you wish."

element. If the psychological conflict Thea personifies has been the stimulus for his creativity, it also becomes the source of the entropy in his work. References to death saturate *The Rite* (among them, a report that a close friend of Les Riens has just died at the age of fifty—Bergman's age when he was writing the play). But the most central, the emblem for all the rest, takes the form of Thea's recurring dream about islands that float up from the riverbed. According to her psychiatrist, these islands are "signs of approaching death. They get bigger and more solid as they rise out of the swirling darkness. One day the stream is choked by the islands." What the stream represents is made evident elsewhere. The same psychiatrist has told her, "You are not solid substance. You are movement. You flow into others, they flow into you. Nothing is constant." And Hans's letter describes "Thea's" games of make-believe as "an unimpeded flowing water." More than a symbol of Thea's life, then, the stream connotes the energy of the artist's imagination; the islands, its increasing paralysis.

Although Les Riens as a corporate entity evince the artist's disintegration, Thea is the locus of their morbidity, the one who carries death within her being. That death, a wasting consciousness of the Nothing which Bergman's fictions dissimulate (and which Alma/Elisabet finally acknowledges with such devastating implications at the end of *Persona*), is also a trope for corrosive guilt. Ostensibly, the legal charge against Les Riens concerns the ritual they stage, but, until the final scene, the Judge's investigation completely ignores that matter, delving instead into the sexual interior of this "conglomerate" artist. And clearly, what makes Les Riens obscene to the Judge emanates from Thea; indeed, the play essentially depicts the conflict between an accusing conscience and this most vulnerable facet of the artist's mind.

Commenting on his intentions in writing *The Birth of Tragedy*, Nietzsche justified art as potentially a Dionysian rite through which the artist assumes the guise of the gods in his dreams and overturns the enslaving, absolute moral dictates of the Christian God: "art, rather than ethics, constitute[s] the essential metaphysical activity of man."[10] The ritual with which Bergman concludes *The Rite* is precisely the assertion of freedom advocated by the philosopher he had idolized in his youth. Magically, what has been the source of the guilt enfeebling the artist is

Clearly, even though it is the "father" who speaks, the secret technique is the projected fantasy of an immature child. Not only does the fantasy avoid mentioning the penis that is the focus of his feelings of inadequacy, but it also satisfies two contradictory needs simultaneously: one, to translate guilt arising from his sexual desire into aggression against its object; the other, to exculpate the mother for her infidelity with the father by showing it to be an involuntary —indeed, brutally enforced—submission.

transformed into a sacred ceremony of deliverance: simultaneously, the creative power arising from Thea again flows and the Judge dies. As, earlier, Sebastian says of art, "The miracle is always the same. Suddenly lilies shoot up from the assholes of corpses."

In revivifying what he had pronounced dead in the Erasmus address, however, Bergman was engaging in wishful fantasy, not expressing genuine conviction. As all of his fictions for the next decade attest, his imagination would remain trapped within its vision of depleted possibility.

A Passion

Even before he began the *Silence of God* trilogy, Bergman had recognized that the era of the black-and-white feature film was drawing to a close, yet he resisted the transition. After dropping plans to shoot *The Wallpaper* (the original version of *Through a Glass Darkly*) in color, he continued to use black and white until *Not to Speak of All These Women*. That experiment left him dissatisfied: technically, he said, the color was textbook perfect—and lifeless. For the next five years, he returned to black and white, but by the end of the decade, a permanent commitment to color had become inevitable.* Confronting necessity, Bergman saw a challenge. In *A Passion*, he and Sven Nykvist would discard the textbook and strive for "a *noch nie da gewesenes*."[1]

Rejecting the "synthetic reality" produced by the emphasis on color in previous color films, Bergman and Nykvist adopted a strategy of general understatement—both to create a more natural effect and to heighten the emotional force of particular passages in which color attracts attention as a dramatic element. Aside from the purely visual effect, this strategy also seems to have influenced the presentation of the story in a radical way. For Bergman, film operates as dream; thus, if muting the color had the desirable result of enhancing realism, that realism could also diminish the film's dreamlike property. The apparent solution was to approximate the workings of a dream through discontinuities in the story itself: most of what "happens" in *A Passion* takes place between scenes, and much of what is seen remains isolated from contextual reference.

---

*One reason Bergman cited was that black-and-white films had no appeal for young people—and in fact, though it was certainly not the sole explanation, that portion of the Swedish audience had long since deserted him.

But if the challenge of color inspired innovation, the film's temper and issues continue to form part of the common denominator which subtends 'sixties Bergman. The filmmaker himself has remarked that *A Passion* follows "a line of development" stretching from *Through a Glass Darkly*, and it is clearly the terminus for that segment of the line, beginning with *Persona* and passing through *Shame*, in which the island settings serve as metaphor for a besieged consciousness. Although any script Bergman might have written in 1968 would probably have shown a basic similarity, *A Passion* evolved directly from *Shame*; indeed, he looked upon it as virtually a sequel.

Once *Shame* had been finished, Fårö's strict environmental code required that the structure built to represent the Rosenbergs' house be razed. Bergman was reluctant to comply, in part, he says, because he thought it a charming building, but also because he could not dismiss *Shame* from his mind. Something in its conception had misfired in the execution, and he wanted to redo that "something." To save the house which stood as symbol of his intention, he advised the authorities that it would soon be used for another film—though, at the time, he did not know what it would be or when he would turn to it. Preparations for his next film were already very far along: the script had been drafted; the cast, chosen and signed. But second thoughts at the last minute caused him to shove that project aside (the script would later be reworked as *The Preserve*) and to write *A Passion* in its stead. Because he had actors under contract, he fitted the story to the characters from the aborted script, even retaining their original names, but its thesis was the interrelationship of humiliation and violence that he had set out to demonstrate in *Shame*. The fact that Max von Sydow plays the lead in both films is significant: Bergman has stated that he thought of Andreas Winkelman, the central figure of *A Passion*, as another Jan Rosenberg. And although Liv Ullmann's role as Anna Fromm in the new film seems quite unlike her role in *Shame*, Bergman felt compelled to associate the two women by having Anna dream of herself as Eva Rosenberg.

Like most of Bergman's films, *A Passion* begins with foreboding. While Andreas Winkelman is repairing his roof, three suns appear in the sky.* Next, a cement pail tumbles from the roof for no discernible reason; after he sets it upright and walks away, it again falls on its side. Shortly thereafter, a woman with a crutch hobbles to the house, introduces

The Seventh Seal also opens with this meteorological phenomenon. "For me, it's an old, familiar omen," Bergman has explained, adding that the appearance of seven suns supposedly augured the Thirty Years' War.[2]

herself as Anna Fromm, and asks to use his phone. While she makes frantic inquiries about her late husband's finances, Andreas eavesdrops.

After she leaves, he notices that she has forgotten her purse. Searching it, he discovers an old letter from her husband—whose name was also Andreas. As he reads, Bergman shows the impact of the dead Andreas's words on him by projecting the letter on the screen in extreme close-up, line by line: "It is best that we not meet. I would just give in to you for, despite everything, I love you. But I don't want to give in because I know that we would only enter into new complications, which in turn would produce frightful spiritual shocks, physical and psychic violence."

Andreas, in retreat from a failed marriage and troubles with the law, has been leading a reclusive life on the island, but the encounter with Anna draws him out of his protective shell. When he returns her purse, he meets Elis and Eva Vergérus, whom Anna is visiting; several weeks later, looking rather out of place in his ill-fitting suit and nooselike tie, he joins them for dinner. The conversation is entirely pleasant—until Eva makes light of her childhood belief in God, and Elis, an eminent architect, deprecates the cultural center he is designing for Milan as "a tombstone over the total meaninglessness in which people of our sort live." Suddenly, Anna shrieks at Eva for her lack of convictions and at Elis for his cynicism. Her own life, she proclaims, has been a pact with truth, and although fate has not been kind to her, a harmonious marriage based on absolute honesty has left her "something to believe in." The fervor is genuine, but at the end of her sermon, the words "physical and psychic violence" from her husband's letter fill the screen.

Staying overnight at the Vergérus house, Andreas hears screams; the next morning, Elis explains that Anna suffers nightmares from her terrible accident. (Eva will subsequently reveal that Anna was driving the family car when it went off the road, killing her husband and young son.) Rather matter-of-factly, Elis adds that Anna loved her Andreas "to the point of madness," even though she knew he was having an affair with Eva. The guest absorbs these bits of information with calm interest, but once he returns home, he drinks himself into a stupor and stumbles about the heath bellowing his own name, as though insisting on his separate identity. Apparently, he has fallen in love with Anna; even more disturbing, he senses a power forcing him to relive Andreas Fromm's experience. That eerie duplication of someone else's past continues when Eva comes to his house and seduces him.

Some time later, Elis, an ardent amateur photographer, is snapping pictures of Andreas in his studio. As he stalks his subject, he whistles archly—as though, more than suspecting that this man has cuckolded him, he had actually been a witness and heard Andreas whistle after sleeping with Eva. The hateful look he gives his wife when she enters the studio to speak briefly with Andreas further confirms that he knows all about their secret. Obviously, Elis is hatching a scheme for revenge. Another uncovered secret seems to set the trap: Elis has learned about Andreas's criminal record, and he uses the information to force this "beaten dog" into accepting a job as his secretary—presumably, to be beaten again.

Strangely, however, Bergman does not develop this well-prepared conflict any further; indeed, neither Elis nor Eva reappears in the film. Instead, without furnishing any explanation of how it came to pass, Bergman next shows Andreas and Anna living together as though they were man and wife. From this point on, the focus is on their relationship —and on the contagion of "physical and psychic violence."

The world's distemper reaches the couple via the flickering televised newsreel of a South Vietnamese officer shooting a bound prisoner in the head. On the island, where some unknown psychopath has been viciously attacking animals, Andreas's friend Johan Andersson is accused of being the torturer solely because he was once in a mental hospital; one day, after being battered and urinated upon by young thugs, Johan commits suicide. The Winkelman-Fromm household initially seems to offer refuge from the raging infection of violence, but, as Bergman's voice on the soundtrack emphasizes, "warnings are beginning to appear on the underside." (One of the "warnings" is Anna's dream from *Shame*.) Anna persists in deluding herself about the nature of her marriage to Andreas Fromm, and she begins to reproach her present mate for lying about his own marriage and divorce, and for denying that he ever slept with Eva. When Andreas tries to explain that he cannot reach her through the wall she has raised around herself, and that life with her is a constant humiliation he can no longer tolerate, Anna, suddenly afraid she will lose him as she lost the first Andreas, momentarily clenches his throat with a murderous look in her eye. The violence welling up from the "underside" soon breaches the surface: after a bitter quarrel, Andreas hurls an ax that narrowly misses her head, then beats her furiously.

An hour or so later, a fire alarm summons Andreas to a neighboring farmstead. As the charred carcass of a horse is dragged from the burning barn, a constable states that the island's elusive maniac poured gasoline over the tethered animal, ignited the straw, and locked the barn door, leaving the horse to a torment prolonged by its "devilish will to live." The fact that, previously, Bergman has repeatedly photographed Andreas through flame—of a bonfire, a match, and a gasoline lamp —makes the analogy between him and the horse unmistakable. Significantly, when Anna arrives by car to fetch him home, he cries, "I want to be free."

Desperate to break his own tether, Andreas at last reveals that he had read Andreas Fromm's letter. The shock to Anna seems to send the car off the road, and Andreas cries out, "Are you thinking of killing me just as you did . . . ?" The inference to be drawn from the unfinished sentence is plain: under similar circumstances, her reaction to her husband's assault on her illusions caused his death.

As Andreas steps out of the car, he asks Anna why she had come searching for him after he had beaten her. "To beg forgiveness," she answers; then, steering the car back onto the road, she drives off alone. Now that these two have been stripped of their masks, forgiveness—or, indeed, any communication—has become impossible. Andreas paces back and forth in his cage of silence until, abandoning even that limited exercise of volition, he drops to his knees on the sandy ground. As the camera fixes on the fallen figure, the color grains composing the picture drift apart; the human image disintegrates and the screen fills with white. "This time," Bergman solemnly intones, "his name was Andreas Winkelman."

Raised to vatic status in this way, the final line is manifestly intended to complete the film's design of meaning. That meaning, however, was far from clear to the small audiences who attended *A Passion* in 1969, and it has remained rather hazy in the critical discussions published since then. Obviously, "This time his name was Andreas Winkelman" refers to the strange replication of the first Andreas's relations with Anna by the second. One cannot help noticing the replication pattern. In a story Bergman has described as more a collection of moods than a filmscript, it is the one element which provides a basis of formal unity. But stopping at that level of interpretation distorts the film into a psychological melodrama, or a preternatural mystery, culminating in a revelation that solves the puzzle. Although *A Passion* is a difficult, sometimes puzzling film, it is not a puzzle. Moreover, that the two Andreases have tracked parallel courses is scarcely an ironic discovery reserved to the drama's last scene.

The seminal role played by *Shame* in the evolution of *A Passion*, coupled wiith Bergman's comment that their main characters reflected a single prototype, suggests another reading of the last line: i.e., this

Elis Vergérus (Erland Josephson), with part of his collection of anguished portraits in the background. Permission from Svenska Filmindustri.

time "Jan Rosenberg" is named Andreas Winkelman. Asked why he inserted the dream identifying Anna with Eva Rosenberg, Bergman stated, "For me it was stimulating to think that this Anna Fromm had a secret background of experience in the war in *Shame*."[3] This Andreas has also emerged from that "secret background." Indeed, the doubling pattern of the two Andreases probably developed from the notion that, in Bergman's mind, Winkelman and Anna had "met" before in the previous film.

To be sure, the specific link between Andreas and Jan Rosenberg is chiefly a matter of private significance—like Bergman's naming the architect "Vergérus" because he thought of him as "a great grandson or something of that sort" to Royal Medical Counselor Vergérus in *The Face*. But Jan is not a unique figure isolated in a single film; rather, he represents Bergman's evolution of that long line of victim-sufferers he has repeatedly (though with varying degrees of explicitness) likened to Christ abandoned on the cross. *A Passion* is not an allegory based on Christ's Passion; nevertheless, its title implicitly indicates Bergman's conception of life as a "crucifixion." In this central respect, the film's final line can be construed to mean that, this time, the Christ figure's name was Andreas Winkelman.

Johan Andersson, the innocent *sparagmos* who is reviled and stoned before his death, comes closest to the role of Christ in this Passion play.

But clearly, the eremitic Johan, trapped by circumstances, is a double of his one friend Andreas Winkelman—whose surname translates as "corner man" (and whose forename, obviously, mirrors "Andersson.") In the script (written in the form of a first-person novel), Andreas describes his situation in terms that will be echoed by Johan's suicide note:

> The world sprawls over me. I no longer have any protection. I have no one to turn to in protest, no one to accuse—not even myself. I am rendered powerless. I can neither affirm nor change what I see and hear. It goes on ceaselessly hour after hour: bleeding, gurgling, shrieking, crawling, and stinking. I look on, dispirited, scared, paralyzed."

In the film itself (where, in four "intermedia," Bergman interrupts the story to ask the actors how they perceive their roles), Max von Sydow speaks of his character as someone bent on effacing his existence by "trying to wipe out his means of expression"—which, again, is precisely what Johan's suicide signifies. And just after paying last respects to Johan, Andreas himself feels dead and debased:

> I live without self-respect. I know that sounds strange, pretentious, because almost all mankind is forced to live without any sense of their own worth. Basically humiliated and half-suffocated, spat upon. They live just because they know of nothing else to do.... Isn't freedom a terrible poison for the humiliated? Or is the word "freedom" just a drug the humiliated must use to be able to endure? I can't go on living with this.

The Passion motif is made more elaborate through the association of Andreas with the animals that are being tortured and killed by an unknown madman. The burned horse may be the most striking example, but the pattern operates throughout the film.

At just the moment Andreas is figuratively putting his head into a noose by getting involved with Eva and Anna, he finds a puppy hanging from a cord around its neck and adopts it. The analogy becomes more overt when Elis uses Andreas's tainted past to force him into his employ. Gloating, Elis says, "You withdraw like a beaten dog"; "I *am* a beaten dog," Andreas replies. Finally, as Anna drives Andreas away from the fire and the reenactment of Andreas Fromm's experience comes full circle, the camera repeatedly fixes on a jerking, small stuffed animal tied at its throat to the rearview mirror.

A more complex analogy is introduced in the midst of Andreas's entanglement with the Vergérus couple. An entire herd of sheep, knifed to death by the madman, lie strewn over a snow-covered heath. There are no clues. Although the police take photographs of the mutilated beasts, one officer remarks that the pictures are only for the records; they can reveal nothing about the mentality responsible for the crime. Beyond providing gory evidence of the maniac's work, the scene seems a pointless digression. But then Bergman makes a jump cut to the Vergérus studio: the arc traced by the men's arms heaving the sheep carcasses into a pit extends, in a continuous movement, into the sweep of Elis's camera as he photographs Andreas. The sheep obviously correspond to Andreas—and perhaps Bergman means to imply a parallel between the twisted mind preying on the animals and Elis's apparently vengeful intentions.

But the juxtaposition of these two scenes also implies a broader point. Elis has filled rows of file cabinets with thousands of photographs of faces; the studio is a veritable morgue of humanity. The portraits being taken of Andreas will be added to that collection, which includes pictures of the first Andreas, Eva, and Anna. Whether Elis knows the subjects of these studies or not, however, is a matter of complete indifference to him; like the police photographs of the sheep, these are only records. Yet that is just what Elis finds fascinating about his hobby: each face hides the suffering behind it and gives no clue as to its cause. If Andreas and the rest of humanity are victims, like the sheep, the humiliation and anger written on their "underside" also make them potential torturers. And in fact, this is precisely what Bergman illustrates as the film draws to a conclusion. When Andreas's resentment against Anna explodes and he beats her to the ground, Bergman locks the camera on her red kerchief, lying on the snow. The evocation of the blood-marked heath in the earlier scene is unmistakable.

For all the stress Bergman places on humiliation as the source of man's passion, however, he never reveals the cause of his protagonist's humiliation in the past, or why he should now feel so humiliated by Anna that he must strike back with murderous rage. Anna's only offense is a monumental hypocrisy which, paradoxically, results from her obsession for a perfect truth. But that paradox finally emerges as the film's crucial issue. Once Andreas shatters the lie on which her system of "truth" depends, there is no turning back—for either of them. Each is brought to the recognition that the only truth is the impossibility of living within truth, that truth is finally Nothingness.

Describing Anna in this way makes her sound like Elisabet Vogler

—and indeed, under its references and resemblance to *Shame*, *A Passion* shows a remarkable similarity to *Persona*. Played by the same actresses, the paired women in the two films are virtually the same characters. Like Nurse Alma, Eva Vergérus is a pliable personality, "selfless" in the radical sense of the word. (Bibi Andersson's commentary in her "intermedium" serves to accentuate the parallel: "Eventually, Eva won't be able to stand the consciousness of her own detachment and the fact of not being someone, of just being a product shaped by others. . . . But suicide is really no solution; what's more, it is an egocentric affair; I hope she'll be saved. . . . And I believe she will then choose to be—for example—a teacher of the deaf, because the deaf live in an even deeper isolation and loneliness than she.") An apparently minor detail further associates her with Alma "the sleepwalker": before going to bed with Andreas, Eva confesses that her one pregnancy was aborted—as a result of taking too powerful a soporific. Morover, by indicating the similarity to Alma, this detail also calls attention to the correspondence between Anna and Elisabet. The accident which killed Anna's husband killed their young son as well; curiously, however, although Anna frequently talks about Andreas Fromm's death, she never mentions the boy—as though, like the child Elisabet wished dead, he has been excluded from her existence. If Eva's "selflessness," like Alma's, renders her symbolically incapable of giving birth to new life, Anna's egocentrism, like Elisabet's, excludes even that most elementary form of love between mother and child.

Just as Bergman has used birth, maternal affection, and even symbolic reentry into the womb as tropes affirming life's goodness, he has used rejection by the mother, expressed through emotional coldness, abortion, or infanticide, to represent despair. The conceit was first implied in *Prison*, where Birgitta-Carolina's complicity in the murder of her baby underlies the demonstration that satanic malevolence, not divine love, governs the world. By the time he wrote *Persona*, this rejection had become the crux of the plot: once Alma's dream penetrates to the horror of Elisabet's hatred for the child who loves her, the actress's ideal of absolute truth crumbles, suddenly revealing (at least in the logic of the film) that all human relationships conceal a universal lie. In *A Passion*, neither Anna's son nor Eva's miscarriage directly affects the story; perhaps they are only triggers for Bergman's imagination, or personal signals of a private meaning. Thematically and structurally at the core of the film, however, is the same terrifying vision of life as Nothingness masked by lies which

Persona had portrayed as the "necessary" concomitant of maternal rejection.

At the level of the obvious, the story revolves around Anna's self-deception about her marriage. Simply told, this story can be reduced to a few phrases: after a harmonious beginning to her domestic arrangement with a new Andreas, her great lie, combined with accusations that he is lying when he denies ever having slept with Eva, eats away at his tolerance; when he feels "humiliated" beyond endurance, violence erupts; finally, in a moment of fear, he destroys her pretensions—and thus any possibility of their reconciliation. But behind the simplicity lurks confusion. Why should Anna's lie, *in itself*, be so humiliating? (Would Andreas feel less humiliated if Anna acknowledged that her husband was a cad yet remained a slave to his memory?) Furthermore, Andreas had known of Anna's obsessive need to delude herself and others long before he became her lover—indeed, according to what the film actually shows of their "courtship," he knew little else about her. If her lie humiliates him, has he not in a sense sought that humiliation? Why is Anna so troubled by her suspicion that he has been to bed with Eva? Presumably, she fears another betrayal by this second Andreas, but the circumstances are quite different: Andreas Fromm carried on the affair while he was married to Anna; when Andreas Winkelman spent the night with Eva, he had barely made Anna's acquaintance. By the same token, why should Andreas lie about it? Certainly not to protect Eva's marriage—as he has already discovered, Elis knows all about it. And why, having spent an entire scene on that sexual encounter, does Bergman avoid any sign of an erotic attraction between Andreas and Anna? Although establishing that two people are lovers need not involve lubricious display, this strange couple almost never touch. Perhaps most puzzling of all (if one takes note of the way the film is canted), why should the devastation of Anna's illusions result in Andreas's annihilation? As is often the case with Bergman's films, the more one ponders over *A Passion*, the more the questions multiply, suggesting that the fiction responds to a hidden agenda.

Bergman provides little information about Andreas's past, but the few details that do emerge indicate a guilt-ridden consciousness—like Johan Borg's, Jan Rosenberg's, and, especially, like the collective mind depicted as Les Riens. Apparently he was to blame for the collapse of his marriage (Hans Winkelmann's first marriage also failed); he forged checks (like Sebastian), defrauded on his taxes (Les Riens have tax debts), and struck a traffic policeman in a moment of panic (when she was arrested for speeding, Thea "attacked" the policeman by removing her clothes). The pattern shown by this brief history—domestic difficulties, dishonesty, panic, and then violence—will be retraced in the course of his relationship with Anna. More than the memory of any particular event in his past, however, it is Andreas's psyche that persecutes him: his retreat to the island represents an attempt to escape from himself, from something shameful bound up with his identity that cries out for punishment. The scene in which Anna and Andreas witness the execution of the Viet Cong prisoner on television underscores this sense of doom. Andreas immediately draws a personal significance from the newsclip: "They will destroy me," he says. The "they," of course, is not some human enemy but Strindberg's *Makterna*, the dark "powers" of Nemesis. Seconds later, a bird crashes against the window. Andreas humanely destroys it. When Anna then asks why was it flying at night, he answers, "Perhaps it was afraid of something." Clearly, he associates himself with the bird and sees its fate as his own.

That Andreas fears destruction because he feels guilty is self-evident, but what accounts for his guilt—for his "passion"? Although Bergman never spells it out, the source is implicit. Here again, guilt has a psychosexual root.

One indication arises from the ungainliness of the plot: the story turns on the axis defined by the relationship between Andreas and Anna, yet, soon after these two meet, Anna is thrust into the background while Andreas becomes implicated with the Vergérus couple. Then, abruptly, Andreas and Anna are living together, and nothing more is heard of Eva and Elis. What justifies the long digression? To argue that the "replication" motif requires Andreas Winkelman to reenact Andreas Fromm's affair begs the question. Why should Eva's sexual liaisons with the two Andreases be part of the replication? Furthermore, even if it is an essential feature, why go to such lengths to develop Eva's character or to involve Andreas with Elis? If Bergman's chief purpose were to convey the eeriness of the replication, a mysterious, silent visit to Andreas's bed one night after the dinner party, followed by a casual social encounter with Eva and Elis at some critical moment in the relationship between Andreas and Anna, would have been far more effective.

The beginning of a solution to the riddle lies in recognizing that Eva and Anna—like Ester and Anna in *The Silence* and, even more pertinently, like Elisabet and Alma in *Persona*—are carefully drawn as complementary opposites, as one woman (or as the image of Woman) divided in two. (Can it be entirely coincidental that all three pairs bear the initials E and A?) Given the obsessive psychological underpinnings of Bergman's other fictions, the inference that this divided woman reflects the ambiguous childhood response to his mother seems logical, perhaps even inescapable. (Which, of course, is not to say that either woman, any more than the mother figures in his other fictions, is an actual portrait of Karin Bergman.)

The first time Andreas meets Eva, she is sleeping at the side of the road, and when she later visits him it is almost as though she were entering a dream. Neither of them has to propose that they make love; they drift toward bed as if obeying an inevitability. The dreamlike quality is enhanced by the soft red light that drenches the scene. Normally, red connotes intense sexual passion, but the eroticism here is tender and liquid. (A comment Bergman offers in his introduction to *Cries and Whispers* may be relevant here: "ever since my childhood I have pictured the inside of the soul as a moist membrane in shades of red.") These lovers meet as fellow victims, childlike in their vulnerability; when Eva leaves, Andreas gives her his puppy as a substitute for himself.

Perceiving this encounter as an Oedipal fantasy gives added meaning to the very next scene, in which humiliation and guilt are figured by the crime against the sheep. It also puts the oddly inconclusive conflict between Elis and Andreas in a new perspective. Although Elis's desire for revenge may accord with the role of cuckolded husband, the means does not: invoking Andreas's past sins to force him to accept a job that will enable him to support himself seems a most peculiar revenge. But if Elis is seen as a father commanding acknowledgment of his hierarchical authority and using his son's dependency to secure it, the scene begins to make a kind of sense. Significantly, Andreas concedes that he is "beaten," and Eva is never seen again.

From this point on, "mother" shows another face—Anna's. Contrary to what her rigid moral code and religious pretensions would lead one to expect, Anna lives with Andreas even though they are not married. Even so, nothing would indicate an erotic basis to their relationship. It is almost as though she were remaining faithful to her husband. Certainly, her requirement that Andreas accept the lie about that marriage as truth comes between them. Moreover, given the indication that she could not tolerate Andreas's having had intercourse with Eva, Anna in effect forces him to deny it. Implicitly, the condition for their living together is observance of the sexual taboo.

What Andreas is compelled to repress is symbolically conveyed in a strange, long scene that, at the story's superficial level, seems only confusing. One day, both "lovers" are writing in the same room—he, making a final copy of something or other; she, typing her translation of a book in a Slavic language. After asking several times whether she is "disturbing" him, he admits to having a headache—whereupon, with maternal solicitude, she offers to warm some milk for "Poor Andreas." As he waits, he either remembers or fantasizes making love with a woman who tells him he has "cancer of the soul" and will die a horrible death, then copulates with him again.* (The cancer presumably represents his sexual sinfulness.) When Anna snaps him out of the reverie by asking what he is thinking about, he replies, "Cancer, and it frightens me." He invites her to reveal her thoughts. "Lies," she answers. Then, as she walks from the kitchen with the milk (the symbol of her motherliness), he notices that it is heaving "violently" in the dish. Suddenly, the dish smashes to the floor.

Another obscure, seemingly extraneous scene, Anna's "Eva Rosenberg" dream, further develops this interior meaning. The dream begins, in black-and-white, as a continuation of *Shame*: the boat carrying the refugees has landed on a beach after drifting across the Baltic. Eva Rosenberg hurries along a deserted road, "longing for fellowship, for an embrace, for rest, yet knowing that these things were gone forever"; when she meets a young woman, she is shunned and told that "all the locks have been changed." Farther down the road, she comes to a bonfire, where an older woman is awaiting word that her son, condemned for some unnamed crime, has been put to death. Eva begs for the woman's forgiveness; instead, she is beaten. As she escapes across a burning landscape, the black-and-white dream changes into full color and Eva instantly turns into Anna. She screams, but there is no sound to her cries.

The identification of Anna with one Eva implies her relationship with the other; once one also recalls the Oedipal subtext in *Shame*, the

---

*The account in the script is much more erotic that what the film shows. There, the vision begins with the naked woman, Katarina, sitting on his chest, then "gliding down"— apparently onto his mouth. The script also associates sex with disease. As she "presses ever deeper into [his] soft fever" and instructs him to "grab my hips hard," he fixes his eyes on her red-painted toenails and comments that they "look like a disease." When she lifts herself from him, she draws up her knees, presses her hands against her inner thighs, and breathes "violently"; "I thought she was sick," Andreas says.

Interestingly, Katarina was the name of Alma's friend who initiated the orgy in *Persona*. Bergman uses the name again for the wife and the prostitute in *From the Life of the Marionettes*.

dream's content becomes rather transparent. The key symbol is the bonfire, which points back to the sexual episode between Eva Vergérus and Andreas. (That scene had begun with a curtain of flame; the "curtain" then "parted," showing Andreas behind a bonfire and, seconds later, Eva's arrival.) Eva's treatment as a pariah at the outset of the dream thus emphasizes guilt, not fear spread by some war. The bonfire sequence further elaborates this guilt through the disclosure that a son is being executed. The execution suggests crucifixion—and Andreas's "passion." (In the scene immediately preceding the dream, Andreas has identified himself with the executed Viet Cong prisoner; in the scene immediately after, Johan, his Christlike alter ego, has hanged himself.) Then, in the dream's most telling moment, Eva acknowledges responsibility for what is happening to the son.

The end of the dream not only equates Anna to Eva (i.e., Eva Vergérus in the guise of Eva Rosenberg) but also foreshadows the film's concluding scenes. Eva's plea for forgiveness is tied to the last line of dialogue in the film: Anna's revelation that she had driven to the fire in order to ask Andreas's forgiveness. What Anna wanted forgiven—and now realizes is beyond forgiving—was what had provoked Andreas to beat her. And, clearly, the meaning of that eruption of "physical and psychic violence" coincides with the underlying significance of the beating in the dream —the point at which Eva becomes Anna. The surest sign that Bergman intended the dream as an emblem for the film, however, is in the script, where, after having beaten Anna, Andreas looks at the sky, sees "the fire glow from Anna's dream over the woods," and rushes to the neighbor's burning barn. Bergman thus expressly links not only the bonfire and the arson but also the "crucified" son and the tortured horse.

How can Andreas remember (much less see) something in Anna's dream? For the same reason Bergman gave an interviewer when he was called upon to justify the dream's scrambling of characters from two different films: "because it is actually I who gives her her dreams."[4] Though facile and cavalier, the truism underscores an important point. More than Anna's dream, *A Passion* is a product of his dream machinery —and after a quarter century of filmmaking, Bergman had cause to wonder whether he really controlled its levers or the machine controlled him. It is not only Andreas who is sucked into reproducing a preexisting pattern. When Bergman was asked to explain his pronouncement at the very end of the film, he replied, "It means a sort of giving up.... You must feel behind the [ostensible] meaning another you cannot define. For me, it expresses a feeling of boredom. I mean, '*This* time his name is Andreas'; but I will be back and *next* time my character will have another name. I don't know what it will be, but this boring character will be back."[5]

"Accelerating Necrosis"

Like the turns of the previous decades, the transition from the 'sixties to the 'seventies was a trying time for Bergman. Trouble dogged *A Passion* from the start, making the summer of 1968 one of the most exasperating in his professional experience. Bergman usually has every scene worked out in his mind before he begins shooting; perhaps no major director sacrifices less footage in the progress toward the final cut. But the script for *A Passion* had been written hastily, and consideration of the "technical" problems was put off until the film was already in production. As a result, many of the scenes had to be redone. Working in color compounded the problem. Costs rose, threatening the limits of the budget, and the director struggled to finish within the tight forty-five-day schedule. Moreover, Bergman later stated, "the film itself infected all of us in a peculiar way, and most of all, of course, it infected me."[1] The morbidity was not just a function of the subject matter. *A Passion* seems a product of an exhausted imagination, a summing-up by an artist who realizes he can only repeat himself.

Breaking with his usual practice, Bergman wrote no script for a new film to be shot the next summer. Instead, in March 1969, he began making a 16mm documentary about Fårö to be broadcast on Swedish television the following New Year's Day. Meanwhile, Liv Ullmann worked with Jan Troell in the film versions of Vilhelm Moberg's novels about Swedish emigration to America. Rumors began to circulate that all was not well between Liv and Ingmar; after Ullmann took their daughter

Linn out of the country, the rumors found their way into print. In an angry blast at meddlesome, irresponsible journalists during a television interview, Bergman denied there was any domestic discord, but a week later he publicly acknowledged that he and Ullmann had agreed to a three-month "trial separation." Almost coinciding with this announcement was the death of his father on April 26. For years, Erik Bergman had suffered from a slow paralysis of his legs, and after his wife's death in 1966 he rapidly became more feeble. During the last months of his life, while he was confined at Sofiahemmet, his son visited frequently. Although Ingmar's psychologically snarled feelings about his parents never stopped being the prime motivation in his films, he had long since established cordial filial relations. Five years later, when the University of Stockholm awarded Bergman an honorary degree, he lamented that his parents, who had been so deeply disturbed by his withdrawal from the university thirty-five years earlier, could not enjoy the richness of the moment.

That the domestic ties with Liv Ullmann were beyond repair soon became evident with reports of his being regularly seen with a new companion—Malin Ek, who, that very season, had scored a triumph in Bergman's production of *A Dream Play*. Given not only her sudden celebrity but also the May-December aspect of the romance and the fact that she was the daughter of Bergman's longstanding friend and co-worker Anders Ek, the tabloids and the weekly magazines kept a steady eye on the couple.* The affair ran its course rather quickly, however, and early the next fall, the press was caught completely unaware by the news that Bergman would wed Ingrid Karlebo, a forty-one-year-old woman with four children who had just been granted a divorce from Count von Rosen. The ceremony was performed in November. Against the odds indicated by Bergman's marital history, this fifth marriage has now lasted longer than all previous four combined.

Bergman's marriage to Gun Grut in 1951 after a period of crisis had ushered his first real success as a filmmaker, and his marriage to Käbi Laretei after another crisis a decade later had been instrumental in his artistic regeneration. Like Grut and Laretei, Ingrid Karlebo had a settling influence on Bergman, and her emotional support would sustain him through the trials that lay ahead, but the 'seventies witnessed no compa-

---

*Anders Ek had played Caligula in Bergman's first production with the Gothenburg City Theater in 1946. His most memorable role in a Bergman film was as Frost, the clown in *Evening of the Jesters*. Ek had also directed *Painting on Wood* at Dramaten. Malin Ek's mother is the renowned Swedish dancer and choreographer Birgit Cullberg.

rable creative burst in cinema. Though *Cries and Whispers* would prompt critics to use superlatives they had not applied to a Bergman film since *Through a Glass Darkly*, and though *Scenes from a Marriage* would prove the greatest popular success he had ever had, neither is on a par with his best. And no run of films in the last third of his career displays the vigorous imagination which, with such few lapses, had distinguished his work from the early 'fifties through *Persona*. Bergman did not neglect cinema after *A Passion*, but it is clear that the theater reclaimed the more vital part of his genius.

In 1969, after a three-year absence, he was back at Dramaten, directing Georg Büchner's *Woyzeck*. (In the interim, he had mounted only one new production—the thunderously acclaimed *Six Characters in Search of an Author* at the National Theater in Oslo.) He had wanted to do the play for quite some time—Frans Woyzeck could almost be a character in a Bergman film, and Büchner's fragmentary text, with no certain conclusion, presented just the kind of interpretive challenge Bergman relished. But the director saw the production as, more than a presentation of Büchner, an opportunity to preach a new gospel about the relationship between the theater and the community—and to do it in the main temple of Swedish drama. To counter the notion of a performance as an occasion for a night on the town, and to stress the audience's role in the making of a theatrical event, he invited the public to participate, free of charge, in open morning rehearsals. It was a bold stroke. *Woyzeck* did not dawn on the public's consciousness on opening night; even before the start of the open rehearsals, everyone was talking about the production.* Bergman also determined that there would be two perfor-

---

*An unintended by-product of the open rehearsals generated even more publicity. Bengt Jahnsson, the drama critic for *Dagens Nyheter*, was leaving the theater by climbing over the stage apron when the director, offended by the invasion of his territory, stopped him with—depending on who told the story—either a shove or a punch. "I am against violence, but this was the exception that proves the rule," the director told the press the next day.

A month earlier, Bergman and Erland Josephson, his successor as chief of Dramaten, had issued a statement chiding Jahnsson for disseminating false information about the *Woyzeck* production. But the roots of the quarrel went even deeper. Bergman saw Jahnsson as the protégé of Olof Lagercrantz, a "notorious theater-hater"—and the critic who had led the attacks on Bergman as a playwright in the 'fifties. Without Lagercrantz's sponsorship, he claimed, it would be "unthinkable" that a major newspaper should employ "this fantastic figure whose mediocrity and ignorance are exceeded only by neurotic aggressiveness."[2] Furthermore, beyond standing as surrogate for a former antagonist, Jahnsson represented the rising generation of critics who were ideologically unsympathetic to Bergman. Both men alluded to the rift in their remarks after the incident: Jahnsson recalled a television broadcast from Oslo a couple of years earlier in which the director had derogated the young Leftists who were becoming the new establishment; Bergman

mances every night and that admission would cost less than the price of a movie ticket. But what provoked the most comment was Bergman's radical alteration of the theater's layout, opening the house to the lobby, removing the separation between audience and stage, and restricting the actors to a 5×3.5 meter playing area. Even though the idea of "liberating" theater from the physical limitations of its post-Renaissance tradition was scarcely new, this, after all, was Dramaten!

The next year, Bergman brought his version of *A Dream Play* to the smaller, satellite theater within Dramaten. He had directed the play once before for Swedish television in 1963, but this was very much *his* version — edited and freely interwoven with distinctively Bergmanian elements. Strindberg was fifty-two when he wrote the play; Bergman was approaching fifty-two when, one could almost say, he rewrote it. Once again, he held open rehearsals, and there was much buzzing about his compact, visually lean, and richly suggestive rendition of this highly problematic Strindberg work, but the premiere exceeded all expectations. *A Dream Play* immediately became the most sought-after ticket in Stockholm, and in the weeks and months that followed, people from every corner of Sweden made the pilgrimage to witness one of the outstanding moments in the nation's theatrical history.*

Over the next five years, Bergman staged five new productions at Dramaten—*Show* (1971), *The Wild Duck* (1972), *The Ghost Sonata* (1973), *To Damascus*, Parts I and II (1974), and *Twelfth Night* (1975)—and a sixth, *The Dance of Death*, was in rehearsal when intervention by the tax authorities forced a cancellation. (In addition, he developed a new *Misanthrope* for the Royal Danish Theater in Copenhagen in 1973.) Except for *Show* (a play by Lars Forsell based on the life of Lenny Bruce), each was by one of the theater's giants; furthermore, he chose four of the most difficult plays by Sweden's national playwright. Clearly, he meant to establish his credentials as the principal Strindberg interpreter of his

sarcastically excused his knocking the critic to the ground as just the sort of "engaged theater" admired by Jahnsson and his fellows.

By the time the case went to court, the director decided he had struck the blow to protect his actors from the critic's tactic of petty, personal humiliation. The judge fined the defendant—a bargain price, Bergman told reporters, for satisfying honor—and the fuss over this mock epic quickly subsided.

A Dream Play opened in Stockholm in March. In May, after restaging his 1964 production of *Hedda Gabler* at the Old Vic with a British cast, he oversaw the installation of the Strindberg drama (in Swedish) in Helsinki. Although Bergman declined a bid to mount *A Dream Play* at the Comédie Française, it was subsequently staged in Belgrade, Venice, and Vienna.

time. Having passed the age of fifty, Bergman said, he now had the confidence and the emotional and intellectual preparation to confront theater's great tests.

In cinema, the circumstances were quite different. If his eminence in film history was unassailable, the 'sixties seemed to confirm that he belonged to the past. *The Communicants*, surely one of his major achievements, had been dismissed as a tiresome mistake. *The Silence* was a financial success for the wrong reasons, and the critics had found almost nothing redeeming in its "obscurantism." Everyone, including Bergman, agreed that *Not to Speak of All These Women* was a huge embarrassment. *Persona*, after receiving respectful (if puzzled) reviews, attracted a small audience, and a couple of years later, critics looked back on it as a symptom of Bergman's disease. *Hour of the Wolf* pleased only those acolytes of New Wave theory who chased allusions to the horror film genre. The controversy *Shame* briefly stirred in Sweden did not enhance box office receipts, and abroad, despite some favorable notices plainly inspired by anti-Vietnam sentiment, the film quickly sank. When *A Passion* had its premiere in the university town of Uppsala, most seats remained empty. It proved an accurate omen.

Viewed against this background, *Fårö Document* seems a strategic withdrawal—as if the filmmaker, like Andreas Winkelman, were retreating to the island to lick his wounds. Bergman cited several reasons for taking on the project. Never having handled the camera during all his years as a director, he said with questionable seriousness, he felt it was about time he should experience this aspect of his profession—if only as insurance against the day when Sven Nykvist might be unavailable; an unpretentious documentary, almost a home movie, offered a good place to begin. (In fact, the credits identify Nykvist as the photographer.) Second, he wanted to pay tribute to his neighbors' hard, humble lives and to the spare natural beauty of his adopted home. Third, at a time when younger Swedish filmmakers were advocating social commitment, the documentary, which was in part a sermon to the mainland about the political and economic problems of a remote community, served as an act of piety by "a good Social Democrat." Perhaps the cardinal reason, however, was that, after laboring in the "oxygen-less" atmosphere of his recent fictions, he longed for an encounter with reality at the ground level of existence. *Fårö Document* resembles virtually every other documentary on Swedish television, but, judged according to its modest ambitions, it was a success: estimates placed the number of viewers at nearly half the country's population.

Of course, *Fårö Document* provided only a brief respite from a problem that loomed larger every year: financing films for a steadily contracting market. The problem went beyond Bergman's artistic malaise. Hollywood's difficulties in the 'fifties—competition from television, the breaking down of the studio system, and the puritanical restrictions of the Production Code, among others—had helped make possible the astonishing resurgence of European cinema, but by the mid-'sixties the Americans had adjusted to the new conditions, in part by absorbing the major European directors into an internationalized film industry. Bergman, among the last to withstand the trend, had already come close to such an arrangement for *Shame*, and plans to begin *Love Duet* in 1969, a two-part film in which he and Fellini were to have joined forces, had proceeded to the point of negotiation with Hollywood actresses before the project was scrapped. By 1970, surrender seemed inevitable; the object now was to arrange the best possible terms.

In May, while in London for the rehearsals of *Hedda Gabler*, he met with executives of the American Broadcasting Company and its newly organized division for theatrical films. Two days after describing the film he wanted to make, he signed the contract to write *The Touch* within the next seventy days and to begin filming in September. ABC congratulated itself on scoring a coup. For only a million dollars plus the salary of an American star, it was launching its venture into motion pictures in association with one of the world's great directors. Moreover, in contrast to the dolorous subjects of Bergman's recent films, *The Touch* would tell a romantic story; in English, and with a "bankable" American actor as the male lead, it seemed a very salable product. All things considered, Bergman also felt pleased by the deal he had struck. Although he had repeatedly stated in the past that he could not imagine filming in a language other than Swedish, the comfort of a million-dollar budget —much more than any of his previous films had cost—offered a strong inducement to climb over the linguistic barrier. If being required to work with an American film star meant forsaking his prized intimacy with his familiar group of actors, he at least had the right to pick the star. (His first choice, reportedly, was Lee Marvin, but he settled for Elliot Gould.) Most important, he retained absolute control of the film through the final cut.

From the day he arrived, Gould stood in awe of Bergman. The director, in turn, went out of his way to praise the American actor and to emphasize the ease with which he had become part of the team. Perhaps to drown his residual misgivings, Bergman declared that an actor's citizenship really did not matter: the theatrical profession was a nationality unto itself. Shooting proceeded without serious hitches. ABC, true to its word, kept at arm's length. Based on the public statements, one would guess that Bergman was wondering why he had so long resisted an international arrangement. When Barbra Streisand visited Gould, Bergman told her he was thinking about a film of *The Merry Widow*, his great popular success at Malmö, and he asked her to star in it.*

ABC viewed *The Touch* in the spring; apparently confident of its appeal, the company set the premiere for August 30, 1971, insuring that it would receive extra press attention as the first major film of the fall season. But the strategy backfired. Led to expect so much more, even the minority of favorably disposed reviewers let their disappointment show. If *The Touch* was not quite the immediate debacle that *Not to Speak of All These Women* had been, it probably did greater damage to the director's reputation. The fact that the film was in English made its faults transparent. The story was thin; the characters, bewildering; the dialogue, stilted and unidiomatic. Of the principal actors, only Bibi Andersson breathed life into her role. As the betrayed husband, Max von Sydow seemed uncertain of what he was supposed to convey. And Gould, the most egregiously miscast actor in any Bergman film, delivered his lines in a way that bespoke no understanding of his character.

While *The Touch* foundered in New York and London, Bergman's struggle to raise money for the film he had written over the summer illustrated how precarious his future in Swedish film had become. *Cries and Whispers* was quintessential Bergman—and thus, given his recent track record, a most unattractive property for commercial investment. But this was a film Bergman felt he had to make. Refusing to accept defeat, he committed his private funds to the project, asked Sven Nykvist and the actresses he had chosen for the major roles to barter their services for a share in future earnings, and finally, in October, applied to the Swedish Film Institute for their investment of the remaining 550,000 crowns (approximately $140,000). The Institute's board of directors quickly approved the request, and Bergman moved into production.

Several months later, the board's decision flared into a national issue.

---

*Streisand subsequently accepted the offer, and in December 1972 Svensk Filmindustri announced it would produce *The Merry Widow* in conjunction with Dino De Laurentiis. Bergman bore down on preparing the adaptation, but when De Laurentiis stipulated that SF would have to assume full financial responsibility if the costs exceeded the four-million-dollar budget, the project was cancelled.

Toward mid-decade, Bergman also engaged in discussions with the Italian television corporation about a series of episodes concerning the Crucifixion.

A public corporation supported by a tax on motion picture tickets, the Institute had been established to promote the art of cinema; that duty, the board maintained, justified advancing the funds to Bergman. An anti-Bergman claque disagreed. Blatant cronyism, they protested, had allowed a raid on the public treasury for funds intended to develop untried filmmakers and to encourage film's exploration of social problems. As an eminent director with access to any number of international film companies—indeed, as the great oak of Swedish film whose shade inhibited the growth of younger talents—Bergman, they insisted, was an inappropriate beneficiary of the state's largesse.

For once, Bergman restrained his phlogistic temperament and countered with a coolly reasoned argument. The costs of filmmaking were escalating, and the highly risky nature of the business made competing for private capital in Sweden increasingly difficult; were he forced to deal with a foreign producer, he would have to use at least one star with international appeal, place himself in a position where he might have to compromise the film, and, possibly, have to work outside of Sweden. Furthermore, half the 1.5 million crown budget had come from Cinematograph—his own company—and from his personal funds; another 200,000 he had raised through loans. Did it not make sense, he asked, for the Institute to provide the difference, thereby insuring not only the filmmaker's artistic freedom but also jobs for Swedish personnel who would otherwise be unemployed? And while he conceded that the Institute was supposed to promote innovation, he submitted that *Cries and Whispers*, particularly in its new approach to color cinematography, qualified as very much an experimental venture. Innovation was not exclusively a function of the socio-political views a film advanced —there should be room for various kinds of films. Besides, Bergman reminded his opponents, the Institute was not a government agency but a publicly funded independent corporation, at liberty to use its discretion in fulfilling the terms of its charter. The money it committed to the project was an investment, not an outright grant; if the film turned a profit, future applicants for assistance would benefit. (Harry Schein, the Institute's chairman, offered a similar explanation of the board's action; he also categorically denied that the board had by-passed any other filmmaker to favor Bergman.)

A deeply rooted political and generational antagonism, not the question of fidelity to the Institute's charter, obviously spurred the dispute. Bergman was still the colossus of Swedish cinema, despite his recent setbacks. Had *Cries and Whispers* been as great a flop as *The Touch*, the charges of favoritism and intellectual corruption would have damaged his allies and thereby undermined him. But just when he appeared to be most vulnerable, *Cries and Whispers* scored an astounding success all over the world. The sale of foreign distribution rights alone more than recovered the entire cost of production. Rushed to a premiere in Los Angeles so it could qualify for Academy Award nominations, it received glorious reviews; within three months, before it was distributed nationally, American gross receipts exceeded two million dollars. In New York, it won the Film Critics' Awards for Best Film, Best Director, and Best Screenplay. Juries in Milan, Warsaw, and Belgrade also cited it as the year's best film. At the Cannes Festival, the director was given an overwhelming emotional reception. Bergman's drooping reputation had bounced back to the heights, and those who had shown their faith in him reaped a handsome profit. The Film Institute found itself fully vindicated as well as much richer. Except for some bleating in *Dagens Nyheter* that Bergman "does not strive to give us a social consciousness" and "is seldom interested in social factors," his detractors withdrew to the sidelines to await a more opportune moment.

During the year before the premiere of *Cries and Whispers*, however, Bergman could not have imagined the magnitude of its success, and even if he had been clairvoyant, he was not about to depend again on the irregular means used to finance that film. Nor was he eager to repeat the experience with *The Touch*. For his next project, he looked to television.

Bergman wrote *Scenes from a Marriage* in the spring of 1972 for production by Cinematograph and presentation on Sveriges Radio-TV's second channel the following spring. The budget for the six fifty-minute episodes, or "scenes," was set at about a third less than what *Cries and Whispers* had cost. (Half of that sum was to be recovered from the Swedish television company; the rest, from sales to foreign counterparts.) Expenses had to be cut to the bone. The series was shot in 16 mm with a skeleton crew, and Bergman kept to a schedule of one week per episode. Fortunately, Liv Ullmann and Erland Josephson fell into their roles with such remarkable ease that the director could dispense with rehearsals.

Cries and Whispers opened in Sweden on March 5, but once the weekly installments of *Scenes from a Marriage* began on April 11, the success of the series eclipsed that of the film. No dramatic program in the history of Swedish television had had as many viewers or provoked as much discussion. Indeed, as the subsequent leap in applications for divorce tended to confirm, no Scandinavian drama since *A Doll's House*

had caused more wives to question their roles and forced more husbands into defensive arguments. Two decades earlier, Swedish women
at the edge of middle age had seen themselves in Eva Dahlbeck's Karin
Lobelius and Marianne Erneman; now their daughters saw a much
more disquieting reflection in Liv Ullmann's Marianne. In homes and
offices throughout the country, each succeeding "Scene" supplied new
material for conversation.

As an artist who took pride in fashioning "articles for use," Bergman
had already far surpassed his modest ambitions for the series when
luck boosted its success to an even more improbable level. An American
distributor—apparently perceiving bright auguries in the acclaim for
Cries and Whispers, the media's recent promotion of Liv Ullmann to the
status of "cinema goddess," and the surge of feminism—proposed conversion of the six episodes into a 35 mm feature film for export. Bergman
was initially cool to the idea. With good reason. Visually, *Scenes from a
Marriage* had been tailored for television; even its color values were
adjusted for the technical peculiarities of electronic transmission.
Dramatically, the shape and tempo of each episode were regulated to
fifty minutes. Furthermore, it seemed impossible to edit the story so
drastically without sacrificing coherence. Nevertheless, he was persuaded
to go along, and to his amazement, this two hours and forty-eight minute version became an enormous hit. *Cries and Whispers* had brought
the "deep," complex Bergman back into vogue; *Scenes from a Marriage*
gratified the public's curiosity by offering a transparently simple story. The
success of the crimped version then created an even larger audience
when national television networks in Western Europe and the United
States ran and reran the original series. All told, probably more people
have seen *Scenes from a Marriage* than the rest of his films combined.*

A second project he hatched for television in 1972 was quite grandiose by Scandinavian standards. Anticipating the fiftieth anniversary of
Sveriges Radio, Bergman proposed a film of *The Magic Flute* to coincide
with the event; the next year, officers of the second channel announced
that it would serve as producer for the opera, scheduled for broadcast
on New Year's Day, 1975. The agreement caused some grumbling.
Sweden's second channel, an emulation of BBC-TV 2, had been launched
at the start of the decade to provide a popular, entertainment-oriented

---

*Bergman added still another chapter to this saga in 1981 by adapting *Scenes from a
Marriage* for the stage. The dramatic version was produced at Munich's Residenztheater
as part of a single program, played in adjacent theaters, which also included *A Doll's
House* and *Miss Julie*.

alternative (initially, *The Preserve*, a Bergman play directed by Jan Molander, was to have been the inaugural broadcast). Whether the production of an opera at a cost between three and four million crowns, a major share of its funds, accorded with its original objective was questioned in some quarters, and the diversion of personnel from other duties further fed concern that too much was being sacrificed to the project. But if Bergman was aware of the treacherous undercurrent, he did not allow it to hinder his enthusiasm. Approximately a year passed between auditions in the summer of 1973 to the completion of shooting in June 1974, and the preparation of the prints in 16 mm for television and in 35 mm for theatrical release took months more. No Bergman film had absorbed as much time and attention. The response to the film, however, amply rewarded all the painstaking work. The New Year's Day broadcast delighted Scandinavia, and its subsequent premieres in country after country completely conquered the skeptics who had believed that opera and film were an impossible match.

By the end of 1974, Bergman fully recognized the interdependence of television and his career in cinema. The theatrical version of *Scenes from a Marriage* had been a happy accident, and the decision to issue *The Magic Flute* in 35 mm was made in 1974, long after the project had gotten under way; *Face to Face*, however, was planned to serve as both a four-part television series in Scandinavia and a theatrical feature in the rest of the world. He finished the script in December. In early 1975, he met in New York with De Laurentiis, who—partly because he had been responsible for the collapse of the *Merry Widow* project, partly because Bergman had just had his third triumph within three years, and partly because a deal with Swedish television provided a safety net—quickly consented to finance the film. Two months later, the cameras were rolling.

Although the production phase was substantially completed by July, Bergman came back to Stockholm to shoot some additional footage in September. He then gave his attention to other matters. On November 30, back on Fårö, he finished writing *The Petrified Prince*, a bitter erotic farce which was to be combined with short films by Fellini and Mike Nichols in a feature film produced by Warner Brothers. His thoughts next turned to theater. Bergman's *Twelfth Night* had made 1975 a memorable year in the Swedish history of Shakespearean productions, and he hoped to equal that gigantic success with *The Dance of Death*, set to begin rehearsals in January. But in 1976, luck suddenly deserted him. *Face to Face* did not fare well, either in Sweden, where it was broadcast between April 28 and May 19, or elsewhere in its theatrical release. By that time, however, Bergman's personal drama overshadowed what he had created for the screen. He had already been arrested for tax evasion, suffered a mental breakdown, and gone into exile.

The Touch

Evidently influenced by American financing and the required use of an American star to try to make a popular "American" film, Bergman seems to have built *The Touch* to the specifications of the "women's pictures" Hollywood pumped out during the 'forties and early 'fifties. Even this overtly commercial product, however, reflects an essential continuity in his fictions. Extracted from the thematically complex scheme of *A Passion*, the brief affair between Andreas Winkelman and Eva Vergérus is recast here as the affair between David Kovacs and Karin Vergérus. Like Andreas, David is an outsider, a coward menaced both by the violence of the world and by a corrosive secret he carries within himself; like Eva, Karin (also played by Bibi Andersson) is a "sleepwalker" waiting to be awakened to life. To be sure, the two stories take different turns, but they derive from the same psychological impulse.

Bergman has said that the genesis of the initial scene, played before the title and credits come up on the screen, was the death of a friend in the 'fifties. Perhaps so, but its emotions imply that the recent deaths of his father and of his mother a few years earlier were much in his mind. Karin has been called to the hospital room where her mother has just died. "Tribulation has engraved deep lines in [the mother's] brow," Bergman notes in the script, "but the face, instead of bearing the mark of pain, suggests a secret smile." In contrast to this serenity attained in death, the daughter feels a rush of anxiety on hearing the clock's ticking, magnified by the silence. When a nurse hands her the double wedding bands, worn thin after fifty years of marriage, that symbolize the sum and justification of the mother's life, Karin is almost reluctant to accept them. Do the rings underscore the futility of the mother's existence from which death has delivered her, or, as a sign of perseverance through hardship, do they reproach the daughter for sinking into material ease? Although nothing more is said about the mother in the film, these questions are the backdrop to subsequent events.

While descending the hospital staircase, Karin bursts into tears; a bearded stranger offers help, then quickly leaves when it is declined.

Some time later, Andreas, a doctor, tells his wife that he has invited one of his patients to their home for dinner. This patient, a foreign archaeologist named David, is the same man who had approached her in the hospital. Andreas proudly shows off his house and grounds, but David is interested only in Karin. At the first opportunity, he tells her he fell in love with her the instant they met, and late in the evening, while Andreas shows family slides, the bored guest crassly asks to see some pictures of Karin nude. Despite this churlish behavior, the unperturbable Andreas goes to bed that night pronouncing David "a fine fellow," not realizing that the dark stranger has "touched" Karin and stirred long-dormant desires in her.

Ostensibly to satisfy her curiosity about archaeology, she visits the Gotland church where David's crew is excavating a medieval Madonna from within the church wall. The mysterious smile on the statue (noted in the script as well as shown in the film) recalls the "secret smile" on the dead mother's face, but the more obvious symbolism associates the statue with Karin, immured in middle-class respectability. When David begins to kiss her, she feebly resists, then proposes an assignation at his apartment.

The ensuing affair, however, brings no contentment. David demands that she give up cigarettes and alcohol, that she behave like his private "Madonna," always at his behest to comfort and inspire. But he also tries to make her into a creature of his lust, and when she responds to his sexual desires, his guilt causes him to degrade her as a whore. The noise of a buzz saw that accompanies their meetings in the dark, shabby room reflects the violent contradictions ripping within David.

This temptestuous first phase of their relationship ends when David leaves Sweden to work in other parts of Europe and Karin travels to Rome to join her husband. In the letters they exchange, the memory of their quarrels is erased, and half a year later, they are hotly anticipating their reunion. But once David arrives on Gotland clean-shaven—i.e., showing his "true" face—truth starts to destroy Karin's illusion about her lover. Andreas discovers the affair and goes to his rival's apartment to confront him; while Karin hides behind the bedroom door, she learns that David had become Andreas's patient as the result of a suicide attempt. When the husband leaves, David refuses to admit that he had ever tried to kill himself, but his lie is transparent. Instead of being the vital lover who can rescue Karin from suffocation, David is a coward who cannot face up to reality.

Another visit to the medieval church emphasizes the corrosive effects of her disillusionment. The Madonna, David informs her, is not at all the priceless, unique piece it had been thought to be; moreover, its removal from the wall has activated five-hundred-year-old larvae which are now consuming the statue from within.

But the full force of the horror that has invaded her life does not hit Karin until some months later. On discovering that she is pregnant, she rushes to David's apartment, only to find it empty except for the sound of the buzz saw and the cast-off mementos of their affair. Frantic, she tracks him to an address in London where he lives with his crippled sister Sara. Receiving the visitor in David's absence, Sara fights for exclusive possession of her brother by disclosing the truth about him. The terrible dystrophy that is destroying her muscles is congenital, and although David does not yet show its symptoms, it will appear in any child he conceives. Sara then relates the history of their family, from the Nazi extermination camp to settlement in Israel, and suggests that David turned his back on his duty to this heritage in having fled from the dangers of war in the Middle East. Her most effective weapon, however, is the revelation of her brother's promise never to leave her. Finally bowing to the gravity of that responsibility, Karin concedes defeat and heads back to her family.

Half a year later, David returns to Gotland with the news that a Danish university has offered him a tenured post. Ever the escapist, he sees this as the happy ending to their romance: any condition she might set for their marrying, he argues, he can now meet. But Karin refuses. Despite her love for him, she says, obligations to her family must take precedence. While David, ironically, accuses her of being a liar and a coward, she holds herself resolutely silent until, in the film's last frames, he walks away.

Even as a sentimental romance, the story is unconvincing, confusing, and, at times, preposterous. Despite Bibi Andersson's superb performance in a role as complex and difficult, in its own way, as that of Alma in *Persona*, one never understands why Karin falls in love with David while he behaves boorishly in the Vergérus home, or why, afterward, she tolerates being humiliated and physically abused. Part of the problem, to be sure, stems from Elliot Gould's inability to reach inside his character and project those qualities that would entice Karin, but the script is itself deficient in this regard.

The concluding scenes are still murkier. The disclosure of the congenital disease in David's family introduces an entirely new element, unrelated to what has been the story's central interest up to this point: David's ambivalence toward Karin. Nor does it explain his desertion. (Obviously, if he were trying to spare her the pain of bearing children with the trait, he would have taken greater precaution against impregnating her, and if his motivation were to avoid becoming a burden to her after the disease had stricken him, he would not later return to Gotland and insist on their marrying.) The events that follow from the disclosure produce more perplexity. When Karin, without ever revealing her meeting with Sara, asserts that her family responsibilities prevent her from seeing David again, is she telling a noble lie? If so, why should the lie be more noble than frankly acknowledging the priority of the sister's claim? If not, how has Sara's plight rekindled Karin's devotion to her family? The pregnancy raises another batch of questions. Karin has apparently rejected the possibility of an abortion, and in doing so, she has made Andreas pay an enormous price for her infidelity. Surely, some indication of his coming to terms with the problem would seem obligatory, yet Andreas has been long out of sight and silent. And what of David in all of this? Since Karin is at least seven months pregnant, he should notice her swollen belly, at least suspect that he is the father, and in some way recognize the implications. Instead, he only rants about her cruelty in thwarting his plans.

More risible than incomprehensible, the business of the Madonna statue involves several unlikely propositions. The statue's chief historical value is said to lie in the mystery of how it found its way to Gotland, but there should be no riddle in this question: medieval Visby (the island's main city) was an important port in early Hanseatic trade. The archaeological team takes months to retrieve the statue, yet the hole through which it is first detected already seems quite large enough for anyone to extract it by sticking in his arm. Still sillier, David watches the beetles emerge from its interior (after a half millenium's dormancy!) and never thinks of sealing the work of art in a chamber of toxic gas or, at the very least, of using his finger to flick away the insects chewing on its surface. Apparently, once Bergman's imagination lit on the idea of the statue, probability fell sacrifice to symbolism.

There is, of course, an obvious analogy between the statue and the middle-class wife: both are damaged (perhaps even destroyed) after their removal from the "oxygen-less" safety of immurement reactivates the life within them. As a simplified synopsis of the story's action, however, this parallel operates at a rather shallow level. The far more important element of the analogy—indeed, its crucial element—is the dualism of the Madonna: an idealized image of the Virgin Mother which, in its physical being, is subject to corruption. Not only does this reflect David's ambivalence toward Karin, but it also strikes at its Oedipal basis.

The initial clue to that underlying meaning arises from two factors in the opening scene. First: the attention Bergman gives to the mother's death much exceeds what its overt relationship to subsequent events might warrant. Even as a way of suggesting the different worlds mother and daughter have experienced, or as an explanation of Karin's desire, whatever the cost, to feel fully alive, the emphasis on the deathbed is disproportionate. Second: David's encounter with Karin on the stairs seems without purpose in terms of the plot; were they not to have met before David's arrival at the Vergérus home, it would change nothing at all—nothing, that is, which concerns the story's ostensible content. If *The Touch* is perceived as a kind of dream, however, both the prominence of the mother's death as prologue to a love affair and the fact that David instantly falls in love with Karin as she leaves the deathbed assume major significance. A decade before writing *The Touch*, Bergman told Vilgot Sjöman that his "interblending" of mother and wife (or sexual partner) had been a "constant" psychological problem, and that the "probable unconscious reason" for his attraction to younger women was "to make the possibility of that substitution as remote as possible." The same logic appears to operate here. In effect, the death of Karin's mother represents the attempt to extract "mother" from the confused (or interblended) image of woman, and thereby free David sexually.*

But that attempt fails. Once the Madonna is unearthed—wearing, like the mother's corpse, a faint smile—David is in conflict with himself.** His carnal desire for Karin fills him with guilt, and when she displays her own sexuality, he hurls his self-disgust at her. In contrast to these "tumultuous feelings," when she plays the role of a comforting mother and calls him her "new-born infant," he floats in a gentle, peaceful dream of escape from the world. But the dream, David knows, is transitory; eventually, consciousness must return—and with it, anguish. In an especially telling passage, David expresses his despair to Karin by linking three of Bergman's recurring cardinal conceits: that life is a prison; that "being" and lies are finally inseparable; and, most important of all within this particular context, that escape to the sanctuary of the womb is a chimera.

> I'll never be able to disappear into you. You can never live within
> me. It is only in the brief, hopelessly brief moments that we imagine

*Karin's final lines in the film also lend themselves to this interpretation. She insists that, even though she has chosen to fulfill her obligations to her family, she loves David *and is free to love him*: "I want to be with you, everything in me wants to be with you. I can leave everything. I am no longer afraid. Perhaps if mother were alive—it would be different."

**That David is an archaeologist, and that the Madonna is found by digging through to a subterranean wall, suggests both a psychoanalytic search into a personal past and a descent to the nether layers of the psyche. Interestingly, Andreas in *A Passion* is a former geologist who speaks of the terror he felt on going down into the French potholes.

the prison has opened. But it isn't true; it's just a lie among all the other lies. Do you know what I think? I think it is some vague memory from the womb. That is the only fellowship there is and then it's over for all eternity.*

The opposed aspects of David's relationship to Karin as mother join at the conclusion. In a sense, her pregnancy represents the insemination of himself into her womb, a re-creation of the "only fellowship" between self and sexual other that is wholly innocent. But there is another side to this metaphor, ironically involving the very guilt he tries to evade. The beetle larvae that feed inside the Madonna, Karin's symbol, obviously correspond to the fetus conceived as a result of their "incest." And just as these perversely "beautiful" insects (as David calls them) are analogous to a wasting disease, the child is dystrophic.

The psychosexual implications of the congenitally afflicted child trace back to the "knot of cells" born to Jan and Ingeborg in *Kamma Noll* and the "wolf-child" in *Dreams*.** The same implications become more arresting when expressed through the metaphor of disease. Mental illness and incest are explicitly related in *Through a Glass Darkly*, implicitly in *Hour of the Wolf*, and cancer (imagistically similar to the gnawing beetles in *The Touch*) serves as a critical link to the Oedipal disturbance underlying *A Passion*. In *The Touch*, however, these allied metaphors are more directly tied to Bergman than in any previous work. The disease which David has kept secret and which brands his affair with "mother" Karin is the same hereditary myotonic dystrophy that crippled Bergman's grandfather, father, and brother.

---

*The script of *The Touch* contains a "scene" (or "chapter"—given that the script takes the form of a story rather than of a screenplay) consisting entirely of a poem by Gunnar Ekelöf. Like the film itself, the poem plays on the image of woman as a mother attracting a lover to refuge in her womb.

Wake me to sleep in you
wake my worlds to you
light my dead stars closer to you.
Dream me out from my world
home to the home of the flames
give birth to me, live me, kill me closer to you.
Closer me to you
closer me to the hearth of birth
take me warmer, take me closer to you.

Although Bergman may initially have considered flashing its words onto the screen, the poem does not enter into the film in any manner.

**A more recent example occurs in *The Rite*, where, for no evident reason, Bergman injects the information that Thea has given birth to a severely retarded child.

Cries and Whispers

Disease—once again cancer—is also central to *Cries and Whispers*, which Bergman called a "self-portrait [*sic*] of my mother, . . . the great beloved of my childhood."[1]

The film evolved from a recurring dream, "pregnant with something needing to be born," in which he saw four white-clad women whispering in a red room.* "Time and again," he comments in the script, "I have rejected this picture, refusing to make it the basis of a film (or whatever it is). But the picture has persisted, and slowly, reluctantly, I have identified it: Three women who are waiting for the fourth to die and who take turns to watch by her."

As seminal as the figures of the four women was the color of the room they occupied. Bergman quickly understood its significance. "As a boy," he explained, "I experienced the soul as a black person without a face whose inside was [a moist membrane] in red tones—rather naively Freudian, one might say."[2] In a sense, then, the story extrapolated from the dream takes place in his own psyche, and the red that not only dominates the film's decor but also saturates every fade-out expresses this "somewhat mystical" personal meaning.

What that meaning involves emerges from Bergman's image of the soul, the "Freudian" interior of which implies the source of the guilt and shame connoted by its black and faceless exterior. Obviously a womb, it suggests a disturbing suspicion that the self is actually female. (Interestingly, at about the time of *Cries and Whispers*, Bergman began to acknowledge a feminine component within himself that he had previously suppressed; as a result, he said, he had rejected his former practice of conceiving characters as solely male or female.) A more pronounced "Freudian" pattern in Bergman's fictions, however, prompts another reading, centered on the self's maleness.** As the object of sexual desire, the "moist membrane" signifies the self's Oedipal guilt; simultaneously, like Joakim's entry into Susanne's womb in "The Fish" and Frost's fantasy at the end of *Evening of the Jesters*, it symbolizes the wish to escape from consciousness of that guilt. The

*The title, nodding to this initial dream-image, was borrowed from Swedish music critic Yngve Flycht's description of Mozart's *21st Piano Concerto* as "whispers and cries." In the English translation of the title, the first and last word were reversed after the film opened in Los Angeles.

**In this regard, there is a notable similarity to the fetus-soul described by Kaj in *Rakel and the Cinema Doorman*.

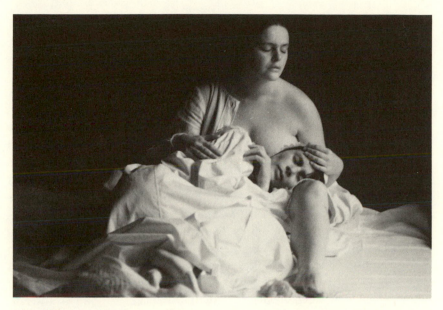

Two of Bergman's prime motifs—regression to infancy and the Crucifixion
—coincide in this Pietà: Anna (Kari Sylwan) holds Agnes (Harriet Andersson).
Permission from Svenska Filmindustri.

film Bergman exfoliated from his recurring dream shows the same
tension.

Agnes, who is dying, represents Bergman, and the cancer swelling
her womb (or soul) represents both his guilt and the film about guilt with
which his dream was "pregnant." Karin and Maria, two of the three
women maintaining the death watch, are sisters: significantly, one bears
the name of Bergman's mother; the other, the script explicitly states, of
the Virgin Mother. The third member of the watch, Anna, is a family
servant utterly devoted to Agnes. Her name, too, is one the filmmaker
has often assigned to his mother figures. Although Bergman introduced
additional characters in the course of transforming his original dream
"picture" into a story, the drama essentially concerns the relationship
between Agnes and these three aspects of mother.*

Cries and Whispers opens with lingering, extreme close-ups of the
clocks in the house. Soon after, as though to hasten the end of her agony,

*The central character's name is also suggestive. Derived from *agnos*, Greek for "pure" or
"chaste," it accords with the emphasis on her innocence—like the white robes of the
women in the dream, a Freudian "reaction formation" against the guilt that drives the
story. Moreover, as virtually a homonym for the Latin *agnus*, "Agnes" calls to mind the lamb
that iconographically represents Christ. This association with the crucified son takes on
critical importance in the latter half of the drama.

Agnes sets the hands of the stopped clock on her mantelpiece in motion; she then begins writing in her diary. The parallel to *Wild Strawberries* is unmistakable. Indeed, in the script, Bergman notes that the text of "Where is the friend whom everywhere I seek . . . "—the same hymn Isak recites at the Golden Otter—is displayed within a frame hanging in Agnes's room. As Agnes's story progresses, one perceives that it is similar to Isak's in other ways as well. Both films evoke a sense of dream; both, in their essentially confessional form, reach into the past to explain the present; and both elaborate the same theme. *Wild Strawberries* shows an old man, near death, confronting the fact that life has left him terribly alone. "What is so important" about the scenes at Agnes's bedside, Bergman explains in the script, is the idea of "death [as] the extreme of loneliness."

In illustrating this idea, Agnes (like Isak) reflects a great deal of the filmmaker himself. For no reason necessary to the story, he makes her an artist. "In the old days," she writes in her diary, "I used to imagine that my creative efforts brought me into contact with the outside world, that I left my loneliness. Nowadays I know that this isn't so at all. In the end all my so-called artistic expression is only a desperate protest against death."* Even to the point of using the same words, Bergman has offered the same explanation for his becoming an artist and for persisting despite his conviction that art is as vital as a sloughed-off snakeskin.

Like the rest of Bergman's "desperate protests," *Cries and Whispers* is rooted in early memories of his mother—here transferred to Agnes. As a "sickly and puny" ten year old, she states in her diary, she loved Mother "because she was so gentle and beautiful and alive." But the child's desire for tenderness met with scorn:

> I was too like Father for her to be able to stand me. When Mother spoke to me in her light, excitable way, I didn't understand what she meant. I tried terribly hard, but never managed to please her. Then she would get impatient. . . . [She could] be cold and indifferent. When I used to come and ask her for affection, she would rebuff me and be playfully cruel, saying she hadn't time. Yet I couldn't help feeling sorry for her, and now that I'm older I understand her much better. I should like so much to see her again and tell her what I have understood of her ennui, her impatience, her panic and refusal to give up.

At this point, Bergman interjects a *laterna magica* performance of "Hansel and Gretel" during Twelfth Night. The other children in the

---

*Like several other passages in the script that evince Bergman's identification with this character, these lines were cut from the film.

audience shriek with delight at the image of the witch, but young Agnes, observing her mother and Maria "sharing secrets," is too disturbed by jealousy to join in the merriment. (Might the fact that the fairy tale deals with children sacrificed by their mother also reflect Agnes's feelings?) The next passage in the diary further illustrates the child's emotional distress.

> I remember once—it was autumn—I came running into the drawing room; I suppose I had something important to do (one always has at the age of ten). Then I saw Mother sitting there . . . in her white dress. . . . I went up to her. She gave me a look so full of sorrow that I nearly burst into tears. But instead I began to stroke her cheek. She closed her eyes and let me do it. We were very close to each other that time.

The flashback ends here in the film, but in the script the closeness of mother and child has most revealing consequences:

> Suddenly she came to herself and said, "Just look at your hands, they're filthy. Whatever have you been up to?" Then, overcome with affection, she took me in her arms and smiled at me and kissed me. I was dazzled by these riches. Just as suddenly, she began to weep and begged my forgiveness over and over. I didn't understand a thing; all I could do was hold her tightly until she freed herself. Her face changed and, giving her little laugh, she dabbed her eyes. "How ridiculous," was all she said, then she got up and left me with my tumult.

Virtually every detail in this memory intimates a hidden drama. Even though Father is never mentioned—here or anywhere else in the film—one surmises that Mother's unexplained sorrow has to do with her marriage.* Sensing an opportunity, the child ventures a caress, which Mother permits while shutting her eyes, as if aware of its illicit motive. This surrender ends abruptly when the mother "comes to herself" and blames the child for having "filthy" hands—a charge plainly reflecting the "unclean" meaning of the caress. Then, as though acknowledging complicity in their forbidden pleasure, Mother kisses the child and begs

---

*Besides Bergman's acknowledgment of the story's autobiographical impulse, two factors lead to this inference: (1) His comment elsewhere in the script that the setting is a house originally built "for a distinguished gentleman's cast-off mistress" suggests an ambience of sexual estrangement. (2) Marital unhappiness is a prominent feature of the other flashbacks, which also concern aspects of mother.

forgiveness. The child protectively claims ignorance, yet clings to the mother while she struggles, literally, to break free from this dangerous emotional entanglement. Finally, Mother steps back and pronounces the pathetic game they have been playing "ridiculous," leaving the bewildered child to deal with the psychological "tumult" it has created.

If one fails to grasp that this daughter is actually a son, Agnes's flashback appears to be the first of several digressions from an account of her death. Once the tumult's psychosexual cause is understood, however, it becomes the integrating motif for the rest of the drama.

The association of death and sexual guilt continues to reverberate in the next pair of scenes. A doctor calls at the house to monitor the progress of Agnes's cancer; after the examination, she holds his hand at her breast for a long moment. Nothing more can be done. Then, just as he is leaving, Maria emerges from the shadows. "When can I come to you?" she asks. He lays his hand on her breast, and she clasps it. (The parallel with Agnes's gesture is surely not coincidental.) As they kiss passionately, it seems Maria will succeed in exploiting her sister's death throes to arrange an assignation, but the doctor's sudden "No!" spoils her plan.

A flashback follows. It is several years earlier, and the doctor has come to the house because Anna's young daughter is ill. While he hurriedly eats his meal, Maria invites him to stay the night; later, she slips into his bedroom. Before they make love, he turns her toward a wall mirror and analyzes her reflection. She is growing old, he says, and makeup does not quite hide "the sharp, almost invisible wrinkles of boredom and impatience"; in her heart, he sees "selfishness, coldness, indifference." When Maria tries to blunt the charge by observing that they are "so alike," the doctor readily admits that she is right. "Are there no extenuating circumstances for people such as you and I?" he asks. She answers: "I've no need of being pardoned."

The next morning, after the doctor has left, Maria's husband Joakim returns from a business trip. In the presence of their daughter (who is approximately the age of Anna's child), Maria conceals her infidelity by chatting casually about an upcoming Easter visit with friends. Minutes later, however, "an obscure fear" sends her into her husband's room, where she discovers that he has plunged a paperknife into his chest. As "the bloodstain spreads on the snow-white shirt," he cries for help "in a clear, childish voice." "From that moment," Bergman states,

Maria is haunted by two conflicting yet completely similar mental pictures. One shows her rushing up to her husband and pulling the knife out of his wound, showering him with kisses and protestations, staunching the flow of blood with tender embraces, and pleading for forgiveness. The other picture, which is equally vivid and occurs just as often, shows her forcing the knife deeper into her husband's chest with all her strength, in a moment of stinging satisfaction.*

Given Bergman's description of *Cries and Whispers* as a multifaceted "portrait of my mother," this bitter tale might be rather simply explained as a fanciful rendering of the affair that had rocked his parents' marriage. Closer scrutiny, however, reveals a psychologically more intricate meaning, manifested through several sets of doubles.

In beginning her childhood recollections, Agnes states, "Mother loved Maria because they were so alike in every way." The observation seems irrelevant, but in the next flashback, the doctor applies the very same words to Maria that Agnes has used in describing her mother. (Liv Ullmann, it should be noted, plays both roles.) If Mother and Maria are doubles, is Bergman not also implying a parallel between the doctor and young Agnes—and between his seduction and the child's "tumult"?

The motif of illness further accentuates the correspondence. In the diary, Agnes (like Bergman) associates her sickliness as a child with the intensity of her love for Mother. In the scene bridging the two flashbacks, the cancer that brings the doctor to the house is also linked to passionate desire: the hand Agnes holds in desperation next fondles Maria until conscience causes the doctor to break away—a variation on young Agnes's stroking her mother's cheek and then being reproached for her "filthy hands."

The same motif establishes another pair of doubles in Maria's flashback, where it is the illness of Anna's daughter that leads to the seduction. Why should Bergman go to the trouble of creating another character when he could have arranged for the doctor's presence in the house through more economical means? The answer rests in the information (supplied elsewhere in the film) that the little girl later died, and in Anna's maternal solicitude towards Agnes in the scenes which follow.

---

*The quoted passage is from the script. In the film itself, the first "mental picture" merely shows Maria's horrified reaction; the second, her cruel smile.

To avoid confusion, it should also be noted here that Joakim will later arrive for Agnes's funeral; thus, either he recovered from the wound or else what Maria sees when she opens the door to the study is a fantasy.

Apparently, this girl serves as a stand-in for the girl in the diary, and her illness corresponds to Agnes's cancer of the womb.*

What underlies the second part of Maria's flashback becomes clearer if it is approached through the climactic scene in "The Fish." There, another Joakim watches through a transparent mirror as his wife's lover remarks on her aging face, then "wills" his wife into stabbing the lover. Here, somehow knowing about the infidelity that followed a similar moment in front of a mirror, this Joakim stabs himself.** To be sure, the knife thrusts in opposite directions in these parallel events, yet one can infer a common significance. In "The Fish," the lover has acted out Joakim's repressed sexual desire for his wife, patently a mother figure; having first willed the affair, Joakim then wills the lover's death to punish himself. That the lover performs as the husband's alter ego in *Cries and Whispers* is less evident, mainly because Joakim is seen only briefly and Bergman provides no means of entering his thoughts. Even so, this interpretation explains not only why the entrance of one of the pair coincides with the exit of the other—as though they were alternating aspects of a single self—but also why Joakim is uncannily aware of what has happened in his absence. More important, it is consistent with the portrayal of "mother" from the Oedipal perspective established in Agnes's childhood memory.*** Both flashbacks may be seen as efforts to shift sexual guilt from the "son" to the "mother": much as the diary stresses the pain brought on by Mother's rejection, Joakim's suicide attempt focuses on his humiliation and helplessness as an undeserving victim of Maria's "cruelty." Furthermore, there is an obvious analogy between Mother's vacillating responses to young Agnes and Maria's

---

*Lending further complexity to these substitutions is the fact that the girl in the photograph of Anna's daughter is Bergman's daughter Linn, who also plays Maria's daughter.

**The aging of the mother figure is a source of tension in both stories. At the start of "The Fish," Joakim pores over pictures of his wife Anne taken when she was a young girl and tries to convince himself that she has not changed during the intervening twenty years; then, tucking the pictures into the depths of his desk drawer as though he were "sharing a delicious secret with a sweetheart," he says, "With me, you are safe, my darling wife." In *Cries and Whispers*, Bergman shows Maria awakening with a doll at her pillow while sunlight dances on a doll house opposite her bed. Like "The Fish" (and other early works, such as *Prison*), the film reflects a conflict between the wish to reduce the mother to the level of a child and the disturbing perception of her adult sexuality.

***Given that the doctor acts as Agnes's double in the scene bridging the two flashbacks, and that the doctor then doubles for Joakim, it follows that Agnes and Joakim are also dual aspects of the Oedipal son.

"two conflicting yet completely similar" reactions to the "dying" Joakim's appeal for help—which is echoed in turn by Agnes's cries at the start of the next scene.

The third sister's flashback, inserted after Agnes's death in the film, is nearly a reverse image of Maria's. (In the script, the two flashbacks appear in inverted order.) Karin and her husband Fredrik, a diplomat twenty years her senior, are seated at the dinner table. In contrast to the sensual intimacy between Maria and her lover during the meal in the corresponding sequence, a wall of mutual hatred separates this couple. When Karin accidentally upsets her wine goblet, the shattered glass and the red pool remain on the tablecloth—in some way, an emblem of a lacerating truth they dare not confront in their marriage. "It's all a tissue of lies," she mutters after he retreats to his study; then, fingering one of the shards, she carries it into her boudoir, where it lies in plain sight while Anna undresses her. As though her nakedness as she stands before a mirror had exposed her thoughts to the servant's eyes, she slaps Anna for her impertinence, then begs forgiveness—which Anna refuses to grant. (One cannot help but recall here the doctor's analysis of Maria's mirrored image and the lovers' acknowledgement that no absolution is possible for them.) Left alone, Karin now executes her plan: picking up the jagged glass, she stabs it deep into her vagina. When Fredrik enters the room to claim his conjugal privileges, she lifts her peignoir, smears the blood from the wound across her mouth, and laughs at his disgust.

An intriguing clue to the meaning of Karin's bizarre revenge, though omitted from the film, figures prominently in the script. There, Karin remembers the episode while staring at a "large Italian painting of St. Teresa in the sacred third stage of prayer" (that complete surrender to God which, the mystic claims, produces "a glorious madness, a celestial wildness where one learns true wisdom.") As the flashback ends, she is still looking at the painting with a "sarcastic, almost obscene smile." Presumably, the self-mutilation has been her own mad, wild experience of "truth." But what does this "truth" imply for Bergman?

Much as "The Fish" helps illuminate Maria's flashback, *Through a Glass Darkly* casts a revealing light on Karin's. Not only does the Karin of the earlier film also feel trapped in hypocrisy, but "The Artistic Haunting," which Minus has written to expose that hypocrisy, involves a similar allusion to St. Teresa. When the Princess (Karin) asks the Artist (intended by Minus to represent their father) to prove his love by accompanying her into St. Teresa's chapel—the realm of death—the Artist fails the test.

But then, in the wrecked schooner, Minus himself faces the choice that had confronted his Artist: by committing incest, he in effect yields to the Princess's appeal. This "mortal" sin ejects him from the innocence of childhood into the consciousness of a terrible new reality. At the film's conclusion, however, his father extends an unexpected reprieve: understanding that God and love, in *all* its forms, are one and the same, he tells his son, is like receiving "a pardon from death."

No incest is actually committed in *Cries and Whispers*, and there is no forgiveness. The perverse triumph Karin gains through sexual mutilation and her "almost obscene" response to the St. Teresa painting are diametrically opposed to Minus's deliverance. But it is precisely the difference between the two films that is significant. *Through a Glass Darkly* marks the last of Bergman's "Willed" happy endings; *Cries and Whispers* is among the bitterest rejections of that "false" resolution. Here, no form of love survives; there is no "pardon from death."

If the film's first half coils around Oedipal guilt, the second represents an elaborate effort to "deny" that guilt, to retreat into innocence. The process begins with the dying woman's cries for Anna—the incarnation of a maternal love wholly divorced from sexual complications. Mystically aware of her role, the servant unbuttons her nightgown, slides under the coverlet, and props her breast against the "infant's" face. Agnes immediately falls asleep. A few hours later, her sisters are at the bedside, holding a cup of water to her lips, washing her fevered body, and dressing her in a fresh nightgown. Further soothing the "child," Maria then reads aloud from *The Pickwick Papers*. (One recalls Karin Bergman's dramatic readings for the family at the parsonage.) Tenderness and solicitude in this dream-like scene have dissolved the punitive aspects of these "mothers" portrayed in the flashbacks. But the illusion of their love evaporates when Agnes dies. At that moment, only Anna will approach the corpse: embracing Agnes, she seems to receive the "child" into herself.

As is often the case in Bergman's films, this intrusion of the womb motif is paired with the metaphor of crucifixion. The episode depicted in Maria's flashback occurs just before Easter; in the scene between Karin and Fredrik, Bergman notes in the script that the couple are dressed in black, "perhaps [because] it is Good Friday." In both instances, the association of Agnes with Christ is indirectly implied; however, upon the arrival of the family's chaplain, Father Isak, to pray for the deceased, it becomes most explicit. The minister begins as though he were reciting a formula: "You submitted to [prolonged suffering] patiently and uncomplainingly, in the certain knowledge that your sins would be forgiven through the death on the cross of your Lord Jesus Christ. May your Father in Heaven have mercy on your soul when you step into His presence." Midway through the prayer, however, Isak casts himself as the sinner and addresses Agnes—who has "gathered our suffering in [her] poor body"—as if she were Jesus. "Pray for us who are left here on the dark, dirty earth under an empty and cruel Heaven," he beseeches her. "Lay your burden of suffering at God's feet and ask Him to pardon us. Ask Him to free us at last from our anxiety, our weariness, and our deep doubt."*

Father Isak's monologue contributes nothing to the plot (such as it is); its function, plainly, is to underscore the crucifixion motif. But here, in contrast to Bergman's typical use of the trope, the father figure admits his error and speaks of their reconciliation. (Apparently alluding to their differences during "long and intimate talks" in her earlier years, the minister now concedes that "her faith was stronger than mine.") Instead, it is the mother—and her "doubles," Maria and Karin—whose failure of love "crucifies" the child.

The next day—in "strong, unmoving sunlight" like that which "drenches my cruelest dreams," Bergman comments in the script—Maria proposes to Karin that they be friends. "After all, we're sisters," she says. "We have so many memories in common—we can talk about our childhood! Karin, my dear, it's so strange that we don't touch one another, that we only talk impersonally." Karin protests that her sister has mis-read her, yet even in this moment of proffered tenderness, she cannot bear the thought of being touched. A long monologue ensues which suggests a battle with some sort of demon within her. (Bergman's presen-tation of the monologue in the film shows a striking resemblance to *Persona*.) With one voice, she spits out her hatred for Maria, greedily argues for a quick sale of Agnes's personal belongings, and confesses that, to satisfy "a dirty itch" and gain revenge on Fredrik, she has been having an affair with Henrik, her lawyer. With the other, alternating voice,

---

*To the extent that Maria and Karin are imaginative transformations of Bergman's mother, Father Isak stands in the place of his father. Realizing at the prayer's conclusion that he has blasphemed, the minister blames his grief: "She was my confirmation child," he explains. Erik Bergman, one remembers, had confirmed his son. But the more intriguing autobiographical connection is suggested by the "blasphemy" itself—evidently a projec-tion of the guilt associated with the "Christ envy" Bergman admits he felt as a child. (In addition, there is probably more than coincidence at work in the fact that this minister is named "Isak": one recalls the strained relations between father and son in *Wild Strawberries*.)

she speaks of the guilt that has consigned her to a hell of "misery and torment" and admits to having contemplated suicide. Finally, the penitent Karin overcomes the demon that "is me, yet not me," and she pleads for a new start. Clasping hands, the sisters smile "openly, with no guile or anxiety."

Why, if the film is about Agnes, does Bergman introduce a scene showing the settlement of a quarrel between Maria and Karin—a quarrel, moreover, which has not previously been mentioned? The answer once again comes from perceiving the film as a sophisticated elaboration of a primitive fantasy. Guilt feelings often stimulate children (or adolescents and, even, adults) to imagine themselves dead. Initially, they may think of their death as deserved punishment for some awful offense, or as an escape from profoundly disturbing conditions they believe they cannot change. Once the thought takes hold, however, it becomes a means of asserting power. The guilt is transferred from the child to the parent or other beloved person who is "responsible" for the fantasied death, and who now, in repentance, responds to the child's wishes. *Cries and Whispers* exhibits the same pattern. Father Isak's prayer for forgiveness marks the first manifestation of the child's newfound power; Karin's emotional capitulation, only a few feet from where Agnes's body lies "on the white, almost luminous bed," is the second. Sensual, seductive Maria and cruelly aloof Karin are extensions of the two aspects of the mother shown in Agnes's childhood memory—and, of course, of the "maddening" vacillations in Karin Bergman's demeanor toward her children. In a sense, their reconciliation in this "home of our childhood" fulfills Agnes's (and young Ingmar's) wish to overcome mother's ambivalence. Still more suggestive is the conflict within Karin. Her fear of being touched, her curious mix of revulsion and pleasure when Maria strokes and kisses her in a manner implying incestual passion, and the reference to her coldhearted affair with Henrik (surely an allusion to the Oedipal pairings in *Smiles of the Summer Night*) all point toward the elementary basis of Bergman's recurring psychosexual drama.* Significantly, when

---

*In the film, Bergman excised the reference to Henrik as her lover; Karin speaks of him only as her able solicitor. Even so, their sexual liaison is suggested. When she mentions his name, she accidentally knocks over the wine glass she has been holding—an obvious association with the broken wine glass in her flashback. One thereby infers what is openly stated in the script: that her relationship with Henrik is meant as revenge against Fredrik.

By repeating Karin's clumsiness with the glass, Bergman also reinforces the Oedipal connection between *Cries and Whispers* and *Smiles of the Summer Night*. Much is made of the wine's arcane erotic properties during the dinner party in that film. After drinking the wine, Henrik, distraught because of his love for his stepmother, accidentally breaks the

Karin finally yields to her emotions in this magical fantasy, anxiety is banished.

Ultimately, however, what Agnes's artistic imagination—i.e., Bergman's—wills into happening cannot erase the "reality" of the mother's rejection. The next scene obviously caused Bergman great discomfort. In the script, he injects an "outburst," two pages long, to justify an outrageous violation of the audience's credulity; then, declaring that imagination must not always be accountable to the intellect, he proceeds. The dead Agnes awakes, weeps like a child, and speaks to Anna! The servant tries to calm her: "It's only a dream," she whispers. "Not for me," Agnes answers "tormentedly."

As though to test the conversion depicted in the previous scene, Agnes summons Karin to the bedroom, asks her to hold her hand and kiss her, and begs that she stay until the horrifying loneliness of death has passed. Karin refuses: "Perhaps if I loved you," she says, "but I don't. What you ask of me is repulsive." After she leaves, Anna escorts the other sister to the bed. Restraining her fright, Maria recalls how, as children, they would cling tightly to each other, and she promises to remain with the dead woman as long as necessary. But when, like a lover, Agnes draws her sister's head down to the bed and kisses her, Maria flees in terror. Anna then reenters the room, where she sees Agnes, coiled in a fetal posture, sucking her thumb. Once again, the servant instantly understands her mistress's need; baring her breast, she holds the woman-child across her lap—an unmistakable evocation of Michelangelo's *Pietá* combining the crucifixion and regression toward the womb motifs which dominate Bergman's works.

The key to the image's meaning rests in Anna—an idealization of Mother, divorced from any Oedipal encumbrance. Bergman describes her as though she were a primitive goddess: "Everything about Anna is weight; her body, her face, her mouth, the expression of her eyes. But she doesn't speak; perhaps she doesn't think, either." Her silence symbolizes the nothingness beyond life (or, stated another way, beyond the guilt Bergman regards as virtually coexistent with consciousness itself). She personifies both the womb and death as a merciful release from the pain of being.

The remaining scenes constitute the coda.

A hasty family council after the funeral reflects the failure of love the

glass. It is as a result of this accident that Fredrik discovers the truth about his wife's romantic affections, and that, shortly thereafter, Henrik's beloved is delivered to him by the trick bed.

two sisters have shown in the dream. Relieved of the burden Agnes has been to them, they now turn their attention to settling the terms of Anna's dismissal as expeditiously as possible. It is a coldly conducted business. When Karin mentions that she has offered the servant a small keepsake, Fredrik reproves his wife for lapsing into "detestable spontaneity." Joakim and Maria think themselves more generous: out of a sense of noblesse oblige, they give Anna a large banknote. Yet this "cash consideration" for twelve years of service is as demeaning as the other couple's stinginess. Still more chilling than the sisters' treatment of Anna, however, is their alienation from each other. Just before parting, Karin reminds Maria of the moment of tenderness they had achieved and of their pledge to make a new start, but Maria is in no mood to listen to sentimental appeals. "I can't possibly remember every silly thing," she replies, "and above all I *won't* be made to answer for them. Goodbye, Karin dear. . . . I'll expect to see you again at Twelfth Night as usual." After Karin, stung by the betrayal, snaps her head away from the perfunctory farewell kiss, Maria makes her exit saying, "How absurd."

The prominence of the crucifixion motif and Bergman's association of the other sisters' flashbacks with Good Friday lend a special resonance to the mention of Twelfth Night. Given the circumstances, there is a piercing irony in this allusion to the Epiphany (the first manifestation to the Gentiles of Jesus as Christ, thus heralding the Gospels' "new commandment" of love). Perhaps the more important function, however, is to link the scene to the relationship between young Agnes and her mother depicted in the flashback which began at Twelfth Night. In effect, the drama derived from the pain and confusion portrayed in that episode has come full circle. Surely it is not just coincidence that Maria's parting words on this occasion replicate Mother's concluding line in the script's version of the "tumult."

The short final scene shows Anna (the transcendent Mother, or Death) as the inheritor of the diary that symbolizes Agnes's life. While she calmly begins reading, Anna and the three sisters appear on the screen. Agnes knows she is dying, but her sisters' return to the family mansion has given her a new surge of strength. "It's wonderful to be together again like in the old days—like in our childhood," Agnes writes. Dressed in white (as in Bergman's dream) and carrying white parasols, they stroll down to the garden swing. As Anna gently rocks them to and fro, Agnes feels all her pain leave her body. "The people I'm most fond of in the world were with me. . . . I closed my eyes tightly, trying to cling to the moment and thinking: Come what may, this is happiness. . . . I can experience perfection. And I feel a great gratitude to my life, which gives me so much."*

Even more conspicuously than the film's opening scenes, this idyllic finale invites comparison to its counterpart in *Wild Strawberries*. The diary provides retrospect over an interval of only a few months—not the lifetime spanned with Isak's last dream.** Nevertheless, Bergman achieves much the same effect. Agnes's feeling that something of the goodness of childhood has been restored to her, the sisters' childlike gambol to the swing, and the virginal white worn by the women all imply a magical leap to a past innocence quite similar to Isak's final vision of a vanished world. The guilt at the core of both films is thus submerged in gentle illusion. It is also significant that the illusion centers on a reunited, loving family. Isak's imaginary sighting of his parents marks the end of a quest—primarily for his father, although the underlying reason Father has been absent from this journey backward in time involves Isak's relationship with his mother. Agnes, too, has been engaged in a quest, which terminates in the "perfection" she experiences with her sisters and Anna. Signaling the meaning of this perfection, a Chopin theme is heard throughout the scene: earlier, the same theme had introduced Agnes's flashback and then accompanied the eruption of wild emotions during the girl's rare moment of intimacy with her mother.

Perhaps the most revealing element in the correspondence of the films' endings, however, lies in their final lines. As Isak calls to his parents across the bay, he realizes that "the warm summer breeze carried away my cries. . . . Yet I wasn't sorry about that; I felt, on the contrary, rather lighthearted." In *Cries and Whispers*, the flashback to the last of summer's days, just before Agnes's autumn of agony, concludes with a close-up of her face and Bergman's own voice saying, "Then the cries and whispers died away." Both instances reflect Bergman's conventional use of the summer theme in contrasting illusion and the reality of hypocrisy and betrayal laid bare by the stories, but they also reach

---

*The script also ends quoting this entry from the diary, but Anna does not read it. In this version, she is last seen moving about from room to room; as though horrified by the import of the events she has witnessed, she repeatedly stifles a scream. Far in the distance, a child is crying. It is the same sound heard at the start of the "resurrection" scene—the dream that is not a dream—but now the crying becomes steadily fainter as, presumably, Agnes speeds toward oblivion in her journey backward into the womb of time.

**Joakim's reference after the funeral to a snowstorm that is threatening to make the roads impassable indicates a late autumn or early winter day; the diary entry is dated September 3.

beyond it in their attempts to strip death of its terrors. Presumably, Isak feels "lighthearted" because he has come to accept his imminent death as a deliverance from the cold life into which he was born from his mother's "cold womb." Bergman's valediction for Agnes conveys the same mercy. Anna's love is finally the kind embrace of death. Abandoned in her need by Karin and Maria, Agnes finds release from life's crucifixion in oblivion.

The Preserve and Scenes from a Marriage

At a meeting with the press in August 1972, Bergman announced that *Scenes from a Marriage* would complete a trilogy begun with *The Preserve* and *The Touch*.[1] The idea that these works should be considered complementary parts of a whole failed to catch on, and Bergman himself never mentioned it again. Indeed, if the three were intended to interlock, why was the first a television drama, the second a film, and the third something not quite a play but six "scenes" televised over a six-week period? Furthermore, no principle of evolution binds them. The *Silence of God* trilogy, despite the discreteness of its individual films, presumed to be a progressive metaphysical "reduction"; here, the "parts" have no order. Even so, they do show similarities of subject and theme—marriage, infidelity, and the sterile conditions of a middle-class existence—and to varying degrees, all three derive from *A Passion*—the first film, Bergman has said, in which he tried to make amends for his previous comic treatment of marriage by "gripping" onto the substance of the relations between a man and a woman."[2]

As a reworking of the script that supplied the characters for *A Passion*, *The Preserve* shows the closest connection.* "Fromm" reappears as the name of the couple who are the main characters: this Anna Fromm is a combination of Anna Fromm and Eva Vergérus from *A Passion*; this Andreas, an architect in the civil service, is half Andreas Winkelman, half Elis Vergérus—and his wife's lover, Elis Andresen, reflects the other halves.

The "preserve" (*Reservatet*, the Swedish title, could also be translated

*Directed by Jan Molander, *The Preserve* was broadcast from Sweden to much of Western Europe in 1970 as the first offering of a consortium called Eurovision. Subsequent productions, in English, were staged for the BBC and for CBS, which used *The Lie* (as it had been retitled) to launch a revival of Playhouse 90. (The American response to this long, slow-moving drama was disappointing, and the "revival" quickly perished.)

as "the reservation," "the sanctuary," or "the refuge") is at once the privileged nation of Sweden and the limited social world the Fromms inhabit, but it is also a state of mind—like the island in *A Passion*, an illusion of safety floating in a sea of guilt and vulnerability. Thus, in the prologue, Andreas announces:

> I don't believe many people are as well off as I. Sometimes I almost feel that an existence so well-protected against discomforts and serious worries is cause for alarm. It happens occasionally that one wonders: when will the storm shift its course? When will it draw over this sheltered island? But then these aren't thoughts to keep one awake nights.

His wife echoes his sentiments: "If the news upsets me, I may feel a queasiness rising, but then it disappears in the daily routine." The first scene illustrates the point. The couple's eight-year-old child wakes them with the news of Martin Luther King's assassination, just reported by the radio, and headlines of battles in Vietnam spread across the newspaper on the table.* As the Fromms sip their breakfast coffee, however, the bloody tide seems too distant to disturb the predictability of their insular lives.

At the office, Andreas has the usual tiff with his secretary, assesses the standing of his faction in departmental politics, eats an insipid meal in the cafeteria, dashes from one conference to another in which the same questions are discussed endlessly. Then, without warning, panic: the proposal he has spent months preparing has been rejected, and he is about to be replaced by two younger men who have the "colossal advantage" of inexperience. Andreas is incredulous—after all, he himself is only forty. His supervisor laughs; "To be forty," he says, "is almost like having a shameful disease."

After work, as if to seek treatment for that disease, Andreas rushes to a doctor's office. Even though the doctor is out, he refuses to leave; when darkness falls and the nurse tells him she must close the office, he persuades her to sit with him a few minutes more while he talks of the lack of tenderness and warmth in his home. Next, taking refuge in a pub, he starts a frantic letter to his wife: "Isn't everything a cruel lie? Can we change things? Can we? Or are we caught? Locked in our preserve?

---

*Bergman had included a reference to the King assassination in the script of *A Passion*, but in the film itself he substituted the newsclip showing the execution of the Viet Cong prisoner.

In our comfortable. . . . " Unable to finish the letter, he tears it to pieces.

The tone of Anna's day is set by a visit to a mental hospital, where her brother Albert, a poet who has lost the ability to write, broods about the death of civilization while feeding plagiarized scraps from Baudelaire to his publisher. "Destruction rules, that is the truth," he declaims. "The lie rules. That is the truth. Hate has clad itself in the clothes of righteousness, that is the truth. . . . The worst is that I once had hope."* This jeremiad seems to pursue Anna to her study at the university, where an angry colleague accuses her of being a consummate liar.** Anna swears the charge is unmerited—and darts to a meeting with Elis, with whom she has been successfully deceiving her husband for eight years. At the end of the day, she has dinner with her father. As she listens to him grumble about the uselessness of old age, one realizes that her daughterly role is also a kind of playacting, another instance of the "damnable parody" of truth cited by Andreas in his anguished letter.

Six days later, on Maundy Thursday, Anna is stunned by the news that Elis and his wife will spend a two month vacation on the Continent to rejuvenate their marriage. That night, in the Fromms' bedroom, Andreas awakens her to confess to having made love to the nurse in the doctor's office the previous afternoon. To his astonishment, Anna dismisses the incident as unimportant and urges him to go to sleep, but Andreas continues to protest that they must reconstruct their relationship on a basis of truth. Finally wearied by his earnestness, she reveals her own affair with Elis—a liaison she insists poses no danger to their marriage. The fact that she has not sought a divorce, despite being economically independent, proves she actually *chooses* to live with her husband.

This absurd reasoning precipitates a desperate farce. They tumble on the bed, kissing clumsily and ardently until, for no apparent cause, Anna panics, scratches herself free, runs to another room, and locks herself in. While Andreas chops at the door with an ax, she unbolts it, whereupon he begs forgiveness, then beats her until her nose bleeds and she vomits. Thus purged of their aggressions, they calmly repent

---

*As a spent artist slipping into madness and a sexual deviate who wears rouge and lipstick, Albert recalls Johan Borg in *Hour of the Wolf*. His name also suggests a link to another despair-ridden "artist," Albert Emanuel Vogler in *The Face*.

**Like the Anna Fromm of *A Passion*, this Anna is a Slavic scholar—a detail which seems to hold a personal significance for Bergman. In addition to being a journalist, Gun Grut had worked toward an advanced degree in Slavic studies at the University of Uppsala. By eerie coincidence (given the prominent role of the car accident in *A Passion*), she died in 1971 in Yugoslavia as the result of an automobile collision.

their confessions. Having blundered into destroying the lie that supported their marriage, they now discover the terror of having nothing to set in its place. In the play's closing lines, Anna says, "No, I don't want to," but when Andreas asks, "What is it you don't want?" she gives no answer, and he, about to say something more, surrenders to silence.

Surely not by coincidence, the removal of the couple's masks, the explosion of violence, and the recognition of truth's devastating effect all occur after midnight—i.e., on Good Friday. It is the maker's mark. Once again, Bergman depicts man as abandoned, "crucified"; *this time* his name was Andreas Fromm.

No iteration of that recurrent conceit, however, is as listless as *The Preserve*. The symbolism of the cross finds no purchase in the events of the drama; in this respect as well as in almost every other, self-quotation has displaced invention. Moreover, the content of any given scene often strays from the narrative design. To illustrate the economy of drama, Chekhov once remarked that a loaded rifle placed on stage in one act must be fired in another. Here, the playwright loads and reloads without discharging the expectations he has created. For example: Andreas, on leaving his office, offers his secretary a lift; then, while maneuvering his car out of its tight parking space, he scrapes the fender of the car in front. Another driver blocks his exit and accuses him of meaning to leave without filing a report of the accident; rather unconvincingly, Andreas protests that he had no such intention. Although the incident is not entirely superfluous—the implied wish for intimacy with the secretary, the blocked car, and the guilty reaction to his attempted escape all relate to his feeling trapped—it has no consequence in terms of the play's action. Similarly, Anna's meetings with her brother, her colleague, and her father promise complications that never emerge.

What the play unfolds is not a story or even a study of its characters but the vision of life announced by the play's subtitle: *A Tragicomedy of Banality*. Again, Bergman argues that even the most elementary social existence is inseparable from hypocrisy; again, he makes disease the metaphor for that existential lie. Unlike his other works conveying the same message, however, *The Preserve* quickly spends its dramatic force in setting forth its despairing thesis. Thereafter, to tedious effect, the play advances chiefly through repetition of its central metaphor. That, on entering the doctor's office, Andreas should complain of feeling as though he were suffocating justifiably extends the motif of asphyxiation within "the preserve"; that he should then spot two dead fish in the doctor's aquarium and be told that "the whole aquarium needs scour-

Bergman on the set with Liv Ullmann and Bibi Andersson (whose back is to the camera). Permission from Svenska Filmindustri.

ing with some disinfectant" chases an analogy which adds nothing to what is already apparent.

What accounts for this flaccidity? Given that *The Preserve* is a revision of a script Bergman had previously rejected, and, in addition, that he chose not to direct it himself, one could assume that he regarded the play as simply work for hire. But its basic fault probably owes to another reason. After acknowledging in *Hour of the Wolf* that the mirror of an art turned inward on the self had shattered, Bergman had three options. As he demonstrated most emphatically in *A Passion*, he could make the fragmentation itself the point of the fiction. Or he could avoid the problem by stepping over the line he had drawn between his interpretive role as a theatrical director and his creative work for the screen. (The aborted film version of *The Merry Widow* represented one such effort; his appropriation of Mozart's *The Magic Flute* would soon be another.) *The Preserve* exemplifies the third option: restatement of the same nihilistic vision which had begun to overpower the filmmaker's works in the early 'sixties, but removed from "the essence of the personal." The results indicated that the strategy was a mistake: by omitting an autobiographical reference point, Bergman had shackled his creativity. The tepid response from audiences on both sides of the Atlantic should have discouraged a similar effort.

After the failure of *The Touch*, however, and with no reason to believe that the painfully personal *Cries and Whispers* would reverse the decade-long decline in his popularity, he renewed the experiment in another marital drama written for television. Indeed, in retrospect one can see that *The Preserve* served as a rehearsal for *Scenes from a Marriage*. Although Andreas and Anna are not prototypes for Johan and Marianne, these two studies of marriage follow basically the same scheme: both begin with the couples' self-congratulatory statements; both conclude with "truth's" devastation when they drop their masks.

Originally, Bergman had planned a stage play about a man's informing his wife that, despite a wholly satisfactory marriage, he wants to leave her for another woman. Once he had settled on that germinal scene, he turned his imagination to other moments in their lives. Had the couple's relationship really been as good as both parties believed? What might happen to them after they separated? And after they met again? Guided by no particular scheme, he claimed, his examination of the different phases of love and marriage produced "six distinct dialogues." Much that enters the dialogues is, of course, an extension of the author: in his prefatory comments to the series, Bergman stated that, although "it took [only] two and a half months to write these scenes, it took an adult lifetime to experience them." Even so, *Scenes from a Marriage* is primarily about a middle-aged couple's discovery of their dreadful freedom; it is not a psychologically motivated investigation of the self. While writing the script, Bergman later commented (apparently having forgotten *The Preserve*), he found to his surprise that, "perhaps for the first time," the two characters formed through his internal colloquy "did not at all speak with my own voice."[3]

"Innocence and Panic," the first episode, introduces Johan and Marianne by means of an interview being conducted by a magazine writer for her article on modern marriages. Only half-jokingly, Johan describes himself as "extremely intelligent, successful, youthful, well-balanced, and sexy; a man with a world conscience, cultivated, well-read, popular, a good mixer"—and, he adds with mock grandness, "a splendid lover." At the age of forty-two, he has achieved a secure place in society: he is a solid citizen who pays his taxes and respects the government; he fulfills his duties as a son, father, and husband. In contrast to Johan's cocklike crowing, Marianne gives a short, self-effacing reply to the same question. Although she is an established divorce lawyer, she defines herself exclusively in terms of the feminine role prescribed by her middle-class background: "I'm married to Johan and have two daughters. That's all I can think of for the moment."

Both have put the follies of youth behind them—she had been briefly married; he, while a bachelor, had had a fling with a pop singer—and they have convinced themselves that immersion in life's dull routine will insure contentment. But even during the polite chatter of the interview, it is apparent that they are engaging in self-deception: for them, marriage is a refuge from the peril of lucidity.

> *Johan*: If I stopped to think I'd be petrified with fear. Or so I imagine. So I don't think. I'm fond of this cozy old sofa and that oil lamp. They give me an illusion of security which is so fragile that it's almost comic. I like "St. Matthew's Passion," though I'm not religious, because it gives me feelings of piety and belonging. Our families see a lot of each other and I depend very much on this contact, as it reminds me of my childhood when I felt I was protected. . . . I think you must have a kind of technique to be able to live and be content with your life. In fact, you have to practice quite hard not giving a damn about anything.

> *Marianne*: [While her husband is out of the room.] St. Paul told us what love is. The trouble is, his definition squashes us flat. If love is what Paul says it is, then it's so rare that hardly anyone has known it. . . . If you can supply [kindness, affection, comradeship, tolerance, a sense of humor, and moderate ambitions for one another,] then love's not so important.

To celebrate the publication of the article extolling their happiness, the couple entertain their good friends Peter and Katarina, who proceed to display a very different picture of marriage. Like Swedish counterparts of George and Martha in *Who's Afraid of Virginia Woolf?*, the guests rip at each other's souls by clawing through the sexual organs. And yet, though they claim that only their tangled financial interests and a symbiotic perversity prevent their divorce, their hatred is a twisted expression of their love. "Right inside Katarina," Peter says, "a little girl is sitting and crying because she has fallen and hurt herself and no one has come to comfort her. And I'm sitting in the corner and haven't grown up, and I'm crying because Katarina can't love me even though I'm nasty to her."

The "peep into the bottom-most pit of hell" the guests have provided only increases the hosts' smugness, but their own descent is about to begin. Soon after, when Marianne discovers she is pregnant, her husband convinces her to have an abortion. To him, the termination of this inconvenient pregnancy represents no more than a slight ripple in the calm sea of their marriage; to her, it is a repudiation of the one traditional role which has given her a sense of fulfillment. In Johan's prattling at the side of her hospital bed about dinner parties and visits to relatives, she recognizes the prevision of a barren future; that night, staring at the ceiling with tear-filled eyes, she is too frightened to sleep.

The second episode, "The Art of Sweeping Under the Rug," focuses on the morbidity that has slowly spread through their lives. Johan, who once fancied a literary career, shows a sheaf of his poetry to Eva, an old friend from his student days. Her judgment that the poems are mediocre injures his pride, but her remark that their set at the university had believed he was the one destined for fame inflicts the deeper hurt. Johan suddenly feels as though he were attending his own funeral, unable to scream his protest that he is not dead. Marianne experiences similar sensations. The same morning, she vows to break the pattern of Sunday dinner with alternating pairs of parents, but the phone call to her mother ends with a confirmation of the routine visit. A few hours later, the grim implications in this comic defeat echo during Marianne's conference with Mrs. Jacobi, a client some twenty years her senior. The time has come to sue for divorce and smash the lie she has lived, Mrs. Jacobi insists: "Comradeship, loyalty, affection, friendship, well-being, [and] security" are inadequate recompense for a loveless marriage. Since these are the very consolations Marianne has raised above love, Mrs. Jacobi's brave resolve to start a new life strikes terror in the younger woman.

What Marianne still fights to deny, Johan is ready to admit: duty and respectability have become a tomb in which "everything has been neatly arranged, all cracks have been stopped up, . . . [and our marriage has] died from lack of oxygen." The story of this marriage has now reached the point at which it originated.

In "Paula," Johan has become sexually involved with a woman years younger than his wife. "Oxidized by the cheerful selfishness of the new infatuation" (Bergman comments), he feels a rush "of vital eagerness to act," and one evening, he abruptly announces that he will move to an apartment with his mistress. Marianne is stupefied. Not knowing how to deal with this new reality, she asks him to make love "for old times' sake" (which brings her a rare orgasm); in the morning, she loyally packs his bags, trims his hangnail, assumes responsibility for canceling his dentist appointment and notifying his father they will not attend his birthday celebration. The full force of what has happened does not hit her until he closes the door. When she telephones her best friend and learns that Johan's affair has been common knowledge for months, she feels bitterly humiliated.

A year later, in "The Vale of Tears," Johan has discovered that he fled one trap to land in another with Paula: the apartment complex where he now lives, he says, "most resembles my idea of hell . . . a place where no one believes in solutions any more." When he arranges to visit Marianne, he wistfully hopes something might come of their meeting —though he seems unsure what that something might be. Marianne, in contrast, is completely sure of what she wants; after reeling through a succession of lovers, she has found strength in her independence. Showing feline assurance, she plays with him until, moved by mercy as much as by desire, she finally invites him to stay the night. Johan gratefully accepts, but soon nods off to sleep on the couch. When he awakes alone in the dark living room, he slips away like a beaten cur.

"The Illiterates" is set in Johan's office on Midsummer Eve. Although the estranged pair have come together to sign the divorce agreement, Marianne seduces her defeated mate on the office carpet, and each confesses that thoughts of a reconciliation still linger. The dreamlike midsummer night seems to be working its benign magic. While reminiscing, however, they rip away the lies and half-truths that had sustained their marriage, and he bloodies her nose. Marianne calls the brutal combat a unique instance of honesty in their long relationship. Had it occurred years earlier, she adds on parting from him, they might still be together.

A decade at most separates the final episode from the first, yet the change in values suggests the passing of an era. "In the Middle of the Night in a Dark House Somewhere in the World" begins with Marianne calling on her mother after her father's death. A bourgeoise of the old school, the mother looks back on a thirty-nine-year marriage in which she gave her husband unswerving loyalty, bore her conjugal obligations with sufferance, and trusted in dignified silence to erode whatever hostilities existed between them; "We had a good life," she concludes. To her daughter, now married to a sexual wonder for whom she has little affection, such serenity seems as remote as the precepts of a nineteenth-century novel. Johan's transformation has been no less great. Like Marianne, he has remarried and adopted a mode of conduct that would have scandalized the faithful spouse and earnest citizen he once was. When the episode opens, he has just discarded the latest of several lovers who have kept him briefly amused (the same woman who pronounced him a mediocre poet in the second episode). Only one affair continues to hold his interest: as the viewer suspects, it proves to be with Marianne.

Not by chance, they tryst at a friend's seaside cottage rather than at their old country house. Theirs is a liaison without commitment, a love affair based on a mutual rejection of the possibility of love; sexual intercourse in their former bed, they agree, would not be "suitably impersonal." Although "everything is still in confusion" and "a heap of wretched compromises" continues to burden their lives, they have found a way to be "citizens of the world of reality in quite a different way from before" by making a principle of egotism. This new realism, however, is actually self-deception in another form. At night, Marianne dreams of reaching for Johan with handless arms while sinking into soft sand. And Johan confesses that he cannot "accept the complete meaninglessness behind the complete awareness," that he aches for "something to long for . . . , something to believe in." The bond between them is not the selfish hedonism they profess but their fright. Midway through this biography of a marriage, Johan had observed that fellowship, at all levels, is a treacherous illusion: "You must live with the realization of absolute loneliness. . . . [and] learn to accept with a certain satisfaction how pointless it all is." But the closing shot, of the reunited couple in bed, seeking a moment's respite from the unconfrontable, belies that stoic nihilism by exposing the illusoriness of life without illusions.

Scenes from a Marriage gathers thematic elements often found in Bergman's writing: abortion as a violation not only of woman's natural purpose but also of her symbolic meaning as hope; the artist's gnawing suspicion that his best efforts are only mediocre; the explosion of mutual humiliation into physical violence; and, most important of all, the proposition that human relationships rest on lies stretched over the maw of nothingness. But only the tiniest fraction of the audience interpreted these elements in Bergman's terms. Clearly, the chief factor in the enormous success of *Scenes from a Marriage* was its timeliness as a social document. To countless husbands and wives experiencing profound shifts in the foundations of modern marriage, the tribulations of Johan and Marianne reflected their own dramas, staged either openly or in hidden theaters of the mind behind masks of conjugal felicity.

That its appeal owed primarily to its content (and to the routinely superb performances of Erland Josephson and Liv Ullmann in the lead roles) is demonstrated by the fact that, initially, it was the version Bergman butchered for theatrical release which won international acclaim. Abridgement of six fifty-minute episodes into a two-hour-and-forty-eight-minute feature film had meant not only sacrificing parts of the story (such as Marianne's abortion) which help explain the marriage's deterioration but also altering the audience's aesthetic perception. For Swedish viewers of the first television version, the installments were weekly visits with their compatriots Johan and Marianne; reinforcing this impression, Bergman's reading of the credits at the close of each while he showed them a picture postcard "beautiful sight on Fårö" (which quickly became a running joke in Sweden) was like a ritualistic "thank you" uttered at the door. Between episodes, the couple and their problems became a subject of discussion and seeped into the viewers' thoughts—much as one's friends and acquaintances in real life do between meetings; in this manner, Johan and Marianne acquired a dimension beyond the one represented on the television screen. And when the next installment began a week later, the audience could easily accept that from one to seven years had passed (even though the characters seem not to age at all over the decade the series spans).

Integration of the episodes, however, makes the visit last too long, especially since these banal "guests" have themselves as their one topic of conversation. Formally, too, the edited version is inferior. In the series, each segment revolves around a single motif; combining the parts disturbs these unities without replacing them with a dramatic structure organic to the whole. Furthermore, as theorists since Aristotle have noted, drama implies change through praxis, but in *Scenes from a Marriage* the change the story traces is mostly external to what the episodes depict; seaming the scenes to form one tapestry accentuates the interruptions in the design.

To argue that the abridged version is a distortion, however, is not to assign the original an especially high position in the Bergman canon. In spite of the excellence of its execution, *Scenes from a Marriage* remains a close cousin to soap opera—not only in its episodic form and serial presentation but also in the nature of its appeal. Soap opera is always in medias res, and because its narrative skein has neither beginning nor end, it concentrates interest in the circumstances of an immediate present, not in the relationship of any event to a meaning made manifest through the design of a greater whole. The fundamental reason the pace of the action in soap opera is so slow is not because the writers are trying to stretch their material but because the evolving story consists in its characters' secret lives; essentially, it feeds a voyeuristic curiosity.

Although, unlike soap opera, *Scenes from a Marriage* has a beginning, a middle, and an end, these are almost arbitrary divisions in that they do not function as necessary components of a structure of meaning. What intrigues the audience is the camera's violation of privacy: the screen becomes both a glass wall of a neighbor's house and a mirror reflecting the audience to themselves. The fascination of these episodes lies in their disclosure of "real life" rather than in the artifice with which a similitude of reality is composed.

Recognizing that he would probably be criticized for catering to popular taste, Bergman jousted against the pretensions of "art." In the preface to the published script of the series, he sarcastically lamented his inability to furnish a happy ending, "if for no other reason [than] to infuriate all artistically sensitive people who, in disgust over this completely understandable work, will already be aesthetically nauseated after the first part of the first scene." But who was the target of the sneer? The aesthetes who snubbed Bergman in his youth had long since faded as a threat; indeed, it was those clamoring for a "completely understandable" art serving to awaken consciousness of social wrongs who constituted his present enemy and the "artistically sensitive" who were his defenders. Moreover, it seems highly disingenuous for the creator of such films as *Persona* and *A Passion* to rail against pessimism and complexity, especially when he was preparing to make *Cries and Whispers*. What this disparagement actually indicates is Bergman at odds with Bergman, the artist in conflict with his perception of reality. Once he had looked to art as a kind of sympathetic magic, a dream on which he could impose happy endings that would lift the dreamer from his despair. The dreams of the artist, however, led ever more deeply into a nightmare of the self which overwhelmed the possibilities of art. In exchanging descent into that horror for an excursion to document the frightening conditions of modern middle-class existence, *Scenes from a Marriage* offered no comfort, but it allowed him to explain art's insufficiency on something other than personal terms. If, as *Hour of the Wolf* proclaimed, the mirror was shattered, so too was the world art had traditionally presumed to reflect.

Recovery of art's magical power required a means not only of averting confrontation with the shattering truth within the self but also of escaping to a more innocent age. Although Bergman plunged once again into the depths of his psyche in *Cries and Whispers*, his next film would float free on borrowed enchantment.

The Magic Flute

As a twelve year old frequenting the cheap, third balcony seats at the
Royal Opera, Bergman had conceived such a fixed fierce loyalty to Wagner
that he could allow himself to enjoy only two other operas. One was
Mignon ("perhaps," he wrote in 1974, "because I found the woman who
sang the title role irresistible"); the other was *The Magic Flute*.[1]

Exactly what it was in Mozart's combination of fairy-tale naiveté and
Masonic ponderousness that captivated him, he did not know, but the
fascination was intense. Preparing the costumes and sketching the sets,
he planned to stage it with his dollhouse theater until he recognized
that the price of the phonograph records to which the dolls would
"sing" lay beyond his means. Two decades later, Bergman considered
fulfilling his delayed childhood ambition while he was theater chief at
Malmö; this time, however, the problem was not lack of funds but the
unavailability of a suitable cast. Another opportunity presented itself in
the early 'sixties when he was invited to direct the opera in Hamburg,
but then his appointment as head of Dramaten forced him to decline
the offer. Finally, in 1972, an agreement with Swedish television enabled
him to launch the project he had waited a lifetime to bring to fruition.

Filming *The Magic Flute* posed a formidable challenge, not only
because it strained the resources available in Sweden but also because
it involved some fundamental aesthetic problems which none of the
various attempts to film opera since the advent of sound had satisfactorily overcome. Aside from the impossibility of exactly reproducing the
singers' voices and re-creating the acoustics of an opera house, the
filmmaker confronted the conflict between the inherent realism of his
medium and the inherent artificiality of his material. A libretto makes a
poor screenplay. On the other hand, treating the opera as though it
were a performance on stage being recorded by the camera embalms it.
Bergman's solution was to blend the disparate elements by playing
against them — and by having them play against each other. Periodically,
the illusion of the fairy tale Schikaneder wrote for Mozart's music is
interrupted by shots backstage which remind the audience that this
"reality" is a product of the imagination, abetted by theatrical machinery;
and between acts, he opposes life to art by showing one singer cramming for his next role while another, a boy, reads a Donald Duck comic
book. Similarly, although he exploits cinema's advantage over theater in
creating a world for the characters to inhabit, he also underscores its
trickery — as when the text being sung "magically" appears on an

unfurled scroll. Neither quite theater nor quite film, Bergman's *Magic Flute* is a hybrid—not a compromise but a witty invention drawing on both.

Even critics who laud his ingenuity invariably regard *The Magic Flute* as an anomaly in the Bergman canon, as an extension of his interpretive role as a theatrical director rather than of the self-revelation manifest in his films. But the assumption is valid only in a narrow, literal sense; figuratively, Bergman appropriates Mozart to make his own statement. Some time before the curtain rises on the opera, the film begins with the audience filling the theater. The tactic has an obvious purpose: through these spectators, the audience in front of the screen also "enters" the theater and prepares to watch not a film as such but a stage performance. This purpose, however, is quickly superseded by another. Panning the spectators, the camera spots Bergman's former wife Käbi Laretei, his daughter Linn, his present wife Ingrid, and—among other members of his professional family—Erland Josephson and Sven Nykvist. Then, half-humorously, it turns to faces representing diverse races and nationalities. The walls of the small Drottningholm theater (the elegant eighteenth-century theater outside Stockholm where the performance is suppos-edly occurring) thus expand to embrace the entire world—just as Bergman's audience of Hälsingborg citizens has grown into an interna-tional following. Implicitly, the production about to begin becomes a personal, artistic testament, offered both to the circle of intimates who have shared his life and to the far-flung public that has peered at his creations from a distance.

But why does he choose *The Magic Flute*? Bergman provided one explanation in discussing his insertion of an extract from the opera in *Hour of the Wolf*. Rapidly approaching death, Mozart, he said, managed to triumph over his mortality through the magnificent art of his music; hence, by presenting a crucial passage from that heroic achievement, the demons mock Johan's surrender to the corrosive powers working to destroy his art, his sanity, and his life. Behind Johan, of course, lay Bergman himself—and the despair he depicted in that film had not diminished in the 'seventies. In making *The Magic Flute*, he was paying tribute not only to a great artist but also to a faith in art he himself could no longer summon.

Yet Mozart and his music may not have been the strongest attraction. Although, compared even to the usual rickety plots in opera, Schika-neder's libretto is a hastily assembled construction which few have taken seriously, Bergman extols this fairy tale as nothing less than a mythic expression of truth. Its very contradictions, he states, belong to "the secretive pattern of the dream" that speaks to the subconscious. His interpretation of that dream, which corresponds to the dream repeatedly expressed through his films, serves as the blueprint to his version of the opera.

To account for the notorious inconsistencies involving Sarastro and the Queen of the Night, Bergman advances a plausible theory: originally, he argues, the composer and his librettist devised a plot about "a couple in love, a martyred and loving mother, and a villain," but when they learned a competing theater was about to present *The Magic Zither*, a play with similar components, they hurriedly changed the story without taking the time to revise what they had already written. Thus, the sympathetic Queen abruptly turns into "a shiny, dark, poisonous snake," and Sarastro, displaced as villain by a new character, the black Monostatos, emerges as a prince of wisdom. A more convincing theory, however, explains the ambiguity in terms of the filmmaker's psyche rather than the circumstances of the opera's composition. As a twelve year old, Bergman believed Sarastro and the Queen had been husband and wife, and although he later discovered that nothing in the opera warranted the assumption, for his film he altered the text to conform with his initial inference. The reason this belief had taken such firm hold in his mind becomes evident when one recognizes in the Queen and Sarastro a child's ambivalent images of his mother and father. Just as clearly, Tamino represents the son.

Like so many of Bergman's films, *The Magic Flute* deals with a quest: Tamino must penetrate Sarastro's Temple of Wisdom (the heart of the drama, Bergman states) and gain acceptance by the powers who control it—in other words, he must contend against, solve, and incorporate into his own being the masculine mastery embodied in Sarastro. But rising in opposition to the father, who is the son's guide to manhood, poses grave psychological danger. Hence the image of the father is split in two: Sarastro becomes the benign influence, and Monostatos, his dark alter ego, is introduced to represent the sexual rival who unfairly uses trickery and superior strength to keep the youth from success —and from his beloved. Learning to distinguish these two figures is a necessary condition for the completion of Tamino's task, which will result in Sarastro's approbation and the elimination of Monostatos.

Correspondingly, the change in the Queen of the Night demonstrates the male child's progress toward independence from the mother. The very first mention of the Queen indicates her role as protector: the

Three Ladies who slay the dragon that is about to destroy the unconscious Tamino act as her agents. But once the Queen physically enters the drama (i.e., once the youth, awakened from his infantile "sleep," becomes aware of her as a separate being who makes demands on him as well as answers his needs), she presents a threat. Bergman's commentary at this point stresses her erotic artfulness:

> Her first words to Tamino are an invitation to come near. She thinks, quite simply, that she can turn the boy's head: she is beautiful, mature, sorrowful, and she plays on a broad register of feminine wiles. Every time I hear the first measures which lead up to her entry, I think I can see someone *approaching*, first at a distance, secretive, then human, near, palpable.

Significantly, this reading is based on an aria in which the Queen addresses the youth as "my dear son," praises him as "innocent, wise, pious" and tries to calm his fears. Nowhere does the Queen sound more softly maternal, yet Bergman senses a perilous seduction in her plea that Tamino, the one "best able to comfort this deeply troubled mother's heart," conquer "the scoundrel" Sarastro. Of course, the Queen is not actually Tamino's mother, nor is Sarastro actually his father, but if the opera is understood in terms of its "dream language," the relationship among the three is transparently Oedipal.

The second time the Queen speaks, in Act II, Bergman accentuates the metamorphosis of "the sorrowing martyr, so soft and feminine," into "a tremendous, dark, shining insect" who is "frightening in her frenzy and—her nearness." To be sure, the Queen directs her rage at the daughter Pamina, not Tamino, but the two adolescents are symbolically dual components of a single personality. In Jungian terms, Tamino's love for Pamina represents the young male's striving for the anima—a view the text supports not only in the conspicuous similarity of their names but also in the fact that, for Tamino to enter the temple gates (i.e., achieve psychological adulthood), the lovers must pass his final test together. Moreover, the Queen's anger is in response to Pamina's failure to murder Sarastro. In light of Bergman's interpretation that Sarastro is Pamina's father (and of Sarastro's evident function as father figure to Tamino), this "betrayal" suggests a male child's attempt to deny Oedipal guilt.

The Queen's last appearance appropriately coincides with Tamino's invitation into the temple as an initiate by the male chorus of priests. "We must really feel the impression of a threat, of emotional surrender,"

Bergman says, indicating that, for him, the psychological burden of this decisive moment is on Tamino. From this perspective, the "dreadful tumult" that ensues, after which the Queen ("the antithesis of light, the ultimate threat") sinks into the earth and a great sun reveals Sarastro elevated above his fellow priests, is only superficially a clash between rival potentates; at a more profound level, it expresses the conflict within the symbolic son as he breaks free of the mother's restraints.

Yet, despite his keen interest in complementing Schikaneder's disjoined portrait of the Queen, Bergman also recognizes that the fairy-tale rendering of the possessive, inhibiting mother omits her side of the story. "In some way," he writes, "I have always felt sorry for the Queen of the Night. . . . Usually the director and stage designer have put the poor woman on a pedestal in the depths of the stage, and there she stands, madly made up, without any possibility of depicting the interesting complications of the queen's character." This sympathetic understanding of the Queen's betrayal and frustration—from the point of view, as it were, not of Tamino during his quest but of Tamino in later years as he might have looked back on his struggle—accords with Bergman's changed perception of his mother toward the end of her life. (Cf. *Cries and Whispers*, where, after describing her mother's "cold cruelty," Agnes insists she has since come to understand and forgive her.) Like the Queen, Karin Bergman was a strong-willed woman who, though thrust into "the depths of the stage," radiated a powerful influence. If much of his writing has been an effort to deal with the real or imagined wrongs he suffered from her, it is equally apparent that she was the prime source of his artistic impulse. Although the opera does not directly promote sympathy for the Queen, Bergman's construction of its meaning indirectly acknowledges the mother's stimulation of the artist through Papageno, the half-fantastic figure who is the Queen's bird-catcher.

Papageno supplies the opera's comedy, but he is not just a buffoon. More than Tamino's companion, he is his double; at the same time, parallel actions in the plot also establish him as Pamina's male alter ego.* For Bergman at least, these dual roles imply a common base: Papageno represents the son who trembles at the thought of Sarastro's

---

*Bergman underscores "the brother-sister feeling" instantly present when Papageno and Pamina meet early in the opera: "they speak openly to one another, like two nice children. [At this point] Pamina is still far from the suffering woman she matures into during the course of the play." Later, this correspondence surfaces most dramatically when, at the same moment but in different locations, they are on the verge of killing themselves over the absence of their beloveds.

paternal might while (as Pamina's "brother") longing for proof of the Queen's maternal love.

One can confidently assume that Bergman has always felt a strong bond with Papageno. Both the punishment he often faced as a child for telling wild stories and the stammer which he says afflicted him in early adolescence find their emblem in the opera's first scene, where a padlock is clapped on Papageno's lips for lying. In addition, the incident reflects a perceived ambivalence in the mother—and the same shift from guilt to reconciliation that Bergman so frequently depicts in his fictions. Much as Karin Bergman's punitive "silent treatment" of her son would give way to sudden, effusive forgiveness, the Queen imposes the penalty (after ordering that Papageno be given water instead of wine and a stone instead of sweetmeats—symbols of the mother's withdrawal of nourishment and love), then pardons him.

The significance of the lock's removal deepens when it is seen within the larger context of the Queen's determination to defeat Sarastro: first, she begs Tamino to take vengeance on her adversary for her sake; next, in unfastening Papageno's lips, she commands him to overcome his fears and hurry to Sarastro's castle; then, she gives Tamino a flute and Papageno a glockenspiel as magic charms against danger. If, initially, Tamino and Papageno are twin agents of her desire, their mission leads toward two fundamentally different ends. At the cost of losing the Queen's favor, Tamino must prove his manhood—indeed, the flute, that obviously phallic symbol which he plays to succeed in his last trial, turns out to have been carved from a mystical ancient oak by Pamina's father (Sarastro, in Bergman's version). In contrast, the glockenspiel symbolizes art, and Papageno himself is the eternal child (as is attested by the fact that he does not take part in Tamino's final test to reach adulthood). Although the Queen enlists him in her cause against Sarastro, she also makes him swear to tell the truth as a condition for restoring his freedom to speak. That truth pertains not to the objective reality of the adult but to the subjective vision of the child; in a sense, Papageno's function in the opera-as-dream is to recover what Tamino must forsake.

This motif leads, in Act II, to Papageno's encounter with an old woman (or, in Bergman's phrase, "a beauty past her prime.") When she tells him she is the promised sweetheart he has never met, he is incredulous, but as soon as he pronounces her name, Papagena, she instantly changes into a young girl—and then vanishes. Cast into despair by the loss, Papageno prepares to hang himself, but at the final moment he remembers the magic power of the glockenspiel. As he plays the chimes,

Bergman says, the "leafless autumnal garden" (according to his interpretation) becomes a nuptial bower of "springtime blossoming" and
Papagena reappears.* Twenty years before filming *The Magic Flute*, Bergman had written his own version of this scene: in *Smiles of the Summer
Night*, Anne (the transformed mother) is wondrously delivered to Henrik
to the accompaniment of music after he botches his attempt to hang
himself.

The similarity of *The Magic Flute* to Bergman's most successful comedy acquires a mordant significance if it is set alongside the homage to
Mozart in the film which followed the courageous and self-devastating
Persona. The bitter irony of *Hour of the Wolf* is concentrated in Tamino's
question, "When will I see the light?" For Tamino, the answer is "Soon";
for Johan, the artist reproved by this performance of his soul's drama, it
is "Never." Merkens Castle is exactly Sarastro's Temple, but inverted
into a dungeon of the self, admitting no light, where feminine demons
rip the artist apart. For the next eight years, Bergman would grope in
vain for an Ariadne's thread to guide him from his labyrinthian despair.
Even *Cries and Whispers*, his most concerted artistic effort of this period,
leads inexorably toward the darkness and concludes with an illusion of
light that only accentuates life's cruel futility. In "inviting" family, friends,
and the world to enjoy his rendition of *The Magic Flute*, Bergman was
holding up a magic glass which, though it reflects the conflicts within
his own psyche, resolves them with a confidence and joy now beyond
the contrivance of his art.

Face to Face

Bergman finished shooting *The Magic Flute* in June 1974. While he
worked with his assistants to prepare a final print of the opera during
the closing months of the year, he wrote the script for his next film. The

---

*Bergman's rearrangement of the material in Act II further indicates that the two-stage
transformation of the old woman into a girl represents a son's wish to convert his mother
into his sweetheart. In the original, Papagena appears just before the opera's close; here,
Bergman moves the scene to a much earlier point, adjacent to Pamina's suicide attempt
—thereby stressing (or creating) the parallel between the two characters.

In addition, the juxtaposition serves to highlight the difference between Papageno and
Tamino. The realization of Papageno's fantasy involves the mother as lover; in contrast,
Pamina's preparations for suicide indict the mother for preventing her union with Tamino.
("Rather die by this blade," she sings, "than be destroyed by love's grief. Mother, mother,
through you I suffer, and your curse pursues me.")

contrast between them could not be more telling. Like *Hour of the Wolf*, *Face to Face* surrenders to the psychic terrors that Mozart—or the Mozart Bergman had fashioned into a counterimage of himself—overcame through the power of his art.

The absence of inspiration can be sensed in a letter to the cast and crew that, as had become his custom, he affixed as a preface to the published script. "If some honest person were to ask me honestly just why I have written this film," he states with a tinge of self-mockery, "I, to be honest, could not give a clearcut answer." The best explanation he can muster is that, having lived for some time "with an anxiety which has no tangible cause," he has decided to investigate his condition methodically; the filmmaker, in short, will act as his own psychiatrist. He claims to have based the story on a woman whose experiences, though similar to his own, "were more obvious, more explicit, and much more painful," but if the woman ever actually existed, little of her survives in Jenny Isaksson, the emotionally ravaged psychiatrist who is the film's central figure. Jenny is transparently a self-portrait.

The weakness of *Face to Face* can be attributed at least in part to this close identification with his protagonist. The title, taken from the next clause of the sentence in 1 Corinthians that furnished the title for *Through a Glass Darkly*, emphasizes the same self-encounter Bergman has made the basis of almost every film since he undertook the trilogy, but here he neglects to situate that preoccupation within a dramatically coherent context. And in offering the "discovery" that life presents a choice between hypocrisy and nothingness, he merely echoes the cry he had been raising with diminishing force after it shuddered a terrific energy through *Persona*. The dulling effect of repetition can also be seen in his protagonist. Although the name "Jenny Isaksson" points back specifically to Jenny in *The Day Ends Early* (a similar character caught in analogous circumstances) and to Isak in *Wild Strawberries* (another doctor drawn into examining the pathology of his soul), her antecedents, male and female, can be found in various places throughout his works. Few of these prior incarnations, however, are as opaque as this character. She is married to a man who evidently cares more about his business career than about her; she has a grown daughter who resents her mother's remoteness; and she is engaged in at least one affair, with a tiresome but sexually adequate lover. Presumably, these relationships play an important part in her mental life, yet her speech and actions fail to indicate it. Nor does Bergman convincingly portray her as a psychiatrist. Even if only to register the irony of her helplessness, a psychiatrist would surely reflect her professional training as she becomes aware of her own emotional collapse. But Jenny does not. Despite Liv Ullmann's sensitive performance, her character is never more than a vehicle for Bergman's self-exposure.

The first scene, set in the office of a mental hospital, recalls Marianne's interview with her client in *Scenes from a Marriage*. Like Mrs. Jacobi, Jenny's patient, Maria, reverses their roles by diagnosing the psychiatrist's problem: existence in an unreality caused by the inability to love. To prove her contention, she lays her hand on Jenny's thigh and offers to fondle her sexually. They both need help, Maria says; therefore they should "share the responsibility—and the risks." Clinging to her clinician's mask as a shield, Jenny refuses to admit her fear and isolation, but Maria's accusations stir subliminal anxieties. That night Jenny meets a startling apparition: a one-eyed woman, dressed in black, carrying a white cane. The specter, who will reappear several times during the film, symbolizes both death and Jenny's blindness to the dreadful import of her circumstances.

These intimations are reinforced by the next scene. Jenny has given up her apartment, but because of delays in the construction of the house she and her husband are having built, she is staying with her grandparents. (Conveniently, the husband is away on business—as usual.) Nothing has changed in the grandparents' flat since World War I, and Jenny—like several of Bergman's other personae—feels disconcerted by this return to the troubled world of her childhood. More than the revival of the past, however, it is the prevision of her future presented by the aged grandparents that shakes her. Once a proud scientist and a haughty lion among Uppsala society, the grandfather has been reduced by a paralytic stroke to poring tearfully over old photograph albums, obsessively winding the clock, and fretting that he will be sent to a home for the aged. Yet, pitiable as he is, Jenny finds the grandmother's fate still sadder. In one of those intimate talks between women that Bergman has made his specialty since *Women's Waiting*, the granddaughter asks whether she ever wanted to escape the marital obligations that have now sentenced her to serve as a nursemaid. Calmly, the old woman confesses that once, early in her marriage, she had considered leaving her husband, but the sight of him walking along their street caused her to dismiss the thought.* "I wouldn't call it love exactly.

---

*The description of this occurrence places it on the same street where Bergman's grandmother lived in Uppsala—just as the furniture Jenny's grandparents have clung to suggests Grandmother Åkerblom's apartment—but it also has overtones of the crisis in his parents' marriage.

Rather a kind of understanding. I suddenly grasped the meaning of all sorts of things: my own life and Grandpa and his life and the children's future and the next life and I don't know what." To Jenny, the values of her grandmother's generation no longer seem to apply: like Marianne during her talk with her mother at the end of *Scenes from a Marriage*, she realizes that the possibility of mooring life to "the meaning of all sorts of things" has been lost. Her sleep that night is restless; just before dawn, the one-eyed woman appears in her room and tries to speak to her, but she cannot make out the words.

In mirroring Jenny's emptiness, the next pair of scenes also imply that the condition is endemic. While reviewing their patients, Jenny reports a slight improvement in Maria, but her colleague, Dr. Helmuth Wankel, sneers at the claim. Psychoanalysis, he asserts, is a hoax; only brutal, mechanistic methods have proved effective—and only to the extent of eradicating symptoms. But if Jenny's adherence to a therapy from which she has excluded the risk of love is a self-serving delusion, so too is Wankel's concept of man as a neurological machine. Within the suit of armor he makes of his cynicism is a man tormented by his love for a fatuous wife who buys the attentions of young men. Later, at a party in the Wankel home, Jenny meets Mrs. Wankel's newest acquisition, a handsome, homosexual actor named Mikael Strömberg who confesses his fear of death and, paradoxically, his urge to rid himself of the "sickly sweet, nauseating" stench of the corpse that is his body. Jenny makes him promise not to commit suicide, yet, significantly, she can offer him no reason to continue living. Her introduction to Dr. Tomas Jacobi at the same party promises a more pleasant acquaintance; when this suave gynecologist invites her to dinner, she cancels a date with her lover to accept. But Tomas, it happens, is Maria's half-brother, and this fact quickly casts a pall over their table conversation. He describes his sister's need to love as a disease, "like elephantiasis"; still worse, he compares her to a wounded dog he once saw that refused to die until someone doused it with gasoline and set it afire. Then, straining to lift the gloom which has descended on their first evening together, he suddenly compliments Jenny on her breasts. But she is neither flattered nor amused by what she takes to be a prelude to seduction. Before leaving him, she asks with bitter sarcasm how he had planned to maneuver her into the bedroom, which sexual technique he had chosen, what strategy he thought would best lessen the awkwardness of saying good-bye after intercourse.

Though broadcast in four installments, *Face to Face* splits into two main parts. The conclusion to the first part is triggered by a mysterious telephone call summoning Jenny to her former apartment, where she finds two men standing over Maria's drugged, unconscious body. Without warning, the younger of the pair seizes Jenny, rips off her pants, sucks her breast "with a desperate sort of hunger," and repeatedly tries to penetrate her; finally, he abandons the effort because she is "too tight and too dry." In some strange, twisted way, it seems, Jenny's humanity, not her assailant's, has failed. Her reaction to the attack reinforces the impression. Instead of informing the police, she telephones Tomas and makes a date for that evening's concert. Not until she has returned to his house does she speak of what happened in the morning—and even then, she is troubled by her puzzling response to the attempted rape rather than by the assault itself. "At first I was frightened," she confesses, "then I thought it was ridiculous, and then.... Suddenly I wanted him desperately to do it.... The strange thing was that I couldn't take him, much as I wanted to."

Late the next day, having awakened in a depressed mood, she phones Tomas to arrange an evening at the movies. But then, in the middle of their conversation, she sees the one-eyed woman staring at her from a mirror. For a moment, she is seized by panic. Through an intense effort of will, however, she quickly calms herself and decides to tape-record a suicide note to her husband Erik. She feels like "a puppet, reacting more or less to external demands and stimuli": their sexual relations have been reduced to cold, mechanical functions; she has lost emotional contact with their daughter Anna. To escape the "great horror" of the emptiness inside her, she will take fifty Nembutal, chancing that it will produce "recovery from a lifelong illness."

The film's second half consists mainly of Jenny's drug-induced dreams, segmented by bedside conversations with Tomas, Erik, and Anna when she slips briefly out of her coma. Scrambling early memories with the events of the previous few days, these hallucinations figure an inward journey into her "great horror."

In the first dream, Jenny, in an embroidered medieval hood, sees herself as a little girl in her grandparents' drawing room. (Like the hood, the girl's red apparel alludes to Little Red Ridinghood—an association that recurs in the final dream.) A guttering candle, obviously a symbol of death, frightens the girl and her grandfather. Dr. Wankel then startles the adult Jenny with the announcement that the masquerade is over; the pungent odor which fills the room, he adds, is the product of the masqueraders' "accelerating necrosis." Suddenly, the room's occupants all cringe in "horror-filled respect" before a grotesquely scarred man with one eye gouged out—apparently Death himself. Jenny spies a door, and despite Wankel's warning that she may awaken with brain damage, she opens it. But the escape does not lead her back to life. Instead, she meets the one-eyed woman—a merciful figure of Death who draws Jenny to her breast in a motherly embrace.

Following a lucid interval during which Tomas, sitting at her bedside, explains how he rescued her, the second dream begins with Jenny's strenuous attempt to close the rift between herself and her parents (who died when she was a child). Now that she is an adult, she says, she understands why they behaved as they did; forgiving them, she asks that she be forgiven. (One cannot fail to note the similarity to Agnes's "forgiveness" of her mother in *Cries and Whispers*.) As soon as the words are out of her mouth, however, she renounces the hypocrisy of her request and lashes out at her parents for their coldness and for instilling a profound guilt in her. The vehemence of the outburst shocks her back to consciousness.

To her surprise, she discovers that her husband Erik has come to visit at the hospital. But even though news of her suicide attempt has brought him from halfway around the globe, they exchange only a few predictable comments before he excuses himself to return to his business duties in America. This display of emotional frigidity apparently triggers the next dream, in which she is confronted with Maria's dead body, propped in a gynecological table, and accused by her fellow physicians of having caused the patient's death through lack of compassion.* Clearly, the dream depicts a double Jenny: she is not only the doctor who rejected Maria's appeal for love but also, as the unloved, would-be suicide whose husband has just turned away from her in her anguish, the victim of her rejection.

In terms of the film's ostensible meaning, the dream's transformation of Jenny from psychiatrist into gynecologist is less easily explained. Tomas, of course, is a gynecologist, and his presence in the hospital room when Jenny awakes reinforces the implication that the two characters are being symbolically equated. But what might the equation signify? Although obviously attracted to Tomas, Jenny had been enraged by his praising her breasts—indeed, her fury was so excessive as to lead

---

*This "trial" rather resembles the dream in which Isak Borg is judged incompetent because he has forgotten a doctor's first duty. Like Isak, Jenny pleads that her human failure is irrelevant: "I don't see the point of all this. If I have broken any of the rules, scientific or ethical, that we have pledged ourselves to respect, then charge me."

one to suspect some deep sexual disturbance. Might the dream's mirror writing then be expressing her wish that she could reach out to him as Maria reached out to her? If so, however, this repressed desire is abruptly dashed by Tomas's confession that he is homosexual, and that he had sought her company to assuage the pain caused by the defection of his lover, Mikael Strömberg, to Mrs. Wankel when she offered him better terms.

Whatever may have initially accounted for the dream's intertwining of Jenny's identity with Tomas's, it is now apparent they are radically alike in their terrible vulnerability and lovelessness. Jenny's next dream proceeds from that recognition of their similarity. Two patients come to her. The first strips off his skin—much as Tomas has figuratively done in his confession. The second, who represents Jenny, draws a paper tape from her mouth on which is written: "They've made an incision in my head and cut away my anguish, but when they sewed up my head they left behind the daily dread." She then meets her grandfather, reduced to inanition by his fear of dying. "Count to ten," Jenny tells him. "If you're still alive when you get to ten, start all over again." The "therapy," of course, is virtually the "disease" in another form, and its failure to help the grandfather sends her scurrying away to attend to the rest of her long list of patients—her own method of "counting to ten." Ironically, what makes death terrifying is not cessation of being but its confirmation of life's meaninglessness. When Jenny opens her eyes, she finds Tomas still sitting beside her. Almost as though he had been privy to her dream and wanted to establish that they are twin souls caught in an unalterable loneliness, he makes another confession. He, too, recently tried to kill himself. The human brain, he says, developed from a cancerous cell at the dawn of evolution; "Man is a wolf to man."

The last dream, a variation on the "accelerating necrosis" motif of the first, plunges deepest into the core of her psychic self. Attending the funeral of herself as a little girl, Jenny hears the minister say that the corpse has begun to stink and must be buried immediately. A heavy coffin lid is carried in by her parents. Once it is set in place, the corpse, terrified of confinement, tries to rise in protest, but the struggle fails and the lid is fastened shut. Her frantic rapping from inside leaves the minister unmoved; indeed, he compounds the horror by directing one of the mourners to trim away the protruding cloth of her red dress which her exertions had caused to spill over the edges of the box. Then, as the corpse repeatedly calls out for her mother, the coffin bursts into flame —the Jenny who has been watching has set it afire.

On recovering consciousness, Jenny speaks at length about the experiences behind the dreams—particularly the last. She first knew death's terror at the age of fourteen, when her cousin Johan died of polio; as they lowered the coffin, she could sense him fighting for breath in the dark grave. To account for her identification with Little Red Ridinghood in the dreams, she recalls a scene from her nursery. Her grandmother had apparently said something that made her mother cry; when Jenny looked into the grandmother's face, she saw the features of "a mad dog that was about to bite." Her most wrenching memory from childhood, however, is of battles of will that ended either in a bad conscience or in submission produced by being locked in a wardrobe. In rebellion against those years of humiliation, Jenny later left home to cohabit with a "crazy artist," but neither that flight from pernicious respectability nor her subsequent accomplishments freed her from profound feelings of personal worthlessness. As a result, she has playacted her way through life, performing the lies demanded by her roles.

Whether Jenny can ever "become real" remains an open question at the film's end, but the "face to face" encounter with herself in her dreams, like the process of psychoanalysis (or, perhaps, like the artist's dredging of his past), has enabled her to acknowledge consciously what she had repressed and, thereby, deal with the conditions under which she lives. The awful fact is that she is essentially alone. Tomas refuses her request to join him on a trip to Jamaica, explaining that she has no place in his fantasies of vice. Her daughter Anna's visit brings a more jolting truth. Shunning her mother's kisses, the girl protests that Jenny has never loved her—and Jenny cannot deny it. Later the same afternoon, after being discharged from the hospital, Jenny learns that her grandfather has suffered another stroke and will probably die. Yet she accepts the evidence of her desolation without panic. In the final scene, she meets the one-eyed woman at a curbside; instead of recoiling in fright, Jenny speaks gently to her, takes her arm, and walks her across the street.

In the letter to his co-workers, Bergman stated that his intent had been to analyze "the causes of the disaster as well as the possibilities available to this woman in the future." Jenny has summarized her understanding of the causes in her final monologues; the possibilities lie wholly outside the text. She may, says Bergman, revert to her "stifling, static combination of mapped-out qualities and patterns of behavior." Or she may modify her conviction "that a human being is a human being" and thereby "let herself be drawn farther and farther in toward the center of her universe [and a discovery that] opens her up to other people in an endless design." Exactly what this second possibility actually means is far from clear. In refuting Tomas's contention that all human relationships are a form of predation (that "man is a wolf to man"), it seems to hold out a basis for hope. But even a frail optimism would be an anomaly amid the bleakness of Bergman's later films. Thus, no sooner than he has mentioned the prospect of revival, he shrouds it with "a consequential alternative: the endlessness becomes unbearable. . . . she tires of her increasingly broadened insight and of the ennui that results. . . . She tires and puts out the light, in the respectable certainty that if you put out the light it will be dark at any rate—and quiet." Finally, it would appear, there are only the same two possibilities to which Bergman's films invariably arrive: routinized existence within an unconscious "seeming," or a state of "being" in which self-knowledge is an incurable affliction leading to suicide or surrender to death.

If *Face to Face* does not quicken because Bergman could not create sufficient distance between his persona and himself, the deeper reason for its artistic failure is a function of his despair. Art and magic have always been inextricably bound in Bergman's mind; after he had firmly rejected the possibility that, through art, he could discover—or conjure—a credible escape from the terrors of his personal prison, his fictions, drained of their vitalizing purpose, steadily lose coherence. Instead of seeking the magic key to pass through the walls of the self into a daylit world, he turns inward to describe the darkness of his cell and its instruments of torture. Dramatically, the problem with *Face to Face* is that Jenny never has a choice to make—and that, despite what Bergman says in his "letter," her future cannot change as a result of any discovery the film has produced. Although the conclusion implies she has become aware of the terms of her life, she remains caught in the same predicament in which she was trapped at the start. What falls between is not a sustained pattern of action developing a dramatic argument but a static "analysis," presented as an aggregation of fragments that show even less unity than the parts of *The Preserve* and *Scenes from a Marriage*.

Jenny's mental troubles originate in her childhood, particularly in the turmoil surrounding her parents, but Bergman does not provide the means to understand why the scars formed, and the parents are too sketchily drawn for the audience to grasp how they made Jenny one of "a vast army of emotional cripples." The grandparents emerge as more distinctive characters, but to what end remains hazy. Although the grandfather demonstrates the humiliating infirmities of old age and the dread of death, the issue of biological frailty does not pertain to Jenny's psychological problem. And if, as his repeated appearance in her dreams would imply, some special bond was forged between them in her past which relates to her present distress, the film neglects to establish what it was; indeed, when the two are together, no currents of emotion seem to pass between them. The grandmother's role, though less prominent, shows even greater ambiguity. In Jenny's childhood, the grandmother was a domineering, cruel tyrant the girl confused with the wolf who menaced Little Red Ridinghood; as an old woman selflessly looking after her husband, she embodies a love Jenny finds as unattainable as it is enviable. How Jenny reconciles these conflicting images should play an important part in her revision of reality, yet the film ignores the question.

Why Bergman should have devised whole scenes to introduce the Wankels and Mikael Strömberg eludes speculation. Dr. Wankel's mechanistic model of human behavior reflects a frightening reductionism that has often intruded into Bergman's fictions, but it does not impinge on the concerns of this story. (Nor, for that matter, does the Freudian theory espoused by Jenny—despite what her dreams are supposed to reveal about her psyche. The premise on which the film rests is that the awareness of what it means to be human is itself the disease, the "accelerating necrosis.") Mrs. Wankel counts for still less: given her husband's irrelevance, the fact that her fatuousness causes him to suffer is a complication without consequence. And what purpose is served by Mikael? Would it make any difference if he were a joyous, faithful homosexual partner? Or if, the night of the party, he did commit suicide? One might argue that each of these characters contributes to Bergman's vision of a world in the throes of spiritual death, but the nature of the story dictates that that vision radiate from Jenny. By multiplying the number of writhing souls without engaging their anguish to the specific conditions of the central figure's struggle, Bergman disperses what he means to intensify.

But the fragmentation is not just the result of minor characters who pull the story from its main interest; that interest itself is inconsistent —and the shorter the focus on Jenny, the more pronounced the confusion becomes. Her dreams are crowded with symbols for private terrors with private meanings that lie beyond the film's confines, even after Jenny has supposedly traced their references to her past. (The remembrance of her grandmother's canine look, for example, seems insufficient explanation for Jenny's repeated identification with Little Red Riding-hood.) And because the dreams shift from fear of death to anger against her parents to anxiety about her helplessness without ever indicating how the various elements connect, the import of the conclusion remains occluded. Still more disconcerting, however, is Bergman's failure to knit the dreams to the outer story—which in its own way presents as much a puzzle as the broken images afloat in Jenny's mind. Why does Jenny's refusal to engage in a lesbian affair with Maria signify that the psychiatrist is spiritually sick? What is implied by the fact that Jenny is raped as a result of her concern for Maria; why, while the rape is occurring, are the two women shown on opposite sides of the same partitioning wall? What accounts for Bergman's contriving that Maria and Tomas be half-siblings? Why make Tomas a homosexual? (Does it matter that his disillusionment results from being cast off by a male lover and not, as Jenny had previously assumed, by a wife?) And why should he loom so large in the story when he seems to serve as little more than a confidant who has casually drifted into Jenny's life and will just as casually drift away?

Although analysis of the film as an autonomous work of art yields no satisfactory solution, the puzzle's pieces do begin to fit together if viewed from Bergman's perspective. Jenny's grandparents reflect both the Åkerbloms and, to a greater degree, Bergman's parents in their old age —particularly during the years just before Karin's death when Erik Bergman's infirmity made him so dependent on her. The film never makes a sufficiently convincing connection between Jenny's guilt and the grandparents who exist in death's shadow to warrant their prominence in the story; if one sees the film as a projection of Bergman's own story, however, that connection is quite apparent.

How closely Bergman ties Jenny to himself becomes most evident at the conclusion, when he has her recall moments from childhood and youth that have affected her dreams. One instantly recognizes the provenance of the wardrobe tale, which has by this time become a Bergman hallmark. The "crazy artist" Jenny takes as a lover in rebellion against her middle-class upbringing surely corresponds to the "nymphomanical" poet who was briefly his mistress during Sagoteatern days. The reference to cousin Johan's burial appears to mix Anna Åkerblom's schizophrenic stepson Johan and the funeral of one of Erik Bergman's colleagues which so upset young Ingmar that he failed his Latin examination. And Jenny's memory of the day she saw a rabid dog in her grandmother's face calls to mind Henrik's old aunt in *Summergame*—that figure of

death to whom Bergman assigned his grandmother's maiden name.*
Although these details do not really explain the dreams, they tend to
confirm that the dreams sprout from tangled roots in Bergman's past.
By itself, of course, this observation adds little to one's interest in the
film. What matters is how it bears on the other parts of Jenny's story,
especially the curious relationship between Jenny and the homosexual
Jacobis which implies so much more than the film ever brings to
realization.

Although the dreams are evidently related to what the three visitors
to Jenny's hospital room disclose when she awakes, the dense symbolism in each overwhelms the adjacent developments; moreover, the reference to "a lifelong illness" in the suicide note indicates that the dreams'
meaning lies much further back than Jenny's adult years. What that
meaning involves can be better understood through the design the five
dreams trace. Since the dreamer has attempted suicide, it seems appropriate that the first and last should be about Jenny's "death," yet, clearly,
her mind is troubled by something other than physical death. The odor
of "accelerating necrosis" in the first dream refers to the masquerade
that is the disease of life—and, as Jenny acknowledges both in her
suicide note and after the effect of the Nembutol wears off, her life has
consisted solely of "playacting." The last dream resumes the metaphor:
Jenny must be buried quickly because her corpse stinks, yet this corpse
protests that she is alive. Equally important is the fact that Jenny appears
as a young girl in both dreams. Whatever it is that has led her to perceive herself as a sham, exuding a powerful stench, is associated with
her childhood.

The second and fourth dreams sound the same theme in minor
chords. One, in exposing the hypocrisy of "forgiveness," blames Jenny's
parents for her guilt. The other pulls away the self's "mask" (its skin) to
reveal, in the next patient, that only dread is left in the self's interior;
Jenny is then guilty of failing her grandfather (her substitute father) by
being unable to give meaning to his life—and to her own. Neither dream,

---

*Bergman has always talked about of his grandmother with great fondness —and every-
where else in *Face to Face*, the grandmother is presented as an admirable person. Yet one
also recalls Margareta's testimony that the basis for her brother's infamous story about
being locked in the wardrobe was actually a punishment by his grandmother. Anna
Åkerblom was a strong-willed woman who spoke her mind; as a boy, Bergman may very
well have witnessed the scene Jenny describes.

Another link to the personal background of *Summergame* is Jenny's memory of cousin
Johan's death: Henrik, Bergman has said, was based in part on a cousin who had died of
polio.

however, indicates what is past forgiveness, what accounts for the emptiness. That terrible message, which ties the dreams not just to each other but also to the rest of the film, is encoded in the middle dream.

Like the first and last, this third dream revolves around death—or, more accurately, guilt represented as death—and although the corpse here is not Jenny's, it is that of her opposing "self," Maria. Two aspects of the self-encounter are especially significant. First, the corpse's legs spread by the gynecological stirrups; as Jenny's indictment for lacking compassion further indicates, it is a reverse image of Maria's earlier attempt to reach her hand between Jenny's thighs. And that allusion, obviously, also relates it to the rape, where Jenny's identity and Maria's seem to cross. Second, another exchange of identities: Jenny's appearance in Tomas's role as gynecologist. Given, in addition to the doubling of Jenny with the lesbian Maria, the subsequent revelation of Tomas's homophilia, should one assume that Jenny's psychic torment owes to a latent homosexuality? Put another way: given Jenny's evident function as Bergman's persona, is the real link between the film's two halves—the inner story consisting of the dreams and the outer story in which Jenny's mirror relationship with the Jacobis provides the only evident structure —finally Bergman's own confession of repressed homosexuality?

The question has arisen before of course: in various guises, homosexuality has intruded into Bergman's fictions ever since the 'forties. During the last decade of the filmmaker's career, however, it becomes a major concern. Four of the five filmscripts that follow *Face to Face* deal with the subject, and in at least two of them (*From the Life of the Marionettes* and *Fanny and Alexander*), it is the key to the protagonist's "discovery" about himself. And yet, in these last films as in the earlier ones, the very evidence which prompts the question points to a different answer. In virtually every instance, the homosexuality occurs in conjunction with sexual anxieties involving either the mother or a readily identifiable mother figure. One can only speculate as to why Bergman mixed the two. Perhaps one taboo surfaced in the shape of another. More likely, he was reflecting the now generally discredited belief that homosexuality results from an untransferred sexual attachment to the mother. (One recalls that, after describing to Vilgot Sjöman his emotionally painful childhood—in which the pain was mostly caused by his mother's swings from tender affection to indifference—he commented, "It's a wonder I didn't turn out a homosexual or a masochist.") But whatever the reason, it is the Oedipal anxiety expressed through homosexual fears, not homosexuality itself, which churns the fiction. So, too, in *Face to Face*.

The names Bergman chooses are usually significant: sometimes they allude to a radical component in his concept of the character; sometimes—as with "Tomas Jacobi"—they suggest an association with previous characters. The first Tomas in a Bergman film is the writer in *Prison*; the second, the minister in *The Communicants*. Symbolically, both are crippled by the mother. The writer's problem is to resolve the conflict in his mind represented by two women: a wife with whom he presumably cannot function sexually and a curiously innocent prostitute who provides a fantasy of returning to childhood. Similarly, the minister's obsession with the purity he idealizes in his dead wife (whose middle name, interestingly, is Magdalena) prevents him from loving his mistress. The surname "Jacobi" links him to the Colonel in *Shame*. Although, from Jan's perspective, Colonel Jacobi assumes the role of the rival father within the psychological pattern of that film, when he asks Eva to be his lover, just once, he behaves like a confused, hurt little boy, offering his mother a gift (his life savings) to prove his love—and, clearly, Eva responds out of motherly solicitude, not because she is erotically aroused. The sexual disturbance implied by these associations becomes more apparent through the imagery Tomas uses to describe the balefulness of existence—just before confessing his homosexuality. "Man is a wolf to man" nods toward *Hour of the Wolf*; the reference to consciousness as the evolutionary product of a cancerous cell evokes *A Passion* and *Cries and Whispers*.

"Maria" implies the same source of anxiety (the allusion would be obvious even if Bergman had not applied the name to a long string of women related in some manner to mother). On the surface, Bergman seems to call greater attention to this character than the story warrants, and nothing in the plot would explain why she is portrayed as a lesbian. Seen from the film's Oedipal underside, however, she takes on major importance—not directly as the mother but as a mirror image of Jenny —the "son" burdened with guilt for his feelings toward the mother. Maria's homosexuality, like her mental illness, is a distorted reflection of "Jenny's" sexual desires. But the converse of this relationship is equally relevant. If Maria is Jenny-as-son, Jenny is also Maria-as-mother: thus, when Jenny stands accused of failing to show compassion, it is really the mother who is being indicted for her aloofness, for the same "indifference" that so wounds Agnes in *Cries and Whispers*. Most significantly, the inverted pairings of both equations are brought together in the rape scene. On complementary halves of what is effectively a split screen, a young man tries to force his penis into Jenny's dry vagina while Maria lies huddled in a fetal position on the other side of the wall. In a sense, Maria has summoned Jenny and willed what is happening in the adjacent room. But what is willed is also being denied: as "fetus," Maria escapes the punishment of consciousness—much like Joakim in reentering the womb at the conclusion of "The Fish."

Seeing the rape in this light transforms it from an overdramatization of Jenny's emotional frigidity into the central event of the film's first half from which all the dreams of the second half radiate. It is especially pertinent to deciphering the final dream: if the rape depicts the Oedipal crime, the funeral represents the trial and sentence. The odor of death young Jenny exudes betrays the guilt she has tried to mask. Though a pose of innocence, her Little Red Ridinghood costume reflects that guilt. (The fairy-tale heroine, after having been warned against the wolf by her mother, seems compelled to meet the fascinating, devouring embodiment of evil that Bergman once called "the devil without horns" —and that Tomas evokes as the figure of the cancerous depravity in the human mind.) When Jenny sets the coffin afire, she repeats what she had tried to accomplish through suicide: destroy her Little Red Ridinghood self—the child in whom the guilt resides. But that inner-most self clings horribly to life—like the horse with "a damnable will to live" in *A Passion*, and like Maria, whom Tomas compares to the dog he saw doused with burning gasoline.

More intriguing than the relationship between the suicide and the rape, of course, is the further connection between this final dream and Bergman. Surely, one need not ponder too long over the derivation of the minister who decrees that young Jenny must be buried, or what is symbolized by her parents' securing the lid to her coffin, or why the corpse cries out to her mother. Although both his parents were in their graves, they continued to preside over his nightmares—as his next filmscript would demonstrate in even more lurid fashion than *Face to Face*.

The Petrified Prince

Sparked by a revival of Bergman's enthusiasm for a joint effort with Fellini, the plan was to make an anthology film for Warner Brothers of the sort the Italians had successfully packaged in the 'fifties and early 'sixties. The addition of Mike Nichols as the third director rounded out the scheme in which each filmmaker, working independently, was to contribute an erotic fantasy. Only Bergman went so far as to write a script, however, and the project died—as he probably knew it would even if his colleagues had completed their assignments. *The Petrified Prince* is not a naughty comedy poking fun at the follies of love but a sexual nightmare in which the most strictly guarded taboos are violated. Despite the permissive climate of the 'seventies, it was most unlikely that a major American studio could commit itself to such a film.[1]

Why, then, did Bergman take the trouble to write the script? Perhaps because of the licence that came from knowing it stood virtually no chance of ever playing before the cameras. The script's sexual content is one expression of that licence, but there is another, equally important: a dialogue with himself about the conflict between the falsifying demands of an art that deals in solutions and his need to release a destructive truth.

The vehicle for this debate is the Director, a comic figure who patently represents Bergman. When the Prince first meets his princess-to-be midway through the story, the Director interrupts. "If this were a fairy tale," he tells the audience, one would only have to say that the couple lived happily ever after and "the film would be over."

> But this isn't a fairy tale. Granted, it isn't documented fact either but a small mirror held up to a dream, a serious game, something both cruel and kind, something mysterious which follows its own laws and goes its own way. So those who think I sit here making it all up are very much mistaken. I listen, and I get an answer —pictures, gestures, words. Then I write it all down. If I tried to interfere, to arrange and create things, I'd soon come to grief—all those figures who now living their own lives would become petrified, wither up, grow lifeless and mute. Far too often, I have played the part of the mass murderer, leaving behind me through the years far too many small lifeless mummies. The temptations in the wonderful world of film are sometimes overpowering, and who doesn't want to earn his living and drive about in limousines twenty yards long? But here at any rate you see a director who for the moment resists all temptations and gives an account of what happens, deplorable and tiresome though it is.

In other words, all Bergman would have to do to earn his "limousine" is supply Hollywood with the kind of film Martin Grandé directs in *Prison*; instead, whether because of choice or compulsion, he holds a mirror to a dream—his dream. With *The Magic Flute*, he had invited the world to rejoice in a fairy tale in which art confirms a forgiving illusion; *The Petrified Prince* pulls away that veil of innocence to disclose the fairy tale's grotesque underside.

The Director introduces the film by stepping in front of the curtain to offer "some sort of explanation" for the performance the audience is about to see. But before he gets very far, a "very obscene" picture of King Maximilian and Queen Katarina of Slavonia engaged in a "Homeric fuck" flashes against the curtain. Apologizing for the mistake, he begins again to describe this film about Napoleon's march across Europe in the summer of 1807—only to be interrupted once more by the sexual earthquake in the royal bedchamber. When the King's exertions bring on a heart attack and Katarina exults over his death, the Director, appalled by the "fiasco," withdraws behind the cameras. From that place of safety, he says, he will "weave a number of unusual spells and perform some trivial conjuring tricks." But, he adds, "if you look carefully, you may catch a glimpse of me in a mirror or even hanging from a chandelier."

This fragmented opening establishes two fundamental motifs. The first—labored and scarcely original—caustically exposes the effect of male sexual anxiety. The King commands the Queen to say that his penis is "bigger than all others"; Napoleon needs to conquer because he is short (later, he responds to the news that he has slain 193,586 men with a lament that his penis "should be so small"). "I have loaded my gun," the King announces on the verge of climax; immediately, Napoleon's cannons discharge, killing thousands. The King's lust marks him as a buffoon; Napoleon's murderous obsession, springing from the same source, earns him the world's homage and the Pope's blessing for his "Great Mission in Imitation of Jesus Christ." Although the King is quickly dispatched and Napoleon will appear only occasionally in an ancillary role, the anxiety their juxtaposition displays becomes the central element of the film.

The second motif emerges from the tension between the Director and the film he cannot control. Despite his effort to present an implicitly political drama about Napoleon (the kind of film the Swedish Left was criticizing Bergman for not making), another film—about which, significantly, he admits he "knows everything"—keeps breaking through. When, finally, the Director surrenders to this irrepressible tale, he retreats into Bergman's familiar role as conjurer. But even though he will do his best to ply the tricks by which art changes reality, an alert viewer (i.e., one who has paid attention to Bergman's previous performances) will spy the Director himself behind the dissimulating mirror.

As is often the case in a Bergman film, the argument is rooted in the protagonist's childhood. Prince Simson (or, as it would be rendered in English, Samson) was a delicate, gifted boy who loved music and wrote songs and poems. For all this, the King despised him. The Queen, on the other hand, doted on him and sheltered him from the unpleasant aspects of life—especially the sexual foulness of women. As a result of her protectiveness, and in reaction to his father's violence and exaggerated virility, Simson immersed himself in study. His only friend was a young abbé. When the abbé's sudden death ended their passionate (and implicitly homosexual) friendship, Simson became mute and paralyzed.

The machinery of the plot is set in motion by the King's death. Determined to share the throne with her son, Katarina must first restore his health. She believes she understands the cause of his strange malady—as the most renowned prostitute in Vienna before she married Maximilian, she learned a great deal about men—and hires a young whore named Elise to cure him. Yet, despite her thirst for power and what seems at times a genuine concern for Simson's well-being, she is still the possessive mother. In choosing Elise, a peasant girl who has just given birth to a bastard daughter, Katarina is convinced she has insured against any possibility that Simson's sexual initiation might lead him to fall in love.

Predictably, she has miscalculated, and the "second act" of this deadly farce consists of her jealous rage against Elise and an unrelenting effort to crush her son. Eventually, however, Elise's patient education of the Prince and Napoleon's arrival in Slavonia produce a happy ending —though not in the conventional manner of the fairy tale. When the Queen's "negotiations" with the French conqueror in her bedchamber convince him of his sexual prowess, he makes her the kingdom's absolute ruler. Katarina's first act is to banish the young lovers. That night, after the exiles pitch a tent in a meadow, Elise pulls the frightened Simson on top of her. To his astonishment and enormous relief, he experiences his first orgasm—and for the first time in his life, he is able to say "I love you."

Even this very brief synopsis makes it quite apparent that *The Petrified Prince* functions as an allegorical autobiography, based less on fact than on the distortion of fact into a personal myth that has had a more powerful impact on his mental life. Simson's paralysis, a psychosomatic manifestation of his emotional crippling by Katarina, patently refers to the psychological disturbance rooted in Bergman's relationship with his mother—to the extent of evoking his comparison of his childhood to life in an iron lung. Katarina is the Queen of the Night who would keep this Tamino bound to herself by preventing him from attaining manhood. Nowhere is the Oedipal terror in Bergman's labyrinth of fictions more furious than in this "fairy tale" depicting mother as a devouring sexual monster. Awakening in Katarina's bed one night, Simson realizes that he is pinned under his mother's body while she is being penetrated from behind by a succession of brutish lovers. (The similarity to Anna's *coitus a tergo* in *The Silence* says a great deal about the psychological meaning of that film.) Suddenly, she spreads her legs wide apart over her son's face, bends backward, thrusts her pudenda forward, and grabs his hair, holding him fast.

> *Katarina*: What is it you see? A hole, that's what you see, nothing else. That is the truth of truths and the reality of realities for ever and ever. That's where impurity comes out, that's where impurity is forced in. In there is the focal point of life, there is pleasure and degradation. Out of that hole *you* came, my young prince. Out of that big hole with its smell of tainted fish you forced your way one early morning, blue in the face and with your umbilical cord round your neck and with muck all over your body and you stank of blood and I hated you just as I hated you from the very moment I knew you were there inside my body, which was the most beautiful body in the world and which you destroyed with your ugly little head and your limp arms and flabby legs. Now I'm going to put you in again. Now I'm going to stifle you in there in the dark, now you're going to feel what it's like to oppose your mother; you're going to be punished for your faithlessness, my darling little prince. You will never come out again, never speak again. I'll stifle your screams.

To free himself from her paralyzing influence, Simson must re-create mother and then develop through her a new perception of women. As a whore from the same bordello where the Queen once practiced her trade, Elise is obviously a younger Katarina. The first step in the Prince's reenactment of his childhood is to strip mother of her "dirty" sexuality —to "Virginize" her. Thus, during his initial encounter with Elise, her baby daughter seems an inseparable part of her physical being; significantly, Simson first breaks his silence to express awe when Elise, in introducing him to a woman's body, shows him her lactating breast. (While she holds his head to her as though her were an infant, he then sucks at her nipple "for a long time, quite still.") Like Mia in *The Seventh Seal*, who, in the company of her child, awakens the Knight to life's meaning when she shares the strawberries and milk with him, Elise embodies the ideal of woman as the unselfish nurturer. But, purified of all sexual threat, she is also a child in woman's guise, a female counterpart of the self. When she and Simson are imprisoned in the Queen's dressing chamber while Napoleon and Katarina copulate in the adjoining bedroom, they paint smiles on their faces and try to dispel fear by playing a children's game in which each challenges the other to name the greatest number of real things—a kind of magical evocation of objects to drive out from the mind thoughts of what is happening in the next room.*

So long as Elise holds to her roles as Virgin Mother and playmate, Simson finds her presence reassuring, but any show of affection that stirs his sexual feelings ignites the volatile confusion of emotions stemming from Katarina. When, moved by compassion, Elise gives Simson a cat and instructs him on how to pet it, a rush of excitement causes his hands to crush the purring creature on his lap.** A subsequent scene, which begins with "the children" (as Bergman calls them) huddling in a dark corner, illustrates the point with still greater force. Assuring Simson that, "for all eternity, nobody knows where we are," Elise kisses his "little and anxious" penis and promises to protect it. Simson feels safe, but when his penis swells, producing mixed sensations of pain and pleasure, the image of mother as a sexual partner displaces that of the playmate, and he screams. Frightened, she hides behind a velvet curtain, but he repeatedly plunges a paper knife through the cloth. Blood drips from the blade. Yet, to his astonishment, Elise emerges unharmed, saying, "You missed. That was lucky, wasn't it? But someone else hid behind the curtain. The Queen. . . . Your mother is dead."

By separating Elise and Katarina, the "lucky" substitution appears to solve the Prince's problem. Up to this moment, he has spoken only a few words, and never more than one short sentence at a time; now he fully recovers his voice:

Take the carcass away. Chuck her on the dunghill. Give her to the dogs. No, come to that, they've never done me any harm, they

---

*Similar magical escapes into childhood from menacing adult "truths," set in rooms that seem not to belong to the rest of the world, occur in several of the 'forties films (most notably in *Prison*).

**A similar conversion of the need for tenderness into sadistic aggression had been a central element as early as *Torment*, where Caligula's account of drowning a cat illustrates his erotic disorientation, and as recently as *A Passion*, where the mutilation of the sheep is implicitly linked with Andreas's sexually incited violence.

might be poisoned. Lay her in the forest, on an anthill, and when only the bones are left, picked nice and clean, put her on the high altar in the cathedral and call her Mother Martyr; let the archbishop kiss her pubic bone and call her The Holy Mother.

His exultation comes to an abrupt end, however. Though blood pours through her fingers as she holds her hand over the deep wound into her heart, Katarina is not dead. "You never could do anything properly," she says with a smile playing on her lips. "You gave me a second of pleasure, I admit. For one short moment, I was impressed." Then she strides triumphantly out of the room.

Given the mother's tenacious spell—which, this scene suggests, continues to thwart her son beyond her death—how is "Tamino" to enter "Sarastro's Temple" and bring the fairy tale to a happy resolution? On the surface, the ending Bergman supplies skirts the problem. Napoleon's entrance immediately after the stabbing seems a deus ex machina; that he then rewards Katarina's performance in the bedroom by making her absolute monarch implies that the drama turns either on the Queen's lust for political control or on her need to prove she has not lost her sensual power—and, of course, neither is the case. The banishment of her son appears still less appropriate: clearly, the story is driven by his struggle to rid himself of her, not the other way around. Nevertheless, the ending does conform to the story's inner logic if Napoleon is seen as Simson's double. In this respect, the short French Emperor's destructive fury at the script's beginning is not an extension of the King's concupiscence but the son's compensation for his sexual inadequacy. While the Emperor marches his army across Europe as though he were a little boy playing with tin soldiers, he worries about the size of his penis, which is no bigger than the Prince's. Only the Queen can ease his doubt about his masculinity. Significantly, once that occurs, the source of the conflict between mother and son is removed: Napoleon now recognizes the Queen as an "injured mother" and, like a son trying to prove that his love for her is superior to his father's, awards her the realm formerly tyrannized by the priapic King. The expulsion of the Prince that leads from this act is actually the start of independence, the arrival at maturity. As the fairy tale would have it, Simson's orgasm signals his ability, at last, to disentangle Elise and Katarina.

Almost a decade and a half earlier, Bergman had described a dream to Vilgot Sjöman in which his mother prevented his making love to a woman in the Sophiahemmet parsonage; the most troubling aspect of the dream was that his mother and his wife Käbi kept changing into one another—a symbolic manifestation, he said, of the "interblending which has been constant with me." Although he may not have had that specific dream in mind while writing *The Petrified Prince*, he was evidently thinking of the problem it depicted. And, also, of Käbi. Elise is the fourth candidate Katarina interviews for the assignment of curing her son when she returns to her former bordello, and the fact that Elise is still nursing her baby daughter gives the Queen assurance that Simson will not fall in love with her; Käbi was Bergman's fourth wife, and the fact that she was married and had a young daughter when he met her brought a scent of scandal to their courtship. Elise begins her tutelage of Simson by coaxing him into discarding his "smelly old top hat" and the strange clothes he has worn ever since the onset of his paralysis; one of the first signs that Käbi had taken Bergman in hand was the sudden change from his bohemian dishabille—especially the distinctive beret which had served cartoonists as an identifying mark—to an almost conservative wardrobe.

The most significant similarity, however, is one which points beyond the strictly personal psychosexual meaning of the fairy tale to the implications of that meaning for Bergman as an artist. Like Käbi, Elise belongs to a circle of distinguished friends in the arts. She speaks of her intimate acquaintance with Hölderlin before he went mad; she once had a liaison with Goethe, who confused her with his first love, Frederike Brion; most important of all, she has maintained especially close ties with Beethoven, who, midway through the story, arrives at the palace. Obviously, Bergman intends Elise to be seen as a conjunction of feminine innocence and sensuality that stimulates the artist to create. Yet nothing in the fairy tale itself warrants the inclusion of this element; its explanation lies behind Simson and Elise in the relationship between Bergman and Käbi. Thus, Simson's introduction to Beethoven through Elise alludes to Käbi's schooling her husband in the masterly composition of the quartets—lessons which he began applying in the Chamber Films. That Simson, on being told by Elise that Beethoven continues to write music even though he is deaf, is inspired to take his first steps since his paralysis evidently refers to Bergman's own emergence from an artistic "paralysis," the new beginning in film which he attributed in large part to Käbi's influence. (*Through a Glass Darkly*, one recalls, carries the dedication "To Käbi"; in *The Petrified Prince*, Beethoven tells of having written "Für Elise" in gratitude for Elise's help in nursing him back to health.) Perhaps the most revealing allusion to Käbi's role in

Bergman's recovery occurs in the fairy tale's key scene. From the moment "the children" begin learning to enjoy each other erotically until Simson stabs at Elise through the curtain and "kills" his mother, Beethoven, alone with his "demons," is trying to compose in an adjoining room. Clearly, the strange drama being accompanied by the "broken music" illustrates the nature of the "demons" tormenting the composer—not only Beethoven, of course, but also Bergman himself. Just as Simson is going through the painful process of separating Elise from Katarina, Bergman, during his years with Käbi, was confronting the parallel problem.

But if the association with Käbi restored the artist in him, it was only to deal more openly with the cause of his disease. Although, like *The Magic Flute*, *The Petrified Prince* is brought to a happy end, the sinister image he had twisted into the shape of the Queen of the Night would continue to resist exorcism.

The Final Phase

When Alan Blair's translation of *The Petrified Prince* reached Warner Brothers on December 30, 1975, two other projects had eclipsed it in Bergman's mind. His next film, *The Serpent's Egg*, a major undertaking in association with DeLaurentiis, was to be shot in the summer. Closer at hand, his version of *The Dance of Death* was scheduled for an April 1 premiere at Dramaten—and at this stage of his career, Bergman regarded productions of the Strindberg masterworks as the instruments by which posterity would measure his achievement in Swedish theater.

Rehearsals began in January; with memories of his dazzling interpretation of *A Dream Play* in 1970 still fresh, the public awaited news of how the director intended to meet one of the most difficult challenges posed by Sweden's national playwright. But the front page headlines in the evening papers of January 30 only indirectly concerned the play. At midday the police had interrupted the rehearsal, ludicrously blocked the theater's exits to prevent their quarry's escape, and arrested Bergman for failure to pay his taxes. Within hours, reports of the state's tragicomic raid against its illustrious citizen flashed around the globe.

If Bergman's fiction reflected his life, life now reflected his fiction. With *Shame*, he had extrapolated his conviction that the existence of society in all its aspects depends on its power to inflict humiliation—a theme already present in *Torment*. But the truly remarkable correspondence with the events of 1976 is to be found in *The Rite* and *A Passion*. Les Riens' tax problems and the Judge's inquiry into the nature of the triune artist function as metaphors of guilt, and although that guilt flows from psychosexual sources, it is manifested through society's oppression of the artist. Society here represents a magnified superego, exerting a constant pressure which threatens to annihilate Les Riens. Similarly, the eventual "dissolution" of Andreas Winkelman is foreshadowed by his legal problems with the tax authorities and the panic, induced by his dread of humiliation, that has led him to withdraw from society. Much as Winkelman discovers that he has retraced the experience of Andreas Fromm, Bergman would reenact that of Andreas Winkelman. Anyone who thought himself an esteemed, law-abiding citizen would be stupefied by an arrest in which he was treated like a common criminal, but the jolt Bergman received was especially severe. It was as though he had suddenly been thrust into a drama he had written—a drama in which the dispute over taxes had a far more profound meaning. The accusation was a judgment against his life.

For different reasons, Sweden looked upon the case in the same way. Although his enemies had not engaged in a conspiracy with the tax office, there was a symbolic connection between the mounting antagonism toward him among his countrymen and his public humiliation. A government official, identified only as "a senior civil servant" in the press, observed at the time of the arrest:

> Bergman is a unique figure here and, in many ways, he's not a modern Swede. He's had five wives. His films—everything he does —are a projection of his own spiritual troubles, his concerns. That's not particularly Swedish now. In Sweden we have no real debate about spiritual problems, the problems of man's nature. Everything is politicized. It's Bergman's uniqueness that makes him a target. He's a symbol of something that threatens people.

Erland Josephson, Bergman's friend and co-worker for many years, expressed the same view: "There's a saying, 'no one's allowed to grow too tall.' Bergman is one of the few totally free people here. . . . He's not a critic of the system, he's just independent of it, and that upsets people." Harry Schein, who had previously been scorched by lightning aimed at Bergman in the Film Institute controversy, also blamed "the Royal Swedish Envy": "One of the reasons Swedish equality is so advanced," he said, "is that the motive behind it is not just socialism, but an active dislike of people who are supposed to be better. You have to cut people down. Everyone must be equal. Make someone who's exceptional feel unexceptional . . . [;] if you are difficult or different in Sweden it's very hard, and Ingmar has made himself too different."[1]

In an odd sort of way, the extraordinary success abroad that had made him the object of envy at home also furnished the means by which he was to be "cut down." With the consent of the Bank of Sweden, Bergman had incorporated Persona Limited in Switzerland in 1967 to receive revenues from the sale of foreign rights to his film properties.* Initially, its purpose was to accumulate capital for *Love Duet*, the two-part film he had originally planned to make with Fellini. But that project collapsed after Bergman visited Cinecittá with a completed draft of his script and discovered that Fellini had only a page of jottings to show him. The funds were then reserved for a serial treating the Gospel accounts of Christ's last days he was to write and direct for Italian television. When that venture, too, came to nothing, he decided to dissolve the corporation and repatriate the money to Sweden, paying a capital gains tax on the aggregate. Although one office in the tax department approved the accounting used in the transaction, a higher level of the bureaucracy later concluded that, since Persona Limited had engaged in no real business, it was a shadow company, and its transferred money should therefore be taxed as ordinary personal income—at more than eight times the capital gains rate.

Eager to recover part of the difference before the statute of limitations would moot the question, the tax office tried to reach the director by telephone to arrange a meeting, but Bergman had instructed his aides to inform all callers he would not be available until after the play's premiere. The bureaucracy interpreted this as an affront to its authority and, puffing itself up with righteous indignation that any citizen should set himself above the state, decided to descend on this obstreperous scofflaw while he was in the theater. (Just before the "raid," evidently motivated by more than a desire to enforce the tax code, someone tipped the press.) But the embarrassment of being arrested in front of his colleagues was only the beginning of the ordeal. Even though, having left management of his intricate financial affairs to others, Bergman could offer little information, he was taken away for three hours of

---

*Sven Harald Bauer, the lawyer who had counseled Bergman on tax matters and arranged the Swiss incorporation, lent his name to Les Riens' theatrical agent in *The Rite*. When the fictional Bauer notifies the artists that they have suffered financial reverses, in part because of their legal problems, Sebastian consents to sell his Swiss apartment to raise tax-free funds. What Bergman had meant as an inside joke was given an ironic twist by the government's action against him in his own tax case.

questioning; then, on returning him to his Stockholm apartment, the police searched the rooms, seized his private papers, and confiscated his passport. Bergman was in a state of shock. Three days later, suffering from the delusion that he was being pursued by a spectral self, he entered a mental ward. His confinement—first at the Karolinska hospital, then at Sophiahemmet—lasted almost two months.

The controversy that rocked Sweden while he lay recuperating in a psychiatric bed also provoked international comment. What did this callous handling of an artist say abut a country that prided itself on the humane treatment of its most violent criminals? What fueled the puritanical zeal that made perfect compliance with a confusing, illogical tax code an article of faith in the secular religion of Social Democracy? Bergman was not the only fish in the taxman's net. Among several others, Bibi Andersson had been apprehended on the suspicion that she had received wages paid through Persona Limited which were then funneled into overseas bank accounts. Her treatment was at least as outrageous as Bergman's: even though no charges had been filed, she was detained for questioning for more than a day, and during that time she was denied permission to notify her home of her whereabouts or to reassure her young daughter. Another case, unrelated to Bergman's, involved Astrid Lindgren, the creator of *Pippi Longstocking* whose children's books had made her the most popular author in Swedish history. After announcing, with an exquisite sense of the ridiculous, that the tax rate on her earnings exceeded the earnings themselves, Miss Lindgren published a satire about a strange utopian land in which such things could happen. Sweden laughed uneasily at itself. But the Bergman fracas was in a category all its own—and not only because of his world fame or because the terrible consequences of his arrest focused attention on the danger posed by arrogant bureaucrats. In a sense, the particulars of the tax dispute were incidental. The "demon director" (as the press loved to call him) had cast himself as the incorrigible outsider from the start of his career; that the weight of authority should one day come down on him was almost inevitable. There was a widespread feeling in Sweden, even among those who were ready to criticize the tax laws or to scorn the police's methods, that Bergman had invited his punishment, that he somehow deserved what had happened. The tax imbroglio bore a curious resemblance to Strindberg's trial for blasphemy in 1884. It would soon have a similar outcome.

In March a criminal investigation arrived at the conclusion that Bergman had been innocent of any wrongdoing; with this exoneration, it seemed the ugly affair was behind him. But the embarrassed tax authorities still had blood in their eyes, and even though there was no longer any question of fraud, a second review of Bergman's financial records produced other claims. The public, however, knew nothing of these developments until a new bombshell exploded on April 22—a week before the first installment of *Face to Face* on Swedish television. In a long letter to *Expressen*, topped by headlines that filled the front page, Bergman announced he had left the country.

He did not go quietly. Far from being a tax evader, he wrote, he had resisted the temptation to follow the lead of other prosperous Swedes who changed their legal residence to a more tax-lenient foreign country. (The tax rate consumed all but thirty- to forty-thousand dollars of his annual income.) Moreover, had he been guilty of the charges initially brought against him, he could have left Sweden for some overseas haven. Or, long before his arrest, he could have hidden the "incriminating" evidence when the state's auditors began their examination. Instead, he had innocently cooperated with the investigators in their requests for the company's books, unaware that he was marked for persecution in a "competition among bureaucrats." Not until his health had improved sufficiently to enable him to meet with the tax authorities did he realize how cruelly stupid their game was. On April 2, he reported, they informed him that the Persona Limited funds were subject to taxation not only as revenues pertaining to the liquidated corporation but also as part of profits earned by Cinematograph in 1975. According to Bergman's reckoning, the same money would thus be taxed twice—at the combined rate of 139 percent. But this crushing blow could be avoided, they said. All he had to do was pay the tax assessed against him *in the original dispute*. Bergman quickly grasped the real issue. Shamed by the publicity given the case at home and abroad, the tax office was now trying to take advantage of his depression and fear of further opprobrium to proclaim its vindication. But the "poker players" overplayed their hand. "I was so furiously angry that I became healthy. The dread and feeling of ineradicable humiliation I had dragged around day and night evaporated in a few hours and never returned."

Upon considering his situation and the events that led to it, the letter continued, he made several hard decisions. "If I don't create, I don't exist"—and having been raped of a sense of security in Sweden, he could no longer work in the country. Therefore, despite the risk that his artistry would prove inseparable from his familiar milieu and native language, resettlement elsewhere had become imperative. So that no

"Conscientious Swedish Taxpayer" should think he sought to escape his obligations, he was leaving all his assets at the disposal of the tax office in case the legal judgment went against him—and if that sum should be insufficient, he pledged to discharge the debt "to the last *ore*." Meanwhile, he was dissolving Cinematograph, abandoning the studio he had been building on Fårö, suspending work on the film he had planned to begin shooting in July *(The Serpent's Egg)*, and canceling Cinematograph's production of a film to have been directed by Kjell Grede; all affected personnel, he promised, would receive full compensation. Finally, he confessed his political disillusionment:

> I have been a convinced Social Democrat. With genuine passion have I believed in this ideology of grey compromise. I thought my country the best in the world, and if I continue to think so, it is perhaps because I have seen so very little of other lands. My awakening was a shock, partly because of my intolerable humiliation, partly because I saw that anyone in this country, whenever and however, can be attacked and abased by a special kind of bureaucracy that grows like a galloping cancer . . . and to which society has given powers exercised by individuals who are in no way mature enough to handle them.

While Sweden read this farewell and buzzed about it, Bergman and his wife were in Paris, resting and slowly trying to appraise their future in exile. That weekend they flew to Los Angeles, where he told the press of his relief at having extricated himself from "a situation which could have been written by Kafka." Later, they visited the studios. A generous guest, Bergman stated that he felt at home because, irrespective of their citizenship, motion picture people belonged to the same great sodality. But resettlement in Hollywood was never really a possibilty. He was a European, and despite his work in cinema, his roots were in theater. For weeks, the Bergmans traveled from hotel to hotel in several European capitals until they arrived in Munich to prepare to shoot *The Serpent's Egg*. They found it a pleasant city, reminiscent of Stockholm in some ways. And theater was a main motor of its throbbing cultural life. After attending a performance of *Hamlet* at the Residenzteater and then meeting with its chief, Kurt Meisel, he decided that he would establish his domicile in Munich and affiliate himself with that theater. Once again, Bergman seems to have been under the influence of Strindberg's star: the playwright's flight from Sweden after the blasphemy trial had also taken him to Bavaria.

Like Les Riens, that fall Bergman may have derived some satisfaction from the consequences of his contest with the state. After unbroken control of the government since 1932, the Social Democrats lost to a coalition of bourgeois parties in the September elections. To be sure, opposition to the ruling party had been gathering strength over the previous six years (in the 1973 election, the bourgeois coalition had pulled to a tie with the socialist left), and Astrid Lindgren's deft attack probably rallied sympathies for change more effectively than the Bergman case. Yet what had happened to Bergman could not easily be expunged from the average Swede's consciousness: it ripped against the self-congratulation in which the nation had swaddled itself for having achieved a "middle way" between full socialism and unbridled capitalism through the West's most highly developed welfare state. If few Swedes cast their ballots for the opposition because they supported Bergman, the events of January and April had nonetheless raised disquieting questions about the state's exercise of power and stiffened resolve to begin curbing it.

Despite the shift in parliament, the tax case would drag through the courts for another three years. It ended, unceremoniously, with the court's ruling that Bergman's obligation amounted to about $35,000—a small fraction of what the tax office had assessed and much less than the lost taxes on his income every single year he resided in Munich. Under Swedish law, the state was required to pay all court costs—a sum thirteen times what it collected from the defendant. Bergman had won vindication.

To the cinema world, of course, the chief concern in 1976 was not the case's legal aspect but the effect Bergman's resettlement in Munich would have on his films. For over thirty years he had insisted that he needed to express himself in his native language among familiar surroundings and to work within an intimate circle of professional associates. How would an artist so firmly rooted in Swedish soil react to transplantation under such unfavorable conditions? His experience with the concept of an "international film" in The Touch did not augur an easy adjustment. On the other hand, there was a feeling, never quite overtly stated, that the uprooting might prove providential. Bergman's reluctance to yield to economic reality and accept the compromises necessitated by foreign investment in his films had meant a continuous struggle for subsistence from the meager financial resources available within Sweden; now he was being flung into the richer possibilities afforded by international film production. In addition, many of his erstwhile foreign admirers assumed that the *huis-clos* despair his films had exuded for over a decade was a product of his national environment.* By lifting him from the confined Swedish parish of Western civilization, they reasoned, exile offered the stimulating influence of new, broader vistas.

In retrospect, it seems evident that the dislocation in his personal life had minimal impact on his filmmaking career. Indeed, it is difficult to imagine what different turn his films might have taken if the tax imbroglio had never occurred. Bergman had realized at the start of the 'seventies that he would have to alternate between low budget "television films" and more ambitious films financed from abroad and made to suit a foreign market. Exile provided no relief from the exigencies that determined that strategy; the films made outside of Sweden only accentuate the pattern which had begun taking form during the first half of the decade. *The Serpent's Egg*, already in the works before Bergman left for Paris, was shot in Germany instead of Sweden, but from the start the producer was Dino De Laurentiis, the language was to be English, and an American actor was to play the principal role. Plans for *Autumn Sonata* were set in 1975, when the filmmaker described the story to Ingrid Bergman and she accepted the starring role. On a much more modest scale, this production—financed through Lew Grade's ITC, a British company, was also an "international" film. Had Ingrid Bergman not insisted that Swedish be used, it would have been made in English. And despite the fact that the Swedish-born star had started her career in Swedish films, her luminescence radiated from Hollywood. His only German-language film, *From the Life of the Marionettes*, takes the alternate route. In its small cast (all drawn from the Residenzteater company), its few, simple sets, and its close, relatively static camerawork, it resembles *The Rite* and *Scenes from a Marriage*. Except for his exile, it would have been a film made for Swedish television.

But the more important evidence that leaving Sweden did not change

---

*Vincent Canby's review of *Face to Face* typifies this interpretation. In Jenny's anxieties, he saw the reflection "of the fury that may exist just below the surface of any perfect state." Bergman's Sweden is a society convinced it has already attained a utopian future "in which all social ills have been cured. There are no political or social causes left, no excuses not to tend to the inner self. . . . In an earlier era, one might have spent a good deal of time in church, on one's knees, going through rituals of atonement, supplication and thanksgiving. But now that that has been denied, what is left?"[3] (Note: *Face to Face* had its New York premiere before Swedish television broadcast the film's first installment on April 28. Canby's review in the *New York Times* appeared on April 18—four days before Bergman's announcement of his departure from Sweden.)

the artist lies in the content of the films themselves. Whether Bergman's living room window looked out at the Alps, Östermalm, or Fårö mattered little to an artist preoccupied with an inner landscape. *The Serpent's Egg* is set in Weimar Germany, *Autumn Sonata* in a Nordic parsonage, and *From the Life of the Marionettes* in the various rooms of a bordello, police headquarters, and the middle-class couple's apartment; but, in a radical sense, these three superficially very different films are all versions of one, complex nightmare. *Fanny and Alexander*, which would mark Bergman's return to Sweden as well as the culmination of his career in cinema, is clearly linked to the last film he made before he left: young Alexander's terrors are another form of the terrors nested within the Jugend surroundings of Jenny's childhood. The intervening films are no less part of the chain.

The Serpent's Egg

Journalists who trekked to Munich in the summer of 1976 repeatedly asked Bergman how it felt to be filming abroad after thirty years within the Swedish system. He had a ready answer: although he had been afraid leaving Sweden would kill him, he found the change stimulating. The $4 million budget provided by De Laurentiis not only made possible an elaborate set but also allowed him to spend fifteen weeks in shooting the film—a luxury he never enjoyed in Sweden, where he had less than two months before the cameras. And working with foreign actors and technicians, he said, presented far less difficulty than he had imagined. Bergman's statements that the film would explore the vulnerability of twentieth-century society to the temptations of totalitarianism also raised expectations that a new chapter in Bergman's career was about to begin. Even if one inferred analogies between his fictional treatment of Germany at the time of the Munich Beer Hall putsch and his denunciation of the Swedish bureaucrats as a peril to individual freedom comparable to the Gestapo, the subject seemed certain to take him beyond his usual preoccupations.

But *The Serpent's Egg* swiftly proved a greater fiasco than *The Touch*. With near-unanimity, the critics throughout Western Europe and the United States could detect almost nothing to commend except the sets and Sven Nykvist's cinematography. Back in Sweden, those who had been jealous of the international deference to Bergman's reputation now voiced a new complaint. The amount of space the press devoted to unfavorable comment on the film was entirely without justification: had *The Serpent's Egg* not been made by "one of the gods," they argued, it would have received *no* attention at all. Even in New York, where he continued to enjoy an awesome reputation despite a decade and a half of less than favorable reviews, the reaction approached derision. With this "windiest, most banal [script] since *The Touch*," wrote the critic of the *New York Times*, Bergman had made a "dead" film about "characters who remain as anonymous as the bodies in a morgue." Perhaps, he speculated, it was Bergman's exile that explained "the peculiar sense of dislocation within his English-language screenplay, a melodrama that never quite makes any connection to the characters within it."[1] The filmmaker obviously saw the language problem as a hurdle—the protagonist is presented as a Canadian only because he is played by an American actor (David Carradine), and the German characters consistently explain why they speak English. But the fundamental fault runs far deeper. *The Serpent's Egg* rattles through the silliest, most muddled story of any Bergman film since *Such Things Don't Happen Here*.

The film begins on the night of November 3, 1923—a week before the putsch. Slightly inebriated, Abel Rosenberg climbs the stairs of his boardinghouse, enters his room, and finds his brother Max seated on a disheveled bed with a pistol in his hand and the back of his head blown off. Under questioning by Inspector Bauer the next day, Abel relates that he, his brother, and Max's divorced wife Manuela were a team of trapeze artists marooned in Berlin by a touring circus when, a little more than a month ago, Max injured his wrist. (Since Abel is neither accused nor suspected of having a hand in Max's death at this point, the interrogation patently serves as a means of exposition.) Upon his release, Abel encounters an old acquaintance, a circus organizer who—conveniently for the film's purposes—translates a newspaper's diatribe against the Jews for him. Abel, who is Jewish, proclaims his indifference; content just "to eat, sleep, and fuck," he avoids worrying about the "stupid Jews" who bring trouble down on themselves. (Can anyone watching this film doubt for a moment that Abel will soon confront his Jewishness?)

Calling on Manuela, who has found work as a cabaret entertainer, he hands her Max's suicide note, a nearly illegible lament that alludes to mysterious "poisonings." But she cannot waste time grieving over her ex-husband's death; she has another number to perform. As she rushes upstairs to the stage, Abel sees a sinister figure outside her door whom he immediately recognizes as Dr. Hans Vergérus—a man once secretly engaged to Abel's sister. Later, he will learn that Manuela has been augmenting her income from the cabaret through prostitution, and that Vergérus is her special client.

The next day, the mutilated corpse of a woman wearing Max's engagement ring is discovered—the seventh person linked in some way with the Rosenberg trapeze act to have died violently within the past month. Inspector Bauer again questions Abel, who, suddenly convinced he is being persecuted because he is a Jew, ferociously battles the police until they beat him into submission. Yet, despite his innocence of the murders, Abel feels guilty of an existential crime interwoven with his Jewishness. "Maybe it's true, what we're accused of," he says to Manuela.

> Deep down there's a morbid spot sending out signals that I can't defend myself against. And then I want to go up to some big, goddamn stupid German policeman and say: "Please hit me, beat me up, punish me, kill me if necessary. But punish me so that at last I'm relieved of the fear that torments me day and night. Hit me hard so that it hurts. It won't hurt half as much as the evil I'm forced to live with day in, day out."

Sensing his vulnerability and agitated by their own fears, even his fellow victims in this society prey on him. At the cabaret, Manuela had given him Max's hoard of dollars; when Abel decides to share Manuela's apartment, the landlady, who is also Jewish, seems to smell the money in his pocket. Taking advantage of his distress, she extorts more than a month's advance rent in dollars, then turns him out, returning the advance not in the original currency but in near-worthless marks.

The film's "first act" has introduced a mystery story, set against the background of a sick society; the second, departing from that plot, uses social decay to illustrate Abel's personal disintegration.

Through Vergérus, Manuela and Abel obtain lodging and employment (she in the laundry, he in the archives) at St. Anna's Clinic, where Vergérus is director. Soon after they have settled into their apartment in a dirty building at the rear of the clinic, she asks Abel to make love to her, but he is so revulsed by their misery and mutual dependency that he cannot summon any erotic desire; pulling free from her embrace, he rushes into the "creeping paralysis" of Berlin. His aimless flight in this "isolated world of heat deep inside a dying organism" leads him to a needlework shop. On noticing that its sign bears his own name, he hurls a rock through the window. An elderly man and a thin, bent woman emerge from the shop's dark interior. Abel seems momentarily paralyzed as he is pounded by the old proprietor's fists, but he quickly recovers and forces his pitiable adversary to the ground. He then grabs the woman, who has been screaming and spitting at him, and kisses her on the lips; overcome by disgust, she falls to the pavement.

The dreamlike nature of this episode extends into the next, which Bergman describes as a vision in a "hectic fever." Lured to a sleazy flat by a streetwalker named Mikaela, Abel witnesses another whore's humiliation of Monroe, a black cocaine dealer. Taunted for being a homosexual, Monroe pathetically tries to deny the truth by insisting that he has often copulated with Mikaela. Abel finds this theater of cruelty fascinating and adds to its horror by offering all his money as a prize if Monroe can prove his boast. Monroe starts to masturbate frantically, but before he can penetrate Mikaela, his erection droops. As the defeated man sobs, Abel throws himself on the other whore. Some time later, he awakes beside the snoring, dead-looking woman; dressing hurriedly, he steals the money he paid her.

The third "act" concludes the mystery begun in the first. Having experienced a resurgence of power by adopting the role of the oppressor, Abel continues to indulge that feeling as he heads home, bragging of his wealth to a group of poor soldiers and smugly berating the Jews. But the respite from fear ends abruptly on his return to St. Anna's: Manuela is staring through vacant, unblinking eyes, lying in a pool of vomit. Noises and a light flashing from the other side of the mirror arouse his suspicion that what has happened to Manuela is part of a fiendish operation. A chair hurled at the glass discloses a movie camera. Climbing through the hole, he then pursues the sound of footsteps into a secret building where perverse medical experiments have been conducted. An unrecognizable figure pounces from the shadows. The hunter now becomes the hunted. Chased to the edge of an elevator shaft, Abel turns on his assailant and wrestles him into the path of the descending car.

Surmising that the answer to the riddle of St. Anna's lies in its archives, Abel returns to his workplace and takes the keys from his supervisor. An iron door leads into a labyrinth of corridors. Somehow intuiting which is the right one, he follows it to a room stocked with film cannisters and switches on a projector. While images of men and women being tortured flicker on the screen, Vergérus enters. These "experiments," he explains, have been conducted under his orders—the work, not of a monster, but of a scientist who has undertaken "the first faltering steps of a necessary and logical development" which, in ten years, will produce a new society "based on a realistic assessment of man's potentialities and limitations." The perfectly formed, terribly beautiful embryo of that future is already visible through the transparent "serpent's egg" of the present moment in history. Max Rosenberg had been among more than three hundred destitute persons paid to be subjects of the study which will hatch the reptile. That the experiments have resulted in forty-six murders and suicides is dismissed as trivial. To this "comparatively small percentage of casualties," Vergérus is prepared to add the sacrifice of his own life. Inspector Bauer, he knows, has blundered onto the true nature of his operation and is on his way to the clinic. As if on cue, the police crash through the iron door, and Vergérus bites the cyanide pellet he has been holding in his cheek.

Two days later, on November 11, Bauer wakes the heavily sedated Abel in the prison infirmary to deliver good news. He has persuaded a circus in Switzerland to employ the trapeze artist. And Manuela, who is not dead after all, has been sent to a mental hospital for what is certain to be a long period of treatment. The horrors of the past week, Bauer advises, would best be forgotten as "just a lot of muddled dreams." Then, in saying good-bye, he adds a final bit of information: "By the way, Herr Hitler failed with his Munich putsch. In fact, the whole thing was a colossal fiasco. Herr Hitler and his gang underrated the strength of the German democracy."

Even judged as a melodrama, *The Serpent's Egg* makes little sense. Why, for example, should Max have sold himself as a human guinea pig—poorly paid employment, Vergérus admits, that appealed only to the most wretched—when he had a cache of dollars? Why, after having been in Germany only a month, must Manuela resort to prostitution instead of using Max's money to find work elsewhere in Europe? Why does Abel wait until Bauer pays his fare to Switzerland to leave the country? Since no restrictions have been placed on his right to travel, he could earlier have bought a ticket with Max's money.

The epilogue seems wholly unnecessary. Since everything Bauer tells Abel could as easily have been told after the police raid on St. Anna's, why devise a scene in the infirmary or sedate Abel for forty-eight hours? (That Bergman wants the end of the story to coincide with the failure of the putsch is no explanation: the police raid could just as well have occurred on November 11.) Why go to the trouble of "resurrecting" a woman Abel has believed to be dead only to report that she has been removed to a hospital for the insane? And why should Bauer counsel Abel to forget what has happened? The only plausible explanation is that he wants Abel to leave the country and remain silent so that the story of Vergérus's experiments can be kept from the German people. Yet, if this is the intention, how does it serve the interests of a strong, democratic German government?

The reference to the putsch strikes the falsest note of all. What makes Bauer's ironic assessment of German political stability relevant to the story it concludes? Does Bergman mean to suggest that Hitler rose to power in the next decade not primarily because of social unrest but because of the evil he depicts nesting in St. Anna's Clinic? Historically, of course, the Nazis did sanction inhuman medical experiments, but the film never connects Vergérus's mentality to the ideology of the Third Reich or to anti-Semitism. Indeed, Vergérus's contempt for that "incredible scatterbrain" Hitler is as great as Bauer's, suggesting that the Nazis would merely be the accidental agents of an historical inevitability. Through Vergérus, Bergman warns of a future in which all "extremely romantic ideas as to man's goodness" will have corroded away, but what acid is at work is never specified—and in the apparent absence of some such thesis, Vergérus remains simply a cliché of the power-crazed scientist found in the most vulgar fiction.

The Serpent's Egg should not be dismissed as just a silly, poorly constructed film, however. Behind the ungainly melodrama and the confusing treatment of Germany's recent history lies Bergman's persistent Ur-script.

Perhaps the chief clue to its private drama leads from the recurrence of the name "Vergérus." Like his antecedents, this Vergérus is a fervid materialist, driven by his own torment to torment others. The still more telling similarity concerns the pattern marked by the Vergérus character. In *The Face*, Royal Medical Examiner Vergérus tries to persuade the magician's wife to become his mistress and offers to install her in the town's bordello. In *A Passion*, Andreas sleeps with Elis Vergérus's wife. Here, for no reason dictated by either the plot or the putative theme, Hans Vergérus shares Manuela with Abel. In each instance, humiliation is the locus of points in a sexual triangle.*

Although this triangular arrangement seems to have a distinctive resonance for Bergman when it is identified by the name "Vergérus," it appears elsewhere as well: in *Evening of the Jesters*, *The Rite*, and, most interestingly, two films remarkably close to *The Serpent's Egg* in several essential respects, *Shame* and *Torment*. Like the conditions in Germany in 1923, the social collapse in *Shame* exposes the vicious instincts that

---

The Touch, the one other "Vergérus" film, also concerns a sexual triangle, but there, uniquely, Anders Vergérus is not a tormentor.

have been concealed by the protocols of decency. Both films present the same despairing vision. Jan Rosenberg and Abel Rosenberg are cut from the same cloth, and though Eva Rosenberg is more admirable and more resilient than Manuela Rosenberg, their functions within the scheme underlying both films almost match. And Colonel Jacobi is virtually a "Vergérus," a father figure onto whom the "son" has projected his own tortured desire for power. Just as Jacobi assumes the role of provider and protector and then extorts affection from Eva, Hans Vergérus proclaims his tender feelings for Abel and Manuela even as he victimizes them.*

Torment, like *The Serpent's Egg* a melodrama in which a mystery revolves around a room under the spell of a sadistic force, presents even more intriguing similarities. Berta's situation between Jan-Erik and Caligula corresponds to Manuela's between Abel and Vergérus; furthermore, Berta's death—a murder that turns out to be no murder at all—is analogous to Manuela's "death" and the peculiar twist given that event at the conclusion.** The link between Caligula and Vergérus extends beyond their personalities and their relationships to the two women. Abel's memory of an incident that occurred during his adolescent friendship with Vergérus almost echoes Caligula's chilling memory of drowning a cat: "Once we caught a cat and tied it down. Hans cut it open—it was still alive—and showed me how its heart beat, fast, fast, fast. Then he poked one of its eyes out with a sharp, little knife and showed me how the pupil continued to react." The elements of this sadistic anecdote are not, of course, exclusively properties of these two films. "A Shorter Tale," for example, had stressed the brutal use of "a sharp, little knife" on a creature who arouses the sadist's tender instincts; more recently, Bergman included a variation on the torturing of a cat in *The Petrified Prince*. What makes the parallel particularly significant is the fact that, in *The Serpent's Egg*, young Abel participates in the cruelty. The alter ego relationship between Jan-Erik and Caligula that exists on the underside of *Torment* becomes much more apparent in their coun-

---

*Perhaps not coincidentally, Bergman cast Max von Sydow as the humiliated protagonist in *The Face, A Passion*, and *Shame*; when Bergman wrote *The Serpent's Egg*, he had von Sydow in mind for the role of Abel Rosenberg.

**In the last scene of *Torment*, Jan-Erik says that, by staying in Berta's flat, he is in some way keeping her alive. Manuela's "reprieve" from death—followed by her sentence to a living death in the asylum—reflects a similar urge on the part of the filmmaker to have it both ways. It is as though the woman must pay the price for her sexual misconduct, yet, because the protagonist is also implicated in her sin, she must also be spared the full penalty.

terparts here. The cat story is only one of several superficially gratuitous details pointing in this direction. Why else, for instance, would Bergman strain probability to portray the German bureaucrat and the Canadian circus performer as boyhood friends, or invent an engagement between Vergérus and Abel's sister? But the strongest evidence that they are psychologically paired rests in the strange matter of the St. Anna's apartment and in Abel's transformation from victim to oppressor in the two scenes which follow.

Why would Vergérus arrange for his mistress to share a bedroom with another man? Presumably, he wants to study them as part of his research, yet the conditions of this experiment do not correspond to those imposed on his other subjects. If, as seems obvious, the motive is really voyeuristic rather than scientific, what does the voyeurism signify? The transparent mirror furnishes the clue. A quarter century earlier, Bergman had employed the very same device in "The Fish," where Joakim, emasculated by the Oedipal implications of sexual intercourse with Anne, spies through the mirror on her tryst with Peter. The situation in the St. Anna's apartment closely approximates that previous triangular relationship. Manuela corresponds to Anne, the wife on whom Joakim has imprinted a mother's image. (Can it be entirely coincidental that "St. Anna" evokes not only "Anne" but also Joakim's strained insistence on venerating his wife as an innocent?) As the symbolic pattern of subsequent events will further indicate, the real reason for Abel's impotence when Manuela asks him to make love is not, as he claims, the squalor of their circumstances, but his Oedipal guilt.* Vergérus's "voyeurism" is also a function of that guilt. In one sense, he is the superego, a father figure who stands ready to punish; in another, he reflects the vitiation which the "son" recognizes within himself.**

Once one understands the veiled significance of Abel's sexual failure, it becomes apparent that his wandering through Berlin's streets is actually a journey inward. In departing from the plot of the

---

*Curiously, the fact that Manuela has been married to Abel's brother has no bearing at all on the melodrama; on the level at which the story operates as dream, however, this detail adds another overtone of incest to her ambiguous relationship with Abel.

**Although Vergérus is the unseen observer in *The Serpent's Egg*, and his counterpart, Peter, is the one spied upon in the corresponding scene of "The Fish," the two characters stand in similar psychological relationships to the protagonists. In the film Joakim is making at the start of "The Fish," the actor who represents Joakim cannot make love to his wife because he knows that Peter is under the bed. In the hotel scene, Joakim sees ("through a glass darkly," as it were) a Peter who reflects Joakim's own repressed sexual feelings toward Anne.

mystery story, these scenes lead into the film's psychosexual center.

Manifestly, smashing the window under the shop sign bearing his name is a form of self-punishment, but it also dramatizes his need to confront the "cause" of his impotence—the parents for whom the old Rosenberg couple patently substitute. When the shopkeeper beats Abel for violating his establishment, Abel at first submits, like a child caught being bad; then, asserting his strength as an adult, he beats "father" in turn. Clearly, the key to the dreamlike incident's meaning is the "mother" who, after execrating Abel for his vileness, faints when he spitefully kisses her.

If "mother" is at the root of his inability to perform sexually with Manuela, the next scene amplifies the implications of that impotence. In offering herself sexually to Abel, Mikaela in effect repeats what Manuela (a part-time whore) had done by asking Abel to be her lover. (The rhyme and near echo in their names accentuate the two women's relationship as doubles.) The red-lit, disordered brothel to which she takes him corresponds to the St. Anna's apartment, where, in the impotent black homosexual Monroe, Abel meets the embodiment of his fears about himself. (Bergman's remark, at the time he was making *Cries and Whispers*, that he "experienced" the soul as a black person takes on added meaning in this context.) In humiliating Monroe by offering a prize if he can achieve coitus with Mikaela and then watching his futile exertions to maintain an erection, Abel "unwittingly" assumes Vergérus's role—not only in paying the desperate subjects of his experiments while he films their agony but also, more directly, in observing Abel's impotence with Manuela. Significantly, once Monroe has admitted failure, Abel asserts his own potency—not with Mikaela (whose association with Manuela, and thus with mother, is too intimidating)—but by leaping onto the second whore. Having proved his manhood, he then pockets the money he has paid the whore—in effect, claiming the prize his homosexual alter ego could not win.

In addition to concluding the mystery story *The Serpent's Egg* pretends to be, the return to St. Anna's also complements the "discoveries" illustrated by the second act. Manuela's apparent death—which nothing in the plot would adequately explain—fulfills the wish to destroy the mother's debilitating influence; in a sense, it is both a parallel to the shopkeeper's wife's fainting and the correlative to Abel's successful copulation with the whore. Smashing the mirror is a reprise of smashing the shopwindow, and the sadistic outcome of the fight with the man inside the building—another unnecessary wrinkle in the plot—corresponds to the tussle with the shopkeeper. Clearly, Abel's exploration of the mazelike interior of the archives is an investigation into the recesses of his own mind, the inevitable culmination of which is his meeting with Vergérus, his final "self-encounter."

In describing his delving into human agony, Vergérus is indirectly commenting on Abel's own tortured psyche, but his assessment embraces more than the characters in this film and has ramifications beyond the state of Germany and the world in 1923. Vergérus's analysis essentially repeats the same message of despair that Bergman has sounded in his films. At the beginning of *Face to Face*, Dr. Hans Wankel (a figure rather like Hans Vergérus) speaks of man as a defective machine; at the conclusion, philosophizing on the reasons human beings cause one another to suffer, Tomas Jacobi says, "Man is a misconstruction." In *The Serpent's Egg*, among the few decipherable phrases Abel's brother writes in his suicide note is the statement, "Man is a misconstruction"; just before biting the cynanide pellet, Vergérus unwittingly repeats the very words his victim had used to justify escaping from the "poisoning" he saw going on everywhere by killing himself.

Since, obviously, Vergérus represents not only Abel's dark side of the self but the filmmaker's as well, this terrible pronouncement has profound implications for Bergman's art. In "The Fish," Mr. Paul, the old bellhop who has installed the transparent mirror, describes his "scientific and systematic" study of human beings as leading "to spiritual death for those who engage in it." There are alternatives—cynicism or belief in God—but, he adds, "That is not the case with me. I am simply a researcher into the human condition. In part, I explore the immeasurable void within myself, and in part I have . . . my collections." Twenty years later, in *A Passion*, Elis Vergérus compiles his own photographic documents in archives recording the "meaninglessness" of human existence. Hans Vergérus's archives, of course, consist of the same material. The inference that, in each case, these pictorial studies of anxiety, cruelty, and pain are equivalent to the fictions manifesting Bergman's "research" is ineluctable. Even more significantly, what Joakim sees through Mr. Paul's transparent mirror, what mystery about Anna Fromm is captured in Elis's archives, and what Hans Vergérus's camera has observed between Abel and Manuela all strike at the heart of Bergman's Oedipal obsession. Surely, it is that unresolved conflict which determines the judgment that "Man is a misconstruction."

From this perspective, the title *The Serpent's Egg* acquires a very different connotation from the one supplied in the film. The Erasmus address, in proclaiming art dead, had compared it to a sloughed-off snakeskin, given the semblance of life only by the antlike agitation of the artist's curiosity. In an extremely complex manner, *Persona*, the film prefaced by the address, had related two women's rejection of their child to the fracturing tensions within an art attempting to deal with that subject. Its conclusion (in both senses of the word) was "*Ingenting*" — "Nothing," or "Nothingness." Given art's presupposition that man and his actions are in some way "construable," what is the consequence of the artist's realization that his subject is a "misconstruction"? Bergman's films since the mid-'sixties, generated no longer by a quest for solutions but by a perverse curiosity, have depicted the answer: art is a splintered mirror, and the self it seeks to reflect disintegrates into the void. The awful, reptilian embryo Vergérus sees perfectly formed in its shell is the monstrous guilt that will leave Bergman's art an "empty snakeskin."

Autumn Sonata

Had Bergman not already completed his next film before the critics lambasted *The Serpent's Egg* and the public ignored it, the problem of financing *Autumn Sonata* might have been insuperable. As it was, the fiasco served as a springboard vaulting the new film to heights of acclaim it probably would not have reached. "The old Ingmar Bergman is back again," an approving Swedish critic began his review. "After his escapade into the world of the international thriller, ...he has returned with *Autumn Sonata* to dissecting souls under our barren Northern sky."[1] Even the minority who found the film a somewhat boring refashioning of his customary motifs seemed relieved to be resuming their quarrel on familiar ground.

Regardless of their different trappings, of course, no two successive Bergman films are ever very different in their interiors. Like the "thriller," *Autumn Sonata* develops a view of man as a "misconstructed" being doomed to futility. Yet, in every obvious respect, the contrast between this Chamber Film—as he advertised it—and the grand production bought by De Laurentiis's money could not be more vivid: in *Autumn Sonata*, Bergman was again working within the confines of a story arranged around himself like a tight ring of mirrors. The script's concentrated intensity extended to conditions on the set. He trimmed his crew to a minimum, partly, of course, because of budgetary restraints but also because he wished to avoid the distractions that had attended the making of *The Serpent's Egg*. To be sure, the new film also featured an international star—and despite the generous compliments she received from reviewers, Ingrid Bergman's acting never fully blends with the director's style. As a native Swede, however, she did not inject the foreign element that had evidently disturbed the collaboration with Elliot Gould and David Carradine. Equally important to Bergman's sense of ease was the fact that he had returned to Scandinavia; although he shot the film in Norway instead of Sweden, he was dealing with characters and an environment he knew and understood thoroughly.

There is virtually no plot in *Autumn Sonata*, and very little actually happens; in the main, its development is a function of the monologues and colloquies which expose the past's effect on the present. As the title and Bergman's allusion to chamber music suggest, the film is a kind of sonata da camera played by four instruments: the melodic line passes back and forth between Eva, a writer and minister's wife living in a remote Norwegian parish, and her mother Charlotte, an internationally celebrated concert pianist; the continuo is supplied through Eva's husband Viktor and her dystrophic sister Lena. On learning second hand of her stepfather's death, Eva invites her mother for a long visit after a seven-year estrangement. When Charlotte arrives unexpectedly early, they greet each other effusively, in part to overcome their nervousness but also because, in their desire for mutual acceptance, they have suppressed their memories of the antagonism that has separated them. The next morning, however, Charlotte phones her agent, begging him to send a telegram that would furnish any invented excuse necessitating her immediate departure. The illusions sustaining hopes of a reconciliation have crumbled, and shortly thereafter she is on the train south.

The story that unfolds between these two events seems to focus on Charlotte. From the outset, it is apparent that she has used her career to escape those who would claim her love; even the rigors of her endless concert tours have provided a defense against invasions of emotion that might threaten her safety. Music substitutes for life; it offers a world she can solve and control. Her pernicious egoism is almost immediately evident when she discovers that Eva has removed Lena from the hospital where she had been wasting to death among strangers and taken her helpless invalid sister into her home. Charlotte panics. Having expunged Lena from her consciousness, she reacts to the prospect of a confrontation with her rejected child as though she were being called upon to face an accusing apparition. Her equally ghastly relationship with Eva seems to pose no such threat. Charlotte has always disdained this frumpy, awkward daughter whom she could dominate with such ease. But the child she thought so weak-willed has grown hard in her loneliness. Although Eva may not be aware of it, the real reason she has invited her mother is to force her to accept blame for the suffering she has caused.

Yet, despite the story's organization as an indictment of Charlotte, its complexity derives from Eva's history. Long before meeting Viktor, she had lived with a man Charlotte found unsuitable; when she became pregnant, her mother intimidated her into having an abortion and breaking off the affair. Eva now openly accuses Charlotte of having wrecked her one chance for happiness, just because she could not control the young man. But the fact that this cast-off lover subsequently robbed their house tends to confirm Charlotte's assessment of him; more significantly, it also indicates that Eva's professions of love were actually a self-deception, a means of blaming her mother for her unhappiness by forcing her to express disapproval. Similarly, although Eva attributes the abortion wholly to Charlotte's interference, the responsibility lies more heavily on herself; as Charlotte is quick to point out, if her daughter had really wanted the child, nothing could have convinced her to end the pregnancy. One begins to suspect that the real reason Eva gave in to her mother's urging and had the abortion was to have greater justification for hating her.

The emerging picture of Eva as an emotional cripple is amplified by the account of her marriage. When Viktor proposed, she confessed that she did not love him—indeed, that she never loved anyone because she was not "permitted" to love. She consented only because his gentleness reminded her of her father—whom Charlotte had deserted to be with her lover. Thus, in marrying Viktor she symbolically assumed Charlotte's place, not merely to make amends to her father through her fidelity to his surrogate but also to prove herself her mother's moral superior.

For several years after the marriage, Eva remained barren—implicitly a reflection of her emotional deadness. Then, just as the couple had given up hope of having a child, Erik was born. This "Isaac" later drowned at the age of four, however, when he pried open the nailed-down lid of the well and plunged into the water. Viktor, a minister, was so crushed by the senselessness of his son's death that he at first rejected the idea of God's existence; only the example of his wife's faith, he says, enabled him to resume his ministry. What he fails to see is that Eva's inability to forgive her mother by letting love overcome hatred makes her faith a sham. Mercifully, he also does not understand that, in effect, the God who corresponds to Eva's desire for retribution has used Erik's death to punish her for destroying her fetus.

Over most of the film's length, to be sure, the perception of Eva as implacably vindictive depends on inferences drawn from accounts of the past. The Eva one meets on the screen, in contrast, is the meek wife of a country parson, a victim who elicits sympathy in her unequal contest with her bullying mother. At the climax, however, she unleashes her resentment with devastating effect, using as her weapon not her own grievances but the suffering of her helpless sister. She reminds her mother of an Easter family gathering, years earlier, when Lena and Leonardo, Charlotte's second husband, had had a brief but intense infatuation. Charlotte crushed it, and that night, after Leonardo left, Lena fell suddenly ill. As Eva repeats the story, Charlotte four times calls it preposterous to blame her for the disease which has been wasting Lena ever since, but Eva keeps pressing. When Charlotte tries to save herself by maintaining that she never *consciously* intended to destroy Lena, Eva is unrelenting: nothing less than an admission of "irrevocable guilt" will satisfy her. At last, Charlotte surrenders and abjectly pleads for mercy:

> Can you not come to me? Can you not hold me? I am so terribly afraid. Darling, can't you forgive me for all I've done wrong? I'll try to change myself. You will teach me, we'll talk to each other, long, a great deal. But help me. I can't stand it any more, *your hate is so horrible.*

Yet, even in this moment of her long-awaited triumph, Eva cannot be moved to charity.

Much of the comment in the press when *Autumn Sonata* was released emphasized its autobiographical reference: through Charlotte, Bergman was presumably assessing the human price he had paid for his artistic achievement. The association is obvious, and one has to believe that, in naming Charlotte's daughters Lena and Eva—the names of two of his own daughters—he was consciously alluding to his faults as a parent. But the "essence of the personal" expressed by the film reaches far beyond sacrifices offered in the service of art to Bergman's tortured relationship with his mother.

The key to this private significance can be found in Lena—curiously, a character often regarded as superfluous by critics. If Eva's emotional paralysis were only the product of her mother's cold-blooded domination, then the critics' objection to Lena's corresponding physical affliction as an obtrusive symbol of what is already patent would be entirely justified. But something else consumes Eva, and her alter ego Lena serves to reflect it. The mutual attraction between Leonardo and his stepdaughter has an unmistakably Oedipal resonance; furthermore, the paralysis that, in some peculiar way, follows from it points not only to the hereditary disorder which has cursed Bergman's family but also to the psychosexual implications of paralysis in *The Touch* and *The Petrified Prince*. If, in Lena (and Eva), Bergman portrays himself as a daughter instead of as a son, Leonardo represents the yielding, sexually alluring aspect of mother. (Interestingly, the event which prompts Eva to believe in the possibility of a reconciliation with Charlotte is Leonardo's death, apparently from cancer—the other wasting disease that implies Oedipal guilt in *A Passion* and *Cries and Whispers*.)

The guilt that stirs *Autumn Sonata*, however, is not manifested in Lena's Christlike agony—which connotes her rejection—but in Eva's inability to forgive. The film opens with a prologue in which Viktor quotes from a book written by his wife: "One must learn to live, I recite the lesson every day. The greatest impediment is that I don't know who I am, I do it blindly. If someone were to love me as I am, perhaps I could finally look at myself." Complementing this confession is an epilogue, also read by Viktor, which takes the form of a letter Eva has written to her mother:

> *I have understood that I wronged you*. I met you with demands instead of with tenderness. I tormented you with an old, sour hate which is no longer real. I was wrong the whole time, and I beg your forgiveness. . . . You must understand that I'll never let go of you or let you disappear from my life. . . . I won't give up, even if it is too late. I don't believe it is too late. It must not be too late.

Yet nothing in the film bracketed by the two quotations sustains this final note of repentance and love. As Charlotte's train speeds away from her daughters, she recites the critics' praises for her "generosity as a musician," for the "warm tone" of her interpretations; then the train enters a tunnel and she is swallowed up by the darkness. The last scene (so labeled in the filmscript) shows Lena having a seizure. Rolling out of her chair, she calls out the only intelligible words she speaks during the entire film: "Mama, come." Of course, the cry is unheeded. If one draws the almost ineluctable inference that Eva's letter expresses the filmmaker's own anguished appeal to his mother's memory, the story to which it is appended offers pungent testimony to the persistence of an "old, sour hate." And his next film would plunge even deeper into the pathology of that relationship.

From the Life of the Marionettes

Once he had passed his sixtieth birthday, Bergman started to plan for the retirement from cinema he had been talking about for some years. Filmmaking was a young man's game, he said; having been at it for half the history of motion pictures, he had reached the point where he should prepare for his exit. On July 8, 1979, he finished the script for *Fanny and Alexander*, a final return to the troubled childhood which had gestated the artist in him. But before he could devote his attention to preparation for shooting that film, two pieces of unfinished business remained. One was *Fårö Document 1979*, a resumption of the chronicle of his island neighbors a decade after the original documentary. He had conceived the film when he returned to Fårö in the summer of 1976; the next fall, his cameraman, Arne Carlsson, began capturing every aspect of the islanders' lives. Over the next two years, twenty-eight hours of material accumulated, from which Bergman quarried the two-hour film presented by Sweden's first television channel on Christmas Eve, 1979. Divided into sections representing the four seasons, *Fårö Document 1979* celebrates the cyclical rhythms of an existence in harmony with nature, isolated in time as well as distance from the cacophony of modern civilization. For Bergman, it served as an assertion of his citizenship in a real community where the bureaucratic machinations that had driven him into exile seemed an alien fantasy. Moreover, it offered a respite from tussling with the destructive demons that gripped his creative imagination. He obviously relished the project: it was, he said, "the most enjoyable film I have made since *The Magic Flute*."

The second film, shot in Munich during the closing months of the same year, bears no resemblance at all to the tribute to the health of the human spirit of Fårö. *From the Life of the Marionettes* is a study of depravity, a "documentary" about Bergman's island of hell within the self. Peter and Katarina, the tormented couple who visit Johan and Marianne in the first part of *Scenes from a Marriage*, so intrigued Bergman that he planned to continue the story of their marital disaster as one of several themes in a film to be called *Love Without Lovers*. After that project foundered, the couple, transpatriated as Germans, reappeared as the subjects of a new film; yet, aside from the retention of the names, they are essentially different characters who show none of the desperate ferocity that energized the pitted couple in *Scenes from a Marriage* for their unending battle. This Peter and Katarina trace more directly to Abel and Manuela in *The Serpent's Egg*, Joakim and Maria in *Cries and Whispers*, Johan and Anna in *The Passion*, Jan and Eva in *Shame*, and, even further back, to Tomas and Sofi in *Prison*.

The story has no plot, and virtually all its action occurs in one scene. The film opens in a porno palace, photographed in garish red, where Peter Egermann bolts from his embrace with a prostitute, stalks the frightened woman through a bedroom-performing stage, and kills her. The conclusion reverts to the minutes preceding the crime, then shifts to the cold green and white interior of a hospital room where Peter, confined for the insane murder, spends his days playing chess against a computer and his nights sleeping beside an old teddy bear. The dozen scenes between, all shot in black and white, take place at various times before and after the murder. Narratively unrelated to each other except as reflections of Peter and his world, these scenes—four of which occur in the police interrogator's office—constitute an inquiry to determine why this comfortably established young business executive has killed the prostitute and then had anal intercourse with the corpse. Unlike the usual detective story, however, here the mystery presumably cannot be solved, even after all the information has been gathered. A solution would have to suppose reasons, and to the extent that the film proposes to make a philosophical point, it is that acts such as Peter's defy rational explanation.

And yet Bergman supplies all the facts necessary to understand the only mystery with which the film deals. The prostitute, called Ka, has the same given name as Peter's wife; the German meaning of her surname, Krafft, suggests Strindberg's *Makterna*—the dark, destructive "Powers," or "Forces," that can take control of a person much as a puppet master pulls the strings of a marionette. For two years before the murder, Peter, even though he maintains that he loves his wife, has been obsessed by the thought of slashing her throat with a razor. The impulse is evidently generated by sexual anxieties: Katarina is openly unfaithful, at least in part because he cannot satisfy her beyond stimulating an occasional orgasmic flutter. Thus, apparently, when Ka arouses a lust in him which he fears will disclose his impotence, and then, on trying to escape, he finds that the one door leading from the bordello's cellar has been bolted shut, the prostitute becomes the target for his pent-up rage against Katarina. But this is only part of the complicated mechanism that triggers his violence.

The key to Peter's mind—and thus to the film—lies in a dream he records for his psychiatrist. It begins with his realization that God is female, and that he is a fetus inside her, unable to decide whether his state implies life or death. Within the dream, he awakens to find Katarina (or someone who "may be" Katarina) beside him on the thick carpet of the womb that has become a closed room. Like several of Bergman's previous protagonists, he is at first comforted by the presence of this twin "fetus," who is both a feminized self and an infantilized version of the mother. Even so, he senses a terrifying danger, and although he tells himself he must not panic, her softness and her indifference (a quality he would associate with his mother) so excite him that he tries, unsuccessfully and against her will, to thrust his penis into her. After they fight, they stroke each other's bruises; when he starts to cry bitterly —like a child—Katarina's resistance to his sexual desires melts and they meet "in a sudden intimacy without reserve." But then, something "ghastly, unbelievable, irrevocable" happens: still inside the dream, he "wakes" a second time to discover that, without knowing why or how, he has killed Katarina "in a cruel and painful way." The existence surrounding the dream within the dream within the dream is itself dreamlike in its triple confusion of wife and mother. In attempting to explain her special bond with her husband, Katarina tells the psychiatrist she carries Peter inside her, that they have the same circulatory system, the same nerves; later, it is implied that she has not had a child because Peter (like Eugen in *Rakel and the Cinema Doorman*) could not tolerate sharing her womb. Yet, as she also recognizes, she is herself essentially a child, and her marriage is a union of two children who refuse to grow up. (Once again, one recalls *Rakel and the Cinema Doorman*—as well as a number of the films—in which Bergman portrays the husband as a *puer eternus* and the wife-mother as his sexually innocent playmate.) Even though Katarina participates in both of these fantasies, they principally express Peter's wish to evade reality. The horror of that reality—a prison from which he cannot escape—is at the core of the third confusion. Once he confronts it, dream turns into nightmare.

Clearly, his erotic failure with Katarina owes to his Oedipal attachment to Cordelia Egermann. Since wife is surrogate for mother (a substitution emphasized by the fact that Peter wears his father's wedding ring), any manifestation of sexual desire for her confirms his foulness. For his libido to function, he must think of her, too, as debased; thus, he favors *coitus a tergo*, apparently because it simulates anal intercourse, and he feels special excitement in lying with her just after she has slept with other men.* In Ka, of course, he finds a thoroughly vitiated Katarina —and Cordelia. The very debauchery which lures him, however, fills him with self-loathing for having corrupted the purity of the idealized mother. (In his dream, one notes, Peter's effort to penetrate Katarina is rapelike. Even when she relents, moved by his tears, he bears the responsibility for the act that, in its description, suggests the breaking of a taboo.) If Peter is not to commit suicide, he must project his guilt onto the symbolic mother and punish her with death.

Yet another aspect of the mystery—one which receives considerable emphasis—points in the same direction. Tomas Isidor Mandelbaum (or Tim, as he calls himself), Katarina's homosexual partner in a fashion business, tells the interrogator midway through the film that he has a guilty conscience over the crime because it was he who introduced Peter to the prostitute. His fondness for Katarina, he says, always concealed an equally strong element of hatred; therefore, he found spiteful amusement in being the instrument in Peter's betrayal of his majestic wife with a common whore. At the same time, he confesses a more urgent motive: he loves Peter, and by promoting the affair with Ka, he had hoped to win him away from Katarina.

At first glance, none of this makes any sense. Not only does one wonder why Tim, a jealous lover, would nudge Peter toward Ka, or why he should expect Ka's bed to lead to his but also why Bergman took the trouble to introduce the character at all. His primary function, to account for Peter's meeting with Ka, is entirely unnecessary. Moreover, his homosexual desire for Peter—unknown to Peter or anyone else—is an isolated detail, disengaged from the rest of the film. But once one understands the Oedipal significance of Ka's murder, Tim fits into a pattern of meaning rather different from that described on the surface. His ambivalence toward Katarina parallels Peter's own love-hate relationship with her, and his sexual pursuits among the "brutal, filthy trade" where he encounters "lust and mad excitement and terror and beastliness, all jumbled up" match Peter's erotic obsession with degradation. From this mirroring, one can infer that Tim's guilty conscience over the murder

---

*Peter's anality is especially evident in the murder scene. Bergman stresses the fecal smell in Ka's dressing room and implies it is instrumental in inciting the violence, which ends in the anal coitus with the corpse.

Peter's need to associate sex with corruption is also attested by his statement that he "sees" his moments of love with Katarina in red—the color of the bordello.

(half-attributable, he says, to his homosexuality) is more deeply lodged than he acknowledges: i.e., that, as Peter's psychological twin self, Tim fantasied the murder and willed Peter to commit it. Further indicating this affinity, Peter's account of his dream that foreshadows the brutal events in the bordello begins with a curious allusion to his femininity: "in some way there was a distinct connection between the lower half of my body and the nice, strong scent of a woman's moistness, sweat, saliva, the fresh smell of thick hair."

Although the correspondence between the psychotic murderer and Tim remains submerged during the course of the film, the inference to which it ineluctably leads is finally voiced by the psychiatrist in his summary remarks:

> As regards our patient, a dominating mother and poor contact with his father have undoubtedly resulted in a latent homosexuality which Peter Egerman himself has hardly been aware of, but which of course has had a disturbing effect on his relations with his wife and other women. This condition, plus a fear evolving from aggressiveness toward the dominating mother, has not found a natural outlet in Egerman's social environment, in which any form of emotional outburst is considered almost obscene. . . . A strongly developed sense of duty and a self-discipline instilled and practiced since childhood, combined with social success, have hindered the patient from giving any kind of natural expression to his feelings. Moreover, he has manifestly been tied to his wife, who, like his mother, is a possessive and strong-willed personality. . . . The disaster is inevitable from the moment he contacts the prostitute. Suddenly everything is possible and Egerman's stored-up aggressiveness toward his wife and mother finds a vent.

Despite Bergman's assertion in the screenplay's preface that the psychiatrist is "farthest away" from understanding the truth, the film Bergman presents confirms the analysis in all its details. (Although the psychiatrist could be said to have missed the truth in not articulating the specifically Oedipal source of Peter's problem with women, the analysis implies it.) Furthermore, the interpretation broadly applies to the basic story Bergman has retold for almost four decades, most recently—and most transparently—in *The Petrified Prince* (where, significantly, the mother is named Katarina) and *The Serpent's Egg*.

But what makes the psychiatrist's hypothesis particularly intriguing is that Bergman goes to greater lengths than in any previous work to identify the protagonist with himself.* Peter, too, was a middle child and his parents' favorite. Timid and sheltered from the world, he suffered from psychosomatic illnesses and was terrified by birds and the dark. He has a younger sister, corresponding to Margareta, with whom he played doll games and staged puppet shows. His elder brother, like Dag, has risen to the top rank in the diplomatic corps; as a boy, this brother, again like Dag, rebelled against his father's discipline and thereby increased the pressure on the next son to conform. The father, like Erik Bergman, showed a special fondness for his second son and relished their intimacy on trips into the countryside, but he also behaved in ways that the son regarded as cruelly repressive. (Peter's statement that he has become a "punctuality neurotic" because of his suppressed aggression also has an autobiographical reference: Bergman attributes his own compulsive punctuality to the corporal punishments for tardiness administered by his father.) Peter confesses to repaying his father with open hatred; yet—just as Bergman's memories of heroic clashes with the "tyrant" may have been mainly imaginary dramatizations of an Oedipal jealousy—Cordelia insists that he has much exaggerated these displays of aggression. The key member of this parallel family portrait, of course, is the mother. Just as Karin Bergman was compelled to give up her nursing career when she married, Cordelia Egermann abandoned the stage to raise children. (The substitution of actress for nurse—a pairing that also occurs in *Persona*—seems less arbitrary if one recalls Bergman's special delight in his mother's dramatic readings of stories in the parsonage living room.) Both women endured unhappy marriages by practicing "self-deceit"; both sought compensation for what they had sacrificed by fastening on sons who inherited their interests, emotional sensitivity, and frail health.

All this information about Peter and his family constitutes the pieces of a puzzle. If the purpose of assembling the pieces is to produce a coherent design that accounts for Peter's crime, then, despite Bergman's statement in the preface, the psychiatrist has solved the puzzle. But the extent of the details, far exceeding the dramatic requirements of the minimal plot, and Bergman's pains to match them to his own personal history raise an alternative possibility: that the film really concerns the failure to solve another puzzle made up of the same pieces.

---

*The effort to establish the connection spills over into minor details. Even though Ka is German and the bordello is in a German city, her dressing room—in a sense, an objectification of Peter's mind—is decorated with photographs of, among others, Björn Borg and the Swedish King and Queen.

Beyond serving as the "detective" summoned to unriddle this psycho-logical mystery at the end, the psychiatrist, Mogens Jensen, is deeply involved in the film's inner meaning. In the second of the black and white scenes, Peter calls on Dr. Jensen to talk about his compulsion to kill Katarina. The psychiatrist is strangely unsympathetic: in disparag-ing Peter as a "proper little bureaucrat. . . . so well behaved, well adjusted, well groomed, well educated, well prospered," he seems to be challeng-ing his patient's manhood—indeed, daring him to commit the murder. After the session is over, Peter pretends to leave; hiding in the shadows, he watches as Katarina enters the office and soon disrobes to "enjoy a fuck" with Jensen. At the last minute, however, she changes her mind because she loves her husband, despite his sexual inadequacy, and she senses that Jensen is trying to come between them. Peter then slinks away.

Even though nothing happens between Jensen and Katarina for the rest of the film, this perplexing scene reveals a great deal about the impulse behind the story. The patient behaves like a little boy. Afraid, burdened with guilt, and seeking reassurance, he approaches the psy-chiatrist as a father—who then fails him. The second part of the scene follows in the same vein. Like a child imagining his parents' sexual activity, Peter seems instinctively to know that Katarina will arrive and for what purpose. What he sees from concealment is a dreamlike enact-ment of an Oedipal drama in which Katarina manages to fight off her attraction to the sexually superior Jensen by invoking a maternal love for Peter.

Several scenes later, despite the fact that Peter has witnessed Jensen's treachery, he writes him the long letter describing his dream. As in the visit to the psychiatrist's office, Peter reveals ambiguous feelings toward this man old enough to be his father. He insists that he likes Jensen, that he bears him no ill will for trying to make love to Katarina, yet he also refers invidiously to this rival male's "indubitable sex appeal," to the ease with which he can slip his "hand between the legs of some willing or attractive patient." In Peter's eyes, Jensen has mastered the masculine role that still confounds Peter. Thus, in part, his relating the dream is motivated by his need for a mentor's help. But the dream also repre-sents the Oedipal complement to the scene in which Jensen and Katarina symbolically portrayed father and mother. At this level, the letter serves as a veiled confession and an appeal for absolution from the father figure.

Significantly, however, the letter is never sent; in a sense, to the extent that Peter and Bergman are interchangeable, the film that is essentially an elaboration of the letter takes its place, and the appeal, encased in the vehicle of art, is turned toward the audience. Bergman implies as much in his preface, where, after proposing "to show why I have written the film," he never supplies a direct answer. As author, he has cast himself "as an outsider, to record the minutes, as it were"; yet (given the obviously personal reference of his story), that pose of "objectivity is nevertheless a pure illusion." Moreover, he continues, "None of the performers [and least of all, the psychiatrist] can claim to elucidate or clarify the drama [because] they are all implicated and thus perplexed." Consequently, he says (still in the logical train of "why I have written this film"), "The intention is that those who want to or think it is exciting should draw their own conclusions; those who don't want to can, it is hoped, view it all as entertainment."

Taken one step further, this very peculiar preface points to another, and finally more important symbolic function for the psychiatrist. Just as the representations of Erik and Ingmar Bergman cross in such films as *Wild Strawberries* and *The Communicants*, Jensen deputizes for Bergman in his role as filmmaker as well as for the "father" this confessional film psychologically addresses. In effect, he is the "outsider" and "minutes-taker," set within the film, who (through his entanglement with Katarina) is too "perplexed" to present an objective solution to the mystery. If Peter manifests that component of Bergman arrested in the little-ease chamber of his childhood, Jensen represents that same child grown to manhood, the conscious artist incapacitated by his recognition of overwhelming futility.*

At the conclusion of his unsent letter, Peter asks Jensen the question that Johan posed at the end of *Hour of the Wolf* and that has been implicit in every film since: "The mirror is smashed, but what do the splinters reflect?" Finally, *From the Life of the Marionettes* is about the impossibility of assembling the splinters—the pieces of the puzzle —into a coherent meaning. Asked by Peter at another point why he goes on in a profession which trades in hopelessness, Jensen can only reply, "Out of curiosity"—the very same answer with which Bergman has justified his continuing in his own profession. As the preface virtu-

---

*The psychiatrist's name also points to Bergman: "Mogens"—not an unusual first name in Denmark and bordering areas of Germany—was evidently chosen to suggest *mogen*, the Swedish word for "mature"; "Jensen," the Danish form of "Jansson," clearly associates him with the long succession of Bergman's personae, beginning with Jan-Erik, tagged by the name "Jan" or its variants.

ally concedes, however, that curiosity is without artistic consequence; ultimately, it leads to the demonstration of art's — or the artist's —impotence. Jensen cannot "elucidate or clarify the drama" because, for Bergman, the drama admits no resolution.

Fanny and Alexander

In public explanations of his decision to withdraw from cinema, Bergman emphasized the physical strain: two months of working all day to capture, at most, three minutes of footage for the final cut had become too taxing a regimen. Making films was no longer the fun it had once been; for the future, he would concentrate on directing in theater, with occasional forays into television. But there were other reasons, at least as forceful.

Since the mid-'sixties, film had become increasingly multinational an industry in its means of financing and in its reliance on foreign sales —and, thereby, in its proclivity toward international casts. Among the major European directors, Bergman had been one of the last to resist the trend, but with his announcement in 1970 that *The Touch* would be financed by ABC Pictures Corporation and star Elliot Gould, he, too, bowed to the new conditions. The production of *Cries and Whispers*, a wholly Swedish venture, required extraordinary measures that raised howls of resentment. Thereafter, Dino De Laurentiis became the producer of *The Serpent's Egg*, and an advance sale of rights to Lew Grade and his American associate furnished the capital for *Autumn Sonata*. (Except for *From the Life of the Marionettes*, the rest of his films were made for Swedish television.)

In each case, much was made of Bergman's retention of full artistic control, yet, if only because a proposed film had to be aimed at an international market in order to attract foreign investment, these new arrangements influenced his work. Furthermore, as the costs of such films rose, they put Bergman at greater risk: although a De Laurentiis or a Grade, eager for the respectability lent by association with Bergman, would profess devotion to art, losses at the box office quickly cooled that ardor. The difficulty in raising money for *Fanny and Alexander* illustrated the problem. After *From the Life of the Marionettes* proved a financial and critical disaster, Grade's interest in Bergman's next film immediately evaporated. Only the nimble efforts of Jörn Donner, then head of the Film Institute, rescued the project which, with a budget almost one hundred times that of *The Seventh Seal*, would set a record for the cost of a Swedish film.

Although it seemed anomalous during the late 'fifties that a country of seven million inhabitants in which the studios operated on the margin of economic survival should produce a Bergman, in retrospect one realizes that a film industry geared to those conditions was essential to the phenomenon. If the tastes of the Swedish audience would not support the typical Bergman film, the production costs were so low that they could usually be recovered abroad, where his real audience lay. No one failure threatened ruin; indeed, his international reputation made it possible for him to survive even a string of failures. But with the erosion of his Swedish economic base in the 'seventies, every film that fell short of a critical triumph made him vulnerable.

Perhaps more wearing than having to contend with economic vicissitude, however, was the strain of writing and directing films in which his nihilism extends beyond his subject matter and undermines the very assumptions on which his art had rested. Bergman first confronted the crisis in *The Face*, where he admitted the impotence of art as a magic means to deny despair; but the real turning point was *Persona*: after Elisabet speaks the single word *ingenting*, the tension between "nothingness" and the effort to posit some meaning to life disappears from his work. Conceptually, his films depart from the conventional foundations of drama and become investigations into the pathology of existence that are motivated by a joyless "curiosity."

Fanny and Alexander was to be a very different film. According to an account widely reported in the Swedish press, Kjell Grede, a prominent filmmaker once married to Bibi Andersson, caused Bergman to shift course when he asked his friend why a man of lusty vitality had persistently given the public such depressing stories. Suddenly, Bergman claims, he realized his cinematic finale should spring free of the morbidity that had seized his imagination since the mid-'sixties. What evolved from this thought was a large "tapestry," originally planned to stretch over five hours in a version for Swedish television and about half that length in a print cut down for theatrical release. A celebration of life, it would re-create the world of Bergman's childhood—so distant from the "twilight world" of the twentieth century's latter decades which he blamed for the enfeeblement of art.

If Bergman's intent had been to coax a final outpouring of affection from his public, he could not have devised better. Even before settlement of the tax dispute almost entirely in his favor in late 1979, he had frequently returned to Stockholm while summering on Fårö, yet the fact remained that, for more than five years, he had neither directed a play nor (except for the documentary) made a film in his native land. Consequently, when shooting for *Fanny and Alexander* began in Uppsala in the fall of 1981, it was regarded as a homecoming. Sweden seemed eager to overcome the embarrassment of having hounded one of its most renowned sons into exile; even the dissenters who had habitually grumbled about his "pernicious" influence on Swedish cinema kept silent. That the film was set in 1910 also contributed to the mood of reconciliation. Despite a national obsession for the modern—or per- haps because human beings long to return to what they have unrelent- ingly destroyed—Swedes have a special nostalgia for the decades before World War I in which the two Oscars reigned. For almost every Swedish critic, the film's evocation of that ambience was its chief glory. In viewing *Fanny and Alexander*, the country reveled in a pleasure much like that which comes from looking through a cousin's family album. Sentiment weighed heavily in its success abroad as well. Although many reviewers may have been predisposed in its favor by Bergman's declaration that this would be his last film, their praise was elevated by surprise at finding an exuberance that had long been absent from his fictions. At the end of his career, Bergman was seen to be reclaiming what they presumed had been the happy ground of *Wild Strawberries*; suddenly, it was possible once again to describe a Bergman film as "charming," "richly textured," "luminous," "magical."*

But *Fanny and Alexander* is actually two films, which, except that they concern members of the same family, are dramatically separate entities. The glow that warmed audiences radiates from only an outer layer; its core is as chilling as any of Bergman's fictions.

Fifty years before the time of the film, in a university town which, though not identified by name, is unmistakably Uppsala, Oscar Ekdahl had bought a theater for Helena Mandelbaum, the eminent actress he had just married. In the novel-like screenplay, eighteen pages of pro- logue encapsulate the subsequent histories of both the theater and the Ekdahls, but the film itself begins with the Christmas festivities in which the dowager gathers her family and her good friend Isak Jacobi, a Jew-

---

*Not every critic was swept along by this tide of good feeling, of course. The most egre- gious exception appeared in *Commentary*, where Richard Grenier not only demonstrated that he had understood almost nothing about the film but also tedded his piece with factual errors which he then raked together to produce the outrageous conclusion that Bergman harbored a Himmler-like anti-Semitism.[1]

ish merchant who was once her paramour. Between scenes of the games and rites that command major attention, a loosely worked narrative thread weaves portraits of her three sons. Life is a carefree gambol for Gustav Adolf, a prospering restaurateur blessed with a wife who not only lifts her skirts whenever he feels a sexual urge but also smiles on his philandering with the maids. In contrast, despair is strangling Carl, the second brother. A failure as a professor at the university, he is so saddled with debts to everyone that he cannot even raise enough money for coal to keep his house warm; still worse, fate has yoked him to an adoring, stupid German wife for whom he feels only disgust. The story's development, however, leads from neither the comic "Gusti" nor the pathetic Carl but from Oscar—the eldest brother, who, though named for his businessman father, has inherited his mother's passion for theater. His death soon after the Christmas gathering leads into the film's central story, which revolves around his widow Emilie's remarriage to Bishop Edvard Vergérus and the cruel treatment of Alexander by his stepfather.

After this Dickensian tale of evil concludes with the Bishop's death, the film returns to the Ekdahl house, where the family is celebrating the double baptism of two daughters—one, Emilie's, fathered by the Bishop; the other, Gustav's bastard child with Maj, the Ekdahls' lame, good-hearted maid. In his toast to the babes, Gustav speaks of "the poison that will strike at everyone, without exception," as the twentieth century unfolds; yet, holding Emilie's baby—like Jof lifting Mikael at the end of *The Seventh Seal*—he professes hope for humanity, embodied in the "little empress" who, as an expression of love, may one day reign over all the world. Meanwhile, life will go on, despite history's gathering darkness: Gustav's twenty-year-old daughter will join Maj in opening a couturier's shop, and the Ekdahls' old theater, which has resisted the introduction of modern drama, will renew itself by presenting a play by "that woman-hating swine, August Strindberg."

Aside from supplying a happy ending, Bergman's chief purpose in relating the Ekdahls' saga seems to have been to revive the pleasant memories of his childhood, but in laying one vignette upon another, he neglected to develop a structure of meaning.* The dramatic incoher-

---

*Although Bergman scrambles places and characters and moves the time of the story back seventeen years, the film is as close to an autobiographical reminiscence as any he has ever made. Helena Ekdahl is a grander version of the widowed Anna Åkerblom (just as the model for the first Oscar Ekdahl seems to be Johan Åkerblom), and most of the film's outdoor scenes were shot within a very small area on the west bank of the Fyris, only a couple of city blocks from his grandmother's apartment. Into this Uppsala setting, Bergman imported the servants from the Sophiahem parsonage in Stockholm—

ence becomes especially obtrusive in the final scenes, where Bergman's message of hope responds to no argument. How—and to whom—does it matter that Maj has borne Gustav's child, or that Maj will sell fashions (instead of cakes as Gustav had intended)? And although it could matter that Emilie has given birth to the odious Bishop's child, the thematic possibilities in that fact are completely ignored; she might as well have been impregnated by the wind. But the most egregious disjunction is that none of these concluding developments bears on the overpowering drama of self-discovery at the center of *Fanny and Alexander*.

Although this inner tale focuses on the bitter antagonism between Alexander and his stepfather the Bishop, its Oedipal significance pivots on Emilie, who, like many of Bergman's previous images of the mother, combines two opposites: virgin and seductress. Vis-à-vis Oscar, she is the virgin. Throughout their marriage, Emilie reveals, he has never shown the least sign of an erotic appetite (thus his role as Joseph in the annual Christmas play presented in one of the film's early scenes is emblematic of his offstage role as well.)* Yet, despite his sexual abstinence (or, in a sense, because of it), they have lived harmoniously. Like the protagonists in Bergman's early films seeking escape from adult reality in a play-house marriage, Oscar is a childlike man, sexually crippled by a domi-

Maj, the lame nursemaid of whom he was especially fond, even retains her own name. Although no model for Isak Jacobi existed within the family circle, the character may have been suggested by the Jewish shopkeeper from whom young Ingmar bought filmstrips —apparently the same man figured as Isak in *To My Terror* ...

The film's title, which elevates Alexander's two-years-younger sister Fanny to an importance unsupported by the story, serves as an autobiographical marker of the very close ties Bergman had with his sister Margareta; that Alexander is a self-portrait is patent from the film's first frame, showing him with his puppet theater. (The actor who plays the role, Bertil Guve, so resembles Ingmar as a boy that one has to surmise he was chosen for that reason.) Numerous details also point to his childhood. The marble statue that Alexander sees move, for example, refers to the statue of Venus in the Åkerblom apartment that Bergman once imagined came to life; the prominence given to the laterna magica recalls young Ingmar's fascination with that toy; the stuffed bear Alexander clutches in several scenes marks another appearance of Baloo, the teddy bear that Bergman had previously resurrected in *The City* and in *From the Life of the Marionettes*.

*The screenplay stresses Oscar's celibacy—and Emilie's erotic hunger—more than does the film. There, Alexander and Fanny—and an older sister, Amanda, who is omitted from the film—are the products of infidelity. According to the prologue, Oscar and Emilie had been childless for ten years when Amanda was conceived during Emilie's guest engagement as an actress with a Helsinki theater. Her pregnancy with Alexander coincided with the arrival of a new leading man in the Ekdahl theater. Two years later, she gave birth to Fanny, a baby "much resembling the archbishop who had been visiting the diocese."

The different "texts" of *Fanny and Alexander* create a problem for interpretive discussion. Not only is the film a reduced version of the screenplay, but the film itself has also undergone successive cuts.

neering mother; in marrying a woman who is like his mother, he has not only re-created his condition of dependency but also raised a barrier against a sexual relationship.*

To Alexander, however, Emilie's sexuality is a disruptive magnetic force, pulling him into a conflict with his father and himself that is foreshadowed, early in the film, when he begs his parents for permission to appear in the Ekdahl theater's *Hamlet*. (Bergman's naming the actor cast as Hamlet in that production Mikael Bergman links Shakespeare's troubled prince not only to himself but also to the boy who so transparently represents the filmmaker.) Oscar's part in this parallel drama is clearly marked by his stage role as King Hamlet's ghost. After suffering a stroke in rehearsal, he tells his wife he is preparing to act the ghost properly—as indeed he will, reappearing to his son until Alexander, in a sense, wreaks vengeance on the "Claudius" his mother has married so hastily. But Oscar's dying also serves to suggest a deeper analogy with the psychological underpinnings of Shakespeare's story. When the father calls his son to his bed for a final word, the boy resists. The other members of the family assume that the child is merely frightened by the strangeness of death, but one can infer from subsequent events that the real reason is guilt for having wished his father were out of the way so he could have his mother all to himself (just as he will later wish his stepfather's death into occurring).** Through Emilie's announcement at Oscar's funeral that the Ekdahl theater will perform *Hamlet* as scheduled, Bergman is clearly intimating more than a gallant observation of stage tradition, and

---

*The "mama's boy's" ambiguous view of women emerges in a strange episode during Christmas Eve. Spinning a fantasy for the children about a chair with the power to glow "mysteriously" in the dark (actually, it is standing in the light of the laterna magica), Oscar says it was an emperor's gift to his empress, who, though no taller than a child, was the world's most beautiful woman; when the empress died, she was buried seated in the chair, and its magical rays gleamed through her body for two thousand years before the chair was brought to the Ekdahl house. He tells the children they must be extremely careful of this delicate relic, the world's dearest chair; but then, after ducking into the wardrobe where he has hidden a brandy flask, he curses the chair, kicks it, accuses it of biting him, and, finally, beside himself with fury, tries to pull it to pieces. Symbolically, the chair is associated with the virginal empress, who in turn represents the mother/wife— first venerated, then recognized as a biting (i.e., castrating) monster.

**In the screenplay, Alexander's request for a part in *Hamlet* is followed by his reciting Macbeth's famous monologue. To his sister, he boasts of knowing all Macbeth's lines by heart and says he is thinking of making his stage debut in the role. Why should Bergman go to such lengths to connect Alexander with Macbeth? One reason may have to identify Alexander with himself (*Macbeth*, one recalls, figured prominently in Bergman's early theatrical career), but he may also have meant to associate the boy with the two Shakespearean regicides.

when, shortly after her remarriage a year later, Emilie warns her son against thinking of himself as the melancholy prince and of her as Gertrude, the thematic implications of the drama about to unfold are unmistakable.

Whatever other reasons Alexander may have for despising Vergérus, the basis of his antagonism is sexual. In one respect, the Bishop represents a surrogate self to be hated and punished for acting out Alexander's desires.* More obviously, he is also the other half of a split father image —not the emasculated Oscar who makes the son feel guilty but the overpowering sexual rival who makes him feel impotent. When Fanny dares her brother to "tell something really horrible," Alexander has a ready answer. On his way to the bathroom one night, he saw His Eminence "lying on Mama with his nightshirt drawn up over his scrawny ass and thumping so that the whole bed shook. Mama screamed for help and prayed to God. 'God, oh God,' she said, in just that tone." This amusing misconstruction is typical of the boy's effort to excuse his mother's betrayal by seeing her as a victim, but deep within himself, he recognizes that the Bishop fills a need in her that the boy cannot satisfy.

Interestingly, Alexander's ambivalent perception of Emilie seems to reflect Bergman's own conflict. As though in dealing with an emotional confusion rooted in his childhood he were thrown back to the use of a child's tropes, he presents this part of the story in fairy-tale terms. Like an innocent, deceived heroine, Emilie quickly discovers she has paid a terrible price in becoming the handsome bishop's wife. His mother, sister, and aunt dominate the austere household and insist that she conform to their rules; her new husband is a self-righteous tyrant; the cold, damp house, set over river rapids, suggests a prisonlike castle. To explain why she does not simply walk away from this dreadful marriage, Bergman provides a set of snares with which the Bishop holds her fast. And yet, when her brothers-in-law enter the house, disclose several means by which they can force the Bishop into submission, and offer to take her away, she refuses. Despite all the reasons she has to hate her captivity, she acquiesces to it because of some weakness inherent in her sex which Alexander senses but cannot fathom and which the author himself seems reluctant to acknowledge.

This ambiguous response to the mother is also the key to Bishop Vergérus's fairy-tale villainy. Although the character would seem to beg

---

*Bergman's peevish response to critics who assumed a simple equation of the filmmaker with Alexander is interesting in this connection. "There's a lot of me in the bishop, rather than in Alexander," he stated. "He's haunted by his own devils."[2]

for an insight into the reasons for his cruelty, Bergman resists all opportunities to supply it. Indeed, the Bishop is drawn as such an inhuman
figure that, apart from the insinuations about his sexual sorcery, Emilie's
attraction to him is scarcely credible. The perspective is entirely
Alexander's. But even more than the one-sided view of the stepfather, it
is the events of the tale that reveal an imagination struggling to deal
with the pain the mother has caused. Thus, the Bishop's locking the
children up as hostages to prevent Emilie from running away not only
exonerates her of blame for sleeping with her husband but also transforms her into a martyr. And when Alexander makes up a story about
having been told by the ghost of the Bishop's first wife that she and her
two daughters died while attempting to escape from the house, his
conscious intent may be to vilify his stepfather but his subconscious
aim is to win his mother from her lover. In paying for the lie with a
bloody flogging and solitary confinement in the attic, he confronts Emilie with the consequences of her "infidelity" and forces her to choose
between the ogre who has inflicted the torture and his victim.

The autobiographical foundations of Alexander's ordeal are, of course,
readily discernible. From their very first meeting, the Bishop vows to
break Alexander of lying—just as Pastor Bergman was determined to
correct his son of the same fault—and the severe punishment in which
these efforts culminate recalls Bergman's accounts of the wardrobe ritual he has made the emblem of his quarrel with his father. That these
"memories," which conflict with everyone else's recollections of Erik
Bergman's kindness toward his favorite child, were probably Oedipally
induced figments is also reflected by the film. Pitiable as Alexander may
be as the victim of a cruel righteousness, the fact remains that his
jealousy has led him to calumniate his stepfather. The guilt for having
told such a terrible lie literally haunts him. During the night he spends
locked in the attic, the ghosts of the Bishop's dead daughters appear to
his troubled conscience, accuse him of torturing their father (who "was
always so kind to us") with his baseless hate, and threaten to hound him
into a madhouse; there, while he lies chained in a padded cell, they will
whisper in his ear the terrible secret they know frightens him "more
than anything else." In a sense, of course, he is already shackled in this
madhouse where dark fantasies seize his mind, and although the secret
that torments him is not spoken aloud, one can infer that it concerns
the same sin inscribed on the walls of Bergman's other depictions of his
"prison."

At this point, Bergman gives his dreamlike fairy tale a most revealing

turn. Trying to extricate himself from his Oedipal trap, Alexander (or
Bergman) in effect creates a new father for himself in Isak Jacobi, the
lovable old Jew who holds that the imagination can realize new possibilities by refusing to recognize the limitations of reality. Entering like a
deus ex machina, Isak calls at the Vergérus house to buy an antique
chest, in which he conceals Fanny and Alexander. But when the Bishop,
suspecting what is afoot, lifts the lid, he finds it empty; still convinced
the Jew means to steal the children, he bounds upstairs to their attic
prison—where he sees them sleeping. Nevertheless, they *are* in the
chest, which is then hauled away to Jacobi's antique shop. Through
magic—symbolically, the magic of art—Alexander has undergone a
kind of rebirth to escape not only from the Bishop but also from his
mother. (Why else should the intervention of magic not rescue Emilie as
well?) The promise of deliverance, however, is deceptive. Wondrous as
the shop filled with mysterious objects from all times and places may
seem at first, Alexander will find its innermost chamber to be the same
prison he believed he had fled.

One night, Alexander has three strange experiences, or dreams, all
tied to his hatred of the man who sleeps with his mother. In the first
—which Bergman indicates is occurring while Emilie and her husband
prepare for bed—Oscar's ghost tries to assuage his son's resentment
against him. But Alexander, blaming his father and God for not redress-
ing injustice, refuses to be comforted. "Why can't you go to God and say
that he must kill the Bishop?" he asks. "That responsibility is his
department." Weeping, the ghost can offer no answer other than to urge
his son to respect life and show greater charity for his fellow man.

Aside from emphasizing the boy's desire for vengeance (which is
already quite evident), this scene further suggests the complex workings
of his guilt. When Oscar asks why his son is so angry, Alexander charges
that he showed the other children greater affection by giving them gifts;
then, after the father protests he gave the boy as many gifts as the others,
Alexander drives closer to the truth by replying that he has always
resented having a father who was so unmanly. Since it is precisely that
unmanliness which had given the boy convenient access to his mother's
bed and the encouragement to think of himself as her secret sweetheart,
he tries to pin the blame for his sinful fantasies onto the father who let
them occur. Realizing that this flimsy rationalization will not hold, he
next turns his anger toward his stepfather. In one respect, the sexual
dominance combined with sadism evinced by the Bishop is a projection of the boy's own confused erotic ideas which he feels should be

punished. At the same time, the Bishop also represents an image of the father—not the bumbler he disdains but the superior rival he imagines mastering his mother behind the bedroom's closed door.* Finally, guilt-ridden and powerless, Alexander shifts his anger toward God. Were God to eliminate the Bishop—i.e., the sexual disturbance he reflects—hatred and recrimination would vanish and something like the "holy family" Bergman extolled in *The Seventh Seal* would be possible. But God does not act, leading to the inference (as in *Prison*) that the deity who presides over the world is Satanic.

A short time later, Alexander again awakens (or has another dream). While wandering the corridors of the antique shop in search of a bathroom, he hears a voice claiming to be God, almighty and all-encompassing. When Alexander calls for proof that such assertions attest anything more than vanity, the strange voice offers the evidence of "God's love. God's Love for Mankind. . . . Is there anything bigger than Love?" To which Alexander answers: "That would be His Eminence the Bishop's hard-on. I can't think of anything else, because I am only ten years old and haven't much experience." Although this rejoinder to the gospel of love Bergman proclaimed in *The Virgin Spring* and *Through a Glass Darkly* may seem only a bit of humorous impertinence, it actually strikes the quick of the boy's problem. Not only does the Bishop's sexual spell on Emilie demonstrate to him the ascendancy of "evil" over "good" but also, in more general terms, the torment he suffers as a result of his mother's betrayal mocks the concept of a loving God.

At the conclusion of the argument with "God," Aron, Isak's twenty-year-old nephew, drops through a hole in the ceiling; an accomplished puppet maker who has been working late into the night, Aron has played a prank to scare Alexander. Now that he has accomplished his purpose, Aron casually announces his atheism: "If one is brought up among magicians and has learned all the tricks in childhood, one respectfully declines the invitation to involve the supernatural! As a magician, I stick to the comprehensible; let the spectators construe the incomprehensible."** Clearly, in this skilled puppeteer who is adept at dissimulat-

---

*If the good-hearted, uxorious Oscar represents Erik Bergman as he is described by friends and family (including, in more generous moments, his son), the Bishop is the despot young Ingmar held accountable for his humiliation. Although these two father-images appear wholly different, Bergman does not completely separate them. Just as Oscar is entangled in apron strings, the Bishop (for reasons the film never develops) is a captive in a family of women—much as Erik Bergman, following his father's death, was raised by his mother, aunt, and grandmother.

**Despite the emphasis on his rational materialism, Aron calls Alexander's attention to a

ing magic, Alexander is meeting an older, more sophisticated double. (The boy's favorite plaything, one recalls, is his puppet theater.)* Frightened of "a shit-and-piss-God," Alexander wants to retaliate by "kicking his behind." Aron, in contrast, has risen above the quarrel: the control he exercises as an artist has displaced the fear that comes from vulnerability. (One is reminded here not only of Vogler's turning the tables on his oppressors in *The Face* but also of Bergman's claims of having overcome his terror of death and his religious anxieties through various films.) This hope of liberation through art, however, is quickly dashed when Aron takes Alexander to meet his younger brother Ismael.

Earlier, upon first entering the sanctuary of the antique shop, Alexander had been led through "a long, dark corridor" to a secret room. "Behind this door," Isak had warned, "lives my other nephew Ismael. He is sick. For that reason, he must be locked in. For that reason, the door must always remain closed." Now that the proscription has been violated, Alexander meets Evil, embodied not as God or even the Bishop but as himself, mirrored in Ismael. After chasing Aron from the room, Ismael commands the boy to write his name; when Alexander reads his signature, it says not "Alexander Ekdahl" but "Ismael Retzinsky." "Perhaps," Ismael says archly, "we are the same person, perhaps we have no limits, perhaps we float into each other, flow through each other, unbounded and magnificent. You bear dangerous thoughts: it is almost painful to be near you, yet, at the same time, enticing." The corridor to the secret room has led Alexander inward into his psyche; the sick creature locked inside is the son who had been punished with confinement (in the attic—or in the wardrobe) for lies motivated by his sinful jealousy over his mother. (Significantly, Bergman cast a female actress in Ismael's role, suggesting, once again, his association of homosexuality with an overdeveloped attraction to the mother.)

Set against Aron, who represents the benign illusions wrought by art's magic, Isak's other nephew embodies the repressed, destructive urges that power the imagination. Like his biblical namesake (and like Jack the Ripper in Bergman's earliest fictions), he is the pariah, the "wild ass" doomed by the circumstances of his birth to constant rebellion. When

mummy in the shop that inexplicably glows. Along with Aron's curious use of feminine pronouns in referring to the mummy, the luminescence links it to the mysterious chair which had previously suggested the mother's dangerous power. (Both the mummy and the chair may be associated in Bergman's imagination with another disinterred symbol of the mother: the statue of the Virgin in *The Touch*.)

*The doubling is also implied by Bergman's casting his son Mats in the role of Aron.

Ismael grasps Alexander and declares that the "ghastly wishes" in the boy's mind are being granted, Alexander tries to break free of his demonic alter ego, but it is too late. In the Bishop's house, Emilie, as though infused with her son's will, has drugged her husband's bouillon; as she makes her escape, Vergérus's aunt sets herself aflame by upsetting the kerosene lamp at her bedside, runs to her sleeping nephew, and—at the very moment Ismael holds Alexander in his arms—wraps him in a fiery embrace as he burns to death.*

The restoration of Emilie and the children to the bosom of the Ekdahl family following this grim scene has the effect of palliating its horror for the audience, but, like the vision of reconciliation at the end of *Wild Strawberries*, it has no real bearing on the meaning of the preceding psychological drama. To create the appearance of continuity, Bergman inserted a brief scene, not found in the screenplay, in which Alexander is visited by the Bishop's ghost and put on notice that he will be haunted for the rest of his life. Yet, although this displacement of Oscar's ghost by the stepfather's further implies the two fathers' common identity and brings an awareness of the boy's guilt closer to the surface, it is essentially a gloss which neither affects the resolution of the central story nor relates that descent into nightmare to the outcome of lovable Uncle Gusti's erotic exuberance. Clearly, Bergman's fascination is with the psychosexual anguish expressed through the nuclear dream; the rest is a conjurer's trick performed both for his own diversion and to enlist an audience's sentimental approval.

Almost inevitably, the last line of the film proffered as the finale to his

---

*The symbolism attached to the Bishop's death grows more complex as one considers the several levels on which the film operates as dream. Had the filmmaker merely wanted to arrange for Vergérus to perish in a fire, it could have been accomplished more economically by having him knock over the lamp in his stupor; instead, Bergman assigned that function to the grotesque aunt, an otherwise superfluous character. In the screenplay, Bergman spews opprobrium at this mentally retarded freak of nature who spends her life confined to her bed. No defense attorney, he says, would take her case: "She is repugnant, she is rotting, a parasite, a monster. Her role is soon played out, it does not pay to waste sympathy on such a defective loaf in the great tray of the world's baking." Thus, one reason for making her the agent of the Bishop's destruction may have been to personify the monstrosity of Alexander's desire. Similar "unfortunates" appear—in some cases, very briefly and without any apparent dramatic justification—in *To My Terror . . .*, *Kamma Noll*, *The Murder in Barjärna*, and *Autumn Sonata*; in each instance, the malformed person seems an emblem of psychological disturbance and may refer to Bergman himself. Here, significantly, the aunt is named Bergius.

Alternatively, if Vergérus is seen not only as a surrogate father but also as an Oedipal projection of Alexander, the death of this nephew—given the equation of Alexander with Isak's nephew Ismael—suggests self-punishment.

cinematic career quotes Strindberg. As Alexander lays his head on Grandmother Ekdahl's lap, she begins reading the well-known paragraph from
the preface to *A Dream Play*: "Anything can happen, all is possible and
probable. Time and space do not exist. On an insignificant foundation of
reality, imagination spins out and weaves new patterns. . . . " In the context of the ending, the quotation appears intended as a comment on the
future, but the passage's continuation implies retrospect: "a mixture of
memories, experiences, free fancies, absurdities, and improvisations.
The characters divide, double, multiply, evanesce, solidify, diffuse, clarify.
Yet, one consciousness reigns above them all—that of the dreamer."
Presumably, Bergman is suggesting that the four decades of films culminating in *Fanny and Alexander* be seen as his own *Dream Play*, that these
various dreams have been forms of one dream, and, most important of
all, that the dream has been a constant revelation of the dreamer.

In a sense, *Fanny and Alexander* is hinged to *From the Life of the
Marionettes* in a diptych that portrays the dreamer stepping out from
his dream to confront it and acknowledge its meaning. In the inquiry
into Peter Egerman's enactment of his murderous fantasy, Bergman executed the motive behind the unmade *The Petrified Prince*, where, with
shocking frankness, he unfurled the Oedipal pathology in a relationship
between son and mother; here, another conjunction of fantasy and
murder results from the rivalry over the mother between son and father.
The psychological tensions wound in childhood had, of course, caused
the buckling and twisting that gave Bergman's fictions their shape from
the very start: the violence associated with Bertha's death began a pattern of hostility against symbolic mothers, and the convolution of guilt
into vengeful accusation depicted through Caligula, a compound image
of father and son, would keep recurring in a variety of forms. In *From
the Life of the Marionettes*, however, the fantasy of matricide is not an
impulse that must be disguised and transformed through the elaborate
agency of artistic metaphor; rather, it is itself the openly declared,
unfiltered subject. Similarly, every step in the central story of *Fanny and
Alexander* leads inexorably to the moment of parricide; once it has risen
through Alexander's mind, Bergman virtually concedes his inability
to construe any further significance. In themselves, like the rest of
his works after *Persona*, both films are inconclusive—perhaps necessarily so; indeed, it could even be said they are artistic failures because they confess the failure of art. From a perspective that encom-
passes the forty-year progression of Bergman's long dream-drama,
however, these films are the climactic lines of the last scene in

which the terrible secret knowledge underlying the drama is finally spoken aloud.

Postlude: *After the Rehearsal*

Many had doubted Bergman's farewell to cinema would be more than an au revoir; thus, when *After the Rehearsal* opened in New York in the summer of 1984, it seemed he had retracted his decision. But the new film, written in the summer of 1980 and already finished well before the American premiere of *Fanny and Alexander*, had been made for Swedish television and was never intended for theatrical release. Indeed, after its producer, Jörn Donner, sold it to an American film distributor, Bergman and his Munich-based corporation tried to prevent its being shown in theaters.

More than a taxonomic technicality separated the two kinds of filmmaking. One difference is reflected by the budget for *After the Rehearsal*: photographed in 16 mm and completed in a ten-day shooting schedule, it cost less than two million crowns (about $260,000 at the then-current rate of exchange). Another, with deeper implications, springs from Bergman's conception of this television film as a drama bound to the conventions of the stage rather than to the idiosyncratic properties of cinema. To be sure, *The Rite*, *Scenes from a Marriage*, and *Face to Face* had all been planned and shot for Swedish television, and Bergman had found no reason to object to their eventual theatrical distribution abroad. But now the circumstances had changed. Having announced that he was through with cinema, he wanted no confusion among the public over whether he honored his word. Furthermore, *Fanny and Alexander* had brought the obsessive pursuit of his demons to an end; the boundary between that long-evolving private drama and whatever else he might write in his remaining years had to be boldly drawn.

Although *After the Rehearsal* bears some resemblance to those parts of *Fanny and Alexander* in which Bergman evokes the theater as a special place, his choice of plays by Moliere and Shakespeare for his two most recent stage productions may be more relevant. The *Don Juan* he presented in Salzburg during the summer of 1983 was such a departure from the traditional interpretation that it perplexed the audience and irritated reviewers. (In one of those inexplicable shifts of judgment that sometimes occur in theater, the same production was received with great enthusiasm when it subsequently moved to Munich; even some of the critics who had given it chilly notices in Salzburg recanted.) Shearing away the satire and wit, Bergman found an introspective drama about an old, wasting lover confronting the mortality in his dissipation. The second play required no such surgery to disclose a similar theme, but the *King Lear* he brought to Dramaten in March 1984 was so unusually powerful it was hailed in *Svenska Dagbladet* as marking nothing less than the rebirth of Swedish theater. One month later, the telecast of *After the Rehearsal* added one more indication that Bergman was taking a cardinal interest in the psychology of aging.

Essentially a one-act for three characters, the drama focuses on Henrik Vogler, a director in late middle age whose fifth production of *A Dream Play* is in rehearsal. Sitting among props from past plays, he is contenting himself with the company of the theater's "angels and demons" when Anna Egerman, the actress cast as Indra's Daughter, interrupts his solitude on the pretext that she is looking for a lost bracelet. Vogler immediately realizes she means to encourage his advances—this is not the first time a young actress has tried to compromise him to further her ambitions. But, in this case, the actress apparently has an additional motive. Before Anna was born, Vogler and her father were best friends, and she suspects the director of having had an affair with her mother, Rakel. Even though Rakel has been dead several years, the hatred Anna had always felt toward her still rankles; presumably, a sexual liaison with Vogler would be a way of spiting her mother.

As Anna, frozen in place on the sofa, turns into her twelve- or thirteen-year-old self, the film flashes back to a scene between Rakel and Vogler about a decade ago in this same theater. More brazen than Anna would later be, she invites her director to make love, and when he declines, she bares her thighs and breasts in a grotesque effort to arouse him with the ruins of her former beauty. Henrik's aversion is not just to her gray hair and alcoholic puffiness; in her desperate bid to trade sex for a better role and, with it, the dream of recapturing the glory days of her youth, he smells decay and death.

Upon Rakel's exit, the time reverts to the present and the conversation between the director and his ingenue resumes. After he admits to being jealous of her boyfriend Johan, Anna makes a startling announcement: she is pregnant with Johan's child and will be in her eighth month by the time of the premiere. Henrik is stupefied. He had chosen to do *A Dream Play* solely because of her; now he will be forced to drop it from the schedule, and she will have lost the chance for recognition as a great young actress. But Anna soon shows herself an even better actress than he believed. When she proposes an abortion, Vogler, driven to acknowledge that life matters more than theater, rejects the offer. Then it dawns on him that she lives for her theatrical ambitions and would not let a baby get in her way; appalled by this insight, he delivers his conclusion that she has already had the abortion. But Henrik has been fooled again: finally, Anna reveals she was never pregnant at all. The little drama into which she has hooked him was an improvisation to test her acting skill—and to pave the way for their affair by overcoming his emotional detachment.

That affair happens only in their imagination, however. As the "lovers" take turns describing how it would progress, they live the experience in their voices and facial expressions. Once this mental substitute for the anticipation, excitement, delight, and sorrow of an actual romance has run its course, Vogler and Anna part—just as they will part after the set of the play is struck: she, to establish a brilliant reputation before, possibly, burning out like her mother; he, to combat his weariness in mounting new productions, including, he speculates, a sixth or even a seventh *A Dream Play*.

Although the design of *After the Rehearsal* traces a love story of sorts, its content consists mainly of reflections upon the world of the theater by one who has spent himself in its service. That it is Ingmar Bergman speaking through Henrik Vogler is undisguised. Small details, such as the bottle of Ramlösa mineral water (well-known to be Bergman's only beverage) conspicuously placed on the director's table, or the fleeting glimpse of Bertil Guve, dressed as Alexander, when Vogler speaks of his seeing his first performance, signal a more extensive correspondence between the author and his central character. Much of the dialogue concerning actors, their craft, and the magic of the stage paraphrases or even directly echoes Bergman's own statements recorded over the years; moreover, Director Vogler shares not only Director Bergman's special affinity for *A Dream Play* but also his other credits: each of Vogler's previous productions was a play Bergman directed as well. And, touching closer to the man than to the artist, Vogler's confession of his spiritual afflictions—"remoteness, indifference, disgust, fear, powerlessness, anger beyond measure"—repeats Bergman's familiar litany of anguish.*

---

*The author may, in a different way, also be linked in his story through Vogler's "affair" with the actress who is the same age as his daughter. After Liv Ullmann left Bergman, he had a brief, much-publicized fling with Malin Ek. As with Anna Egerman's promotion by Vogler, Malin Ek was a young actress given a major boost when Bergman cast her in his 1970 production of *A Dream Play*, and just as Mikael Egerman, Anna's father, had been Vogler's

And yet, despite the personal associations, Bergman seems unwilling to peer within the character. *The Deception*, the filmscript Bergman wrote in the 'sixties but never took before the cameras, had a protagonist, much like Vogler, whose sense of futility was illustrated through meetings with women similar to Anna and Rakel. But there one knew why Axel Andersson suffered; here, only that Vogler lives with recrimination. What has given rise to his feelings of "remoteness and disgust, remoteness and anxiety"? Are they the result of something in his past? Except for the affair with Rakel in his youth (about which he indicates no guilt), nothing said or done even hints at what that might have been. Or, given the emphasis on Vogler's being full of years, is it his experience of humanity that has led to his sealing himself into the "little world of the theater" to escape life's invasions? If so, then Bergman undercuts the proposition, for what is discomfiting in Anna and repellent in Rakel emerges in a specifically theatrical context.

Bergman seems just as unclear as to the meaning served by the two women. As the main structural device, the parallel between Anna's dropping in on Vogler and Rakel's visit in the flashback would appear crucial to any interpretation; furthermore, Bergman stresses its importance by prefacing the flashback with Anna's venomous attack on her mother and then making the child a mute witness to Rakel's abasement. Yet neither the parallel nor the daughter's hatred has a significant effect in terms of the play's design. If, as one must assume, Anna's interest in Vogler is rooted in the rivalry with her mother, does the imaginary affair indicate a victory or a defeat? And over or by what? In addition, how does the women's relationship bear on the central question of Vogler's weariness?

Even if Rakel's antagonism toward her mother is set aside, the thematic function of these two characters remains nebulous. Bergman seems to be recalling instead of composing. Although Rakel's maundering about her rotting flesh echoes Ester's lament about her sexual nature in *The Silence*, the issue in that earlier film does not enter here. Her self-loathing makes her more of a gargoyle, but whether Vogler sees in that repugnant figure a reflection of something horrifying within himself or the product of a consuming egotism that is foreign to him is

best friend, Malin's father was Anders Ek, Bergman's very close friend from the time they were both starting their careers. (Among many appearances with Bergman, Ek had the title roles in Bergman's second *Macbeth* and in the *Caligula* which inaugurated his term as director at the Gothenburg City Theater; perhaps Ek's most memorable role in a Bergman film was as Frost in *Evening of the Jesters*.)

undeterminable. Another echo can be be heard in Anna's deception about her pregnancy—which calls to mind Alma's discovery in *Persona* that her abortion equals Elisabet's egotistical wish for her child's death. Like the boy "outside" that film who groped at the photograph of Alma/Elisabet to understand the mystery behind the face, Vogler, similarly outside this piece of drama, tries to unriddle Anna as woman/actress, but what bore implications of a devastating encounter with truth in *Persona* here dissolves into a game.

After the Rehearsal is dominated by voices and faces. Once again, Bergman proves himself without peer in drawing superlative performances from his cast, and because the actors express the subtlest nuance of their roles, the viewer is captivated by the characters. What they unfold, however, has no dramatic consequence. Both the film's power as theater and its weakness as a play become most evident when Vogler and Anna surrender the moment to collude in their imaginary relationship as lovers. One tries to understand how this illusion explains or resolves what has gone before. Has Vogler learned something that will either dispell his mood of resignation or lift him out of it? Is Anna condemned or saved by her devotion to her career? Now that they have proleptically experienced their affair, will they reenact it in actuality? Bergman supplies no basis for answers—perhaps because, having lost confidence in the capacity of art to arrive at answers, he has locked his aim to a different goal.

Early in the film, Vogler tells of his first having been smitten by the magic of theater when, as a boy, he watched an actor illustrate a mystery. The actor began by describing a hairpin as an example of doubleness; then, bending it straight, as a single thing; and finally, after breaking the wire, as a different kind of "two." The hairpin, which is ultimately as much (or as little) a mystery as ever, may be seen as corresponding to the line transcribed by the film—from the opposed presence of the director and the actress at the start, to their becoming one entity through the play they are rehearsing (and their "affair") and then parting. But the wonder the boy had felt was not in the metaphor illustrated by the hairpin; it lay instead in the actor's ability to make what had after all been an imaginary piece of wire seem to exist. Thus, the only "meaning" of the fantasy affair that concludes the film may be in its exhibition of the power of theater—in which respect, it also becomes the emblem of the seventy minutes of theater that precede it.

As Bergman approached his sixty-eighth birthday, his fascination with the theater seemed as keen as ever. After ending his contractual obligation to Munich's Residenztheater with Ibsen's *John Gabriel Borkman* in June 1985, he returned "home" to Dramaten, where two Strindberg productions, *Miss Julie* and *A Dream Play*, were scheduled for the spring and *Hamlet*—at long last—for the fall. And in retiring from "the world of cinema," he has not forsworn the camera. In 1985 he filmed Ulla Isaksson's dramatization of her novel *The Blissful Two* for television, and two subsequent collaborations with Isaksson have been planned. In addition, there have been reports, which Bergman will not at present confirm, of his directing three Ibsen dramas for German television, and Placido Domingo has publicly stated that he has agreed to appear in a Bergman version of *The Tales of Hoffmann*. That some of Bergman's "filmed drama" will follow the path from television to the motion picture theater is highly probable. His decision to have *Fanny and Alexander* stand as "the last Bergman film" seems firm, however—although he recently added a very small but most appropriate coda to this dream life in cinema: at the Gothenburg Film in January 1986, he presented "Karin's Face," a short film consisting entirely of photographs of his mother.

Translation of Titles

Films and Filmscripts

Note: Titles are listed alphabetically as they appear in the text; unless otherwise noted, these are literal translations. Next in order is the original title, followed by other titles in English under which the film has been distributed.

After the Rehearsal (*Efter repetitionen*).

Autumn Sonata (*Herbstsonat*; Swedish title: *Höstsonaten*).

Close to Life (*Nära livet*). Also known as *Brink of Life* and *So Close to Life*.

The Communicants (*Nattvardsgästerna*). *Winter Light*.

Cries and Whispers (*Viskningar och rop*). First released in Los Angeles as *Whispers and Cries*—which corresponds to the order in Swedish.

Crisis (*Kris*).

The Deception (*Falskspelet*). *Att spela falskt* means "to deceive"; *falskspelet* implies an act of cheating, as at a game.

The Devil's Eye (*Djävulens öga*).

Divorced (*Frånskild*).

Dreams (*Kvinnodröm*). British title: *Journey into Autumn*. The Swedish title cannot be easily rendered in English: *kvinno* is the combining form of *kvinna*, "woman"; *dröm* is "dream."

Eva.

Evening of the Jesters (*Gycklarnas afton*). Released in the United States as *The Naked Night* and in Britain as *Sawdust and Tinsel*. Aware of the fact that neither of these comes close to the original, several critics have referred to the film as *The Night of the Clowns*—an exact translation of its French title, though a shade away from the Swedish.

The Face (*Ansiktet*). Also known, only in the United States, as *The Magician*.

Face to Face (*Ansikte mot ansikte*).

Fanny and Alexander (*Fanny och Alexander*).

From the Life of the Marionettes (Original title, in German: *Aus dem Leben der Marionetten*).

Fårö Document (*Fårö-dokument*).

Fårö Document 1979 (*Fårö-dokument 1979*).

The Garden of Eden (*Lustgården*). Though usually translated as *The Pleasure Garden*, the Swedish term signifies "Eden."

Hour of the Wolf (*Vargtimmen*).

It Rains on Our Love (*Det regnar på vår kärlek*).

Karin's Face (*Karins ansikte*).

Last Couple Out (*Sista paret ut*). The Swedish title is the name of a children's game.

A Lesson in Love (*En lektion i kärlek*).

The Magic Flute (*Trollflöjten*).

Music in the Dark (*Musik i mörker*). Also known as *Night Is My Future*.

Not to Speak of All These Women (*För att inte tala om alla dessa kvinnor*). Usually referred to as *All These Women*.

A Passion (*En passion*). *The Passion of Anna*, the title it acquired at the last minute in the United States when it was discovered that *A Passion* duplicated an existing title, is obviously misleading, not only because of its sexual connotations but also because the story is about Andreas's passion.

Persona.

The Petrified Prince

Port of Call (*Hamnstad*).

Prison (*Fängelse*). *The Devil's Wanton*.

The Rite (*Riten*). Also known as *The Ritual*.

Scenes from a Marriage (*Scener ur ett äktenskap*).

The Serpent's Egg (Original title, in German: *Das Schlangenei*; Swedish title: *Ormens ägg*).

The Seventh Seal (*Det sjunde inseglet*).

Shame (*Skammen*).

Ship to India (*Skepp till Indialand*). Also known as *A Ship Bound for India* and *The Land of Desire*.

The Silence (*Tystnaden*).

Smiles of the Summer Night (*Sommarnattens leende*). Although the film is known as *Smiles of a Summer Night*, substitution of the indefinite for the definite article creates a different nuance. A still more literal translation of the Swedish would be *The Summer Night's Smiling*.

Such Things Don't Happen Here (*Sånt händer inte här*). In addition to *This Can't Happen Here* and similar variants of the original, the film is also known as *High Tension*, the title under which it was first released outside of Sweden.

The Summer with Monika (*Sommaren med Monika*). Also known as *Monika*.

Summergame (*Sommarlek*). Although it is known in the United States as *Illicit Interlude* and in Britain as *Summer Interlude*, neither the original title nor the film itself conveys the notion of an interlude—and there is no hint of illicitness. Some critics have translated Bergman's title as *Summerplay*; though accurate, this rendering introduces an ambiguity not present in the original.

Thirst (*Törst*). *Three Strange Loves*.

Through a Glass Darkly (*Såsom i en spegel*). Literally: *As in a mirror* (or *As Through in a mirror*).

To Joy (*Till glädje*).

Torment (*Hets*). The British title, *Frenzy*, is an equally valid rendering of the Swedish.

The Touch (*Beröringen*).

The Virgin Spring (*Jungfrukällan*).

While the City Sleeps (*Medan staden sover*).

Wild Strawberries (*Smultronstället*). Literally: *The Wild Strawberry Patch* (or *Place*).

Woman Without a Face (*Kvinna utan ansikte*).

Women's Waiting (*Kvinnors väntan*). Also known in the United States as *Secrets of Women* and in Britain as *Women Waiting*.

Bergman's Plays and Stories

The City (*Staden*).

The Day Ends Early (*Dagen slutar tidigt*).

The Death of Punch (*Kaspers död*). As in German, "Kasper" is the name for Punch ("Kasperina" = Judy).

"The Fish: A Farce for Film" ("Fisken. Fars för film").

Jack Among the Actors (*Jack hos skådespelarna*).

Kamma Noll. Literally "to rake (or comb) zero," this gambling term has no precise English equivalent. It could loosely be translated as "to come up empty," "to draw blank," or "winner take nothing."

The Murder at Barjärna: A Passion Play (*Mordet i Barjärna. Ett passionspel*).

"Painting on Wood: A Morality" ("Trämålning. en moralitet").

The Preserve: A Tragicomedy of Banality (*Reservatet. En banalitetens tragikomedi*).

Rakel and the Cinema Doorman (*Rakel och biografvaktmästaren*).

"A Shorter Tale of One of Jack the Ripper's Earliest Childhood Memories" ("En kortare berättelse. Om ett av Jack Uppskärens tidigaste barndomsminnen).

"Story of the Eiffel Tower" ("Sagan om Eiffeltornet").

Tivoli (*Tivolit*).

To My Terror . . . (*Mig till skräck* . . .).

Recurrent Names

Agnes
Agnes Vergérus (Karin's daughter), *The Touch*
Agnes, *Cries and Whispers*

Albert
Albert (who plays the betrayed husband), "The Fish"
Albert Johansson, *Evening of the Jesters*
Albert Emanuel Vogler, *The Face*
Albert Emmanuel Sebastian Fischer (or Fisher), *The Rite*
Albert (Anna Fromm's brother), *The Preserve*

Alma
Alma Frost, *Evening of the Jesters*
Nurse Alma, *Persona*
Alma Borg, *Hour of the Wolf*
Alma Ekdahl (Gustaf Adolf's wife), *Fanny and Alexander*

Anders (also *Andreas, Andersson*)
Gösta Andersson, *Port of Call*
Anders (the divinity student), *Wild Strawberries*
Anders Ellius, *Close to Life*
Harry and Stina Andersson, *Close to Life*
Anders Vergérus, *The Face*
Johan Andersson, *A Passion*
Andreas Winkelman, *A Passion*
Andreas Fromm, *The Preserve*
Andreas Vergérus (Karin's husband), *The Touch*
Anders Vergérus (Karin's son), *The Touch*

Anna (also *Anne, Anita, Susanne*)
Susanne Karlberg, *Kamma Noll*
Anne (Joakim's wife), *The City*

Anita Lobelius, *Women's Waiting*
Susanne (eventually Joakim's surrogate mother), "The Fish"
Anne (Joakim's wife), "The Fish"
Anne (Albert's mistress), *Evening of the Jesters*
Susanne (David's mistress), *A Lesson in Love*
Susanne, *Dreams*
Anne Egerman, *Smiles of the Summer Night*
Anita, *Last Couple Out*
Anna (Fanny's daughter, the ingenue in *The Garden of Eden*)
Anna, *The Silence*
Anne, *The Deception*
Anna Fromm, *A Passion*
Anna Fromm, *The Preserve*
Anna, *Cries and Whispers*
Aunt Anna (played by Käbi Laretei), *Fanny and Alexander*
Anna Egerman, *After the Rehearsal*

Borg
Isak Borg, *Wild Strawberries*
Johan Borg, *Hour of the Wolf*

David
David Lindell, *It Rains on Our Love*
David Nyström, *Summergame*
David Erneman, *A Lesson in Love*
David Franzén, *The Garden of Eden*
David, *Through a Glass Darkly*
David Kovacs, *The Touch*
David (the doctor who is Maria's lover), *Cries and Whispers*

Egerman (also *Egermann*)
Fredrik Egerman, *Smiles of the Summer Night*
Consul Abraham Egerman, *The Face*
Peter Egermann, *From the Life of the Marionettes*
Anna Egerman, *After the Rehearsal*

Elis (also *Ellius*)
Anders Ellius (Cecilia's husband), *Close to Life*
Elis Vergérus, *A Passion* (Note: like Anders Ellius, Elis Vergérus is played by Erland Josephson. The relationship to Anders Ellius is also reflected by a second figure in *A Passion*, Andreas.)

Emanuel (also *Emmanuel, Manuela*)
Albert Emanuel Vogler, *The Face*
Albert Emmanuel Sebastian Fisher (or Fischer), *The Rite*
Manuela, *The Serpent's Egg*

Erik
Jan-Erik Widgren, *Torment*
Stig Eriksson, *To Joy*
Tomas Eriksson, *The Communicants*
Dr. Erik Isaksson, *Face to Face*
Erik (Eva's dead son), *Autumn Sonata*

Eva
Eva, *Eva*

Eva Rosenberg, *Shame*
Eva Vergérus, *A Passion*
Eva (eventually Johan's mistress), *Scenes from a Marriage*
Eva, Autumn *Sonata*

Fredrik
Bo Fredriksson, *Eva*
Fredrik Lobelius, *Women's Waiting*
Fredrik Egerman (+ Fredrik, Desireé's son), *Smiles of the Summer Night*
Fredrik (Minus), *Through a Glass Darkly*
Fredrik Blom (the organist), *The Communicants*
Fredrik (Karin's husband), *Cries and Whispers*

Grandé
Martin Grandé, *Woman Without a Face*
Martin Grandé, *Prison*

Hans (see also: *Johan*)
Hans Dahlin (the protagonist's father), *Last Couple Out*
Hans Winkelmann (the leader—and "father figure"—of Les Riens), *The Rite*
Hans Vergérus, *The Serpent's Egg*

Henrik
Henrik (Marie's lover), *Summergame**
Henrik Lobelius (the callow lover), *Women's Waiting**
Professor Henrik Erneman, *A Lesson in Love**
Henrik Lobelius, *Dreams*
Henrik Egerman, *Smiles of the Summer Night**
Henrik Vogler, *After the Rehearsal*

Isak (also *Isaksson*)
Isak (the old Jew), *To My Terror . . .*
Isak Borg, *Wild Strawberries*
Pastor Isak, *Cries and Whispers*
Jenny Isaksson and Dr. Erik Isaksson (Jenny's father), *Face to Face*
Isak Jacobi, *Fanny and Alexander*

Jack (also *Jacqueline*)
Jack Kasparsson, *Jack Among the Actors*
Jack the Ripper, "A Shorter Tale of One of Jack the Ripper's Earliest Childhood Memories"
Jack, *Crisis*
Jacqueline (called Nix), *A Lesson in Love*

Jacobi
Colonel Jacobi, *Shame*
Mrs. Jacobi (who wants to end her loveless marriage), *Scenes from a Marriage*
Tomas Jacobi, *Face to Face*
Isak Jacobi, *Fanny and Alexander*

*Fredrik and Henrik are paired as father and son in *Smiles of the Summer Night*; though not father and son, the characters with the same names in *Women's Waiting* play very similar roles: Fredrik is the worldly middle-aged man; Henrik, the love-struck naïf.

"Henrik" is also paired with "David." In *A Lesson in Love*, Henrik Erneman is the wise old father, and David is his middle-aged son. In *Summergame*, Henrik is Marie's young first lover; David, his "older" (and tougher) successor.

The two names linked to "Henrik" are also linked to each other: in *Through a Glass Darkly*, David and Fredrik (called Minus) are father and son.

Jenny (also *Jens*, *Jöns*, *Jensen*; see also: *Johan*)
Jenny, *Crisis*
Jenny, *The Day Ends Early*
Jens, *Evening of the Jesters*
Jöns, *The Seventh Seal*
Jenny Isaksson, *Face to Face*
Mogens Jensen, *From the Life of the Marionettes*

Joakim
Joakim, *The City*
Joakim Naked, "The Story of the Eiffel Tower"
Joakim Naked, "The Fish"

Johan (also Jan, Johansson, Johannes, Jenny, Jens)
Jan-Erik Widgren, *Torment*
Johannes (the son), *Ship to India*
Jan Karlberg, *Kamma Noll*
Albert Johansson, *Evening of the Jesters*
Johan Spegel, *The Face*
Johan Åkerblom (old man at Mittsunda mass), *The Communicants*
Johan (the boy who has given up confirmation class), *The Communicants*
Johan (Anna's son), *The Silence*
Johan Borg, *Hour of the Wolf*
Johan (the young soldier mothered by Eva), *Shame*
Johan Andersson, *A Passion*
Johan, *Scenes from a Marriage*

Karin
Karin (who kills her baby), *The Murder in Barjärna*
Karin, *Women's Waiting*
Karin, *The Virgin Spring*
Karin, *Through a Glass Darkly*
Karin Persson, *The Communicants*
Karin Vergérus, *The Touch*
Karin, *Cries and Whispers*

Katarina
Nurse Katarina (Alma's friend, who initiates the orgy), *Persona*
Katarina Egerman, *Scenes from a Marriage*
Katarina Egermann, *From the Life of the Marionettes*
Katarina Krafft, called Ka (the prostitute), *From the Life of the Marionettes*

Lobelius
Eugen Lobelius, *Women's Waiting* (and *Rakel and the Cinema Doorman*)
Henrik Lobelius, *Dreams*
(There is also a minor character named Lobelius in *Shame*)

Maria (also *Marie*, *Mia*)
Marie (Jack's girlfriend), "A Shorter Tale"
Mia, *Rakel and the Movie Theater Doorman*
Marie, *The City*
Marie, *Summergame*
Mari (Jonas's wife), *The Murder in Barjärna*
Mia, *The Seventh Seal*
Britt-Marie, *The Devil's Eye*

Maria, *Cries and Whispers*
Maria, *Face to Face*

Marianne (see also *Marie, Anne*)
Marianne Berg, *Divorced*
Marianne Erneman, *A Lesson in Love*
Marianne, *Dreams*
Marianne Borg, *Wild Strawberries*
Marianne, *Scenes from a Marriage*

Marta (also *Märta, Martha, Märeta*)
Marta, *To Joy*
Märta, *Women's Waiting*
Martha, "The Story of the Eiffel Tower"
Märeta, *The Virgin Spring*
Märta Lundberg, *The Communicants*

Mikael (also *Mikaela*)
Mikael Bro, *To Joy* (also *Jack Among the Actors*)
Mikael (Mia's baby), *The Seventh Seal*
Mikael Strömberg (Tomas's homosexual lover), *Face to Face*
Mikaela (the prostitute), *The Serpent's Egg*
Mikael Bergman (the actor who plays Hamlet), *Fanny and Alexander*
Mikael Egerman (the actor, corresponding to Mikael Bro, who is Anna's father), *After the Rehearsal*

Rosenberg
Jan and Eva Rosenberg, *Shame*
Abel, Max and Manuela Rosenberg, *The Serpent's Egg*

Tomas
Tomas, *Prison*
Tomas Eriksson, The *Communicants*
Tomas Jacobi, *Face to Face*

Vergérus
Elis and Eva Vergérus, A *Passion*
Dr. Anders Vergérus, The *Face*
Andreas and Karin Vergérus, The *Touch*
Hans Vergérus, *The Serpent's Egg*
Bishop Edvard Vergérus, *Fanny and Alexander*

Vogler
Albert Emanuel Vogler, *The Face*
Elisabet Vogler, *Persona*
Veronica Vogler, *Hour of the Wolf*
Henrik Vogler, *After the Rehearsal*

Filmography

Hets (*Torment*)
Script: IB. Director: Alf Sjöberg. Photography: Martin Bodin. Music: Hilding Rosenberg. Art Direction: Arne Åkermark. Editing: Oscar Rosander. Production Company: Svensk Filmindustri. 101 minutes. Swedish premiere: October 2, 1944.

Cast: Stig Järrel (Caligula), Alf Kjellin (Jan-Erik Widgren), Mai Zetterling (Bertha Olsson), Gösta Cederlund (Pippi), Olof Winnerstrand (the principal), Stig Olin (Sandman), Jan Molander (Pettersson), Olav Riego (Jan-Erik's father), Märta Arbiin (Jan-Erik's mother), Hugo Björne (the doctor), Gunnar Björnstrand (a teacher), Birger Malmsten (a student).

Kris (*Crisis*)
Script: IB, from the play, *Moderdyret*, by Leck Fischer. Photography: Gösta Roosling. Music: Erland von Koch. Art Direction: Arne Åkermark. Editing: Oscar Rosander. Artistic Adviser: Victor Sjöström. Production Manager: Harald Molander. Production Company: Svensk Filmindustri. 93 minutes. Swedish premiere: February 25, 1946.

Cast: Dagny Lind (Ingeborg Johnson), Inga Landgré (Nelly), Marianne Löfgren (Jenny), Stig Olin (Jack), Allan Bohlin (Ulf), Ernst Eklund (Uncle Edvard), Signe Wirff (Aunt Jessie), Svea Holst (Malin), Arne Lindblad (major), Julia Caesar (mayor's wife).

Det regnar på vår kärlek (*It Rains on Our Love*)
Script: IB and Herbert Grevenius, from the play, *Bra mennesker*, by Oskar Braaten. Photography: Göran Strindberg, Hilding Bladh. Music: Erland von Koch, with extracts from Richard Wagner and Bernhard Flies. Art Direction: P. A. Lundgren. Editing: Tage Holmberg. Producer: Lorens Marmstedt. Production Company: Sveriges Folkbiografer, distributed through Nordisk Tonefilm. 95 minutes. Swedish premiere: November 9, 1946.

Cast: Barbro Kollberg (Maggi), Birger Malmsten (David Lindell), Gösta Cederlund (man with the umbrella), Ludde Gentzel (Håkansson), Douglas Håge (Andersson), Hjördis Pettersson (Mrs. Andersson), Julia Caesar (Hanna Ledin), Sture Ericsson, Ulf Johansson (peddlers), Gunnar Björnstrand (Mr. Purman), Åke Fridell (assistant vicar), Torsten Hillberg (vicar), Benkt-Åke Benktsson (prosecutor), Erik Rosén (the Judge), Magnus Kesster (bicycle repairman), Sif Ruud (his wife), Erland Josephson (clerk in vicar's office).

Kvinna utan ansikte (*Woman Without a Face*)
Script: IB. Director: Gustaf Molander. Photography: Åke Dahlquist. Music: Erik Nordgren.

Art Direction: Arne Åkermark. Editing: Oscar Rosander. Production Company: Svensk Filmindustri. 100 minutes. Swedish premiere: September 16, 1947.

Cast: Gunn Wållgren (Rut Köhler), Alf Kjellin (Martin Grandé), Stig Olin (Ragnar Ekberg), Anita Björk (Frida, Martin's wife), Olof Winnerstrand (Martin's father), Marianne Löfgren (Charlotte), Georg Funkquist (Victor), Åke Grönberg (Sam Svensson, the chimney sweep), Linnea Hillberg (Martin's mother).

Skepp till Indialand (*Ship to India*)

Script: IB, from the play, *Skepp till Indialand*, by Martin Söderhjelm. Photography: Göran Strindberg. Music: Erland von Koch. Art Direction: P. A. Lundgren. Editing: Tage Holmberg. Production Manager: Allan Ekelund. Producer: Lorens Marmstedt. Production Company: Sveriges Folkbiografer, distributed through Nordisk Tonefilm. 102 minutes. Swedish premiere: September 22, 1947.

Cast: Holger Löwenadler (Alexander Blom), Birger Malmsten (Johannes), Gertrud Fridh (Sally), Anna Lindahl (Alice, his wife), Lasse Krantz (Hans), Jan Molander (Bertil), Erik Hell (Pekka), Naemi Briese (Selma), Hjördis Pettersson (Sofie), Åke Fridell (director of variety theater), Peter Lindgren (foreign sailor), Kiki (the dwarf).

Musik i mörker (*Music in the Dark*)

Script: Dagmar Edqvist, from her novel with the same title. Photography: Göran Strindberg. Music: Erland von Koch, with extracts from Chopin, Beethoven, Badarczewska-Baranowska, Schumann, Handel, Wagner, and Tom Andy (pseudonym for Thomas Andersen). Art Direction: P. A. Lundgren. Editing: Lennart Wallén. Production Manager: Allan Ekelund. Producer: Lorens Marmstedt. Production Company: Terraproduktion, distributed through Terrafilm. 85 minutes. Swedish premiere: January 17, 1948.

Cast: Mai Zetterling (Ingrid Olofsdotter), Birger Malmsten (Bengt Vyldeke), Bibi Skoglund (Agneta Vyldeke, his sister), Olof Winnerstrand (Kerrman, the minister), Naima Wifstrand (Mrs. Schröder), Åke Claesson (Mr. Schröder), Hilda Bergström (Lovisa), Douglas Håge (restaurant owner), Gunnar Björnstrand (Klasson, violinist).

Hamnstad (*Port of Call*)

Script: Olle Länsberg, IB. Photography: Gunnar Fischer. Music: Erland von Koch. Art Direction: Nils Svenwall. Editing: Oscar Rosander. Production Manager: Harald Molander. Production Company: Svensk Filmindustri. 99 minutes. Swedish premiere: October 11, 1948.

Cast: Nine-Christine Jönsson (Berit Holm), Bengt Eklund (Gösta Andersson), Erik Hell (Berit's father), Berta Hall (Berit's mother), Mimi Nelson (Gertrud), Sture Ericson (her father), Birgitta Valberg (Agnes Vilander, social worker), Hans Strååt (Vilander), Harry Ahlin (man from Skåne), Nils Hallberg (Gustav), Sven-Eric Gamble ("the Oak"), Stig Olin (Tomas), Sif Ruud (Mrs. Krona), Nils Dahlgren (Gertrud's father), Kate Elffors (Berit Holm as a child).

Eva

Script: IB and Gustaf Molander. Director: Gustaf Molander. Photography: Åke Dahlquist. Music: Erik Nordgren. Art Direction: Nils Svenwall. Editing: Oscar Rosander. Production Company: Svensk Filmindustri. 97 minutes. Swedish premiere: December 26, 1948.

Cast: Eva Stiberg (Eva), Birger Malmsten (Bo), Eva Dahlbeck (Susanne), Stig Olin (Göran), Åke Claesson (Fredriksson), Wanda Rothgardt (Mrs. Fredriksson), Inga Landgré (Frida), Hilda Borgström (Maria), Lasse Sarri (Bo, aged twelve).

Fängelse (*Prison*)

Script: IB. Photography: Göran Strindberg. Music: Erland von Koch, Alice Tegnér, Oscar Ahnfelt. Art Direction: P. A. Lundgren. Editing: Lennart Wallén. Production Manager: Allan Ekelund. Producer: Lorens Marmstedt. Production Company: Terraproduktion, distributed through Terrafilm. 80 minutes. Swedish premiere: March 19, 1949.

Cast: Doris Svedlund (Birgitta-Carolina Söderberg), Birger Malmsten (Tomas), Eva Henning (Sofi), Hasse Ekman (Martin Grandé), Stig Olin (Peter), Irma Christensson (Linnéa), Anders Henrikson (Paul, professor of mathematics), Marianne Löfgren (Signe Bohlin), Curt Masreliez (Alf), Carl-Henrik Fant (Arne, an actor), Inger Juel (Greta, an actress), Åke Fridell (Magnus), Ulf Palme (man in dream), Birgit "Bibi" Lindqvist (Anna Bohlin), Arne Ragneborn.

Törst (*Thirst*)
Script: Herbert Grevenius, from the collection of short stories, *Törst*, by Birgit Tengroth. Photography: Gunnar Fischer. Music: Erik Nordgren. Choreography: Ellen Bergman. Art Direction: Nils Svenwall. Editing: Oscar Rosander. Production Manager: Helge Hagerman. Production Company: Svensk Filmindustri. 88 minutes. Swedish premiere: October 17, 1949.

Cast: Eva Henning (Rut), Birger Malmsten (Bertil, her husband), Birgit Tengroth (Viola), Mimi Nelson (Valborg), Hasse Ekman (Rosengren), Bengt Eklund (Raoul), Gaby Stenberg (Astrid, his wife), Naima Wifstrand (Miss Henriksson, ballet teacher), Sven-Eric Gamble (worker in glass factory), Gunnar Nielsen (Rosengren's assistant), Estrid Hesse (patient), Helge Hagerman (Swedish minister), Calle Flygare (Danish minister), Monica Weinzierl (girl on train), Inga Gill (lady in hotel), Ingmar Bergman (passenger).

Till glädje (*To Joy*)
Script: IB. Photography: Gunnar Fischer. Editing: Oscar Rosander. Music: Beethoven, Mozart, Mendelssohn, Smetana, Sam Samson, and Erik Johnsson. Art Direction: Nils Svenwall. Production Manager: Allan Ekelund. Production Company: Svensk Filmindustri. 98 minutes. Swedish premiere: February 20, 1950.

Cast: Maj-Britt Nilsson (Marta), Stig Olin (Stig Eriksson), Victor Sjöström (Sönderby), Birger Malmsten (Marcel), John Ekman (Mikael Bro), Margit Carlqvist (Nelly Bro), Sif Ruud (Stina), Erland Josephson (Bertil), Ernst Brunman (janitor at concert house), Allan Ekelund (vicar at wedding), Maud Hyttenberg (toyshop clerk), Berit Holmström (Lisa), Eva Fritz-Nilsson (Lisa as a baby), Björn Montin (Lasse), Staffan Axelsson (Lasse as a baby), George Skarstedt (flutist), Svea Holst (nurse), Ingmar Bergman (himself), Rune Stylander (Persson), Carin Swensson (Anna), Svea Holm (Märta), Dagny Lind (Grannie).

Medan staden sover (*While the City Sleeps*)
Script: Lars-Eric Kjellgren and Per Anders Fogelström, from a synopsis by IB of a story by Per Anders Fogelström. Director: Lars-Eric Kjellgren. Photography: Martin Bodin. Art Direction: Nils Svenwall. Production Manager: Helge Hagerman. Production Company: Svensk Filmindustri. 101 minutes. Swedish premiere: September 8, 1950.

Cast: Sven-Erik Gamble (Jompa), Inga Landgré (Iris), Adolf Jahr (Iris's father), John Elfström (Jompa's father), Märta Dorff (Iris's mother), Ulf Palme (Kalle Lund), Harriet Andersson.

Sånt händer inte här (*Such Things Don't Happen Here*)
Script: Herbert Grevenius, from the novel *I løpet av tolv timer*, by Waldemar Brøgger (Bergman's collaboration uncredited). Photography: Gunnar Fischer. Editing: Lennart Wallén. Music: Erik Nordgren (music in export version by Herbert Stéen-Ostling). Art Direction: Nils Svenwall. Production Manager: Helge Hagerman. Production Company: Svensk Filmindustri. 84 minutes. Swedish premiere: October 23, 1950.

Cast: Signe Hasso (Vera), Alf Kjellin (Björn Almkvist), Ulf Palme (Atkä Natas), Gösta Cederlund (doctor), Yngve Nordwall (Lindell), Hannu Kompus (priest), Els Vaarman (female refugee), Sylvia Tael (Vanja), Edmar Kuus (Leino), Helena Kuus (another refugee), Rudolf Lipp ("Shadow"), Stig Olin (young man).

Frånskild (*Divorced*)
Script: IB, Herbert Grevenius. Director: Gustaf Molander. Photography: Åke Dahlquist. Production Company: Svensk Filmindustri. 103 minutes. Swedish premiere: December 26, 1951.

Cast: Inga Tidblad (Gertrud Holmgren), Alf Kjellin (Dr. Bertil Nordelius), Doris Svedlund (Marianne Berg), Hjördis Pettersson (Mrs. Nordelius), Håkan Westergren (P. A. Beckman), Holger Löwenadler (Tore Holmgren), Marianne Löfgren (Ingeborg), Stig Olin (Hans).

Sommarlek (*Summergame*)

Script: IB, Herbert Grevenius, from a story by IB entitled "Marie." Photography: Gunnar Fischer. Editing: Oscar Rosander. Art Direction: Nils Svenwall. Music: Erik Nordgren, Delibes, Chopin, and Tchaikovsky. Production Manager: Allan Ekelund. Production Company: Svensk Filmindustri. 96 minutes. Swedish premiere: October 1, 1951.

Cast: Maj-Britt Nilsson (Marie), Birger Malmsten (Henrik), Alf Kjellin (David Nyström), Georg Funkquist (Uncle Erland), Renée Björling (Aunt Elisabeth), Mimi Pollak (Henrik's aunt), Annalisa Ericson (Kaj, a ballerina), Stig Olin (ballet master), Gunnar Olsson (pastor), John Botvid (Karl, a janitor), Douglas Håge (Nisse, a janitor), Julia Caesar (Maja, a dresser), Carl Ström (Sandell, stage manager), Torsten Lilliecrona (lighting man), Marianne Schuler (Kerstin), Ernst Brunman (boat's captain), Olav Riego (doctor), Fylgia Zadig (nurse), Sten Mattsson (boat hand), Carl-Axel Elfving (man with flowers), Eskil Eckert-Lundin (orchestra conductor), and the ballet corps of the Royal Opera.

Kvinnors väntan (*Women's Waiting*)

Script: IB. Photography: Gunnar Fischer. Music: Erik Nordgren. Art Direction: Nils Svenwall. Editing: Oscar Rosander. Production Company: Svensk Filmindustri. 107 minutes. Swedish premiere: November 3, 1952.

Cast: Anita Björk (Rakel), Jarl Kulle (Kaj), Karl-Arne Homsten (Eugen Lobelius), Maj-Britt Nilsson (Märta), Birger Malmsten (Martin Lobelius), Eva Dahlbeck (Karin), Gunnar Björnstrand (Fredrik Lobelius), Gerd Andersson (Maj), Björn Bjelvenstam (Henrik), Aino Taube (Anita), Håkan Westergren (Paul), Naima Wifstrand (Mrs. Lobelius), Torsten Lilliecrona (host at nightclub), Douglas Håge (porter), Märta Arbiin (Nurse Rit), Kjell Nordensköld (Bob), Carl Ström (anesthetist), Ingmar Bergman.

Sommaren med monika (*The Summer with Monika*)

Script: IB, P. A. Fogelström, from a novel by Fogelstrom. Photography: Gunnar Fischer. Music: Erik Nordgren, with the waltz "Kärlekens hamn," by Filip Olsson. Art Direction: P. A. Lundgren, Nils Svenwall. Editing: Tage Holmberg, Gösta Lewin. Production Manager: Allan Ekelund. Production Company: Svensk Filmindustri. 96 minutes. Swedish premiere: February 9, 1953.

Cast: Harriet Andersson (Monika), Lars Ekborg (Harry), John Harryson (Lelle), Georg Skarstedt (Harry's father), Dagmar Ebbesen (Harry's aunt), Naemi Briese (Monika's mother), Åke Fridell (Monika's father), Gösta Eriksson (manager of glass shop), Gösta Gustafsson, Sigge Fürst, Gösta Pŕuzelius (employees in glass shop), Arthur Fischer (vegetable manager), Torsten Lilliecrona (driver), Bengt Eklund (first man), Gustaf Färingborg (second man), Ivar Wahlgren (villager), Renée Björling (his wife), Catrin Westerlund (his daughter), Harry Ahlin (other villager), Wiktor Andersson and Birger Sahlberg (two men in street), Hanny Schedin (Mrs. Bohman), Åke Grönberg (foreman), Magnus Kesster and Carl-Axel Elfving (workmen), Anders Andelius, Gordon Löwenadler, Bengt Brunskog.

Gycklarnas afton (*Evening of the Jesters*)

Script: IB. Photography: Hilding Bladh, Göran Strindberg, Sven Nykvist. Music: Karl-Birger Blomdahl. Art Direction: Bibi Lindström. Editing: Carl-Olov Skeppstedt. Costumes: Mago. Producer: Rune Waldekranz. Production Company: Sandrews. 92 minutes. Swedish premiere: September 14, 1953.

Cast: Harriet Andersson (Anne), Åke Grönberg (Albert Johansson), Hasse Ekman (Frans), Anders Ek (Frost), Gudrun Brost (Alma), Annika Tretow (Agda, Albert's wife), Gunnar Björnstrand (Mr. Sjuberg), Erik Strandmark (Jens), Kiki (the dwarf), Åke Fridell (officer), Majken Torkeli (Mrs. Ekberg), Vanjek Hedberg (Ekberg's son), Curt Löwgren (Blom).

En lektion i kärlek (*A Lesson in Love*)
Script: IB. Photography: Martin Bodin. Music: Dag Wirén. Art Direction: P. A. Lundgren. Editing: Oscar Rosander. Production Manager: Allan Ekelund. Production Company: Svensk Filmindustri. 95 minutes. Swedish premiere: October 4, 1954.

Cast: Eva Dahlbeck (Marianne Erneman), Gunnar Björnstrand (Dr. David Erneman, her husband), Yvonne Lombard (Suzanne), Harriet Andersson (Jacqueline, called Nix), Åke Grönberg (Carl-Adam), Olof Winnerstrand (Professor Henrik Erneman), Renée Björling (Svea Erneman), Birgitte Reimar (Lise), John Elfström (Sam), Dagmar Ebbesen (nurse), Helge Hagerman (traveling salesman), Sigge Fürst (minister), Gösta Prüzelius (guard on train), Carl Ström (Uncle Axel), Arne Lindblad (hotel manager), Torsten Lilliecrona (porter), Yvonne Brosset (ballerina).

Kvinnodröm (*Dreams*)
Script: IB. Photography: Hilding Bladh. Art Direction: Gittan Gustafsson. Editing: Carl-Olov Skeppstedt. Production Manager: Rune Waldekranz. Production Company: Sandrews. 86 minutes. Swedish premiere: August 22, 1955.

Cast: Eva Dahlbeck (Susanne), Harriet Andersson (Doris), Gunnar Björnstrand (Consul Sönderby), Ulf Palme (Henrik Lobelius), Inga Landgré (Mrs. Lobelius), Sven Lindberg (Palle), Naima Wifstrand (Mrs. Arén), Benkt-Åke Benktsson (Magnus), Git Gay (lady in studio), Ludde Gentzel (Sundström, the photographer), Kerstin Hedeby (Marianne), Inga Gill (shopgirl), Axel Düberg (photographer in Stockholm), Ingmar Bergman.

Sommarnattens leende (*Smiles of the Summer Night*)
Script: IB. Photography: Gunnar Fischer. Music: Erik Nordgren. Art Direction: P. A. Lundgren. Costumes: Mago. Makeup: Carl M. Lundh. Editing: Oscar Rosander. Production Manager: Allan Ekelund. Production Company: Svensk Filmindustri. 108 minutes. Swedish premiere: December 26, 1955.

Cast: Gunnar Björnstrand (Fredrik Egerman), Eva Dahlbeck (Desirée Armfeldt), Ulla Jacobsson (Anne Egerman), Harriet Andersson (Petra, the maid), Margit Carlqvist (Charlotte Malcolm), Jarl Kulle (Count Carl-Magnus Malcolm), Åke Fridell (Frid, the groom), Björn Bjelvenstam (Henrik Egerman), Naima Wifstrand (Madame Armfeldt), Jullan Kindahl (the cook), Gull Natorp (Malla, Desirée's maid), Birgitta Valberg, Bibi Andersson (actresses), Anders Wulff (Desirée's son), Gunnar Nielsen (Niklas), Gösta Prüzelius (footman), Svea Holst (dresser), Hans Strååt (Almgren, the photographer), Lisa Lundholm (Mrs. Almgren), Sigge Fürst (policeman), Lena Söderblom, Mona Malm (chambermaids), Josef Norman (elderly dinner guest).

Sista paret ut (*Last Couple Out*)
Script: IB and Alf Sjöberg. Director: Alf Sjöberg. Photography: Martin Bodin. Music: Erik Nordgren, Charles Redland, Bengt Hallberg. Art Direction: Harald Garmland. Editing: Oscar Rosander. Production Company: Svensk Filmindustri. 104 minutes. Swedish premiere: November 12, 1956.

Cast: Eva Dahlbeck (Susanne Dahlin), Olof Widgren (Hans Dahlin), Björn Bjelvenstam (Bo Dahlin), Johnny Johansson (Sven Dahlin), Märta Arbiin (Grandmother), Jullan Kindahl (Alma, the Dahlins' maid), Harriet Andersson (Anita), Bibi Andersson (Kerstin), Jarl Kulle (Dr. Farell), Aino Taube (Kerstin's mother), Hugo Björne (lecturer), Nancy Dalunde (Mrs. Farell).

Det sjunde inseglet (*The Seventh Seal*)
Script: IB. Photography: Gunnar Fischer. Music: Erik Nordgren. Art Direction: P. A. Lundgren. Editing: Lennart Wallén. Choreography: Else Fisher. Costumes: Manne Lindholm. Makeup: Carl M. Lundh (Nils Nittel). Production Manager: Allan Ekelund. Production Company: Svensk Filmindustri. 95 minutes. Swedish premiere: February 16, 1957.

Cast: Max von Sydow (the Knight, Antonius Block), Gunnar Björnstrand (Squire Jöns), Bengt Ekerot (Death), Nils Poppe (Jof), Bibi Andersson (Mia), Åke Fridell (Plog, the blacksmith), Inga Gill (Lisa, Plog's wife), Maud Hansson (witch), Inga Landgré (Knight's wife), Gunnel Lindblom (girl), Bertil Anderberg (Raval), Anders Ek (Monk), Gunnar Olsson (Albertus, the painter), Erik Strandmark (Skat), Benkt-Åke Benktsson (tavern owner), Ulf Johansson (leader of the soldiers), Lars Lind (young monk), Gudrun Brost (woman in tavern), Ove Svensson (corpse on hillside).

Smultronstället (*Wild Strawberries*)
Script: IB. Photography: Gunnar Fischer. Music: Erik Nordgren. Art Direction: Gittan Gustafsson. Editing: Oscar Rosander. Costumes: Millie Ström. Makeup: Carl M. Lundh (Nils Nittel). Production Manager: Allan Ekelund. Production Company: Svensk Filmindustri. 90 minutes. Swedish premiere: December 26, 1957.
    Cast: Victor Sjöström (Professor Isak Borg), Bibi Andersson (Sara), Ingrid Thulin (Marianne), Gunnar Björnstrand (Evald), Folke Sundquist (Anders), Björn Bjelvenstam (Viktor), Naima Wifstrand (Isak's mother), Jullan Kindahl (Agda, the housekeeper), Gunnar Sjöberg (Alman), Gunnel Broström (Mrs. Alman), Gertrud Fridh (Isak's wife), Åke Fridell (her lover), Max von Sydow (Åkerman), Sif Ruud (aunt), Yngve Nordwall (Uncle Aron), Per Sjöstrand (Sigfrid), Gio Petré (Sigbritt), Gunnel Lindblom (Charlotta), Maud Hansson (Angelica), Anne-Marie Wiman (Mrs. Åkerman), Eva Norée (Anna), Lena Bergman, Monica Ehrling (twins), Per Skogsberg (Hagbart), Göran Lundquist (Benjamin), Prof. Sigge Wulff (rector, Lund University).

Nära livet (*Close to Life*)
Script: IB, Ulla Isaksson, based on the short story, "Det vänliga, värdiga," in her book, *Dödens faster*. Photography: Max Wilén. Art Direction: Bibi Lindström. Editing: Carl-Olov Skeppstedt. Production Company: Nordisk Tonefilm. 84 minutes. Swedish premiere: March 31, 1958.
    Cast: Eva Dahlbeck (Stina Andersson), Ingrid Thulin (Cecilia Ellius), Bibi Andersson (Hjördis), Barbro Hiort af Ornäs (Nurse Brita), Erland Josephson (Anders Ellius), Inga Landgré (Greta Ellius), Max von Sydow (Harry Andersson), Gunnar Sjöberg (Dr. Nordlander), Anne-Marie Gyllenspetz (welfare worker), Sissi Kaiser (Nurse Marit), Margareta Krook (Dr. Larsson), Lars Lind (Dr. Thylenius), Monica Ekberg (Hjördis's friend), Gun Jönsson (night nurse), Inga Gill (woman), Gunnar Nielsen (a doctor), Maud Elfsiö (trainee nurse), Kristina Adolphson (assistant).

Ansiktet (*The Face*)
Script: IB. Photography: Gunnar Fischer. Music: Erik Nordgren. Art Direction: P. A. Lundgren. Editing: Oscar Rosander. Costumes: Manne Lindholm, Greta Johansson. Makeup: Börje Lundh, Nils Nittel. Production Manager: Allan Ekelund. Production Company: Svensk Filmindustri. 100 minutes. Swedish premiere: December 26, 1958.
    Cast: Max von Sydow (Albert Emanuel Vogler), Ingrid Thulin (Manda Vogler), Åke Fridell (Tubal), Naima Wifstrand (Vogler's grandmother), Gunnar Björnstrand (Dr. Anders Vergérus), Bengt Ekerot (Spegel), Bibi Andersson (Sara Lindqvist), Gertrud Fridh (Ottilia Egerman), Erland Josephson (Consul Abraham Egerman), Lars Ekborg (Simson, the coachman), Toivo Pawlo (Frans Starbeck), Ulla Sjöblom (Mrs. Starbeck), Axel Düberg (Rustan, the butler), Birgitta Pettersson (Sanna, the maid), Oscar Ljung (Antonsson), Sif Ruud (Sofia Garp).

Jungfrukällan (*The Virgin Spring*)
Script: Ulla Isaksson, based on a fourteenth-century legend, "Töres dotter i Wänge." Photography: Sven Nykvist. Music: Erik Nordgren. Art Direction: P. A. Lundgren. Production Buyer: Karl-Arne Bergman. Editing: Oscar Rosander. Costumes: Marik Vos. Makeup: Börje Lundh. Production Manager: Allan Ekelund. Production Company: Svensk Filmindustri. 88 minutes. Swedish premiere: February 8, 1960.
    Cast: Max von Sydow (Töre), Birgitta Valberg (Märeta), Birgitta Pettersson (Karin), Gunnel Lindblom (Ingeri), Axel Düberg (thin herdsman), Tor Isedal (mute herdsman), Allan Edwall (beggar), Ove Porath (boy), Axel Slangus (Odin worshipper), Gudrun Brost (Frida), Oscar Ljung (Simon), Tor Borong, Leif Forstenberg (farm hands).

Djävulens öga (*The Devil's Eye*)
Script: IB, based on the Danish radio play, *Don Juan vender tilbage*, by Oluf Bang. Photography: Gunnar Fischer. Music: Erik Nordgren, with extracts from Domenico Scarlatti, played by Käbi Laretei. Art Direction: P. A. Lundgren. Production Buyer: Karl-Arne Bergman. Editing: Oscar Rosander. Costumes: Mago. Makeup: Börje Lundh. Production Manager: Allan Ekelund. Production Company: Svensk Filmindustri. 86 minutes. Swedish premiere: October 17, 1960.

Cast: Jarl Kulle (Don Juan), Bibi Andersson (Britt-Marie), Stig Järrel (Satan), Nils Poppe (pastor), Gertrud Fridh (Renata, the pastor's wife), Sture Lagerwall (Pablo, Don Juan's servant), Gunnar Björnstrand (narrator), Georg Funkquist (Count Armand de Rochefoucauld), Gunnar Sjöberg (Marquis Giuseppe Maria de Maccopazza), Torsten Winge (old man), Axel Düberg (Jonas), Kristina Adolphson (veiled woman), Allan Edwall (Ear Devil), Ragnar Arvedson (Devil in Attendance), Börje Lundh (hairdresser), Lenn Hjortzberg (enema doctor), Tom Olsson (black masseur), Inga Gill (housemaid).

Lustgården (**The Garden of Eden**)
Script: IB and Erland Josephson under the pseudonym "Buntel Eriksson." Director: Alf Kjellin. Photography: Gunnar Fischer. Music: Erik Nordgren. Art Direction: P. A. Lundgren. Editing: Ulla Ryghe. Production Company: Svensk Filmindustri. 93 minutes. Swedish premiere: December 26, 1961.

Cast: Sickan Carlsson (Fanny), Gunnar Björnstrand (David Samuel Franzén), Bibi Andersson (Anna, Fanny's daughter), Per Myrberg (Emil), Stig Järrel (Ludvig Hesekial Lundberg), Hjördis Petterson (Ellen Franzén), Torsten Winge (Wibom), Gösta Cederlund (Liljedahl), Fillie Lyckow (Berta), Jan Tiselius (Ossian, a schoolboy).

Såsom i en spegel (*Through a Glass Darkly*)
Script: IB. Photography: Sven Nykvist. Music: Erik Nordgren, with extracts from Bach, played by Erling Blöndal Bengtsson. Art Direction: P. A. Lundgren. Editing: Ulla Ryghe. Production Buyer: Karl-Arne Bergman. Costumes: Mago. Production Manager: Allan Ekelund. Production Company: Svensk Filmindustri. 89 minutes. Swedish premiere: October 16, 1961.

Cast: Harriet Andersson (Karin), Gunnar Björnstrand (David, her father), Max von Sydow (Martin, Karin's husband), Lars Passgård (Fredrik, David's son, known as Minus).

Nattvardsgästerna (*The Communicants*)
Script: IB. Photography: Sven Nykvist. Music: from *The Swedish Hymnal*. Art Direction: P. A. Lundgren. Production Buyer: Karl-Arne Bergman. Editing: Ulla Ryghe. Costumes: Mago. Makeup: Börje Lundh. Production Manager: Allan Ekelund. Production Company: Svensk Filmindustri. 80 minutes. Swedish premiere: February 11, 1963.

Cast: Ingrid Thulin (Märta Lundberg), Gunnar Björnstrand (Tomas Eriksson), Gunnel Lindblom (Karin Persson), Max von Sydow (Jonas Persson), Allan Edwall (Algot Frövik), Kolbjörn Knudsen (Knut Aronsson), Olof Thunberg (Fredrik Blom, organist), Elsa Ebbesen-Thornblad (Magdalena Ledfors), Tor Borong (Johan Åkerblom), Bertha Sånnell (Hanna Appelblad), Helena Palmgren (Doris), Eddie Axberg (Johan Strand), Lars-Owe Carlberg (local police officer).

Tystnaden (*The Silence*)
Script: IB. Photography: Sven Nykvist. Music: Ivan Renliden, R. Mersey, J. S. Bach (*Goldberg Variations*). Art Direction: P. A. Lundgren. Production Buyer: Karl-Arne Bergman. Editing: Ulla Ryghe. Costumes: Marik Vos-Lundh, Bertha Sånnell. Makeup: Gullan Westfelt. Production Manager: Allan Ekelund. Production Company: Svensk Filmindustri. 95 minutes. Swedish premiere: September 23, 1963.

Cast: Ingrid Thulin (Ester), Gunnel Lindblom (Anna), Jörgen Lindström (Johan, her son), Håkan Jahnberg (old waiter), Birger Malmsten (waiter in bar), the Eduardinis (seven dwarfs),

Eduardo Gutierrez (the dwarfs' manager), Lissi Alandh and Leif Forstenberg (couple in the theater), Karl-Arne Bergman (newsboy), Olof Widgren (old man in hotel corridor), Kristina Olansson (stand-in for Gunnel Lindblom in sex scene).

För att inte tala om alla dessa kvinnor (*Not to Speak of All These Women*)
Script: Erland Josephson and IB, under pseudonym "Buntel Eriksson." Photography (Eastmancolor): Sven Nykvist. Music: Erik Nordgren, with extracts from Bach. Art Direction: P. A. Lundgren. Production Buyer: Karl-Arne Bergman. Editing: Ulla Ryghe. Costumes: Mago. Makeup: Börje Lundh, Britt Falkemo, Cecilia Drott. Production Manager: Allan Ekelund. Production Company: Svensk Filmindustri. 80 minutes. Swedish premiere: June 15, 1964.

Cast: Jarl Kulle (Cornelius), Bibi Andersson (Bumble Bee, Felix's mistress), Harriet Andersson (Isolde, Felix's chambermaid), Eva Dahlbeck (Adelaide, Felix's wife), Karin Kavli (Madame Tussaud), Gertrud Fridh (Traviata), Mona Malm (Cecilia), Barbro Hiort af Ornäs (Beatrice, Felix's accompanist), Allan Edwall (Jillker, Felix's impresario), Georg Funkquist (Tristan), Carl Billquist (young man), Jan Blomberg (English radio announcer), Göran Graffman (French radio announcer), Jan-Olof Strandberg (German radio announcer), Gösta Prüzelius (Swedish radio announcer), Ulf Johansson, Axel Düberg, Lars-Erik Liedholm (men in black), Lars-Owe Carlberg (chauffeur), Doris Funcke (first waitress), Yvonne Igell (second waitress).

Persona
Script: IB. Photography: Sven Nykvist. Music: Lars Johan Werle, with extract from Bach. Art Direction: Bibi Lindström. Production Buyer: Karl-Arne Bergman. Editing: Ulla Ryghe. Costumes: Mago. Makeup: Börje Lundh, Tina Johansson. Sound Effects: Evald Andersson. Production Manager: Lars-Owe Carlberg. Production Company: Svensk Filmindustri. 84 minutes. Swedish premiere: October 18, 1966.

Cast: Bibi Andersson (Nurse Alma), Liv Ullmann (Elisabet Vogler), Margaretha Krook (psychiatrist), Gunnar Björnstrand (Mr. Vogler), Jörgen Lindström (Elisabet's son).

"Daniel"
Direction, Idea, and Photography (Eastmancolor, 16 mm.): IB. Editing: Ulla Ryghe. Music: Käbi Laretei, playing piano. One of eight short films gathered as *Stimulantia*; other segments directed by Hans Abramson, Jörn Donner, Lars Görling, Arne Arnbom, Hans Alfredson and Tage Danielsson, Gustaf Molander, and Vilgot Sjöman. Production Company: Svensk Filmindustri. Swedish premiere: March 28, 1967.

Cast: Daniel Sebastian Bergman, Käbi Laretei (themselves).

Vargtimmen (*Hour of the Wolf*)
Script: IB. Photography: Sven Nykvist. Music: Lars Johan Werle, with extracts from Mozart and Bach. Art Directon: Marik Vos-Lundh. Production Buyer: Karl-Arne Bergman. Editing: Ulla Ryghe. Costumes: Mago, Eivor Kullberg. Makeup: Börje Lundh, Kjell Gustavsson, Tina Johansson. Production Manager: Lars-Owe Carlberg. Production Company: Svensk Filmindustri. 89 minutes. Swedish premiere: February 19, 1968.

Cast: Max von Sydow (Johan Borg), Liv Ullmann (Alma Borg, his wife), Ingrid Thulin (Veronica Vogler), Georg Rydeberg (Archivist Lindhorst), Erland Josephson (Baron von Merkens), Gertrud Fridh (Corinne von Merkens), Naima Wifstrand (demon who removes her face), Bertil Anderberg (Ernst von Merkens), Ulf Johansson (Curator Heerbrand), Lenn Hjortzberg (Kapellmeister Kreisler), Agda Helin (maid at Merkens castle), Mikael Rundquist (boy in jeans), Folke Sundquist (Tamino in puppet theater). Cut: Mona Seilitz (corpse in mortuary).

Skammen (*Shame*)
Script: IB. Photography: Sven Nykvist. Art Direction: P. A. Lundgren. Production Buyer: Karl-Arne Bergman. Editing: Ulla Ryghe. Costumes: Mago. Production Manager: Lars-Owe

Carlberg. Production Company: Svensk Filmindustri / Cinematograph. 102 minutes. Swedish premiere: September 29, 1968.

Cast: Liv Ullmann (Eva Rosenberg), Max von Sydow (Jan Rosenberg), Gunnar Björnstrand (Jacobi), Birgitta Valberg (Mrs. Jacobi), Sigge Fürst (Filip), Hans Alfredson (Lobelius), Ingvar Kjellson (Oswald), Frank Sundström (interrogator), Ulf Johansson (doctor), Frej Lindqvist (stooped man), Rune Lndström (stout gentleman), Willy Peters (older officer), Bengt Eklund (orderly), Åke Jörnfalk (condemned man), Vilgot Sjöman (interviewer), Lars Amble (an officer), Björn Thambert (Johan), Barbro Hiort af Ornäs (Mrs. Jacobi), Karl-Axel Forsberg (secretary), Gösta Pruzelius (pastor), Brita Oberg (woman in interrogation room), Agda Helin (woman in shop), Ellika Mann (prison warden), Monica Lindberg, Gregor Dahlman, Nils Whiten, Per Berglund, Stig Lindberg, Jan Bergman, Nils Fogeby, Brian Wikström, Georg Skarstedt, Lilian Carlsson, Börje Lundh, Eivor Kullberg, Karl-Arne Bergman.

Riten (*The Rite*)
Script: IB. Photography: Sven Nykvist. Art Direction: Lennart Blomkvist. Editing: Siv Kanälv. Costumes: Mago. Production Manager: Lars-Owe Carlberg. Production Company: Svensk Filmindustri/Sveriges TV/Cinematograph. 74 minutes. Swedish premiere (on Swedish television): March 25, 1969.

Cast: Ingrid Thulin (Thea Winkelmann), Anders Ek (Albert Emmanuel Sebastian Fischer), Gunnar Björnstrand (Hans Winkelmann), Erik Hell (Judge Abramsson), Igmar Bergman (priest in confessional).

En passion (*A Passion*)
Script: IB. Photography (Eastmancolor): Sven Nykvist. Music: extracts from Bach, and Allan Gray's song, "Always Romantic." Art Direction: P.A. Lundgren. Production Buyer: Karl-Arne Bergman. Editing: Siv Kanälv. Costumes: Mago. Hairstyles: Börje Lundh. Production Manager: Lars-Owe Carlberg. Production Comapny: Svensk Filmindustri/Cinematograph. 101 minutes. Swedish premiere: November 10, 1969.

Cast: Liv Ullmann (Anna Fromm), Bibi Andersson (Eva Vergérus), Max von Sydow (Andreas Winkelmann), Erland Josephson (Elis Vergérus), Erik Hell (Johan Andersson), Sigge Fürst (Verner), Svea Holst (Verner's wife), Annika Kronberg (Katarina), Hjördis Pettersson (Johan's sister), Lars-Owe Carlberg, Brian Wikström (policemen), Barbro Hiort af Ornäs, Malin Ek, Britta Brunius, Brita Oberg, Marianne Karlbeck, Lennart Blomkvist.

Fårö-Dokument (*Fårö Document*)
Photography (part Eastmancolor): Sven Nykvist. Editing: Siv Kanälv. Production Manager: Lars-Owe Carlberg. Production Company: Cinematograph. Narrator: IB. 78 minutes. Swedish premiere (on Swedish television); January 1, 1970.

The Touch / Beröringen
Script: IB. Photography (Eastmancolor): Sven Nykvist. Music: Jan Johansson. Art Direction: P. A. Lundgren. Editing: Siv Kanälv-Lundgren. Title Sequence Photography: Gunnar Fischer. Production Manager: Lars-Owe Carlberg. Production Company: ABC Pictures (New York)/Cinematograph (Stockholm). 113 minutes. Swedish premiere: August 30, 1971.

Cast: Elliott Gould (David Kovac), Bibi Andersson (Karin Vergérus), Max von Sydow (Dr. Andreas Vergérus), Sheila Reid (Sara Kovac), Barbro Hiort af Ornäs (Karin's mother), Staffan Hallerstam (Anders Vergérus), Maria Nolgård (Agnes Vergérus), Åke Lindström (doctor), Mimmi Wahlander (nurse), Else Ebbesen (matron), Anna von Rosen, Karin Nilsson (neighbors), Erik Nyhlen (archeologist), Margareta Byström (Dr. Vergérus's secretary), Alan Simon (museum curator), Per Sjöstrand (another curator), Aino Taube (woman on staircase), Ann-Christin Lobraten (museum worker), Dennis Gotobed (British immigration officer), Bengt Ottekil (London bellboy), Harry Schein, Stig Björkman (guests at party).

Viskningar och rop (*Cries and Whispers*)
Script: IB. Photography (Eastmancolor): Sven Nykvist. Music: Chopin, played by Käbi Laretei;

Bach, played by Pierre Fournier. Art Direction: Marik Vos. Editing: Siv Lundgren. Production Manager: Lars-Owe Carlberg. Production Company: Cinematograph, in association with Svenska Filminstitutet. 91 minutes. Swedish premiere: March 5, 1973.

Cast: Harriet Andersson (Agnes), Kari Sylwan (Anna), Ingrid Thulin (Karin), Liv Ullmann (Maria), Erland Josephson (David, Maria's lover), Henning Moritzen (Joakim), Georg Åhlin (Fredrik), Anders Ek (Pastor Isak), Inga Gill (Aunt Olga), Malin Gjörup, Rosanna Mariano, Lena Bergman, Monika Priede, Greta Johanson, Karin Johanson.

Scener ur ett äktenskap (*Scenes from a Marriage*)
Script: IB. Photography (Eastmancolor, 16 mm.): Sven Nykvist. Art Direction: Björn Thulin. Editing: Siv Lundgren. Production Manager: Lars-Owe Carlberg. Executive Producer: Lars-Owe Carlberg. Production Company: Cinematograph. 168 minutes (theatrical version). Swedish premiere (on television, in six weekly parts): April 11 through May 16, 1973.

Cast: Liv Ullmann (Marianne), Erland Josephson (Johan), Bibi Andersson (Katarina), Jan Malmsjö (Peter), Anita Wall (interviewer), Gunnel Lindblom (Eva), Barbro Hiort af Ornäs (Mrs. Jacobi), Bertil Norström, Arne Carlsson. (Wenche Foss plays Marianne's mother in the TV version.)

Trollflöjten (*The Magic Flute*)
Script: IB, based on the opera by Mozart and libretto by Schikaneder. Photography (Eastmancolor): Sven Nykvist. Sound: Helmut Muhle, Peter Hennix. Musical Direction: Eric Ericson. Art Direction: Henny Noremark. Editing: Siv Lundgren. Costumes: Karin Erskine. Choreography: Donya Feuer. Production Manager: Måns Reuterswärd. Production Company: Sveriges TV 2. 135 minutes. Swedish premiere (on television): January 1, 1975.

Cast: Josef Köstlinger (Tamino), Irma Urrila (Pamina), Håkan Hagegård (Papageno), Elisabeth Eriksson (Papagena), Ulrik Cold (Sarastro), Birgit Nordin (Queen of the Night), Ragnar Ulfung (Monostatos), Erik Saeden (speaker), Britt-Marie Aruhn, Birgitta Smiding, and Kirsten Vaupel (ladies), Gösta Prüzelius and Ulf Johanson (priests), Urban Malmberg, Ansgar Krook, and Erland von Heijne (boys), Hans Johansson, Jerker Arvidsson (armed men).

Ansikte mot ansikte (*Face to Face*)
Script: IB. Photography (Eastmancolor): Sven Nykvist. Music: Mozart, played by Käbi Laretei. Art Direction: Anne Terselius-Hagegård, Anna Asp, Maggie Strindberg. Set Decoration: Peter Krupenin. Editing: Siv Lundgren. Producers: IB, Lars-Owe Carlberg. Production Manager: Katinka Faragó. Production Company: Cinematograph. 136 minutes. Swedish premiere (on television, in four weekly parts): April 28 through May 19, 1976.

Cast: Liv Ullmann (Dr. Jenny Isaksson), Erland Josephson (Dr. Tomas Jacobi), Gunnar Björnstrand (grandfather), Aino Taube (grandmother), Kari Sylwan (Maria), Sif Ruud (Elisabeth Wankel), Sven Lindberg (Dr. Erik Isaksson), Tore Segelcke (lady), Ulf Johanson (Dr. Helmuth Wankel), Helene Friberg (Anna), Kristina Adolphson (Veronica), Gösta Ekman (Mikael Strömberg), Käbi Laretei (concert pianist), Birger Malmsten (rapist), Göran Stangertz (second rapist), Marianne Aminoff (Jenny's mother), Gösta Prüzelius (clergyman), Rebecca Pawlo, Lena Ohlin (boutique girls).

Das Schlangenei (Swedish title *Ormens ägg; The Serpent's Egg*)
Script: IB. Photography (Eastmancolor): Sven Nykvist. Additional Photography: Peter Rohe, Dieter Lohmann. Music: Rolf Wilhelm. Production Designer: Rolf Zehetbauer. Art Direction: Erner Achmann, Herbert Strabel. Editing: Jutta Hering, Petra von Oelffen. Choreography: Heino Hallhuber. Costumes: Charlotte Fleming. Producer: Dino De Laurentiis. Executive Producer: Horst Wendlandt. Production Manager: Georg Föcking. Production Executive: Harold Nebenzal. Production Company: Rialto Film (West Berlin)/Dino De Laurentiis Corporation (Los Angeles). 119 minutes. Filmed in English. German premiere: October 26, 1977.

Cast: Liv Ullmann (Manuela Rosenberg), David Carradine (Abel Rosenberg), Gert Froebe

(Inspector Bauer), Heinz Bennent (Hans Vergérus), James Whitmore (priest), Glynn Turman (Monroe), Georg Hartmann (Hollinger), Edith Heerdegen (Mrs. Holle), Kyra Mladeck (Miss Dorst), Fritz Strassner (Dr. Soltermann), Hans Quest (Dr. Silbermann), Wolfgang Weiser (civil servant), Paula Braend (Mrs. Hemse), Walter Schmidinger (Solomon), Lisi Mangold (Mikaela), Grischa Huber (Stella), Paul Burks (cabaret comedian), Toni Berger (Mr. Rosenberg), Erna Brunell (Mrs. Rosenberg), Hans Eichler (Max Rosenberg).

Herbstsonat (Swedish title: *Höstsonaten; Autumn Sonata*)
Script: IB. Photography (Eastmancolor): Sven Nykvist. Music: Chopin, played by Käbi Laretei; Bach, performed by Claude Genetay; and Handel, performed by Frans Brüggen, Gustav Leonhardt, and Anne Bylsma. Set Design: Anna Asp. Editing: Sylvia Ingemarsson. Costumes: Inger Pehrsson. Production Supervisors: Ingrid Karlebo Bergman, Lars-Owe Carlberg. Production Manager: Katinka Faragó. Production Company: Personafilm for ITC. 92 minutes. Swedish premiere: October 8, 1978.

Cast: Ingrid Bergman (Charlotte), Liv Ullmann (Eva), Lena Nyman (Helena), Halvar Björk (Viktor), Arne Bang-Hansen (Uncle Otto), Gunnar Björnstrand (Paul), Erland Josephson (Josef), Georg Løkkeberg (Leonardo), Linn Ullmann (Eva as a child), Knut Wigert (professor), Eva von Hanno (nurse), Marianne Aminoff, Mimi Pollak.

Fårö-Dokument 1979 (*Fårö Document 1979*)
Script: IB. Photography (color): Arne Carlsson. Music: Svante Pettersson, Sigvard Huldt, Dag and Lena, Ingmar Nordström, Strix Q, Rock de Luxe, Ola and the Janglers. Editing: Sylvia Ingemarsson. Production Manager: Lars-Owe Carlberg. 103 minutes. Swedish premiere (on television): December 24, 1979.

Narrator: Ingmar Bergman. Cast (themselves): Richard Ostman, Ulla Silvergren, Annelie Nyström, Per Broman, Irena Broman, Inge Nordström, Annika Liljegren, Arne Eriksson, Adolf Ekström, Victoria Ekström, Anton Ekström, Valter Broman, Erik Ekström, Ingrid Ekman, Per Nordberg, Gunilla Johannesson, Herbert Olsson, Rune Nilsson, Joe Nordenberg, Jan Nordberg.

Aus dem Leben der Marionetten (*From the Life of the Marionettes*)
Script: IB. Photography (part Eastmancolor): Sven Nykvist. Music: Rolf Wilhelm; Song, "Touch Me, Take Me" (in English, singer uncredited). Production Design: Rolf Zehetbauer. Art Direction: Herbert Strabel. Set Decoration: Rolf Zehetbauer. Editing: Petra von Oelffen (English-language version: Geri Ashur). Costumes: Charlotte Flemming, Egon Strasser. Makeup: Mathilde Basedow. Production Managers: Paulette Hufnagel, Irmgard Kelpinski. Producers: Horst Wendlandt, Ingrid Karlebo Bergman, Richard Brick (English-language version). Production Company: Personafilm (Munich) in collaboration with Bayerische Staatsschauspiel. 104 minutes. Premiere: 1980.

Cast: Robert Atzorn (Peter Egermann), Martin Benrath (Professor Mogens Jensen), Christine Buchegger (Katarina Egermann), Rita Russek (Katarina Krafft, known as Ka), Lola Müthel (Cordelia Egermann), Walter Schmidinger (Tomas Isidor Mandelbaum, known as Tim), Heinz Bennent (Arthur Brenner), Ruth Olafs (nurse), Karl-Heinz Pelser (police investigator), Gaby Dohm (Peter Egermann's secretary), Toni Berger (brothel doorman), Erwin Faber, Doris Jensen.

Fanny och Alexander (*Fanny and Alexander*)
Script: IB. Photography (Eastmancolor): Sven Nykvist. Music: Daniel Bell. Art Direction: Anna Asp. Set Decoration: Kaj Larsen. Editing: Sylvia Ingemarsson. Wardrobe: Marik Vos-Lundh. Makeup: Leif Qviström, Anna-Lena Melin, Barbro Holmberg-Haugen. Production Manager: Katinka Faragó. Administration: Lars-Owe Carlberg, Ingrid Karlebo Bergman, Fredrik von Rosen, Hellen Igler. Executive Producer: Jörn Donner. Production Company: Svenska Film-institutet (Stockholm) / Sveriges TV 1 (Stockholm) / Personafilm (Munich) / Gaumont (Paris). 199 minutes (first version in theatrical release). Swedish premiere: Christmas, 1982.

Cast: Gunn Wållgren (Helena Ekdahl), Allan Edwall (Oscar Ekdahl), Ewa Fröling (Emilie Ekdahl), Bertil Guve (Alexander), Pernilla Allwin (Fanny), Börje Ahlstedt (Carl Ekdahl), Christina Schollin (Lydia Ekdahl), Jarl Kulle (Gustav Adolf Ekdahl), Mona Malm (Alma Ekdahl), Maria Granlund (Petra), Emelie Werkö (Jenny), Kristian Almgren (Putte), Angelica Wallgren (Eva), Majlis Granlund (Miss Vega), Svea Holst-Widén (Miss Ester), Siv Ericks (Alida), Inga Ålenius (Lisen), Kristina Adolphson (Siri), Eva von Hanno (Berta), Pernilla Wallgren (Maj), Käbi Laretei (Aunt Anna), Sonya Hedenbratt (Aunt Emma), Erland Josephson (Isak Jacobi), Mats Bergman (Aron), Stina Ekblad (Ismael), Gunnar Björnstrand (Filip Landahl), Anna Bergman (Hanna Schwartz), Per Mattson (Mikael Bergman), Nils Brandt (Morsing), Heinz Hopf (Tomas Graal), Åke Lagergren (Johan Armfeldt), Lickå Sjöman (Grete Holm), Sune Mangs, (Mr. Salenius), Maud Hyttenberg (Mrs. Sinclair), Kerstin Karte (prompter), Tore Karte (administrative director), Marianne Karlbeck (Mrs. Palmgren), Gus Dahlström (set decorator), Gösta Prüzelius (Dr. Fürstenberg), Georg Årlin (colonel), Ernst Günther (dean of the university), Jan Malmsjö (Bishop Edvard Vergérus), Kerstin Tidelius (Henrietta Vergérus), Marianne Aminoff (Mrs. Blenda Vergérus), Marrit Olsson (Malla Tander), Brita Billsten (Karna), Harriet Andersson (Justina), Krister Hell (young man 1), Peter Stormare (young man 2), Linda Krüger (Pauline), Pernilla Wahlgren (Esmeralda), Carl Billquist (police inspector), Anna Rydberg (Rosa).

Efter repetitionen (*After the Rehearsal*)
Script: IB. Photography: Sven Nykvist. Art Direction: Anna Asp. Executive Producer: Jörn Donner. 72 minutes. Swedish premiere: 1984. Cast: Erland Josephson (Henrik Vogler), Lena Ohlin (Anna Egerman), Ingrid Thulin (Rakel).

Notes

The Early Years

The Depths of Childhood

1 Quoted in Jean Béranger, "Renaissance du cinéma suedois," *Cinéma 58*. No. 29 (July-August, 1958), 32.

2 Quoted in Maud Webster, "I tjugofem år har det stormat kring Bergman," *Veckojournalen*, No. 15 (April 8, 1970), 7. (Hereafter referred to as Webster.)

3 Interview with Stig Björkman, Torsten Manns, and Jonas Sima, "Ingmar Bergman: 'Man kan ju göra vad som helst med film,'" *Chaplin*, 10 (1968). This is the same interview which appears in *Bergman om Bergman*, but it contains several questions and answers that were cut when it appeared in the book. Reprinted in a French translation in *Cahiers du Cinéma*, and in English in *Movie*, 16 (Winter, 1968–69), 2–8, and in *Evergreen Review*, XIII, 63 (February, 1969), 43, 45, 78–82. The quotation here is from the *Evergreen Review* translation (page 45); subsequent quotations are from the version that appeared in *Movie*, a British journal appearing at irregular intervals. Hereafter referred to as *Movie* 16 interview.

4 Letter, Margareta Bergman Britten Austin to Frank Gado, August 15, 1985.

5 *Karin: A Novel* (London, 1985), pp. 156–57. First appeared in Swedish as *Karin vid havet* (Stockholm, 1980).

6 Letter, Margareta Bergman Britten Austin to Frank Gado, November 23, 1985.

7 "Ingmar Bergman berättar om sin mor," *Husmodern*, No. 29 (August 20, 1971), 65, 67. Hereafter referred to as "Bergman berättar.")

8 Letter, Margareta Bergman Britten Austin to Frank Gado, August 15, 1985.

9 "Det att göra film," lecture given at University of Lund, November 25, 1954. Published in *Filmnyheter*, No. 19–20 (December, 1954).

10 "Bergman berättar," 65.

11 Letter, Margareta Bergman Britten Austin to Frank Gado, November 23, 1985.

12 Letter, Margareta Bergman Britten Austin to Frank Gado, August 15, 1985.

13 "Bergman berättar," 65.

14 Letter, Margareta Bergman Britten Austin to Frank Gado, November 23, 1985.

15 Letter, Else Fisher-Bergman to Frank Gado, November 17, 1985.
16 Letter, Margareta Bergman Britten Austin to Frank Gado, August 15, 1985.
17 Quoted in Marianne Höök, *Ingmar Bergman* (Stockholm, 1962), p. 23. (Hereafter referred to as Höök.)
18 "Det att göra film," lecture given at the University of Lund, November, 1954. Published in *Filmnyheter*, No. 19–20 (December, 1954). (Hereafter referred to as "Det att göra film."
19 "Bergman berättar," 19.
20 "Bergman berättar," 19.
21 Quoted in *Il Nuovo Spettatore Cinematografico*, No. 5, 1959, iii.
22 "Erasmus address." Reprinted as Introduction to *Persona* (Stockholm, 1966). (Hereafter referred to as "Erasmus address.")
23 Quoted in Eric Rohmer, "Presentation d'Ingmar Bergman," *Cahiers du Cinéma*, No. 61 (July, 1956), 17–18.
24 "Erasmus address."
25 Quoted in Webster, 7.
26 Quoted in Fritiof Billquist, *Ingmar Bergman: teatermannen och filmskaparen* (Stockholm, 1960), p. 128. (Hereafter referred to as Billquist.)

A Foothold in Theater
1   Webster, 7.
2   Quoted in Höök, p. 36.
3   Billquist, pp. 26–27.
4   Bergman's program note is reproduced in Billquist, p. 26.
5   Quoted in Billquist, p. 35.
6   Letter, Else Fisher-Bergman to Frank Gado, October 25, 1985.
7   Letter, Else Fisher-Bergman to Frank Gado, October 25, 1985.
8   Letter, Else Fisher-Bergman to Frank Gado, November 17, 1985.
9   Letter, Else Fisher-Bergman to Frank Gado, October 25, 1985.
10 Letter, Else Fisher-Bergman to Frank Gado, October 25, 1985.
11 Letter, Else Fisher-Bergman to Frank Gado, October 25, 1985.
12 Billquist, p. 48.
13 Letter, Else Fisher-Bergman to Frank Gado, October 25, 1985.
14 Letter, Else Fisher-Bergman to Frank Gado, October 25, 1985.
15 *Sydsvenska Dagbladet*, quoted in Billquist, p. 62.
16 Quoted in Billquist, p. 65.
17 Henrik Sjögren, *Ingmar Bergman på teatern* (Stockholm, 1968), p. 41. (Hereafter referred to as Sjögren.)
18 Reprinted in Billquist, p. 67.
19 Quoted in Billquist, pp. 75–76.
20 The program note is reprinted in Sjögren, p. 45.

The 'Forties Films

Learning to Make Movies
1   May 13, 1946, lecture presented before the Uppsala Student Film Club, reported in *Upsala Nya Tidning* of the next day.
2   Billquist, p. 119.
3   Billquist, pp. 70–71.
4   Stig Björkman, Torsten Manns, and Jonas Sima, *Bergman om Bergman* (Stockholm, 1970), p. 52. *Bergman on Bergman*, English translation by Paul Britten Austin (New

York, 1973), p. 46. (Hereafter referred to as *Bergman om Bergman*.) Note: In my text, I have translated directly from the Swedish. The first page number in subsequent citations to this work refers to the Swedish edition; the second to the American.

5   *Bergman om Bergman*, p. 51 / 45.
6   *Bergman om Bergman*, p. 51 / 45.
7   Quoted in Billquist, p. 138.

Fictions About the Self: "A Shorter Tale"

1   Risto Fried, "The Dream Content of Ingmar Bergman's 'A Shorter Tale About One of Jack the Ripper's Earliest Childhood Memories,'" unpublished manuscript.

Torment

1   Billquist, p. 71.

Crisis

1   Quoted in Billquist, p. 68.
2   Bergman, "Om att filmatisera en pjäs," *Filmnyheter*, No. 4 (1946), 6 ff.

Woman Without a Face

1   Bergman, "Rut," *SF Filmblad till Kvinna utan ansikte*, n.p. Quoted in Billquist, p. 113.

Prison

1   Bergman, "Filmen on Birgitta-Carolina," *Stockholms-Tidningen* (March 18, 1949), 4.
2   *Bergman om Bergman*, p. 11 / 10.

Eva

1   *Bergman om Bergman*, p. 32 / 29.

To Joy

1   *Bergman om Bergman*, p. 52 / 46.

Playwright Bergman

1   Sjögren, p. 307.
2   Sjögren, p. 307.
3   Vilgot Sjöman, *L 136* (Stockholm, 1963), p. 24. *L 136: Diary with Ingmar Bergman*, English translation by Alain Blair (Ann Arbor, 1978), p. 20. (Hereafter referred to as Sjöman.) Note: In my text, I have translated directly from the Swedish. The first page number in subsequent citations to this work refers to the Swedish edition; the second to the American.
4   Sjögren, p. 307.
5   Sjöman, p. 23 / 19.
6   "Ingmar Bergman ser på film," *Chaplin*, No. 18 (March, 1961), 61.

Rakel and the Cinema Doorman

1   Vernon Young, *Cinema Borealis* (New York, 1971), p. 49. (Hereafter referred to as Young.) See also: Birgitta Steene, *Ingmar Bergman* (New York, 1968), p. 28. (Hereafter referred to as Steene.)

The Day Ends Early, To My Terror . . . , Kamma Noll

1   Ingmar Bergman, *Moraliteter* (Stockholm, 1941).

Joakim Naked: *The City*, "The Story of the Eiffel Tower," "The Fish"
1 Interview in *Röster i Radio* (May, 1951); quoted in Billquist, pp. 142–43.

The Murder in Barjärna
1 Sjögren, pp. 124, 128–29.

The Lengthening Shadows of Summer

1 Quoted in Lise-Lone Marker and Frederick J. Marker, *Ingmar Bergman: Four Decades in Theater* (Cambridge, Mass., 1982) p. 239.
2 *Bergman om Bergman*, p. 55 / 51.

Summergame
1 Quoted in Billquist, p. 148.
2 Quoted in Billquist, p. 149.
3 Interview with Elof Hellqvist in Swedish Radio, November 28, 1952. Printed in subsequent issue of *Hörde Ni*.
4 Wood, p. 32.

The Early Comedies: *Women's Waiting* and *A Lesson in Love*
1 Quoted in Billquist, p. 158.
2 *Bergman om Bergman*, p. 83 / 79.
3 Höök, p. 108.

Evening of the Jesters
1 "Filmson" (pseudonym), *Aftonbladet*, September 15, 1953. Quoted in *Bergman om Bergman*, p. 87 / 82.
2 "Det att göra film."
3 *Bergman om Bergman*, p. 89 / 84.
4 *Bergman om Bergman*, p. 99 / 93.

Dreams
1 Young, p. 139.
2 John Russell Taylor, *Cinema Eye, Cinema Ear* (London, 1964), p. 156.

Smiles of the Summer Night
1 *Bergman om Bergman*, p. 105 / 99.

Quests

1 Quoted in Billquist, pp. 176–78.
2 *Bergman om Bergman*, p. 109 / 102.
3 *Bergman om Bergman*, p. 109 / 103.

The Seventh Seal
1 Billquist, p. 186.
2 Program notes to *The Seventh Seal*.
3 Program notes to *The Seventh* Seal.
4 Steene, p. 65.
5 Norman Holland, "*The Seventh Seal*: The Film in Iconography," in Julius Bellone, editor, *Renaissance of the Film* (New York, 1970), p. 239.
6 Young, p. 154.

7   Wood, p. 88.
8   *Bergman om Bergman*, p. 125 / 117.

Wild Strawberries

1   *Bergman om Bergman*, pp. 139–41 / 131–32.
2   *Bergman om Bergman*, p. 156 / 146.
3   *Hedvig Eleonora Forsamlingsblad* (Christmas, 1971), 10.
4   *Bergman om Bergman*, p. 160 / 148.
5   Jörn Donner, *The Personal Vision of Ingmar Bergman*, translation of *Djävulens ansikte*: *Ingmar Bergmans filmer* (Stockholm, 1962) by Holger Lundbergh (Bloomington, Ind., 1964), p. 160. (Hereafter referred to as Donner.)
6   *Bergman om Bergman*, p. 157 / 147.
7   *Bergman om Bergman*, pp. 151, 156 / 140–41.
8   *Bergman om Bergman*, p. 159 / 148.
9   "Ingmar Bergman and Ludvig Jönsson discuss guilt," *Utmaningen*, Sveriges Radio Program 2, June 11, 1973.
10 Hans Åkerblom, obituary for Erik Bergman, *Hedvig Eleonora Forsamlingsblad* (May-June, 1970), 4.

The Face

1   *Bergman om Bergman*, pp. 130–31 / 123.
2   *Bergman om Bergman*, p. 134 / 127; John Simon, *Ingmar Bergman Directs* (New York, 1972), p. 33. (Hereafter referred to as Simon.)
3   Young, p. 175.

The Virgin Spring

1   *Bergman om Bergman*, p. 165 / 150.
2   Sjöman, p. 46 / 43.
3   *Bergman om Bergman*, p. 41 / 35.
4   *Bergman om Bergman*, p. 128 / 120.
5   Interview on Sveriges Radio; quoted in Billquist, p. 206.
6   Quoted in Billquist, p. 206.
7   Ulla Isaksson, Preface, *The Virgin Spring* (New York, 1960), p. *vii*.
8   Isaksson, p. *vi*.
9   Höök, p. 148.
10 *Bergman om Bergman*, p. 130 / 123.
11 Wood, p. 103.

The Devil's Eye

1   Bergman, Commintary on Series Ö (circular published by the Swedish Film Institute for a 1973 Bergman retrospective), n.p.
2   Bergman, "Kära skrämmande publik," *SF Filmblad till Djävulens öga*, n.p.
3   *Bergman om Bergman*, pp. 160–61 / 149–50.
4   *Bergman om Bergman*, p. 161 / 150.
5   "Kära skrämmande publik."

God's Silence

1   Martin Lamm, *August Strindberg*, translated and edited by Harry Carlson (New York, 1971), p. 477.
2   Letter to Adolf Paul, quoted in Lamm, p. 477; Strindberg, *Samlade skrifter* (Stockholm, 1912–1919) L, p. 11.

3 Sjöman, pp. 82–83 / 80.
4 *Bergman om Bergman*, p. 186 / 172.
5 *Bergman om Bergman*, p. 165 / 151.
6 Sjöman, pp. 127 / 127–28.
7 Sjöman, pp. 134–35 / 135.
8 Sjöman, pp. 160–61 / 161–62.

Through a Glass Darkly
1 *Bergman om Bergman*, p. 178 / 163.
2 Wood, p. 107.
3 Wood, pp. 108–09.
4 Sjöman, p. 25 / 22.
5 Sjöman, p. 30 / 26–27.
6 Quoted in Derek Prouse, "Ingmar Bergman: A Problem Genius," *Washington Post*, April 15, 1964. Reprinted from the *Sunday Times* (London), March 15, 1964.
7 *Bergman om Bergman*, pp. 180–81 / 167.

The Communicants
1 Sjöman, p. 9 / 5.
2 *Bergman om Bergman*, p. 186 / 173. See also Sjöman, p. 16 / 12.
3 *Bergman om Bergman*, pp. 188–89 / 173–74.
4 *Bergman om Bergman*, pp. 189–90 / 174.
5 Sjöman, p. 63 / 60.
6 Sjöman, p. 17 / 13–14.
7 Sjöman, pp. 124, 169 / 125, 170.
8 Sjöman, p. 18 / 14.
9 Sjöman, pp. 41, 201 / 37–38, 203.
10 Sjöman, pp. 42–43 / 38–39.
11 Sjöman, pp. 7, 67, 36 / 3, 64–65, 32.
12 Sjöman, p. 49 / 46.

The Silence
1 Sjöman, p. 61–62 / 58–59.
2 Sjöman, p. 220 / 222.
3 Charles Thomas Samuels, *Encountering Directors* (New York, 1972), p. 201. (Hereafter referred to as Samuels.)
4 Samuels, p. 200.
5 Bosley Crowther, "Brooding and Grim Bergman," *New York Times* (February 4, 1964), 28. Brendan Gill, "No Contest," *New Yorker*, XXXIX (February 8, 1964), 108.
6 Young, p. 213.
7 Peter Cowie, *Ingmar Bergman: A Critical Biography* (New York, 1982), p. 214. (Hereafter referred to as Cowie.)

Not to Speak of All These Women
1 *Bergman om Bergman*, pp. 21–22 / 21.

A Twilight World

1 Interview with Annika Holm in *Dagens Nyheter*; reprinted in *Theater Heute* (June, 1976).
2 Interview with Bo Strömstedt, *Söndags Expressen* (February 16, 1969), 2. (Hereafter referred to as Strömstedt interview.)

3 *Movie* 16 interview, 6.
4 Bergman, *Four Screenplays* (New York, 1960), pp. *xxi - xxii*.
5 *Four Screenplays*, p. *xxii*.
6 Interview with Nils Petter Sundgren, broadcast on Swedish television (February 21, 1968). (Hereafter referred to as Sundgren interview.)
7 Interview with Gunnar Oldin on Sveriges Radio, broadcast October 26, 1966. (Hereafter referred to as Oldin interview.)

Persona
1 *Bergman om Bergman*, pp. 213–14 / 196.
2 Samuels, p. 186.
3 Oldin interview.
4 *Bergman om Bergman*, p. 232 / 211.
5 Erasmus address.
6 *Bergman om Bergman*, p. 218 / 199.
7 *Bergman om Bergman*, p. 218 / 199.
8 *Bergman om Bergman*, p. 219 / 199.
9 Simon, p. 30.
10 Stig Ahlgren, *"Persona,"* *Idun-Veckojournalen* (December 2, 1966).
11 Simon, p. 215.
12 Cowie, p. 231.

Hour of the Wolf
1 *Bergman om Bergman*, p. 233 / 215.
2 Samuels, pp. 206–07.
3 *Movie* 16 interview, 2.
4 Interview on PBL program, Public Broadcasting Service on the eve of the American premiere of *Hour of the Wolf* on April 14, 1968. (Hereafter referred to as PBL interview.)
5 Sundgren interview.
6 *Movie* 16 interview, 5.
7 *Movie* 16 interview, 5.
8 *Movie* 16 interview, 4.

Shame
1 Young, p. 247.
2 *Bergman om Bergman*, p. 254–55 / 234.
3 *Bergman om Bergman*, p. 247 / 228.
4 TV interview with Nils Petter Sundgren, September 29, 1968.
5 PBL interview.
6 PBL interview.
7 Sundgren interview (9/29/68).
8 *Bergman om Bergman*, p. 258 / 235.

The Rite
1 *Bergman om Bergman*, p. 261 / 238.
2 *Bergman om Bergman*, pp. 262–63 / 238.
3 *Bergman om Bergman*, p. 265 / 240.
4 *Bergman om Bergman*, p. 262 / 238.
5 *Bergman om Bergman*, p. 265 / 241.
6 *Bergman om Bergman*, p. 262 / 238.
7 *Bergman om Bergman*, p. 262 / 238.

8   *Bergman om Bergman*, p. 264 / 239.
9   *Bergman om Bergman*, p. 277 / 251.
10 Friedrich Nietzsche, *The Birth of Tragedy and the Genealogy of Morals*, translated by Francis Golffing (New York, 1956), p. 9.

A Passion
1   *Bergman om Bergman*, p. 291 / 261.
2   *Bergman om Bergman*, p. 282 / 255.
3   *Bergman om Bergman*, p. 282 / 253.
4   *Bergman om Bergman*, p. 282 / 253.
5   Samuels, p. 198.

"Accelerating Necrosis"

1   *Bergman om Bergman*, p. 290 / 261.
2   Quoted in *Aftonbladet* (February 28, 1969), 1.

Cries and Whispers
1   Quoted by Arne Reberg, *Expressen* (March 5, 1973), 4.
2   Quoted by Britt Larsson, *Göteborgs Posten* (May 29, 1973).

The Preserve and *Scenes from a Marriage*
1   Quoted in *Dagens Nyheter* (August 20, 1972), 12.
2   *Bergman om Bergman* p. 194 / 178.
3   Bergman's statement on the book jacket of *Scener ur ett äktenskap* (Stockholm, 1973).

The Magic Flute
1   Bergman, pamphlet included in the boxed album of *The Magic Flute* (SR Records).

The Petrified Prince
1   I am indebted to Marsha Kinder for alerting me to the importance of *The Petrified Prince*. (See her essay in *Film and Dreams: An Approach to Bergman*, edited by Vlada Petrić (South Salem, N.Y., 1981). I am also most grateful to Professor Kinder for her assistance in making it possible for me to read a copy of that unpublished filmscript.

The Final Phase

1   *New York Times* (March 16, 1976), 4.

The Serpent's Egg
1   Vincent Canby, "Slouching Towards Berlin," *New York Times* (January 27, 1978), Section C, 8.

Autumn Sonata
1   Hanserik Hjertén, "Ingmar Bergmans *Herbstsonat*: Ingrid Bergmans bästa film," *Dagens Nyheter* (October 9, 1978), 14.

Fanny and Alexander
1   Richard Grenier, "Bergman Discovers Love," *Commentary* (September, 1983), pp. 64–67.
2   Quoted in Cowie, p. 359.

Index

Library of Congress Cataloging-in-Publication Data
Gado, Frank.
The passion of Ingmar Bergman.
Filmography: p.
Bibliography: p.
Includes index.
1. Bergman, Ingmar, 1918–   —Criticism and inter-
pretation. I. Title.
PN1998.A3B4634 1986   791.43'0233'0924   86-19731
ISBN 0-8223-0585-2
ISBN 0-8223-0586-0 (pbk.)